Karin Papp

ACCOUNTING FOR MANAGEMENT

ACCOUNTING FOR MANAGEMENT
Planning and Control

Richard M. Lynch
Professor of Accountancy
University of Notre Dame

Robert W. Williamson
Associate Professor of Accountancy
University of Notre Dame

SECOND EDITION

McGRAW-HILL BOOK COMPANY
New York   St. Louis   San Francisco   Auckland
Düsseldorf   Johannesburg   Kuala Lumpur   London
Mexico   Montreal   New Delhi   Panama   Paris
São Paulo   Singapore   Sydney   Tokyo   Toronto

ACCOUNTING FOR MANAGEMENT
Planning and Control

34567890 **FGFG** 7987

This book was set in Bodoni Book
by Ruttle, Shaw & Wetherill, Inc.
The editors were J. S. Dietrich and Annette Hall;
the designer was Nicholas Krenitsky;
the production supervisor was Charles Hess.
Kingsport Press, Inc., was printer and binder.

Library of Congress Cataloging in Publication Data

Lynch, Richard M
    Accounting for management.

    Includes index.
    1. Costs, Industrial. 2. Cost control. I. Williamson, Robert W.,
joint author. II. Title.
HD47.L92   1976   657′.42   75-16432
ISBN   0-07-039217-X

CONTENTS

Theory of Pricing; Limitations of Marginal Analysis / Full Cost Pricing / *ROI Pricing; Full Cost Pricing and Government Regulation* / Contribution Approach to Pricing / *Differential Costs and Pricing; Relationship of Full-Cost and Contribution Pricing* / Transfer Prices / *Economics of Transfer Pricing; Transfer Price with an Outside Market; Transfer Price with No Outside Market; Dilemma of Transfer Pricing* / Summary / Key Words and Phrases / Discussion Questions / Problems.

PREFACE

Modern accounting renders its services to a wide variety of users: investors, government agencies, the public, and management of enterprises to mention but a few. Until recently, however, the immense potential of service to management has been relegated to the technical courses on cost accounting and budgeting in our college curricula.

The main objective of this book is to present to the undergraduate student, in an introductory manner, the usefulness of accounting for informing management decisions in the realm of planning and control. It is intended for use in a one-semester or one-quarter core course following a basic course in introductory financial accounting. Typically, it will precede the student's choice of a major. For one group of students it will add another element to the foundation of a major in accounting. For the larger group, however, it will be a terminal course in accounting as well as a bridge to broader, management-oriented courses.

In the light of this purpose, accounting technique is made subordinate to management uses of the end products of accounting analysis. A certain skill at accounting analysis is, of course, essential to effective management decision making. Hence, a second objective—to sharpen the analytical and problem-solving skill of the student—is placed in close conjunction with the first.

In summary, this book stresses two things: the acquisition on the part of students of substantive knowledge pertaining to the management functions of planning and control, and the increase of their intellectual skill at problem analysis.

In the area of substantive knowledge, students need to know something of the economics of management: how costs behave under various operating conditions; the techniques of constructing a detailed, comprehensive planning budget; cost-volume-profit relationships; the use of standard costs and flexible budgets in appraising performance in controlling costs; the meaning of variable costing and relevant costs; the kinds of motivational and human relations problems that are inevitably encountered in management planning and control; how management uses methods of quantitative analysis to appraise capital expenditure decisions; the practical uses of measures of return on capital.

Analytical skills are sharpened by rigorous problem materials involving concepts and subject matter impinging on a variety of management decisions. Included are such techniques as the determination of the break-even point under a variety of conditions; the organization of the parts of a planning budget and the projection of financial statements into the future; the analysis of cost factors to determine the nature and causes of variances from standards; the differentiation of relevant from irrelevant costs in arriving at decisions to replace equipment, make or buy, add or drop a product line; the application of certain quantitative techniques to the appraisal of capital expenditure proposals. Problems range from the most elementary to the CPA examination level of difficulty.

The material is organized into four sections. The first consists of three chapters which are introductory in nature. Chapters 2 and 3 are an exposition of basic cost concepts, the notion of cost flow, and all methods of cost determination. This section can be used as an introduction for students whose earlier accounting courses included no treatment of cost and manufacturing accounting, or as a brief review of such fundamentals for students who covered them previously.

The Section 1 may be by-passed if the instructor believes the student's background in the subject warrants it. However, the review contained in Chapter 2 will likely prove beneficial in any case. It has been the authors' classroom experience that costs are best explained and understood, at the outset at least, in a manufacturing context. This seems to result from the fact that the manufacturing enterprise is familiar and typifies the modern American business firm, that most of the pioneering developments of cost accounting concepts and techniques occurred in the manufacturing area, and that the manufacturing firm contains most of the elements of cost. The treatment of the flow of costs through a manufacturing company, then, together with the elaboration of the basic technique of input-output analysis, has invariably proved beneficial in establishing the foundation for what is to follow in the course.

Section 2 concerns planning. In Chapter 4 cost-volume-profit analysis is introduced, its relevance to profit planning is explained, and its limitations are pointed out. Chapter 5 elaborates the comprehensive budget process for detailed operational planning.

Section 3 focuses on control. In Chapter 6 the notion of standard costs is introduced. Cost factors are identified, and their influence on variances of actual from standard costs is analyzed. Chapter 7 builds the notion of flexible budgeting for cost control on the concepts of standard costs and the so-called fixed budget. Variance analysis is amplified to include the element of manufacturing overhead, with its fixed as well as variable cost components. Chapter 8 interprets cost control from a human and an organizational point of view. This vital subject, so long neglected in the technical accounting literature, is integral to the entire question of management planning and control. The authors believe that the problem of balancing the personal objectives of the members of the organization with company goals, coupled with the importance of the proper handling of motivational factors in the organizational environment, deserves as much attention as the quantitative aspects of planning and control. While an attempt has been made to write the entire book in a humanistic vein, this chapter attempts to focus specifically on the fundamental concepts of organizational behavior and their relevance to the particular problem of the measurement of management performance.

Section 4 examines a number of special decisions common to management in many segments of business and industry. Chapter 9 treats of the usefulness of variable costing analysis for certain fundamental decisions, stressing the importance of accuracy in the reporting of income. Chapter 10 applies the basic notion of return on investment to the motivation and measurement of management's performance in the various segments of a firm. Chapter 11 elaborates the concept of relevant costs, with emphasis on the analysis of the economic effects of such decisions as make or buy, replacement of equipment, adding or dropping a product line, acceptance of a special order. Chapter 12 discusses various techniques useful in making pricing decisions, with emphasis given to the economic factors involved. Chapter 13 examines alternative methods of analyzing the economic effects of capital expenditure decisions.

It is of the essence of the students' learning process in this course that problems be prepared and discussed by them. All discussion questions and problem materials have been classroom-tested and deemed effective for such purposes. A wide variety of business situations is included, and a spectrum of difficulty is available. Selected problems in each chapter (marked with a †) are solved for the student. The solutions for these problems appear after the glossary at the end of the text.

Members of the faculty and students at Marquette University, Boston College, and the University of Notre Dame have contributed valuable comments and insights, as well as actual materials, toward the improvement of the quality of this book. To attempt a complete listing of their names would certainly result in some inadvertent omissions which would be most unjust, so we offer to each and all, anonymously, a heartfelt thank-you.

There are, of course, some who deserve special mention. At Marquette, to both Walter Gast, who encouraged the undertaking of what at the time was a radical idea, and graduate assistant Hart Klee, who helped organize and administer the pilot course, an especially fond acknowledgment. To James O. Dunn at Boston College, whose cogent observations served to nourish a barely viable embryo, this grateful mention in the finished product. At Notre Dame, a sincere salute to Ray Powell, Chairman of the Department of Accountancy, and to Bill Gould and Vicki Allen, our course assistants.

The critical comments of Norton Bedford, Robert K. Jaedicke, and the late Charles E. Johnson were invaluable in shoring up many weak spots. Charles T. Horngren, whose ideas influenced ours before the thought of a book ever arose, was especially generous in his early encouragement and tough-minded comments.

We are especially indebted to Maxine Semprini and Sheryl Rossow for their patience and excellent work in typing the manuscript.

Numerous individuals and organizations have generously allowed the use of copyrighted material and are cited at appropriate places throughout the text. However, the following rate special appreciation: the American Institute of Certified Public Accountants; the Financial Executives Institute; Intercollegiate Case Clearing House; the National Association of Accountants; the Graduate School of Business Administration, Harvard University; Ernst and Ernst; Touche Ross; and Arthur Andersen and Company.

Richard M. Lynch
Robert W. Williamson

ACCOUNTING
FOR MANAGEMENT

INTRODUCTION

CHAPTER 1

ACCOUNTING ANALYSIS AND MANAGEMENT DECISION MAKING

THE PLAN OF THIS CHAPTER
Management accounting is a subject that is both practical and intellectually satisfying. Its structure is too complex to be reduced easily to simple terms. Our approach to understanding it, therefore, will be to take a close look at management—first as an economic function and then as an administrative one. Topics to be discussed are the following:

How accounting provides and analyzes economic information

The difference between a controller and a CPA

The role of cost accounting and the flow of costs

What costs are and what elements go into their making

ECONOMIC FUNCTION

Economics is the study of the way limited resources are used to produce and distribute commodities that satisfy needs. In a free society, the bulk of these activities is carried on by privately managed entities called business firms. The means of production are (1) natural resources, (2) accumulated capital, and (3) human effort (physical and mental).

Management attempts to put these means together in the combination that best satisfies all interested parties. These parties are:

1. *The users of the output of production* who are willing to pay a certain price

2. *The providers of the natural resources* who require a sufficient return on their money to extract further resources for future use

3. *The workers* who do the actual production and ask a fair compensation to satisfy their needs as family providers and consumers

4. *The savers* who provide the productive capital and expect a fair return on their investment

5. *Members of the general public* who are affected by the firm's production methods, advertising policies, and the exercise of its corporate citizenship

Management derives its legal right to manage a business from the delegated property rights of investors of ownership capital, that is, the stockholders of a corporation. In a profit-seeking enterprise, the effectiveness of management is measured ultimately by the profits realized. It is only from profits that owner-investors can be compensated for risking their capital. Profits also ensure jobs for workers, customers for suppliers of raw materials, and end products for consumers. Hence, management recognizes as its primary obligation the maximization of the firm's profits over the long term in a way that is consistent with its social responsibility.

The achievement of these economic goals carries with it both certain privileges and responsibilities for the future. The privileges are to continue in business as a going concern and to realize profits. The responsibilities are fourfold:

1. To continue to provide useful goods and services to customers at a price they are willing to pay

2. To continue to provide employees with jobs at an appropriate level of compensation

3. To preserve the financial well-being and the profit-making capacity of the firm in order to provide a fair return on its capital to the owners

4. To exercise its economic function with a "sensitive awareness of changing social values and priorities"[1]

---

[1] Committee for Economic Development, *Social Responsibility of Business Corporations*, Washington: 1971, p. 15.

The multiple nature of this responsibility is basic to management; failure to meet this responsibility in any of its aspects for a protracted period will affect the health of the firm and jeopardize its long-term ability to perform in its economic function as a going concern.

ADMINISTRATIVE FUNCTION

The administrative function of management develops from its economic function. Management activity centers on what is to be managed—the business firm. In the simplest but broadest terms, management *plans*, *organizes*, and *controls*. Each of these three activities encompasses a large number of complex and inter-related day-to-day actions, mostly intellectual in character.

In a going concern, these activities are usually carried on simultaneously, often under conditions of such urgency that the manager does not stop to answer his or her own unspoken question, "Which am I doing now—planning, organizing, or controlling?" Most of the specific actions taken by a manager will imply all three. Nevertheless, logically analyzed, all meaningful management actions rest on this tripod.

1. *Planning* consists in setting goals for the firm, both immediate and long range; considering the various means by which such goals may be achieved; and deciding which of any available alternative means would be best suited to the attainment of the goals sought under the conditions expected to prevail.

2. *Organizing* consists in deciding how best to put together the scarce human and nonhuman resources available to the firm, in some orderly fashion best suited to carrying out established plans.

3. *Controlling* consists in checking the performance of activities against the plan, noting deviations from it, and deciding what corrective action, if any, ought to be taken.

These three administrative activities have one thing in common: Each requires that *decisions* be made. Decision making is the motor that makes management go.

Decisions are of all kinds, and they are made at all levels of an organization. But whatever their form or impact, all decisions have two characteristics in common: (1) They involve choosing among available alternatives, and (2) they culminate in action (or meaningful nonaction) from which certain consequences flow.

Because a decision involves choosing, it follows that some rational activity has preceded it. The decision maker chooses what he or she perceives to be the greatest good in a given situation. Rational men and women appraise the various "goods" available for choice on the basis of the information provided by their minds. Thus, the better the information supplied by the mind, the better is the choice likely to be. Management—the decision maker—chooses a particular action because it believes the consequences will further the attainment of sought-after goals. Management, therefore, seeks constantly for the best available information concerning goals and the consequences of alternative actions.

ACCOUNTING PROVIDES ECONOMIC INFORMATION

Accounting has been described succinctly and accurately as "the measurement and communication of financial and economic data."[2] The accountant is the major channel through which quantitive information flows to management.

The position of the management accountant is unique with respect to information about the firm. Apart from top management, probably no one in the organization can know more about all the functions of a given business. The management accountant must gather information from every function, area, and level of the company. This person must also keep abreast of happenings outside the firm, in the business world.

However, gathering information is only the first step. The accountant must *analyze* it, that is, break it down, sift it out, and organize it into meaningful categories. The accountant must *evaluate* it, that is, decide first what is relevant and what is irrelevant, and discarding the irrelevant, rank the relevant according to its degree of importance to management. He or she must then *report* relevant information in an intelligible form, so that it will enlighten the decisions of responsible management and frequently those of interested persons outside the company as well. Thus it is clear that accountants are more than "reporters" of information—they "editorialize." In this way, they are able to influence the decision makers toward achieving better results.

CONTROLLER AND CERTIFIED PUBLIC ACCOUNTANT

The field of accounting is broad and diversified. Of the many different types of activity engaged in by persons trained in accounting, two stand out as major. The first is carried on by accountants who serve exclusively the firm employing them, and it is known as management accounting. The top management accounting executive in a firm is usually called the controller.[3] The other major type of accounting practice is an independent one, and it is carried on by certified public accountants who serve a wide variety of clients on accounting and management matters.

The difference between the work of the controller and that of the CPA (certified public accountant) in public practice is roughly the same as that between the chief legal counsel of a large corporation and the attorney conducting a private law practice. The controller, like the corporate legal counsel, devotes his or her entire time and energy to the needs of one company, the employer. The CPA, like the practicing attorney, serves many clients in an advisory and often confidential capacity. This role is that of an objective outsider, expressing expert opinion as to the financial condition and operating results of the clients'

[2] Herman W. Bevis, "The Accounting Function in Economic Progress," *Journal of Accountancy*, August 1958.

[3] The more archaic term "comptroller" is still used occasionally. For all practical purposes, the two terms have the same meaning.

business. Third parties, such as banks, government agencies, and stockholders, rely on the fairness of such financial reports by CPAs in making certain decisions about a given company.

For this reason, the CPA is bound by a set of rigid professional regulations, which include an examination on technical competence and adherence to a code of ethical conduct. As with other established professions whose activities involve the public interest, these standards are intended to inspire confidence in the work of the professional and to offer a measure of protection to those who rely upon it. In addition to auditing the clients' records and rendering an opinion on financial reports, the CPA also offers them advice on matters involving their income tax and problems concerning their internal systems of information and control.

Thus the CPA and the controller employ the same body of accounting knowledge in their work, but the emphasis with which it is applied varies according to the difference in the fundamental purpose of the two fields. The CPA, in pursuing the audit function, tends to emphasize the historical results of the client company as a whole. The controller, in addition to processing historical data, must supply a good deal of information concerning *future* operations, in line with management's planning needs. Besides serving top management with information concerning the company as a whole, this professional must supply detailed information to managers in different functional areas and at different levels of the organization.

In short, the type of service rendered by CPAs and controllers is geared to the needs of those being served. CPAs, although serving client management, must remember their principal responsibility to *third parties*. Controllers, although reporting frequently to various outsiders, must exert their greatest efforts toward the service of management *within their own organization*.

ROLE OF THE CONTROLLER

The role of the controller has been described in a most definitive manner by the Financial Executives Institute, a national organization whose membership consists of top-level financial and accounting executives. It emphasizes that the controller should be an integral part of management, performing duties in the following areas.

Planning

The controller should establish, coordinate, and administer an adequate plan for the control of the firm's operations. This plan would include profit planning, programs for capital investing, and financing, sales forecasts, expense budgets, and cost standards.

Control

The controller is expected to compare performance with operating plans and standards and to report and interpret the results of operations to all levels of management and to the owners of the business, through the compilation of appropriate accounting and statistical records and reports.

Other Information

The controller should consult with all segments of management responsible for policy or action. Such consultation might concern any phase of the operation of the business having to do with attainment of objectives and the effectiveness of policies, organization structure, and procedures. He or she is generally charged with the responsibility for the protection of the assets of the firm, both through proper internal controls and through insurance coverage. This responsibility generally extends also to tax matters, reporting to government agencies, and interpreting economic and social forces as they affect the business.[4]

ROLE OF COST ACCOUNTING

One of the important characteristics of the management accountant's work is concern with costs. This is a direct reflection of the central role played by costs in management's pursuit of the economic goals of the firm. Essentially, *cost consists in value forgone for the purpose of achieving some economic benefit which will promote the profit-making ability of the firm.*

Costs are generally reckoned in terms of cash (or its equivalent) expended to acquire bundles of various services capable of accomplishing the economic purposes of the company, for example:

The compensation of production employees for performing their assigned manufacturing operations provides a measure of the cost of direct labor.

Insurance cost is determined by the amount of the premium, which represents a measure of the cost of the service rendered by the insurance company in providing protection for the firm's assets.

When a building is purchased, the total value represented by the purchase price constitutes a measure of the cost of the services the building will render over its useful life.

Cost is the monetary measure of the value of economic services acquired by the firm. At any given time, costs can be either unexpired or expired. An unexpired cost represents *asset value*, or stored-up service potential to be realized as economic benefit in the future. When a cost expires, it becomes an *expense*, which is the measure of an economic service which was used up during a fiscal period and which helped produce the firm's revenue during that period. In the accounting sense, the measure of the net profit for a fiscal period is the excess of revenue realized in that period over the expenses incurred to produce that revenue.

Thus it is clear that costs are *tools of profit*, either as assets whose economic benefits lie in the future or as expenses whose economic benefits were realized in the production of past revenue.

Applied to the preceding three examples, the flow of costs is as follows:

The direct labor cost in a manufacturing company becomes part of the asset

---

[4] Adapted from "Concept of Modern Controllership" as defined by the Financial Executives Institute.

value of inventory, which expires and becomes expense when the manufactured goods are sold.

The insurance premium, usually paid in advance, buys protection for a specified period of time, and its service expires with the passage of time.

The cost of the building is the measure of the service of housing certain business operations over an extended period of time, and the expiration of these services is usually reckoned in terms of the passage of time.

Elements of Cost

One of the more difficult problems in the measurement and reporting of economic data has been the orderly classification of the almost-infinite variety of costs incurred by business and economic entities. One of the earliest of the management purposes served by accounting in developing cost information was income determination. In accordance with this purpose, costs are first classed according to *object*, i.e., the nature of the economic service being provided — such as wages of factory workers, rent of building, advertising, or office supplies.

Next, costs are collected into groups called *elements*. These elements are established in accordance with the broad economic functions common to many types of business activity, as mentioned at the beginning of the chapter. These functions include manufacturing (production), sales (distribution), and administration (management).

The interrelationship of the functions and their corresponding cost elements may be discerned in the operations of a manufacturing company. Throughout this book there will be a decided emphasis on the manufacturing firm for illustrative purposes. There are several reasons for this: (1) The manufacturing firm embodies most of the elements of cost; (2) it is widely regarded as typical of the modern American business enterprise; and (3) it has provided the historical framework within which modern management accounting concepts and techniques have been developed. It is believed that most of these fundamental concepts and techniques, once grasped in a manufacturing context, are readily transferable to nonmanufacturing environments, such as wholesale and retail trade, service industries, nonprofit institutions, and government agencies.

In the manufacturing firm, then, management combines various types of materials, machinery, tools, labor skills, and scientific techniques to produce an often-astonishing variety of goods capable of satisfying an ever-widening assortment of human needs and wants. The costs of the different factors needed to produce such goods, to sell them, and to administer the firm must be measured and reported in a manner which will enable management to regulate all factors in the interest of maximizing profits.

Exhibit 1-1 contains an analysis of the broad operating functions in a manufacturing firm; the cost elements which reflect their measurement in monetary terms; and a series of examples, by object, of the expense types which might be found in each. This arrangement of cost elements has evolved over the years into the conventional order in which costs are reported on the income statement, and it is generally acceptable for the purpose of income determination.

EXHIBIT 1-1
COST ELEMENTS IN A MANUFACTURING FIRM

Function	Cost Element	Examples of Expenses by Object
Manufacturing	Direct material	Raw materials; purchased parts
	Direct labor	Productive labor
	Factory overhead (or burden)	Indirect labor; factory supplies; expendable tools
		Inspection; supervision; maintenance; toolroom labor
		Heat; light; power
		Depreciation, machinery; material handling; factory engineering
Sales	Selling expense	Commissions; advertising; delivery expense; sales order writing
Administration	General and administrative expense	Officers' salaries; office salaries; office supplies; depreciation, office building
Extraoperational	Financial expense	Interest expense
	Income tax	Federal income tax expense

Relevant Costs

Income determination is but one of many information services rendered by the management accountant. The diversity of these services requires that he or she be able to distinguish the relevant from the irrelevant in the data he uses. "Relevant" means pertinent to, or having a direct bearing on, the matter at hand. Thus for the management accountant, relevant costs are indispensable tools of information service.

Management accountants have at their command a knowledge of the basic cost structure of the company; they know intimately the different management problems and the cost concepts which may apply to them; they know the methods for data analysis which are likely to be pertinent to the decisions which confront management. In any problem situation, then, management accountants must construct their cost analyses to suit the nature of the problem involved. *The relevance of the cost and other data used will be determined by the purpose management is seeking to achieve.* One author sums it up thus: "We need different cost constructions and different income concepts for different purposes — a *relevant costing* approach."[5]

ILLUSTRATIVE EXAMPLES

Perhaps a few examples of problems involving the use of management accounting cost analysis will help to clarify the purpose and scope of this book. Consider each of the following problems which management might encounter:

[5] Charles T. Horngren, *Cost Accounting: A Managerial Emphasis*, Englewood Cliffs, N.J.: Prentice-Hall, Inc., 1962.

1. *Inventory valuation.*   Management wants to know the fair value to place upon its ending inventory of finished goods so as to report an acceptable asset value on the balance sheet and a proper figure for net income on the income statement.

2. *Profit planning.*   Management wants to know what profit it can plan on earning next year in view of an anticipated drop of 10 percent in sales volume.

3. *Cost control.*   Management wants to know the reason for a sharp increase in the cost of operating its assembly department in October over September.

4. *Return on capital.*   Management wants to know whether the plant manager of plant A is earning an adequate profit on operations.

5. *Make or buy.*   Management wants to know whether it would be better, in terms of profit improvement, to subcontract a manufactured part which the company is presently making.

6. *Special order.*   Management wants to know whether it would be profitable to accept a special order for one of its products at a lower price than that customarily charged.

7. *Dropping a product line.*   Management wants to know whether or not to eliminate from its line a product which, according to income statement figures, is losing money.

8. *Capital expenditures.*   Management wants to know whether or not to invest a substantial sum of money in a piece of labor-saving equipment which promises to lower the direct labor cost in production appreciably.

It will be the purpose of the remainder of the book to explore some of the ways in which management accounting can help management to reach profitable decisions in problem situations such as those just suggested. It may be helpful at this point to demonstrate, very briefly and simply, the type of approach which might be used in some of these management problems.

Inventory Valuation

Assume the following costs to have been incurred in the year 19x1 to produce 100,000 units of product A:

Direct material	$ 80,000
Direct labor	50,000
Factory overhead	70,000
Total cost to manufacture	$200,000

The cost to produce a single unit is determined to be

$$\$200,000/100,000 = \$2$$

A count of the finished goods in the shipping department at the end of 19x1 revealed 10,000 units of product A on hand in inventory. It was decided that the unit cost of $2—the average cost during the year—would be a fair basis for valuing the ending inventory. The value of finished goods inventory shown on the balance sheet at the end of 19x1 was thus determined to be

10,000 units, product A
  ×$2
$20,000

Management's Purpose   To present a fair value for the finished goods inventory on the balance sheet (this figure is an integral factor in the determination of cost of goods sold and therefore net income as well).

Relevant Cost   The unit manufacturing cost, based on the total manufacturing costs actually incurred during the period.

Decision   To value finished goods ending inventory at $2 per unit.

Profit Planning

Consider a filling-station operator who leases a station, sells only gasoline, employs one helper, and had the following income statement for the year 19x1:

Net sales (1 million gal @ $0.45)		$450,000
Cost of gasoline (including taxes and		
delivery of 1 million gal @ $0.38)		380,000
Gross margin		$ 70,000
Other expenses:		
Rent on station	$ 4,800	
Wages (self and one helper)	20,000	
Other	10,200	
Total other expenses		35,000
Net income for year		$ 35,000

Assume further that, because of increased competition in the locality, the operator expects to sell 10 percent fewer gallons of gasoline in 19x2. The other expenses are not expected to change. In making plans for 19x2, the operator sets up the following data in income statement form:

Net sales (900,000 gal @ $0.45)	$405,000
Cost of gasoline (900,000 gal @ $0.38)	342,000
Gross margin	$ 63,000
Other expenses	35,000
Net income for year	$ 28,000

Management's Purpose   To determine the effect of a 10 percent drop in volume on its planned profit for the coming year, and to consider possible remedies.

Relevant Costs   Costs which change as a result of a change in volume (variable), and costs which tend to remain stable as volume fluctuates (fixed).

Decision It is unlikely that the station operator can either increase prices (competition would prevent this) or reduce the cost of gasoline (a variable cost). The operator might try to recruit new customers by offering inducements other than lower prices, by expanding his activities to include selling items besides gas, and by cutting his fixed costs. He decides to find a way to cut $1,000 out of fixed costs other than rent and wages, and to take on a line of tires, batteries, and accessories.

Cost Control

Assume that a manufacturer of window shades operates, among other production departments, a department for the assembly and packing of finished shades. The supervisor of this department is required to control costs within the limits of a budget established before the beginning of a month's operations. The assembly department supervisor agrees that she should be able to control certain costs incurred in the department as follows:

Direct material (cartons) used: one per shade, plus 5 percent scrap

Direct labor time (i.e., efficiency): 3 worker-hours per shade at $4 per hour

Factory overhead costs: indirect labor, $1.50 per shade; indirect material, $2 per shade

In September, the assembly supervisor incurred costs only $25 over her budget. In October, however, she finished and packed 1,000 shades with the following cost results:

Direct material (1,010 cartons @ $0.50)	$ 505
Direct labor (3,400 worker-hours @ $4)	13,600
Indirect labor (1,000 shades @ $1.70)	1,700
Indirect material (1,000 shades @ $1.90)	1,900
Total controllable costs incurred	$17,705

The management accountant analyzes the control of assembly department costs for October as follows:

	Controllable Costs Incurred	Budget Allowance*	(Over) Under Budget
Direct material	$ 505	$ 525	$ 20
Direct labor	13,600	12,000	(1,600)
Indirect labor	1,700	1,500	(200)
Indirect material	1,900	2,000	100
Total controllable costs	$17,705	$16,025	$(1,680)

*Budget allowances determined as follows:
1,000 shades produced:

Direct material (1,000 + 5% scrap = 1,050 @ $0.50)	$ 525
Direct labor (1,000 units @ 3 = 3,000 worker-hours @ $4)	12,000
Indirect labor (1,000 units @ $1.50)	1,500
Indirect material (1,000 units @ $2)	2,000

Management's Purpose To set limits within which responsible managers are expected to control costs properly assigned to them, and to measure actual performance against these preestablished standards.

Relevant Costs Controllable costs incurred compared with budgeted standard costs.

Decision Interpretation of the cost difference from budget indicates that the assembly supervisor did a good job of controlling direct material usage (allowed carton usage, 1,050; used, 1,010; savings on 40 cartons at 50 cents each, $20) and indirect material usage (allowed, $2 per shade; incurred, $1.90 each; savings on 1,000 shades, $100). It seems that direct labor efficiency lagged significantly (allowed hours, 3,000; hours used, 3,400; excess, 400 hours at $4, $1,600). Finally, indirect labor was incurred at a higher-than-standard rate (allowed, $1.50 per shade; incurred, $1.70 each; excess on 1,000 shades, $200). The supervisor will be commended for good material usage; she will be asked to explain the cause of poor labor performance; and she will be admonished to correct the cause as soon as possible.

Return on Capital

Assume that Mr. A. is the general manager of Division X of the Apex Manufacturing Company. His divisional income statement shows a net income of $100,000 on sales of $1 million in 19x1. The consolidated income statement for the Apex Company shows a net income of $1 million on sales of $10 million for the same period. Thus in both cases the percentage of net income to net sales is 10 percent. The Apex Company has total operating assets of $5 million, of which $2 million is invested in Division X. The management accountant analyzes the results thus:

	Division X	Apex Company
Net sales	$1,000,000	$10,000,000
Net income	100,000	1,000,000
Percentage of net income to net sales	10%	10%
Operating assets used	2,000,000	5,000,000
Turnover of assets in sales (net sales/operating assets)	0.5 times	2.0 times
Return on operating assets (percent net income to net sales times asset turnover)	5%	20%

Management's Purpose To appraise the effectiveness of Mr. A.'s performance in attaining profit goals in line with those of the company.

Relevant Costs Cost controllable by and identified with Division X; total Apex Company operating costs. Also relevant factors: net sales, Division X and total company; operating assets assigned to and usable by Division X; total company operating assets.

Decision Evaluation of percentage of net income to net sales indicates that Division X performance is equal only to that of the company as a whole. When related to the comparative investment in operating assets of Division X and total company, however, it is apparent that divisional performance falls far short of total company performance (5 percent return compared with 20 percent return on assets used). Since the cause lies in a slow turnover of assets in the sales of Division X, it may be decided that there is considerable idle capacity and that investment in this division could be reduced without affecting the volume or profitability of its sales. Accordingly, a portion of Division X fixed asset investment is liquidated; and Mr. A. is advised to reduce inventories, to put pressure on the collection of receivables, and to increase sales promotion in an effort to increase sales volume to fill unused capacity.

Special Order

Assume that the B Manufacturing Company, makers of a specialized line of toys, receives an order for 2,000 units of a certain type of truck from a large mail-order house at a price of $3 per unit. The B Company sells this type of truck to its other customers at $5 each, but its present operating volume is low, and it could take on the special order without impairing its regular operations for the coming month. Its income statement for the preceding month shows:

Net sales (10,000 units @ $5)	$50,000
Costs:	
Direct material ($1.50/unit)	15,000
Direct labor ($1/unit)	10,000
Factory overhead	10,000
Selling and administrative	10,000
Total costs	$45,000
Net profit	$ 5,000

The management accountant, in analyzing the costs, reasons that direct material and direct labor costs will have to be incurred on the special order at the same amount per unit as for the regular line, and that $500 will have to be spent for special tooling to meet the specifications of the mail-order house. Since the company is operating below normal capacity, and because the sale to the mail-order house will not require the payment of sales commissions, the accountant concludes that no additional factory overhead, selling, or administrative costs will be incurred if the order is accepted.

Management's Purpose To utilize idle capacity and to maximize profits.

Relevant Costs Incremental (or differential) costs, i.e., those which must be incurred as a result of taking on an additional piece of business, that would be avoided if that piece of business were forgone. Costs which do not differ between the two alternatives are therefore irrelevant.

Decision   Other qualitative factors favoring it, the order should be accepted, because it maximizes profits. The analysis shows:

	Present Operations	Special Order	Revised Operations
Net sales (10,000 @ $5; 2,000 @ $3)	$50,000	$6,000	$56,000
Costs:			
Direct material ($1.50/unit)	15,000	3,000	18,000
Direct labor ($1/unit)	10,000	2,000	12,000
Factory overhead (plus special tooling)	10,000	500	10,500
Selling and administrative	10,000		10,000
Total costs	$45,000	$5,500	$50,500
Net profit	$ 5,000	$ 500	$ 5,500

The three-column analysis is helpful, but the relevant costs are to be found in the middle, or "special order," column. Therein are found the revenue and cost factors which are the difference between the two alternatives, and the positive net profit indicates that the order will contribute to the overall net profit of the company for the period. Other factors, such as the likely effect on the price to regular customers and the possibility of future business from the mail-order house, will likewise influence the final decision.

The foregoing examples are merely indicative of the variety of ways in which accounting cost analysis — suiting different costs to different purposes — may be useful in assisting management to make informed decisions.

ART VERSUS SCIENCE IN MANAGEMENT

Management is said to be an art because business operates in a changing world, fraught with uncertainty. On the other hand, there has arisen in the past few decades a system of concepts and techniques based on mathematics, statistics, and accounting that has come to be called "management science." Generally speaking, the *science* of management seeks to organize the *quantitative* factors of a business decision, while the *art* of management consists in weighing the *qualitative* factors in the scale of the manager's judgment, experience, and insight to produce the best decision in the circumstances.

If management functioned in a world of *complete uncertainty*, any decision would be difficult to make however well developed the art, and quantitative analysis would be of little assistance. Fortunately, such is not the case. Human behavior is somewhat predictable — history does repeat itself, and thus many useful quantitative data are available. Sales managers plan their marketing campaigns and engineers design the automobiles, shoes, detergents, furniture, and washing machines in anticipation of what they believe large numbers of people want to buy.

Because of the predictability of many of the factors which impinge upon the business decision, it has been suggested that ultimately all factors in a business decision might be quantified. This idea postulates a world of *perfect certainty*, in which quantitative indices could be developed to cover all conceivable situations, and any business decision could rest on the secure basis of quanti-tative analysis.

Perfect certainty remains a myth, however. One need but recall how in-adequately prepared the automobile industry was for the large-scale shift in consumer preference to compact cars in the middle 1950s and again in the late 1960s and early 1970s, a fact which underscored the presence of a substantial degree of uncertainty in a generally stable and well-managed industry and which served to catapult American Motors and Volkswagen to new heights of economic stature.

The importance of quantitative analysis in management, then, lies not in the elimination of uncertainty, but in *minimizing* its weight in a problem. The greater the number of factors which can be quantified, the greater the attention management is able to devote to those which cannot be quantified. Although it remains doubtful that uncertainty can ever be eliminated, there are no apparent limits to the possibility of reducing its unfavorable effects in decision making.

Herein lies the challenge to the management accountant:

To establish systems of information and control within the business organi-zation

To provide relevant information for all functions and levels of management within the organization

To master existing techniques of analysis and develop new, improved meth-ods which will narrow still further the boundaries of uncertainty in manage-ment decision making

For this process to be sucessful, two other conditions are essential:

The *management accountant* must strive constantly to increase his or her own insight into management problems.

The *manager* must strive to understand the uses of the management accoun-tant's analysis in informing and improving management decisions.

SUMMARY

Management performs an administrative function which develops from its eco-nomic function. Management must engage in planning, organizing, and control-ling. *Planning* means setting goals for the firm, considering various ways of meeting those goals, and picking out what appears to be the best way to meet the goals. *Organizing* means putting together the economic resources of the firm in the way best suited to carrying out established plans. *Controlling* means evalu-ating the firm's activities against the plan and deciding what should be done if the plan is not being followed.

Accounting provides information to management so that planning, organiz-ing, and controlling can be done in an orderly and rational manner. The manage-ment accountant must provide a system which allows management to receive this necessary information in a useful form. The top management accountant, the controller, is thus responsible for gathering, analyzing, evaluating, and reporting data.

The management accountant characteristically is concerned with costs. Cost consists in value forgone for the purpose of achieving some economic benefit which will promote the profit-making ability of the firm. Costs are tools of profit, either as assets whose economic benefits lie in the future (unexpired costs) or as expenses whose economic benefits were realized in the production of past revenues (expired costs).

Management relies on accounting data to supply information helpful in a wide range of decisions—a few of which were illustrated in this chapter. An important part of the management accountant's responsibilities is to determine what information is relevant to specific management decisions.

KEY WORDS AND PHRASES

planning   cost
organizing   unexpired cost
controlling   expired cost
controller   relevant cost
CPA

DISCUSSION QUESTIONS

1. Distinguish between the economic function and the administrative function of management.
2. What are the basic means of production in the economic order?
3. Is it sufficient, from the economic standpoint, for management to pay a wage high enough to satisfy the wishes of its employees? Why?
4. How important is profit in meeting the economic goals of a free society?
5. What is the meaning of planning as a management function?
6. What is the meaning of organizing as a management function?
7. What is the meaning of controlling as a management function?
8. It has been said that the job of management is to make decisions. What does this mean?
9. What is the essential relation between information and decision making?
10. What has accounting to do with management?
11. In drawing the analogy between the journalist and the accountant, it is noted that accountants do not merely "report" information to management—they "editorialize." Does this responsibility give the accountant the somewhat dangerous power to "manage the news"—to decide what facts to provide and what to withhold? Discuss the implications of the accountant's function in this area.
12. Why is it necessary to make a distinction between management accounting and general (financial) accounting?
13. Does the CPA, by virtue of membership in a recognized profession, belong to a higher order of accountant than his or her counterpart in management?
14. How does controllership serve management?
15. Why are costs important to the management accountant?
16. In what way are costs different before and after they expire?

17. What is the basic scheme which underlies the accountant's grouping of cost elements?
18. What determines the relevancy of costs?
19. Distinguish between "art" and "science" in management.
20. The accountant's record-keeping function has long been regarded by many as a "necessary evil." If the art of management is essential and enduring, is there any real need for the management accountant's function?
21. Is it likely that the science of management will ever become so perfect as to eliminate the need for the art? Why?

CHAPTER

2

COST DETERMINATION AND FLOW

THE PLAN OF THIS CHAPTER
How are costs, particularly in a manufacturing firm, determined? To answer this question we shall explore the following topics in this chapter:

Costs for a manufacturing firm compared with those for a merchandising concern

The flow of costs through a manufacturing firm and how they are measured

Sources of cost information

The special problems in accounting for factory overhead and the use of predetermined rates

The accumulation of costs by centers of activity and the use of departmental rates

MERCHANDISING AND MANUFACTURING COMPARED

In the study of elementary accounting, it is customary to use the merchandising firm as the entity by which to introduce the subject, because its operations are basically simple.

A manufacturing firm is similar to the merchandising firm in the function of selling goods. To the extent that it must apply productive human effort, through the medium of equipment and tools, to the conversion of materials to suit the specific needs of its customers, it is considerably more complex. Hence the costs in a manufacturing firm are more numerous and varied than those in a merchandising firm, with the result that the form for reporting manufacturing net income is also more complex.

Exhibit 2-1 shows a conventional form of income statement for a merchandising firm, A Stores, Inc. Exhibit 2-2 does likewise for a manufacturing firm, X Manufacturing Company. The latter is distinctive in its cost of goods sold section in two respects:

The input of three cost elements—direct material, direct labor, and factory overhead—is required in contrast to a single element—purchases of merchandise—in the case of A Stores.

There are three classes of inventory—raw materials, work in process, and finished goods—in X Manufacturing, but only one—merchandise inventory—in A Stores.

EXHIBIT 2-1
A STORES, INC.
Income Statement
For the Month Ended January 31, 19x1

Net sales		$70,500
Cost of goods sold:		
Merchandise inventory, 1/1/x1	$10,000	
Add: Net purchases—merchandise	55,000	
Cost of goods available for sale	$65,000	
Less: Merchandise inventory, 1/31/x1	5,000	
Cost of goods sold		60,000
Gross margin on sales		$10,500
Operating expenses:		
Selling expenses	$ 1,500	
Administrative expenses	2,500	
Total operating expenses		4,000
Income from operations		$ 6,500
Interest expense		500
Income before taxes		$ 6,000
Income tax expense		3,000
Net income		$ 3,000

In all other respects, the reporting of net income is the same for the two types of business.

Exhibit 2-3 demonstrates schematically the essential sameness of the two operating cycles in terms of the flow of current assets through the business. In both cases, cash is expended to acquire the goods which will be sold to customers; these goods, in turn, are converted to receivables upon being sold; the cycle back to cash is completed by the collection of receivables.

The basic difference between the two types of business lies in the fact that, in the manufacturing firm, cash is expended not only for the purchase of materials but also for direct labor payrolls and all the many and varied factory over-

EXHIBIT 2-2
X MANUFACTURING COMPANY
Income Statement
For the Month Ended January 31, 19x1

Net sales			$58,500
Cost of goods sold:			
Raw materials inventory, 1/1/x1		$ 5,000	
Add: Net purchases		21,000	
Cost of material available		$26,000	
Less: Raw materials inventory, 1/31/x1		3,000	
Cost of direct material used		$23,000	
Direct labor		7,500	
Factory overhead;			
Indirect labor	$9,400		
Factory supplies	2,000		
Factory rent	3,000		
Depreciation	600	15,000	
Manufacturing costs incurred		$45,500	
Add: Work in process inventory, 1/1/x1		8,500	
Cost of work in process		$54,000	
Less: Work in process inventory, 1/31/x1		4,000	
Cost of goods manufactured		$50,000	
Add: Finished goods inventory, 1/1/x1		7,000	
Cost of goods available for sale		$57,000	
Less: Finished goods inventory, 1/31/x1		9,000	
Cost of goods sold			48,000
Gross margin on sales			$10,500
Operating expenses:			
Selling expenses		$ 1,000	
Administrative expenses		3,000	
Total operating expenses			4,000
Income from operations			$ 6,500
Interest expense			500
Income before taxes			$ 6,000
Income tax expense			3,000
Net income			$ 3,000

I. MERCHANDISING

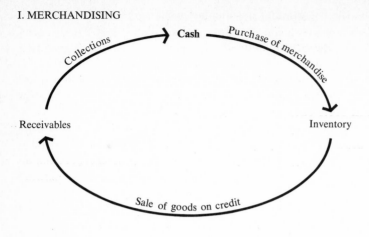

II. MANUFACTURING

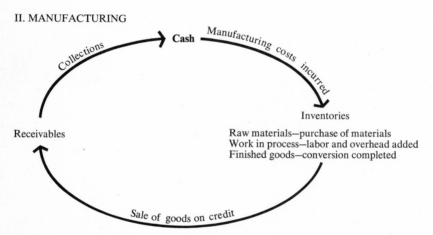

EXHIBIT 2-3 Flow of current assets through the operating cycle of business

head expenses incurred in the production process. The sum of all such cash expenditures for the incurrence of manufacturing costs represents investment in an asset—the three classes of inventory—until the time of sale.

COST ELEMENTS FOR PRODUCT COSTING

Manufacturing costs are usually accumulated in a form which facilitates product costing for income determination and inventory valuation. The major elements of manufacturing costs are direct material, direct labor, and factory overhead (or burden).

The term "direct" used in connection with material and labor is understood to mean "directly identified with the manufactured product." Generally speaking, if a material becomes part of the finished product, it is considered *direct material.*[1] Likewise, if a productive worker performs an operation directly on any part of the product which contributes to its finished form, it is considered *direct labor.* These two direct production costs, material and labor, are often referred to as the *prime cost.*

Factory overhead is a summary classification which includes a wide variety of other expenses incurred in connection with operating the factory. It may include indirect payroll costs such as the wages and salaries of machine helpers, inspectors, truckers, timekeepers, maintenance employees, toolroom employees, shipping department employees, guards, supervisors, and superintendents. It will also include a great many costs of the non-payroll type, such as rent on the factory building; machinery depreciation; heat, light, and power; factory supplies; property taxes; and insurance.

The sum of direct labor and factory overhead is frequently referred to as *conversion cost.* This term is based on the notion that manufacturing activity is undertaken to convert raw materials and component parts into useful products and that the cost of providing the facilities (factory overhead) and human productive effort (direct labor) is actually the cost of such conversion.

To summarize, then, the basic terminology applying to elements of manufacturing costs may be viewed thus:

$$\text{Prime cost}\begin{cases}\text{Direct material} \\ \text{Direct labor} \\ \text{Factory overhead (or burden)}\end{cases}\text{Conversion cost}$$

It should be noted that direct labor is a component of both prime cost and conversion cost, so one may conclude that these two convenient terms should never be used simultaneously with reference to the same set of cost elements.

FLOW OF COSTS

Production typically takes place in a three-stage cycle. To secure the most accurate costing of products possible, the flow of costs is traced through each of these three stages. In the first, purchased materials are received and stored in the stores warehouse. Stage 2 begins when needed materials are introduced into the manufacturing process (i.e., requisitioned from stores into the factory) and the performance of productive operations is begun. The final stage is accomplished when finished units of product are transferred from the factory to the finished goods warehouse to await shipment to customers.

For costing purposes, measuring points are established to coincide with each of the three stages. At any given time the cost of materials remaining at the first stage of production, not yet introduced into manufacturing, is recorded as stores (i.e., the raw materials inventory account). Upon delivery to the producing

---

[1] Exception is made to this rule if the item in question is so small that its cost in the finished product is insignificant or extremely difficult to measure. Therefore, screws, nuts, welding materials, electroplating materials, and the like are often classed as supplies (indirect materials) even though they actually become part of the finished product.

departments at the beginning of the second stage of production, the cost of the requisitioned materials is transferred to work in process (likewise an inventory account). There it will be combined with direct labor and factory overhead costs. When all production is completed and the finished units arrive at the third stage of production, which is the finished goods warehouse, their cost is transferred from work in process to finished goods inventory.

It is important to note that at all three stages of the cycle, the costs are still regarded as unexpired (each of the three accounts used to trace the flow of costs is an *inventory* account). It is not until the finished goods are shipped (i.e., sold) that the costs *expire* and take the form of *expense* as cost of goods sold.

Input-Output Analysis

A simple form of "input-output" analysis, similar to that used to determine cost of goods sold for income statement purposes, will facilitate the description of the flow of costs through the three stages of the production cycle.

Take a simple, familiar example: If the gas in the tank of your car is getting low, you stop at a filling station. You tell the attendant to "fill 'er up." If the capacity of the tank is 20 gallons, then 20 gallons is the amount of gas available when the tank is full. If you have 2 gallons left in the tank when you stop, the input will be 18 gallons.

Suppose you plan to make a trip and wish to check average gas mileage. Upon arrival at your destination, you will fill the tank again. This second input should be a close measure of the output of gas consumed on the trip. Suppose the filling at the end of the trip amounts to 15 gallons. This indicates an unconsumed balance of 5 gallons in the tank at the end of the trip. By using simple input-output analysis, you can determine the gas consumed on the trip in the same way in which a merchant determines the cost of goods sold, thus:

Beginning balance in tank	2 gal
Add: Fill at beginning of trip (input)	18 gal
Amount available (full tank)	20 gal
Less: Balance in tank—end of trip	5 gal
Gas consumed on trip (output)	15 gal

This simple method of analysis is useful for many applications in management accounting. In its general form, it proceeds from beginning to ending balance thus:

Beginning balance
Add: Input

Amount available

Less: Output

Ending balance

Obviously, if any three of the four basic factors (input, output, beginning balance, and ending balance) are known, the fourth can be determined. By rearranging the factors slightly, then, the cost of materials used (i.e., the output factor for stores) is determined thus:

GENERAL FORM	SPECIFIC: STAGE 1—STORES
Beginning inventory	Stores—beginning balance
Add: Input	Add: Purchases
Available	Cost of material available
Less: Ending inventory	Less: Stores—ending balance
Output	Cost of material used

For factory operations the specific factors would be:

GENERAL FORM	SPECIFIC: STAGE 2—FACTORY
Beginning inventory	Work in process—beginning balance
Add: Input	Add: Cost of material used
	Direct labor
	Factory overhead
Available	Cost of work in process
Less: Ending inventory	Less: Work in process—ending balance
Output	Cost of goods manufactured

It should be noted that the cost flow from the first to the second stage of the production cycle is the cost of material used. If stores and the factory were separate companies, the cost of material used would be the cost of goods sold (output) for stores and purchases (one of the input factors) for the factory.

For the finished goods stage, the specific factors in the input-output formula are as follows:

GENERAL FORM	SPECIFIC: STAGE 3—FINISHED GOODS
Beginning inventory	Finished goods—beginning balance
Add: Input	Add: Cost of goods manufactured
Available	Cost of goods available for sale
Less: Ending inventory	Less: Finished goods—ending balance
Output	Cost of goods sold

Again, if the factory and finished goods warehouse were separate companies, the output for the factory (cost of goods manufactured) would be the input factor for finished goods, as if the factory had purchased the goods from another company.

Output at this third stage is the cost of goods sold for the company as a whole and marks the point at which the product costs expire and become expenses of the period in which the products were sold.

The schematic view of the flow of manufacturing costs through a manu-

EXHIBIT 2-4
X MANUFACTURING COMPANY
Schematic View of Flow of Costs through a Manufacturing Plant

Unexpired Costs (Inventory)

	Stage 1 Stores Warehouse	Stage 2 Factory Operations	Stage 3 Finished Goods Warehouse	Sale of Finished Goods (Point of Cost Expiration)	Expired Costs (Cost of Goods Sold, Jan.)
A.					
Formula:					
Beginning inventory	Jan. 1 balance $ 5,000	Jan. 1 balance $ 8,500	Jan. 1 balance $ 7,000		
Input	Mat. purchases 21,000	Mat. used $23,000 / Dir. labor 7,500 / Fac. overhead 15,000 = 45,500	Cost of goods mfd. 50,000		
Available	Cost of mat. avail. $26,000	Cost of work in process $54,000	Cost of goods av. for sale $57,000		
Ending inventory	Jan. 31 balance 3,000	Jan. 31 balance 4,000	Jan. 31 balance 9,000		
Output	Cost of mat. used $23,000	Cost of goods mfd. $50,000	Cost of goods sold $48,000		→ $48,000

B.
T-Account Illustration:

Stores		Work in Process		Finished Goods		Cost of Goods Sold	
1/1 $ 5,000	Mat. into production 1/31 $23,000	1/1 $ 8,500	Goods completed 1/31 $50,000	1/1 $ 7,000	Goods sold 1/31 $48,000	1/31 $48,000	
Purchases 21,000		Mat. 23,000		Cost of goods mfd. 50,000			
	3,000	Labor 7,500		9,000			
		Overhead 15,000	4,000				

facturing plant, in three stages, is shown in Exhibit 2-4. The movement of costs from one stage to the next is also portrayed in Exhibit 2-4 by means of T-accounts, a familiar accounting device.

With the earlier example of X Manufacturing Company, activity for the month of January 19x1, is reflected in the following facts:

Inventories at January 1:	
Stores	$ 5,000
Work in process	8,500
Finished goods	7,000
Input:	
Material purchases	21,000
Direct labor payroll	7,500
Factory overhead	15,000
Inventories at January 31:	
Stores	3,000
Work in process	4,000
Finished goods	9,000

In Exhibit 2-4 it can be seen that the cost flow for the X Company can be traced step by step from the raw material stage to cost of goods sold simply by inserting the above data in the input-output formula for each stage of the production cycle and determining the unknown output factor of each. Each output, in turn, becomes input for the following stage.

For example, the output of stores (cost of material used, $23,000) is transferred to the factory (work in process), where it is combined with the other input factors (direct labor, $7,500; and factory overhead, $15,000). Next, the output for the factory (cost of goods manufactured, $50,000) is transferred to finished goods warehouse, where it becomes the input factor. The final step is the transfer of $48,000 (output) from finished goods inventory to cost of goods sold.

SOURCES OF COST INFORMATION

The determination of product costs is the job of cost accounting. The cost accountant must understand the physical flow of production and then establish efficient means of recording and analyzing cost information which reflects accurately this production activity. The first step is to gather information from its source, which identifies it as belonging to one of the three manufacturing cost elements, that is, according to its nature and function in the production process.

Information as to quantities and prices paid for the raw materials and parts is found on the purchase invoices which suppliers send in connection with shipments of such materials. This purchase information, *together with the cost of freight on the shipment* (freight in), constitutes the basis for the determination of direct material cost. A simplified sample invoice is shown in Exhibit 2-5. Such invoices are usually prepared with several copies. One copy would be mailed

EXHIBIT 2-5
SALES INVOICE

Invoice

Sherman Steel Warehouse, Inc.
809 South Ferrous Blvd.
Steelvale, Maryland

No. 1386

Date: March 13, 19 —

Terms: Net 30 Days

Sold to: X Manufacturing Co.
987 South 6th Street
Factorytown, Maryland

Item	Size	Description	Quantity	Unit Price	Amount
X916	36" × 48"	12 ga. 1014 carbon steel sheets	1,200 lb	0.082/lb	$ 98.40
L242	24" × 96"	20 ga. 1050 carbon steel sheets	2,000 lb	0.085/lb	170.00
A2140	1" × 200"	24 ga. 1160 carbon steel — coil	800 lb	0.100/lb	80.00
		Total			$348.40

to the X Company's accounting department, where prices and quantities would be compared with the original order and the extensions and additions would be recomputed. Another copy would be included with the goods shipped, so that the X Company's receiving department could verify quantities and the condition of the goods. Additional copies of the invoice would be retained by the supplier for its records.

Information concerning the movement of direct material into production is recorded on a stores requisition. When notified of the production schedule, the supervisor of the department where the material will receive its first processing will ordinarily fill in the prescribed requisition form, designating the department, the production order number, and the specification, description, and quantity of the materials that will be needed to meet this schedule. The storeskeeper, when issuing the material, will confirm the quantities issued and send a copy of the requisition to the cost accounting department. When the cost department has applied the proper price to the quantities on the requisition, the information for direct material cost is available. A simplified sample stores requisition is shown in Exhibit 2-6.

Information for the direct labor cost in production is conveyed by means of the worker's timecard. Each employee working on productive operations will record daily the amount of time spent on each lot of product, according to the operation performed and the department in which it took place. The cost department will usually summarize this information weekly when the worker's pay

EXHIBIT 2-6
STORES REQUISITION

	X Manufacturing Company Stores Requisition			
Date _____			Number _____	
Production Order No. _____				
Store No. _____			Department _____	
Specification	Description	Quantity	Unit Price	Total
	Total			
I have received the above material. Signed _____			Authorized by: _____ Department Supervisor	

is determined and will distribute the direct labor cost thus calculated to the products and departments indicated. A simplified sample of a timecard is shown in Exhibit 2-7.

EXHIBIT 2-7
TIMECARD

Name _____ Date _____
Clock No. _____
Department _____

Clock Time	Elapsed Time		Job. No.	Operation
		Stop		
		Start		
		Stop		
		Start		
		Stop		
		Start		
		Stop		
		Start		
		Stop		
		Start		

Job. No.	Hours	Rate		Cost
Total				

Information for factory overhead derives from a number of sources, in view of the great variety of types of cost which make it up. Indirect material and expendable tools, for instance, will be reported first on purchase invoices and then on requisitions, in the same way as direct material. Indirect labor, inspection, maintenance labor, and all the other forms of the payroll type of overhead will be reported on timecards in one form or another. Invoices from utilities, outside contractors, taxing bodies, etc., provide appropriate information, and depreciation charges are generally found on worksheets prepared previously by the accounting department. Essentially, all cost information flows from its source to cost records via some variation of the few simple documents described herein.

Accumulation in Accounting Records

Subsidiary ledgers may be kept for the elements of manufacturing cost, depending on the degree of detail desired in a given company. For instance, there may be hundreds of different types of direct material used in manufacturing a firm's product line. A stores ledger will provide a page for each type of material and part, with the total of all direct material balances reflected in the stores control account in the general ledger.

In lieu of subsidiary-ledger treatment for direct labor, information is more often accumulated in the form of a direct labor distribution, which summarizes labor cost according to product and department. A brief description of the flow of direct labor, along with direct material and factory overhead, costs through the general ledger accounts will be given later in the chapter.

The most common way of handling the various types of overhead cost consists in recording them in individual accounts according to object in a factory overhead expense subsidiary ledger. The total of the accounts in this ledger is shown as the balance in the factory overhead control account in the general ledger.

PROBLEMS IN ACCOUNTING FOR FACTORY OVERHEAD

For a great many years, both accountants and managers have considered it desirable that all manufacturing costs be assigned as product costs. This practice results from the historic accounting emphasis on income determination. It was generally conceived that *all* costs incurred to manufacture the goods ought to be taken into account in the apportionment of costs between the goods sold and those which remain in inventory. This approach naturally raised problems when it came to the handling of factory overhead. It may be recalled that although prime costs are directly identifiable with products, factory overhead as a whole is not.

Conceived as a single cost element, factory overhead needs first to be determined in total for the fiscal period (i.e., recorded in the factory overhead ledger and summarized in the factory overhead control account) and then apportioned to the products which were manufactured during that period.

For example, assume that the X Manufacturing Company cited in Exhibit 2-2 produces a single product, a steel fishing-tackle box.

The factory overhead ledger reveals that the following overhead costs were incurred for the X Manufacturing Company in January 19x1:

Indirect labor	$ 4,000
Inspection	2,000
Factory supplies	2,000
Factory rent	3,000
Machinery depreciation	600
Factory superintendence	3,400
Total overhead incurred	$15,000

Suppose further that the cost of direct labor for the month was $7,500 and that 5,000 units of product were produced. What is the conversion cost per unit for January production? It might be determined thus:

Direct labor	$ 7,500
Factory overhead	15,000
Total conversion cost	$22,500

Conversion cost per unit: $22,500/5,000 units = $4.50

Predetermined Overhead Rates

The above calculation is conceptually sound but poses certain practical difficulties. First, the $15,000 total factory overhead represents the costs actually incurred. These costs obviously cannot be known until after the completion of the period. When product cost must be known before actual information is available, another method must be used.

In the example cited, the information can be analyzed further:

	Total	Per Unit	Percent
Direct labor	$ 7,500	$1.50	100
Factory overhead	15,000	3.00	200
Total conversion cost	$22,500	$4.50	

The additional information with respect to factory overhead, shown here, is that it amounted to $3 per unit, representing 200 percent of direct labor cost.

If we assume for the moment that these relationships are approximately what management thinks they ought to be, then it might be possible to use the information for a number of purposes where waiting for the accumulation of actual data at the end of the period might be impractical.

For example, management may want to know how much to bid for a contract to produce 1,000 units of its product for a government agency. Suppose the management knows that its costs for direct material and direct labor ought to be $5,000 and $1,200 respectively, and that it ought to provide for selling and administrative cost plus profit at a combined rate of 15 percent of total manufacturing cost. What price ought the firm bid for the contract? If the above relationship of factory overhead to direct labor cost (200 percent) is considered acceptable, the bid would be made as follows:

Direct material	$5,000
Direct labor	1,200
Factory overhead (200 percent of direct labor)	2,400
Total manufacturing cost	$8,600
Selling, administrative, profit (15 percent of manufacturing cost)	1,290
Selling price bid	$9,890
Price per unit (÷ 1,000)	$ 9.89

In addition to setting prices, factory overhead rates are useful for determining income on interim (e.g., monthly) operating statements; for determining the profitability of particular jobs, orders, or product lines; for valuing inventory for balance sheet purposes; and for estimating future costs.

The idea of a predetermined rate includes not only the rate (e.g., 200 percent) but the base to which it is applied (e.g., direct labor cost). A variety of bases are used in practice, including:

> Direct labor hours (rate: dollars per hour)
>
> Machine hours (rate: dollars per hour)
>
> Prime cost (rate: percentage of total dollars)
>
> Units of product (rate: dollars per unit)

The simple notion of a predetermined factory overhead rate by which to apply costs to products has been predicated on a single, plantwide rate in the preceding examples. There are many weaknesses in this approach. Attention should now be turned to some of the advantages of the more complex but more accurate method of using departmental overhead rates.

DEPARTMENTALIZATION OF COSTS

It is the second stage of the production cycle—the factory—at which direct materials are removed from storage and at which direct labor and the bulk of factory overhead costs are incurred as productive operations are performed.

It is common practice in a manufacturing plant to bring together operations in groups according to their nature, placing each group under the supervision of a supervisor and designating each group as a *department*. For instance, in a company which manufactures stamped metal products (e.g., toolboxes, fishing-tackle boxes, steel office equipment), there might be:

A press department in which sheet, tube, or bar steel is cut, bent, and given form for certain components parts

A plating department in which parts may be coated by an electrolytic process with zinc or some other material for the purpose of preventing rust

A machine shop in which metal parts are cut to more intricate shapes and fine dimensions

A painting department in which parts are given their decorative finish

An assembly department in which parts are riveted, bolted, or welded together into finished form for shipment to customers

These operational units are known as *productive* departments, and are established in terms of the types of operations, machinery, and labor skills which form the core of each.

In addition to productive departments, most manufacturing plants have a number of *service* departments. Their function is to make productive operations more efficient, thus to facilitate the achievement of company goals. Such a company as we are now considering might have:

A maintenance department, charged with the responsibility of keeping the buildings and all machinery and equipment in good operating condition

A toolroom, responsible for keeping in good operating condition all special tools, dies, jigs, and fixtures used in conjunction with manufacturing equipment

A scheduling department, responsible for keeping a smooth and efficient flow of work moving through the plant and seeing that shipment deadlines are met

A shipping department, handling finished products from finished goods warehouse to truck or boxcar

A company cafeteria

A plant personnel department

A timekeeping department

Because of the typical complexity of manufacturing operations and associated costs, it has long been found advantageous by management accountants to pattern their information systems upon the basic organization of the plant operations.

Hence the department—productive or service—often can be a natural *cost center.* Units of product are worked upon in the productive departments. Those costs which can be identified directly with the products themselves (direct material and direct labor) can usually be associated as well with the departments through which they pass.

Meaning of "Direct"

A problem of terminology is encountered when costs are related to the department as a costing unit, in addition to being identified with the unit of product.

It has already been pointed out that the original classification and naming of costs were done with income determination and product costing in mind. Thus, the term "direct" as used with reference to prime costs meant "direct as to product." Similarly, the term "indirect" as applied to indirect material or indirect labor (classed as factory overhead) meant "indirect as to product."

Costs can also be direct or indirect when identified with the department as a costing unit. For instance, the press department in a metal fabricating plant may initiate the productive operations for the plant. It requisitions metal from stores, performs a series of press operations upon it, and transfers it to subsequent productive departments. The following costs could probably be identified *directly* with the department through the source documents mentioned:

Direct material (e.g., steel, by requisition from stores)

Direct labor (e.g., the time of its press-operator employees, as evidenced by their timecards)

Factory supplies (e.g., metal prep fluids, lubricating oils, and gloves, requisitioned by or for departmental employees)

Indirect labor (e.g., machine helpers and hand truckers whose time is spent working in the department, as evidenced by timecards)

Maintenance (e.g., work on the presses by employees of the maintenance department, as evidenced by timecards)

Depreciation (e.g., of presses located in the department, or the dies used in the presses, as evidenced by a plant ledger)

Inspection (e.g., inspectors who give final approval to parts leaving the department, as evidenced by their timecards)

In addition, the press department benefits *indirectly* from services that give rise to the following types of cost:

Building depreciation	Production control
Power plant	Personnel
Property taxes	Plant cafeteria

In short, the term "direct," when used to designate prime cost (i.e., direct material and direct labor), refers to indentification with *product*. The same is true of the term "indirect" when used to designate certain overhead costs not directly incorporated into the product.

Identification of costs directly with a department or cost center depends on the individual situation. The name of the individual account ordinarily is no guide to direct identification of cost with department. This is especially true where certain costs, indirect as to product (such as indirect material or indirect labor), are directly identifiable with the department.

Distribution of Overhead

In the earlier discussion of the plantwide predetermined overhead rate, the advantage of such a rate over an actual rate for purposes of pricing and interim determination of income (among others) was suggested. Now that some of the ramifications of cost accumulation by departments have been explored, the possibility of developing departmental overhead rates can be taken up.

When departmental rates are being considered, certain problems must be faced which are not present when plantwide overhead rates are used. Three distinct and significant characteristics of costs accumulated by departments have an influence on their relationship to product costs: (1) Some costs can be identified directly with departments, both productive and service; (2) some costs are general in nature and not suitable for direct identification with departments; and (3) service department costs, whether direct or indirect as to the department, cannot be identified with units of product, since no production is performed in such departments.

The essential problem of determining departmental overhead rates consists in deciding how best to assign all factory overhead costs to productive departments. The conventional approach to the assignment of factory overhead costs to products proceeds according to the following steps:

1. *Charge directly* those costs which can be identified with all departments, productive and service.

2. *Allocate* the indirect costs to all departments—productive and service—which benefit from their incurrence. Distribute on the basis of some reasonable measure of the relative benefit received by each (e.g., factory rent on the basis of the square feet of floor space occupied by each department).

3. *Distribute* the total cost of each *service* department to all the departments which use its service, until all service department costs reside in productive departments. Use whatever basis of distribution may be appropriate to the department (e.g., maintenance department on the basis of the total hours worked by maintenance men in each department).

4. *Compute* the overhead rate for each *productive* department in terms of some base which reflects departmental activity (e.g., worker-hours of direct labor).

In thus relating all factory overhead to some gauge of productive activity, all manufacturing costs are assigned—directly or indirectly—to products.

Determination of Departmental Overhead Rates

In connection with the example of the X Manufacturing Company begun earlier in the chapter, additional data with respect to the assignment of factory overhead to products are presented in Exhibits 2-8 to 2-10.

Throughout this example, it is assumed that X Company has two productive departments (press and assembly) and one service department (maintenance). In Exhibit 2-8, the distinction is made between direct departmental costs and indirect costs. The direct overhead is shown by departments, both productive and service. The indirect overhead, not identified with any of the departments, is shown only in total.

In Exhibit 2-9 four different distribution bases are presented: square feet of floor space, acquisition cost of machinery, number of employees, and maintenance worker-hours. In addition, the factors for each of the depart-

EXHIBIT 2-8
X MANUFACTURING COMPANY
Departmental Cost Data
January 19x1

| | | Departments | | |
	Total	Press	Assembly	Maintenance
Direct departmental overhead:				
Indirect labor	$ 4,000	$1,000	$1,000	$2,000
Inspection	2,000	800	1,200	
Factory supplies	2,000	1,100	550	350
Total direct departmental				
overhead	$ 8,000	$2,900	$2,750	$2,350
Indirect overhead:				
Factory rent	$ 3,000			
Machinery depreciation	600			
Factory superintendence	3,400			
Total indirect overhead	$ 7,000			
Total overhead incurred	$15,000			

EXHIBIT 2-9
X MANUFACTURING COMPANY
Basis of Overhead Distribution
January 19x1

| | | Departments | | |
	Total	Press	Assembly	Maintenance
Basic data:				
Square feet of floor space	50,000	25,000	20,000	5,000
Acquisition cost of machinery	$60,000	$40,000	$15,000	$5,000
Number of employees	34	12	17	5
Maintenance worker-hours	800	520	280	
Direct labor worker-hours	2,394	1,010	1,384	
Departmental distribution factors:				
Square feet	100%	50%	40%	10%
Machinery cost, fraction	1	$\frac{2}{3}$	$\frac{1}{4}$	$\frac{1}{12}$
Number of employees, fraction	$\frac{34}{34}$	$\frac{12}{34}$	$\frac{17}{34}$	$\frac{5}{34}$
Maintenance worker-hours	100%	65%	35%	

EXHIBIT 2-10
X MANUFACTURING COMPANY
Distribution of Indirect Overhead and Service Department Cost, and Calculation of Departmental Overhead Rates
January 19x1

Step	Type of Cost	Basis of Distribution	Total	Press	Assembly	Maintenance
a	Indirect labor	Direct	$ 4,000	$1,000	$1,000	$2,000
a	Inspection	Direct	2,000	800	1,200	
a	Factory supplies	Direct	2,000	1,100	550	350
b	Factory rent	Square feet of floor space	3,000	1,500	1,200	300
b	Machinery depreciation	Acquisition cost of machinery	600	400	150	50
b	Factory superintendence	Number of employees	3,400	1,200	1,700	500
	Total overhead costs incurred		$15,000	$6,000	$5,800	$3,200
	Distribution of service department cost:					
c	Maintenance department	Maintenance worker-hours		2,080	1,120	(3,200)
	Total overhead in production departments		$15,000	$8,080	$6,920	-0-
d	Direct labor worker-hours		2,394	1,010	1,384	
d	Incurred overhead rate (dollars per direct labor hour)		$ 6.27	$ 8	$ 5	

ments are developed for these four bases. Finally, the direct labor worker-hours for the productive departments are listed for use later as an activity base for applying departmental overhead rates.

In Exhibit 2-10, all the data are brought together for the determination of the overhead rates in the two productive departments. First, the direct departmental costs are assigned (step a). Next, the indirect costs are distributed (step b): factory rent on the basis of square feet of floor space occupied by each department; machinery depreciation on the basis of acquisition cost of machinery by departments; and factory superintendence on the basis of the number of employees in each department. This step is followed by the totaling of departmental costs.

Next, the total overhead for the maintenance department, found to be $3,200, is distributed to the productive departments on the basis of their respective usage of the worker-hours of maintenance department personnel (step c).

Finally, the departmental overhead rates are determined (step d). In this particular case, the rates for both productive departments are expressed in dollars per worker-hour of direct labor in the department. The total of $8,080 of assigned overhead cost in the press department is divided by the 1,010 worker-hours of direct labor in that department to establish a rate of $8 per direct labor worker-hour. In the assembly department, the same procedure indicates a rate of $5 per direct labor hour.

Earlier, it was mentioned that departmental overhead rates could be related to several possible activity bases, such as dollars per unit of product, dollars per machine hour, percentage of direct labor cost, and percentage of prime cost. Management's choice of an activity base is generally geared to the nature of productive activity in the department. For instance, where productive operations are predominantly manual, direct labor hours or direct labor cost may be used; if operations are largely automated, machine hours may prove to be the logical base. The point is that a choice of base for applying departmental overhead is a matter for managerial discretion.

PLANTWIDE VERSUS DEPARTMENTAL OVERHEAD RATES

By now it should be clear that the simplest method of applying overhead to products is the use of a plantwide rate. On the other hand, the use of departmental rates, though a more complex method, results in greater refinement and precision in costing.

Product costing will generally yield different results depending on whether factory overhead is applied at a plantwide rate or at departmental rates. Consider a simple example:

A firm manufactures many different products, two of which are designated A and B. Products A and B receive all their processing in two departments, designated 1 and 2. Other data are given as follows:

Overhead Rates	Per Direct Labor Hour
Department 1	$5
Department 2	$1
Plantwide	$2

	Product	
Direct Labor (DL) Hours	A	B
Department 1	3	1
Department 2	1	3
Total	4	4
Prime cost per unit of product	$10	$10

	Product	
Costing with Overhead Applied at Plantwide Rate	A	B
Prime cost	$10	$10
Overhead ($2/DL hour):		
Product A (4 hr)	8	
Product B (4 hr)		8
Total manufacturing cost per unit	$18	$18

Costing with Overhead Applied at Departmental Rates		
Prime cost	$10	$10
Overhead:		
Product A (3 hr @ $5; 1 hr @ $1)	16	
Product B (1 hr @ $5; 3 hr @ $1)		8
Total manufacturing cost per unit	$26	$18

The difference in the results of costing a unit of product by the two alternative methods is evident. Product A spends more time in the department with the higher overhead rate. The effect of the higher rate in department 1 is lost in the plantwide rate, its effect diluted by the much lower rate in department 2. Thus product A, which spends three times as long in department 1 as in department 2, is undercosted by $8 when the plantwide rate is used.

The danger of using the plantwide rate should be obvious, particularly where the product cost is a major factor in setting the price of the product. If the product A price is set to make a moderate profit on a manufacturing cost of $18, the fact that $26 is a more accurate manufacturing cost could mean that losses will result.

NONMANUFACTURING COSTS

This chapter has emphasized the distinction between manufacturing and merchandising concerns by focusing on the nature of manufacturing costs. Direct material, direct labor, and factory overhead are of course important factors only in a manufacturing concern. Every type of company, however, has a basic concern about management and control of costs. A review of the illustrative examples given at the end of Chapter 1 will reveal that almost all are applicable to every kind of company.

The income statement on page 23 lists five categories of costs and expenses, generally based on a functional classification:

1. Cost of goods sold

2. Selling expenses

3. Administrative expenses

4. Interest expense

5. Income tax expense

The cost of goods sold relates to the manufacturing function, the selling expenses relate to the marketing and distribution functions, the administrative expenses relate to the management function, and interest and income tax expenses relate to the financial function of the organization. A manufacturing or merchandising concern will incur all five types of the costs listed, and other kinds of organizations will usually incur all those costs except cost of goods sold. A bank or dry cleaner or TV repair shop, as examples, will incur selling and administrative expenses as well as interest and income tax expense in the normal course of carrying on business.

Although this book concentrates on the management and control of costs incurred by manufacturing concerns, it must be remembered that all firms have the same kinds of problems in controlling costs. Almost every technique to be discussed will be equally applicable to the control of nonmanufacturing costs as well as manufacturing costs, and the general principles of cost measurement and control are the same for nonmanufacturing costs as for manufacturing costs.

SUMMARY

Apart from the fact that the manufacturing firm combines three elements of cost in its cost of goods sold — direct material, direct labor, and factory overhead — whereas only one — merchandise — is found in the merchandising concern, the flow of costs is essentially the same.

The direct cost elements — material and labor — are commonly referred to as *prime cost*. Direct labor and factory overhead combined are frequently called *conversion cost*.

In the typical manufacturing process, costs follow the flow of production through three stages: stores, work in process, and finished goods. These three stages mark the flow of costs *within* the company; therefore each marks a different form of inventory, that is, unexpired product cost. When the goods are sold, the costs expire and become expenses under the heading cost of goods sold.

The familiar input-output analysis form used for reporting cost of goods sold for income statement purposes is extremely useful in accumulating costs at each of the three stages of the production cycle. It also depicts the flow of costs from one step to the next, highlighting the fact that output at one stage becomes input for the next stage.

Information about direct material comes from two basic source documents: the *purchase invoice* and the *stores requisition*. The former provides information about the quantities and prices of materials purchased. The latter tells the quantity and cost of material put into production, as well as the department and product with which it is identified. Direct labor information is gathered from the *timecard*. This document provides information concerning worker, department, operation, product, time, and cost. Factory overhead information is derived from a variety of sources, but especially from invoices, requisitions, and timecards.

It is customary to organize manufacturing operations into groups of activity according to the nature of the product, part, type of machinery, and labor skills involved. These groupings are known as *departments*. For the purpose of cost accumulation, such departments frequently make the most natural and convenient cost centers.

Departments are classified as *productive* and *service*. Productive departments contribute directly to the final form of the product, while service departments exist to promote the efficiency of the plant as a whole, as well as all its productive operations.

Since product costing generally aims at the assignment of all manufacturing costs as product costs, and since not all costs are directly identifiable with products, some means must be employed to assign the indirect costs to productive departments and then to the products processed within them. Since prime costs can usually be assigned directly, the problem essentially involves the manner in which factory overhead is assigned to products. The generally accepted approach proceeds according to the following four steps:

1. Charge directly those costs which can be identified as direct departmental costs.

2. Allocate indirect costs to all departments.

3. Distribute the service department costs to the appropriate productive departments.

4. Compute the overhead rate for each productive department on the basis of some measure of that department's productive activity.

Factory overhead rates can be either plantwide or departmental. Because of their somewhat greater precision, departmental rates are generally preferable for product costing. On the other hand, plantwide rates are considerably easier to develop, and in some instances may yield a satisfactory degree of accuracy for most costing purposes.

Overhead rates, whether plantwide or departmental, may be either *incurred rates* or *predetermined rates*. The latter will be discussed more fully in the next chapter.

KEY WORDS AND PHRASES

direct material	input-output analysis
direct labor	invoice
factory overhead	predetermined overhead rates
conversion cost	productive department
prime cost	service department

DISCUSSION QUESTIONS

1. What is the essential difference between the income statement for a manufacturing firm and that for a merchandising firm?
2. Explain the similarities and differences in the flow of current assets through the operating cycle of the manufacturing firm and the merchandising firm.
3. Why can factory overhead not be considered a prime cost?
4. Why can direct material not be considered a conversion cost?
5. How can direct labor be both prime cost and conversion cost?
6. What is meant by the "flow of costs" through a manufacturing plant?
7. Suppose your bank account showed a balance of $156.15 at April 30 and deposits for April of $865. The balance at April 1 had been $62.85. Of what use might input-output analysis be to you in this situation? Identify each of the factors in the general form of the analysis as it applies to this particular case.
8. What is a predetermined overhead rate?
9. Identify each of the following as a productive (P) or service (S) department:
   a. Glassblowing department, x-ray factory
   b. Grinding and welding department, metal fabricating plant
   c. Forklift truck repair department, appliance factory
   d. Tool crib and maintenance department, metal fabricating plant
   e. Corrugating machine, paperboard manufacturer
   f. Product research and development shop, appliance factory
   g. Plant employees' cafeteria, heavy-machinery manufacturer
   h. Toolmaking department, tool and die manufacturer
   i. Tasting department, distillery
   j. Packaging material stores, food processing plant
   k. Kitchen, commercial restaurant
   l. Pattern- and template-making department, foundry
   m. Packaging and container finishing department, manufacturer of packaging materials
   n. Factory cost accounting department, furniture manufacturer
   o. Testing kitchen, soup manufacturer
   p. Cost accounting department, large CPA firm
10. Explain the difference, if any, between the assignment of a cost using *product* as the costing unit and that using a *department* as the costing unit.
11. What is the difference, if any, between an indirect departmental cost and a service department cost?
12. Identify four methods or bases used in applying or allocating overhead expenses. What are the advantages and disadvantages of each method? (American Institute of Certified Public Accountants, or AICPA, adapted.)
13. In the distribution of factory overhead, is it possible for an item of cost to be distributed more than once? Give an example.

14. A company leases 10,000 square feet of floor space at $850 per month. It uses 7,000 for production and 3,000 for warehousing and storage. It apportions this cost as follows:

To productive departments (7,000 sq ft) $595
To warehouse (3,000 sq ft)   255
    Total rent (10,000 sq ft) $850

Is this an equitable allocation of factory rent?

15. Suppose that in the example given in question 14, the company needs to expand production floor space and is able to rent warehouse space a block away at 5 cents per square foot per month. In order to convert the 3,000 square feet of warehouse space to production space in the present building, certain structural strengthening must be undertaken. The landlord is willing to do this, but will raise the rent for the building to $1,000 a month. In what way would the cost of rent apportioned between production and warehouse space differ from the example in question 14? Which method is right?

16. It is the express purpose of a plantwide overhead rate to recover the total factory overhead cost at the normal operating level in a given period. The use of departmental overhead rates at the normal level of operations should accomplish the same thing. Why, then, bother with the considerably more complex departmental rates?

17. The general manager is discussing overhead rates with you, the controller. "Last month our overhead rate for the plant was 150 percent of direct labor. But you insist that we should figure costs at 200 percent. A lot of my customers already think I'm a bandit. Maybe this confirms it. Hadn't we better cost out our products at our true rate of 150 percent?" As controller, explain the advantages of the predetermined rate for costing.

PROBLEMS

2-1. Listed below are several types of costs and expenses incurred by the typical manufacturing concern. Classify each of these costs and expenses as selling (S), administrative (A), direct manufacturing (DM), or indirect manufacturing (IM).

a. Shipping supplies   S
b. Factory power   IM
c. Salespersons' commissions   S
d. Glue for product labels   IM
e. Depreciation on administration building   A -
f. Salary of stores clerk   S   IM.
g. CPA fees   A   A.
h. Machine maintenance   IM.
i. Supervisors' salaries   IM
j. Salespersons' salaries   S
k. Freight out   S
l. Depreciation on factory building   IM
m. Advertising   S
n. Assembly labor   DM

    o.   Salespersons' samples $\quad$ S

    p.   Executive training program $\quad$ AD

    q.   Property taxes on machinery $\quad$ iM

    r.   Factory rent $\quad$ IM

    s.   Raw materials used $\quad$ DM

    t.   President's salary $\quad$ AD

2-2.†   Given below are the income statements of the Y Company for 19x1 and 19x2. Certain amounts have been omitted. You are to compute the missing amounts, using input-output analysis.

	19x1	19x2
Net sales	$100,000	?
Stores, beginning inventory	1,000	?
Purchases	?	$12,000
Cost of material available	11,000	?
Stores, ending inventory	2,000	?
Cost of materials used	?	13,000
Direct labor	25,000	?
Factory overhead	?	41,000
Manufacturing costs incurred	74,000	?
Work in process, beginning inventory	15,000	?
Cost of work in process	?	95,000
Work in process, ending inventory	?	16,000
Cost of goods manufactured	75,000	?
Finished goods, beginning inventory	20,000	?
Cost of goods available for sale	?	?
Finished goods, ending inventory	25,000	24,000
Cost of goods sold	?	?
Gross margin on sales	?	30,000
Operating expenses	20,000	?
Income from operations	?	12,000
Interest expense	1,000	1,000
Income before taxes	?	?
Income tax expense	4,500	5,500
Net income	?	?

2-3.   The following accounts of a manufacturing company appeared in its balance sheets of December 31, 1975, and December 31, 1976:

	1975	1976
Raw material inventory	$30,000	$45,000
Work in process inventory	17,000	17,500
Finished goods inventory	23,000	18,000
Accrued factory payroll	3,100	3,500
Accrued interest on receivables	120	150

The following amounts appeared in its income statement for 1976:

Raw material used	$300,000
Cost of goods sold	920,000
Direct labor	205,000
Indirect labor	70,000
Interest income	400

Required:

From these accounts, calculate:

    a.   Raw material purchased in 1976

    b.   Cost of goods manufactured for 1976

    c.   Amount actually paid for factory labor in 1976

    d.   Interest received in 1976

2-4.   On January 1, 1975, the James Company had on hand raw materials which cost $10,600, finished goods in the warehouse of $16,000, and work in process with a cost of $11,300. The purchases journal showed a total of $27,000 worth of raw materials had been bought. A total of $24,000 of raw material had been put into process during the year.

   The payroll journal showed labor costs of $25,000, of which $22,000 was factory payroll and $3,000 was selling payroll. Factory supplies of $1,000, depreciation on machinery of $9,000, factory taxes of $1,500, and heat, light, and power of $3,000 had been incurred. At the end of the year, the incompleted work in process included $1,000 of material, $800 of direct labor, and $400 of manufacturing expenses. Finished goods sold during the year had a cost of $65,000.

Required:
Prepare a statement of the cost of goods manufactured and sold for 1975.

2-5.   The following are taken from the records of the Amherst Company for the year 19x1:

	Dec. 31, 19x0	Dec. 31, 19x1
Inventories		
Raw materials	$56,250	$ 47,620
Work in process	19,280	23,810
Finished goods	95,660	115,070
Other Balances		
Purchase of raw materials		$126,100
Depreciation—machinery		17,000
Indirect labor		28,900
Heat, light, power		12,120
Supervision		19,870
Direct labor		84,620
Inspection		9,850
Factory supplies used		13,230
Insurance and taxes		5,690
Depreciation—building		11,200
Miscellaneous manufacturing expense		3,240

134,730 cost of du mat.

Required:
1.   Prepare a schedule of cost of goods sold for the year 19x1.
2.   Determine a plantwide overhead rate (as incurred in 19x1) based on direct labor cost.

2-6.   *Part A.* Listed below in alphabetical order are certain accounts of the Stable Manufacturing Company with balances for the year ending December 31, 19x1. You are asked to prepare a detailed income statement on the basis of this information.

Administrative expense	$ 35,000
Customer returns and allowances	54,400
Depreciation—plant and equipment	38,800
Depreciation—selling	4,300
Direct labor cost	164,500
Dividends paid	14,000
Factory heat, light, and power	91,500
Factory supplies expense	24,100
Finished goods inventory, 1/1/x1	74,400

Finished goods inventory, 12/31/x1	71,500
Freight in	9,800
Goods in process inventory, 1/1/x1	20,800
Goods in process inventory, 12/31/x1	45,600
Indirect labor	25,750
Insurance and taxes – factory	8,900
Interest expense	9,000
Profit on disposal of machinery	11,500
Provision for income tax	24,500
Purchases	270,500
Raw materials inventory, 1/1/x1	158,300
Raw materials inventory, 12/31/x1	169,290
Sales	792,500
Selling expense	41,500

Part B. Multiple choice, based on data in Part A

1. If the cost to manufacture a complete unit in 19x1 was $10, how many units were manufactured: (*a*) 62,286; (*b*) 60,096; (*c*) 67,246; (*d*) 59,806; or (*e*) 64,366?

2. If the unit cost was $10 (and if the beginning finished goods inventory was valued on the same basis), how many units were sold in 19x1: (*a*) 62,286; (*b*) 60,096; (*c*) 67,246; (*d*) 59,806; or (*e*) 64,366?

3. If a unit cost of $10 was applied consistently to both beginning and ending finished goods inventories, the net change in finished goods between January 1 and December 31, 19x1, was: (*a*) an increase of 2,480 units; (*b*) an increase of 290 units; (*c*) an increase of 67,246 units; (*d*) a decrease of 290 units; or (*e*) a decrease of 2,480 units.

4. In 19x2, if cost of work in process is $728,260, the manufacturing costs incurred are: (*a*) $656,760; (*b*) $773,860; (*c*) $622,860; (*d*) $682,660; or (*e*) $799,760.

5. In 19x2, if cost of goods available for sale is $694,360, the cost of goods manufactured is: (*a*) $656,760; (*b*) $773,860; (*c*) $622,860; (*d*) $682,660; or (*e*) $799,760.

2-7. The Con-Mor Manufacturing Company makes one model of a product known as Brand X. At January 1, 19x1, there were 500 units of finished product in finished goods inventory. Other inventories at January 1 were:

Work in process	$ 5,740
Raw materials	11,620

Among the data available for December 31, 19x1, were the following:

Indirect labor	$ 12,160
Direct labor	32,640
Freight in	5,570
Raw materials inventory	9,640
Other factory overhead expenses	31,730
Work in process inventory	7,820
Sales (15,000 units)	360,000
Indirect material	21,390
Total manufacturing costs incurred	194,080

There were 1,500 units of Brand X in the finished goods inventory at December 31, 19x1.

Required:

1. Determine the purchases of raw materials for the year.

2. Determine the incurred rate of factory overhead for the year, based on direct labor cost incurred.
3. Determine the proper unit cost at which to value finished goods inventory, beginning and ending (assuming the same cost to be used for both).
4. Prepare schedule of cost of goods sold and an income statement showing determination of gross profit.

2-8. The Horace Corporation makes 100 meters each workday and incurs the following costs on each day of production:

Direct labor	$500
Direct material	100
Overhead	100

Its budget for the year shows the following *additional* overhead costs per month:

	Overhead Cost per Month	Workdays per Month
January	$ 600	21
February	600	20
March	600	22
April	400	22
May	400	20
June	400	22
July	800	22
August	475	21
September	400	22
October	500	22
November	600	20
December	600	21
Total	$6,375	255

Required:
1. What is the predetermined factory overhead cost per unit?
2. What is the actual overhead cost in each month, assuming that actual costs and production were equal to the budget?
3. Assume that the company produces 25,000 units during the year and that actual overhead costs total $30,000. Using the predetermined rate above, was overhead over- or underapplied? By how much?

2-9.† The Wilson Corporation was formed in 1974 for the purpose of manufacturing a single product. During 1974 it maintained only summaries of the various cost elements. At the end of 1974, the following cost data were available from its records:

Number of units manufactured and sold	30,000
Sales price per unit	$11
Total material costs	$150,000
Total labor costs	$75,000
Total manufacturing overhead	$60,000

On January 1, 1975, the company appointed a new president. He immediately made several shifts in production methods which created additional overhead costs, but eliminated the need for several employees. He also altered the type of materials used in the manufacturing process and changed the sales price of the product to $10 per unit in an attempt to increase the sales volume. The following data summarize the company's operations in 1975:

Number of units manufactured and sold	40,000
Sales price per unit	$10
Total material costs	$160,000
Total labor costs	$90,000
Total manufacturing overhead	$110,000

The sales manager was very happy with the results of the new president's decisions because sales increased from 30,000 to 40,000 units. The production manager was not so pleased since her total manufacturing costs were higher.

Required:

You are requested by the president to ascertain the results of his decision on profits.

1. Prepare an income statement comparing 1974 with 1975.
2. Prepare an analysis showing the per unit cost of each element of manufacturing cost in the first year and in the second year.

2-10. The manufacturing costs of the Edmund Company for 1974 were as follows:

Factory labor	$280,000
Raw materials purchased	320,000
Factory insurance expired	8,000
Factory building depreciation	18,000
Factory equipment depreciation	12,000
Factory supplies	4,000
Heat, light, and power	8,000
Equipment repairs	60,000

The company had no beginning inventory of work in process or finished goods because changes in its product, beginning in 1974, had necessitated clearing out all old models. There were no beginning or ending raw material inventories. During 1974, a total of 10,000 new units were started and completed, and 6,000 were sold.

John Elson, the company's sales manager, had been instrumental in changing the company's product and was not disturbed when the company reported net income of $90,000, which was only two-thirds that of the previous year. He stated, "We actually had a good year, even though profits are down, because our factory insurance and repair costs were almost $50,000 more than in previous years. If it had not been for these costs, our net income would have been $50,000 greater and would thus be higher than that of the previous year."

Required:

1. Prepare a statement of the cost of goods manufactured and sold.
2. Comment briefly on the correctness of the statement made by Elson, wherein he claimed the $50,000 additional cost reduced profit by that same amount.

2-11. The Pre-Aft Manufacturing Company has two production and two service departments. The factory overhead expenses incurred for the month of August were as follows:

	Production Departments		Service Departments	
	Mixing	Packaging	Maintenance	Personnel
Indirect labor	$18,750	$ 9,630	$ 8,700	$ 900
Indirect material	6,540	5,620	2,600	350
Heat, power	4,110	2,750	3,400	250
Total	$29,400	$18,000	$14,700	$1,500
Bases for distribution:				
Number of employees	53	27	20	2
Maintenance worker hours	17	8		

Required:
Prepare a distribution of service department overhead to production departments.

2-12. The Kirschner Manufacturing Company makes several product lines, which are processed through three production departments, designated X, Y, and Z. Estimates of key data for the coming year include:

	Factory Overhead (including Share of Service Departments)	Direct Labor Hours	Direct Labor Cost
Department X	$124,000	80,000	$160,000
Department Y	230,000	115,000	241,500
Department Z	546,000	105,000	199,500
Total	$900,000	300,000	$601,000

Production records at the end of the year indicated the following for the product line Krish:

Units produced   20,000

	Department X	Department Y	Department Z
Prime cost	$45,000	$10,500	$59,500
Direct labor hours	10,000	5,000	30,000

Required:
1. Calculate departmental and plantwide overhead rates, based on direct labor hours.
2. Cost the Krish line for the year by (*a*) applying overhead at the plantwide rate; (*b*) applying overhead at departmental rates.
3. Comment on the results.

2-13. John Adcock, Inc., has three production departments and two service departments. Expenses are budgeted for the year 19x2 as follows:

	Production Departments			
	Stamping	Grinding	Assembly	Total
Direct overhead:				
Indirect labor	$22,000	$15,000	$ 82,200	$119,200
Indirect material	33,400	17,800	87,400	138,600
Power and heat	8,600	3,200	6,400	18,200
Total direct overhead	$64,000	$36,000	$176,000	$276,000

	Service Departments		
	Maintenance	Production Control	Total
Direct expenses:			
Indirect labor	$ 90,000	$21,000	$111,000
Indirect materials	7,300	1,500	8,800
Power and heat	2,700	1,500	4,200
Total direct expenses	$100,000	$24,000	$124,000
Indirect expenses:			
Factory rent			$200,000
Miscellaneous indirect expense			100,000
Total indirect expenses			$300,000

Other statistics are as follows:

	Departments					
	Total	Stamp-ing	Grind-ing	Assem-bly	Mainte-nance	Production Control
Number of em-						
ployees	200	72	58	46	20	4
Square feet of						
floor space	120,000	60,000	18,000	24,000	12,000	6,000
Cost of machinery	$150,000	$70,000	$27,000	$50,000	$3,000	
Maintenance worker						
hours	42,000	21,000	7,000	14,000		
Shop work orders	10,000	3,000	2,000	4,500	500	
Machine hours	250,000	88,500	21,500	130,800	9,200	
Direct labor hours	360,000	144,000	120,000	96,000		

Required:
Determine the departmental overhead rates for 19x2 on the basis of machine hours. (Select what you believe to be the best bases for allocating indirect and service department expenses. Indirect expenses are assumed to be allocable to both production and service departments as appropriate.)

2-14. Following are selected data for the Milani Company for January 1974:

	Productive Departments		Service Departments	
	A	B	X	Y
Direct labor	$20,000	$10,000		
Indirect labor	4,000	6,000	$ 4,500	$ 3,100
Supplies	2,000	3,000	1,500	1,500
Maintenance	7,000	2,000	5,500	1,000
Depreciation	5,000	5,000	1,500	2,200
Utilities	10,000	6,000	12,000	2,200
	$48,000	$32,000	$25,000	$10,000

Service department X is to be allocated on the relative amount of floor space. Service department Y is to be allocated on the basis of total labor and overhead cost before allocation. Relative floor space is as follows: department A, 20,000 square feet; department B, 20,000 square feet; department X, 5,000 square feet; and department Y, 10,000 square feet.

Required:
1. Calculate burden rates for departments A and B, assigning service department costs directly to productive department.

2. Calculate overhead rates for the Milani Company for January 1974, allocating department X costs to both productive departments and department Y first. Then allocate department Y to productive departments.

3. The direct labor costs for January on four selected parts are as follows:

Part	Department A	Department B
101	$1	$2
103	2	1
107	1	1
108	4	5

Calculate the overhead costs for each part, based on the information developed above, on the following bases:

a. Using the overhead rates developed in item 1
b. Using the overhead rates developed in item 2
c. Using a single overhead rate for the entire plant

2-15. The Parker Manufacturing Company has two production departments (fabrication and assembly) and three service departments (general factory administration, factory maintenance, and factory cafeteria). A summary of costs and other data for each department prior to allocation of service department costs for the year ended June 30, 1975, appears below.

The costs of the general factory administration department, factory maintenance department, and factory cafeteria are allocated on the basis of direct labor hours, square footage occupied, and number of employees, respectively.

	Fabrication	Assembly	General Factory Administration	Factory Maintenance	Factory Cafeteria
Direct labor costs	$1,950,000	$2,050,000	$90,000	$82,100	$87,000
Direct material costs	$3,130,000	$ 950,000	–	$65,000	$91,000
Manufacturing overhead costs	$1,650,000	$1,850,000	$70,000	$56,100	$62,000
Direct labor hours	562,500	437,500	31,000	27,000	42,000
Number of employees	280	200	12	8	20
Square footage occupied	88,000	72,000	1,750	2,000	4,800

Required:
(Round all final calculations to the nearest dollar.)

1. Distribute the service department costs to the producing departments, assuming that Parker elects to make this distribution directly, without interservice department cost allocation.

2. Distribute the service department costs to the producing departments, assuming that Parker elects to distribute service department costs to other service departments as well as producing departments. (Start with the service department with the greatest total costs.)

(AICPA adapted)

2-16. The Mix-Max Company has two producing departments, A and B, and two service departments. The costs of the service departments during a typical month are stated below:

	Power Department	Materials Handling Department
Labor and material	$10,000	$ 40,000
Overhead	80,000	80,000
Total	$90,000	$120,000

The power department's output is typically distributed as follows: 30 percent to A, 50 percent to B, and 20 percent to the materials handling department. The materials handling department distributes its workload evenly to departments A and B.

Required:
1. Distribute the costs of the service departments directly to the producing departments.
2. Distribute the costs of the power department to the other three departments and then distribute the costs of the materials handling department to the producing departments.
3. Which of these two approaches to distributing service department costs will give more meaningful results? Why?

2-17.† The Pipe Company has been in operation for one year. It manufactures concrete pipe in lengths of 4 feet and has the necessary equipment to produce 18-, 24-, 30-, and 36-inch pipe. The company has one basic machine to produce pipe. Only one size is made during each working day of eight hours, the last hour of which is used by the crew for cleanup and, as necessary, for changing the machine so that a different size can be made the following day. Production during the first year was limited to sizes from 18 to 30 inches inclusive. You are informed that there is a ready outlet for 36-inch pipe if it were to be produced. The company has prepared the following schedule of profit and loss for the year just ended:

Sales		$58,000
Raw material purchases	$17,657	
Direct labor	13,255	
Freight in	2,447	
Delivery expense	3,582	
Depreciation:		
Factory building	600	
Office building	280	
Factory machinery	3,000	
Office furniture and fixtures	200	
Electric power purchased — factory	1,519	
Shop supplies	2,550	
Office supplies and expense	1,000	
Office salaries	5,200	
Telephone and telegraph	375	
Repairs and maintenance — factory	2,175	
Commissions on sales	2,700	
Other factory expense	760	
Miscellaneous general expense	200	
Raw material inventory — year-end		1,630
Finished goods inventory — year-end		
(at estimated cost per ton of $10)		5,990
Profit for year	8,120	
	$65,620	$65,620

Your review of records discloses the following data as to production and sales:

Pipe Diameter	Feet Produced	Feet Sold	Feet Unsold	Pounds per Foot	Total Weight, lb	Production per Day, ft	Selling Price per Foot
18	7,200	6,200	1,000	150	150,000	120	$2.20
24	10,200	8,120	2,080	250	520,000	100	3.00
30	6,320	5,000	1,320	400	528,000	80	4.00
					1,198,000		

Material cost in finished pipe is found to be the same per ton throughout the year. The plant supervisor tells you that test runs have indicated that 36-inch pipe would weigh 500 pounds per foot and that production should average 64 feet per day. The 36-inch pipe will sell for $5 per foot.

Required:
1. *a.* Compute the cost of each size of pipe produced during the year on a per-foot basis including material, labor, and manufacturing overhead.
   b. Prepare a schedule showing which size of pipe would be most profitable to produce.
   c. Compute the value for the closing inventory of pipe of each size.
2. Prepare an estimate of the cost of producing 36-inch pipe, and compare the gross profit from producing it with that from producing other sizes.

(AICPA adapted)

2-18. The plant manager of one of the divisions of General Statics Corporation, just back from a visit to a good customer, called in his plant controller. "What's wrong with our efficiency around here?" he demanded. "I was talking to the purchasing agent at Ajax, and he tells me that our plant burden rates are 80 percent higher than Consolidated [a leading competitor]. This guy knows what he's talking about—he's done business with both of us for years. I can't understand it. Consolidated's plant is no newer than ours, practically the same size, same kinds of equipment and methods, wage rates about the same—what in the devil is wrong with us? How can I compete? How do I explain to the guys at headquarters?"

As plant controller, how would you answer him?

CHAPTER

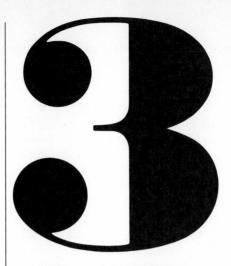

JOB ORDER COST AND PROCESS COST ACCUMULATION

THE PLAN OF THIS CHAPTER
In Chapter 2 we explored the manner in which costs are determined. Now we shall consider the two basic techniques for accumulating manufacturing costs: job order costing and process costing. Each of these methods is a variation of the fundamental technique discussed in Chapter 2 as adapted to particular types of industrial activity. Nearly all modern cost methods have their roots in these two techniques. Topics to be discussed in this chapter are the following:

When, where, and how to use job order costing and process costing

The use of predetermined rates

The treatment of underapplied overhead

Determining equivalent production for different elements of cost

A four-step procedure for determining units of equivalent production

APPLICATIONS OF JOB ORDER COSTING AND PROCESS COSTING

Techniques of assigning costs to manufactured products are ordinarily tailored to the particular nature of the products and manufacturing operations involved. Some types of manufacturing activity are characterized by the production of certain items to the unique specifications of the customer or by the performance of some specified activity under a negotiated contract. Examples of this type of producer are manufacturers of machine tools; construction contractors; machine shops; tool and die manufacturers; commercial printers; builders of special types of truck bodies; and manufacturers of electronic components for rockets under contract with the National Aeronautics and Space Administration. For such types of productive activity, the technique of accumulating costs is termed *job order* or *job lot costing*. Job order costing suits the needs of the custom-made item, or the stipulations of a special contract, where the quantity may be small and the unit cost fairly high.

Process costing, on the other hand, is better adapted to the production of large quantities of similar or identical units of standardized products. Examples of such applications will be found in the petroleum, plastics, paint, chemical, brewing, or salt processing industries, to mention but a few.

ILLUSTRATIVE PROBLEM USING JOB ORDER COSTING: THE CUSTOMCRAFT BOAT COMPANY

For job order costing, the job itself is the focal point for cost identification, and incurred costs are recorded on a job cost sheet or job cost card. From an accounting standpoint, the job cost sheets represent individual pages in a subsidiary-cost ledger, with work in process acting as a general ledger control account. A simplified sample of a job cost sheet is shown in Exhibit 3-1.

Material requisitions and labor timecards provide the basis for charging prime costs to a job, and predetermined overhead rates enable the management accountant to apply the appropriate amount of factory overhead cost to the job. The operation of job order costing will probably best be understood within the context of a simplified example.

Assume that a small manufacturer of pleasure boats—the Customcraft Boat Company—builds only custom boats, using all-wood construction. The owner employs two people for construction work and rents a building. He owns all the machinery and equipment, which is quite modest, consisting primarily of certain power tools and some specialized jigs and fixtures.

The owner purchases basic lumber and plywood supplies locally, and all other materials on special order, to be assembled into the boats according to specifications in each customer's order. Thus purchases of such items as Plexiglas, plumbing equipment, upholstery, and special attachments are made only after the customer's order is in. The business is too small to employ a management accountant full time, but it uses the services of a CPA for cost analysis purposes.

EXHIBIT 3-1
A JOB COST SHEET

Customcraft Boat Company
Job Cost Sheet

Job Order No. _____

Customer:
Name _____
Address _____

Description _____

Price _____
Delivery Date _____

Material

Date	Description	Quantity	Price	Amount
	Total			

Labor

Operation	Hours	Rate	Amount
Total			

Overhead Applied

Base	Rate	Amount
Total		

Summary

Sales
Manufacturing costs:
  Direct material
  Direct labor
  Manufacturing overhead applied
Total manufacturing costs
Gross margin

As of March 1, 19x1, the company had four boats under construction:

Job No. 221, a 16-foot skiff
Job No. 222, a 22-foot cruiser
Job No. 223, a 30-foot special cruiser
Job No. 224, a 45-foot luxury cruiser

The job sheets showed the following costs as of March 1:

	Jobs			
	221	222	223	224
Direct material	$923	$3,823	$6,422	$2,300
Direct labor	265	856	1,722	527
Factory overhead applied	265	856	1,722	527

The balances in the inventory accounts at March 1 were:

Stores	$ 5,430
Work in process	20,208

The following transactions in summary form provide the manufacturing cost information for the month of March:

1. Purchases of direct material and supplies for the month of March totaled $14,900.

2. Requisitions of direct material in March for jobs in process were as follows:

Job No. 221	$ 270
Job No. 222	210
Job No. 223	2,740
Job No. 224	12,580
Total	$15,800

3. The summary of the timecards for March indicated direct labor incurred on jobs as follows:

Job No. 221	$ 38
Job No. 222	140
Job No. 223	513
Job No. 224	709
Total	$ 1,400

4. Factory overhead is applied to jobs in process at a single, plantwide pre-determined rate of 100 percent of direct labor cost.

5. Jobs 221 and 222 were completed during March, and their costs were transferred to cost of goods sold.

6. Customers were billed as follows: for 221, $2,500; for 222, $8,000.

7. By the end of March, the following information was compiled concerning factory overhead costs incurred:

Requisitions for supplies	$ 335
Timecards showing indirect labor	150
Monthly rent on factory building	500
Monthly depreciation of machinery	320
Monthly electric bill	165
Total factory overhead incurred	$ 1,470

Required:

1. Journal entries to reflect March activity

2. Posting to T-accounts to show flow of costs

3. Determination of gross margin on jobs 221 and 222

4. Explanation of factory overhead incurred and applied

Solution:

1. Journal entries:

   a.
Stores	14,900	
Accounts payable		14,900

   To record purchases of direct material and supplies.

   b.
Work in process	15,800	
Stores		15,800

   To record requisitions of direct material to jobs, to be posted to job sheets as follows:

Job No. 221	$ 270
Job No. 222	210
Job No. 223	2,740
Job No. 224	12,580
Total	$15,800

   c.
Work in process	1,400	
Accrued payroll		1,400

   To record direct labor cost incurred on jobs, to be posted to job sheets as follows:

Job No. 221	$ 38
Job No. 222	140
Job No. 223	513
Job No. 224	709
Total	$ 1,400

62

EXHIBIT 3-2
CUSTOMCRAFT BOAT COMPANY
Summary of Activity in T-Accounts
March 19x1

Stores

Bal. 3/1	$ 5,430	(b)	$15,800
(a)	14,900	(g)	335
		Bal. 3/31	4,195
	$20,330		$20,330
Bal. 3/31	$ 4,195		

Accrued Payroll

	(c)	$ 1,400
	(g)	150

Factory Overhead Applied

	(d)	$ 1,400

Factory Overhead Control

(g)	$ 1,470

Work in Process

Bal. 3/1	$20,208	(e)		$ 7,824
(b)	15,800			
(c)	1,400			
(d)	1,400	Bal. 3/31		30,984
	$38,808			$38,808
Bal. 3/31	$30,984			

Finished Goods

(e)	$ 7,824	(f)	$ 7,824

Sales

	(f)	$10,500

Cost of Goods Sold

(f)	$ 7,824

Accounts Payable

	(a)	$14,900
	(g)	165

Accounts Receivable

(f)	$10,500

Accumulated Depreciation – Machinery

	(g)	$ 320

Prepaid Rent

	(g)	$ 500

Manufacturing Expense Ledger

Factory Supplies

(g) $335

Indirect Labor

(g) $150

Factory Rent

(g) $500

Machine Depreciation

(g) $320

Heat, Light, Power

(g) $165

Job Cost Ledger

Job No. 221

Bal. 3/1	$ 1,453
(b)	270
(c)	38
(d)	38
	$ 1,799

(e) $1,799
$1,799

Job No. 223

Bal. 3/1	$ 9,866
(b)	2,740
(c)	513
(d)	513
Bal. 3/31	$13,632

Job No. 222

Bal. 3/1	$ 5,535
(b)	210
(c)	140
(d)	140
	$ 6,025

(e) $6,025
$6,025

Job No. 224

Bal. 3/1	$ 3,354
(b)	12,580
(c)	709
(d)	709
Bal. 3/31	$17,352

d. Work in process   1,400
       Factory overhead applied   1,400
To record factory overhead applied to jobs at
a predetermined rate of 100 percent of direct
labor cost, as follows:

Job No. 221	$ 38
Job No. 222	140
Job No. 223	513
Job No. 224	709
Total	$ 1,400

e. Finished goods   7,824
       Work in process   7,824
To record the cost of completed Jobs 221 and
222, sold in March, and closing out job sheets
as follows:

Job No. 221	$ 1,799
Job No. 222	6,025
Total	$ 7,824

f. Accounts receivable   10,500
       Sales   10,500
Cost of goods sold   7,824
       Finished goods   7,824
To record the sale of two boats, Jobs 221 and
222.

g. Factory overhead control   1,470
       Stores   335
       Accrued payroll   150
       Prepaid rent   500
       Accumulated depreciation—machinery   320
       Accounts payable   165
To record factory overhead incurred, to be
posted to the manufacturing expense subsidiary ledger as follows:

Factory supplies	$ 335
Indirect labor	150
Factory rent	500
Machinery depreciation	320
Heat, light, power	165
Total	$ 1,470

2. Summary of March activity in T-accounts: See Exhibit 3-2.

3. Summary of completed Jobs 221 and 222:

	Job 221	Job 222
Sales	$2,500	$8,000
Manufacturing costs:		
Direct material	1,193	4,033
Direct labor	303	996
Factory overhead applied	303	996
Total manufacturing costs	$1,799	$6,025
Gross margin	$ 701	$1,975

4. Explanation of factory overhead: Factory overhead in a firm using a job order costing system is typically applied to work in process and to the individual jobs by the use of a predetermined overhead rate. Such a rate can be either a single plantwide rate, as in this case, or a set of departmental rates. Predetermined rates can be applied to one of several possible bases of activity: direct labor worker-hours, prime costs, etc. In this case, management has decided to use direct labor cost as the base and is using a predetermined rate of 100 percent.

REASONS FOR USING PREDETERMINED RATES

There are a number of reasons for using a predetermined rate in preference to an incurred rate. First, the incurred rate is not available until after the end of the period. Second, if the rate were computed each month, it would probably fluctuate widely over a year's time, obscuring the cost relationships between jobs and between months. Finally, it is subject to all the unusual events and operating inefficiencies which may occur during the period, leaving management without a way of knowing whether the rate is too low or too high, and by how much.

A predetermined rate, on the other hand, is available when it is most needed: for pricing jobs and for current costing of jobs, especially those completed during the period. Moreover, the predetermined rate irons out month-to-month fluctuations in the incurred rate, permitting improved comparability of job costs between months.

Furthermore, the predetermined rate, not being subject to the unusual events and operating inefficiencies which cause the activity in many periods to deviate from normal, comes closer to reflecting what factory overhead costs ought to be than does the incurred rate. When incurred costs exceed the predetermined rate, management is warned that cost performance is unfavorable, suggesting that the cause be looked into. (This idea—cost control—will be developed at greater length in Chapters 6 and 7, which deal with standard costs and flexible budgets.)

ACCOUNTING TREATMENT OF UNDERAPPLIED OVERHEAD

From an accounting standpoint, the use of a predetermined rate introduces the question of what to do with the difference which arises between the overhead applied to production and the overhead costs actually incurred.

In the case of Customcraft, overhead applied was $1,400, whereas the overhead costs actually incurred amounted to $1,470. In other words, the predetermined rate applied $70 less overhead to jobs than was incurred during the period. Should this $70 difference be reflected on the financial statements as additional cost of goods sold or as additional inventory value? The problem is significant from the standpoint of income determination, for the $70 is just as much incurred cost as the $15,800 of direct material requisitioned and the $1,400 direct labor paid during the month.

Underapplied overhead will tend to fluctuate from month to month, being sometimes underapplied and sometimes overapplied but tending to balance out over the year. There will inevitably remain some difference between overhead incurred and overhead applied at the end of the year, however. In the interest of reporting net income for the year on the basis of the costs actually incurred, the final net difference (either over- or underapplied) will be considered an adjustment to cost of goods sold on the income statement.

This same procedure would be followed when income is reported on a quarterly basis. However, when management wishes to have monthly or weekly income statements and balance sheets prepared for its own internal use only, over- or underapplied overhead may be carried as an adjustment of the asset value in inventory. The income statement would then be based on normal overhead cost (i.e., overhead applied at the predetermined rate).

If the figures in the problem for Customcraft had represented a year instead of a month, the following entries would be in order:

Underapplied overhead	70	
Factory overhead applied	1,400	
Factory overhead control		1,470
To close overhead applied and overhead incurred, and to record the amount of overhead underapplied for the period		

Cost of goods sold	70	
Underapplied overhead		70
To close underapplied overhead to cost of goods sold		

As indicated by the second entry, the over- or underapplied overhead account is an adjustment to cost of goods sold, and is generally shown on the income statement as a separate factor of overhead cost in order to highlight the degree to which overhead costs in the operations of the period deviated from normal.

PREDETERMINED OVERHEAD RATES: JOB ORDER AND PROCESS COSTING

The application of factory overhead, under job order and process costing, is essentially an averaging process. Total overhead incurred (or budgeted, in the case of predetermined rates) is distributed to producing departments and then to individual products. Job order costing focuses on the job itself, and overhead is applied to individual jobs—frequently on the basis of a predetermined rate. Factory overhead applied to the job, as well as direct material and labor charges related to that job, is posted on the job cost sheets.

Under process costing, the department is considered to be the costing unit. Direct material and labor are accumulated by departments, and factory overhead is applied to the individual departments, using much the same methods as are used in job order costing. The application of overhead is based on some measure of the department's productive activity, such as direct labor or machine hours. Again, overhead is frequently applied using a predetermined rate. The point is that overhead costs are incurred by all manufacturing companies and must be distributed to units produced, regardless of the technique used for accumulating costs.

ILLUSTRATIVE PROBLEM USING PROCESS COSTING: DYNAPLASTICS, INC.

Because quantities typically are small and unit costs relatively high in situations utilizing job order costing, the focal point for cost accumulation is the job or contract. The emphasis is different in process costing, however. Large quantities of homogeneous product with relatively low unit costs render it not only difficult but unnecessary to cost by small lots. Instead, the focal point for process cost accumulation is usually the department or process center.

The fundamental problem is to match the total departmental costs with the total number of units processed in any given period. Since it is a basic assumption of process costing that we are dealing with identical units, a simple averaging technique is sufficient. The accuracy of the resulting unit costs must rest, therefore, on the accuracy of the two factors of the calculations: total costs and total units processed.

The task of accumulating the major manufacturing cost elements is no different under process costing than under job order costing. Essentially the same source documents and bookkeeping techniques will develop the input of direct material, direct labor, and factory overhead. The chief differences lie in the method of measuring units produced, reporting the product costs, and valuing work in process inventories. If each department in a processing plant were to start and finish its production runs in a given period, so that all units were completely processed and no partially completed units were in process at the beginning or at the end of the period, the measurement of unit cost would be rather simple.

Consider as an example a small plastics manufacturer—Dynaplastics, Inc. —turning out one type of plastic substance to be sold to other manufacturers for molding into various consumer products. The process is completed in one department, all the material being introduced at the beginning of the process, and the conversion cost (direct labor and factory overhead) being added uniformly throughout the process.

Assumption 1

In January 19x1, there were no work in process inventories, and all units started in production were completed during the month. The quantity produced was 50,000 units, the direct material cost incurred was $35,000, and the conversion cost amounted to $65,000.

The solution to the costing problem under these conditions is:

Manufacturing costs:	
Direct material	$ 35,000
Conversion cost	65,000
Total manufacturing costs	$100,000
Total units produced	50,000
Cost per unit ($100,000/50,000)	$ 2

Assumption 2

Suppose that, in February, 60,000 units were started in production, that 45,000 units were completed, and that 15,000 units remained in process at the end of the month. Direct material cost incurred was $42,000, and conversion cost amounted to $65,000. If we performed the same analysis as in January, the following would be the results:

Manufacturing costs:	
Direct material	$ 42,000
Conversion cost	65,000
Total costs in process	$107,000
Total units in process	60,000
Cost per unit ($107,000/60,000)	$ 1.783

The first question that comes to mind is: What caused the unit cost to decline so much? Reference to the January figure reveals that material cost ($35,000/50,000) averaged $0.70 per unit and that conversion cost ($65,000/50,000) averaged $1.30 per unit. In February, material cost remains at $0.70 per unit ($42,000/60,000), but conversion cost is $1.083 ($65,000/60,000).

The next question likely would be: Are the figures accurate? Inasmuch as the records from which the total incurred costs were taken are generally reliable, there should be little reason to doubt their accuracy.

But is 60,000 units the proper figure to reflect the month's production? In the case of material, since it is introduced at the beginning of the process, any units started during the month must have incurred their full material cost; therefore, 60,000 units is correct for material.

On the other hand, conversion costs are incurred uniformly over the process. Therefore, full conversion cost is not incurred until the units are completed and transferred out. At the end of February, there were 15,000 units still in process, therefore *not* completed. Undoubtedly, if they had been, there would have been more than $65,000 total conversion cost incurred, and the cost per unit would have been closer to the $1.30 realized in January.

Still, to divide the $65,000 by the 45,000 units that were completed would ignore the fact that the 15,000 units in process had some conversion costs connected with bringing them to partial completion. The question then becomes: What was the degree of completion which the 15,000 units had reached by the end of February? Suppose investigation reveals them to be about one-third complete. If conversion costs are incurred *uniformly* over the process, then it would seem that, having one-third of the costs on 15,000 units, we could have *completed* one-third as many, or 5,000 units, for the same conversion costs.

Here we have the notion of *equivalent completed units*. If we know, in this instance, that conversion costs are incurred uniformly over the process, it follows that, for the cost to complete a given number of units, we could bring *three times* that many units to a stage of one-third of completion. Therefore, we can determine the number of equivalent completed units by multiplying the number of partially completed units by the fraction or percent which represents their average stage of completion.

Recasting the February figures on this basis, then, we first determine the equivalent units by cost element, and determine the unit cost in terms of each cost element. Equivalent units for February are:

For material (material being introduced at the beginning of the process, all units started in production are complete as to material cost)	60,000
For conversion cost:	
Units completed and transferred out	45,000
Equivalent complete units in ending work in process (15,000 units, one-third complete)	5,000
Total equivalent units	50,000

Unit costs for February, then, are computed as follows:

	Total Cost	Equivalent Units	Unit Cost
Material cost	$ 42,000	60,000	$0.70
Conversion cost	65,000	50,000	1.30
Total costs in process	$107,000		$2.00

Clearly, this is the superior approach to the analysis of the unit costs. Insofar as the cost elements are incurred in a different manner, or at a different rate, so as to result in different equivalent units in process at any given time, the unit costs for each element may have to be computed separately. Hence, it will not be possible to divide *total* costs by any one figure for *total* units and expect to get a meaningful unit cost figure. Accurate total unit cost will result only from computing separately the unit costs per element of cost and then totaling those unit costs.

The distribution of manufacturing costs between units completed in February and units in process at February 28 would be made as follows:

Units completed and transferred out (45,000 @ $2)		$ 90,000
Work in process—ending balance:		
Material (15,000 units @ $0.70)	$10,500	
Conversion (5,000 units @ $1.30)	6,500	
Total work in process—ending balance		17,000
Total costs in process as distributed		$107,000

Assumption 3

In March, we begin with 15,000 units in process, all complete as to material cost and one-third complete as to conversion cost. During the month, 35,000 are started in process. Forty thousand units are completed and transferred out, leaving 10,000 units in process, complete as to material cost and one-half complete as to conversion cost. Costs incurred in March were: material, $24,500; conversion, $52,000.

With the additional factor of beginning work in process inventory, we now have a further degree of complication. Perhaps it would be best at this point to formulate an approach which would apply to any set of conditions.

Once again, the key is equivalent units, and the tool is the now-familiar input-output formula. The procedure can be organized in four steps toward the development of equivalent costs:

Step 1. Physical Flow of Units

	Total Units
Work in process—beginning	15,000
Started in production	35,000
Total units in process	50,000
Units completed and transferred out	40,000
Units in work in process—ending	10,000
Total units in process distributed	50,000

In this step, the application of the input-output formula is clear: The units started constitute the input; units completed and transferred out constitute output; the pivot point, or "available" factor, is the number of units in process. The purpose of step 1 is simply to demonstrate the accumulation of units in process and then to account for their distribution between completed units transferred out and units remaining in process at the end.

Step 2. Equivalent Units

	Total Units	Equivalent Units	
		Material	Conversion
Units completed and transferred out	40,000	40,000	40,000
Work in process—ending:	10,000		
Material (complete)		10,000	
Conversion (one-half complete)			5,000
Total equivalent units in process		50,000	45,000

Here only the second half of the input-output formula is relevant, since it is the total of equivalent units transferred out and remaining in process at the *end* of the period to which the costs in process for the period will attach. Step 3 will demonstrate the accumulation of these costs, which attach to the units of equivalent production determined in step 2.

Step 3. Accumulation of Costs in Process

	Total	Material	Conversion
Work in process—beginning	$17,000	$10,500	$ 6,500
Current costs incurred	76,500	24,500	52,000
Total costs in process	$93,500	$35,000	$58,500

Since process costing is essentially a matter of averaging costs, it should be clear that the pool of costs representing total costs in process will comprise those carried over from the prior period in beginning work in process inventory and the costs incurred in the current period. This pool will attach, through the averaging procedure, to the equivalent units which emerge from the period's productive activity, as determined in step 2. Notice also in step 2 that units completed and transferred out (40,000) are not separated into units from the beginning inventory (15,000) and units started *and* completed in this period (35,000 minus 10,000 equals 25,000). For the averaging process to be complete, costs carried forward from the last period are added to this period's costs to determine total costs in process.

In summary, then, the purpose of step 2 is to develop an accurate figure for the number of equivalent units, that is, complete units that the period's activity would have produced had none but complete units been processed; the purpose of step 3 is to accumulate the total costs (from the prior as well as the current period) matched to the period's output of production.

Step 4. Cost per Equivalent Unit

	Total	Material	Conversion
Total costs in process (step 3)	$93,500	$35,000	$58,500
Equivalent units in process (step 2)		50,000	45,000
Cost per equivalent unit	$2.00	$0.70	$1.30

The final distribution of these costs between units completed and transferred out and those which remain in process at the end of the period will usually be reported to management on a form called a departmental production cost report (see Exhibits 3-5 and 3-6). The essential facts for such a report have been generated in the four steps for developing the cost per equivalent unit, and the results for March would be summarized as follows:

DEPARTMENTAL PRODUCTION COST REPORT

Units completed and transferred out (40,000 @ $2)		$80,000
Work in process—ending balance:		
Material (10,000 units @ $0.70)	$7,000	
Conversion (5,000 units @ $1.30)	6,500	
Total work in process—ending balance		13,500
Total costs in process distributed		$93,500

ILLUSTRATIVE PROBLEM USING PROCESS COSTING: THE KOOKIE KOLA BOTTLING COMPANY

The Kookie Kola Bottling Company produces a single soft-drink product, processing it through a mixing department and a bottling department.

In the mixing department, the materials, consisting mainly of syrup, sugar, and water, are introduced at the beginning of the process, while conversion costs are incurred uniformly over the process.

In the bottling department, the materials consist principally of throwaway bottles and caps, which are introduced at a more or less constant rate in advance of the actual bottling operation, so that at any given time there is always a backlog of bottles and caps in the bottling machine. Here also, the conversion costs are incurred at a uniform rate. Units of production are reckoned in terms of 100 bottles equaling 1 unit.

At the beginning of the month of August 19x1, there were 500 units in process in the mixing department, complete as to material and one-fifth complete as to conversion cost. There were 100 units in process in the bottling department, one-half complete as to material cost and one-fifth complete as to conversion cost.

There were 3,000 units started in production in the mixing department and 3,200 completed and transferred to the bottling department in the month of August. There were 3,150 units completed and transferred to finish goods from the bottling department during the month.

	Total Cost	Trans-ferred-in Cost	Material Cost	Conversion Cost
Inventories of work in process, August 1:				
Mixing department	$ 575		$ 500	$ 75
Bottling department	$ 235	$ 175	$ 25	$ 35
Costs incurred in the current period:				
Mixing department	$ 5,475		$3,000	$2,475
Bottling department	$12,765	$5,600	$1,600	$5,565

At August 31 there were 300 units in process in the mixing department, complete as to material and two-thirds complete as to conversion costs. In the bottling department, there were 150 units in process, two-thirds complete as to material and one-third complete as to conversion costs.

Required:

1. Development of cost per equivalent unit for each department by a four-step procedure.

2. Completion of separate departmental production cost report for each department for the month of August 19x1.

Solution:
It will be noted, first of all, that where there are two departments in sequence in a processing plant, the total unit cost of the preceding department follows the units transferred from it to the succeeding department. Thus, in this case, the cost incurred in the mixing department attaches to the units transferred from it to the bottling department, and appears as another element of cost in the latter, entitled transferred-in costs.

This new element will be treated in the same manner as material and conversion costs. All units in process at any time in the bottling department are complete as to transferred-in costs by definition. The total and unit costs for the bottling department will be cumulative, i.e., will contain the costs transferred from the mixing department as well as its own.

EXHIBIT 3-3
KOOKIE KOLA BOTTLING COMPANY
Process Cost Analysis in Four Steps, Mixing Department
August 19x1

	Cost Elements		
	Total	Material	Conversion
1. *Physical flow*			
Work in process, Aug. 1	500		
Units started or transferred in	3,000		
Units in process	3,500		
Units completed and transferred out	3,200		
Work in process, Aug. 31	300		
Units in process distributed	3,500		
2. *Equivalent units*			
Units completed and transferred out	3,200	3,200	3,200
Work in process, Aug. 31	300		
(Material complete; conversion, two-thirds complete)		300	200
Equivalent units in process		3,500	3,400
3. *Total costs*			
Work in process, Aug. 1 (Material complete; conversion, one-fifth complete)	$ 575	$ 500	$ 75
Current costs incurred	5,475	3,000	2,475
Total costs in process	$6,050	$3,500	$2,550
4. *Cost per equivalent unit*			
Total costs in process	$6,050	$3,500	$2,550
Equivalent units in process		3,500	3,400
Cost per equivalent unit	$1.75	$1.00	$0.75

EXHIBIT 3-4
KOOKIE KOLA BOTTLING COMPANY
Process Cost Analysis in Four Steps, Bottling Department
August 19x1

	Cost Elements			
	Total	Trans- ferred-in	Material	Conversion
1. Physical flow				
Work in process, Aug. 1	100			
Units started or trans- ferred in	3,200			
Units in process	3,300			
Units completed and transferred out	3,150			
Work in process, Aug. 31	150			
Units in process distributed	3,300			
2. Equivalent units				
Units completed and transferred out	3,150	3,150	3,150	3,150
Work in process, Aug. 31	150			
(Material, two-thirds complete; conversion, one-third complete)		150	100	50
Equivalent units in process		3,300	3,250	3,200
3. Total costs				
Work in process, Aug. 1 (Material, one-half complete; conversion, one-fifth complete)	$ 235	$ 175	$ 25	$ 35
Current costs incurred	12,765	5,600	1,600	5,565
Total costs in process	$13,000	$5,775	$1,625	$5,600
4. Cost per equivalent unit				
Total costs in process	$13,000	$5,775	$1,625	$5,600
Equivalent units in process		3,300	3,250	3,200
Cost per equivalent unit	$4.00	$1.75	$0.50	$1.75

The solution is worked out in its entirety in the four related exhibits as follows:

1. Cost per equivalent unit—see Exhibits 3-3 and 3-4.

2. Departmental production cost reports—see Exhibits 3-5 and 3-6.

EXHIBIT 3-5
KOOKIE KOLA BOTTLING COMPANY
Departmental Production Cost Report, Mixing Department
August 19x1

	Equivalent Units	Cost per Equivalent Unit	Total Cost
A. *Accumulation of costs*			
1. Work in process—beginning:			
Material			$ 500
Conversion			75
Total work in process—beginning			$ 575
2. Current costs incurred:			
Material			$3,000
Conversion			2,475
Total current costs			$5,475
3. Total costs in process			$6,050
B. *Equivalent unit costs*			
1. Material costs in process	3,500	$1.00	$3,500
2. Conversion costs in process	3,400	0.75	2,550
3. Total costs in process		$1.75	$6,050
C. *Distribution of costs in process*			
1. Costs transferred out	3,200	$1.75	$5,600
2. Work in process—ending			
Material	300	$1.00	$ 300
Conversion	200	$0.75	150
Total work in process—ending			$ 450
3. Total costs in process distributed			$6,050

EXHIBIT 3-6
KOOKIE KOLA BOTTLING COMPANY
Departmental Production Cost Report, Bottling Department
August 19x1

	Equivalent Units	Cost per Equivalent Unit	Total Cost
A. *Accumulation of costs*			
1. Work in process — beginning:			
Transferred-in costs			$ 175.00
Material			25.00
Conversion			35.00
Total work in process — beginning			$ 235.00
2. Current costs incurred:			
Transferred-in costs			$ 5,600.00
Material			1,600.00
Conversion			5,565.00
Total current costs			$12,765.00
3. Total costs in process			$13,000.00
B. *Equivalent unit costs*			
1. Transferred-in costs in process	3,300	$1.75	$ 5,775.00
2. Material costs in process	3,250	0.50	1,625.00
3. Conversion costs in process	3,200	1.75	5,600.00
4. Total costs in process		$4.00	$13,000.00
C. *Distribution of costs in process*			
1. Costs transferred out	3,150	$4.00	$12,600.00
2. Work in process — ending:			
Transferred-in costs	150	$1.75	$ 262.50
Material	100	$0.50	50.00
Conversion	50	$1.75	87.50
Total work in process — ending			$ 400.00
3. Total costs in process distributed			$13,000.00

SUMMARY

There are two fundamental methods of accumulating costs. Where products are made to the customer's special order or under contract, where units differ significantly and are ordinarily small in quantity and relatively high in unit cost, the job order system of costing is suggested. Where the product and process are typified by the mass production of standardized product, units being large in quantity, indistinguishable one from another, and generally low in unit cost, the process method of costing is favored.

Job order costing focuses on the job or order. Direct material and labor charges, as well as applied overhead, are accumulated on job cost sheets. These cost sheets function as subsidiary ledger accounts with work in process as the general ledger control. When the units in the job or order are completed, the costs recorded on the job cost sheets are totaled. A per-unit cost figure can then be obtained by dividing these total costs by the number of units in the order.

Overhead applied to individual orders under job order costing or to departments under process costing can be based on incurred rates or on predetermined rates. The incurred rate carries with it certain serious drawbacks:

It is not available until the end of the fiscal period.

It is subject to the effects of inefficient performance and of unusual and nonrecurring events which result in distortions and inconsistencies.

It may vary considerably from month to month because of volume fluctuations and seasonal influences.

The overhead rate which serves management best ought to be:

Available for pricing, for costing jobs finished before the end of the fiscal period, and for determining profits in connection with products or jobs

Free of the undesirable influence of past inefficiencies or unusual, nonrecurring events which distort experience

Free of the distortions inherent in month-to-month fluctuations in volume of activity

A carefully worked-out, predetermined overhead rate possesses the timeliness and stability necessary to produce such advantages.

Overhead applied to jobs or departments in any period will invariably total more or less than the overhead incurred. For internal management purposes in interim (e.g., monthly) reports, such over- or underapplied overhead may be allowed to remain in inventory, with income thus being reported in accordance with the normal amount of overhead applied. At year-end, however, it is generally recommended that over- or underapplied overhead be written off to income as part of cost of goods sold.

Whereas the job is the focal point for costing under the job order method, the department is the costing unit under a process cost system. The total costs in process for a department in a given period are averaged over the units produced during that period to arrive at a cost per unit. However, there are two complicating factors. Beginning and ending work in process inventories contain uncompleted units and make difficult the measurement of units produced in any period. Also, different elements of cost may be incurred at a different rate or with different timing. The problem is to determine *equivalent* production for the different elements of cost.

The key to the difficulty is the determination of equivalent units. If units in process are not complete, it is because they lack a portion of one or more elements of cost. The degree of partial completion is the clue to the equivalent units in the work in process. A four-step procedure is suggested for determining the units of equivalent production in a period, as well as the related cost per equivalent unit. The four steps are:

1. Analyze the physical flow of units for the period.
2. Determine the equivalent units in the production for the period.
3. Accumulate the costs in process for the period.
4. Calculate the cost per equivalent unit in the production for the period.

When the cost per equivalent unit is known, the total costs in process may be distributed properly between completed units which were transferred out and the uncompleted units which remain in work in process at the end of the period.

The input-output formula once again proves useful in developing the necessary data. Its form will also be recognized in the departmental production cost report to management, in which the pertinent information concerning departmental and product cost is summarized.

KEY WORDS AND PHRASES

job order costing	work in process
process costing	finished goods
equivalent units	raw materials

DISCUSSION QUESTIONS

1. Under what conditions is a job order cost system appropriate?
2. Under what conditions is a process cost system appropriate?
3. In what ways are job order costing and process costing alike? In what ways are they dissimilar?
4. Job order costing is said to apply where a product or service must be supplied in accordance with *unique* specifications of the customer. Explain.
5. The following types of business, although quite similar to one another, may or may not find job order costing appropriate to their purpose. For each pair, select the one which might be more likely to utilize job order costing and explain why.
   a. A commercial printer and a daily newspaper publisher
   b. A builder of prefabricated garages and a contractor building homes for several architects
   c. A manufacturer of engine lathes and a tool and die manufacturer
   d. A truck manufacturer and a builder of specialized truck bodies
   e. Henri Du Fault exclusive tailors and Hobart Rawl men's clothing manufacturers
   f. MacDougal's Hamburger Heaven and The Lamp Room, Consul North Hotel
6. "The job cost sheets constitute a subsidiary ledger." What is the meaning of this statement, and how does the cost information reach the financial statements under such a system?
7. "Whereas the job is the focal point for costing under the job order method, the department is the costing unit under a process cost system." Explain.
8. "Process costing is essentially an averaging procedure." Explain.
9. Explain the notion of equivalent units.

10. Suppose that a particular job is finished before the actual overhead for the year can be determined. How is the cost of such a job determined?
11. What is underapplied burden (overhead)?
12. What is overapplied burden (overhead)?
13. What should be management's reaction to underapplied burden? Explain.
14. Should management always be pleased with overapplied burden? Why?
15. "Why keep such careful track of costs? Competition sets our prices—we couldn't charge more even if the costs indicate we should." Would you care to tell this speaker how to run her business?

PROBLEMS

 3-1. The Rossow Building Company constructs modular houses. It currently has three contracts, which have been assigned contract-order nos. 1253, 1254, and 1256. The following information relates to these contracts:

	Job No. 1253	Job No. 1254	Job No. 1256
Materials used	$4,000	$3,000	$6,000
Direct Labor hours	1,000	800	1,250
Average wage rate/hour	$10.50	$10.25	$11.00

The company assigns overhead on the basis of direct labor dollars. The Rossow Company expects to have a direct labor payroll of $65,000 this year and estimates total overhead will be $208,000.   *320%*   *3*

Required:
Assign overhead to each contract and compute the total cost for each contract.

3-2. The Veith Company employs a job order cost system. Summarized transactions for the month of June are as follows:

 a. Materials and supplies purchased on account, $300,000
 b. Materials and supplies used in production, $225,000
 c. Materials and supplies used for general factory purposes, $15,000
 d. Labor used: direct, $300,000; indirect, $25,000
 e. Factory overhead applied at the rate of 120 percent of direct labor cost
 f. Repairs and maintenance of factory, paid for in cash, $55,000
 g. Depreciation: on factory building, $80,000; on factory equipment, $125,000
 h. Other miscellaneous factory overhead items, paid for in cash, $20,000
 i. Products finished and transferred to stock, $450,000
 j. Goods sold on account: cost, $485,000; selling price, $650,000
 k. Factory wages paid, $330,000

Required:
Prepare entries in general journal form to record these summarized transactions. Assume the Veith Company uses perpetual inventory records and closes overhead over- or underapplied to cost of goods sold only on December 31.

3-3.   The Pulaski Company completed the following transactions during the year:

a.   Purchased raw materials costing $15,010.

b.   Issued $10,120 of the raw materials to production. Of this amount, $720 was in indirect materials which could not be traced directly to jobs.

c.   Labor costs for the period were $7,625, all of which were paid in cash. Of these, $1,125 were indirect and could not be charged directly to jobs.

d.   Paid $5,100 of manufacturing overhead costs in cash and recorded $1,500 depreciation on factory equipment.

e.   Manufacturing overhead was applied to work in process, using a rate of 130 percent of direct labor cost.

f.   Jobs with a total cost of $22,330 were completed and transferred to finished goods inventory.

g.   Finished goods costing $20,200 were sold on account for $35,000.

h.   Selling and administrative expenses of $12,420 were incurred.

Required:

1.   Compute the amount of the ending inventories for raw materials, goods in process, and finished goods.

2.   Compute the over- or underapplied overhead.

3.   Prepare an income statement for the year.

 3-4.   The Ahab Company uses a job order cost system. The following data refer to the month of April:

1.   Balances of open jobs, April 1:

	Job No. 410	Job No. 411	Total
Direct material	$ 80	$ 420	$ 500
Direct labor	150	450	600
Factory overhead applied	200	400	600
Work in process inventory, April 1	$430	$1,270	$1,700

2.   Direct material requisitions, April:

Job No. 410	$ 120
Job No. 411	280
Job No. 412	225
Job No. 413	300
	$ 925

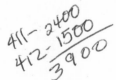

3.   Direct labor distribution:

Job No. 410	400 hr	$ 600
Job No. 411	200 hr	450
Job No. 412	300 hr	675
Job No. 413	100 hr	225
		$1,950

4.   Factory overhead is applied to production on the basis of $2 per direct labor hour.

5.   Factory overhead incurred in April is $2,100.

6.   Jobs 411 and 412 were completed during the month. They were billed

to customers at a price which included 15 percent of the price for selling and administrative expense and 10 percent of the price for profit.

$$3900 + .15x + .10x = x$$
$$3900 + .25x = x \qquad 3900 = .75x$$
$$x = 5200$$

Required:

1. Prepare journal entries for the month's transactions (summary).
2. Determine the billing price for jobs 411 and 412.
3. Determine the work in process inventory balance, April 30.
4. Determine the gross margin (profit) for the month of April.

3-5.† The Snappy Tool and Die Company makes special tools for manufacturers. Job No. 682 was started in May and finished in June. On June 1, the job card showed manufacturing costs incurred to date:

Direct material	$ 75
Direct labor	20
Factory burden	23
Total	$118

In June the following data are recorded in connection with finishing the job:

Material used, department 1	$350
Direct labor hours, department 1	20
Direct labor hours, department 2	25
Machine hours, department 1	13
Machine hours, department 2	18
Direct labor rate, department 1	$2.50/labor hr
Direct labor rate, department 2	$3.00/labor hr
Rate for applying burden, department 1	$2.10/labor hr
Rate for applying burden, department 2	$5.00/machine hr

Customers are billed for a job after it has been completed and manufacturing costs have been accumulated. The price is set to allow 10 percent of the price for selling and administrative expenses, and a net profit of 15 percent of the billing price.

Required:
Compute the billing price for Job No. 682.

3-6. The Lawrence Company uses job order costing with predetermined departmental overhead rates. The rate is based on machine hours in department Bob and on prime cost in department Ray. At the beginning of the year, the following data were projected:

	Department Bob	Department Ray
Material cost	$150,000	$ 50,000
Direct labor cost	$ 90,000	$220,000
Factory overhead cost	$480,000	$405,000
Direct labor hours	30,000	176,000
Machine hours	120,000	6,000

The cost sheet for Job No. 666, completed during April, showed the following information at the end of April:

	Department Bob	Department Ray
Material used	$13.50	$ 2.50
Direct labor	$15.00	$12.50
Direct labor hours	5	10
Machine hours	6	2

Required:

1. What are the predetermined overhead rates for departments Bob and Ray, respectively?
2. What operating characteristics might cause the projected data for the two departments to differ as they do? How might these characteristics affect the choice of bases for overhead rates?
3. How much overhead should be charged in total to Job No. 666?
4. What is the manufacturing cost per unit if Job No. 666 consists of twenty-five units?
5. The following are certain actual results as reflected on the company books at the end of the year:

	Department Bob	Department Ray
Factory overhead incurred	$465,000	$412,000
Direct labor hours worked	28,000	177,000
Machine hours recorded	115,000	6,500
Prime cost incurred	$240,000	$274,000

Determine over- and underapplied overhead for each department and the total for the plant.

3-7. The following information is from the general ledger of the Rebmun Company, a manufacturer of heavy equipment, at the end of July 19x2, the first month of operations in its fiscal year (all figures shown with 000 omitted):

Sales	$813
Raw materials inventory, 7/31/x2	112
Work in process inventory, 7/31/x2	204
Finished goods inventory, 7/31/x2	115
Materials purchased	135
Direct labor	71
Factory overhead control	150
Selling expense	50
Administrative expense	75
Factory overhead applied	142

Additional information:

Raw materials inventory, 7/1/x2	87
Work in process inventory, 7/1/x2	164
Finished goods inventory, 7/1/x2	372

Jobs in process, July 1, 19x2:

Job No.	Material	Labor	Overhead Applied	Total
201	$15	$ 8	$16	$ 39
202	22	13	26	61
203	46	6	12	64
	$83	$27	$54	$164

Charged to jobs in July 19x2:

Job No.	Material	Labor
201	$ 12	$ 6
202	8	14
203		17
204	36	21
205	54	13
	$110	$71

Overhead is applied at 200 percent of direct labor cost. Jobs 201, 203, and 204 were completed in July. Jobs 201 and 204 were sold during July. The cost of jobs in July 1 finished goods, sold in July, was $372.

Sales prices on jobs sold in July:

From July 1 finished goods	$558
Job No. 201	110
Job No. 204	145
Total	$813

Required:
1. Prepare an income statement for the month of July, assuming that over- or underapplied overhead is deferred until year-end.
2. Prepare an analysis of costs on each job, 201 through 205.
3. Determine the gross profit percentages on jobs sold in July.

3-8.† The controller of the newly formed Wen Company was asked to establish a predetermined rate for applying overhead to the jobs moving through the shop and to check results periodically. After consulting various officials of the company, he came up with the following estimated data for the year 19x3:

Factory supervision	$ 50,000
Indirect labor	115,000
Inspection	70,000
Maintenance	35,000
Indirect material	25,000
Heat, light, power	20,000
Depreciation	35,000
Miscellaneous factory overhead	10,000
Total factory overhead	$360,000
Direct labor worker-hours	144,000

At the end of 19x3, the first year of operations, the following results were recorded:

Factory supervision	$ 51,000
Indirect labor	99,000
Inspection	73,000
Maintenance	39,000
Indirect material	20,000
Heat, light, power	18,000
Depreciation	35,000
Miscellaneous factory overhead	3,000
Total factory overhead	$338,000
Direct labor worker-hours	121,500

Required:
1. Compute the controller's predetermined rate, based on direct labor hours.
2. Determine the over- or underapplied overhead for the year.
3. Prepare journal entries to record all information pertaining to overhead, both in the general ledger and in the manufacturing expense subsidiary ledger (use vouchers payable to record credits for expenses incurred).
4. Explain the causes for over- or underapplied overhead. What was the incurred overhead rate?

Sources of Information	General Ledger Control	Raw Materials	Store Supplies	Work in Process Total	Service Depts. Power Plant	Service Depts. General Plant	Producing Depts. Pattern Foundry	Producing Depts. Machine Shop
From voucher register:								
Purchases	$(27,150)	$20,000	$ 7,150					
Direct labor	(6,150)			$ 6,150	$300	$ 350	$ 2,200	$ 3,300
Direct manufacturing expenses	(2,300)			2,300	50	175	730	1,345
Assets acquired	(9,400)							
Prepaid insurance	(3,000)							
From general ledger entries:								
Depreciation	(1,100)			1,100	140	80	*	*
Property taxes	(250)			250	40	20	*	*
Expired insurance	(500)			500	100	25	*	*
Repairs to power plant	(320)			320	320			
From requisitions:								
Raw materials	150	(27,000)		27,000	500	1,000	15,500	10,000
Store supplies			(15,150)	15,000	150	1,350	9,000	4,500
From cost of finished jobs report:								
Shipped to customers	45,000			(45,000)				
For company's own use	2,460			(2,460)				
Bases for distribution of costs:								
Power plant							50%	50%

General plant — store supplies issued to producing departments.
Indirect costs of producing departments — direct labor costs of each department.
* Balance to be distributed on basis of direct labor costs.
Debit/(credit).

Work in Process

3-9.   The president of Small Corporation has requested your assistance in reconstructing a summary of factory operations during April for a job order cost system that has been maintained inadequately since the book-keeper left for another position early in the month.

   The corporation's cost system includes a general ledger and a factory production ledger with reciprocal control accounts. A trial balance of the factory production ledger at April 1, 1974, showed the following:

	Debits	Credits
Raw materials	$30,000	
Store supplies inventory	10,000	
Work in process	20,000	
General ledger control		$60,000
	$60,000	$60,000

   After reviewing the work done up to April 1, you gathered the following information for the month of April from the sources indicated in the table shown on page 84.

Required:
Prepare a summary worksheet for the month ended April 30, 1974, to compute:

1.   Direct, indirect, and total costs that should be debited to work in process for the month
2.   The distribution of service department costs
3.   The April 30, 1974, balances of the following accounts in the factory production ledger:
   a.   General ledger control
   b.   Raw materials
   c.   Store supplies
   d.   Work in process

(AICPA adapted)

3-10.   Given below are certain data relating to two departments of the Scanlon Company for the month of January 19x1. You are to complete the equivalent units of production for each department.

	Department X	Department Y
Beginning inventory (percentage complete)	0	10,000 (80%)
Units started	100,000	90,000
Units completed	90,000	?
Ending inventory (percentage complete)	10,000 (80%)	5,000 (20%)
Material A added to process	At beginning	At beginning
Material B added to process	None	When process is 50% complete

3-11.   The Clancy Company produces a single product requiring only one complex manufacturing process. At the end of March, the company's work in process account had a balance of $7,500, composed of the following debits and credits:

Debits:	
Beginning inventory, materials	$ 3,000
Beginning inventory, conversion	3,000
Materials added, March	23,000
Conversion costs, March	39,000
Total debits	$68,000
Credits:	
Goods completed and transferred out, March	60,500
Balance, end of March	$ 7,500

The beginning inventory consisted of 3,000 units, and 10,000 additional units were started during March. The ending inventory consisted of 2,000 units which were complete as far as material cost but only one-half done with respect to conversion costs. Eleven thousand units were transferred to finished goods during March.

Required:

Show how the cost accountant computed the cost of the goods transferred out, and prove the balance in the work in process account at the end of March.

3-12.   The Ammo Chemical Company produces a single product in a continuous process, completing it in one department. All material is introduced at the beginning of the process, conversion cost being incurred continuously throughout. In June, 8,000 gallons were started in process. At June 30, 1,200 gallons remained in process, 25 percent complete. There were no beginning inventories of work in process. Costs incurred in June were:

Material	$16,000
Conversion	14,200
Total	$30,200

Required:

1. Prepare a summary of costs applied to completed production and ending work in process inventory.
2. Prepare a second summary, assuming the following changes in the above situation:

   Beginning inventory of work in process of 1,000 gallons, 50 percent complete:

Material	$2,000
Conversion	1,000

   Ending inventory of work in process of 2,000 gallons, 30 percent complete.

3-13.   The Incredible Gadget Corporation manufactures a single product. Its operations are a continuing process carried on in two departments, the machining department and the assembly and finishing department. Materials are added to the product in each department without increasing the number of units produced. Labor and overhead are incurred continuously throughout the process in both departments.

In the month of May 19x6, the records showed that 75,000 units were put in production in the machining department. Of these, 60,000 were completed and transferred to assembly and finishing, and 15,000 were left in process with all materials applied but with only one-third of the required labor and overhead. In the assembly and finishing department, 50,000 units were completed and transferred to the finished stockroom during the month, and 10,000 units were in process on May 31. All required materials and four-fifths of the labor and overhead had been applied to the 10,000 units.

There was no work in process in either department at the first of the month. Cost records showed the following charges during the month:

	Materials	Labor	Overhead
Machining department	$120,000	$ 87,100	$36,400
Assembly and finishing department	42,000	101,700	54,900

Required:

1. Prepare in good form a statement showing the unit cost for the month.
2. Prepare a schedule showing the details of the work in process inventory in each department. (AICPA adapted)

3-14.† The Biltimar Company manufactures gewgaws in three steps or departments. The finishing department is the third and last step before the product is transferred to finished goods inventory. All material needed to complete the gewgaws is added at the beginning of the process in the finishing department. Labor and manufacturing overhead are added uniformly throughout the process in this department. The company has accumulated the following data for July for the finishing department:

1. Production of gewgaws:

	Units
In process, July 1 (labor and manufacturing overhead three-fourths complete)	10,000
Transferred from preceding departments during July	40,000
Finished and transferred to finished goods inventory during July	35,000
In process, July 31 (labor and manufacturing overhead one-third complete)	15,000

2. Cost of work in process inventory, July 1:

Cost from preceding departments	$ 38,000
Costs added in finishing department prior to July 1:	
Material	21,500
Labor	39,000
Manufacturing overhead	42,000
Cost of work in process inventory, July 1	$140,500

3. Gewgaws transferred to the finishing department during July had costs of $140,000 assigned from preceding departments.
4. During July, the finishing department incurred the following production costs:

Material	$ 70,000
Labor	162,500
Manufacturing overhead	130,100
Total	$362,600

Required:

1. Determine the cost of the gewgaws transferred to finished goods inventory in July.
2. Determine the cost of the work in process inventory at July 31.

(AICPA adapted)

3-15. You are engaged in an audit of the ABC Manufacturing Company's financial statements as of December 31, 19x9, and are in the process of verifying the pricing of the company's inventory of work in process and finished goods, which is recorded on the company's books as follows:

Finished goods inventory, 110,000 units	$504,900
Work in process inventory, 90,000 units (50% complete)	330,480

You learn that materials are added to the production line at the start of the process and that overhead is applied to the product at the rate of 75 percent based on direct labor dollars, which are incurred uniformly over the process.

A review of the company's cost records shows the following information:

	Units	Costs Materials	Labor
Beginning inventory, Jan. 1, 19x9			
(80 percent complete)	100,000	$100,000	$ 160,000
Additional units started in 19x9:	500,000		
Material costs incurred		560,000	
Labor costs incurred			1,045,200
Units completed in 19x9:	510,000		

Required:

1. Prepare schedules indicating (*a*) effective or equivalent production; (*b*) unit costs of production of material, labor, and overhead; (*c*) pricing of inventories of finished goods and work in process.
2. Prepare the necessary journal entry (or entries), if any, to correctly state inventory valuation of finished goods and work in process.

(AICPA adapted)

3-16. The Bemann Company manufactures two products: Dingbat and Warfal. They are processed through three departments: grinding, mixing, and pasteurizing. The process in each department is the same regardless of the product which emerges. The difference is that Dingbat is processed through all three departments, whereas Warfal passes through only grinding and mixing.

During the month of February, expenses were incurred as follows (assume no beginning work in process):

Expense	Grinding	Mixing	Pasteurizing
Material	$210,250	$ 1,500	
Labor	35,000	141,000	$22,000
Overhead	70,000	141,000	66,000
Total	$315,250	$283,500	$88,000

Production for the month:

Liters started	520,000	450,000	240,000
Liters finished (assume no spoilage)	450,000	360,000	200,000

Of the 360,000 liters finished in grinding and mixing, 120,000 liters became Warfal. The product finished in pasteurizing became, of course, Dingbat.

Unfinished production in each department is estimated to be one-half finished, including material, labor, and overhead.

Required:

1. Prepare an analysis of the cost per equivalent unit by department.
2. Prepare a summary of production for each department, showing costs in process distributed between units completed and transferred and uncompleted units in ending work in process.
3. Prepare a summary of total costs attached to completed Warfal and Dingbat production for February.
4. Prepare analyses of the cost per liter for Warfal and Dingbat.

3-17. The Walsch Company manufactures a single product, a mechanical device known as Klebo. The company maintains a process cost type of accounting system. The manufacturing operation is as follows: Material K, a metal, is stamped to form a part which is assembled with one of the purchased parts, X. The unit is then machined and cleaned, after which it is assembled with two units of part Y to form the finished device known as a Klebo. Spray priming and enameling is the final operation.

Time and motion studies indicate that, of the total time required for the manufacture of a unit, the first operation requires 25 percent of the labor cost, the first assembly an additional 25 percent, machining and cleaning 12.5 percent, the second assembly 25 percent, and painting 12.5 percent. Manufacturing overhead is considered to follow the same pattern by operations as does labor.

The following data are presented to you as of October 31, 19x9, the end of the first month of operation:

Material K purchased, 100,000 lb	$25,000
Part X purchased, 80,000 units	16,000
Part Y purchased, 150,000 units	15,000
Primer and enamel used, cost	1,072
Direct labor cost	45,415
Manufacturing overhead cost	24,905

	Unit quantities
Units finished and sent to finished goods warehouse	67,000
Units assembled but not painted	5,000
Units ready for second assembly	3,000
Inventories at the end of the month:	
Finished units	7,500
Material K, lb	25,000
Part X, units	5,000
Part Y, units	6,000
Klebos in process, units	8,000

It takes 1 pound of material K to make one Klebo. Assume no spoilage in production.

Required:

1. Prepare a schedule of equivalent labor production.
2. Prepare a schedule of total and unit costs incurred in production for (*a*) each kind of material; (*b*) labor cost; (*c*) manufacturing overhead; and (*d*) total cost of production.
3. Prepare a schedule of detailed material, labor, and overhead costs assigned to the units left in process.   (AICPA adapted)

3-18. The King Process Company manufactures one product, which goes through two processes, #1 and #2. For each unit of process #1 output, two units of raw material X are put in at the start of processing. For each unit of process #2 output, three cans of raw material Y are put in at the end of processing. Two pounds of process #1 output are placed in at the start of process #2 for each unit of finished goods started. In-process accounts are maintained for raw material, conversion costs, and prior department costs.

   Data for March are as follows:

   1. Units transferred:

From process #1 to process #2	2,200 lb
From process #2 to finished goods	1,000 gal
From finished goods to cost of goods sold	900 gal

   2. Raw material unit costs: X, $1.51 per unit; Y, $2 per can
   3. Conversion costs: process #1, $3,344; process #2, $4,010
   4. Inventory data:

	Process #1		Process #2		Finished goods	
	Initial	Final	Initial	Final	Initial	Final
Units	200	300	200	300	700	800
Fraction complete conversion costs	$\frac{1}{2}$	$\frac{1}{3}$	$\frac{1}{2}$	$\frac{2}{3}$		
Valuation:					$13,048	
Material	$604					
Conversion costs	106		$ 310			
Prior department costs			$1,808			

Required:

Journalize March entries to record the transfer of costs from process #1 to process #2, from process #2 to finished goods, and from finished goods to cost of goods sold. Prepare schedules of computations to support entries.   (AICPA adapted)

3-19. Bisto Corporation manufactures valves and pumps for liquids. On December 1, 19x4, Bisto paid $25,000 to the Poplen Company for the patent for its Watertite Valve. Bisto planned to carry on Poplen's procedure of having the valve casing and parts cast by an independent foundry and doing the grinding and assembling in its own plant.

   Bisto also purchased Poplen's inventory of the valves at 80 percent of its cost to Poplen. The purchased inventory was comprised of the following:

	Units
Raw material (unfinished casings and parts)	1,100
Work in process	
Grinding (25% complete)	800
Assembling (40% complete)	600
Finished valves	900

Poplen's cost accounting system provided the following unit costs:

	Cost per Unit
Raw material (unfinished casings and parts)	$2.00
Grinding costs	1.00
Assembling costs	2.50

Bisto's cost accounting system accumulated the following costs for the month of December, which do not include cost of the inventory purchased from Poplen:

Raw material purchases (casings and parts for 5,000 units)	$10,500
Grinding costs	2,430
Assembling costs	5,664

Bisto's inventory of Watertite Valves at December 31, 19x4, follows:

	Units
Raw material (unfinished casings and parts)	2,700
Work in process	
Grinding (35% complete)	2,000
Assembling (33⅓% complete)	300
Finished valves	2,250

No valves were spoiled or lost during the manufacturing process.

Required:
1. Prepare a schedule to compute the equivalent units produced and costs incurred per unit for the month of December 19x4.
2. Prepare a schedule of inventories on the FIFO (first in/first out) basis as of December 1 and 31, 19x4, setting forth by layers the number of units, unit costs, and amounts. Show all supporting schedules in good form.

(AICPA adapted)

 3-20. The Vatter Company manufactures a chemical product which passes through two processes. The materials are started into production at the beginning of process A and are passed directly to process B. Operating data for two months are given below:

June:
Process A: No beginning work in process. During June, 800 units were put into process and $8,000 of material costs were charged to this account, along with $2,800 of other costs; 600 units were completed and transferred to process B. The work in process on June 30 was one-half complete.

Process B: No beginning work in process. The units transferred from process A were received, and conversion costs of $2,000 were incurred to complete 300 units. At the end of June, 300 units, one-third completed, remained in the process.

July:
Process A: In this month, 600 units of material were put into process at a material cost of $6,000. Other costs incurred during the month totaled $2,540. At the end of July, there were 300 units, two-thirds finished, remaining in the process.

Process B: Conversion costs for July totaled $2,860. On July 31, the work in process was two-thirds complete and consisted of 300 units.

Required:

1. Develop the cost per equivalent unit for each department for the month of June, using the four-step procedure. Using the cost per unit figures, compute the ending inventories for each department.
2. Develop the cost per equivalent unit for each department for the month of July, using the four-step procedure. Using the cost per unit figures, compute the ending inventories for each department.

3-21. In the course of your examination of the financial statements of the Zeus Company for the year ended December 31, 1974, you have ascertained the following concerning its manufacturing operations:

a. Zeus has two production departments (fabricating and finishing) and a service department. In the fabricating department, polyplast is prepared from miracle mix and bypro. In the finishing department, each unit of polyplast is converted into six tetraplexes and three uniplexes. The service department provides services to both production departments.

b. The fabricating and finishing departments use process cost accounting systems. Actual production costs, including overhead, are allocated monthly.

c. Service department expenses are allocated to production departments as follows:

Expense	Allocation Base
Building maintenance	Space occupied
Timekeeping and personnel	Number of employees
Other	One-half to fabricating, one-half to finishing

d. Raw materials inventory and work in process are priced on a FIFO basis.

e. The following data were taken from the fabricating department's records for December 1974:

Quantities (units of polyplast):	
In process, December 1	3,000
Started in process during month	25,000
Total units to be accounted for	28,000
Transferred to finishing department	19,000
In process, December 31	6,000
Lost in process	3,000
Total units accounted for	28,000
Cost of work in process, December 1:	
Materials	$ 13,000
Labor	17,500
Overhead	21,500
	$ 52,000
Direct labor costs, December	$154,000
Departmental overhead, December	$132,000

f. Polyplast work in process at the beginning and end of the month was partially completed as follows:

	Materials	Labor and Overhead
December 1	66⅔%	50%
December 31	100 %	75%

g. The following data were taken from raw materials inventory records for December:

	Miracle Mix		Bypro	
	Quantity	Amount	Quantity	Amount
Balance, December 1	62,000	$62,000	265,000	$18,550
Purchases:				
December 12	39,500	49,375		
December 20	28,500	34,200		
Fabricating department usage	83,200		50,000	

h. Service department expenses for December (not included in departmental overhead above) were:

Building maintenance	$ 45,000
Timekeeping and personnel	27,500
Other	39,000
	$111,500

i. Other information for December 1974 is presented below:

	Square Feet of Space Occupied	Number of Employees
Fabricating	75,000	180
Finishing	37,500	120
	112,500	300

Required:

1. Compute the equivalent number of units of polyplast, with separate calculations for materials and conversion cost (direct labor plus overhead), manufactured during December.

2. Compute the following items to be included in the fabricating department's production report for December 1974, with separate calculations for materials, direct labor, and overhead. Prepare supporting schedules.

   a. Total costs to be accounted for.

   b. Unit costs for equivalent units manufactured.

   c. Transfers to finishing department during December and work in process at December 31. Reconcile to your answer to part 2*a*.

   (AICPA adapted)

PLANNING

CHAPTER

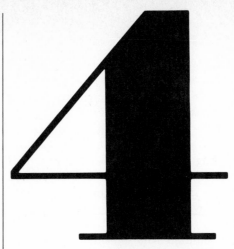

COST-VOLUME-PROFIT ANALYSIS

THE PLAN OF THIS CHAPTER
How do changes in the volume of activity affect the behavior of the firm's costs and ultimately its profits?

In suggesting answers to this question, the following topics will be discussed:

How management approaches the job of planning its profits

The behavior of costs in relation to volume

The calculation and meaning of the break-even point

The effects of changes in the underlying factors of profit

The assumptions upon which cost-volume-profit analysis rests

The limitations of cost-volume-profit analysis for profit planning

Management uses of cost-volume-profit analysis

PROFIT PLANNING

Usually, profits do not just happen. Profits are managed. Before we can make an intelligent approach to the managerial process of profit planning, it is important that we understand the management concept of profit. There are, after all, several different interpretations of the term "profit." An economist will say that profit is the reward for entrepreneurship—for risk taking. A labor leader might say that it is a measure of how efficiently labor has produced and that it provides a base for negotiating a wage increase. An investor will view it as a gauge of the return on his or her money. An internal revenue agent might regard it as the base for determining income taxes. The accountant will define it simply as the excess of a firm's revenue over the expense of producing revenue in a given fiscal period.

Using the accountant's measuring stick, management thinks of profit as:

A tangible expression of the goals it has set for the firm

A measure of the performance toward the achievement of its goals

A means of maintaining the health, growth, and continuity of the company

It is the ultimate objective of management to maximize profits over the long term, consistent with its social responsibility. To plan profits intelligently, management needs to know:

The economic characteristics of the firm's operations

The nature of the market for its products

The nature and severity of its competition

The costs of its factors of production: the material, the labor, the productive capacity, the capital

The relationship of the price it can get for its goods to the expense of producing and selling them

Suppose that management in a small manufacturing concern looked at the summary of its operating results for a period and saw the following:

Net sales	$500,000
Total expense	450,000
Net profit	$ 50,000

Whether this performance is considered good, bad, or indifferent, it is now in the past, and nothing further can be done about it. However, it is necessary to plan the next period's operations, and in the process, certain questions arise:

What condition existed which caused the period's operations to be profitable?

Could profits have been improved? If so, how?

Can the conditions which enabled profitable performance be expected to prevail in the period ahead?

What would be the effects of the following changes in the next period?

An increase or reduction in the selling price of the product

An increase or decrease in wage rates in the factory

An increase or decrease in the cost of materials

An increase or decrease in the efficiency of production

Increased property taxes; increased depreciation due to the addition of new equipment; salary increases to key people in the organization, etc.; or a decrease in expenses as a result of a successful cost-reduction program in the company

An increase or decrease in the volume of goods produced and sold

Clearly, the preceding summary information on profits will answer none of these questions. As a further step in analysis, management might try the following: Assume that the company makes only one product, all units alike, selling at $10 per unit, and that it sold 50,000 units:

	Total	Per Unit	Percent
Net sales	$500,000	$10	100
Total expenses	450,000	9	90
Net profit	$ 50,000	$ 1	10

It is clear that during the past period, it cost $9 per unit to make and sell the product, and that a profit of $1 each, representing 10 percent of net sales was realized. Now management wants to know whether it can expect $40,000 profit if it sells only 40,000 units, and whether it can plan on $60,000 profit if it sells 60,000. This would be the conclusion if expenses were incurred uniformly at $9 each from the first to the last unit in any given period.

BEHAVIOR OF EXPENSES IN RELATION TO VOLUME

Elementary knowledge of how expenses are incurred, however, leads to a ready rejection of the idea that a unit will cost $9 at all volume levels.

Some expenses, such as real estate taxes, insurance, straight-line depreciation on the factory building, the plant superintendent's salary, and many similar factory overhead expenses, are incurred on the basis of a certain amount per period of time, independently of the number of units that might be produced during that period. Because such costs are generally incurred in order to provide a certain capacity for the firm's production and sales activities, they are often referred to as *capacity (or fixed) costs.*

On the other hand, there are certain types of expense, directly identified with each unit of product, which will be incurred if a unit is made and avoided if it is not. The major expenses of this type are the direct materials in the product, the cost of the productive labor operations on the product (these two constituting the prime cost of manufacturing), and certain factory overhead expenses, such as indirect labor, indirect material, and power. These product costs are usually designated as *variable costs*, inasmuch as their total will change in direct relation to the change in the level of volume.

Suppose a study of the $450,000 total expenses in the last example reveals that those which are incurred directly with each unit of product—the variable costs—amount to $6 per unit. Further, assume that those costs which are independent of changes in the volume of production—the fixed costs—amount to $150,000. An income statement can be set up to reflect the costs thus classified:

	Total	Per Unit
Net sales	$500,000	$10
Variable costs	300,000	6
Margin—sales over variable costs	$200,000	$ 4
Fixed costs	150,000	3
Net profit	$ 50,000	$ 1

If the company can produce as many as 60,000 units without adding to its fixed costs, the following comparison can be made of the results to be expected if operations are carried on at levels of 40,000, 50,000, and 60,000 units per period, assuming the same selling price and variable costs as before:

	40,000 Units	50,000 Units	60,000 Units
Net sales ($10/unit)	$400,000	$500,000	$600,000
Variable costs ($6/unit)	240,000	300,000	360,000
Margin—sales over variable costs	$160,000	$200,000	$240,000
Fixed costs	150,000	150,000	150,000
Net profit	$ 10,000	$ 50,000	$ 90,000
Percentage of net profit to net sales	2.5%	10%	15%

This comparison should answer management's question as to whether an increase or decrease in volume will change profit expectations. The fact that 10 percent was earned on sales of $500,000 is obviously no assurance that $40,000 will be earned on $400,000 of sales or that $60,000 will be realized on $600,000. For this to be true, *all* costs would have to be variable, and this clearly is not the case.

As can be inferred from this simple comparison, it is likely that 10 percent will be earned only at the sales volume of 50,000 units if factors of fixed costs, unit variable costs, and unit selling prices remain unchanged.

BREAK-EVEN POINT

The margin of sales over variable costs, as in the preceding profit summaries, will henceforth be called the *contribution margin.* Conceptually, this is the con-

tribution made by the sales of any period, after payment of all applicable variable costs, toward the recovery of the fixed costs of that period and the realization of profit (in that order).

Like the revenue and cost factors, contribution margin can be expressed
per unit or in total. In the example, the contribution margin per unit is the excess
of the unit selling price ($10) over the unit variable cost ($6), and it amounts to
$4. Since fixed costs are stable, enough sales revenue (units sold times unit sell-
ing price) must be realized in each period for these fixed costs to be met out of
the total contribution margin (units sold times unit contribution margin) before a
profit is earned. Once the fixed costs are recovered in a period, however, all
additional contribution margin becomes profit.

Regarded in this way, the operations in the early part of any period are
carried on at a loss, and profits are earned only later in the period, when and if
enough volume is realized to recover the fixed costs. Thus, if the small manufacturer in the previous example did a volume of business totaling 50,000 units
for a calendar year and if sales were made uniformly over that period, profits for
the year actually were not realized until about October. It was then that the sales
totaled 37,500 units, the level at which the total contribution margin was sufficient to recover $150,000 of capacity costs.

Here is the way it is determined:

$$\frac{\$150,000 \text{ fixed costs}}{\$4 \text{ contribution margin per unit sold}} = 37,500 \text{ units}$$

After 37,500 units are sold, profit is earned at the rate of $4 per unit:

$$\$4 \times 12,500 \text{ units} = \$50,000$$

The quantity of 37,500 units in this instance constitutes the *break-even*
point, that is, the level of volume at which total expenses equal total revenue,
and profit is zero. The income statement at 37,500 units would appear thus:

Net sales	(37,500 × $10)	$375,000
Variable costs	(37,500 × $ 6)	225,000
Contribution margin	(37,500 × $ 4)	$150,000
Fixed costs		150,000
Net profit		$ -0-

Calculation of the Break-even Point

The calculation of the break-even point in number of units may be expressed in
the very simple formula:

$$\frac{\text{Fixed costs (total \$)}}{\text{Contribution margin (expressed as \$ per unit)}}$$

which is the same as

$$\frac{\text{Fixed costs (total \$)}}{\text{Unit selling price} - \text{unit variable cost}}$$

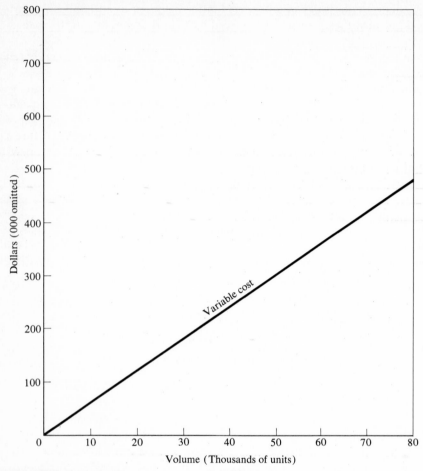

EXHIBIT 4-1   Variable cost

Frequently it is necessary to calculate the break-even point in total dollar volume of sales, especially where different kinds of units may be sold at different selling prices. In this case, the percentage of contribution margin to sales is substituted for the contribution margin (dollars per unit) in the formula above, and it becomes

$$\frac{\text{Fixed costs (total \$)}}{\text{Contribution margin (\% of net sales)}}$$

which is the same as

$$\frac{\text{Fixed costs (total \$)}}{1 - \dfrac{\text{total variable costs (\$)}}{\text{net sales (\$)}}}$$

The expression

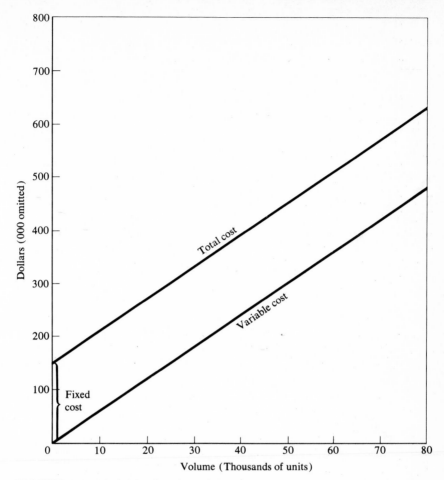

EXHIBIT 4-2   Variable, fixed, and total cost

$$1 - \frac{\text{total variable costs (\$)}}{\text{net sales (\$)}}$$

should thus be recognized as the percentage of contribution margin to net sales. Using the figures in the example:

Break-even point (units):

$$\frac{\$150,000}{\$10 - \$6} = \frac{\$150,000}{\$4} = 37,500 \text{ units}$$

Break-even point ($ of net sales):

$$\frac{\$150,000}{1 - \dfrac{\$300,000}{\$500,000}} = \frac{\$150,000}{1 - 0.60} = \frac{\$150,000}{0.40} = \$375,000$$

The concept of break-even analysis may be even more readily grasped if

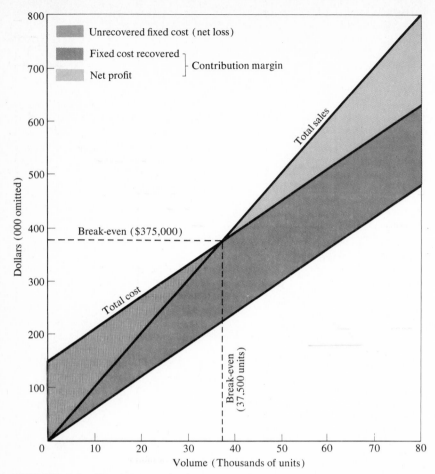

EXHIBIT 4-3   Break-even chart

portrayed graphically. A break-even chart consists of three basic lines drawn on a two-dimensional scale, with the horizontal axis scaled for volume and the vertical axis scaled for dollars. The first step is to plot the variable cost line as shown in Exhibit 4-1.

Next, the fixed cost line is superimposed parallel to the variable cost line. The space between the two represents $150,000, and is the same across the full range of volume, denoting the assumption that the amount of fixed cost does not change as volume changes. The top of the fixed cost line represents the line of total cost, which is $150,000 greater than variable cost at any level of volume (see Exhibit 4-2). Finally, the total sales line is added (see Exhibit 4-3). Note that, while it varies in direct relation to volume, the slope of the total sales line is steeper than that of the variable cost line, because for every additional unit sold, more dollars of revenue are added ($10 unit selling price) than dollars of variable cost ($6 unit variable cost).

The space between the total variable cost and the total sales lines represents the contribution margin. The nature of the contribution margin is readily

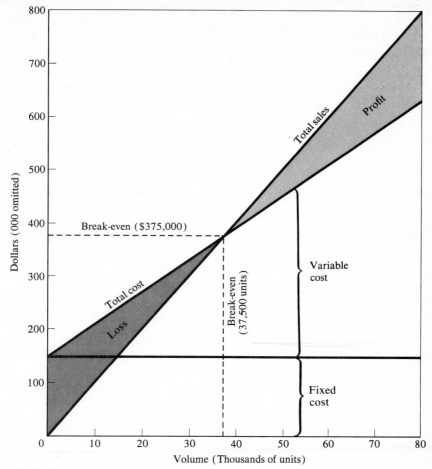

EXHIBIT 4-4   Break-even chart

apparent as it pursues the total cost line up the scale as volume increases. When
it overtakes the total cost line and intersects it, the break-even volume has been
reached.

Below and to the left of the break-even point, the space between the total
cost and total sales lines (medium gray) denotes the amount of fixed cost not yet
recovered by the contribution margin, which equals the net loss for the period at
any volume short of the break-even point.

By the same token, the space between the total sales and total cost lines
(light gray) and to the right of the break-even point represents net profit for the
period at any volume beyond the break-even point.

Another popular form of presenting the break-even chart is shown in Exhibit 4-4. It will be noted that the positions of the fixed and variable cost lines are
reversed, but that their sum — the total cost line — is the same as in Exhibit 4-3.
The two charts *are alike in every respect* except for the positions of the fixed and
variable cost lines.

The distinct advantage of the form depicted in Exhibit 4-3 is that it conveys so clearly the role of contribution margin in the relationship of volume to profit. Hence its use is preferred in this book. Although they are called break-even charts, the most vital aspect of either of the graphs presented in Exhibits 4-3 and 4-4 lies in the portrayal of the net profit or net loss at *any* volume, as well as the contribution margin at all levels. Also, by application of one or the other break-even formula to the relevant cost and sales figures in any given situation, the profit for most levels of volume can be approximated.

It must be emphasized, however, that the relationships portrayed by the break-even chart are static, and there is the implicit assumption that no changes will occur in any of its factors other than volume. But business is quite dynamic, and the factors are changing constantly. The consequent limitations of break-even analysis are noted later in the chapter.

CHANGES IN UNDERLYING FACTORS

As stated earlier, profit as measured in accounting terms is the excess of revenue over expenses. Management, however, must look behind the summary figures to the factors which *cause* revenues and expenses to be what they are.

For example, the net sales figure signifying revenue for the period (e.g., $500,000) results from multiplying the physical quantity of goods sold by the appropriate selling price (e.g., 50,000 units times $10). Here it is evident that *quantity* is only one factor; *price* is of equal importance.

The same process underlies the determination of most variable costs. For example, the total incurred cost of material is based on the multiplication of the physical *quantity* of each kind of material used by its appropriate purchase *price* per unit (e.g., pounds of steel times price of steel per pound). This cost, in turn, must be converted to a cost per unit of finished product by applying the engineering specifications of the quantity of each kind of material used in the product (e.g., 2 pounds of steel in each unit of product times price per pound of steel $0.075 equals $0.15 cost of steel per unit of product).

Total direct labor cost incurred is determined in much the same way, by multiplying hours worked by the hourly wage rate. The labor cost per unit of finished product is the result of dividing the hourly wage rate by the expected labor production rate per hour (e.g., $2.50 wage rate per hour divided by expected production of 25 units per hour equals $0.10 labor cost per unit).

Fixed costs, on the other hand, are generally measured in terms of some definite amount per period, such as factory rent per month, engineers' salaries per year, and security guards' salaries per week. Management will determine the limits of the productive capacity of the firm for a given period, which, in turn, will govern the amount of such costs.

A series of questions which management might be expected to ask regarding the factors affecting the profits of a future period was given earlier in the chapter. At this point, it may be helpful to examine the effects on the planned profit in a future period of certain possible changes in the factors of profit.

Change in Selling Price

1. Suppose that management wishes to know the effect on break-even

point (BE) and profit, at a volume of 50,000 units, of a 10 percent increase in selling price (assuming that other factors will remain the same as given previously).

		Original
Net sales (50,000 @ $11)	$550,000	$500,000
Variable costs (50,000 @ $6)	300,000	300,000
Contribution margin ($5 per unit)	$250,000	$200,000
Fixed costs	150,000	150,000
Net profit	$100,000	$ 50,000
Percentage of net profit to net sales	18.2%	10%
Percentage of contribution margin to net sales	45.5%	40%

$$BE = \frac{\$150,000}{\$5} = 30,000 \text{ units} \qquad\qquad 37,500 \text{ units}$$

$$BE = \frac{\$150,000}{0.455} = \$330,000 \text{ (rounded)} \qquad\qquad \$375,000$$

2. What would be the effect of a 20 percent decrease in selling prices, assuming no change in the other factors?

		Original
Net sales (50,000 @ $8)	$400,000	$500,000
Variable costs (50,000 @ $6)	300,000	300,000
Contribution margin ($2 per unit)	$100,000	$200,000
Fixed costs	150,000	150,000
Net profit (loss)	($ 50,000)	$ 50,000
Percentage of net profit to net sales	(12.5%)	10%
Percentage of contribution margin to net sales	25.0%	40%

$$BE = \frac{\$150,000}{\$2} = 75,000 \text{ units} \qquad\qquad 37,500 \text{ units}$$

$$BE = \frac{\$150,000}{0.25} = \$600,000 \qquad\qquad \$375,000$$

These analyses demonstrate rather dramatically the sensitivity of profit and break-even point to changes in selling price. A doubling of net profit is observed in analysis 1 by simply increasing the selling price 10 percent under existing conditions. It should be noted also that the break-even point in units dropped by 7,500 — a decrease of 20 percent. Although break-even in total dollars also decreased, it was in smaller proportion, being partly offset by the increased selling price.

The effect of an opposite change in price should give pause to the over-zealous sales manager. Analysis 2 indicates that a 20 percent reduction in selling price at a volume of 50,000 units wipes out the profit, causes a $50,000 loss, and doubles the volume which must be sold to break even — from 37,500 to 75,000.

The key to this extreme reaction lies in the effect on contribution margin. At a selling price of $10, the margin was $4, or 40 percent. The $2 reduction in selling price comes directly out of the contribution margin, since variable costs do not change. The result is that the new contribution margin of $2 represents only 25 percent of the new selling price of $8. Since it is this margin which has to do the work of covering fixed costs and profit, drastic things happen to profit when it is cut in half. This "leverage" effect constitutes a vital factor in cost-volume-profit relationships.

Change in Variable Costs

1. Assume that management anticipates an increase in factory wage rates which will result in an increase of 5 percent in total variable costs. (Other factors will be assumed to remain the same as before.)

		Original
Net sales (50,000 @ $10)	$500,000	$500,000
Variable costs (50,000 @ $6.30)	315,000	300,000
Contribution margin ($3.70)	$185,000	$200,000
Fixed costs	150,000	150,000
Net profit	$ 35,000	$ 50,000
Percentage of net profit to net sales	7%	10%
Percentage of contribution margin to net sales	37%	40%

$$BE = \frac{\$150,000}{\$3.70} = 40,540 \text{ units} \qquad\qquad 37,500 \text{ units}$$

$$BE = \frac{\$150,000}{0.37} = \$405,400 \qquad\qquad \$375,000$$

2. Assume that management anticipates a decrease of 10 percent in total variable costs, due to reductions in the purchase prices of various materials.

		Original
Net sales (50,000 @ $10)	$500,000	$500,000
Variable costs (50,000 @ $5.40)	270,000	300,000
Contribution margin ($4.60)	$230,000	$200,000
Fixed costs	150,000	150,000
Net profit	$ 80,000	$ 50,000
Percentage of net profit to net sales	16%	10%
Percentage of contribution margin to net sales	46%	40%

$$BE = \frac{\$150,000}{\$4.60} = 32,610 \text{ units} \qquad\qquad 37,500 \text{ units}$$

$$BE = \frac{\$150,000}{0.46} = \$326,100 \qquad\qquad \$375,000$$

Once again the cost-volume-profit analysis reveals a sensitivity in profit and break-even point to change in unit factors, this time in the area of variable costs. For example, in analysis 1 an increase of only 30 cents per unit in variable costs results in a $15,000 drop in net profit (30 percent of its former level) and indicates the need of selling approximately 3,000 more units to break even. On the other hand, in analysis 2 the 10 percent reduction in variable costs boosts profit by 60 percent ($30,000) and effects a reduction of nearly 5,000 units in the break-even point.

The factors assumed to change in these illustrations were the unit rate factors of cost: wage rates and material prices. The same type of effect would be realized if, for example, changes were made which increased labor efficiency, increased machine output per hour, or decreased the quantity of material per unit through redesign of the product. Since most variable costs are determined by the multiplications of a given rate by a given quantity, a change in either the rate or the quantity factor would have significant effects on expenses, profit, and break-even point.

Change in Fixed Costs

1. Management would like to know the effect on profit and break-even point if increased property taxes, depreciation of new equipment, and increased salaries to key people in the organization should cause total fixed costs to increase $10,000. As before, other factors remain unchanged.

		Original
Net sales (50,000 @ $10)	$500,000	$500,000
Variable costs (50,000 @ $6)	300,000	300,000
Contribution margin ($4)	$200,000	$200,000
Fixed costs	160,000	150,000
Net profit	$ 40,000	$ 50,000
Percentage of net profit to net sales	8%	10%
Percentage of contribution margin to net sales	40%	40%

$$BE = \frac{\$160,000}{\$4} = 40,000 \text{ units} \qquad\qquad 37,500 \text{ units}$$

$$BE = \frac{\$160,000}{0.40} = \$400,000 \qquad\qquad \$375,000$$

2. What would be the effect of a companywide cost-reduction program which resulted in a reduction of $15,000 in total fixed costs?

		Original
Net sales (50,000 @ $10)	$500,000	$500,000
Variable costs (50,000 @ $6)	300,000	300,000
Contribution margin ($4)	$200,000	$200,000
Fixed costs	135,000	150,000
Net profit	$ 65,000	$ 50,000
Percentage of net profit to net sales	13%	10%
Percentage of contribution margin to net sales	40%	40%

$$BE = \frac{\$135,000}{\$4} = 33,750 \text{ units} \qquad\qquad 37,500 \text{ units}$$

$$BE = \frac{\$135,000}{0.40} = \$337,500 \qquad\qquad \$375,000$$

Dollar changes in fixed costs, when other factors remain unchanged, are translated directly into equal and opposite changes in dollars of net profit. Because the contribution margin per unit is unchanged, the leverage effect is limited. Thus break-even points react somewhat sluggishly to such changes, in contrast to their sensitivity to changes in variable cost and selling price factors. For example, in analysis 1, an increase of $10,000 in fixed costs caused the break-even point to go up only 2,500 units. This is not to underrate changes in fixed costs. Changes in break-even point can be significant if the changes in fixed costs are substantial.

Change in Volume

Generally, management will be cautious about raising or lowering selling prices in view of the sensitivity of the profit and break-even point to such changes. Nevertheless, it is often believed that the level of volume can be manipulated by means of price changes or that competitive conditions may require it. Economists offer the concept of *elasticity of demand* as a tool of analysis in such circumstances. Essentially, this concept holds that demand is relatively elastic if lowering the price of the product causes an increase in its sales volume sufficient to increase the total revenue over that realized at the former (higher) price, or if raising the price causes volume to decrease sufficiently to cause a reduction in total revenue. Thus it is interesting to observe the profit effect of volume changes brought about by changes in selling prices.

1. Suppose that management believes that an increase of 10 percent in selling price will result in the loss of 10,000 units of volume. (All expense factors are assumed to remain unchanged.)

		Original
Net sales (40,000 @ $11)	$440,000	$500,000
Variable costs (40,000 @ $6)	240,000	300,000
Contribution margin ($5)	$200,000	$200,000
Fixed costs	150,000	150,000
Net profit	$ 50,000	$ 50,000
Percentage of net profit to net sales	11.4%	10%
Percentage of contribution margin to net sales	45.5%	40%

$$BE = \frac{\$150,000}{\$5} = 30,000 \text{ units} \qquad\qquad 37,500 \text{ units}$$

$$BE = \frac{\$150,000}{0.455} = \$330,000 \text{ (rounded)} \qquad\qquad \$375,000$$

2. What would be the effect of a 15 percent price reduction which would stimulate a 20 percent increase in volume?

		Original
Net sales (60,000 @ $8.50)	$510,000	$500,000
Variable costs (60,000 @ $6)	360,000	300,000
Contribution margin ($2.50)	$150,000	$200,000
Fixed costs	150,000	150,000
Net profit	-0-	$ 50,000
Percentage of net profit to net sales	-0-	10%
Percentage of contribution margin to net sales	29.4%	40.0%

$$BE = \frac{\$150,000}{\$2.50} = 60,000 \text{ units} \qquad\qquad\qquad 37,500 \text{ units}$$

$$BE = \frac{\$150,000}{0.294} = \$510,000 \text{ (rounded)} \qquad\qquad \$375,000$$

Percentage changes exhibit rather peculiar behavior, as the data just given will indicate. At first glance, neither change seems advantageous.

In the case of analysis 1, despite relative elasticity of demand, the substantial reduction of volume is cushioned by the increased contribution margin. Under these conditions, net dollar profit is preserved. A definite advantage may be seen, however, in the improved percentage of profit to net sales, the lowered break-even point, and the likelihood that this lower volume can be managed on a smaller investment in operating assets, thus improving the return on capital used.

In the case of analysis 2, again despite relative elasticity of demand, the advantage of increased volume is more than wiped out by the decreased contribution margin. Here, profit is eliminated and the break-even point is increased substantially.

Generally speaking, there is considerable hazard in attempting to increase volume by reducing selling prices, elasticity of demand notwithstanding. Not only are contribution margin diminished and break-even point increased, but there is the serious risk of incurring competitive retaliation in the form of similar price cutting, with the result that little, if any, additional volume is gained.

ASSUMPTIONS AND LIMITATIONS

Cost-volume-profit analysis, as explained in this chapter, constitutes a very useful tool for management planning. Certain underlying assumptions upon which it rests, however, place definite limitations on the conclusions which can be drawn from its results.

To begin with, this type of analysis is static, whereas business is dynamic. No sooner has the analyst gotten a "fix" on the various pertinent factors than they begin to drift away from him. The following are some of the static assumptions upon which this analysis is based.

1. *All costs can be classified as fixed or variable.* It is exceedingly difficult, if indeed it is possible, to classify all costs as variable or fixed. Some, such as those associated with a work stoppage due to a strike, a fire, or some other unusual circumstance, are distinctly erratic.

Others may bear an inverse relationship to volume—machinery maintenance, for instance, which is often postponed while the plant is operating at a high level of activity, only to be increased in a slack period when volume has decreased.

Another difficulty arises from the traditional accounting practice of recording expenses in accounts according to their object, with the result that certain accounts contain a mixture of fixed and variable parts. Where supervisors are paid a base salary plus a production bonus, with both parts recorded in one account for supervisors' compensation, the result is a mixture of variable (the bonus) and fixed (the base salary) costs. There are ways of separating mixed costs into their variable and fixed constituents, but this condition does pose analytical difficulties.

2. _Fixed costs will not change over the entire capacity range._ The assumption that fixed costs will remain the same from zero volume to peak activity does not conform to reality.

Under shutdown conditions of any significant duration, management will cut the cost of capacity to the bone. Even short of complete curtailment of production, management has been known to reduce executive salaries or rent its idle facilities to other firms.

At the other end of the volume scale, sustained high volume may necessitate adding shifts, with increases in supervision cost, factory engineering staff, clerical employees, and the like. Frequently it becomes necessary to rent additional space and buy or rent more equipment to accommodate added volume. When such moves are made to expand capacity temporarily, activity reaches a point in volume where fixed costs move up abruptly in a pattern which would appear as a step on a break-even chart.

For the purpose of realistic cost-volume-profit analysis, the relevant range of volume is the space between two steps on the fixed cost line.

Since such a range of activity is established by management decision and cannot be measured precisely, it is usually described as the range over which the cost of capacity remains fixed. It follows that the lower limit of such a relevant range is the level of volume at which management would make drastic reductions in the cost of capacity, and its upper limit would represent the point at which no more volume can be squeezed out of existing capacity, necessitating a definite, if temporary, expansion. The graphic description of relevant volume range and its steplike behavior may be seen in Exhibit 4-5.

3. _The behavior of costs will be linear (i.e., will show as straight lines on a chart), and variable costs will change in direct proportion to changes in volume._ As explained in the foregoing paragraphs, there are a number of reasons why the variable and fixed costs will not exhibit a linear relationship in a volume analysis.

To these reasons the typical economist will add the fact that unit variable costs do not remain constant at all levels of volume, but tend to be greater at low volume, to decrease as volume increases to the level of greatest efficiency, and to increase again when volume exceeds that point of optimum efficiency. On a chart, the total of these variable costs would describe an ascending curve with two bends, instead of the straight line we see on the typical management break-even chart (see Exhibit 4-6).

As in the case of fixed costs, however, there is a range of volume levels over which the total variable cost line is approximated rather closely by a

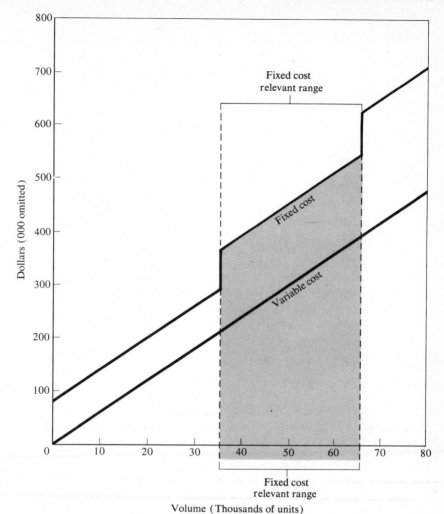

EXHIBIT 4-5   Fixed cost in steps (with relevant range indicated)

straight line. This is illustrated in Exhibit 4-6. Thus, there is a relevant range
for fixed costs and a relevant range for variable costs—and they typically
would not be exactly the same.

4. *Units of product and selling prices are homogeneous (i.e., all alike), or*
the proportions of different types of products with different prices will not
change in the "sales mix." It can be said with a great deal of truth that, in
a company with a diversified product line, there is no single break-even point
for the company—only for the major product divisions or segments.

The assumption of a constant sales mix for a company is one of the
most tenuous of all assertions. For the company which has progressed beyond the single-product–single-price composition of sales (and most modern companies have), there is greater benefit in cost-volume-profit analysis
for the major product segments than for the company as a whole.

The greatest difficulty here is to identify fixed cost accurately with each

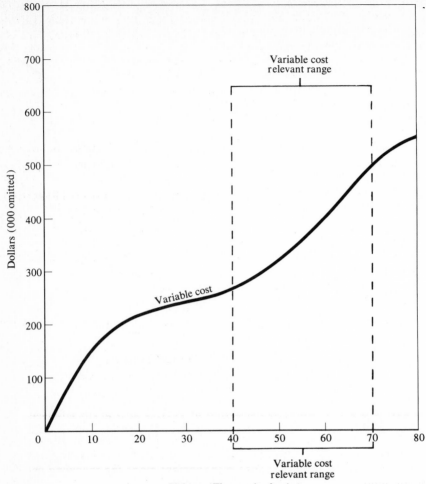

EXHIBIT 4-6   Curvilinear variable cost

segment. This task is more difficult for the company which produces a variety
of products in the same plant and markets them through the same channels.
However, such difficulties have been overcome with some degree of precision and reliability by some companies; and where it can be done, it is worth
the trouble.

5. *There is no significant difference between production and sales in the
period being analyzed.* Great care must be exercised to measure revenue
and expense in terms of the same volume base. Almost never are the volume
of production and that of sales the same for any given period of a company's activity. Either sales will exceed production, or vice versa.

Because expenses are most easily measured as they are incurred, it is
frequently found that the easiest and safest way to put revenue and expense
on the same volume base it to calculate the sales value of production volume
for use as the revenue factor. A widely used alternative is variable costing,
which will be treated in some detail in Chapter 9.

6.   *There are no changes in material prices or wage rates, no design changes in the product, no methods changes in manufacture, nor any significant changes in the efficiency or productivity during the period being analyzed.* Changes in product design, methods, efficiency, wage rates, and other rate factors in cost are occurring constantly in a dynamic business.

The best that any analyst can do when studying the cost-volume-profit relationships of a past period is to average the changes over the period, if they were not too radical. For important changes which would distort the ordinary revenue-expense relationships, appropriate adjustments must be made.

When this analysis is applied to planning for a future period, such changes in the factors as may be foreseeable should be introduced into the analysis to show their proper effect. As a general rule, however, only a continuous process of updating the analyses, giving recognition to factor changes as they occur, can ensure the reliability of the conclusions drawn from them.

Let it be repeated that cost-volume-profit analysis can be extremely useful as a planning tool, but it is subject to definite limitations by virtue of its static nature and the many underlying assumptions upon which it rests.

MANAGEMENT USES OF COST-VOLUME-PROFIT ANALYSIS

Now that the mechanics of cost-volume-profit analysis have been illustrated and its assumptions and consequent limitations explained, it is possible to describe in greater detail its usefulness to management.

1.   *Management plans future operations with cost-volume-profit analysis.* As was stated earlier, profits do not just happen — they must be managed and planned. By estimating what the selling price, unit variable cost, total fixed costs, and sales volume will be next month, for example, management can estimate next month's profit. Suppose management made the following estimates for June:

Sales (55,000 units @ $10 each)	$550,000
Variable costs (55,000 units @ $6 each)	330,000
Contribution margin ($4 each)	220,000
Fixed costs ($150,000/month)	150,000
Estimated net profit for June	$ 70,000

Management can now use this estimated or budgeted net profit statement in several ways. Assuming that management believes that the estimates of selling price, unit variable cost, total fixed cost, and sales volume are all reasonable, the estimated net profit for June itself can then be examined. Is it high enough? Should management be earning more profit for its stockholders, considering the amount of investment in the firm? Is net profit too high? Is management earning such high profits that it will encourage the development of competing products which will hurt its profit in the future?

If management believes profits are too low or too high, then cost-volume-profit analysis can be used to determine the likely effects of changes it may wish to make in any of the variables. For example, management may decide to improve profits by increasing the advertising expenditures (part of fixed costs) from $10,000 to $15,000 per month. Sales volume is expected to increase to 60,000 units per month as a direct result of this change. The revised budgeted net profit for June would then be as follows:

Sales (60,000 units @ $10 each)	$600,000
Variable costs (60,000 units @ $6 each)	360,000
Contribution margin ($4 each)	240,000
Fixed costs (now $155,000/month)	155,000
Estimated net profit for June	$ 85,000

In making this revised estimate, management assumed that the increased volume would not affect unit variable costs or fixed costs other than advertising expenditures. It also assumed that all 60,000 units expected to be sold in June would be sold at the same price of $10. Management will, of course, develop budgets in much greater detail than those shown here, but cost-volume-profit analysis can be used as a starting point and as a quick and easy way to determine the likely effects of management policy changes.

2. *Management uses the budgeted amounts to control operations through-out the month.* Management should not now just sit back and wait until the end of June to see if it was right or wrong. During the month, sales and cost figures actually incurred should be compared with those expected to see if any additional action should be taken. Suppose, for example, that the advertising campaign was not as effective as was originally expected. Management should then use cost-volume-profit analysis to determine the probable effects of various alternatives which may be considered.

3. *Management uses cost-volume-profit analysis to analyze past performance.* Suppose that the actual results for June turned out as follows:

Sales (60,000 units)	$594,000
Variable costs	363,000
Contribution margin	231,000
Fixed costs	153,000
Actual net profit for June	$ 78,000

Management should determine the reason for differences, or variances, between budgeted and actual results. An accounting report summarizing these differences is often called a variance report:

	June, Budgeted	June, Actual	Variance (Budget-Actual)
Sales	$600,000	$594,000	$6,000 (1)
Variable cost	360,000	363,000	3,000 (2)
Contribution margin	240,000	231,000	9,000
Fixed costs	155,000	153,000	2,000 (3)
Net profit	$ 85,000	$ 78,000	$7,000

Explanation of variances:
1. There is a $6,000 sales variance because some discounts were given to certain customers in order to meet the 60,000 units budgeted to be sold.
2. The $3,000 variable cost variance is a result of reduced efficiency in the plant.
3. Fixed costs were $2,000 lower than expected because some planned maintenance and repairs were postponed until next month.

The most important part of a variance report is the explanation of the variances. The numbers involved in the calculation of the variance give management a good indication of where to look for explanations, but the numbers themselves are not as useful to management as are the explanations. It is the explanations which indicate to management whether any additional action can and should be taken. Once the variances have been explained, management must decide what changes, if any, should be made in succeeding months. Necessary corrective actions can be planned to bring actual results in line with future plans (budgets), or future plans can be made to reflect items management cannot control. These variances and their explanations can also be used to evaluate the performance of submanagers. Part of their job is to ensure that things go according to plan, so comparing the budget with actual results gives management a good idea of how well the submanagers are performing this part of their job.

It can be seen that cost-volume-profit analysis is an integral part of management's administrative function. Chapter 1 described this function as including planning, organizing, and controlling. Cost-volume-profit analysis can make an important contribution to each of these activities. It provides a framework for planning future operations and a means for determining the likely effects of various ways of organizing those operations. In addition, cost-volume-profit analysis can be used to control current operations by comparing actual results with planned results. This entire process will be described in much more detail in later chapters, but it is important to note now that it is a cyclical and continuous process:

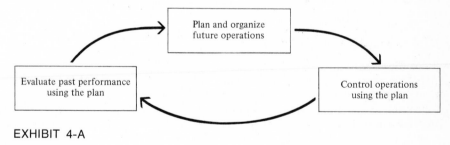

EXHIBIT 4-A

SUMMARY

Management plans profits. Although the results of operations in a given period may show a certain profit per unit sold, it must be recognized that such a figure is an average profit per unit sold that prevailed only under the conditions of volume for that period. The volume at which a firm operates is an integral factor in its profit plan. Because of the behavior of fixed costs, which remain stable over a broad, relevant range of normal operating volume, profits will vary depending on the volume achieved.

There is no profit from a period's operations until the fixed costs of the period have been recovered. Variable costs claim the first portion of the selling price of every unit sold. The residual amount of sales over variable costs is called the contribution margin. In effect, this factor is the dollar contribution of sales to the recovery of fixed costs and profits, in that order. Thus, when volume is sufficient to boost the contribution beyond the level of fixed costs, a profit is earned.

The level of volume at which enough units have been sold to accumulate contribution margin equal to fixed costs is called the break-even point—the point of zero profit. When factors of unit selling price, unit variable cost, unit contribution margin, and total fixed costs are known, the break-even volume can be established and the profits for different levels of forecast volume can be determined.

When changes are expected in selling prices, in rates of variable cost factors, in efficiency, or in the amount of fixed costs, an analysis of the cost-volume-profit relationship can determine the effects of such changes on the period's profit under the conditions forecast. In this way profit planning is sharpened considerably.

The value of cost-volume-profit analysis is limited by its static character and the assumptions on which it is based; but used with discretion by a skillful management accounting analyst, it becomes a potent weapon in management's strategic arsenal.

KEY WORDS AND PHRASES

capacity costs	elasticity of demand
fixed costs	mixed costs
variable costs	relevant range
contribution margin	sales mix
break-even point	

DISCUSSION QUESTIONS

1. "Don't confuse me with all the theoretical folderol about profit concepts. There's only one workable concept—take all you can get for as little cost as you can get by with." Do you agree? Why?
2. What must management know to plan profits intelligently?
3. Why, if management prices a product to yield $1 profit per unit, cannot management plan as many dollars of profit as units sold, regardless of volume?
4. Why are fixed costs often referred to as capacity costs?
5. What makes fixed costs fixed?
6. Can fixed costs be controlled?
7. What makes variable costs variable?
8. Explain the concept of contribution margin.
9. Explain the break-even concept.
10. How is the break-even point determined in terms of sales of physical units? Of total dollar volume of sales? How are these methods alike?
11. Why should there be two methods of calculating the break-even point?
12. "In a profit-motivated industry or economy, nobody operates to break even—so why bother with break-even charts?" Do you agree? Why?
13. Discuss the effect on profit of changes in the following: (a) selling price; (b) unit variable cost; (c) total fixed cost; (d) volume.
14. What is meant by elasticity of demand? Give examples.
15. When management is contemplating an increase or decrease in selling

prices, what factors affecting profits must be considered besides elasticity of demand?

16. Can all costs be classified as fixed and variable? Elaborate.
17. Explain what is meant by "the relevant range."
18. Will cost behavior be linear over the entire range of volume applicable to a given firm? Explain.
19. What has sales mix to do with break-even analysis and profit planning?
20. What effect do changes in wage rates, material prices, product design, manufacturing methods, efficiency, and the like have on break-even analysis and profit planning?
21. "We price our product to incur a loss on each unit we sell, but we intend to make it up on the volume." Comment.

PROBLEMS

4-1. *Part A.* After reading an article you recommended on cost behavior, your client asks you to explain the following excerpts from it:

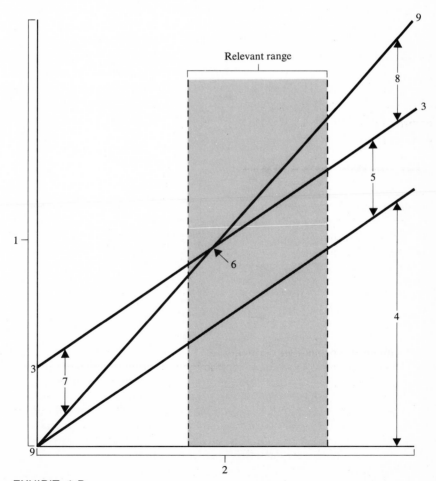

EXHIBIT 4-B

    1. "*Fixed costs* are variable per unit of output and *variable costs* are fixed per unit of output (though in the long run all costs are variable)."

    2. "*Depreciation* may be either a fixed cost or a variable cost, depending on the method used to compute it."

Required:

For each excerpt:

1. Define the italicized terms. Give examples where appropriate.
2. Explain the meaning of the excerpt to your client.

Part B. A break-even chart, as illustrated in Part A, is a useful technique for showing relationships between costs, volume, and profits.

Required:

1. Identify the numbered components of the break-even chart.
2. Discuss the significance of the concept of the "relevant range" to break-even analyses.

(AICPA adapted)

4-2. On a lined sheet of paper, number the first ten lines from 1 through 10. Select the graph which matches the numbered factory cost or expense data and write the letter identifying the graph on the appropriate numbered line. The vertical axes of the graphs represent total dollars of expense and the horizontal axes represent production. In each case the zero point is at the intersection of the two axes. The graphs may be used more than once.

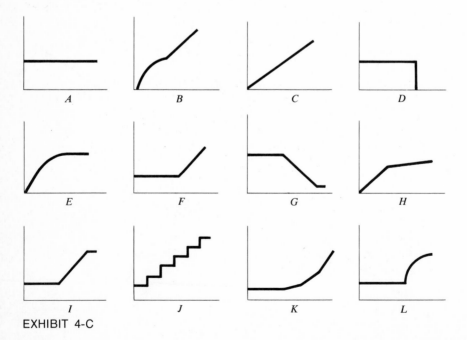

EXHIBIT 4-C

1. Depreciation of equipment, where the amount of depreciation charged is computed by the machine-hours method.
2. Electricity bill, a flat fixed charge plus a variable cost after a certain number of kilowatthours have been used.
3. City water bill, which is computed as follows:

First 1,000,000 gal or less	$1,000 flat fee
Next 10,000 gal	0.003/gal used
Next 10,000 gal	0.006/gal used
Next 10,000 gal	0.009/gal used

4. Cost of lubricant for machines, where cost per unit decreases with each pound of lubricant used (for example, if 1 pound is used, the cost is $10; if 2 pounds are used, the cost is $19.98; if 3 pounds are used, the cost is $29.94; minimum cost per pound is $9.25).
5. Depreciation of equipment, where the amount is computed by the straight-line method. When the depreciation rate was established, it was anticipated that the obsolescence factor would be greater than the wear-and-tear factor.
6. Rent on a factory building donated by the city, where the agreement calls for a fixed fee payment unless 200,000 worker-hours are expended, in which case no rent need be paid.
7. Salaries of repair personnel, where one repairer is needed for every 1,000 hours of machine hours or less (that is, 0 to 1,000 hours requires one repairer, 1,001 to 2,000 hours requires two repairers, etc.).
8. Federal unemployment compensation taxes for the year, where labor force is constant in number throughout the year (average annual salary is $6,000 per worker).
9. Cost of raw material used.
10. Rent on a factory building donated by the county, where the agreement calls for rent of $100,000 less $1 for each direct labor hour worked in excess of 200,000 hours, but minimum rental of $20,000 must be paid. (AICPA adapted)

4-3.† The Timeless Instrument Company makes Fletcher Rabbit watches for children. Management plans profits around the following set of conditions:

Selling price of watches	$2.00
Variable costs per unit	$1.60
Fixed costs	$150,000
Sales volume	500,000 units

Required:
Determine the profit in each case as a result of the following changes (assume other factors to remain the same as the original case):

1. Increase of 10 percent in selling price
2. Decrease of 25 cents in selling price
3. Increase of 20 cents in variable cost

4. Decrease of 10 percent in variable cost
5. Increase of $20,000 in fixed cost
6. Decrease of 10 percent in fixed cost
7. Increase of 10 percent in sales volume
8. Decrease of 20 percent in sales volume
9. Decrease of 10 percent in selling price and 10 percent increase in sales volume
10. Increase of 10 percent in selling price and 10 decrease in sales volume
11. Decrease of 20 cents in selling price and decrease of 4 cents per unit in variable cost
12. Increases of 10 percent in fixed costs and 10 percent in sales volume
13. Increase of $50,000 in fixed costs and 10 percent decrease in variable cost per unit

4-4. The Dietzl Company has annual fixed costs of $120,000. In 19x2, sales amounted to $600,000 as compared with $450,000 in 19x1, and profit for 19x2 was $50,000 higher than in 19x1.

Required:
1. If there is no need to expand the company's capacity, what should profits be in 19x3 on a forecast sales volume of $840,000?
2. At what dollar volume does Dietzl Company break even?

 4-5. The Frosty-Dip Ice Cream Company operates a chain of drive-ins selling only ice-cream products. The company is considering opening a new drive-in stand at a desirable location. The following data pertain to the typical stand:

Average selling price per gallon of ice cream	$1.20
Variable costs per gallon:	
Ice cream	$0.67
Supplies (cups, cones, toppings, etc.)	0.29
Total unit variable costs	$0.96
Fixed costs per month:	
Rent	$ 400
Utilities	120
Wages (including fringe costs) of employees	1,330
Manager's base salary	400
Other fixed costs	150
Total fixed costs	$2,400

Required:
Develop the basis for a decision to open a new drive-in. Consider each of the following separately, based on the above set of data:

1. What is the monthly break-even point, expressed both in gallons of ice cream and in dollars of sales?
2. If the rent were increased to $1,000 per month, what would be the new break-even point in dollars and gallons?
3. If the cost of ice cream increased to 71 cents, what would be the new break-even point in dollars and gallons?

4. If the manager were to be paid a commission of 1 cent per gallon for each gallon sold beyond the break-even point, what profit would the stand earn at a volume of 25,000 gallons?

4-6. The Dawn Mining Company mines selum, a commonly used mineral. Following is the company's report of operations:

THE DAWN MINING COMPANY
Report of Operations
For the Years Ended December 31, 19x4 and 19x3

	19x4	19x3	Increase (Decrease)
Net sales	$891,000	$ 840,000	$ 51,000
Cost of goods sold	688,500	945,000	(256,500)
Gross profit (loss)	$202,500	$(105,000)	$307,500

The following information pertains to the company's operations:
1. The sales price of selum was increased from $8 to $11 per ton on January 1, 19x4.
2. New Mining machinery was placed in operation on January 1, 19x4, which reduced the cost of mining from $9 to $8.50 per ton.
3. There was no change in ending inventories, which were valued on the LIFO (last in/first out) basis.

Required:
Prepare an analysis accounting for the change in the gross profit of the Dawn Mining Company. The analysis should account for the effects of the changes in price, volume, and volume-price factors upon (1) sales, and (2) cost of goods sold. (AICPA adapted)

4-7. The Wilnot Company needs a machine with the capacity to produce 200,000 units of a particular product. Two equipment suppliers have submitted bids. The Do-All machine will generate $100,000 fixed cost per year; but if the capacity of 200,000 units is reached, profit for this product will amount to $60,000. The Do-Some machine will have a fixed cost of only $60,000 per year and will yield a profit of $40,000 at 200,000 units. The product is priced at $2 per unit.

Required:
1. Determine the break-even point for each machine in sales dollars.
2. Determine the sales volume at which the two machines produce equal profit.
3. Determine the range in sales dollars in which (*a*) Do-All is more profitable than Do-Some; (*b*) Do-Some is more profitable than Do-All.

4-8. The Luxom Company produces a single product. Fixed costs have been budgeted for a normal range of operations of 160,000 to 200,000 units per year. Seldom is there any significant change in inventories.

Net income at the high and low points of the normal range has been budgeted as follows:

	Low	High
Units	160,000	200,000
Sales revenue	$80,000	$100,000
Cost of sales and expenses	$78,000	$ 90,000
Net income	$ 2,000	$ 10,000

Required:
Determine the following:

a. The contribution margin per unit
b. The fixed cost per year
c. The break-even point in *units*
d. Profit budgeted for 180,000 units

4-9. The Xonit Company has budgeted its sales at $56,000 and its total costs at $44,000 for 1975. Its sales and total costs for the past five years have been as follows:

	Sales	Costs
1970	$46,000	$37,000
1971	40,000	34,500
1972	54,000	40,000
1973	50,000	38,000
1974	48,000	37,000

Required:
Analyze the company's projected operations for the current year, and determine if cost-volume-profit relationships of prior years are being maintained. If they are not, speculate as to possible causes.

4-10. The following article appeared on page 60 of the South Bend *Tribune* on April 21, 1971:

The baseball officials point out that baseball profits, which aren't limited by the small number of home games the way they are in football, can explode once attendance for a team passes 1.5 million.

The Cincinnati Reds, who drew 1.8 million, are believed to have made $2½ million, and the New York Mets, who drew 2.7 million, made even more.

Success Controls Profits

Profits can rise and fall depending on the success of the team. The Atlanta Braves announced a profit of $346,899 on revenue of $8,089,922 in 1969 when the team won the division crown but only $120,097 on revenue of $6,780,148 in 1970 when the team slumped. But the club picture is still good because a major expense each year

—$680,142 in 1969 and $566,536 in 1970—
was for the "amortization of player contracts and bonuses."

Required:

1. At what sales revenue will the Braves break even, assuming no change in its cost-volume-profit (CVP) relationships? (Round to nearest $1,000.)
2. If the Reds' CVP relationship had been the same as those of the Braves, what would have been the Reds' average price per ticket sold? (Round to nearest cent.)

4-11. Liza Fletcher, president of Gamma Delta Iota Honor Society, is making plans for a gala dinner dance to be held at a local country club. She is trying to decide on the price to ask for the tickets. Each ticket will admit one couple to the dance and entitle each partner to enjoy a buffet supper, and allow them to receive certain party favors. Aware of your reputation on campus, she approaches you for advice and furnishes you with the following information:

Service charge for use of club	$700.00 *Fixed*
Additional club charge per person passing through the buffet serving line	$ 2.25 *Variable*
Fee to be paid Jimmy Bigtime's Swinging Jazz Ensemble	$210.00 *Fixed*
Ticket printing charges—Frescoe Press (500 tickets)	$ 25.00 *F.*
Party favors, per couple (extra favors may be returned for a full refund from the Party Shoppe)	$ 0.75 *Var.*
Advertisement in newspaper	$ 15.85 *F.*
Gratuity paid to waitresses	10% of the club's bill *Var.*
Cost of newsletter sent to society members only	$ 18.65 *F.*

Required:

Answer the following questions posed by Liza:

1. If the price set is $9 per ticket, how many tickets must be sold to break even on the dance?
2. The Society vice president, Glen Williams, has suggested that a floral arrangement be placed on each of the 72 tables at the club. Each arrangement will cost $3. The overall delivery charge will be $12.50. Glen is certain that, with this added attraction, all 720 seats will be filled. What will the ticket price have to be in order for the society to earn a profit of $100 on the dance under this alternative, assuming that 360 tickets are indeed sold?

4-12.† The Carey Company sold 100,000 units of its product at $20 per unit. Variable costs are $14 per unit (manufacturing costs of $11 and selling costs of $3). Fixed costs are incurred uniformly throughout the year and amount to $792,000 (manufacturing costs of $500,000 and selling costs of $292,000). There are no beginning or ending inventories.

Required:

Determine the following:

1. The break-even point for this product
2. The number of units that must be sold to earn an income of $60,000 for the year (before income taxes)
3. The number of units that must be sold to earn an after-tax income of $90,000, assuming a tax rate of 40 percent
4. The break-even point for this product after a 10 percent increase in wages and salaries (assuming labor costs are 50 percent of variable costs and 20 percent of fixed costs).

(AICPA adapted)

4-13.

X MANUFACTURING COMPANY
Income Statement
For the Year Ended December 31, 19x1

Sales (100,000 units at $5)		$500,000
Variable cost:		
Direct material	$ 90,000	
Direct labor	100,000	
Factory burden	50,000	
Total manufacturing variable cost	$240,000	
Selling expense	10,000	
Total variable cost		250,000
Contribution margin		$250,000
Fixed cost:		
Factory burden	$100,000	
Selling expense	30,000	
Administrative expense	70,000	
Total fixed cost		200,000
Net profit		$ 50,000

Given:

Forty percent of variable factory burden is indirect labor. There is additional indirect labor payroll amounting to $20,000 contained in fixed factory burden.

    The union has negotiated a 10 percent increase in wage rates for all workers classified as direct and indirect labor, effective January 1, 19x2. The sales for 19x2 are forecast at the same level as 19x1. No other changes are anticipated for the coming year.

Required:

1. Compute the break-even point for 19x1 in units and in dollars.
2. Prepare a forecast income statement for 19x2, including changes as given. Compute the break-even point for 19x2 in units and in dollars.
3. What selling price must management set in 19x2 if their goal is to realize the same dollar amount of profit as in 19x1? The same percentage of profit?
4. Assume that selling price is to remain at $5 per unit. What sales volume (dollars and units) must be attained if management wishes to realize the same dollar amount of profit as in 19x1? The same percentage of profit?

4-14. The president of Beth Corporation, which manufactures tape decks and sells them to producers of sound reproduction systems, anticipates a 10 percent wage increase to the manufacturing employees (variable labor) on January 1 of next year. There are no other changes in costs expected. Overhead will not change as a result of the wage increase. The president has asked you to assist him in developing the information needed to formulate a reasonable product strategy for next year.

You are satisfied by regression analysis that volume is the primary factor affecting costs and have separated the semivariable costs into their fixed and variable segments by means of the least-squares criterion. You also observe that the beginning and ending inventories are never materially different.

Below are the current-year data assembled for your analysis:

Current selling price per unit	$80
Variable cost per unit:	
Material	$30
Labor	12
Overhead	6
Total	$48
Annual volume of sales	5,000 units
Fixed costs	$51,000

Required:
Provide the following information for the president, using cost-volume-profit analysis:

1. What increase in the selling price is necessary to cover the 10 percent wage increase and still maintain current profit-volume-cost ratio?
2. How many tape decks must be sold to maintain the current net income if the sales price remains at $80 and the 10 percent wage increase goes into effect?
3. The president believes that an additional $190,000 of machinery (to be depreciated at 10 percent annually) will increase present capacity (5,300 units) by 30 percent. If all tape decks produced can be sold at the present price and the wage increase goes into effect, how will the estimated net income before capacity is increased compare with the estimated net income after capacity is increased? Prepare computations of estimated net income before and after the expansion.
(AICPA adapted)

4-15. The Carrigan Corporation produces three products: Car, Rig, and Gan. The planned cost and price data are as follows:

	Car	Rig	Gan
Selling price	$ 1.00	$ 0.50	$ 2.50
Variable cost per unit	$ 0.95	$ 0.20	$ 1.85
Fixed cost per month	$5,000	$7,800	$5,200

Required:
1. Determine the break-even point in dollars for each product.
2. Determine the break-even point in dollars for total company, assuming that an equal number of units of each product is sold.

3. For May, sales were $96,000 and profit was $4,000. How does this result compare with profits on a planned basis at that sales volume? What factors might account for the difference?

4. Project the profit for the total company for each of the following years, assuming the same planned cost and price data as given above, based upon the following forecasts of sales in units:

	19x1	19x2	19x3
Car	1,500,000	1,300,000	1,200,000
Rig	350,000	370,000	400,000
Gan	110,000	120,000	130,000

4-16. The Smith Company produces and sells two products, A and B. Selected data on these products show the following:

	A	B
Selling price	$5.00	$6.00
Total variable costs	$2.50	$5.00
Direct fixed costs	$125,000	$100,000
Unallocated company fixed costs	$55,000	

Required:
1. If these products are sold in the ratio of 4A to 3B, what is the break-even point?
2. The sales manager asks you to show the effect on the break-even point of a change in the sales mix to 3A to 4B.
3. Explain to the sales manager which of these two sales mixes should be pushed.

4-17.† A client has recently leased facilities for manufacturing a new product. Based on studies made by his staff, the following data have been made available to you:

Estimated annual sales   24,000

Estimated costs:	Amount	Per Unit
Material	$ 96,000	$4.00
Direct labor	14,400	0.60
Overhead	24,000	1.00
Administrative expense	28,800	1.20
Total	$163,200	$6.80

Selling expenses are expected to be 15 percent of sales, and profit is expected to amount to $1.02 per unit.

Required:
1. Compute the selling price per unit.
2. Project a profit and loss statement for the year.
3. Compute a break-even point expressed in dollars and in units, assuming that overhead and administrative expenses are fixed but that other costs are fully variable. (AICPA adapted)

4-18. The ABC Company produces its own power. Basic data for the month of April are as follows:

Schedule of Horsepower Hours

	Production Departments		Service Departments	
	A	B	X	Y
Needed at capacity production	10,000	20,000	12,000	8,000
Used during the month of April	8,000	13,000	7,000	6,000

During the month of April the expenses of operating the power service department amounted to $9,300; of this expenditure, $2,500 was considered to be fixed cost.

Required:
1. What dollar amounts of the power service department expense should be allocated to each production and service department?
2. What are the reasons for allocating the costs of one service department to other service departments as well as to production departments? (AICPA adapted)

CHAPTER

THE USE OF BUDGETS IN PLANNING

THE PLAN OF THIS CHAPTER

In this "how-to" chapter, we shall view in great detail the planning process and its implementation by the use of budgets. The process of putting together a comprehensive planning budget will be described in an illustrative problem. The essential points of the problem will include:

The sales forecast

The production, purchasing, material, labor, and overhead cost budgets and supporting schedules

The budgeted cash-flow statement

The pro forma (projected) financial statements

PLANNING

The Role of Management Planning and Control Systems

Management planning and control begins with the establishment of the fundamental objectives of the organization, and continues as the process by which necessary resources are provided and employed effectively and efficiently toward achievement of the goals. A management planning and control system provides the comprehensive framework within which this process is carried out. Such a system encompasses all aspects of an organization's operations, and thus is seen as a "total" system.

To help reduce this massive concept to workable proportions, it is convenient to view it in terms of three subsystems:

1. Strategic planning

2. Management control

3. Operational control

Strategic planning is long range in its time perspective, and complete in its breadth of scope and depth of penetration. Involving as it does the determination and periodic change of organizational objectives, the acquisition and use of the resources required for their attainment, and the establishment of the basic policies which guide the goal-oriented activities of the organization, strategic planning is necessarily a top management function. It is highly creative, and therefore relatively unstructured in character. Its timing is irregular and opportunistic. It must be tuned in to the external environment within which the organization presently functions, as well as to the direction in which that environment is heading and to the changes that are likely to occur. Thus, there must be a strong external orientation, with sensitivity to social, economic, political, international, and myriads of other influences.

Plans, policies, and decisions for an industrial concern might typically involve selection of plant sites; acquisitions and mergers; new-product development; changes in markets and distribution channels; changes in fundamental capital structure; formulation of long-range policy; expanding into multinational business activities. Indeed, it might be said that strategic planning establishes the fundamental internal environment within which all the activities of the organization will be carried on.

Management control is carried on within the environment established by strategic planning. Its primary emphasis is on carrying out the policies resulting from strategic planning, rather than on setting them. Its time span tends to be short to intermediate term. The activity is somewhat rhythmic in its patterns of activity and scheduling. Because of the pervasive nature of this function, the participation of management at all levels of the organization is usually required. Its goals are tangible within the broad framework of overall organizational objectives, and its focus is on line management which participates in the formulation of near-term plans and the criteria by which the line managers' performance is to be measured.

Thus, within the scope of the total operations of the organization, the management control system must comprise an integrated structure of related subsystems, setting forth the plans and standards of measurement for each and all functioning units of the organization. In contrast with the creative approach to planning characteristic of strategic planning, management control requires administrative and persuasive skills in its successful implementation. Typical of the form taken by the plans flowing from the management control system are the detailed budgets for all units of the organization for the next year, and the three- to five-year plans as an extension thereof.

Operational control is employed to assure that management planning is carried to fruition effectively and efficiently in the operations of the organization. Its scope and focus involve the operating unit. It is executed principally at the level of front-line supervision. Its goals are invariably short term and rather rigidly structured, as are the criteria for measuring performance toward their achievement. Its activity patterns are highly repetitive, and they are characterized by the close adherence to directions, with little exercise of initiative. Some of the typical ways in which operational control systems are implemented are inventory control systems, sales quotas and sales personnel's reports, credit and collection systems, production scheduling, departmental overhead reports, daily production reports, daily reports of bank balances, responsibility-reporting systems measuring actual costs incurred against budget allowances by departments, and the like.

Perhaps it will be helpful in clarifying certain distinctions between strategic planning, management control, and operational control if all three are examined in terms of certain fundamental characteristics. To summarize:

Characteristic	Strategic Planning	Management Control	Operational Control
Level	Top management	All levels—top to front-line supervision	Supervisory
Scope	Total	Overall, consisting of related subsystem	Operating unit
Time frame	Long range	Short to intermediate (1 to 5 years)	Short periods—day to day, weekly, monthly
Environment	External, toward developing internal	Internal, adjusting to external factors	Internal only
Goals and objectives	Basic objectives	Tangible goals, within framework of overall objectives	Short-term, tangible to operating unit
Structuring	Relatively unstructured	Fairly highly structured but flexible	Quite rigid, preestablished
Activity patterns	Irregular	Rhythmic, regular	Highly repetitive
Character of activity	Creative	Administrative, persuasive	Following directions, little initiative
Focal point	Entire organization	All operations, line management	Operating unit

Strategic planning is a subject whose sophisticated development is beyond the scope of this book. The main focus here will be directed to the role of the detailed budget in management planning and control, to be followed in Section 3 (Control) by a consideration of the role played by standard costs and responsibility accounting in carrying out operational control.

The Budget in Management Planning and Control

In the going concern, top management is assumed to have done much strategic planning which has set the stage for dynamic management planning on a continuing basis. Thus, as each new period of operations approaches, it usually feels the need to apply this general knowledge of the business and its environment to the particular problems anticipated in the immediate future. What it wants is a budget—a detailed, quantitative plan to guide its operations in the near future.

The concept of a comprehensive budget covers its use in planning, organizing, and controlling all the financial and operating activities of the firm in the forthcoming period.

Planning   Planning begins with the setting of general goals, proceeds to the cost-volume-profit analysis of various alternatives, and ends with the preparation of a detailed, quantitative plan of action—the budget.

Organizing   The budget in turn provides a motive and guide to action for all responsible managers in all segments of the firm.

Controlling   When the results of actual performance become available, they are tabulated and compared with the budget for purposes of highlighting off-standard performance as a basis for instituting corrective action.

In this chapter, we shall consider the use of the budget only in its application to the first of these functions—planning. Aptly termed "accounting in the future," this type of budgeting summarizes the estimated results of future transactions for the entire company in much the same manner as the accounting process records and summarizes the results of completed transactions.

With a forecast of sales as a foundation, the budget for a manufacturing concern includes estimates covering such things as:

Production

The use of materials

The purchase of materials

The manning and cost requirements for direct labor

The incurrence of factory overhead costs

The incurrence of operating expenses

The levels and values of the various inventories

The flow of cash

The need for borrowing

Expenditures for capital assets[1]

The budget culminates in a projection of the income statement and balance sheet at the end of the budget period for the company as a whole. A budget of this type is called a *comprehensive* or *planning* budget. We shall see in Chapter 7 that there are other types of budgets which can be prepared for other purposes.

In his fine book on management accounting,[2] Robert N. Anthony develops the analogy between a planning budget used by a business firm and the flight plan prepared and used by the captain of a commercial airliner. No matter how often he or she has flown that particular aircraft or that route before, the pilot realizes that changing conditions may require flight modification. Given the benefit of the meteorologist's forecast of temperature, wind, and other pertinent weather conditions, the pilot works out what she or he considers to be the best way to get from starting point to destination.

So, too, with the business executive. With the aid of a carefully constructed forecast of sales, the expert molds the company's plan of operations from January through December, fully aware that, despite having been over this ground many times before, management may reasonably expect changing conditions to suggest modification in the executive's approach. Anthony concludes by stressing a fundamental but frequently overlooked maxim: "It should be noted that the (flight) plan itself does not fly the plane. Similarly, the budget is an aid to management, not a substitute for management."[3]

FORECAST OF SALES

In a company which operates under a formal budget system, the preparation of the annual comprehensive planning budget typically follows a series of well-defined steps through a well-placed timetable. The starting point must generally be the forecast of sales. Methods of sales forecasting range all the way from the president's "seat-of-the-pants" guess to complex techniques involving mathematical and statistical manipulations of economic and market research data.

In a typical situation, the top sales executive might begin by analyzing past sales data in terms of products, customers, territories, and sales personnel. Then, in the belief that those closest to the market — the sales personnel and the district managers — are in the most strategic position, the executive may issue instructions for all salespersons to submit estimates for their sales by product lines for the coming year. This approach also has the psychological advantage of letting each person have a prime voice in setting the standard by which subsequent performance may be measured, rather than having it imposed unilaterally from above.

---

[1] Amounts of planned capital expenditures, for purposes of this chapter, will be assumed as handed down in final form by top management. The specialized nature of capital budgeting, and the particular analytical techniques useful to top management in arriving at capital budgeting decisions, will be elaborated in Chapter 13.

[2] R. N. Anthony, *Management Accounting: Test and Cases,* Homewood, Ill.: Richard D. Irwin, Inc., 1960.

[3] *Ibid.,* p. 454.

The summation of the sales representatives' own estimates is not likely to constitute the best basis upon which to plan the entire operations of the company, however. The sales manager may wish to modify the estimates in a number of ways:

By consideration of general economic and industrial conditions

By the projected sales trends of specific products

By the anticipated results of advertising and promotional campaigns

By the expected effects of a proposed price change

By the entry into the market of a formidable competitor

By the expected shift of a big customer's business to a competitor

By the anticipated introduction of new, improved, or substitute products by the company or its competitors

By the limits imposed by the company's productive capacity

Finally, when the sales manager's forecast is complete, a budget committee (made up of top executives from the major functional areas of the organization), or perhaps the president may wish to modify it along somewhat more conservative lines, by way of tempering the characteristic optimism of salespeople.

For purposes of illustration, let us assume a company which sells two products, designated O and P, in two territories, known as territory East and territory West. As the first step in its annual budgeting procedures, the sales manager asks the two territory managers to confer with their sales representatives and present a "grass roots" forecast of the two products in their respective territories for the coming year, assuming the same general conditions that prevailed in the preceding year. On receiving these forecasts from the field, the sales manager applies a correction for the long-term growth or decline trends for each product. Next, he or she adjusts the tentative forecasts for the expectation of general business conditions in the coming year. With the forecasts in such form, the manager presents them to the president, who may wish to make some revision on the basis of a personal appraisal of the sales picture for the coming year.

Consider the following simple example. In preparation for the 19x1 budget, the sales manager receives the following forecast from the field staff:

	East	West
Product O	1,200 units	1,800 units
Product P	900	2,100
Total	2,100 units	3,900 units

Previous study of product growth trends indicates the following changes in 19x1:

Product O—East   5 percent increase

Product O—West   10 percent increase

Product P—East   8 percent decrease

Product P—West   4 percent decrease

There has been a general pattern in the company's sales which indicated a tendency to follow the cycle of general business conditions, but the effect on the company's sales is only 50 percent of that in the economy as a whole. For 19x1, most reliable forecasts indicate a decline of 10 percent in general business from the level of the preceding year.

After adjusting for the foregoing factors, the sales manager shows the results to the president. It is the judgment of the latter that the forecast still looks too high by about 10 percent. The sales manager applies the suggested correction, and the president approves the forecast as a basis for budgeting. The sales manager's procedure is illustrated as follows:

		Total	East		West	
			O	P	O	P
Step 1:	Salespersons' estimates	6,000	1,200	900	1,800	2,100
Step 2:	Adjustment for		+5%	−8%	+10%	−4%
	product growth	6,084	1,260	828	1,980	2,016
Step 3:	Adjustment for general business conditions (50% of expected general decline of 10% equals 5%)	5,780	1,197	787	1,881	1,915
Step 4:	President's correction (reduction by 10%); final forecast	5,202	1,077	708	1,693	1,724

The procedure for obtaining the sales forecast just described is generally referred to as a *bottom-up* forecast. That is, its genesis is with those closest to the customer—the sales representatives. From there it works up the organization, through the sales manager, and eventually to the president. An alternative procedure, the *top-down* forecast, would begin with the president establishing sales goals, perhaps by setting a desired share of the market or a desired rate of growth in dollar sales. This goal would then work down through the sales manager to the sales force, with each successive organizational level attempting to convince the next higher level of the necessity of any desired revision. However it is established, the sales forecast is the basis for almost all other estimates and projections to be made. It deserves a good deal of care and effort in its preparation.

STEPS IN BUDGET PREPARATION

Once the sales forecast is official, requests will be sent by the controller or budget director to responsible members of the organization for estimates of cost within their respective functional areas and segments of the business. The data-gathering phase of budget preparation is carried out by the budget director's staff and usually proceeds in steps similar to the following:

1. Bills of material and parts lists are secured from the design engineering department; these provide information about quantities and types of material used to build a unit of product.

2. Operation sheets are received from the industrial engineering department; these provide information on productive operations and estimated labor times on all products.

3. Material price information is made available by the purchasing department.

4. Inventory and scheduling information is provided by the production control department.

5. Wage rate information is found in the payroll department.

When the budget information has been processed and assembled in terms of the forecast volume of business for the period, it is submitted in preliminary form to the budget committee or the president, either of whom may wish to make certain adjustments to the information thus compiled. This series of steps, from original sales estimates to the first submission of the comprehensive budget to top management, may cover a period of two months or more, depending on the size and complexity of the firm and its operations. After the schedules, including plans for capital expenditures during the budget period, have been approved at the top management level, the material is made ready for final publication by the controller's or budget director's staff.

In final form, the comprehensive budget will contain detailed schedules appropriate to each of the key functions in the organization, together with the entire company's plan summarized in a projected cash-flow budget and *pro forma* (literally, "according to form"; projected) financial statements. About three weeks to a month before the start of the budget period, copies of the final budget schedules are distributed to responsible members of the organization in accordance with the individual needs of each.

ILLUSTRATIVE EXAMPLE

The development of the planning budget, involving as it does a series of steps and considerable numerical detail, is probably best studied in the form of a simplified example. The particulars of this case are based on the operations of a hypothetical manufacturer — the Projecto Manufacturing Company — which produces two models of standardized product, identified respectively as model X and model Y.

Problem

In October 19x0, the president asked a CPA (the company was too small to employ a management accountant) for an income statement and balance sheet for the year 19x0, based on the actual results for the first nine months and an estimate for the fourth quarter. The president received the following:

INCOME STATEMENT
FOR THE YEAR ENDING DECEMBER 31, 19x0
(Nine Months Actual—Three Months Estimated)

Net sales	$240,000
Cost of goods sold	204,000
Gross margin	$ 36,000
Operating expense	30,400
Income from operations	$ 5,600
Interest expense	600
Income before taxes	$ 5,000
Income tax (30%)	1,500
Net income to shareholders	$ 3,500

BALANCE SHEET
AS OF DECEMBER 31, 19x0 (ESTIMATED)

Assets

Current assets:			
Cash		$ 10,000	
Accounts receivable		25,000	
Inventories:			
Raw materials	$ 4,500		
Work in process	4,500		
Finished goods	24,000	33,000	
Other current assets		2,000	
Total current assets			$ 70,000
Property, plant, and equipment:			
Acquisition cost		$100,000	
Less: Accumulated depreciation		25,000	
Net book value—property, plant, and equipment			75,000
			$145,000

Equities

Current liabilities:		
Accounts payable	$30,000	
Accrued payroll	1,000	
Accrued income taxes	1,500	
Other current liabilities	2,500	
Total current liabilities		$ 35,000
Shareholders' equity:		
Common stock	$80,000	
Retained earnings	30,000	
Total shareholders' equity		110,000
		$145,000

The president looked at the figures and made a few quick calculations:

Percentage of net income after taxes to net sales:

$3,500 ÷ $240,000 = 1.46%

Percentage of net income on shareholders' equity:

$3,500 ÷ $110,000 = 3.18%

("I could do better than that if I invested in government bonds," he thought.)

Percentage of net income on total assets:

$3,500 ÷ $145,000 = 2.41%

("I pay 6 percent to borrow money at the bank," he reflected.)

He concluded that it would not take much to wipe out this meager profit. It could happen

If competition forced him to reduce selling prices

If he gave a small increase in the hourly wage paid to his employees

If it became necessary to work more overtime to compensate for a decline in productive efficiency

If property taxes or insurance rates were to increase substantially

Or if any of many other possibilities should arise

He called in his CPA. He discussed the situation and his concern over his precarious profit position. The CPA pointed out that, on several occasions in the past, she had recommended that the president establish a profit plan, implemented by a detailed budget. The president countered with the opinion that the company was too small to warrant such elaborate procedures. He added that, ironically, the cost of such a program would probably wipe out the small profit which remained.

The CPA agreed that, in the last analysis, the only justification for incurring a cost was to increase revenue or to save other costs. If a sound but simple budget program would not more than pay for itself in the maximizing of profits, the CPA concluded, it ought not be used. She then pointed out several factors contributing to the current year's poor performance which she thought might have been avoided had there been a carefully constructed budget to guide the operations according to plan.

1. There had been no systematic forecast of sales; a "seat-of-the-pants" guess of $300,000 sales for the year resulted in overproduction in the first quarter, followed by a severe cutback in production in the second quarter

as unsold inventory piled up. When the expected surge occurred in the third quarter, the company was caught short and had to work overtime. The added production still fell short of enough to meet customer orders, with the result that order cancellations amounting to more than $20,000 were received.

2.   In the second quarter, the severe cutback in production resulted in a good deal of idle capacity; the cost of this unused capacity cut sharply into profits for the period.

3.   Employment ranged from a low of seven factory workers to a high of twenty, while sudden shifts in production necessitated working a great deal of overtime; employment and training costs were excessive because of the necessity for unplanned layoffs and hiring during the year.

4.   On two different occasions, it became necessary to borrow money from the bank on extremely short notice because of unexpected shortages of cash. Because of the emergency nature of the situation and the lack of sufficient information to satisfy the bank as to the reliability of the loan, it was necessary to pay higher than the prime rate of interest, and it is likely that more money was borrowed for longer periods than might have been necessary if proper plans had been laid.

The CPA persuaded the president to let her try to put together the elements of a fairly simple budget which would portray in a systematic manner the president's plans for the company in the coming year. She began by asking the president to establish his profit goal for the year. The president expressed his desire to achieve an after-tax profit figure of 7 percent on sales. The CPA suggested that he might like to set his sights on a certain return on the average shareholders' equity as well. The president pondered this; considering the much greater *risk* attaching to the investment of capital in a small business such as this one, in contrast to government bonds or "blue chip" stocks, the *return* to shareholders ought to be commensurately higher. He answered that a rate of 15 percent after taxes on average shareholders' equity should be a reasonable target.

The CPA then explained what her approach would be:

1.   She would confer with the company's one salesperson in the formulation of a carefully detailed forecast of sales, which she would then submit to the president for approval; such a forecast, she added, provides the necessary starting point for any planning budget.

2.   She would secure all the product specifications from the company's engineer by way of developing material cost and raw material inventory data.

3.   She would secure manufacturing information, including labor times, wage rates, and overhead cost data, from the plant superintendent.

4.   She would check out all preliminary information, as well as the estimates for selling and administrative expense and short-term financing arrangements, with the president himself.

The president agreed that the approach seemed to be sound, and upon receiving the CPA's estimate for the cost of the job, he decided he would try it, at least for the coming year, and then appraise the results the following year. The CPA promised to confer with him again late in November, when she expected to have her preliminary figures ready.

Gathering of Information

The CPA conferred with the company sales representative concerning the latter's estimate, by quarters, of the sales for the coming year, by units of product, and the selling price of each. She received the following information:

	X	Y	Total
Selling price	$ 5	$ 10	
Sales forecast by quarters (units):			
1Q	4,000	1,500	5,500
2Q	8,000	3,000	11,000
3Q	12,500	6,500	19,000
4Q	3,500	2,000	5,500
Total	28,000	13,000	41,000

Next she talked to the company engineer regarding material specifications for the two products. She was given the following:

Material Type	Material Unit	Material Units per Unit of Product		Material Unit Price	Material Cost per Unit of Product	
		X	Y		X	Y
A	Foot	2	2	$0.25	$0.50	$0.50
B	Pound		2	0.50		1.00
C	Part	1	3	1.00	1.00	3.00
Total direct material cost per unit of product					$1.50	$4.50

The next source was the plant superintendent, who gave her the following information concerning direct labor times and wage rates by product and by department:

Department	Production Units per Hour		Hours per Unit of Product		Departmental Wage Rate	Direct Labor Cost per Unit of Product	
	X	Y	X	Y		X	Y
Press	10	5	0.1	0.2	$2.50	$0.25	$0.50
Assembly	$2\frac{1}{2}$	2	0.4	0.5	2.50	1.00	1.25
Total			0.5	0.7		$1.25	$1.75

The plant superintendent's estimates of the factory overhead expenses for the coming year were as follows:

	Total
Indirect labor	$10,000
Factory supplies	8,000
Heat, light, power	2,800
Supervision	10,000
Maintenance	6,000
Engineering	7,200
Taxes and insurance	4,500
Depreciation	10,000
Total estimated factory overhead expense	$58,500
Assigned to departments:	
Press department	$13,500
Assembly department	45,000
Total factory overhead expense assigned	$58,500

From personal knowledge of the company's organization and operations, the CPA made an estimate of the selling and administrative expenses. Subject to whatever minor corrections the president might later make, these estimates were as follows:

Selling expense:		
Sales salaries	$ 7,500	
Freight out	2,000	
Advertising	3,000	
Total selling expense		$12,500
Administrative expense:		
Administrative salaries	$10,000	
Office supplies	1,500	
Telephone	500	
Professional fees	2,500	
Total administrative expense		14,500
Total operating expense		$27,000

At this point, the CPA decided to set down all the other information which might have a bearing on the company's plans for the coming year, before proceeding with the construction of the detailed schedules for the comprehensive planning budget, including the following facts:

1. Projecto produces its two models of product to stock. Inventory of finished goods to begin the budget period (i.e., January 1, 19x1) was expected to be as follows: model X, 2,000 units; model Y, 2,000 units. The plant superintendent stated that there should be an inventory of finished goods at the end of the budget period (i.e., December 31, 19x1) as follows: model X, 4,000 units; model Y, 1,000 units. Also, ideally, the ending inventory of finished goods for each of the first three quarters should equal one-fourth the forecast sales for the *following* quarter for each model.

2. Materials expected to be on hand at January 1, 19x1, were as follows:

material A, 4,000 units; material B, 1,000 units; material C, 3,000 units. Purchases of material are planned so as to leave one-fifth of the expected material usage for the *following* quarter in the raw material inventory at the end of the first three quarters. It was desired that inventories of raw material for December 31, 19x1, be as follows: material A, 3,200 units; material B, 1,200 units; material C, 2,600 units.

3. Work in process inventories were expected to remain constant. Thus the number of units in work in process at the end of any quarter would not be significant, and the value shown on the balance sheet at December 31, 19x1, was not expected to change.

4. Direct labor was expected to be incurred by quarters according to the production schedule (i.e., it would be variable with production volume). Factory overhead expenses were expected to be incurred in *equal* amounts each quarter (i.e., they would be fixed). All direct labor and cash factory overhead expenses were to be paid in the quarter in which they were incurred.

5. Depreciation on property, plant, and equipment averaged 10 percent of acquisition cost, or $10,000 for the year.

6. All operating expenses were expected to be incurred in *equal* amounts each quarter (i.e., they would be fixed) and would be paid in cash in the quarter in which they were incurred.

7. Accounts receivable were generally collected 70 percent in the quarter in which the sales were made and 30 percent in the following quarter.

8. The president had already discussed plans for the acquisition of fixed assets, to be paid in cash, as follows:

1Q	$12,000
2Q	7,000
3Q	
4Q	1,000
Total	$20,000

There was to be no depreciation recognized on these assets during the year 19x1.

9. Accrued income taxes (i.e., for the year 19x0) were expected to be paid in equal quarterly installments. The normal tax rate of 30 percent was assumed on profit budgeted for 19x1.

10. Projecto Company has a line of short-term credit with the local bank at 6 percent, for the purpose of meeting seasonal needs for inventory and receivable financing. Borrowing is in multiples of $1,000 and is assumed to be effective at the *beginning* of the quarter in which it is needed. Payment of interest in cash is assumed to take place at the *end* of the quarter of repayment, based on the principal outstanding since the date of the loan or the last payment. Projecto wishes to maintain a minimum cash balance of $8,000.

Schedules

The CPA assembled the information in the form of the following schedules:

Schedule I. Sales Forecast by Quarters (units and dollars)

Schedule II. Budgeted Production by Quarters (units only)

Schedule III. Budgeted Material Usage by Quarters (units only)

Schedule IV. Budgeted Material Purchases by Quarters (units and dollars)

Schedule V. Budgeted Direct Labor by Quarters (hours and dollars)

Schedule VI. Budgeted Factory Overhead Cost by Quarters (dollars and rate)

Schedule VII. Budgeted Raw Materials Inventory (for year, units, and dollars)

Schedule VIII. Budgeted Finished Goods Inventory (for year, units, and dollars)

Schedule IX. Budgeted Operating Expense (for year, dollars only)

Schedule X. Budgeted Cost of Goods Sold (for year, dollars only)

Schedule XI. Budgeted Cash Flow (by quarters, dollars only)

Schedule XII. Budgeted Income Statement (for year, dollars only)

Schedule XIII. Budgeted Balance Sheet (year-end, dollars only)

Sales All budget planning begins with the forecast of sales. Using the information supplied by the salesperson, the CPA put together the sales forecast by quarters shown in Schedule I.

Production Production, while based on estimated sales, must be geared to the production cycle, i.e., the time required to produce an item from raw material to its finished form. Thus, if the production cycle is three weeks, then at least three weeks' work must precede the sale of a unit of product. In other words, production must be planned to allow sufficient time to manufacture the products before the estimated date of sale.

Typically, prudent management will provide a buffer in the form of fin-

SCHEDULE I
PROJECTO MANUFACTURING COMPANY
Sales Forecast by Quarters
For Budget Year 19x1

		1Q	2Q	3Q	4Q	Year
A.	Units of product					
	Model X	4,000	8,000	12,500	3,500	28,000
	Model Y	1,500	3,000	6,500	2,000	13,000
B.	Dollars					
	Model X ($5)	$20,000	$40,000	$ 62,500	$17,500	$140,000
	Model Y ($10)	15,000	30,000	65,000	20,000	130,000
	Total sales	$35,000	$70,000	$127,500	$37,500	$270,000

ished goods inventory, to ensure that goods will be on hand and thus available to sell at any time. In a company like Projecto, which produces to stock, the objective is constantly to replenish finished goods inventory in the light of the sales forecast.

In Schedule II, the CPA has budgeted production by quarters for the year 19x1. Her reasoning proceeds thus:

Management wishes to protect itself by having on hand at the end of each quarter a quantity (units) of goods equal to one-fourth of the sales forecast for the following quarter.

It must also provide enough units to meet the requirements of the sales forecast for the current quarter.

Thus the total needs for the current quarter will be the sum of the desired ending inventory and the sales for the quarter.

These needs can be met from two (and only two) sources: the inventory of finished goods on hand at the beginning of the quarter, and the production of the quarter.

In Chapter 2 we saw that input-output analysis, used in the computation of cost of goods sold, can also be used in accumulating costs throughout the

SCHEDULE II
PROJECTO MANUFACTURING COMPANY
Budgeted Production by Quarters
For Budget Year 19x1

Units of Product	1Q	2Q	3Q	4Q	Year
A. Model X					
Desired ending inventory of finished goods*	2,000	3,125	875	4,000	4,000
Add: Sales	4,000	8,000	12,500	3,500	28,000
Total needs	6,000	11,125	13,375	7,500	32,000
Less: Beginning inventory of finished goods	2,000	2,000	3,125	875	2,000
Production required	4,000	9,125	10,250	6,625	30,000
B. Model Y					
Desired ending inventory of finished goods*	750	1,625	500	1,000	1,000
Add: Sales	1,500	3,000	6,500	2,000	13,000
Total needs	2,250	4,625	7,000	3,000	14,000
Less: Beginning inventory of finished goods	2,000	750	1,625	500	2,000
Production required	250	3,875	5,375	2,500	12,000

* One-fourth of following quarter forecast sales for 1Q, 2Q, and 3Q.
NOTE: Input-output formula employed, reversing the usual order to find the unknown input—production required.

production cycle. If any three of the four basic factors (input, output, beginning balance, ending balance) are known, the fourth can be easily computed. This relationship is extremely useful in the preparation of budgets.

By means of the input-output analysis demonstrated in Schedule II, we see, for example, that the production requirement for model X for the first quarter is determined as follows:

Desired ending inventory (one-fourth of second-quarter forecast of 8,000 units)	2,000
Sales forecast for first quarter (from Schedule I)(estimated output)	4,000
Total needs for first quarter	6,000
Units on hand in finished goods inventory at beginning of first quarter	2,000
Required production in first quarter (required input)	4,000

The fact that the first-quarter production requirements and the sales forecast for the first three quarters are the same (4,000) is entirely coincidental: in the other quarters, these amounts will differ for both models of product. The fluctuating sales forecast calls for differing amounts of quarterly ending inventory, reflecting the importance of production-cycle planning.

Material Usage   The next step in the budget process involves the determination of material usage. Schedule III demonstrates the buildup of the quantities

SCHEDULE III
PROJECTO MANUFACTURING COMPANY
Budgeted Material Usage by Quarters
For Budget Year 19x1

	1Q	2Q	3Q	4Q	Year
Production in product units (see Schedule II):					
Model X	4,000	9,125	10,250	6,625	30,000
Model Y	250	3,875	5,375	2,500	12,000
A. Material A, ft					
Units of material per unit of product:					
Model X — 2	8,000	18,250	20,500	13,250	60,000
Model Y — 2	500	7,750	10,750	5,000	24,000
Total usage	8,500	26,000	31,250	18,250	84,000
B. Material B, lb					
Units of material per unit of product:					
Model Y — 2	500	7,750	10,750	5,000	24,000
C. Material C, parts					
Units of material per unit of product:					
Model X — 1	4,000	9,125	10,250	6,625	30,000
Model Y — 3	750	11,625	16,125	7,500	36,000
Total usage	4,750	20,750	26,375	14,125	66,000

of each material to be used, by quarters, based on the production budget in Schedule II. For example, the number of feet of material A needed in the first quarter is determined thus:

From engineering specifications, it is determined that model X uses 2 feet, and model Y also uses 2 feet, of material A in each unit of product. (Caution: Keep the distinction between units of product and units of material clearly in mind at all times: e.g., a toolbox is made of sheet steel, but a toolbox is a toolbox, while a pound of steel is a pound of steel.)

From Schedule II, it is seen that production of 4,000 units of model X is scheduled for the first quarter, while 250 units of model Y are scheduled for the same period.
 Combine this information:

Model X—4,000 units × 2 ft per unit = 8,000 ft
Model Y— 250 units × 2 ft per unit =   500 ft
   Total usage of material A, 1Q   8,500 ft

The same procedure is applied to the other materials for all four quarters.

Material Purchases   The determination of material usage leads to the solution of the problem of when and how much to purchase of each material. Schedule IV will be recognized as input-output analysis of the same sort as that used to determine the production budget.
 In this instance, the desired ending inventory of *raw materials* is projected as one-fifth of the following quarter's forecast usage of that material in production. Thus, in the case of material A in the first quarter, the desired ending inventory is one-fifth the forecast usage for the second quarter (26,000), which is 5,200 feet. To this quantity is added the budgeted usage for the first quarter (8,500) to obtain total first quarter needs of 13,700 ft. There were 4,000 feet on hand at the beginning of the first quarter, meaning that the difference (9,700 feet) will have to be purchased during the first quarter. Material A costs 25 cents per foot, so the required purchases will cost $2,425.
 The same process applied to all three materials for the four quarters results in the material purchases budget, seen as Schedule IV.

Direct Labor   The direct labor budget is developed in a manner similar to that of the material usage and material purchase budgets. The chief difference lies in the fact that labor is not purchased and stored in inventory the way raw materials are. Direct labor is used at the time of purchase (i.e., it is incurred only at the time of production). Thus, to develop the direct labor *input* (i.e., incurred), it is necessary only to know the amount of time required by productive departments and the wage rate prevailing in the productive departments. Thus, a three-step procedure is demonstrated in Schedule V.
 The production budget (Schedule II) provides the information concerning budgeted production by models in units (e.g., first quarter: model X, 4,000; model Y, 250).

The plant superintendent has provided information regarding the amount of productive time required in each department for a unit of each model of product; from this information is determined the total direct labor hours required by the production budget (e.g., first quarter: press department — model X, 0.1 hour per unit × 4,000 units = 400 hours; model Y, 0.2 hour per unit × 250 units = 50 hours; total, 450 hours).

By applying the appropriate departmental wage rates to the budgeted time by departments, the input of direct labor cost is determined (e.g., first quarter: press department, 450 hours × $2.50 per hour = $1,125).

SCHEDULE IV
PROJECTO MANUFACTURING COMPANY
Budgeted Material Purchases by Quarters
For Budget Year 19x1

	1Q	2Q	3Q	4Q	Year
A. Material A					
Desired ending inventory*	5,200	6,250	3,650	3,200	3,200
Add: Material usage					
(Schedule III)	8,500	26,000	31,250	18,250	84,000
Total needs	13,700	32,250	34,900	21,450	87,200
Less: Beginning inventory	4,000	5,200	6,250	3,650	4,000
Required purchases, units	9,700	27,050	28,650	17,800	83,200
Price per unit	$ 0.25	$ 0.25	$ 0.25	$ 0.25	$ 0.25
Total purchases	$ 2,425	$ 6,762	$ 7,163	$ 4,450	$20,800
B. Material B					
Desired ending inventory*	1,550	2,150	1,000	1,200	1,200
Add: Material usage					
(Schedule III)	500	7,750	10,750	5,000	24,000
Total needs	2,050	9,900	11,750	6,200	25,200
Less: Beginning inventory	1,000	1,550	2,150	1,000	1,000
Required purchases, units	1,050	8,350	9,600	5,200	24,200
Price per unit	$ 0.50	$ 0.50	$ 0.50	$ 0.50	$ 0.50
Total purchases	$ 525	$ 4,175	$ 4,800	$ 2,600	$12,100
C. Material C					
Desired ending inventory*	4,150	5,275	2,825	2,600	2,600
Add: Material usage					
(Schedule III)	4,750	20,750	26,375	14,125	66,000
Total needs	8,900	26,025	29,200	16,725	68,600
Less: Beginning inventory	3,000	4,150	5,275	2,825	3,000
Required purchases, units	5,900	21,875	23,925	13,900	65,600
Price per unit	$ 1.00	$ 1.00	$ 1.00	$ 1.00	$ 1.00
Total purchases	$ 5,900	$21,875	$23,925	$13,900	$65,600
Total purchases — all materials	$ 8,850	$32,812	$35,888	$20,950	$98,500

* One-fifth of following quarter forecast of material usage for 1Q, 2Q, and 3Q (per Schedule III).
NOTE: Input-output formula employed, reversing the usual order to find the unknown input — required purchases.

SCHEDULE V
PROJECTO MANUFACTURING COMPANY
Budgeted Direct Labor by Quarters
For Budget Year 19x1

		1Q	2Q	3Q	4Q	Year
A.	Units in production					
	Model X (Schedule II)	4,000	9,125	10,250	6,625	30,000
	Model Y (Schedule II)	250	3,875	5,375	2,500	12,000
B.	Hours in production					
	Press department:					
	Model X (0.1)	400	913	1,025	662	3,000
	Model Y (0.2)	50	775	1,075	500	2,400
	Total press department	450	1,688	2,100	1,162	5,400
	Assembly department:					
	Model X (0.4)	1,600	3,650	4,100	2,650	12,000
	Model Y (0.5)	125	1,938	2,687	1,250	6,000
	Total assembly department	1,725	5,588	6,787	3,900	18,000
	Total direct labor hours	2,175	7,276	8,887	5,062	23,400
C.	Direct labor cost in production					
	Total press department hours	450	1,688	2,100	1,162	5,400
	× departmental wage rate	$ 2.50	$ 2.50	$ 2.50	$ 2.50	$ 2.50
	Direct labor cost – press	$1,125	$ 4,220	$ 5,250	$ 2,905	$13,500
	Total assembly department hours	1,725	5,588	6,787	3,900	18,000
	× departmental wage rate	$ 2.50	$ 2.50	$ 2.50	$ 2.50	$ 2.50
	Direct labor cost – assembly	$4,312	$13,970	$16,968	$ 9,750	$45,000
	Total direct labor cost	$5,437	$18,190	$22,218	$12,655	$58,500

Factory Overhead Schedule VI presents the budget of factory overhead cost by type of expense, by quarters. This budget was assembled in accordance with the plant superintendent's estimate for the year 19x1 and was apportioned to the four quarters on the assumption that these expenses would be incurred in equal amounts each quarter.

For the purpose of developing departmental overhead rates, the plant superintendent made an assignment[4] of the total budgeted overhead for the year to the two productive departments, as shown at the bottom of Schedule VI. Dividing the departmental overhead thus assigned by the total direct labor hours budgeted for the year for the two departments provided the departmental overhead rates of $2.50 per direct labor hour, as shown.

Raw Materials Inventory Schedule VII applies input-output analysis to the raw materials information — beginning inventory, material purchases, and mate-

---

[4] Details of the method for developing departmental overhead rates are found in Chapter 2. For simplicity in this case, it is assumed that the plant superintendent used such a method, with results as shown.

SCHEDULE VI
PROJECTO MANUFACTURING COMPANY
Budgeted Factory Overhead Cost by Quarters
For Budget Year 19x1

Expense	1Q	2Q	3Q	4Q	Year
Indirect labor	$ 2,500	$ 2,500	$ 2,500	$ 2,500	$10,000
Factory supplies	2,000	2,000	2,000	2,000	8,000
Heat, light, power	700	700	700	700	2,800
Supervision	2,500	2,500	2,500	2,500	10,000
Maintenance	1,500	1,500	1,500	1,500	6,000
Engineering	1,800	1,800	1,800	1,800	7,200
Taxes and insurance	1,125	1,125	1,125	1,125	4,500
Depreciation	2,500	2,500	2,500	2,500	10,000
Total factory overhead cost	$14,625	$14,625	$14,625	$14,625	$58,500

	Press	Assembly	Total
Total factory overhead assigned:			
Overhead cost	$13,500	$45,000	$58,500
Total direct labor hours (Schedule V)	5,400	18,000	23,400
Overhead rate (overhead cost/direct labor hours)	$2.50	$2.50	$2.50

SCHEDULE VII
PROJECTO MANUFACTURING COMPANY
Budgeted Raw Materials Inventory
For Budget Year 19x1

	Material			
	A	B	C	Total
A. Units				
Raw materials inventory, 1/1/x1	4,000	1,000	3,000	
Add: Purchases (Schedule IV)	83,200	24,200	65,600	
Available for production	87,200	25,200	68,600	
Less: Material usage (Schedule III)	84,000	24,000	66,000	
Raw materials inventory, 12/31/x1	3,200	1,200	2,600	
B. Cost per unit	$ 0.25	$ 0.50	$ 1.00	
C. Total value — raw materials inventory, 12/31/x1	$ 800	$ 600	$ 2,600	$4,000

NOTE: Input-output formula employed, reversing the usual positions of the output — material usage — and the ending inventory to suit purposes of the schedule.

rial usage—to derive the amount and value of the raw materials inventory at December 31, 19x1. The analysis of the flow of units by types of material yields the information as to amounts. To these unit totals are applied the respective unit purchase prices to determine the asset values. The sum of these—$4,000— will be used in the projected balance sheet and income statement.

Finished Goods Inventory   What was done to determine the ending inventory of raw materials in Schedule VII is repeated in Schedule VIII for the purpose of valuing the ending inventory of finished goods. The input-output analysis of the flow of units provides the quantity base, which, in turn, is multiplied by the appropriate cost of the finished unit of product by model. The inventory pricing factor (product cost) for finished goods is a bit more complex than the unit purchase price of raw materials, however.

Schedule VIII provides a summary of unit product cost by models, wherein these pricing factors are developed. The rationale of the cost summary is to show the buildup of the product cost by key cost elements. Step by step, the manufacturing cost elements are developed as follows:

The quantity and unit value of each of the three types of direct material in each model of product (e.g., model X: 2 feet of material A @ $0.25 = $0.50; one piece of material C @ $1 = $1; total material cost per unit of model X, $1.50)

The productive time by department times the departmental wage rate, for the unit direct labor cost (e.g., model X: press department, 0.1 hour @ $2.50 = $0.25; assembly department, 0.4 hour @ $2.50 = $1; total direct labor cost per unit of model X, $1.25)

The application of factory overhead cost at the predetermined departmental rates (e.g., model X: press, 0.1 hour @ $2.50 per hour = $0.25; assembly, 0.4 hour @ $2.50 per hour = $1; total, $1.25)

Thus, the unit cost for model X is summarized as follows:

Direct material	$1.50
Direct labor	1.25
Factory overhead	1.25
Total manufacturing cost	$4.00

The product cost thus determined is applied to the number of units of that model in the projected ending inventory (4,000 units), and the asset value is established (4,000 units @ $4 = $16,000).

Operating Expenses   The final information to be included in the preliminary schedules consists of the estimates of selling and administrative expenses. As mentioned earlier, the CPA set them down from her own knowledge of the firm's operations. It remained only to construct the schedule, which would list these estimates by expense type on an annual basis, and to compute an average amount per quarter which would be used in the cash budget. This information is shown in Schedule IX. Although the CPA did not do so in this case, she could have taken the additional step of classifying these costs as fixed or variable. (She could have done this in Schedule VI, Factory Overhead,

SCHEDULE VIII
PROJECTO MANUFACTURING COMPANY
Budgeted Finished Goods Inventory
For Budget Year 19x1

| | Product | | |
	X	Y	Total
A. Units			
Finished goods inventory, 1/1/x1	2,000	2,000	
Add: Goods completed in production			
(Schedule II)	30,000	12,000	
Goods available for sale	32,000	14,000	
Less: Goods sold (Schedule I)	28,000	13,000	
Finished goods inventory, 12/31/x1	4,000	1,000	
B. Manufacturing cost per finished unit (see below)	$ 4	$ 8	
C. Total value—finished goods inventory, 12/31/x1	$16,000	$ 8,000	$24,000

	X				Y			
	Element		Product Unit Cost		Element		Product Unit Cost	
	Unit Cost	Quantity	Detail	Summary	Unit Cost	Quantity	Detail	Summary
Direct material A, ft	$0.25	2	$0.50		$0.25	2	$0.50	
Direct material B, lb	0.50				0.50	2	1.00	
Direct material C, parts	1.00	1	1.00		1.00	3	3.00	
Total direct material				$1.50				$4.50
Direct labor— Press, hr	2.50	0.1	$0.25		2.50	0.2	$0.50	
Direct labor— Assembly, hr	2.50	0.4	1.00		2.50	0.5	1.25	
Total direct labor				1.25				1.75
Factory overhead— Press, hr	2.50	0.1	$0.25		2.50	0.2	$0.50	
Factory overhead— Assembly, hr	2.50	0.4	1.00		2.50	0.5	1.25	
Total factory overhead				1.25				1.75
Total manufacturing cost per finished unit				$4.00				$8.00

NOTE: Input-output formula is employed, reversing the usual order of output and ending inventory to suit the needs of the schedule.

too.) For the purposes of the comprehensive or planning budget, however, such classification is not necessary. In Chapter 7 we will see the advantages of classifying these costs as fixed or variable for budgeting purposes as well as for cost-volume-profit analysis.

Summary Schedules   At this point, the CPA had all the basic information necessary to complete a comprehensive budget for the operations of the Projecto

SCHEDULE IX
PROJECTO MANUFACTURING COMPANY
Budgeted Operating Expense
For Budget Year 19x1

Selling expense:		
Sales salaries	$ 7,500	
Freight out	2,000	
Advertising	3,000	
Total selling expense		$12,500
Administrative expense:		
Administrative salaries	$10,000	
Office supplies	1,500	
Telephone	500	
Professional fees	2,500	
Total administrative expense		14,500
Total operating expense		$27,000
Average per quarter		$ 6,750

SCHEDULE X
PROJECTO MANUFACTURING COMPANY
Budgeted Cost of Goods Sold
For Budget Year 19x1

Raw materials inventory, 1/1/x1 (balance sheet, 12/31/x0)	$ 4,500	
Add: Material purchases (Schedule IV)	98,500	
Material available for production	$103,000	
Less: Raw materials inventory, 12/31/x1 (Schedule VII)	4,000	
Cost of direct materials used	$ 99,000	
Cost of direct labor (Schedule V)	58,500	
Factory overhead cost (Schedule VI)	58,500	
Total manufacturing costs incurred	$216,000	
Add: Work in process inventory, 1/1/x1 (balance sheet, 12/31/x0)	4,500	
Cost of goods in process	$220,500	
Less: Work in process inventory, 12/31/x1 (unchanged)	4,500	
Cost of goods manufactured		$216,000
Add: Finished goods inventory, 1/1/x1 (balance sheet, 12/31/x0)		24,000
Cost of goods available for sale		$240,000
Less: Finished goods inventory, 12/31/x1 (Schedule VIII)		24,000
Cost of goods sold		$216,000

Company for the year 19x1. It remained for her to assemble the information from the first nine schedules into:

Budgeted Cost of Goods Sold	Schedule X
Budgeted Cash Flow	Schedule XI
Budgeted Income Statement	Schedule XII
Budgeted Balance Sheet	Schedule XIII

SCHEDULE XI
PROJECTO MANUFACTURING COMPANY
Budgeted Cash Flow
For Budget Year 19x1

	1Q	2Q	3Q	4Q	Year
Beginning balance—Cash (balance sheet, 12/31/x0)	$10,000	$13,963	$ 8,211	$28,745	$ 10,000
Add: Receipts:					
Accounts receivable, 12/31/x0	$25,000				$ 25,000
70% of current sales (Schedule I)	24,500	$49,000	$ 89,250	$26,250	189,000
30% of previous quarter sales (Schedule I)		10,500	21,000	38,250	69,750
Total receipts	$49,500	$59,500	$110,250	$64,500	$283,750
Total cash available	$59,500	$73,463	$118,461	$93,245	$293,750
Less: Expenditures:					
Purchase (Schedule IV)	$ 8,850	$32,812	$ 35,888	$20,950	$ 98,500
Direct labor payroll (Schedule V)	5,437	18,190	22,218	12,655	58,500
Factory overhead (excluding depreciation, Schedule VI)	12,125	12,125	12,125	12,125	48,500
Operating expense (Schedule IX)	6,750	6,750	6,750	6,750	27,000
Income tax payments (12/31/x0 balance sheet)	375	375	375	375	1,500
Fixed assets (given)	12,000	7,000		1,000	20,000
Total expenditures	$45,537	$77,252	$ 77,356	$53,855	$254,000
Ending balance—cash (before borrowing)	$13,963	$ (3,789)	$ 41,105	$39,390	$ 39,750
Add: Proceeds of short-term loans		12,000			12,000
Less: Repayment of loan:					
Principal			12,000		12,000
Interest (6% annual rate)			360		360
Ending balance—cash	$13,963	$ 8,211	$ 28,745	$39,390	$ 39,390

NOTE: The input-output formula is employed, detailing input (receipts) and output (expenditures) for purposes of clarifying the factors of flow.

It is in these last schedules that the concept of budgeting as "accounting in the future" becomes clear. The basic statements are identical in form to those which report the results of completed transactions—historical accounting. The difference lies, of course, in the source of the budget figures—the forecast of future events as conditioned by the intelligent estimates of persons experienced in the business they are operating.

Schedules X, XII, and XIII thus are virtually self-explanatory. Schedule XI, Budgeted Cash Flow, however, is not a formal financial statement as such. Nevertheless, its form and function are logical and significant. The form—input-output analysis—closely resembles the analysis of a personal bank checking account. The function is to highlight the highs and lows in the short-term flows of cash through the business. Foreknowledge of shortages of cash will faciliate borrowing arrangements; anticipation of the timing of large cash balances will permit timely repayment of loans and minimization of interest cost, as well as the temporary investment of large idle cash balances in marketable securities.

In the budget period 19x1, the cash flow depicted in Schedule XI indicates Projecto's need to borrow money in the second quarter to finance seasonally high investments in inventory and accounts receivable and to maintain a minimum cash balance of at least $8,000.

Certain other facts in connection with the budgeted cash flow are noteworthy:

1.   The amount of interest cost is set forth separately; this amount will be transferred to the income statement as an expense of the budget period (see Schedule XII).

2.   The proposed purchases of fixed assets, although they do not affect the income statement, must be included because they will require the outlay of cash in the budget period.

3.   Depreciation, although a proper expense item on the income statement, does not require the outlay of cash in the budget period and therefore is not shown in the budgeted cash flow.

SCHEDULE XII
PROJECTO MANUFACTURING COMPANY
Budgeted Income Statement
For Budget Year 19x1

Net sales (Schedule I)	$270,000
Cost of goods sold (Schedule X)	216,000
Gross margin	$ 54,000
Operating expense (Schedule IX)	27,000
Income from operations	$ 27,000
Interest expense (Schedule XI)	360
Income before taxes	$ 26,640
Estimated income tax (30%)	8,000
Net income to shareholders	$ 18,640

SCHEDULE XIII
PROJECTO MANUFACTURING COMPANY
Budgeted Balance Sheet
As of December 31, 19x1

Assets				Equities			
Current assets:				Current liabilities:			
Cash (Schedule XI)		$ 39,390		Accounts payable (unchanged)		$30,000	
Receivables (30% of 4Q sales)		11,250		Accrued payroll (unchanged)		1,000	
Inventories:				Accrued income taxes			
Raw materials (Schedule VII)	$ 4,000			(Schedule XII)		8,000	
Work in process (unchanged)	4,500						
Finished goods							
(Schedule VIII)	24,000	32,500					
Other current assets				Other current liabilities			
(unchanged)		2,000		(unchanged)		2,500	
Total current assets			$ 85,140	Total current liabilities			$ 41,500
Plant, property, and equipment				Shareholders' equity:			
Acquisition value		$120,000		Common stock		$80,000	
Less: Accumulated				Retained earnings, 1/1/x1	$30,000		
depreciation		35,000		Add: Budget net income, 19x1	18,640		
Net book value—plant,				Retained earnings, 12/31/x1		48,640	
property, equipment			85,000	Total shareholders' equity			128,640
			$170,140				$170,140

4. Most of the cash outflows are derived directly from previous budget schedules; the regular cash inflows, however, are from the collection of receivables, the source of which is the forecast sales. The problem here is timing — where sales are on account, *there is a time lag between the recognition of the sale transaction and the receipt of cash.* The typical collection period for the firm will ordinarily establish the pattern for anticipating the cash inflow for budget purposes. In the case of Projecto, it is expected that 70 percent of the sales are collected in the period of the sale and that the remaining 30 percent are not collected until the following quarter. This pattern, applied to the forecast of sales for 19x1, provides the information concerning cash receipts in the budget cash flow in Schedule XI.

Acceptance

Armed with the thirteen schedules of the 19x1 comprehensive budget for the Projecto Company, the CPA held a late November meeting with the company president. After explaining the function of each schedule, together with the source of information used, she asked whether the president wished to make any corrections. The latter replied that the budget sounded pretty logical; he thought he would let it stand for the year 19x1, but probably make some corrections the following year, based on the experience in the first year of using it.

The president concluded that the information contained in the budget schedules ought to prove extremely helpful. Never before had the trouble been taken to assemble a detailed sales forecast in such a systematic manner. Thus production could never be planned very far ahead. Because so many details of the operation depended on the fluctuating volume of sales and production, previous practices in the realm of material purchases and the hiring and laying off of plant personnel had been pretty haphazard.

The president was certain that he formerly had incurred excessive employment and worker training costs, to say nothing of the cost of inefficient labor operations while new employees were learning the operations. Because of his fears of running out of materials, as well as of not having enough stock of finished product to meet customer orders, he had consistently overinvested in inventory, a rather costly practice. Finally, he had never paid too much attention to the level of factory overhead and selling and administrative costs, having felt that the periodic accounting reports would tell him how much such costs had been. Now he saw that thinking about these costs ahead of time was the first step in trying to control them.

"Incidentally," the CPA pointed out, "the budgeted financial statements show you where you will be a year from now if you operate according to plan: your profit goals are built in, and will be achieved insofar as operations conform to the budget plan. The forecast net income after taxes of $18,640 represents 6.9 percent of the forecast sales of $270,000 [the president had set a target of 7 percent]. In terms of an average shareholders' equity ($110,000 at 12/31/x0 and $128,640 at 12/31/x1 gives an average of $119,320) for the year 19x1, the return is 15.6 percent [as compared with the president's goal of 15 percent]."

The president agreed that if the budgeted results are achieved, the cost of preparing a budget is well repaid. Indeed, after working for a year with such a budget based on his profit goals and the systematic development of operating plans from carefully prepared sales forecasts, he seriously doubted that he could go back to his former habit of "seat-of-the-pants" planning.

SUMMARY

Planning is a basic management function. The budget is a detailed, quantitative expression of management's plans for the near-term future.

The preparation of a comprehensive budget begins with a forecast of sales. Sales forecasts cover a broad range of complexity and sophistication. Generally they originate with the estimates of sales personnel. These estimates may then be subjected to a variety of adjustments in contemplation of product growth trends, anticipated general and industrial business conditions, advertising programs, price changes, changes in competitive climate, product or process innovation, and many other possible influential factors. Finally, top management judgment may suggest certain modifications before final approval.

The timing and volume of sales as indicated by the sales forecast will establish the basis for the detailed planning of production. Following the production schedule, the detailed plans for material usage and purchases, direct labor manning and cost, factory overhead and operating expense incurrence, and levels of inventory are derived in an appropriate sequence. Basic information for these budget schedules is usually available from bills of material, operation sheets, purchase pricing data, inventory and production control records, and wage rate schedules. These data are processed in a manner similar to the procedures used for conventional historical accounting, but in summary form rather than through the recording of detailed transactions.

The detailed budget schedules provide the basis for the projection of planned results in the form of financial statements and a budget of cash flow. The latter is not one of the conventional financial statements, but it provides some of the most sensitive information available for management planning. It highlights the highs and lows of short-term cash flows through the business during the period ahead. Foreknowledge of shortages of cash will facilitate borrowing arrangements. On the other hand, the anticipation of the timing of large cash balances will permit timely repayment of loans or temporary investment in marketable securities. In short, this valuable device provides information about the prime asset of the firm—cash—not directly available from the conventional income statement and the balance sheet, which have been developed by accrual accounting methods to serve a different purpose.

The pro forma (according to form) financial statements consist of a projected income statement, with supporting projected costs of goods sold schedule, and a projected balance sheet. The comprehensive budget plan is thus summed up in statements which look just like their accounting counterparts. The difference lies solely in the fact that accounting statements are based on completed transactions (historical), while planning budgets are based on estimates tempered by executive judgments—truly "accounting in the future."

KEY WORDS AND PHRASES

sales forecast   strategic planning
budget   management control
pro forma financial statements   operational control

DISCUSSION QUESTIONS

1. What role is played by a budget in management planning?
2. What is meant by a comprehensive budget?
3. "The budget is an aid to management, not a substitute for management." Comment.
4. "The sales forecast is the starting point of the planning budget." Why?
5. Who is in the best position to make a sales forecast?
6. Describe the steps in the budget preparation process.
7. "We can't afford a formal budget system." Explain the internal economics of budgeting.
8. "Budget preparation is essentially the job of the management accountant." Comment.
9. Explain the function of the production budget.
10. Explain the function of the material usage and purchase budgets.
11. Explain the function of the direct labor budget.
12. Explain the function of the factory overhead budget.
13. Explain the function of the inventory budgets.
14. Explain the function of the operating expense budget.
15. Explain the concept of budgeting as "accounting in the future."
16. What is the unique function of the budget of cash flow?

PROBLEMS

5-1. *Part A.* Arrange the following budgets in the order they would probably be prepared:

1. Cost of goods sold
2. Cash flow
3. Sales forecast
4. Balance sheet
5. Production
6. Factory overhead

Part B. Using the following data, prepare a material purchases budget:

Predicted sales	10,000 units
Units of raw material required per unit of finished goods	6
Current finished goods inventory	2,500
Desired finished goods inventory	4,500
Current raw materials inventory	23,000
Desired raw materials inventory	30,000

5-2. The Way Production Company makes and sells one basic product which is manufactured by a process where all direct materials are added at the very beginning of the process and then converted to the finished product. The expected unit cost information is as follows:

Material (4 lb @ $4)	$16.00
Direct labor (1 hr @ $8.25)	8.25
Overhead (3 hr @ $2.25)	6.75
Total	$31.00

The company estimates the next month's sales at 28,000 units and also desires the following inventory levels at the end of the month:

Raw material (lb)	80,000
Work in process (units)	10,000
Finished goods (units)	22,000

Present inventories at the beginning of the month are:

Raw material (lb)	70,000
Work in process (units)	15,000
Finished goods (units)	16,000

Required:
Assume that material purchases are paid for at time of purchase. What will cash requirements be for material in order to meet the sales estimate and desired inventory levels?

5-3.† Tomlinson Retail seeks your assistance to develop cash and other budget information for May, June, and July 1973. At April 30, 1973, the company had cash of $5,500, accounts receivable of $437,000, inventories of $309,400, and accounts payable of $133,055.

The budget is to be based on the following assumptions:

1. *Sales*
   a. Each month's sales are billed on the last day of the month.
   b. Customers are allowed a 3 percent discount if payment is made within ten days after the billing date. Receivables are booked gross.
   c. Sixty percent of the billings are collected within the discount period, an additional 25 percent are collected by the end of the first month, another 9 percent are collected by the end of the second month, and 6 percent prove uncollectible.

2. *Purchases*
   a. Fifty-four percent of all purchases of material and selling, general, and administrative expenses are paid in the month purchased and the remainder in the following month.
   b. Each month's units of ending inventory is equal to 130 percent of the next month's units of sales.
   c. The cost of each unit of inventory is $20.
   d. Selling, general, and administrative expenses of which $2,000 is depreciation, are equal to 15 percent of the current month's sales.

Actual and projected sales are as follows:

1973	Dollars	Units
March	$354,000	11,800
April	363,000	12,100
May	357,000	11,900
June	342,000	11,400
July	360,000	12,000
August	366,000	12,200

Required:
Prepare data showing:

1. Budgeted cash disbursements during the month of June
2. Budgeted cash collections during the month of May
3. Budgeted number of units of inventory to be purchased during July
(AICPA adapted)

5-4. The Dilly Company marks up all merchandise at 25 percent of gross purchase price. All purchases are made on account with terms of 1/10, net/60. Purchase discounts, which are recorded as miscellaneous income, are always taken. Normally, 60 percent of each month's purchases are paid for in the month of purchase and the other 40 percent are paid during the first ten days of the first month after purchase. Inventories of merchandise at the end of each month are kept at 30 percent of the next month's projected cost of goods sold.

Terms for sales on account are 2/10, net/30. Cash sales are not subject to discount. Fifty percent of each month's sales on account are collected during the month of sale, 45 percent are collected in the succeeding month, and the remainder are usually uncollectible. Seventy percent of the collections in the month of sale are subject to discount, and 10 percent of the collections in the succeeding month are subject to discount.

Projected sales data for selected months follow:

	Sales on Account—Gross	Cash Sales
December	$1,900,000	$400,000
January	1,500,000	250,000
February	1,700,000	350,000
March	1,600,000	300,000

Required:
Prepare data showing:

1. Budgeted gross purchases for January
2. Budgeted inventory at the end of December
3. Budgeted payments to suppliers during February
4. Budgeted sales discounts to be taken by customers making remittances during February
5. Budgeted total collections from customers during February
(AICPA adapted)

 5-5. The sales manager of the Newport Company receives the following estimates from the company's regional managers for 19x6 sales based on 19x5 results:

| | Sales in Units | | |
	Widgets	Gismos	Shards
New England	7,130	3,910	2,070
Southeast	6,210	5,520	2,300
Middle West	9,660	4,370	2,530
Total	23,000	13,800	6,900

Before presenting a complete sales forecast to the president, the sales manager believes that certain refinements ought to be made. The following factors are considered relevant:

1. Regional sales managers tend to be somewhat unrealistic (on the high side) in forecasting their own sales. The sales manager feels he must "wring out the water," which he estimates at 15 percent of the realistic figure.
2. Long-term product growth trends among the products are somewhat divergent. Projected changes for 19x6 from 19x5 results are:

Widgets	10% increase
Gismos	5% decrease
Shards	5% increase

3. General business conditions in 19x6 are expected to improve by 10 percent over 19x5. The impact of such changes upon the company is generally assumed to be in the same direction and double that on the general economy.
4. A special promotion of Widgets in the Southeast regional market is expected to boost sales of this item there by 40 percent of the adjusted estimate.

Required:
Prepare a sales forecast of units by products, by regions, for presentation to the president.

5-6. The Vinson Company is considering pricing policies in connection with the sales budget currently being developed. The current selling price of the principal product is $10.50 per unit. The sales department believes that the price should be reduced to $10; the manufacturing department maintains that this decrease in price would not be offset by increased volume, as is claimed. As a result of the discussions concerning the various alternatives that exist, a rather complete study has been made. The following data were developed:

1. Sales price–volume data:

Assumed Selling Price	Estimated Market at Given Price (Units)
$10.00	12,000
10.20	11,500
10.40	11,300
10.50	11,000
10.60	10,600
10.80	9,500
11.00	9,000

2. Total fixed costs $30,000. (It is assumed this cost will be constant at all the volumes listed above.)
3. Estimated total variable cost per unit of product, $7.

Required:

Assume you developed these data. You are asked to prepare a volume-price forecast in a form suitable for submission to the executive committee, supplementing it with comments or graphs if these would add to the effectiveness of the presentation.

5-7.† The Jazbo Company produces three product models: X10, X20, and X30. Four kinds of material are used: sheet steel, handles (purchased), paint, and cartons. All three products use the same gauge of steel and type of handles, but in varying amounts. Two of the models are painted, using the same type and color of paint but in varying quantities. Each of the three uses a different carton.

The following is an analysis of the material specifications for the products by models:

	Model No.		
	X10	X20	X30
Steel sheet, lb	2	3	5
Paint, pints	1		2
Handles, units	2	4	4
Cartons (1 each)	model p	model r	model s

Inventories of raw materials at September 30, 19x1 (quantities) are:

Sheet steel	10 tons
Paint	1,200 gal
Handles	9,000 units
Cartons, model p	4,000 units
Cartons, model r	6,000 units
Cartons, model s	4,000 units

Inventories of finished goods at September 30, 19x1, are:

Model X10	1,200 units
Model X20	1,600 units
Model X30	900 units

The sales forecast for the fourth quarter, 19x1, is:

Model X10	26,000 units
Model X20	32,000 units
Model X30	18,000 units

Management wishes to maintain minimum inventory quantities as follows:

Raw Materials		Finished Goods	
Sheet steel	8 tons	Model X10	1,000 units
Paint	900 gal	Model X20	1,500 units
Handles	7,000 units	Model X30	800 units
Cartons, model p	2,000 units		
Cartons, model r	2,000 units		
Cartons, model s	2,000 units		

There are no beginning or ending inventories of work in process.

Required:
Prepare production and purchasing budgets, expressed in appropriate units, for the fourth quarter of 19x1.

5-8. The Parseghian Company's budget director is preparing her schedules for the comprehensive budget for 19x2. She has assembled the following data:

	Projected, Jan. 1, 19x2	Required, Dec. 31, 19x2
Inventories:		
Raw materials:		
Material Q, lb	55,000	40,000
Material R, gal	6,700	8,000
Material S, each	19,500	15,000
Material T, ft	2,500	10,000
Finished goods (in units):		
Product Bill	1,200	3,800
Product Pete	6,400	5,000
Product Ivan	4,000	8,000
Sales forecast (in units):		
Bill	15,000	
Pete	40,000	
Ivan	25,000	

Bills of materials:	Bill	Pete	Ivan
Material Q, lb	2	1	5
Material R, gal	5		3
Material S, each		3	1
Material T, ft	3	4	

Purchase prices of raw materials:	
Material Q	$2.50/lb
Material R	$4.00/gal
Material S	$0.50 each
Material T	$1.00/ft

Labor operations analysis (in hours):	Bill	Pete	Ivan
Department 1 ($2.00/hr)	2	3	1
Department 2 ($2.20/hr)	1	4	3

Factory overhead rates:	
Department 1	$3/direct labor hour
Department 2	200% of direct labor cost

Required:
Prepare the following:

1. Product budget (quantities)
2. Direct material budget (quantities)
3. Direct material purchase budget (dollars)
4. Direct labor budget (dollars)
5. Analysis of unit costs by products
6. Valuation of finished goods inventory, December 31, 19x2

5-9. The Johnson Company sells two products, X and Y, for $10 and $20 per unit, respectively. The company's monthly selling expenses have been analyzed as follows:

	Fixed	Variable (per Unit)
Depreciation	$6,000	
Taxes	1,000	
Supplies	1,000	$0.20
Telephone and telegraph	500	0.30
Delivery expenses	2,000	0.10
Salaries	4,000	1.00
Advertising	2,000	

Beginning inventories were 2,000 units of product X at a cost of $5 each and 500 units of Y at $10 each. The company wishes to maintain inventories at these same levels throughout the year; raw materials are purchased each month for that month's production and cost $1 per pound. One pound is required for X and three for Y. One hour of labor is required for a unit of X and two hours for Y, and costs $3 per hour. Factory overhead is $1 for each unit of X and $2 for each unit of Y.

The company expects to sell units as follows:

January	4,000 units of X, 1,000 units of Y
February	4,500 units of X, 1,200 units of Y
March	5,000 units of X, 1,500 units of Y

Required:
Prepare a pro forma income statement for the three-month period, with supporting schedules.

5-10. The Wayside Motel is located in a medium-sized university town just off a major highway in the southeastern United States. The manager is planning the operation for the fourth quarter of 19x1.

The motel consists of 100 sleeping rooms, a restaurant, and a cocktail lounge. A family plan is in effect whereby children under twelve may occupy a room with parents at no charge. In planning, the manager assumes that whether a room is occupied by adults or children, it will yield either the single or double rates, which are respectively $9 and $14 per night.

In forecasting revenue, the manager begins with an estimate of the occupancy rate. He uses an average of thirty days per month, which, applied to the 100 rooms available, gives a base of 3,000 rooms as 100 percent occupancy for a month. Considering past experience, the scheduling of football weekends, holidays, travel habits of sales representatives, etc., the manager estimates occupancy percentages for the fourth quarter:

	October	November	December
Total occupancy	65%	70%	55%
Double occupancy (percentage of total occupancy)	50%	60%	40%

Food and beverage revenue averages 120 percent of room revenue. Certain room costs, such as extra maids, laundry, and supplies, vary with occupancy and are estimated at 10 percent of room revenue. Cost of food and beverage sales is variable and is estimated at 40 percent of food and beverage revenue. Fixed costs per month are estimated as follows:

Room:		
Salaries and meals	$ 5,000	
Linens and cleaning	800	
Miscellaneous	200	$ 6,000

Food and beverage:		
Salaries and meals	$12,000	
China, glassware, utensils, etc.	2,000	
Laundry and cleaning	2,500	
Miscellaneous	1,500	18,000

Promotion, general and administrative:		
Administrative salaries	$ 4,000	
Heat, light, power	1,500	
Promotion	1,000	
Depreciation	5,000	
Other	500	12,000
Total fixed costs		$36,000

Required:

1. Prepare a forecast of revenue by months for the fourth quarter (show calculations). *$6,5,675 + Food 'n beverage per month*
2. Prepare a pro forma income statement by months for the fourth quarter.
3. Determine the break-even point, by month and quarter, in dollars of revenue.
4. Using an average of $12 per room as a revenue factor, at what percentage of occupancy does the Wayside Motel break even?

61,190'

5-11. The controller of the Cape Odd Cranberry Packing Company prepares a cash budget by quarters each year as part of the company's overall planning program.

The company's operations consist solely in processing and canning the annual cranberry crop, a highly seasonal commodity. All manufacturing operations take place in the quarter of October through December, although sales are made throughout the year. The company's fiscal year runs from July 1 through June 30.

The sales forecast for the coming year shows (all figures in thousands):

First quarter (July–September 19x1)	$390
Second quarter (October–December 19x1)	750
Third quarter (January–March 19x2)	390
Fourth quarter (April–June 19x2)	390

All sales are on account. The beginning balance of receivables is expected to be collected in the first quarter. Subsequent collections are made two-thirds in the quarter in which sales take place and one-third in the quarter following.

Purchases of materials (the cranberries) are scheduled as follows: $120,000 in the first quarter, $360,000 in the second quarter, and none in the third and fourth quarters. Payment is made in the same quarter in which the berries are purchased.

Direct labor of $350,000 is incurred and paid in the second quarter.

Factory overhead cost, paid in cash during the quarter in which it is incurred, is $430,000 in the second quarter. This overhead cost is at a standby level of $100,000 during the other three quarters.

Selling and administrative expenses are incurred and paid in an amount of $50,000 per quarter throughout the year.

The company has a line of short-term credit with the Usury State Bank for financing its seasonal working capital needs. The company plans to maintain a minimum cash balance of $8,000. It borrows only in multiples of $5,000 and repays as soon as it is able without impairing the minimum cash balance. Interest is at 6 percent. It is assumed that all borrowing is made at the *beginning* of a quarter, and the repayments are made at the *end* of a quarter. (Round interest calculations to the nearest $1,000.)

The company plans to spend the following amounts on fixed assets: third quarter, $150,000; fourth quarter, $50,000.

Account balances, July 1, 19x1, are:

Cash	$ 8,000
Accounts receivable	25,000

Required:
Complete the following schedule:

CASH BUDGET AND FINANCING REQUIREMENTS
(Figures in Thousands)

	1Q	2Q	3Q	4Q	Total
Beginning balance	$ 8				$ 8
Add: Receipts:					
Accounts receivable, 7/1	$25	$—	$—	$—	$25
Two-thirds of current sales					
One-third of previous quarter sales					
Total receipts					
Cash available					
Less: Expenditures:					
Material purchases					
Direct labor					
Factory overhead					
Selling and administrative					
Purchase of fixed assets					
Total expenditures					
Ending balance before borrowing					
Add: Cash borrowed					
Less: Principal of loan repaid					
Interest paid					
Ending balance of cash					
Loan balance—end of period					

5-12.† A client submits the following details about an appliance business to be formed:

Estimated sales in terms of units by month:

January	100
February	160
March	180
April	220
May	380
June	360

Each appliance will be sold for $200. It is anticipated that 25 percent will be sold for cash and the balance on an installment contract. The installment contract requires a down payment of 10 percent and ten monthly payments of $20 each, which includes the finance charge. The finance charge is assumed to be earned in proportion to the collections on installment contracts.

The appliances cost $125 each. Their purchase can be financed by paying 20 percent down with a non-interest-bearing floor-plan note for the balance. This balance must be paid at the end of the month in which the appliance is sold. An average inventory of 200 units should be maintained. The same purchase terms will be available for all replacements.

The installment contracts will be pledged as collateral for loans of 60 percent of the unpaid balance. These loans will be reduced, monthly, by 60 percent of all installment collections received. The client agrees to maintain a minimum bank balance of $15,000.

Salespersons will be allowed a commission of $20 per unit, to be paid during the month of the sale. Other variable expenses will be approximately $30 per unit sold. Other fixed expenses are estimated at $1,200 per month. Interest expense on bank loans will be 6 percent per annum on loans outstanding at the end of the previous month.

Assume that the payments to the manufacturer and monthly advances from the bank will be consummated on the last day of each month. Bank interest will be payable monthly following the date the loan is received. For budgeting purposes all computations should be made to the nearest $10.

Required:

From the foregoing information you are to prepare a cash budget by month, with appropriate supporting schedules, which will summarize cash receipts, cash disbursements, and additional cash investments required to comply with the terms of the bank loan.   (AICPA adapted)

5-13. The Standard Mercantile Corporation is a wholesaler and ends its fiscal year on December 31. As the company's CPA, you have been requested, in early January 19x4, to assist in the preparation of a cash forecast. The following information regarding the company's operations is available:

1. Management believes the 19x3 sales pattern is a reasonable estimate of 19x4 sales. Sales in 19x3 were as follows:

January	$ 360,000
February	420,000
March	600,000
April	540,000
May	480,000
June	400,000
July	350,000
August	550,000
September	500,000
October	400,000
November	600,000
December	800,000
Total	$6,000,000

2. The accounts receivable at December 31 total $380,000. Sales collections are generally made as follows:

During month of sale	60%
In first subsequent month	30%
In second subsequent month	9%
Uncollectible	1%

3. The purchase cost of goods averages 60 percent of the selling price. The cost of the inventory on hand at December 31 is $840,000, of which $30,000 is obsolete. Arrangements have been made to sell the obsolete inventory in January at half the normal selling price on a c.o.d. basis.

   The company wishes to maintain the inventory as of the first of each month at a level of three months' sales as determined by the sales forecast for the next three months. All purchases are paid for on the 10th of the following month. Accounts payable for purchases at December 31 total $370,000.

4. Recurring fixed expenses amount to $120,000 per month, including depreciation of $20,000. For accounting purposes, the company apportions the recurring fixed expenses to the various months in the same proportion as that month's estimated sales bears to the estimated total annual sales. Variable expenses amount to 10 percent of sales. Payments for expenses are made as follows:

	During Month Incurred	Following Month
Fixed expenses	55%	45%
Variable expenses	70%	30%

5. Annual property taxes amount to $50,000 and are paid in equal installments on December 31 and March 31. The property taxes are in addition to the expenses in item 4.

6. It is anticipated that cash dividends of $20,000 will be paid each quarter on the 15th day of the third month of the quarter.

7. During the winter, unusual advertising costs will be incurred which will require cash payments of $10,000 in February and $15,000 in March. The advertising costs are in addition to the expenses in item 4.

8. Equipment replacements are made at the rate of $3,000 per month. The equipment has an average estimated life of six years.

9. The company's income tax for 19x3 is $230,000. A Declaration of Estimated Income Tax was filed for 19x3: The declaration estimated the company's total 19x3 tax as $210,000. The tax liability is extinguished as follows:

19x3 tax	$230,000
Less: Payments on declaration of estimated tax made in September and December 19x3 ($210,000 less $100,000 exemption	110,000
Unpaid tax liability to be paid in equal installments in March and June 19x4	$120,000

For 19x4 the company will file a declaration estimating the total tax as $220,000.

10. At December 31, 19x3, the company had a bank loan with an unpaid balance of $280,000. The loan requires a principal payment of $20,000 on the last day of each month plus interest at $\frac{1}{2}$ percent per month on the unpaid balance at the first of the month. The entire balance is due on March 31, 19x4.

11. The cash balance at December 31, 19x3, is $100,000.

12. The client understands that the ethical considerations involved in preparing the following statement will be taken care of by your letter accompanying the statement. (Do not prepare the letter.)

Required:

Prepare a cash-flow budget by months for the first three months of 19x4 for the Standard Mercantile Corporation. The statement should show the amount of cash on hand (or deficiency of cash) at the end of each month. Present supporting calculations.

(AICPA adapted)

5-14. The following is information pertaining to the Pesky Manufacturing Company as of January 1, 19x2, along with certain estimates to be used in establishing the planning budget for the first quarter.

Balances as of January 1, 19x2:	
Cash	$ 4,000
Accounts receivable	11,000
Raw material inventory	14,000
Work in process inventory	12,000
Finished goods inventory	18,000
Accounts payable	20,000
Sales forecast:	
January	50,000
February	60,000
March	40,000
April	60,000

All sales are on account. It is expected that the entire beginning accounts receivable balance will be collected in January. Subsequent collections are made one-half in the month of sale and one-half in the month following.

Direct material cost amounts to 40 percent of sales. Purchases are planned so as to provide raw material at the *end* of each month equal to the material cost in the *following* month's sales. Payment for materials is made in the month *following* the purchase. Assume that the beginning balance of accounts payable is paid in January.

Direct labor cost amounts to 15 percent of sales. Direct labor payroll is paid in the month in which it is incurred.

Factory burden is estimated at 25 percent of the *total* sales for the first quarter, to be paid in equal amounts in each month.

Selling and administrative expenses are estimated at 10 percent of the *total* sales for the first quarter, to be paid in equal amounts in each month.

Each month's production is planned at a level just sufficient to meet the estimated sales for the month. Thus there is no planned change in the amounts of work in process and finished goods inventories throughout the quarter.

Pesky Company has a line of short-term credit with the Shylock State Bank for financing its working capital needs. Pesky Company wishes to maintain a minimum cash balance of $4,000. It borrows in multiples of $1,000 and repays as soon as it is able without impairing the minimum cash balance. (Ignore interest.)

Required:

Fill the blanks in the following schedules and questions.

1. *Schedule A: Estimated receipts*

	Jan.	Feb.	Mar.	Total
Accounts receivable, Jan. 1	$11,000			$11,000
One-half current month's sales				
One-half previous month's sales				
Total receipts				

Schedule B: Purchases

	Jan.	Feb.	Mar.	Total
Raw material—ending inventory required				
Add: Material in cost of goods sold				
Total material needed				
Less: Raw material—beginning inventory	$14,000			$14,000
Required purchases				

Schedule C: Payments on accounts payable

	Jan.	Feb.	Mar.	Total
Accounts payable, Jan. 1	$20,000			$20,000
Previous month's purchases				
Total payments				

Schedule D: Operating expenditures

	Jan.	Feb.	Mar.	Total
Direct labor				
Factory burden				
Selling and administrative				
Total operating expenditures				

Schedule E: Cash budget and financial requirements

	Jan.	Feb.	Mar.	Total
Cash balance—beginning	$ 4,000			$ 4,000
Add: Receipts (Schedule A)				
Cash available				
Less: Expenditures:				
Accounts payable (Schedule C)				
Operating expenditures (Schedule D)				
Total expenditures				
Ending cash balance before borrowing				
Add: Cash borrowed				
Less: Loans repaid				
Ending cash balance				

Schedule F: Projected income statement for first quarter, 19x2

Sales		$
Cost of goods sold:		
Direct material	$	
Direct labor		
Factory burden	———	
Total cost of goods sold		
Gross margin		$
Selling and administrative		
expenses		
Net income		$

Schedule G: Projected condensed balance sheet as of March 31, 19x2

Assets

Cash		$
Accounts receivable		
Raw materials inventory		
Work in process inventory		
Finished goods inventory		
Other assets		
Total assets		$

Equities

Accounts payable		$
Bank loan payable		
Other liabilities		
Capital stock		$20,000
Retained earnings, Jan. 1, 19x2	$19,000	
Add: net income, first quarter	———	———
Total equities		$

2. Contribution margin for the first quarter is $ ———
3. Capacity costs for the first quarter total $ ———
4. Break-even sales volume for the first quarter is $ ———

5-15. Thorne Transit, Inc. has decided to inaugurate express bus service between its headquarters city and a nearby suburb (one-way fare, 50 cents) and is considering the purchase of either 32- or 52-passenger buses, on which pertinent estimates are as follows:

	32-Passenger Bus	52-Passenger Bus
Number of each to be purchased	6	4
Useful life	8 years	8 years
Purchase price of each bus (paid on delivery)	$80,000	$110,000
Mileage per gallon	10	$7\frac{1}{2}$
Salvage value per bus	$6,000	$7,000
Drivers' hourly wage	$3.50	$4.20
Price per gallon of gasoline	$.30	$.30
Other annual cash expenses	$4,000	$3,000

During the four daily rush hours, all buses would be in service and are expected to operate at full capacity (state law prohibits standees) in both directions of the route, each bus covering the route twelve times (six round trips) during that period. During the remainder of the 16-hour day, 500 passengers would be carried and Thorne would operate only four buses on the route. Part-time drivers would be employed to drive the extra hours during the rush hours. A bus traveling the route all day would go 480 miles and one traveling only during rush hours would go 120 miles a day during the 260-day year.

Required:
1. Prepare a schedule showing the computation of estimated annual revenue of the new route for both alternatives.
2. Prepare a schedule showing the computation of estimated annual drivers' wages for both alternatives.
3. Prepare a schedule showing the computation of estimated annual cost of gasoline for both alternatives.
4. Which alternative appears most profitable?

(AICPA adapted)

5-16. The Rocky Gravel Company mines and processes rock and gravel. It started in business on January 1, 19x1, when it purchased the assets of another company. You have examined its financial statements at December 31, 19x1, and have been requested to assist in planning and projecting operations for 19x2. The company also wants to know the maximum amount by which notes payable to officers can be reduced at December 31, 19x2.

The adjusted trial balance follows:

THE ROCKY GRAVEL COMPANY
Adjusted Trial Balance
December 31, 19x1

Cash	$ 17,000	
Accounts receivable	24,000	
Mining properties	60,000	
Accumulated depletion		$ 3,000
Equipment	150,000	
Accumulated depreciation		10,000
Organization expense	5,000	
Accumulated amortization		1,000
Accounts payable		12,000
Federal income taxes payable		22,000
Notes payable to officers		40,000
Capital stock		100,000
Premium on capital stock		34,000
Sales		300,000
Production cost (including depreciation and depletion)	184,000	
Administrative expense (including amortization and interest)	60,000	
Provision for federal income taxes	22,000	
	$522,000	$522,000

You are able to develop the following information:

1. The total cubic yards of material sold is expected to increase 10 percent in 19x2, and the average sales price per cubic yard will be increased from $1.50 to $1.60.
2. The estimated recoverable reserves of rock and gravel were 4 million cubic yards when the properties were purchased.
3. Production costs include direct labor of $110,000, of which $10,000 were attributed to inefficiencies in the early stages of operation. The union contract calls for 5 percent increases in hourly rates effective

January 1, 19x2. Production costs, other than depreciation, depletion, and direct labor, will increase 4 percent in 19x2.

4. Administration expense, other than amortization and interest, will
   increase $8,000 in 19x2.

5. The company has contracted for additional movable equipment,
   costing $60,000, to be in production on July 1, 19x2. This equip-
   ment will result in a direct labor hour savings of 8 percent as compared with the last half of 19x1. The new equipment will have a
   life of twenty years. All depreciation is computed on the straight-
   line method. The old equipment will continue in use.

6. The new equipment will be financed by a 20 percent down payment
   and a 6 percent three-year chattel mortgage. Interest and principal
   payments are due semiannually on June 30 and December 31, beginning December 31, 19x2. The notes payable to officers are demand notes dated January 1, 19x1, on which 6 percent interest is
   provided for and was paid on December 31, 19x1.

7. Acccounts receivable will increase in proportion to sales. No bad
   debts are anticipated. Accounts payable will remain substantially
   the same.

8. Percentage depletion allowable on rock and gravel is to be computed at 5 percent of gross income and is limited to 50 percent of
   net income before depletion.

9. It is customary in the rock and gravel business not to place any
   value on stockpiles of processed material which are awaiting sale.

10. Assume an income tax rate of 50 percent.

11. The company has decided to maintain a minimum cash balance of
    $20,000.

12. The client understands that the ethical considerations involved in
    preparing the following statements will be taken care of by your
    letter accompanying the statements. (Do not prepare the letter.)

Required:

1. Prepare a statement showing the net income projection for 19x2.

2. Prepare a statement which will show cash-flow projection for 19x2
   and will indicate the amount that notes payable to officers can be
   reduced at December 31, 19x2.

NOTE: Round all amounts to the nearest $100. If the amount to be
rounded is exactly $50, round to the next highest $100.

(AICPA adapted)

5-17. Modern Products Corporation, a manufacturer of molded plastic con-
tainers, determined in October 1974 that it needed cash to continue operations. The corporation began negotiating for a one-month bank loan
of $100,000, which would be discounted at 6 percent per annum on No-
vember 1. In considering the loan, the bank requested a projected income
statement and a cash budget for the month of November.

The following information is available:

1. Sales were budgeted at 120,000 units per month in October 1974, December 1974, and January 1975, and at 90,000 units in November 1974.

   The selling price is $2 per unit. Sales are billed on the 15th and the last day of each month on terms of 2/10 net 30. Past experience indicates sales are even throughout the month and 50 percent of the customers pay the billed amount within the discount period. The remainder pay at the end of thirty days, except for bad debts, which average $\frac{1}{2}$ percent of gross sales. On its income statement, the corporation deducts from sales the estimated amounts for cash discounts on sales and losses on bad debts.

2. The inventory of finished goods on October 1 was 24,000 units. The finished goods inventory at the end of each month is to be maintained at 20 percent of sales anticipated for the following month. There is no work in process.

3. The inventory of raw materials on October 1 was 22,800 pounds. At the end of each month, the raw materials inventory is to be maintained at not less than 40 percent of production requirements for the following month. Materials are purchased as needed in minimum quantities of 25,000 pounds per shipment. Raw material purchases of each month are paid in the next succeeding month on terms of net 30 days.

4. All salaries and wages are paid on the 15th and the last day of each month for the period ending on the date of payment.

5. All manufacturing overhead and selling and administrative expenses are paid on the 10th of the month following the month in which incurred. Selling expenses are 10 percent of gross sales. Administrative expenses, which include depreciation of $500 per month on office furniture and fixtures, total $33,000 per month.

6. The average manufacturing cost of a molded plastic container, based on "normal" production of 100,000 units per month, is as follows:

Materials — $\frac{1}{2}$ pound	$0.50
Labor	0.40
Variable overhead	0.20
Fixed overhead	0.10
Total	$1.20

   Fixed overhead includes depreciation on factory equipment of $4,000 per month. Over- or underapplied overhead is included in cost of sales.

7. The cash balance on November 1 is expected to be $10,000.

Required:
Prepare the following for Modern Products Corporation, assuming the bank loan is granted. (Do not consider income taxes.)

1. Schedules computing inventory budgets by months for
    a. Finished goods production in units for October, November, and December
    b. Raw material purchases in pounds for October and November
2. A projected income statement for the month of November
3. A cash forecast for the month of November showing the opening balance, receipts (itemized by dates of collection), disbursements, and balance at end of month.   (AICPA adapted)

5-18.* Mr. George Wilton received his M.B.A. from California University in June 19x7. He was interested in staying in the vicinity of the university, so he had looked at various local job opportunities. In addition, he considered establishing his own business. An investigation of the market indicated that a duplicating service, primarily for students, should be a good business venture.

His analyses led to the following conclusions:

He determined that the business would have large fluctuations in activity. The university operated on a quarter system, with lower enrollments in the summer quarter. Peak periods would occur at the end of each quarter. A major difficulty with the proposed business would be that the number of copies for each customer would be small.

His analyses led to the following conclusions:

1. A suitable building space was available for $350 per month including all utilities. Rent was payable the first of each month.
2. He could hire a student at $200 per month to work half-time.
3. He estimated that $2,000 would be left in his savings account on September 1 and that he needed $400 per month for living expenses.
4. Rental of a machine for direct reproduction from typed, printed, or handwritten copy would cost $120 per month basic rental, with a charge of $0.04 per copy for the first 25,000 copies, $0.035 for the next 25,000 copies, $0.03 for the next 25,000 copies, $0.025 for the next 25,000 copies, and $0.0225 for all copies over 100,000, with a minimum monthly charge of $1,500 including the basic rental. Rental charges were to be paid the last day of each month.
5. Paper to be used in the machine could be obtained for $.0025 per sheet.
6. Competition in the area was charging $.05 per page, and Mr. Wilton believed that he should start with the same price. All sales would be for cash.
7. The first year he planned to do most of the work himself and maintain hours from 8:00 A.M. to 6:00 P.M. six days a week. He planned to hire a student to work from 11:30 A.M. to 1:30 P.M. on weekdays and all day Saturday.

8. His sales estimates for 19x7 and 19x8 were:

Month	Copies
September	30,000
October	70,000
November	84,000
December	122,000
January	76,000
February	88,000
March	106,000
April	80,000
May	112,000
June	124,000
July	42,000
August	34,000

Required:

1. On the basis of Mr. Wilton's estimates, would you advise him to establish the duplicating service?
2. What other factors would you suggest that he consider?
3. Prepare appropriate statements to show the projected results of the operation of the business.

CONTROL

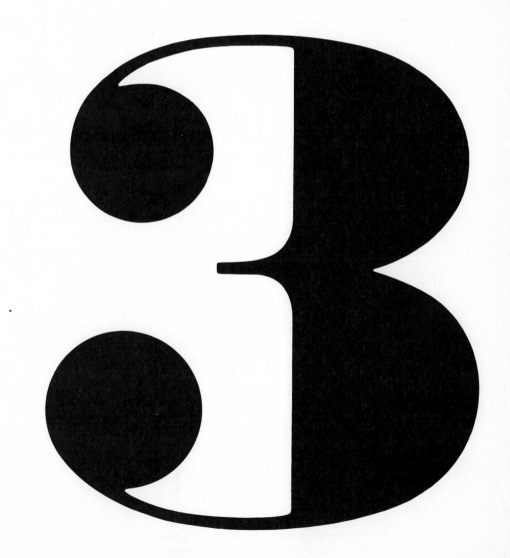

CHAPTER

STANDARD COSTS: MATERIAL AND LABOR

THE PLAN OF THIS CHAPTER
The control of costs (particularly prime cost
—direct material and direct labor) and the
role played by standard costs are particularly
important in management accounting. In this
chapter we shall take up the following topics:

The need for standards

The development of standards

Who sets standards?

The analysis of variances of actual from
standard costs

The accounting treatment of standard costs

Revising standards

NEED FOR STANDARDS

In Chapter 3 we examined methods for determining what it actually costs to produce a job or a unit of product or to operate a department. These actual costs become a factor in the determination of the net income for the period. Such actual cost information can also be useful in establishing a basis for product costing and pricing, insofar as it reflects a desirable level of performance. However, it possesses limited value for controlling costs. It cannot ordinarily answer the question: Did the product, job, or departmental operation cost *too much?* Clearly, management also wants to know how much it *should* cost.

Precise measurement requires standards. A standard is understood to be a rule of measurement established by authority. An inch, an ounce, a gallon, a mile, a dollar — each is an elementary example of a standard of measurement, established by duly constituted authority, undeviating, accepted by all to whom it applies.

Management, in assigning responsibility for the actual results of operations, wants to know that those results were measured accurately. But before there can be a fair judgment concerning good or poor performance, the measure of acceptable performance — a standard — must be applied to actual results. Since a meaningful standard must bear the stamp of duly constituted authority, the standards used to measure performance must have been promulgated by management and recognized and accepted by those whose performance is being evaluated. A *standard cost*, therefore, is *a measure of acceptable performance, established by management as a guide to certain economic decisions.* It is, in short, a reflection of what management thinks a cost *ought to be.*

Consider a simple example. Assume that the purchasing department of a manufacturing concern bought 1,000 units of a certain type of gear for $1.10 per unit along with its other purchases for the month. At the end of the month, management raised a question concerning what appeared to be excessive material costs on its income statement. In this case, let us suppose that the purchasing department, lacking the precise means of determining the causes of excessive costs (if indeed they were excessive), countered with indecisive answers. Typical evasions might be:

"Last year we paid $1.12 for these gears."

"Our assembly department ruined a lot of them."

"The costs of other materials were probably a little high."

"This was a busy month in the plant."

Under these conditions, it might be very difficult to determine why or, for that matter, even whether material costs were excessive.

As one alternative, management could instruct the accountant to look into the matter and report back. Upon investigation, the accountant might report the following:

The $1.12 price paid last year was for a special rush order for 25 units; the regular price on invoices for 1,000 units or more was $1.

The assembly department spoiled 3 percent of the gears this month, but the normal spoilage rate for gears in the department had been running 5 percent.

The costs of some other materials were a little high, but were approximately offset by others that were somewhat lower than expected.

The "busy month in the plant," while resulting in a *total* material cost that was a little higher than usual, actually caused the *unit* cost to be a bit lower than usual, because of more efficient use of materials.

Such an investigation as the one just described is time-consuming and therefore expensive. Furthermore, it might have to be undertaken again next month, and repeatedly in the future. If an information system could be established which would provide such information regularly, highlighting out-of-line conditions so that management could concentrate on correcting and preventing such conditions, cost control would be improved and would also prove less costly. For instance, if a *standard cost* of $1 per unit had been established for the gear in question, the management accountant, in the normal course of reporting, could inform all concerned that this month a purchase of gears resulted in an excess material cost of $100, the result of paying 10 cents each over standard cost for 1,000 units.

It is true that the actual price paid ($1.10 per unit) will be a factor in the determination of income for the period; but because it was excessive, it would be a poor criterion for judging the quality of performance of the purchasing department, for establishing the selling prices of the products using it, and for planning the costs of a future period. The conclusion is clear: *Actual costs* have limited value (the principal one being income determination); for the purpose of decision making in the realm of product costing, pricing, planning, and cost control, standard costs are definitely superior.

DEVELOPMENT OF STANDARDS

Developing standards can be a rather large and detailed task, depending on the size of the company or segment and the complexity and diversity of the product design and manufacturing operations. Before standards can be developed, a thorough understanding is needed of three things:

1. The fundamental *factors* of cost.

2. The design and material specifications of the product

3. The nature of productive labor operations and their departmental locations

Prime cost—direct material and direct labor—is determined by the multiplication of a physical factor by a monetary factor. In the example of the gears, the physical factor was the quantity purchased (1,000 units) and the monetary factor was the price paid ($1.10 per unit). The multiplication of the two produced an actual material cost of $1,100 for this item.

Because of the variety of component parts and productive operations in a unit of a given product, the cost factors must be examined in detail before a standard cost for a unit of product can be determined. In essence a standard cost for a unit of completed product is put together somewhat in the way the physical product is assembled, namely, in detail according to its constituent elements and in sequence according to the flow of operations. In other words, the specified quantity of each type of material for each component part is combined with appropriate prices to determine material cost; the operating time for each operation, from initial fabrication to final assembly, is combined with the appropriate labor rate to determine labor cost. Each "molecule" of material and labor cost in a unit of product is made up of "atoms" of quantity and rate (or price). We prefer to call quantity and rate the *factors* of cost, and it is for these factors that standards are set.

WHO SETS STANDARDS?

Earlier in the chapter, it was mentioned that a standard is to be set by duly constituted authority. In small and medium-sized companies, this authority would mean top management. In large companies, it is likely to be the general manager of a division or a branch plant. It is seldom possible for busy top executives such as these to participate directly in the establishment of standards, however. The actual detailed work is properly delegated to members of the organization in direct possession of the data needed. After tentative standards have been developed, top management will grant its final approval, either personally or through a standards committee, when satisfied that they are right.

This capsule description of the process of establishing a set of standards should make it clear that it is a task requiring the cooperation of many responsible people within the organization. It is the management accountant (and the accounting staff) who must collect and process the data and formulate the standard costs for top management approval, but most of the information on which standards are based will be found in sources outside the accounting department.

The standard quantities for materials will usually be provided by the design engineering department. After the design of the product has been finalized and blueprints have been approved for production, the engineers will compile a bill of materials or parts list, which will act as a guide to the purchasing department. Such a list specifies in complete detail the kinds and amounts of material and purchased parts necessary to manufacture the product. With due adjustments for manufacturing scrap, it provides the best source of information for the establishment of material quantity standards.

Standard prices for materials and purchased parts can usually be established from information available in the current records of the purchasing department. Taking into account the cost of freight, the standard ordering quantity, and whatever price differences may exist between alternative suppliers, the accountant sets standard prices which, in his or her opinion, will reflect realistic current conditions. On new materials for which invoice information is not yet available, firm price quotations from prospective suppliers may be used.

Labor quantity standards are expressed as standard time per operation. These standards, like material quantities and specifications, are most useful when they are the result of sound engineering studies. In modern factories, provision is made in the organizational structure for an industrial engineering function which studies the manufacturing operations; the equipment, tools, and methods used; the machine rates of production; and the pace of the productive worker. When a time study is made of an operation, the industrial engineer attempts to determine how much production can be achieved by the average operator, working under normal conditions at a moderate pace, taking into account such factors as the length of the production run, machine setup time, breakdowns, delays due to waiting for material, interruptions for personal needs, and fatigue. Such analysis requires considerable skill and judgment on the part of the engineer, and the results, by their nature, cannot be set down as precisely as can design engineering information. Nevertheless, operations analysis provides one of the best bases available for setting labor standards.

Labor wage rate standards, on the other hand, are more objectively established and quite readily available. If there is no union in the plant, management usually sets wage rates for the various operations and departments in accordance with prevailing rates in the local labor market and the industry. In a unionized plant, these rates will be established by bargaining between union and company representatives, based largely on the same factors. In either case, the prevailing wage rates are available to the management accountant in the payroll department, the personnel department, or the plant superintendent's office.

STANDARDS: TIGHT, REALISTIC, OR LOOSE?

Before standards are drafted for the approval of higher management, consultation is ordinarily undertaken with the operating personnel most directly affected by them. Departmental supervisors, factory superintendents, and purchasing agents are closest to the day-to-day facts of their own operations and can express an intelligent opinion as to the realism of the standards proposed.

Since such responsible people will be subject to praise or blame, depending on how well their performance stacks up against the standards, enlightened management believes it only fair that they have a voice in how these standards are established. It is generally conceded that standards are most effective as a cost control tool if they are attainable—not too easy to reach, but not impossible either. Such standards become motivating devices even before any formal analysis of performance is made. They provide employees with a rough guide to what is expected of them and should motivate them to perform in such a way as to meet or beat the standards. To be effective, standards must be accepted as reasonable by those being evaluated as well as by top management. Attainable standards stand a good chance of being accepted by all concerned because they should represent a challenge—but not an insurmountable one—to operating personnel.

USING STANDARD COSTS: VARIANCE ANALYSIS

The setting of standards and the establishment of a standard cost system allow managers to follow the *exception principle*,[1] which specifies that the manager will maximize his or her efficiency by concentrating on those operational factors which are deviations from the plan. Management by exception is especially effective in the area of cost control. As we shall see in the next chapter, realistic standard costs should be used in budgeting future costs. When they are so used, deviations from standard costs represent deviations from the plan; significant deviations should be investigated because they point out areas where the budget plan is not being followed.

The difference between standard cost and actual cost is called *variance*. The expression of this relationship is seen in the simple formula

Actual cost = standard cost + variance

We have already seen this concept embodied in the accounting for over- and underapplied overhead (Chapter 2). In that case the applied overhead is analogous to standard cost, the over- and underapplied overhead to variance, and overhead incurred to actual cost.

By rearranging the terms in the formula, we can determine the variance if we know standard and actual costs:

Variance = actual cost − standard cost

Variance can be either plus or minus, depending on whether actual cost is greater or less than standard cost. Since standard cost is a measurement of what a particular cost ought to be, any deviation from it can be interpreted as either good or bad—favorable or unfavorable to the attainment of the company's profit goals. In the example of the purchase of gears discussed early in this chapter, a variance of 10 cents per unit was realized, determined as follows:

Variance ($0.10) = actual cost ($1.10) − standard cost ($1.00)

This variance is to be regarded as *unfavorable* because the company paid 10 cents more per unit than it should have, and profits were lower as a result.

The importance of variances lies primarily in the use management can make of them in determining the causes of off-standard performance and in taking corrective action. Since variances can reflect performance which is either better or worse than standard, it is clear that they can be the basis for praise or criticism of the managers responsible for the control of the particular costs. Thus it is important that (1) standards be carefully set, realistic, and attainable; (2) variances reflect clearly and correctly the causes for deviations of actual from standard performance.

[1] Harold Koontz and Cyril O'Donnell, *Principles of Management*, 5th ed., New York: McGraw-Hill Book Company, 1972.

ILLUSTRATIVE EXAMPLE: MATERIAL VARIANCES

To illustrate variance analysis, let us consider a small factory that manufactures aluminum awnings. It has established standards for both the quantity and the price of the materials which go into the awnings. For the particular size and model of awnings produced during the month of April, the standards were:

Quantity—2 lb aluminum per awning

Price—$0.45/lb

Production information for the press department for April was as follows:

Awnings produced—500

Aluminum used in production—1,100 lb

Aluminum purchased—1,200 lb

Price paid—$0.50/lb

Variances from standard can be attributed essentially to two factors: price (rate) and quantity. For the awning plant in April, then, two questions ought to be answered:

1. How much direct material variance arose as a result of the deviation of price paid from standard price?

2. How much direct material variance arose as a result of the deviation of actual use of material from standard usage?

Two distinct activities must be analyzed here: (1) purchasing; (2) production.

Material Price Variance

Effectiveness of purchasing is measured by comparing the amount paid for a certain quantity of material against the total that would have been paid had standard price been charged for the quantity purchased. In the example cited:

Actual quantity purchased × actual purchase price:	
1,200 lb × $0.50 =	$600
Less: Actual quantity purchased × standard purchase price:	
1,200 lb × $0.45 =	540
Variance due to price (actual price greater than standard)	$ 60

Clearly, the quantity is the constant factor if we are to measure the cost difference due solely to price. The reason we use actual quantity is that we base our incurred cost on this amount. An alternative calculation, based on the recognition of actual quantity as the constant factor, is as follows:

Actual price paid per pound	$0.50
Less: Standard price per pound	0.45
Variance per pound (unfavorable)	$0.05
× Actual quantity purchased (constant)	1,200
Total price variance	$ 60

Material Usage Variance

The variance due to nonstandard usage is based on the deviation of the actual quantity consumed in production from the standard quantity in the production realized. The pricing factor is, of course, the standard price, since the price variance has previously been isolated and the material introduced into production is valued at the standard price. The standard price thus is the constant in the determination of the usage variance. The calculation of the usage variance is as follows:

Actual quantity used × standard price:	
1,100 × $0.45 =	$495
Less: Standard quantity in production realized	
(500 awnings × 2 lb = 1,000 lb) × standard price:	
1,000 × $0.45 =	450
Variance due to usage (actual usage in excess of standard)	$ 45

The alternative calculation here is as follows:

Actual quantity used in production	1,100
Less: Standard quantity in production realized	1,000
Variance in quantity used (unfavorable)	100
Standard price per pound (constant)	$0.45
Total usage variance	$ 45

It should be emphasized that the price and usage variances for direct material are almost invariably based on different quantities. This is quite understandable when the purchasing and production cycles are taken into consideration. Material must be ordered in contemplation of "lead time." For aluminum this may be from four to six weeks. Then the raw material will reside in inventory (stores) for another month or two. By the time the material is requisitioned for production, therefore, one, two, or more months may have elapsed since its purchase was recorded on the books. Furthermore, the quantities requisitioned are likely to be different from those on any particular purchase invoice. The distinction between quantities purchased and quantities requisitioned is emphasized at this point to avoid possible confusion with the direct labor variances, where no such distinction exists. It further emphasizes the fact that the responsibility for purchasing any quantity at standard price is quite distinct from the responsibility in the plant to use the standard quantity of material in relation to realized production, regardless of price paid.

Nevertheless, the two direct material variances may be combined schematically as follows:

Data:

Actual production realized in April — 500 awnings

Actual quantity purchased (AQP) — 1,200 lb

Actual quantity used (AQU) — 1,100 lb

Actual price (AP) — $0.50/lb

Standard price (SP) — $0.45/lb

Standard quantity per awning — 2 lb

Standard quantity used (SQU) based on April
   realized production — 1,000 lb

AQP $\times$ AP
1,200 $\times$ $0.50 = $600
AQP $\times$ SP $ 60 U *price variance*
1,200 $\times$ $0.45 = $540

AQU $\times$ SP
1,100 $\times$ $0.45 = $495
SQU $\times$ SP $ 45 U *usage variance*
1,000 $\times$ $0.45 = $450
Budget variance $105 U

(NOTE: "U" after the variance indicates unfavorable; favorable variances may be designated "F.")

CONTROL THROUGH VARIANCE ANALYSIS

The major purpose of variance analysis is to enable management to measure performance against predetermined norms, to seek out the causes for off-standard results, and to institute corrective action. In the case of the material cost variances just developed, it should be recognized that control over the price and quantity factors of material cost is usually delegated to different persons or departments in an organization.

In our illustration, the responsibility for the $60 unfavorable *price* variance would very likely be assigned to the purchasing department, while the supervisor of the press department would probably be answerable for the $45 unfavorable *usage* variance. In the case of the price variance, we recognize that the purchasing department probably did not determine the *amount* to be purchased; the purchase requisition probably came from the production control department or the plant superintendent. The responsibility of purchasing would be to purchase the quantity requested at *standard price* or better.

The standard in this case was 45 cents per pound; the invoice price turned out to be 50 cents. Management will want to know why. It could be that, because of poor planning or because of the small quantity involved, the purchasing department missed the opportunity to purchase directly from the aluminum mills and bought instead from an aluminum warehouse. On the other hand, it may be that the aluminum mills have raised their prices 5 cents per pound and the purchasing department can do nothing about it. Obviously, the corrective action will depend on the cause. If poor planning, inadequate quantities, or failure to investigate enough suppliers to find the most advantageous price is the reason for the unfavorable price variance, the purchasing department will be criticized, and appropriate corrective action will be urged. If a basic and permanent price increase is responsible, the standard itself is obsolete and should probably be changed. Here, as always, the question of ability to control the cost factor is crucial.

The causes for an unfavorable usage variance will be quite different. Although department supervisors usually have no control over the price paid for the material, they are generally responsible for using it efficiently in the operations in their departments. In the present example, the press department supervisor is charged with all quantities of aluminum at 45 cents per pound—the standard price. It is up to the supervisor to see that only 2 pounds of aluminum are used up for each awning he produces. The standard (2 pounds per unit) probably contains an allowance for normal scrap. If more than this allowance is used it shows up as an unfavorable usage variance, as it did in this case in the amount of $45. This could be due to sloppy work on the part of press operators, worn-out dies which will not produce pieces to specified dimensions, scrap generated by setup personnel when they change dies and test-run a few pieces ahead of production, or poor-quality material from the supplier.

Here again, the cause will determine the corrective action. Sloppy work calls for better supervision; worn dies must be detected by worker, inspector, or supervisor before much scrap is run; too many die changes may be due to poor scheduling, and the production control department may be at fault; poor-quality material is ordinarily the fault of the supplier, and the purchasing department may have to initiate action to correct the situation. Again, it may be that the standard itself is at fault either because of an engineering design change in the product or because the standard was poorly set in the first place. In this case, the standard may need revision.

It should be pointed out, however, that a favorable variance in one area can be related to an unfavorable one in another area. For example, the purchasing department may be able to acquire material at a substantial saving because it is of subnormal quality. Such an action will result in a favorable purchase price variance. When the material is used in production, however, the low quality may cause higher-than-normal spoilage rates. The loss would show up as an unfavorable material usage variance. Obviously, the company as a whole is concerned with the material budget variance. Only if the unfavorable usage variance is less than the favorable price variance will the purchasing department's actions turn out to be beneficial.

Whatever the cause, it is important that management assess the responsibility accurately, both in the interest of fairness to those held accountable for control of specific cost factors and to ensure that appropriate corrective action will be taken. If standards are realistic and attainable, variances can be favorable as well as unfavorable. When favorable variances occur, it is important that praise be accorded the right person. It may also be possible, by discovering the reasons for such variances, to institute effective means for cost savings in other areas.

ACCOUNTING TREATMENT: MATERIAL

Standard costs probably find their most useful application in the area of cost control, but they serve an important purpose in the areas of product costing, income determination, inventory valuation, and budgeting as well. Thus the most efficient way to adapt them to a variety of management purposes is to incorporate them into the books of account. This can be accomplished rather simply by implementing the fundamental equation:

Actual cost = standard cost + variance

by the addition of two material variance accounts, material price variance and material usage variance. The revised awning example would then be recorded as follows:

1. Stores $540
   Material price variance   60
          Accounts payable $600
   To record the purchase of 1,200 pounds of aluminum @ $0.50 per pound to stores at standard price (1,200 @ $0.45) and to debit material price variance for the excess over standard price (1,200 @ $0.05).

2. Work in process $450
   Material usage variance   45
          Stores $495
   To record the requisition of 1,100 pounds of aluminum from stores at standard price (1,100 @ $0.45), to debit work in process for the standard quantity required to produce 500 awnings (500 units @ 2 lb) at standard price (1,000 @ $0.45), and to debit material usage variance for the excess quantity used at standard price (100 @ $0.45).

The effect of these entries in T-accounts would be reflected thus:

Stores		Work in Process		Accounts Payable	
(AQP @ SP) 540	(AQU @ SP) 495	(SQ @ SP) 450			(AQP @ AP) 600

Material Price Variance		Material Usage Variance	
Excess (AP − SP) @ AQP 60		Excess (AQU − SQ) @ SP 45	

With this method, all entries in and out of stores will be actual quantities at standard price. All price variances are recorded to the material price variance account at the time the purchases themselves are recorded. All entries in and out of work in process are standard quantities at standard price. Ordinarily these entries, together with the material usage variances, will not be recorded until the end of the period (e.g., month), when production has been reported and the standard material quantities for realized production have been determined.

There are other methods, variations on the one shown, which are used by cost accountants in practice. Such alternative methods, while fit subject matter for a technical text in cost accounting, are beyond the scope of this book. The method shown is generally accepted, and sufficient to demonstrate the application of the concept.

ANALYZING THE LABOR COST VARIANCE

Continuing with the example of the awning factory, assume that the standard labor quantity factor in the press department has been set at two awnings per hour, or a standard time per unit of 0.5 hour. The standard hourly wage rate in the department is $4. For the month of April, production operations yielded 500 units of the awning referred to in the material cost example, requiring 260 hours of direct labor time at an average hourly wage rate of $4.05.

The variances for direct labor can be computed in the same manner as those for direct material. By applying the same schematic process to the labor data, the following variances are developed:

Data:

Actual production realized in April—500 awnings

Actual quantity (AQ)—260 labor hours

Actual rate (AR)—$4.05 average hourly wage rate

Standard rate (SR)—$4 per hour

Standard quantity per awning—0.5 hour standard time

Standard quantity (SQ) based on April realized production—250 hours

$$AQ \times AR$$
$$260 \times \$4.05 = \$1,053$$
$$\$13 \text{ U } rate \text{ } variance$$

$$AQ \times SR$$
$$260 \times \$4.00 = \$1,040$$

$$\$40 \text{ U } efficiency \text{ } variance$$

$$SQ \times SR$$
$$250 \times \$4.00 = \$1,000$$

Budget variance $53 U

By now the mechanics of the rate and efficiency (quantity) variances are familiar. Their significance from the standpoint of control of labor costs is somewhat different from that of material cost, however. First of all, the rates paid to the workers in a department are generally beyond the control of the supervisor. The basic rates are either those set forth in the union agreement or those established by higher management. Furthermore, periods of peak production sometimes require that workers be provided on a temporary basis from other parts of the plant. When such shifts are necessary, those assigned by the personnel department or the plant superintendent will bring their own rates with them from their home departments, sometimes higher and sometimes lower than those which prevail in the supervisor's own department. The labor rate variance, then, is likely to be of greater concern to the plant superintendent or the personnel department by way of appraising the effectiveness of their deployment of workers throughout the plant.

The labor efficiency variance, however, will generally be of direct concern to the supervisor. As a measurement of the deviation of actual from standard time in achieving the production of the period, this variance is a gauge of the productivity of labor in the department. That the department supervisor has a responsibility for the efficiency of the work force in producing their schedule is axiomatic.

ACCOUNTING TREATMENT: LABOR

The accounting entries for the labor costs under a standard cost system will be quite similar to those for material cost. Variance accounts will be provided for labor rate variance and labor efficiency variance. In the awning example, only one entry will be necessary, as follows:

Work in process	$1,000	
Labor rate variance	13	
Labor efficiency variance	40	
Accrued payroll		$1,053

To record direct labor at standard time and standard rate to work in process (250 hr @ $4), the labor rate variance for the excess of actual over standard rate for the actual time worked (260 hr @ $0.05), and the labor efficiency variance for the excess of actual over standard time at standard rate (10 hr @ $4).

The effect on T-accounts is reflected thus:

Work in Process		Accrued Payroll	
(SQ @ SR) 1,000			(AQ @ AR) 1,053

Labor Rate Variance		Labor Efficiency Variance	
Excess (AR − SR) @ AQ 13		Excess (AQ − SQ) @ SR 40	

As is the case with material cost, all entries in and out of work in process for direct labor cost are standard quantities (time) at standard rate. These entries, as well as the labor rate and labor efficiency variances, usually are not recorded until the end of the period (e.g., month), when production has been reported and the standard time for realized production has been determined.

TREATMENT ON INCOME STATEMENT

The main purpose of the awning example is to demonstrate variance analysis, so we have shown the accounting for production only as far as the work in process stage. However, the logical culmination of these productive operations will be the sale of the awnings. As production is completed in the plant, awnings are transferred from work in process to finished goods inventory at standard cost; when sold, they are transferred from finished goods to standard cost of goods sold at their standard cost. Thus, under the cost accounting method shown, inventories are valued at standard cost at all stages of the production cycle, and variances of actual from standard are recorded in the respective variance accounts according to the cause.

Assuming standards are realistic, most management accountants believe it is desirable to show variances as adjustments to cost of goods sold on the income statement of the period in which they are incurred, and to show as asset values the stores, work in process, and finished goods inventories at *standard cost*. In other words, all price variances related to purchases will be written off as expense in the period of purchase, even though some of the materials on which they were incurred remain in stores at the end of the year; also, in the case of the labor rate and efficiency variances, they will be considered an expense of the period even though some of the basic labor cost remains in the work in process and finished goods inventories at the end of the year.

Thus, a condensed income statement might appear as follows:

AB COMPANY
Income Statement
For the Year Ended December 31, 19x1

Net sales		$100,000
Standard cost of goods sold		60,000
Standard gross margin		$ 40,000
Less: Variances from standard:		
Material price variance	$545	
Material usage variance	(135)*	
Labor rate variance	(620)*	
Labor efficiency variance	510	
Net variance from standard		$ 300
Actual gross margin		$ 39,700

* Parentheses indicate favorable variances.

REVISING STANDARDS

One of the fundamental characteristics of standard costs is their stability. Regardless of inefficiencies, seasonal ups and downs, and unusual and nonrecurring events which affect actual costs, standard costs hold up a steady target for acceptable performance. Nevertheless, because they are used to evaluate good or poor performance, they must be fair. In order to continue to be useful, they must be adapted to changes in the conditions which they are supposed to reflect. Management and the management accountant must exercise skilled judgment in maintaining equilibrium between the need for stability and the need for change in standard costs.

It is frequently recommended that all standards be reviewed approximately once a year, in recognition of the constantly changing environment within which the firm operates. In addition, however, specific standards might be subject to change at any time under such circumstances as the following:

Suppliers of a basic raw material (e.g., steel, aluminum) announce a general price increase.

The design engineering department introduces basic changes in product design which substantially alter the material content of the product.

The company and the union reach an agreement which calls for an 8 percent increase in the basic wage rates for the coming year.

The factory introduces new equipment which substantially changes the method of certain productive operations, increasing output and reducing the number of productive workers needed.

Knowing when and under what conditions to change standards, then, is an art, but management will generally follow the two basic principles suggested by the foregoing:

1. Do not change too frequently, lest comparability of costs between periods be seriously weakened.

2. Change standards promptly when fundamental conditions of cost incurrence are permanently changed.

SUMMARY

Actual costs are essential factors in income determination, but leave much to be desired for other management purposes. Because they reflect the inefficiencies of the period's operations, are subject to seasonal fluctuations, and are influenced by any number of unusual and nonrecurring events, they are decidedly poor guides for planning, control of costs, product costing, and establishment of selling prices.

A standard cost tells what a job, unit of product, or departmental operation should cost. A standard is a rule of measurement established by authority. When management establishes standards, it is seeking a workable means by which to appraise the actual performance of those in the organization who have the responsibility for control of certain costs. While it would be possible for the management accountant to investigate all out-of-line conditions reflected in the accounting results of the period, it is far more efficient to incorporate standards into the accounting system and the regular reports to management.

Standards are developed in relation to the basic factors of cost. With prime costs there are two: quantity and rate. The best information for the establishment of standards typically is found outside the accounting department. The design engineering department can provide material quantity specifications by means of parts lists. The purchasing department should be able to supply current material price information. The industrial engineering department will generally supply information regarding the standard time for the productive operations from the results of its time studies and operations analyses. When the management accountant has assembled all the pertinent information, discussed it with the appropriate operating personnel, and formulated the tentative standard costs, they are submitted to higher management for approval.

The difference between standard cost and actual cost is *variance.* Variances are deemed favorable or unfavorable, depending on whether they reflect performance above or below standard. Variances are analyzed according to their cause and the person responsible. There are four prime cost variances:

Material price variance

Material usage variance

Labor rate variance

Labor efficiency variance

The material price variance is generally considered the responsibility of the purchasing department. The supervisors of the productive departments are usually accountable for their material usage and labor efficiency variances. Labor rate variances are generally beyond the scope of control of the departmental supervisor, but of considerable interest to the plant superintendent and personnel department.

From the accounting standpoint, variances are recorded in special variance accounts as soon as they become known. The variances are generally considered to be expenses of the period in which incurred, and are written off to cost of goods sold on the income statement. The raw materials, work in process, and finished goods inventories thus are carried at standard cost values at all times.

It is generally recommended that standards be revised when operating conditions are sufficiently altered to render the old ones inadequate. One of the advantages of standard costs is their stability, so changing them too frequently is undesirable. However, a general review about once a year, and specific revisions when substantial changes occur in material prices, product design, wage rates, or manufacturing methods may be necessary to keep them current and realistic.

KEY WORDS AND PHRASES

standard cost	attainable standards
actual cost	standard price or rate
factors of cost	standard quantity
exception principle	price or rate variance
variance	usage or efficiency variance
budget variance	

DISCUSSION QUESTIONS

1. "Aren't two sets of costs for the same thing apt to be confusing? You can keep your standard costs. Personally, I'll stick to the *true* [incurred] costs." Do you agree? Explain.
2. Define a standard.
3. Distinguish between the use of actual costs for income determination and their use for cost control.
4. Explain the interaction of quantity and rate in the determination of costs.
5. Who sets standards?
6. Explain the development of a standard cost for direct material.
7. Explain the development of a standard cost for direct labor.
8. Classify the following standards as tight, realistic, or loose, and defend your choice:
   a. The 4-minute mile in track
   b. A 60-mile-an-hour speed limit on an interstate toll road
   c. Five dollars for a sirloin steak dinner
   d. A family of four children
   e. A 50 percent completion percentage for a quarterback in professional football
   f. A 560-mile-an-hour cruising speed for commercial aircraft
   g. A .300 batting average in major league baseball
9. What is a variance?
10. What information does a set of variances convey to management?
11. For variances to be meaningful, what conditions must exist?
12. From the standpoint of management control, how useful is a total material variance?
13. Distinguish between a material price variance and a material usage variance.
14. The machining department shows an unfavorable material usage variance of $500 for the month of May. As plant superintendent, what would you do?
15. Explain how the recording of standard costs and variances for direct material in the books of account affects the reporting of:
   a. Raw materials inventory
   b. The material element in work in process and finished goods inventory
   c. Direct material in cost of goods sold
   d. Material price and material usage variances
16. Compare the variances for direct labor with those for direct material.
17. Who is likely to be responsible for the labor rate variance? The labor efficiency variance?
18. How often should standards be revised?
19. Under what conditions ought standards to be revised?
20. "It's not a question of *whether or not* to use standards; the only question is *how good* are the standards you use." Comment.

PROBLEMS

6-1. Standard costing procedures are widely used in manufacturing operations and recently have become common in many nonmanufacturing operations.

Required:
1. Define standard costs.
2. What are the advantages of a standard cost system? *let's goods advance price question*
3. Present arguments in support of each of the following three methods of treating standard cost variances for purposes of financial reporting:

Is not accurate a. They must be carried as deferred charges of credits on the balance sheet *is an asset, will be written off in several yrs.* *@ liability)*

Reference b. They may appear as charges or credits on the income statement.
   c. They may be allocated between inventories and cost of goods sold. *Is acceptable w/ accurate breakdown.*

(AICPA adapted)

6-2. The Irwin Company produces one product. The following material standards have been set for this product:

Quantity—3 pounds of raw material per unit
Price—$2.50 per pound

During the month of June, the company produced 2,000 units of finished product, using 6,050 pounds of raw material. The company purchased on account 7,000 pounds of raw material, for a total of $17,000.

Required:
Compute the following material variances:

a. Price
b. Usage
c. Budget

6-3. The labor standards for the Irwin Company's one product are as follows:

Quantity—45 minutes per unit
Rate—$6 per hour

During June the company produced 2,000 units of finished product, using 1,440 hours of direct labor, which cost a total of $8,940.

Required:
Compute the following labor variances:

a. Rate
b. Efficiency
c. Budget

6-4. Refer to problems 6-2 and 6-3. Make the required journal entries for the following items:

a. The purchase of raw materials on account
b. The accrued payroll
c. The withdrawal of raw material from stores and its use in production
d. The cash disbursements to pay for June's purchases and accrued payroll

6-5.† The Siegfried Company produces three basic products: Ein, Zwei, and Drei. The bill of materials is as follows:

Material	Ein	Zwei	Drei
A, kilograms	12	40	25
B, liters	4		8
C, meters		1	20
D, each	5	10	

Materials can be purchased as follows:

	Under 15,000	15,000 to 50,000	50,000 to 100,000
Quantities:			
A, per kilogram	$ 1.25	$1.05	$0.90
B, per liter	2.50	2.00	1.90
C, per meter	10.00	9.75	8.00
D, each	4.50	4.25	4.00

The forecast of sales in units is as follows:

Ein	20,000
Zwei	10,000
Drei	2,000

Required:
1. Set up material price standards.
2. Determine standard material cost per unit by products.

6-6. The Bradford Company produces three products in two departments. Industrial engineers time-studied the jobs, with the following results:

	Average Hourly Production	
Product	Fabricating Department	Assembly Department
1	80	20
2	50	110
3	60	150

Bradford operates on a piece-rate system. The results of the time studies are adjusted for the workers' personal needs, fatigue, etc., by a reduction factor of 20 percent of the timed rate. This adjusted rate, in turn, is reduced to 75 percent of itself to provide an incentive to the operator. The result is standard pieces per hour. Piece rates are based on average hourly wage rates as follows:

Fabricating	$3.00
Assembly	$4.62

Required:

1. Determine standard time per unit of product by department (i.e., decimal hour per unit — three decimal places).
2. Establish piece rates (round at three decimal places).
3. Determine standard labor cost per unit by product (round at three decimal places).

6-7. The Cedar Manufacturing Company makes three products: X, Y, and Z. The standard prime costs per unit, according to the cost cards, are these:

	X	Y	Z
Material	$11	$8	$2
Labor	2	1	5

There were no beginning or ending work in process inventories. Completed production for the month, in units, was:

X	3,000
Y	8,200
Z	5,600

Prime costs incurred for the month were:

Material	$115,000
Labor	41,000

Required:

1. Prepare journal entries to record the information given.
2. What additional information might management wish to have concerning prime costs for the month?

6-8. A processing department turns out one product. The prime cost standards have been established as follows:

	Per Completed Lot
Material (5 lb @ $4.20)	$21
Labor (3 hr @ $3.00)	9

The production schedule for the month had called for completion of 5,000 lots; 5,120 lots were actually completed.

Purchases for the month came to 30,000 pounds, in total invoice amount of $126,445.

Production records for the month revealed the following actual results:

Material requisitioned and used	25,672 lb
Direct labor (15,150 hr)	$46,210

Required:

1. Prepare journal entries to record the above information.
2. Supply supporting detail for calculation of variances for material and labor.
3. Interpret the variances.

6-9.† The records of the Osberger Corporation indicate the following for the month of October:

Standards	Factors	Unit Cost
Direct material	4 gal @ $1.20	$ 4.80
Direct labor	3 hr @ $1.80	5.40
Factory overhead	$0.60 per labor hour	1.80
Total manufacturing cost		$12.00

Month of October activity:	
Sales	6,000 units
Production	6,500 units, with no beginning or ending work in process inventories
Materials:	
Purchased	32,000 gal @ $1.18/gal
Used in production	25,600 gal
Labor:	
Hours worked	20,000
Average hourly wage rate	$1.75
Factory overhead:	
Total overhead cost incurred	$12,500

Selling price is set to allow a markup of 40 percent on selling price.

Required:

1. Analyze the variances, determining one total variance for factory overhead.
2. Prepare an income statement for October to the level of actual gross margin.

6-10. The Groomer Company manufactures two products, Florimene and Gly-oxide, used in the plastics industry. The company uses its standard cost system to develop variances. Selected data follow:

	Florimene	Glyoxide
Data on standard costs:		
Raw material per unit	3 lb @ $1 per lb	4 lb @ $1.10 per lb
Direct labor per unit	5 hr @ $2 per hr	6 hr @ $2.50 per hr
Units produced in September	1,000	1,200
Costs incurred for September:		
Raw material (purchased and used)	3,100 lb @ $.90 per lb	4,700 lb @ $1.15 per lb
Direct labor	4,900 hr @ $1.95 per hr	7,400 hr @ $2.55 per hr

Required:

1. Compute the total standard pounds allowed and the total standard hours allowed for September's actual production.
2. Compute the material and labor variances for September.

(AICPA adapted)

6-11. Tolbert Manufacturing Company uses a standard cost system in account-ing for the cost of production of its only product, product A. The stan-dards for the production of one unit of product A are as follows:

a. Direct materials: 10 feet of item 1 at $.75 per foot and 3 feet of item 2 at $1.00 per foot

b. Direct labor: 4 hours at $3.50 per hour
c. Manufacturing overhead: applied at 150 percent of standard direct labor costs

There was no inventory on hand at July 1, 1974. Following is a summary of costs and related data for the production of product A during the year ended June 30, 1975:

d. 100,000 feet of item 1 were purchased at $.78 per foot
e. 30,000 feet of item 2 were purchased at $.90 per foot
f. 8,000 units of product A were produced which required 78,000 feet of item 1, 26,000 feet of item 2, and 31,000 hours of direct labor at $3.60 per hour

Required:
1. Compute the total standard allowances for material and labor for the year's actual production.
2. Compute the material and labor variances for the year.
(AICPA adapted)

6-12. The following is a partial income statement for the Bergstrom Company for the month of March 19x1:

Sales (30,000 units @ $15)		$450,000
Standard cost of goods sold:		
Material	$120,000	
Labor	90,000	
Burden	90,000	300,000
Standard gross margin		$150,000
Variances from standard—over (under):		
Material price	($3,300)	
Material usage	12,000	
Labor rate	(4,800)	
Labor efficiency	6,000	
Burden	3,100	13,000
Actual gross margin		$137,000

Given:

Standard material, weight per unit of product	1 lb
Standard labor, time per unit of product	1.5 hr
Material purchased, March 19x1	33,000 lb
Material used, March 19x1	33,000 lb
Labor hours worked, March 19x1	48,000 hr

Required:
Determine:
1. Actual price paid per pound for material in March 19x1.
2. Actual material cost of goods sold in March 19x1.
3. Average actual hourly wage rate paid for labor in March 19x1.
4. Actual labor cost of goods sold in March 19x1.

6-13. The Delta Company, producer of a single product, made the following summary entries during October 1975:

Raw materials inventory	$50,000	
Material purchase price variance	250	
Accounts payable		$50,250
Work in process inventory	30,000	
Material efficiency variance		200
Raw materials inventory		29,800
Work in process inventory	12,000	
Direct labor efficiency variance	400	
Direct labor rate variance		62
Wages payable		12,338
Work in process inventory	6,000	
Overhead applied		6,000
Overhead control	6,100	
Accumulated depreciation		2,500
Accounts payable		2,000
Prepaid insurance		100
Wages payable		1,500
Finished goods inventory	48,000	
Work in process inventory		48,000

The standard cost card for the Delta Company's product is as follows:

Raw material (15 lb @ $2/lb)	$30.00
Direct labor (3 hr @ $4/hr)	12.00
Overhead (4 mh @ $1.50/mh)	6.00
Total standard cost per finished unit	$48.00

Required:
(Show all computations!)

1. How many units were produced?
2. How many pounds of direct material were purchased?
3. What was the average price per pound paid for the direct material purchased?
4. How many pounds of direct material were actually used?
5. How many direct labor hours were actually worked?
6. What was the average wage rate for the hours actually worked?
7. What was the total overhead over- or underapplied? Was it overapplied or underapplied?

6-14.† The Dearborn Company manufactures product X in standard batches of 100 units. A standard cost system is in use. The standard costs for a batch are as follows:

Raw materials	60 lb @ $0.45/lb	$ 27.00
Direct labor	36 hr @ $2.15/hr	77.40
Overhead	36 hr @ $2.75/hr	99.00
		$203.40

Production for April 19x0 amounted to 210 batches. The relevant statistics follow:

Standard output per month	24,000 units
Raw material used	13,000 lb
Cost of raw material used	$6,110.00
Direct labor cost	$16,790.40
Overhead cost	$20,592.00
Average overhead rate per hour	$2.60

The management has noted that actual costs per batch deviate some-what from standard costs per batch.

Required:
Prepare a statement which will contain a detailed explanation of the difference between actual costs and standard costs.
(AICPA adapted)

6-15. A new product of Elise Toiletries, Inc., is Lano-Lov Skin Lotion, to be sold in 4-ounce bottles at a suggested retail price of $1. Cost and production studies show the following costs:

Container

Item No.	Description	Cost	Comments
2147	4-oz bottle	$5.50/gross	Allow 2% for waste and breakage.
315	Label	$3.30/1,000	Allow 3% for waste and breakage.

(Product will be reshipped in bottle cases.)

Raw Materials

Item No.	Description	Cost	Quantity Used per 125-gal Batch, lb
4247	Compound 34A	$40/cwt	70.0
3126	Alcohol and glycerin	$40/cwt	76.0
4136B	Perfume oil*		3.5

* Perfume oil is mixed by the company according to its secret formula. Standard costs of a 90-pound batch are as follows:

Ingredients	$2,169.95
Direct labor (4.4 hr @ $2.28/hr)	$10.03

Manufacturing overhead $7.50 per batch plus $1.95 per standard labor hour.
(NOTE: A gallon contains 128 ounces.)

Allowance for Lost Material

Overfilling, waste, and breakage: Allow 4 percent of standard material cost.

Direct Labor per Gross

Compounding	0.12 hr @ $1.90
Filling and packing	1.00 hr @ $1.60

Manufacturing Overhead

Compounding	$3.00/standard labor hour
Filling and packing	$1.50/standard labor hour plus $0.90 per gross

Required:
1. Prepare a standard cost sheet for 1 gross bottles of this product, arranging the data under the five subheadings listed. Calculations should be made to the nearest cent per gross.
2. The company expected to produce 1,000 gross of Lano-Lov Lotion in its first week of production, but actually produced only 800 gross. Its direct labor cost of filling and packing was 780 hours, $1,263.60. Prepare an analysis of the labor cost variance from standard, showing the causes of the variance.
(AICPA adapted)

6-16. A company maintains a historical cost accounting system. It produces a single product. Below are data for two months of operation for which the unit costs are identical. There was no work in process inventory at either the beginning or the end of the month.

January 1975

Units produced	1,000
Raw material: X (1,000 lb @ $0.40/lb)	$ 400
Raw material: Y (2,000 lb @ $1/lb)	2,000
Direct labor (4,000 hr @ $2/hr)	8,000
Variable overhead	8,000
Fixed overhead	4,000
Cost per unit	$22.40

February 1975

Units produced	1,500
Raw material: X (1,450 lb @ $0.42/lb)	$ 609
Raw material: Y (3,100 lb @ $0.90/lb)	2,790
Direct labor (6,200 hr @ $1.90 per hr)	11,780
Variable overhead	14,421
Fixed overhead	4,000
Cost per unit	$22.40

Required:

Do the above data mean that the plant was equally efficient in both months? If not, why not?

6-17. The James Company showed the following quarterly production of its product for the year 1974.

Quarter	Units Produced	Materials Used (in Pounds)	Direct Labor Hours
1	900	3,595	890
2	750	3,003	760
3	750	2,990	745
4	600	2,405	605

Quarter	Material Purchased (in Pounds)	Cost of Material	Direct Labor Costs
1	4,000	$1,600	$1,600
2	3,300	1,485	1,370
3	3,100	1,457	1,340
4	2,300	1,196	1,090

Material prices have been climbing for several periods, but it now appears that they have stabilized. A systems engineer has made a study of the company's manufacturing process and concluded that usage could be cut by one-half. However, this would require a better grade of material, which would cost about 15 cents more per pound than the most recent price paid for material.

If the company uses the better grade of material, other changes in the production process would be necessary, and on the average, it would probably take one-third longer to produce the same amount of output.

Required:

1. Develop new standards for the James Company, assuming that there will be a 10 percent increase in hourly wages and that the company makes the changes suggested by the systems engineer.
2. Should the company make the suggested changes? Show supporting computations.

6-18. The Nelson Company has two products, Plain and Fancy. The unit material and labor standards for the two products are as follows:

Plain			Fancy		
Material:			Material:		
A	3 units @ $1	$3.00	Y	3 units @ $2	$6.00
B	2 units @ $1	2.00	Z	2 units @ $3	6.00
Labor:			Labor:		
Assemble	1 hour @ $2	$2.00	Paint	$\frac{1}{2}$ hour @ $2	$1.00
Pack	$\frac{1}{2}$ hour @ $1	0.50	Crate	1 hour @ $1	1.00

During the month of September, the company completed the following transactions:

Purchased materials as follows:
2,000 units of A for $2,070
1,000 units of B for 1,980
   700 units of Y for 1,450
   500 units of Z for 1,460

Consumed materials as follows:
2,550 units of A and 1,460 units of B, to complete 800 units of Plain
   310 units of Y and 190 units of Z, to complete 100 units of Fancy

Employees' time tickets showed the following labor costs:

Assembling   800 units of Plain— 790 hours @ $2.10/hour
Packing   800 units of Plain— 410 hours @ $1.10/hour
Painting   100 units of Fancy— 46 hours @ $1.90/hour
Crating   100 units of Fancy—105 hours @ $1.01/hour

Required:
Compute the materials price variance, materials efficiency variance, labor rate variance, and labor efficiency variances for September.

CHAPTER 7

FLEXIBLE BUDGETING AND OVERHEAD VARIANCE ANALYSIS

THE PLAN OF THIS CHAPTER
Earlier we explored the concept of budgeting and incorporating standard cost and cost-volume-profit concepts for the purpose of developing a better technique for cost control. Now we shall examine these concepts further, placing particular emphasis on the following factors:

Controlling costs as volume changes

Reporting performance against the flexible budget

The concept of capacity

The distinction between standard overhead rate and flexible budgeting.

The analysis of three overhead variances — spending, efficiency, and capacity — and the accounting treatment

PLANNING BUDGETS ARE FIXED

Cost control presupposes planning. Some idea of how much each of the functions in a period's operations ought to cost is applied to the forecast of the volume expected from the period's operations. The notion that actual performance should be compared with the predetermined costs in assessing responsibility for cost control is by now well established.

The *planning budget* may be used conveniently in its original form for cost control purposes if attained volume for the period coincides with forecast volume. This seldom happens, however. The result is that the budget remains fixed at the one volume for which it was planned, and no provision is made for the completely proper deviations of cost necessary to adapt to the attained volume of activity. Under these conditions, it is exceedingly difficult to separate cost variances caused by good or poor cost control from those caused by a deviation of attained volume from forecast volume. Some companies use the planning budget for evaluating actual performance in controlling costs, either because attained volume comes reasonably close to that which was forecast or because it is the least complicated approach to cost control.

If the latter is the reason, the company's management is using an approach which may prove in the long run to be very expensive indeed. That method of control which permits responsible managers to hide poor cost control behind fluctuations of attained and forecast volume of activity actually encourages laxity. What is suggested instead is a method of budgeting for cost control which permits *allowed* costs to be adjusted to the attained level of volume. Such a method is called *flexible budgeting,* in contrast to the practice of comparing incurred costs with the single *fixed budget* established primarily for planning purposes.

COST CONTROL AS VOLUME CHANGES

In Chapter 4, the concept of the behavior of cost in relation to volume was discussed at some length. A simple method whereby costs were classified as variable, fixed (or capacity), or mixed was described. The purpose in that chapter was to emphasize the usefulness of such analysis for profit planning and break-even determination. Now the same classification of costs provides a means of comparing realized cost performance with allowed costs at virtually any level of volume, not just the level forecast in the planning budget.

Prime Cost

Take, for example, the prime cost—direct material and direct labor—in the manufacture of an awning (see Chapter 6). If the standard cost per unit for all the material in a completed awning is $1 and that for labor is $2, and if the forecast volume for the month of January is 5,000 units, the prime cost for planning budget purposes would be:

Direct material (5,000 units × $1)	$ 5,000
Direct labor (5,000 units × $2)	10,000
Total prime cost	$15,000

Suppose, however, that attained volume came to 4,000 units and that material cost incurred amounted to $4,000, while labor cost incurred was $8,000. A performance report using the planning budget as a cost control budget would show:

	Incurred	Budget	Variance
Direct material	$ 4,000	$ 5,000	($1,000)
Direct labor	8,000	10,000	(2,000)
Total prime cost	$12,000	$15,000	($3,000)

NOTE: Parentheses indicate favorable variances.

Obviously, such a performance report is misleading. Incurred cost was lower than budget because *attained* volume fell 1,000 units short of *forecast* volume, not because of any spectacular control by the managers responsible for cost incurrence. The report should have read:

	Incurred	Budget	Variance
Direct material	$ 4,000	$ 4,000	$-0-
Direct labor	8,000	8,000	-0-
Total prime cost	$12,000	$12,000	$-0-

This report makes it clear that costs were controlled at the allowed amount for the volume level attained.

Observe that we are assuming a realistic set of material and labor standard unit costs as budget factors applied to attained volume. Where a standard cost system is in effect in a company, good standards provide the ideal unit prime cost factors for budgeting purposes. In this case, the same standard unit cost factors are used both for establishing the planning budget costs at 5,000 units of *forecast* volume and for constructing the cost control budget for performance reporting at the *attained* volume of 4,000 units.

Factory Overhead

From this example it is evident that the construction of a cost control budget for variable costs like direct material and direct labor is fairly simple. By their nature these costs tend to move up with volume because each additional unit requires the specified quantities of material and labor operations. These unit costs are incurred if a unit is produced and they are avoided if a unit is not produced.

Factory overhead, however, requires somewhat different treatment. Because of the varied character of the many expense items which comprise it, some variable, some fixed, some mixed, they need to be grouped according to their behavior in relationship to volume and listed in the amounts appropriate to the different levels of volume which might be expected. Thus the variable costs (including the variable portion of mixed costs) will be different for different levels of volume, while fixed costs (including the nonvariable base in mixed costs) will remain the same in total amount over a broad range of volume — the *relevant range* (see Exhibit 4-5).

Assume the following set of budgeted factory overhead costs for the awning manufacturer at a planned level of 5,000 units:

Indirect material	$ 8,000
Indirect labor	15,000
Inspection	8,000
Heat, light, power	2,000
Expendable tools	8,000
Supervision	5,000
Equipment depreciation	2,000
Factory rent	2,000
Total factory overhead	$50,000
Overhead per unit ($50,000/5,000)	$ 10

FLEXIBLE BUDGETING FORMULA

The budgeting of costs, from the standpoint of both planning and cost control, would be vastly simplified if all factory overhead costs were variable; and an average unit cost conveys the impression that overhead should be the same ($10, in the above example) at any level of volume. For instance, you would expect to incur $40,000 at 4,000 units and $60,000 at 6,000 units of volume.

Examining the individual overhead accounts, however, we observe certain costs which, by their nature, cannot be expected to vary in direct relation to volume. For instance, it is highly unlikely that plant superintendents will be paid by the unit; typically they are paid a monthly salary which is independent of the number of units produced in any month. Likewise, for factory rent to be variable, the lease would have to provide that it be determined each month on the basis of each month's production. This provision is rarely made, if ever; the lease will usually provide for equal payments each period, regardless of activity.

Suppose, instead, that a detailed analysis of the eight overhead accounts listed revealed that indirect material, indirect labor, inspection, and expendable tools were entirely variable. Further, suppose that supervision, equipment depreciation, and factory rent were strictly fixed costs. Finally, suppose that heat, light, power was a mixed account.

Fuel costs for heat and steam-generated power would always be incurred at some minimum level over a year's time, just by virtue of operating the boilers when the plant is open; power purchased from an electricity-producing public utility generally carries a minimum charge merely for having the service available to the customer; thus the heat, light, and power account will always carry a fixed cost base. Above the activity level necessary to absorb the minimum cost, the cost of steam and electricity will vary as activity varies — hence, in a range of activity near the normal volume, this cost has both fixed and variable factors.

Cost factors for flexible budgeting purposes, then, would be developed as follows:

	Variable Cost Rate, per Unit	Fixed Cost Amount, per Month
Indirect material	$1.60	
Indirect labor	3.00	
Inspection	1.60	
Heat, light, power	0.20	$ 1,000
Expendable tools	1.60	
Supervision		5,000
Equipment depreciation		2,000
Factory rent		2,000
Total factory overhead	$8.00	$10,000

When we reduce these relationships to a formula, we find the following:

Budget allowance = total fixed cost + (unit variable cost × units)

or

$$BA = FC + (UVC \times Q)$$

Although this is the formulation of the general concept of *flexible budgeting*, it applies equally well to the determination of allowed cost for:

A single *mixed cost* item (or account)

A single *department's* costs

The total *factory overhead cost* for a factory

The total *manufacturing cost* for a factory

The total of *all costs* for a firm

In other words, this formula is universal for any mixed cost structure containing fixed and variable portions.

In the case of a forecast volume of 5,000 units, the flexible budget allowance for total factory overhead indicated by the cited budget factors would be:

$$BA = \$10,000 + (\$8 \times 5,000) = \$10,000 + \$40,000 = \$50,000$$

Now a cost control budget for factory overhead at the *attained* level of 4,000 units would be constructed as follows:

	Total Variable Cost	Total Fixed Cost	Total Budget Allowance
Indirect material (4,000 × 1.60)	$ 6,400		$ 6,400
Indirect labor (4,000 × 3.00)	12,000		12,000
Inspection (4,000 × 1.60)	6,400		6,400
Heat, light, power (4,000 × 0.20)	800	$ 1,000	1,800
Expendable tools (4,000 × 1.60)	6,400		6,400
Supervision		5,000	5,000
Equipment depreciation		2,000	2,000
Factory rent		2,000	2,000
Total factory overhead	$32,000	$10,000	$42,000

This approach places the spotlight on the inadequacy for cost control purposes of a single overhead rate, such as $10 per unit, which treats all overhead costs as though they were variable. Application of the $10 rate at the level of 4,000 units would have provided a budget allowance of only $40,000. The flexible budget allowance shown here indicates that the more realistic expectation of overhead costs at 4,000 units is $42,000 (which averages $10.50 per unit).

The flexible budget gives recognition to the fact that over a given relevant range of activity, fixed costs tend to remain stable in total amount, *causing a rise in overhead cost per unit* at the *lower volume* levels and, conversely, *a decrease as volume rises*. This idea may be illustrated as follows:

Relevant Range of Activity—Units:	3,000	4,000	5,000	6,000	7,000
Flexible budget					
Total variable overhead ($8 per unit)	$24,000	$32,000	$40,000	$48,000	$56,000
Total fixed overhead (amount per month)	10,000	10,000	10,000	10,000	10,000
Total factory overhead	$34,000	$42,000	$50,000	$58,000	$66,000
Cost per unit					
Variable overhead	$ 8.00	$ 8.00	$ 8.00	$ 8.00	$ 8.00
Fixed overhead	3.333	2.500	2.000	1.667	1.428
Total factory overhead	$11.333	$10.500	$10.000	$ 9.667	$ 9.428

COST CONTROL THROUGH FLEXIBLE BUDGETING

The preceding example was set in the context of costs for an entire plant, and it served to emphasize the contrasting behavior of variable and fixed overhead costs over a given relevant range of activity. However, the implementation of flexible budgeting for cost control requires that costs be analyzed within the framework of organizational responsibility for such control over specific costs within individual cost centers. If the supervisor of a productive department is to make effective use of a budget for control purposes, it not only must be flexible (i.e., give effect to changes in the level of activity) but must give recognition to the extent to which *he* or *she is able to influence costs* identified with the department.

In Chapter 6, for example, it is indicated that the supervisor of a productive department might well be held responsible for the effective use of direct materials and the efficient performance of the productive workers, but that the supervisor is seldom able to influence either the price paid to suppliers for the materials used or the wage rate paid to the workers.

In the realm of factory overhead costs, the supervisor might be in a position to influence indirect material; indirect labor; inspection; heat, light, power (the variable portion); and the expendable tool costs. On the other hand, certain costs identified directly with the department might be quite beyond the supervisor's control, such as his or her own salary or the depreciation on equipment. Even more remote from supervisory influence are those indirect and service department costs allocated to the productive department by the accounting department.

Although the assignment of such noncontrollable costs to productive departments may serve a definite *product costing* purpose, they tend only to obscure the *cost control* picture unless a positive distinction is made between those for which the supervisors may properly be held responsible and those beyond their scope of control. Thus a performance report ought to present variances between incurred and budgeted costs only for those items which are controllable by the supervisors.

There may be considerable psychological benefit to be gained from reporting the noncontrollable costs assigned to the department by way of reminding supervisors of the magnitude of the cost of their *entire* operation, and just how dependent they are on the services of others in the organization. But these costs should be reported separately, not in comparison with any budget figures.

The costs imposed upon the supervisor from outside the department are not the only factors of operation beyond the control of the productive department chief. The level of his or her activity in any given period is largely determined by the production schedule, which in turn is dependent on the ability of the sales department to sell or the limits imposed by higher management on the buildup of inventory. This, of course, is another reason for judging the supervisor's performance in the light of the specific department's activity level attained in any given period.

EVALUATING PERFORMANCE

Suppose the awning company uses a flexible budgeting approach to the evaluation of its press department supervisor, utilizing the following performance report for the month of January:

	Incurred	Budget	Variance
Controllable Costs			
Indirect material	$ 975	$1,000	($ 25)
Indirect labor	1,750	1,700	50
Inspection	1,060	1,000	60
Heat, light, power	325	300	25
Expendable tools	990	1,000	(10)
Total controllable costs	$5,100	$5,000	$100

NOTE: Parentheses indicate favorable variances.

Noncontrollable costs	
Supervision	$ 400
Equipment depreciation	500
Share of service departments	2,100
Total noncontrollable costs	$3,000
Total costs assigned to department	$8,100

This report is quite informative as it stands, but the supervisor might have two questions about it:

1.   On what measure of volume is the budget allowance based?

2.   To what extent were the controllable cost variances the result of the relative efficiency of the department's operations (working more or fewer hours than we should have) or my own "spending" (carelessness in the use of indirect materials, excessive use of expendable tools, waste of light and power, etc.)?

VOLUME BASE

In general, there is considerable latitude in the choice of a base for the measurement of activity. Units of product manufactured, quantity of material used, direct labor hours worked, or machine hours spent may be appropriate in different situations. Earlier, the activity of the awning plant as a whole was measured in terms of the number of units produced in a given period. Considering the multiplicity and diversity of products and productive operations in modern industrial plants, however, such a measure will generally be found to be impractical.

On the other hand, regardless of design differences, virtually all products are processed through some sort of machinery, contain some sort of material, and require a certain amount of direct labor time. Thus machine hours, direct labor worker-hours, quantity of material, direct material cost, or direct labor cost might prove to be the common denominator in a given department or plant.

Suppose the awning company chose direct labor hours as an index of activity for its press department. Should they be standard hours in the production attained in the period, or the hours actually worked? It is likely that not all the hours worked in a month were equally productive. If the company operates a standard cost system, it probably keeps fairly accurate records on the production of all departments each month. Using these records, the cost accounting department can determine rather readily the standard hours contained in the production of any department for the period.

Upon being informed that, say, 50,000 of a certain size of top panel (among others during the month) were fabricated in January, and checking the standard cost card to find a time factor of 0.01 standard hour per panel, the cost accountant determines the standard time in these panels to be 500 standard hours. This is to say that the press department supervisor is allowed 500 standard hours for the production obtained. Whether more or less than 500 hours were required to get it will be a measure of the department head's productive efficiency. But the 500 *standard* hours will be the index of the supervisor's activity for those 50,000 panels.

ANALYSIS OF VARIANCES

To answer the supervisor's second question will require some sort of variance analysis akin to that for direct material and direct labor in Chapter 6. Essentially, the supervisor is asking, "How much of my variance is due to the *rate* factor (spending), and how much is attributable to the *quantity* factor (efficiency)?"

Whereas prime cost is generally a variable cost, factory overhead, taken as a whole, is a mixture of variable and fixed costs. Examination of the foregoing performance report for the press department reveals that the *controllable* departmental costs tend to be the *variable* costs, while the costs which are *noncontrollable* in the plant are fundamentally *fixed*.[1] This cost behavior is generally characteristic of productive departments in a manufacturing plant. If this be true, we should explore the possibility of using the same approach to overhead analysis that we used in connection with prime cost.

It has already been stated that the relatively simple base of direct labor hours will be used as the *quantity* factor in the press department. The *rate* factor, however, is a little more difficult. With material, it was merely a question of the price for a particular material; with labor, it was the wage rate for different labor classifications and operations; for variable overhead, some common denominator must likewise be found between the several types of cost represented by the list on the supervisor's performance report.

Since the quantity factor in this case is to be the direct labor hour, something similar to an hourly wage rate would seem logical. If, for example, it takes only one worker in the indirect labor category for each two productive workers in the department, and this worker is paid $3 per hour, then one hour of indirect labor at $3 is incurred for each two hours of direct labor, amounting to $1.50 per direct labor hour. For indirect material, a cost analysis may indicate that $500 is incurred every 1,000 direct labor hours. The rate for indirect material, then, would be 50 cents per direct labor hour. The same approach will yield similar rates for each of the variable costs. When added, they yield a single rate for the total of the variable overhead costs.

---

[1] This is not to say that fixed costs generally are noncontrollable. All costs are controllable at some level of the organization. Fixed costs are usually controlled at higher management levels. Management and supervisory salaries, for example, are usually established and approved above the plant level. Depreciation results from the original top management decision to invest in fixed assets, together with the determination of what method of depreciation to use.

For our awning press department example, let us assume that the standard rates for controllable overhead costs have been established as follows:

	Rate per Standard Hour
Indirect material	$0.50
Indirect labor	0.85
Inspection	0.50
Heat, light, power	0.15
Expendable tools	0.50
Total controllable overhead	$2.50

With this as a basis, a flexible budget of controllable costs for the press department can be constructed as follows:

Allowed standard direct labor hours:	Rate	1,000	1,500	2,000	2,500	3,000
Indirect material	$0.50	$ 500	$ 750	$1,000	$1,250	$1,500
Indirect labor	0.85	850	1,275	1,700	2,125	2,550
Inspection	0.50	500	750	1,000	1,250	1,500
Heat, light, power	0.15	150	225	300	375	450
Expendable tools	0.50	500	750	1,000	1,250	1,500
Total controllable costs	$2.50	$2,500	$3,750	$5,000	$6,250	$7,500

Reference to the performance report presented earlier in the chapter reveals that the budget was established at an activity level of 2,000 allowed standard hours. Assume now that 2,100 hours were *actually worked* in the month. Now let us analyze the variances, both in total and by individual account, in order to determine their causes. Beginning with the controllable (budget) variance, we find that we can break it down by identifying the cost factors as follows:

Data:

Actual quantity (AQ) × actual rate (AR) = $5,100 (incurred cost per performance report)

Standard quantity (SQ) – 2,000 allowed hours

Actual quantity – 2,100 actual hours

Standard rate (SR) – $2.50 per hour

AQ × AR
Incurred cost = $5,100
                  Spending (rate) variance
AQ × SR $150 F
2,100 × $2.50 = $5,250
                  Efficiency (quantity) variance
SQ × SR $250 U
2,000 × $2.50 = $5,000

Budget variance – controllable $100 U

NOTE: "F" designates favorable; "U" indicates unfavorable.

The analysis of these variances reveals some interesting facts about the supervisor of the press department and the January performance. While the performance report simply shows that the department exceeded its budget for the month's activity in total—$100—we now discover that the production realized actually cost $250 more than it should have, because of the inefficiency of labor in taking 100 hours more than standard (2,100 actual quantity—2,000 standard quantity) to finish it. On the other hand, the supervisor saved the company $150 by careful spending during the 2,100 worker-hours that the department actually worked during the month.

If we label the deviation due to rate a *spending variance* and that based on quantity an *efficiency variance*, we add a useful degree of refinement to the information provided to the supervisor and thus are able to answer the second question, concerning the causes of the variances. This analysis can also be applied to the individual accounts that make up controllable overhead costs if such an analysis is found to be desirable and useful. By performing the same calculations on each of the cost categories subject to the supervisor's control, the following performance report can be constructed:

Controllable costs	Incurred Costs	Budget at Standard Time Allowance	Budget Variance	Spending Variance	Efficiency Variance
Indirect material	$ 975	$1,000	$ 25 F	$ 75 F	$ 50 U
Indirect labor	1,750	1,700	50 U	35 F	85 U
Inspection	1,060	1,000	60 U	10 U	50 U
Heat, light, power	325	300	25 U	10 U	15 U
Expendable tools	990	1,000	10 F	60 F	50 U
Total controllable costs	$5,100	$5,000	$100 U	$150 F	$250 U

CAPACITY

In Chapter 2, we explored the development and use of factory overhead rates —plantwide and departmental—for product costing. Product costs are used by management for pricing, valuing finished goods inventories, and costing sales.

We have seen further that actual unit product costs are different at different levels of volume because fixed costs are spread more thinly to product units as volume increases. Therefore, if management is to have a product cost which is typical of its general expectations of business activity, the overhead rates must be set at one level of volume—the one which management regards as the *normal capacity* of the firm. This concept is extremely important, since normal capacity is the level at which management sets the prices which are expected to recover *all* costs and yield a reasonable profit.

We have become acquainted with the term "capacity" in earlier chapters. It is now time to examine the notion of capacity in greater detail in preparation for the work to follow. The capacity of a company to produce and sell goods is conditioned by the manner in which management combines the variety of scarce human and nonhuman resources which possess the capability to make and sell those goods and to maintain the firm as a going concern.

The human resources include all members within the organization, from top management through sales, engineering, production, personnel and accounting executives, and skilled technical specialists and factory workers possessing assorted productive skills, as well as many outside the organization, such as customers, suppliers, and lenders of capital. The nonhuman resources include the factory and office buildings; machinery and equipment; special tooling; inventories of productive materials; factory, engineering, and office supplies; and cash.

Among these resources available to the firm, the costs of those directly connected with the product which rise and fall over short periods of time along with the volume of activity (i.e., variable costs) are not regarded as costs of the firm's basic capacity. The cost of everything else is. While the firm's basic capacity remains stable, its cost tends to remain stable in total. When capacity is expanded or contracted in line with changes in the firm's longer-range objectives, the cost of that capacity increases or decreases accordingly.

But what is the concrete substance of this capacity we are talking about? Does it mean you can produce 50,000 units a year, 100,000, or 200,000? How is it measured?

Theoretical Capacity

Engineers can calculate space, time, machine capacities, tool and material speeds and feeds, operator work pace, etc., and add them up to a *theoretical capacity*. In effect, this is the maximum production of which the plant is capable, running full tilt, no interruptions. It goes without saying that this capacity is unattainable for all but the shortest periods of time. It does, however, serve as a measuring point from which to establish other capacity levels.

Practical Capacity

This notion of capacity simply applies the facts of factory life to the measure of theoretical capacity. *Practical capacity* is theoretical capacity less the ordinary and expected interruptions, delays, machine and tool breakdowns, variability in worker productivity, Sundays, holidays, vacations, inventory shutdowns, etc. The limits on practical capacity are determined by *internal constraints* within the factory itself.

Normal Capacity

Probably the most commonly used but elusive concept is that of *normal capacity*. This notion begins with practical capacity, which is based purely on *in-plant factors*, and adjusts for medium-range *market considerations*. When the plant was first established, it undoubtedly conformed to top management's idea of the long-run prospects of the business — say forty or fifty years — with all its uncertainties about growth, expansion, diversification of products, and the like. At any intermediate point in its history, however, the prospects over the duration of a business cycle — possibly three, four, or five years — are unlikely to coincide with such long-run capacity. Hence, normal capacity will generally be conceived in terms of the *market* prospects for the firm over a period of years sufficiently long to iron out the high and low years in a complete cycle, and short enough to be reasonably foreseeable. Thus it is that *external constraints* establish the limits of normal capacity.

Estimated Annual Volume

More useful than either theoretical or practical capacity, but less widely used than normal capacity, is the *estimated annual volume.* Its essential meaning is in the name—the capacity is determined *each year* in the light of forecast volume. Although it is useful for planning material purchases, workforce needs, and cash requirements, it usually provides a rather unstable base for product costing and pricing.

To establish standard overhead rates in this book, the concept of normal capacity will be used. As an index of activity, it is the target level toward which the department or plant is constantly striving. It should therefore be expressed in terms of the most appropriate units of activity: direct labor worker-hours, machine hours, direct labor cost dollars, etc.

DEVELOPMENT OF THE STANDARD OVERHEAD RATE

The standard overhead rate, then, is determined by dividing *total* overhead cost budgeted at normal capacity by the normal capacity. This standard *total* overhead rate provides for the inclusion of all departmental or plantwide overhead costs, variable and fixed alike, in a single factor for product costing purposes.

There is one important thing to note, however. Because fixed costs are incurred in approximately the same total amount over a given relevant range of activity above and below normal capacity, the standard overhead rate based on normal capacity is expected to recover the *exact* total overhead costs *only* at that level of activity.

Thus, if the attained level of volume in a given period falls below normal capacity, the total overhead applied to such subnormal volume will be less than the amount actually incurred, indicating a condition of idle capacity. On the other hand, if attained level exceeds normal capacity, the total applied overhead will be greater than that actually incurred, indicating greater-than-normal efficiency in the use of capacity.

An example of how this works in the case of a single department may be taken from the figures given earlier in the chapter for the press department of the awning manufacturer. On page 216, a flexible budget for the department lists the accounts which make up its variable costs and shows the budget factor for total variable costs to be $2.50 per standard direct labor hour. In a well-integrated standard cost and flexible budget system, the *budget* factor and the *unit standard cost* will be the same for *variable overhead* (as well as for material and labor, which are also variable costs). Hence we may assume a standard variable overhead cost of $2.50 per labor hour in the press department.

No budget for fixed costs is shown, however, nor is the normal capacity indicated. To complete our analysis of the standard overhead cost for this department, let us assume that normal capacity is 2,000 direct labor worker-hours per month and that the fixed overhead costs for a relevant range of volume 50 percent above and below normal consist of the following:

Supervision	$ 400
Equipment depreciation	500
Share of service departments	2,100
Total estimated fixed costs	$3,000

The standard overhead rate for the press department is computed thus:

	Total Cost at Normal 2,000 Hr	Standard Overhead Rate
Variable overhead	$5,000	$2.50
Fixed overhead	3,000	1.50
Total overhead	$8,000	$4.00

It will be realized that, for purposes of cost control budgeting, the cost *amounts* are listed by individual accounts according to expense categories by object. For product costing purposes, however, a detailed breakdown of the standard overhead *rate* by individual accounts is unnecessary. The total rate of $4 per hour is sufficient. To relate the figures in this example to the theory stated previously, we interpret 2,000 worker-hours of labor per month (the normal capacity) to be as accurate a forecast for the press department as can be justified by market analysis for a period of the next three to five years. An average total overhead cost of $8,000 per month will be necessary to sustain the normal level of activity at 2,000 worker-hours. Products costed at the resulting $4 per worker-hour rate, therefore, ought to come fairly close to recovering incurred overhead costs over such a period, and prices based on it should enable the firm to achieve its profit goals.

STANDARD OVERHEAD RATE VERSUS FLEXIBLE BUDGETING

We now return to the problem of reconciling the use of standard costs for product costing with their use for flexible budgeting. The problem is made simpler if we bear in mind one fundamental distinction between the two: *their differing treatment of fixed overhead.*

The standard overhead rate combines fixed and variable costs into a single rate based on some index of activity, with the result that it treats *all overhead as if it were variable.* Flexible budgeting, on the other hand, separates variable and fixed overhead factors, treating variable overhead as a *rate* and fixed overhead as an unchanging *total amount* over a broad range of volume.

In summary, then, a company which maintains a current, realistic set of standards will use its standard costs for both product costing and flexible budgeting for all variable elements of manufacturing cost (i.e., material, labor, variable overhead). However, it will combine a standard fixed overhead rate with its standard variable overhead rate to develop a *total* standard overhead rate for product costing, but for cost control it will budget fixed overhead at the stable total dollar amount expected to prevail over the relevant range of volume.

Earlier in the chapter, when variances in overhead were being analyzed, fixed costs were deliberately omitted, since the purpose was to pinpoint the areas of cost control for the departmental supervisor, and fixed costs were considered beyond the scope of control. Nevertheless, from the standpoint of the company as a whole, fixed costs are not to be ignored; and where standard cost accounting is employed, standard overhead, including fixed cost, is applied to the period's activity. If the attained level of activity is anything other than normal (and it invariably is), another variance arises — a *capacity variance*.

ANALYSIS OF THREE OVERHEAD VARIANCES

The addition of this third overhead variance and its method of calculation probably will best be understood by illustration. Turning once again to the awning company's press department, let us reconstruct the activity for the month of *February*. The following data are given.

```
Normal capacity — 2,000 direct labor worker-hours
Standard overhead rate (per worker-hour of direct labor)
    Variable      $2.50 (used also as variable budget allowance per hour)
    Fixed          1.50
      Total       $4.00
```

Budget allowance for fixed cost	$3,000
Standard direct labor worker-hours allowed in production realized	1,700
Actual worker-hours worked	1,800

```
Factory overhead incurred:
    Variable    $4,400
    Fixed        3,000
      Total     $7,400
```

The formulas for the three overhead variances are:

1. Incurred overhead − [(actual quantity × budget allowance for variable cost) + budget allowance for fixed cost] = *spending variance*.

2. [(Actual quantity × budget allowance for variable cost) + budget allowance for fixed cost] − [(standard quantity × budget allowance for variable cost) + budget allowance for fixed cost] = *efficiency variance*.

3. [(Standard quantity × budget allowance for variable cost) + budget allowance for fixed cost] − [(standard quantity × standard variable cost rate) + (standard quantity × standard fixed cost rate)] = *capacity variance*.

Spelled out thus, the process appears to be very complicated. Analyzed by means of the now-familiar variance analysis diagram, however, it is much simpler. Observe how the separation of fixed (F) and variable (V) portions of the overhead cost is emphasized:

	Variable	Fixed	Total	
Incurred	$4,400	$3,000	$7,400	
				Spending variance $100 F
AQ × BA				
V (1,800 × $2.50)	4,500			
F ($3,000)		3,000	7,500	Budget variance $150 U
				Efficiency variance $250 U
SQ × BA				
V (1,700 × $2.50)	4,250			
F ($3,000)		3,000	7,250	
				Capacity variance $450 U
SQ × SR				
V (1,700 × $2.50)	4,250			
F (1,700 × $1.50)		2,550	6,800	
Total overhead variance			$600 U	

This three-step analysis is more complex than the two-way analysis of the supervisor's controllable variances, not only because of the new variance which is added but because it is necessary to divide total overhead into variable and fixed factors. This procedure is necessary, however, to complete the picture of standard costing and flexible budgeting.

Let us look at the meaning of, and causes behind, these overhead variances in the press department. By way of review, we note that the supervisor has achieved in February another favorable *spending* variance, this time of $100. This is due to sparing use of certain of the variable items of overhead cost which a budget for his actual 1,800 worker-hours would have allowed (spent, $4,400; allowed for 1,800 hours, $4,500). On the other hand, production was inefficient, because it took 100 hours longer to achieve than it should have (1,800 actual against 1,700 allowed); the result was an unfavorable efficiency variance of $250 (100 excess hours at $2.50).

CAPACITY VARIANCE

We have already said that the supervisor's activity level is set by those who prepare the production schedule, and this in turn is determined by how much of the product the sales department has sold. Hence, the failure of the February activity (1,700 allowed hours in the production realized) to reach the normal level of 2,000 worker-hours is beyond the supervisor's control. Yet this fact is highly significant to top management. Idle capacity costs money, for which no revenue is produced. Such a cost is especially disturbing, and management wants to know its amount.

The amount of idle capacity cost in the press department is relatively simple to determine with the information provided by a good standard cost system. First of all, the standard overhead rate was set at a normal activity level of 2,000 standard worker-hours. The level of production actually reached required 1,700 allowed standard hours of capacity. Thus the idle capacity for February was 300 standard worker-hours. In terms of the prevailing standard fixed overhead rate for the press department, the cost of such idle capacity is $450 (300 hours at $1.50).

The converse of this condition will occur when the level of activity exceeds 2,000 standard hours of allowed activity. In such an event, the stable amount of fixed cost will be spread over more than the hours of normal productive capacity, resulting in a favorable capacity variance. Fluctuations between favorable and unfavorable capacity variances are common in seasonal businesses like awning manufacture, and if the normal capacity level has been set accurately, these variances will tend to offset over the period of a year, as well as over the term of the business cycle.

INVESTIGATION OF VARIANCES

This chapter and the previous one have discussed the calculation of standard cost variances and the fact that they may indicate to management that operations are deviating from the plan or budget. The initial step management should take in response to a given variance, however, depends largely on management's assessment of the *significance* of the variance. An insignificant variance should be ignored, whereas a significant one should be investigated to determine its cause and to determine if any additional managerial action should be taken.

The whole idea of the significance of a variance rests on the fact that standard costs are management's estimates of what costs should be under normal operating conditions. Thus, the standard cost for variable overhead in the awning company's press department is estimated to be $2.50 per worker-hour of direct labor, but management probably would not be overly surprised to see an actual rate of $2.52 or $2.49 or some other rate fairly close to the estimate. As with any deviation from an estimate, a standard cost variance can be viewed as one of two possibilities:

1. The variance is a random event within expected limits.

2. The variance indicates that operations did not fall within expected limits.

There are several techniques that management can use to assess the significance of variances. An informal and simple procedure, and one used widely in practice, is to consider only the absolute size of the variance and investigate only those variances greater than some arbitrarily chosen amount. For example, the awning company's management may decide to investigate all variances greater than $200. In that case, the press department's efficiency variance ($250 U) and capacity variance ($450 U) would be investigated, while its spending variance ($100 F) would not be investigated.

This method recognizes that small variances are bound to occur and that the cost of investigating small variances, even if they are not random events, is likely to outweigh any possible benefits. The disadvantage of this method, however, is that it ignores the fact that a given dollar variance may be significant for one type of cost but not for another—a $100 variance for heat, light, and power may be quite significant, but the same variance for indirect labor may be considered within normal limits. Recognizing this variation, some companies will look at the relative size of the variance in addition to (or instead of) its absolute size. For example, the awning company may decide to investigate only those variances which are greater than 10 percent of standard costs. Then the press department's capacity variance ($450/$3,000 = 15 percent) would be investigated, but the spending variance ($100/$4,500 = 2 percent) and the efficiency variance ($250/$4,250 = 6 percent) would not be. The difficulty with looking at relative size alone, of course, is that it may cause management to investigate small (in absolute terms) variances, and the costs of so doing may be considerably greater than any possible benefits. Thus, a combination of the two approaches—absolute size and relative size—is probably better than either one alone.

The major drawback of the informal methods just described is that generally management picks the cutoff points arbitrarily, using intuition, hunches, and guesses. More formal procedures have been developed using statistical techniques.[2] For the purposes of this book, however, it is sufficient to point out that management must set up some methodology for deciding when variances should be investigated. Ignoring the fact that standard costs are only estimates will lead to large demands on management's time. The end result will be hit-or-miss approaches which may vary from month to month and from manager to manager. A much better approach is to evaluate the company's operations and standard cost system and to set down specific rules and guidelines to be followed in the investigation of variances.

ACCOUNTING TREATMENT

The accounting procedure for recording standard overhead costs is virtually the same as that for material and labor (see Chapter 6). The first step is the determination of the variances for the period. Next, the overhead is applied to work in process at standard rate for standard allowed hours in production. Finally, variances are recorded in their respective accounts as factory overhead applied is closed to factory overhead control.

For the press department in February, the entries are as follows:

[2] N. Dopuch, J. G. Birnberg, and J. Demski, "An Extension of Standard Cost Variance Analysis," *Accounting Review*, July 1967, pp. 526–536.

1. Factory overhead control $7,400
     Stores control   ⎫
     Accrued payroll   ⎪
     Accounts payable   ⎬ $7,400
     Other accounts   ⎭
   To record the incurrence of the various factory overhead
   costs of the period (summary entry).

2. Work in process $6,800
     Factory overhead applied $6,800
   To record application of overhead to work in process based
   on 1,700 standard allowed hours at standard rate of $4 per
   hour.

3. Factory overhead applied $6,800
   Overhead efficiency variance   250
   Overhead capacity variance   450
     Factory overhead control $7,400
     Overhead spending variance   100
   To close factory overhead control and factory overhead ap-
   plied, and to record variances as follows:

Efficiency: 1,800 actual − 1,700 standard hours = 100 × standard variable rate
   $2.50 = $250 unfavorable
Capacity: 2,000 normal − 1,700 allowed hours = 300 × standard fixed rate $1.50 =
   $450 unfavorable
Spending: $7,400 incurred − $7,500 (1,800 actual hours × $2.50 standard variable
   + $3,000 budget fixed cost) = $100 favorable

   Many companies do not choose to close the factory overhead applied and
factory overhead control accounts monthly. In that case, since the natural procedure would be to record variances at the time of closing these accounts, the
variance analysis will be developed monthly in memorandum form and reported
to the proper parties, and the general journal entries will be deferred until the
year-end closing. Since the variance analyses demonstrated in Chapter 6 and in
this chapter constitute a form of worksheet, it is not necessary to have a formal
closing of the books in order to develop the information for reporting purposes.

   The handling of the overhead variances for financial statement reporting
will be the same as for material and labor variances. That is, they will be treated
as adjustments to the standard cost of goods sold on the income statement for
the year. They may also be written off on interim monthly income statements,
but some accountants prefer to take only the standard overhead applied into
monthly cost of goods sold, with the result that the favorable or unfavorable
variances remain as additions to or reductions from the month-end inventories.

SUMMARY

Standard costs are versatile tools for management purposes. They are used for
planning, cost control, and product costing. The different purposes require
different adaptations, however.

For planning purposes, a sales forecast will establish the expected activity level, and all costs will be projected in terms of that single level. For all the variable cost elements, standard cost will serve to adapt the totals to the forecast level of volume. A separate estimate is made of the total fixed costs, which can be expected to remain stable over a broad, relevant range of volume.

Since the attained level of operations in a period is nearly always above or below the forecast level of volume, budgets for cost control purposes usually need to be revised in line with the deviation of the attained from planned level of volume. This means that the total variable costs will be adjusted upward or downward in accordance with the rise or fall of attained volume, while fixed costs will stay about the same, within a given range of activity.

Again, standard costs applied to the attained level of volume for the variable cost elements will accomplish this adjustment, while the total dollar amount for fixed overhead within the relevant range will remain at the same level as it was for planning purposes. This characteristic of adapting a budget for cost control purposes to the attained level of volume is known as flexible budgeting. The flexible budget, in turn, provides the basis for preparing performance reports for persons responsible for cost control. In these reports, incurred costs are compared with budgeted costs, and the variances noted.

A single standard overhead rate, which combines both a variable and a fixed rate of overhead at a predetermined normal capacity level of activity, is used for product costing purposes. Among the various notions of capacity which can be used for this purpose, the one which matches the productive capabilities of the plant with the reasonable volume prospects in the market over the approximate period of a business cycle seems the most logical, and is in general use. The use of a standard total overhead rate for product costing results in a capacity variance whenever attained volume goes over or under the normal capacity level at which it was set. Analysis is required to segregate its effects from those arising from other causes.

Where a standard cost system provides for both the recording of costs at standard on the books for product costing purposes and the use of flexible budgeting for performance reporting, a method of analyzing variances may be used which pinpoints the causes for off-standard performance as follows:

A spending variance. This variance represents the difference between the controllable (principally variable) costs actually *incurred* and the budget *allowance* for these costs in terms of the time the department actually worked. The supervisor of the department is generally held responsible for this variance.

An efficiency variance. This variance places a cost (at the standard *variable* rate) on the difference between *actual* hours worked and the allowed standard hour content of the production realized. The supervisor of the department is generally held responsible for the efficiency of the department's operations, measured by the time taken versus what should have been taken to achieve the expected production for the period.

A capacity variance. This variance applies the standard *fixed* cost rate to the difference between the standard hours in realized production and the hours at normal capacity. If standard hours in realized production were below normal, the resulting variance represents the cost of idle capacity. If standard hours were greater than normal, this variance represents additional profits resulting from better-than-normal use of the plant's capacity. Credit or blame for these conditions rests not with the supervisor, who has no control over the level of activity, but with the sales department for fruitful or unproductive selling effort, as the case may be; with the production control department for skilled or inept scheduling; with top management for effective or deficient planning; or perhaps with a combination of these and external factors, such as market shifts or economic recession.

Thus, for purposes of cost control in the area of factory overhead costs, the combination of flexible budgeting and variance analysis based on a sound standard cost system provides one of the most incisive and useful tools which accounting can offer as a service to management.

KEY WORDS AND PHRASES

planning budget	total overhead variance
forecast volume	significance of a variance
attained volume	overhead budget variance
flexible budget	theoretical capacity
controllable cost	practical capacity
standard hours allowed	normal capacity
overhead spending variance	estimated annual volume
overhead efficiency variance	capacity variance

DISCUSSION QUESTIONS

1. Distinguish the fixed and flexible budgets vis-à-vis management planning and control.
2. What types of allowed costs ought to be adjusted to attained levels of volume? Why?
3. Why are standard costs considered good budget factors for material and labor?
4. Why is budgeting for factory overhead different from that for prime cost?
5. Explain the flexible budget formula.
6. What has the concept of relevant range of activity to do with flexible budgeting?
7. What are the criteria of a meaningful cost control performance report?
8. Are *variable* costs and *controllable* costs synonymous?
9. Compare spending and efficiency variances for overhead with material and labor variances.
10. Explain the concept of capacity and the characteristics of its related costs.
11. Explain the concept of *theoretical* capacity. How might it be useful in management accounting?
12. Explain the concept of *practical* capacity and its usefulness in management accounting.

13. Explain the concept of *normal* capacity and its usefulness in management accounting.
14. How does *estimated* annual volume fit into the capacity concept?
15. Explain the establishment of a standard overhead rate.
16. "The *standard* unit overhead cost and the *actual* unit overhead cost can be the same only if *attained* volume equals *normal capacity*." Explain.
17. Since the standard cost is used as the flexible budget factor for material and labor, why can it not be used likewise for overhead?
18. Explain the form, function, and meaning of the *capacity* variance for overhead.
19. Is there any essential difference between the overhead capacity variance under a standard cost system and the over- and underapplied overhead discussed in earlier chapters? Explain.
20. Explain the meaning of the cost of idle capacity.
21. The plant superintendent complains to the plant controller: "Why is it in this plant that we dole out prime cost with an eyedropper and then spread burden with a shovel?" As controller, give an explanation.
22. Comment on the use of standard costs for each of the following: (a) product pricing; (b) inventory valuation; (c) costing sales; (d) evaluating cost control performance; (e) profit planning.

PROBLEMS

7-1.† Refer to problem 6-9. Assume that Osberger's factory overhead rate of 60 cents per labor hour is based on a normal capacity of 7,000 units per month and that fixed overhead represents $33\frac{1}{3}$ percent of total overhead at that level of activity.

Required:
1. Prepare the flexible budget formula for factory overhead.
2. Determine the overhead spending, efficiency, and capacity variances.

7-2. Excel Company operates under a standard cost system. Factory burden is applied to products on a direct labor hour basis. At normal operating level, the company ought to utilize 360,000 direct labor hours in a year, and it budgets overhead cost at that level as follows:

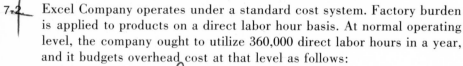

| Variable burden | $720,000 |
| Fixed burden | 180,000 |

During the year 19x1, it took 370,000 direct labor hours to get production that should have required only 350,000 hours.

Required:
Calculate and explain (1) burden variance for efficiency; (2) cost of idle capacity.

7-3. Work out the indicated manufacturing cost variances under the following sets of conditions:

Standards	A	B
Material, per unit	5 lb @ $0.50 = $2.50	4 lb @ $0.50 = $2.00
Labor, per unit	2 hr @ $2.20 = $4.40	3 hr @ $2.20 = $6.60
Burden, per labor hour	$3.00	$2.40
Flexible budget formula for burden	$75,000 + $1.50/ labor hour	$138,000 + $1.25/ labor hour
Normal capacity	25,000 units	40,000 units
Actual results for June		
Attained volume, units	24,000	42,000
Purchases	(140,000 lb) $67,200	(150,000 lb) $78,000
Material used, lb	122,000	170,000
Labor hours	46,000	125,000
Average hourly wage rate	$2.25	$2.10
Burden incurred	$145,000	$293,600

Variances
Material:
  Price
  Usage
Labor:
  Rate
  Efficiency
Burden:
  Spending
  Efficiency
  Capacity
Net manufacturing variance

7-4. The budget manager for the Johnsco Manufacturing Company is preparing a flexible budget for the year 19x3. The company produces one product: DETX-2. She uses the following estimated data: Material costs $7 per unit. Direct labor averages $2.50 per hour and requires 1.6 hours to produce one unit of DETX-2. Sales representatives are paid a commission of $1 per unit sold. Fixed selling and administrative expenses amount to $85,000 per year. Manufacturing overhead is estimated in the following amounts under specified conditions of volume:

Volume of Production, Units:	120,000	150,000
Expenses		
Indirect material	$264,000	$ 330,000
Indirect labor	150,000	187,500
Inspection	90,000	112,500
Utilities	84,000	102,000
Supervision	198,000	234,000
Depreciation—plant and equipment	90,000	90,000
Engineering	94,000	94,000
Total manufacturing overhead	$970,000	$1,150,000

Normal capacity is designated as 125,000 units.

Required:
1. Prepare a budget of total cost at 140,000 units of production.
2. Determine the standard unit cost of DETX-2.

7-5. The Vatter Office Equipment Company has established standard costs for the filing cabinet department, in which one size of a single four-drawer style of cabinet is produced. The standard cost of producing one of these cabinets is shown below:

Standard Cost Card

Materials:
6 sheets 18-gauge steel @ $0.35 each	$2.10	
2 sheets 14-gauge steel @ $0.30 each	.60	$2.70

Direct labor:
3 hours @ $0.60 per hour		1.80

Indirect costs:
Variable charges, 3 hours @ $0.50	$1.50	
Fixed charges, 3 hours @ $0.70	2.10	3.60
Total		$8.10

The costs of operating the department which produced 600 of these cabinets during January are stated below (there were no initial inventories):

Materials purchased:
4,000 sheets 18-gauge steel, $1,360
1,500 sheets 14-gauge steel, $480
Materials appropriated:
3,614 sheets 18-gauge steel
1,182 sheets 14-gauge steel
Direct labor:
1,900 hours @ $0.58, $1,102
Indirect costs:
Variable charges, $935
Fixed charges, $1,490

The budget for January had called for 1,950 direct labor hours, $975 of variable overhead, and $1,500 of fixed overhead.

Required:
Compute the following variances from standard cost:

Materials: price, usage
Direct labor: rate; efficiency
Variable overhead: spending; efficiency
Fixed overhead: spending; efficiency; capacity

7-6. The Traviata Company produces one product—spaghetti. The product unit is 100 pounds (cwt) of spaghetti.

Volume in Units of Product	15,000	25,000
Flexible budget data		
Material	$ 30,000	$ 50,000
Labor	45,000	75,000
Factory burden:		
Indirect material	$ 15,000	$ 25,000
Indirect labor	30,000	50,000
Supervision	26,250	33,750
Heat, light, power	15,250	22,750
Depreciation	63,000	63,000
Insurance and taxes	8,000	8,000
Total factory burden	$157,500	$202,500
Total manufacturing costs	$232,500	$327,500

Other data
Standard time: 1.5 direct labor hours per unit of product
Normal capacity: 30,000 direct labor hours
Units produced, June 19x1: 22,000
Direct labor hours worked, June 19x1: 32,000
Factory burden incurred, June 19x1: $191,000
Standard factory burden rates are based on direct labor hours.

Required:

1. Prepare a factory burden variance analysis (three variances) for June 19x1. Interpret these variances.
2. Determine the selling price per pound, if 30 percent of the price is added to standard manufacturing cost to cover selling and general expenses and profit.

7-7.† The Jones Furniture Company uses a standard cost system in accounting for its production costs. The standard cost of a unit of furniture follows:

Lumber (100 ft @ $150/1,000 ft)		$15
Direct labor (4 hr @ $2.50/hr)		10
Manufacturing overhead:		
Fixed (30% of direct labor)	$3	
Variable (60% of direct labor)	6	9
Total unit cost		$34

The following flexible monthly overhead budget is in effect:

Direct Labor Hours	Estimated Overhead
5,200	$10,800
4,800	10,200
4,400	9,600
4,000 (normal capacity)	9,000
3,600	8,400

The actual unit costs for the month of December were as follows:

Lumber used (110 ft @ $120/1,000 ft)	$13.20
Direct labor (4¼ hr @ $2.60/hr)	11.05
Manufacturing overhead ($10,560 ÷ 1,200 units)	8.80
Total actual unit cost	$33.05

Required:
Prepare a schedule which shows an analysis of each element of the total variance from standard cost for the month of December.

(AICPA adapted)

7-8. The Smith Company uses a standard cost system. The standards are based on a budget for operations at the rate of production anticipated for the current period. The company records, in its general ledger, variations in material prices and usage, wage rates, and labor efficiency. The accounts for overhead expenses reflect variations in activity from the projected rate of operations, variations of actual expenses from amounts budgeted, and variations in the efficiency of production. Current standards are as follows:

Materials:
Material A	$1.20/unit
Material B	2.60/unit
Direct labor	$2.05/hr

	Special Widgets	Deluxe Widgets
Finished products (content of each unit):		
Material A, units	12	12
Material B, units	6	8
Direct labor, hr	14	20

The general ledger does not include a finished goods inventory account; costs are transferred directly from work in process to cost of sales at the time finished products are sold.

The budget and operating data for the month of August, 19x6, are summarized as follows:

Budget		
Projected direct labor hours		9,000
Fixed overhead expense		$ 4,500
Variable overhead expense		$13,500
Selling expenses		$ 4,000
Administrative expenses		$ 7,500
Operating data		
Sales:		
500 special Widgets		$52,700
100 deluxe Widgets		$16,400
Purchases:		
Material A	8,500 units	$ 9,725
Material B	1,800 units	$ 5,635
Material requisitions:		
Issued from stores:	Material A	Material B
Standard quantity, units	8,400	3,200
Over standard, units	400	150
Returned to stores	75	
Direct labor hours:		
Standard		9,600
Actual		10,000
Wages paid:		
500 hr @ $2.10		
8,000 hr @ $2.00		
1,500 hr @ $1.90		
Expenses:		
Overhead		$20,125
Selling		$ 3,250
Administrative		$ 6,460

Required:

1. Prepare journal entries to record operations for the month of August, 19x6. Show computations of the amounts used in each journal entry. Raw material purchases are recorded at standard.
2. Prepare a statement of profit and loss for the month, supported by an analysis of variances.

(AICPA adapted)

7-9. The Carberg Corporation manufactures and sells a single product. The cost system used by the company is a standard cost system. The standard cost per unit of product is shown below:

Material, 1 lb plastic @ $2	$ 2.00
Direct labor, 1.6 hr @ $4	6.40
Variable overhead cost	3.00
Fixed overhead cost	1.45
	$12.85

The overhead cost per unit was calculated from the following annual overhead cost budget for a 60,000-unit volume.

Variable overhead cost		
Indirect labor, 30,000 hr @ $4		$120,000
Supplies – oil, 60,000 gal @ $0.50		30,000
Allocated variable service department costs		30,000
Total variable overhead cost		$180,000
Fixed overhead cost		
Supervision		$ 27,000
Depreciation		45,000
Other fixed costs		15,000
Total fixed overhead cost		$ 87,000
Total budgeted annual overhead cost at 60,000 units		$267,000

The charges to the manufacturing department for November, when 5,000 units were produced, were:

Material	5,300 lb @ $2.00	$10,600
Direct labor	8,200 hr @ $4.10	33,620
Indirect labor	2,400 hr @ $4.10	9,840
Supplies – oil	6,000 gal @ $0.55	3,300
Allocated variable service department costs		3,200
Supervision		2,475
Depreciation		3,750
Other		1,250
Total		$68,035

The purchasing department normally buys about the same quantity as is used in production during a month. In November, 5,200 pounds were purchased at a price of $2.10 per pound.

Required:
1. Calculate the following variances from standard costs for the data given:

   a. Materials purchase price
   b. Materials quantity
   c. Direct labor wage rate
   d. Direct labor efficiency
   e. Overhead budget

2. Prepare a report which details the overhead budget variance. The report, which will be given to the manufacturing department manager, should display only that part of the variance that is the responsibility of the manager and should highlight the information in ways that would be useful to that manager in evaluating departmental performance and when considering corrective action.

            (Institute of Management Accountants (IMA) adapted)

7-10. An analysis of the standard costs and variances for the press department of the Strong Manufacturing Company for the month of July is shown below. Some of the information is missing. From the data available, complete the variance analysis and answer the questions that follow.

Basic data
Standard quantities per unit of product:
  Direct material – 4 lb
  Direct labor – 5 hr
Standard rates:
  Direct material – $1/lb
  Direct labor – $2/hr
Normal capacity: 3,000 direct labor hours
Quantity produced in July: 525 units
Budget for factory overhead at 3,000 direct labor hours:

Variable	$ 9,000
Fixed	3,000
Total factory overhead	$12,000

Variances
A. Material

Actual quantity × actual price	Actual quantity × standard price	Standard quantity × standard price
(2,000 × _____)	(_____ × _____)	(_____ × _____)
$2,100	$_____	$2,100
Price variance	Usage variance	
$_____	$_____	

Budget variance = $_____

B. Labor

Actual quantity × actual rate	Actual quantity × standard rate	Standard quantity × standard rate
(_____ × _____)	(_____ × _____)	(_____ × _____)
$_____	$_____	$_____
Rate variance	Efficiency variance	
$260 U	$50 F	

Budget variance = $210 U

C. Factory Overhead

	Actual overhead incurred	Actual hours @ budget	Standard hours @ budget	Standard hours @ standard rate
Variable	$ 8,000	$7,800	$7,875	$7,875
Fixed	3,000			
Total	$11,000	_____	_____	_____
	Spending variance	Efficiency variance	Capacity variance	
	$_____	$_____	$_____	

Total variance = $500 U

NOTE: The letter "U" denotes an unfavorable variance; "F" means a favorable variance.

Questions:

1. What was the actual price per pound paid for material?   _____

2. What is the material price variance?   _____

3. What is the material usage variance?   _____

4. What is the total material cost variance?   _____

5. What is the direct labor cost for the July production at *standard* rate for the *standard* time allowed?   _____

6. What was the actual time needed to achieve July production?   _____

7. What was the actual average wage rate paid in the press department in July?   _____

8. What is the standard variable overhead rate?   _____

9. What is the standard fixed overhead rate?   _____

10. What is the standard total overhead rate? _____

11. What would the budgeted fixed overhead cost
have been (*a*) at 500 units? _____

  (*b*) at 650 units? _____

12. Explain the capacity overhead variance.

13. As plant superintendent for Strong, how would you rate the press
department supervisor on his cost control performance in July?

7-11. Bull O'Woods, plant superintendent for the Microcosm Division of the
Macrobilt Corporation, pointed proudly to his total factory overhead for
November compared with his budget. "Right on the nose," he gloated.
"How's that for cost control?"

  His cost accountant, Meek N. Mild, cleared his throat. "May I see
the figures, sir?" he ventured, quiveringly.

  "Sure," his boss snapped. "Here—look for yourself!"

  These were the key figures which Mild noted:

	Actual	Budget	Variance
Total factory overhead	$132,624	$132,624*	$ -0-
Machine hours	44,620	44,208	
Standard time per unit of product, hr		2	
Normal capacity, unit of product		22,104	
Units produced this month	21,862		

  * One-third fixed.

Required:

What is likely to befall Mild when he tells O'Woods the truth? (*Hint:*
First determine the truth.)

7-12. The A Company, engaged in production of heavy equipment, had applied factory overhead to its product on the basis of an average rate of
115 percent of direct labor cost. This rate, at the time it was established,
was based on the following information as to expected operations:

Direct labor hours		136,000
Direct labor cost		$163,200
Average rate per hour		$1.20
Fixed overhead	$ 57,936	
Variable overhead	129,744	
Total overhead		$187,680

At December 31, 19x4, the end of the first accounting period, the
records disclosed the following information:

Direct labor hours		130,000
Direct labor cost		$183,040
Average rate per hour		$1.408
Fixed overhead	$ 75,400	
Variable overhead	145,600	
Total overhead (actual expense)		$221,000
Underabsorbed overhead		$ 10,504

The management is concerned with the fact that it failed to absorb overhead of $10,504 in the year's operations.

Required:

1. Discuss and criticize the system currently being used to absorb overhead.
2. Prepare an explanation for management showing why the $10,504 underabsorption existed. Compute and show the effect of variation in direct labor rates and direct labor hours on the absorption of both fixed and variable overhead. Support your conclusions with computations and explanatory comments setting forth the significance of each item in the analysis. (Computations should be corrected to the nearest dollar.)

(AICPA adapted)

7-13.† The Bronson Company manufactures a fuel additive which has a stable selling price of $40 per drum. Since losing a government contract, the company has been producing and selling 80,000 drums per month, 50 percent of normal capacity. Management expects to increase production to 140,000 drums in the coming fiscal year.

In connection with your examination of the financial statements of the Bronson Company for the year ended September 30, you have been asked to review some computations made by Bronson's cost accountant. Your working papers disclose the following about the company's operations:

1. Standard costs per drum of product manufactured:

Materials:
8 gal of miracle mix	$16
1 empty drum	1
	$17
Direct labor – 1 hr	$ 5
Factory overhead	$ 6

2. Costs and expenses during September:

Miracle mix:
500,000 gal, costing $950,000; 650,000 gal used
Empty drums:
94,000, costing $94,000; 80,000 used
Direct labor:
82,000 hr worked at cost of $414,100
Factory overhead:
Depreciation of building and machinery (fixed)	$210,000
Supervision and indirect labor (semivariable)	460,000
Other factory overhead (variable)	98,000
	$768,000

3. Other factory overhead was the only actual overhead cost which varied from the overhead budget for the September level of production; actual other factory overhead was $98,000 and the budgeted amount was $90,000.
4. At normal capacity of 160,000 drums per month, supervision and indirect labor costs are expected to be $570,000. All cost functions are linear.
5. None of the September cost variances is expected to occur proportionally in future months. For the next fiscal year, the cost standards

department expects the same standard usage of materials and direct labor hours. The average prices expected are: $2.10 per gallon of miracle mix, $1 per empty drum, and $5.70 per direct labor hour. The current flexible budget of factory overhead costs is considered applicable to future periods without revision.

Required:
Compute variances for September's production.

(AICPA adapted)

7-14. Ross Shirts, Inc., manufactures short- and long-sleeve men's shirts for large stores. Ross produces a single quality shirt in lots to each customer's order and attaches the store's label to each. The standard costs for a dozen long-sleeve shirts are:

Direct materials	24 yd @ $0.55	$13.20
Direct labor	3 hr @ $2.45	7.35
Manufacturing overhead	3 hr @ $2.00	6.00
Standard cost per dozen		$26.55

During October Ross worked on three orders for long-sleeve shirts. Job cost records for the month disclose the following:

Lot	Units in Lot	Material Used	Hours Worked
30	1,000 dz	24,100 yd	2,980
31	1,700 dz	40,440 yd	5,130
32	1,200 dz	28,825 yd	2,890

The following information is also available:

1. Ross purchased 95,000 yards of material during the month at a cost of $53,200. The material price variance is recorded when goods are purchased and all inventories are carried at standard cost.
2. Direct labor incurred amounted to $27,500 during October. According to payroll records, production employees were paid $2.50 per hour.
3. Overhead is applied on the basis of direct labor hours. Manufacturing overhead totaling $22,800 was incurred during October.
4. A total of $288,000 was budgeted for overhead for the year, based on estimated production at the plant's normal capacity of 48,000 dozen shirts per year. Overhead is 40 percent fixed and 60 percent variable at this level of production.
5. There was no work in process at October 1. During October, lots 30 and 31 were completed and all material was issued for lot 32, which was 80 percent completed as to labor.

Required:
1. Prepare a schedule computing the standard cost for October of lots 30, 31, and 32.
2. Prepare a schedule computing the materials price variance for October and indicate whether the variance is favorable or unfavorable.
3. Prepare schedules computing (and indicating whether the variances

are favorable or unfavorable) for each lot produced during October, the:

    a. Material quantity variance in yards
    b. Labor efficiency variance in hours
    c. Labor rate variance in dollars

4. Prepare a schedule computing the total controllable (budget variance) and noncontrollable (capacity) manufacturing overhead variances for October. Indicate whether the variances are favorable or unfavorable.

(AICPA adapted)

7-15. Conti Pharmaceutical Company processes a single-compound product known as Nulax and uses a standard cost accounting system. The process requires preparation and blending of three materials in large batches, with a variation from the standard mixture sometimes necessary to maintain quality. Conti's cost accountant became ill at the end of October, and you were engaged to determine standard costs of October production and to explain any differences between actual and standard costs for the month. The following information is available for the blending department:

1. The standard cost card for a 500-pound batch shows the following standard costs:

	Quantity	Price	Total Cost	
Materials:				
Mucilloid	250 lb	$0.14	$35	
Dextrose	200 lb	0.09	18	
Ingredients	50 lb	0.08	4	
Total per batch	500 lb			$ 57
Labor:				
Preparation and blending	10 hr	3.00		30
Overhead:				
Variable	10 hr	1.00	10	
Fixed	10 hr	0.30	3	13
Total standard cost per 500-pound batch				$100

2. During October, 410 batches of 500 pounds each of the finished compound were completed and transferred to the packaging department.

3. Blending department inventories totaled 6,000 pounds at the beginning of the month and 9,000 pounds at the end of the month. (Assume both inventories were completely processed but not transferred and consisted of materials in their standard proportions; inventories are carried in the accounts at standard cost prices.)

4. During the month of October the following materials were purchased and put into production:

	Pounds	Price per Pound	Total Cost
Mucilloid	114,400	$.17	$19,448
Dextrose	85,800	.11	9,438
Ingredients	19,800	.07	1,386
Totals	220,000		$30,272

5. Wages paid for 4,212 hours of direct labor at $3.25 per hour amounted to $13,689.
6. Actual overhead costs for the month totaled $5,519.
7. The standards were established for a normal production volume of 200,000 pounds (400 batches) of Nulax per month. At this level of production, variable factory overhead was budgeted at $4,000 and fixed factory overhead was budgeted at $1,200.

Required:
1. Prepare a schedule presenting the computation for the blending department of:
   a. October production in both pounds and batches
   b. The standard cost of October production itemized by components of materials, labor, and overhead
2. Prepare schedules computing the differences between actual and standard costs and analyzing the differences as:
   a. Materials variances (for each material) caused by
      (1) Price differences
      (2) Usage differences
   b. Labor variances caused by
      (1) Rate difference
      (2) Efficiency difference
   c. Overhead variances caused by
      (1) Controllable factors (budget variance)
      (2) Volume factors (capacity variance)
3. Explain how the materials variances arising from usage differences could be further analyzed (no computations are necessary).

(AICPA adapted)

7-16. Refer to problem 7-7. The management of the Jones Furniture Company is searching for a rule to use in deciding whether a particular variance should be investigated. It has been determined that such investigations on the average cost $500. From past experience, the company knows that a 10 percent variance from standard cost allowed indicates that there is a 50 percent probability that the variance is a random event within expected limits.

Required:
1. Which variances will be investigated under the rules decreeing investigation in the following categories:
   a. All variances greater than $500
   b. All variances greater than 10 percent of standard costs allowed
   c. All variances which are both greater than 10 percent of standard costs allowed and greater than $500
2. Is there a better rule that the company should consider?

7-17. The Brand Name Company began operations on June 1, 1975. Although operations were not at full strength until the final week of the month, it was still possible to produce 2,000 units of their one product, Brand X. Brand X requires two types of raw material, A and B, in its production. The records on purchases and usage of A and B during June show:

Material	Purchases	Usage
A	10,000 lb for $12,000	4,000 lb
B	8,000 lb for $77,000	2,100 lb

The standard material cost for Brand X is as follows:

Material A: $2\frac{1}{4}$ lb @ $1.12/lb	$ 2.52
Material B: 1 lb @ $10/lb	10.00
Total standard material cost per unit	$12.52

Required:
1. Calculate the material usage variances for A and B.
2. Calculate the material price variances, assuming they are recorded at time of purchase.
3. Calculate the material price variances, assuming they are recorded at time of usage.
4. How can your answers in 2 and 3 be reconciled?

7-18. Refer to problem 7-17. Make the necessary journal entries for requirements 1, 2, and 3.

CHAPTER

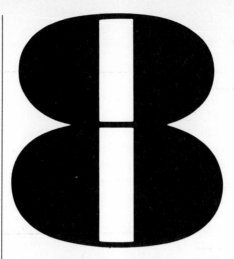

HUMAN RELATIONS AND RESPONSIBILITY ACCOUNTING

THE PLAN OF THIS CHAPTER
Having examined the need for and mechanics of cost control through standards and flexible budgets, we come now to a consideration of the human problems involved in organizational control. These problems include:

"Management by objectives" versus "management by domination"

Motivation

Responsibility accounting

DELEGATION AND ACCOUNTABILITY

The art of administration, so goes the old maxim, is the process of getting things done through people.

The simplest form of economic activity is the one-person business. As long as all the elements of an operation are in the hands of one person, this individual alone is responsible for how the working time is divided among the different jobs in order to minimize costs and maximize profits for the business. As soon as the firm adds an employee, division of labor occurs and an organization is formed. As a business grows in size and complexity, its organizational problems mount. Division of labor takes the form of allocation not only of productive activities but of management as well.

The authority to manage a business, in our legal and economic system, stems from ownership. This power is passed downward—delegated—from the owners to responsible members of the organization charged with the attainment of the economic goals of the company. Concomitant with the power to manage is *accountability* for results. The larger and more complex the organization, the greater is the reliance of top management on an effective system of delegation of authority and accountability for results. This concept of accountability attaching to delegated duties forms the basis of responsibility accounting and budgetary control.

APPROACH TO CONTROL

W. T. Jerome[1] views executive control as "some sort of systematic effort to compare current performance to a predetermined plan or objective, presumably in order to take any remedial action required. To speak of executive control apart from performance standards or some plan of action is impossible." He continues:[2]

The simplicity of this definition, however, belies the host of problems which three innocent questions can quickly raise:

1. Whose plans are used as a basis of comparison and how are they formulated (e.g., are the plans legislated by superiors or developed jointly with subordinates)?
2. How are the deviations from plans being reported (e.g., how quick and effective is the feedback)?
3. What action is taken on the basis of the reported deviations (e.g., is the purpose of getting this information to assess blame or to help those responsible for performance do their jobs better)?

Jerome's pointed questions open the door to the subject of human relations—a problem area upon which accounting impinges at many points, but nowhere as directly as in the realm of cost control budgeting. In the past, failure on the part of well-qualified management accountants to understand the role of

---

[1] William Travers Jerome, III, *Executive Control: The Catalyst,* New York: John Wiley & Sons, Inc., 1961, p. 24.
[2] Ibid.

human relations in cost control has caused serious breakdowns in the best-conceived and technically excellent budget systems.

A great many responsible people seem to dislike budgetary control as it applies to them, although they are quick to agree that costs must be controlled and that budgets are necessary. Since cost control seems so obvious a need, why the difficulty in making it work in practice? Human behavior continues to perplex the most sophisticated of scholars and practitioners who specialize in the study of it. All the questions concerning human problems of cost control have yet to be asked, let alone answered, but a great deal has been learned and written on the subject. A brief review of some of the more prominent human-relations aspects of budgeting may prove worthwhile before looking into the technical side of responsibility accounting.

HUMAN RELATIONS IN BUDGETING

In a significant study of the human problems in budgeting, Chris Argyris[3] reports a high degree of negative reaction to control budgets on the part of frontline factory supervisors, which he attributes in large part to the following:[4]

1. Budgets are, first of all, evaluation instruments. Because they tend to set goals against which to measure people, they naturally are complained about.
2. Budgets are one of the few evaluation processes that are always in writing and therefore concrete. Thus, some of the supervisors tend to use budgets as "whipping posts" in order to release their feelings about many other (often totally unrelated) problems.
3. Budgets are thought of as pressure devices. As such they produce the same kind of unfavorable reactions as do other kinds of pressure regardless of origin.

Argyris reports major problems to include the frequent use of budgets as pressure devices; the tendency to reckon the budget supervisor's success in terms of the factory supervisor's failure; and the tendency for the budget to center the supervisor's attention upon his or her own department, to the exclusion of the well-being of other departments and the plant as a whole.[5]

Is there something in the basic nature of budgeting, then, which brings out the worst in a human being? Is it necessary that the human problems negate the good effects aimed at in the use of budgets for cost control? Simple, universal answers to these questions would be impossible in view of the massive evidence both of successful use of budgets for cost control in some companies and of failure and abandonment of budget systems in others. Rather, an examination of cause and effect may reveal to some extent why budget systems fail when they do, as well as the conditions upon which successful budgeting is based.

---

[3] Chris Argyris, "Human Problems with Budgets," *Harvard Business Review*, January–February 1953, pp. 97–110. The article was based on a field study of three small plants (i.e., less than 1,500 employees) which focused primarily on the effects of manufacturing budgets on front-line supervisors.
[4] Ibid.
[5] Ibid.

MEANING OF CONTROL

In an earlier chapter we looked at the meaning of control in an administrative context. Now let us give it a slightly different slant. Peter Drucker, an eminent writer on management subjects, has this to say about it:[6]

"Control" is an ambiguous word. It means the ability to direct oneself and one's work. It can also mean domination of one person by another. [Management] objectives are the basis of "control" in the first sense; but they must never become the basis of "control" in the second, for this would defeat their purposes. Indeed, one of the major contributions of management by objectives is that it enables us to substitute management by self-control for management by domination.

If we accept Drucker's distinction, it would seem that the problems found by Argyris are related to budgeting which is based on the "domination" form of control. From the most ancient times, human beings have resented and rebelled against domination, whether in the form of out-and-out slavery or in the more refined forms of economic and political coercion.

On the other hand, some of our most significant achievements have been realized when, acting as free persons, we are convinced of the worthiness of the objectives being sought; when we can interpret the success of our efforts at least partially in terms of personal benefit; when we have attained such a level of maturity and integrity as to exercise effectively that "ability to direct oneself and one's work" of which Drucker speaks.

COMPANY OBJECTIVES

But what about the "management by objectives" which, according to Drucker, should provide the basis for "management by self-control"? Presumably, the objectives referred to are those set for the company by top management, which include short- and long-term profit goals, product lines, markets, plant capacity and location, volume of activity, and industry position.

In the modern industrial organization, most individuals are unable to function in the classical economic tradition, running their own business, setting its goals, performing all its activities, and reaping all the rewards. Instead, they bring with them certain work skills and job qualifications useful to the organization in the pursuit of *its* objectives. However, the objectives of the organization seldom coincide exactly with those of its members. One of the foremost tasks of management is to reconcile the differing objectives of the company and its employees in a mutually satisfactory manner.

PERSONAL NEEDS AND OBJECTIVES

As a person, the employee, at whatever organizational level, has certain needs which condition his or her own objectives. As employees:

[6] Peter F. Drucker, *The Practice of Management,* New York: Harper & Row, Publishers, Incorporated, 1954, p. 131.

1. We seek *compensation* for our work which will enable us to provide some desired standard of material welfare for ourselves and our families.

2. We need outlets for our physical and intellectual energies which will provide both *stimulation* and *satisfaction*.

3. We seek *self-realization* — a sense of our own worth and usefulness.

4. We are pursuing further *growth* and greater *personal effectiveness*.

5. We seek the *recognition* of our fellows, whether they be organizational equals, superiors, or subordinates.

6. We cherish an *identification* with a worthwhile and successful undertaking.

FAILURE OF CONTROL BY DOMINATION

Symptoms

The failure of control by domination begins with the failure on the part of top management and all other members of the organization to harmonize personal with business objectives. The logical progression from bad to worse may exhibit some of the following symptoms:

1. Management imposes budgets unilaterally on those whom they expect to control costs. Those expected to "live within" these budgets bristle under the restrictions, feeling that since they are not allowed to participate in the construction of the budgets, doubt is being cast upon their intelligence, their trustworthiness, or both.

2. The production supervisor whose take-home pay is affected by the working of a bonus plan tied to the budget may put off certain machinery maintenance in a period in which department costs are "out of line," when due regard for the longer-term well-being of the company would indicate that incurring the cost now would prevent the need for major repair or replacement in the future.

3. Management, embarking on a cost-reduction program, decides that all budgets will be "cut to the bone," and responsible managers are admonished to "get tough" with all subordinates to "meet the budget" (experience indicates that costs thus artificially and coercively reduced tend to bounce back to the same or higher levels in later periods when the pressure is eased).

4. The supervisor, being thoroughly familiar with departmental operations, takes the worker's side in an argument over a time standard or machine rate; higher management becomes suspicious that the supervisor is collaborating with workers in an attempt to get the standards relaxed so that the budget report will not look so bad and so that the workers will not have to work so hard.

5. Budget supervisors (or members of their staffs) find that they can make themselves look good by making factory supervisors look bad. They become ferrets, snooping for trouble spots, reporting to the boss first instead of tipping off the supervisor involved, hatching ideas for improvement of methods

or removal of bottlenecks in a productive department, but, instead of suggesting them to the supervisor who might implement them directly, bringing them to the attention of their own superiors for the sake of whatever glory might be in it for them.

6. Controllers (or their staffs) unaware of or minimizing the importance of human factors in the functioning of the budget system, will hint darkly at the punishments which might follow a supervisor's failure to "meet" the budget; or even worse, they will attempt to interpose themselves between the supervisor and his or her rightful superior in criticizing poor performance and prescribing corrective action for control of future costs.

Effect on Subordinates

Such conditions, again, are merely suggestive of the infinite varieties of organizational ills which stem from a prevailing management philosophy of control by domination. These ills can be traced to the failure of either top management or its organizational subordinates to adapt personal to company objectives. For example:

1. *Desired compensation.* In the short run, the managers or supervisors may lose a bonus if their performance is below budget; over the long term, failure to meet budget consistently may result in their being deprived of raises and promotions, possibly even the loss of their positions. Is it surprising, then, that they will take steps, however devious and detrimental to company welfare, to protect their livelihood?

2. *Stimulation and satisfaction.* When managers are treated as though their opinions are unimportant in setting the standards by which their performance will be measured, when budget supervisors persist in looking over their shoulders, and when they get saddle-sore from "riding herd" on their subordinates, their stimulation and satisfaction will probably seem pretty thin.

3. *Self-realization.* When managers conclude that top management is suspicious of their motives, dependability, and intelligence, how high is their estimate of their own worth and usefulness likely to stand?

4. *Personal growth.* When managers are deprived of most of the responsibility for setting their departmental objectives and standards, are expected only to "crack the whip" over subordinates, and may expect to be "chewed out" whenever they fall short of standards which they think are too tight, how much growth and increase in personal effectiveness may they reasonably be expected to have achieved over the last year? How much will they progress over the next year?

5. *Recognition.* Can managers who are constantly on their subordinates' backs to "get costs down" expect to be respected? Can they command the respect of their peers when they seem interested only in "slitting their throats" — trying to shift the blame for their own shortcomings while trying to outshine the subordinates' performance? Can they expect to dazzle their superiors with their loyalty and promotability when they are constantly grousing about the unreasonableness of budget standards, alibiing for poor performance, and making decisions calculated to make the short-term record

look good while costing the company many times the spurious cost savings in the long run?

6. *Identification.* How are managers, particularly front-line supervisors, going to identify with:
   a. Employees, since managers are supposed to be boss and are not allowed to join the union
   b. Other supervisors, when they are both involved in a mutual battle for survival
   c. "Management," when they are looked upon as not having the intelligence or reliability to be consulted concerning work or cost standards and are sometimes suspected of being "in cahoots" with the workers for the purpose of inhibiting productive efficiency
   d. "The Company," which they see only as a confusing blend of people sitting in paneled rooms studying *The Wall Street Journal* — and a group of miserly, idle, yacht-plying stockholders whose sole purpose in life is to collect fabulous dividends (which result from the managers' cost-cutting efforts)

Top Management at Fault

Such attitudes on the part of budget-ridden front-line and middle management are generally the reflection of an ill-advised top management philosophy of control by domination. The chief characteristic of such a philosophy is the neglect on the part of top management, as well as the controller, of the human-relations aspect of the control process. This neglect can result from ignorance, preoccupation with the nonhuman technical aspects of managing the business, or just plain inability to "get through" to their subordinates on a human level.

Thus controllers who have designed and set in operation a technically flawless system of responsibility accounting and budgeting are headed for trouble if they allow the following conditions to exist:

1. Managers of cost centers are not consulted about the type or amount of cost assigned to them.

2. Managers are assigned some costs over which they exercise no control.

3. The controller or the department staff have the final say as to the level of budgeted costs.

4. The controller or the department staff take it upon themselves to criticize managers for poor cost control.

5. The controller encourages or condones surreptitious attempts by staff members to "get the goods" on certain managers for the purpose of making them look bad.

6. The controller and his or her staff word their reports and verbal explanations of budget and cost matters with enough technical jargon to keep other members of the organization off balance — the idea being to emphasize how important and complex the controllership function is.

Moreover, the president, although not directly involved in the functions of the system of budgetary control, can stifle its effectiveness by personal ineptness in the realm of human relations. Such a president could be characterized by:

1.   Being jealous of the "figures" (profits), sharing their dark secret only with the controller but expecting everyone else in the organization to be cost-conscious, reminding them constantly that "a dollar of cost saving is a dollar of profit" but failing to disclose the fact that the company's after-tax profits are closer to 4 percent than the 40 percent of sales which many otherwise intelligent people believe them to be

2.   Kicking off a big cost-reduction program by declaring that there will be a 15 percent slash "across the board," without regard for the havoc this could play in some areas where costs are already well managed and further reductions would interfere with the attainment of certain of the president's cherished profit goals

3.   Demanding boldness, ingenuity, and initiative in the company's managers but unquestioning conformity to the president's every turn of mind ("Now I want *you* to make the decisions in your area — but clear them with me, just in case.")

Such a president as this clearly has made no attempt to mesh the personal objectives of subordinates with company goals, and has substituted domination for true delegation. The predictable failure of the control system in such a case will be due to human, not technical, causes.

CONTROL THROUGH OBJECTIVES

After the foregoing analysis of how to fail at budgetary control without really trying, it might be assumed that success will be ensured simply by turning the domination formula upside down. The catch in such a panacea is found in the basic assumption about human beings upon which the concept of management by objectives rests, namely, that human beings are free agents, vastly more responsive to motivation than to domination.

The achievement of success in budgetary control can probably be attributed to the *existence* of a certain favorable set of conditions, but to *cause* these conditions in a particular organization requires considerable management skill in human relations. Nevertheless, it is important to know just what conditions are being sought, since such knowledge provides the guidelines for purposeful effort toward their achievement.

The conditions favorable to the acceptance and successful functioning of a good budgetary control system should include:

1.   Top management's sharing with its subordinates the short-, intermediate-, and long-term objectives of the company as they provide the direction for overall planning. Emphasis should be placed on the consonance of the profit and other goals of the firm with the individual career aspirations of all members of the organization.

2.   A climate of true delegation of authority and responsibility, beginning with top management itself. The emphasis here should be the positive one

of allowing each responsible person maximum opportunity to make decisions within the scope of his or her authority, as a means of achieving personal growth, self-realization, and recognition. It should be self-evident in this regard that the company objective of developing management talent and the manager's personal goal of growth and promotion are two sides of the same coin.

3.   With specific reference to cost control, an employee shall be consulted about where his or her operations fit in the framework of plans for the budget period and what a reasonable expectation of costs will be. Company superiors may not be able to allow department managers all they think they need, but they will at least have had the opportunity to participate in the determination of their budgets, and the reasons for any reduction shall be explained thoroughly.

4.   The budget system shall not be used as a basis for immediate reward or punishment. This means that the manager's paycheck should not be tied directly to his performance against budget in any period, nor should he feel the "heat" if his performance misses the target in a given period. Obviously, this is not to be interpreted as license to exceed the budget capriciously, whenever, however, and by whatever amount he will. His performance should show a consistency over a period of time, and this indeed should be a factor in raises or promotions over the longer term.

5.   Supervisors shall not be *held responsible* for costs over which they have no control. This is simply consistent with proper delegation. On the other hand, it may be beneficial for the controller *to report* to the supervisor such costs assigned to the specific cost center if they are clearly segregated from his or her controllable costs and serve only to emphasize the supervisor's dependency on the rest of the organization for the smooth functioning of his or her own unit.

6.   The controller and all staff members shall serve *only* in a service capacity and shall *never* interpose themselves, directly or by innuendo, between subordinate managers and their superiors. The service rendered is vital: to compile accurate information; to report it quickly; to help educate all members of the organization in the use of budgetary techniques in order that *they* — not the controller's group — may control costs more effectively; to assist in the explanation of deviations from budget; and to offer suggestions for improved control *to the managers themselves* — never acting purely as "watchdogs" for higher management.

The successful functioning of a control system under the conditions thus assumed will be realized to the extent that such a set of conditions creates the type of organizational climate within which its members are motivated to satisfactory levels of performance. This motivation depends on the individual's recognizing the harmony between personal objectives and those of the company.

MOTIVATION

For the individual managers who recognize this harmony, the way is clear to pursue those objectives on all fronts:

1.   Their immediate *compensation* will be secured by their fulfillment of assigned duties; their prospective compensation will be limited only by their long-term performance and ability to grow and become more valuable to the company.

2.   Their understanding of the plans and goals of the company and their own roles in them will provide the *stimulation* to make the job interesting, and their progress toward achievement of these goals will yield a measure of *satisfaction.*

3.   Performance of a responsible job which they know contributes to the progress of the organization as a whole provides a source of *self-esteem* and sense of *personal worth.*

4.   In learning to handle small amounts of responsibility successfully, they are paving the way for the assumption of greater responsibility in the future, and this *personal growth,* they realize, helps strengthen the organization as well.

5.   Not being constrained to "keep the pressure on" their subordinates, highly motivated managers function as motivator, teacher, counselor, and collaborator in keeping the activities of their units efficient. If the law of the jungle does not prevail in the company, they are free to cooperate more fully with others at their same organization level. Moreover, since their performance is not inhibited by the fear of the budget as a weapon in the hands of their superiors or the inquisitorial controller, it is more likely to attract favorable attention in these quarters. In the case of all three—subordinates, equals, and superiors—the way is clear for well-motivated managers to achieve the *recognition* they crave to the extent that they earn it.

6.   Where an organization which possesses real managerial and productive talent operates in the type of climate provided by sound management by objectives, profits are the general result; in such a setting, managers are not likely to find it difficult to *identify* with the organization.

Lest the bemused reader be seriously misled, it should be emphasized that these conditions constitute the ideal toward which human relations in management is aimed. Its achievement in this imperfect world is seldom, if ever, completely realized. Nevertheless, if such an ideal were lacking, so also would be our direction. Moreover, the measure of success already achieved by well-managed companies with their control systems would be significantly less than it is; so too would be our aspirations for the future.

COST, PROFIT, AND INVESTMENT CENTERS

A necessary step in establishing an effective system of management by objectives is to determine the range of discretion and influence the manager is permitted to have over revenues, costs, and investment. Some managers have little or no authority to control their revenues or the investment made in their area of operations. Such divisions or departments are *cost centers*—the division manager is essentially responsible for minimizing costs subject to some output constraints. An example of a cost center is the maintenance department which does not "charge" other departments for its services and thus has no revenues. Budgets and variance analysis performance reports will be the major control devices for a cost center.

A *profit center* is a segment of a company where the manager has control over revenues as well as costs but does not have control over the amount of investment in the segment. An example of a profit center is the division which produces and markets one of a company's products. Decisions as to sales price, advertising strategies, and other marketing policies are made by the division manager. Decisions as to which investment projects are accepted in this division, however, are made by top company management — perhaps by a central committee including various company officers. Focusing on maximizing profit, rather than on minimizing costs, may have motivational benefits as far as the division manager is concerned. Budgets and performance reports continue to play an important role in the control of a profit center.

Those divisions or departments where the manager controls revenues, costs, and investment are called *investment centers.* In addition to the budgets and performance reports, profits as a percentage of invested capital (return on capital used) can be used to control investment centers. This concept of the return on capital used as it relates to investment centers is discussed in Chapter 10. The remainder of this chapter will concentrate on responsibility accounting, a system which can be used advantageously in all types of cost, profit, and investment centers.

WHY RESPONSIBILITY ACCOUNTING?

The ideal of management by objectives might, at first blush, be expected to be reached better if there were no form of budgetary control or responsibility accounting. If, under control by domination, the budget is the symbol of pressure — the bludgeon over the heads of hapless front-line and middle management — should not its abolition be the first step in the elimination of such domination?

It should be emphasized here that it is the *domination*, not the *control*, which must be abolished. The type of control being sought under management by objectives is self-control (by all responsible members of the organization). This implies a motivation toward self-control, as well as a knowledge of the norms of control in the individual situation. How can intelligent managers control their operations if they do not know, explicitly, what is expected of them and how well they are doing? In the realm of cost control, they need to know two things: (1) what their costs *should be;* (2) what their costs *were.* It is the function of the budget to provide the first set of information. Responsibility accounting will provide the second.

RESPONSIBILITY ACCOUNTING

To be effective, the use of standard costs and budgets for cost control must be tied into a system of reporting managerial performance which is at the same time accurate and fair. Many conventional accounting systems are not readily

adapted to the needs of evaluating responsibility for cost control. Some years ago
Arthur Andersen & Co., an international firm of certified public accountants,
came to grips with the problem of responsibility accounting. The following is an
excerpt adapted from a report on the method the company advocates as a result
of its study of the problem, reprinted here with its permission.[7]

This new approach to accounting and reporting is the development of an
accounting system designed to control expenditures by directly relating the
reporting of expenditures to the individuals in the company organization who
are responsible for their control. This system results in the preparation of
accounting statements for all levels of management, designed primarily so
that they can be effectively used by the operating people as a tool in controlling their operations and their costs.

This approach also makes possible the operation of a good budget system. No budget system is fully effective unless it is built around one basic
philosophy, namely that each responsible individual in an organization must
feel that the budget is *his* budget and not something forced upon him which
he might feel is unrealistic and unworkable. Unless the responsible individual does feel that it is *his* budget, he will only make a superficial attempt to
live within it or use the information as a means of controlling his operations.

Now if one will accept this philosophy in his approach to budgeting,
one more step must be taken to complete the picture. One must put the reporting of expenditures (cost accounting) in phase with the budget performance responsibility, which is another way of saying that expenditures
must be reported on the basis of where they were incurred and *who* had responsibility for them. Hence comes the term *responsibility accounting*.

In effect, the system personalizes the accounting statements by saying,
"Joe, this is what you originally budgeted and this is how you performed for
the period with actual operations as compared against your budget." By
definition, it is a system of accounting which is *tailored to an organization* so
that costs are accumulated and reported by levels of responsibility within the
organization. Each supervisory area in the organization is charged only with
the cost for which it is responsible and over which it has control.

There are two major objectives of cost accounting in manufacturing
companies: (1) cost control; (2) product cost. The cost systems of most companies meet the latter objective, but for the most part fall on their faces when
it comes to the objective of real cost control. Practically all of them have systems that emphasize the development of product cost instead of emphasiz-
ing the controlling of costs at the centers where the costs are incurred.
Under responsibility accounting it is possible to meet both of these objectives by first summarizing cost on the basis of "who did it" and then reshuffling the deck, so to speak, or blending the costs to arrive at product cost.
In effect what we are doing is putting the emphasis on the objective of cost
control for the purposes of management reports but also arriving at the
normal cost statements—but on a greatly de-emphasized basis.

A series of charts has been prepared to illustrate a system of responsibility accounting in a hypothetical company named the ABC Manufacturing
Company. It is a multiproduct metal manufacturing firm with annual sales of
approximately $4,000,000 and some 300 employees.

[7] John A. Higgins, "Responsibility Accounting," *The Arthur Andersen Chronicle*, April 1952, vol. 12, no. 2.

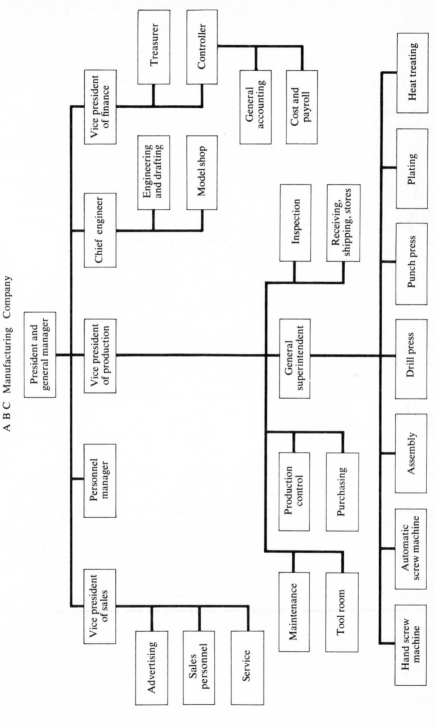

A B C Manufacturing Company

EXHIBIT 8-1 Organization chart

President and general manager			

4th level

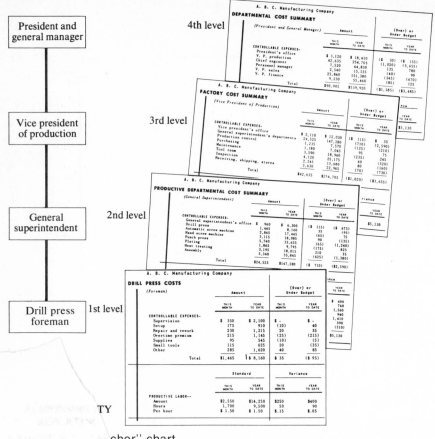

A. B. C. Manufacturing Company

DEPARTMENTAL COST SUMMARY

(President and General Manager)

	Amount		(Over) or Under Budget	
	THIS MONTH	YEAR TO DATE	THIS MONTH	YEAR TO DATE
CONTROLLABLE EXPENSES-				
President's office	$ 3,120	$ 18,410	($ 30)	($ 155)
V. P. production	42,635	254,705	(1,020)	(3,655)
Chief engineer	7,520	44,830	135	780
Personnel manager	2,540	15,135	(40)	90
V. P. sales	25,860	151,380	(345)	(670)
V. P. finance	9,230	55,460	(85)	125
Total	$90,905	$539,920	($1,385)	($3,485)

A. B. C. Manufacturing Company

FACTORY COST SUMMARY

(Vice President of Production)

	Amount		(Over) or Under Budget		nce
	THIS MONTH	YEAR TO DATE	THIS MONTH	YEAR TO DATE	YEAR TO DATE
CONTROLLABLE EXPENSES.					$5,130
Vice president's office	$ 2,110	$ 12,030	($ 115)	$ 35	
General superintendent's departments	24,525	147,280	(710)	(2,590)	
Production control	1,235	7,570	(125)	(210)	
Purchasing	1,180	7,045	95	75	
Maintenance	3,590	18,960	(235)	245	
Tool room	4,120	25,175	(65)	(320)	
Inspection	2,245	13,680	60	(160)	
Receiving, shipping, stores	3,630	22,965	80	(730)	
			(70)		
Total	$42,635	$254,705	($1,020)	($3,655)	

A. B. C. Manufacturing Company

PRODUCTIVE DEPARTMENTAL COST SUMMARY

(General Superintendent)

	Amount		(Over) or Under Budget		riance
	THIS MONTH	YEAR TO DATE	THIS MONTH	YEAR TO DATE	YEAR TO DATE
CONTROLLABLE EXPENSES-					$5,130
General superintendent's office	$ 960	$ 6,300	($ 115)	($ 675)	
Drill press	1,465	8,160	35	(95)	
Automatic screw machine	2,845	17,445	(65)	75	
Hand screw machine	3,115	18,085	90	(135)	
Punch press	5,740	33,635	(65)	(1,240)	
Plating	1,865	9,795	(175)	825	
Heat treating	3,195	18,015	210	35	
Assembly	5,340	35,845	(625)	(1,380)	
Total	$24,525	$147,280	($ 710)	($2,590)	

A. B. C. Manufacturing Company

DRILL PRESS COSTS

(Foreman)

	Amount		(Over) or Under Budget		nce YEAR TO DATE
	THIS MONTH	YEAR TO DATE	THIS MONTH	YEAR TO DATE	
					$ 400
					740
					1,560
CONTROLLABLE EXPENSES-					940
Supervision	$ 350	$ 2,100	$ -	$ -	1,410
Setup	175	910	(10)	40	390
Repair and rework	230	1,215	20	35	(310)
Overtime premium	215	1,145	(25)	(215)	$5,130
Supplies	95	545	(10)	(5)	
Small tools	115	625	20	(35)	
Other	285	1,620	40	85	
Total	$1,465	$ 8,160	$ 35	($ 95)	

	Standard		Variance	
	THIS MONTH	YEAR TO DATE	THIS MONTH	YEAR TO DATE
PRODUCTIVE LABOR--				
Amount	$2,550	$14,250	$250	$400
Hours	1,700	9,500	50	90
Per hour	$ 1.50	$ 1.50	$.15	$.05

Vice president of production	

3rd level

General superintendent	

2nd level

Drill press foreman	

1st level

...TY

..."chor" chart

Organization Chart

Inasmuch as the backbone of any responsibility accounting system is the organization chart of the company, an organization chart of the imaginary ABC Manufacturing Company is presented first [see Exhibit 8-1].

This organization chart shows a president and general manager of a single company. Three vice-presidents are indicated to head up the basic divisions of a normal manufacturing business organization: production, sales, and finance. In addition to these three vice-presidents, there is a chief engineer and a personnel manager reporting directly to the president and general manager. It is assumed that the vice-president in charge of production has a general superintendent who is responsible for seven productive departments, each in charge of an individual foreman. Also indicated are typical service departments responsible directly to the vice-president in charge of production.

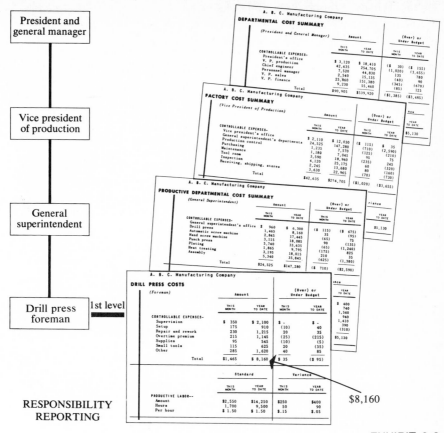

EXHIBIT 8-3

"Anchor" Chart

In Exhibit 8-2, that segment of the organization around which these illustrative responsibility statements have been built has been set out separately. The four levels of responsibility in the organization have been indicated and numbered. Of course, in a practical application, there could be more or less than these four levels, depending on the complexity of the company organization. This chart will serve two purposes:

1. It tends to emphasize the parallel relationship of the levels of responsibility and the reports which are directed at each of the levels.

2. It will serve as an anchor chart in that it will enable one to refer back to this chart as each of the reports is discussed through the various levels of responsibility.

Responsibility Report

Exhibit 8-3 focuses attention on the first level of responsibility reporting, which in this case is the foreman in charge of the drill press department.

The report itself is found in Exhibit 8-4. The top section of the report consists of a listing of certain controllable expenses for which the foreman is to be held fully responsible. These costs have been previously budgeted by the foreman and now the budgeted costs are being compared with the actual costs.

It will be noted that these controllable expenses do not represent the full burden of the department. They are confined to the expenses for which the management holds the foreman completely and directly responsible. It is very important that the foreman be made to feel that he can have the breakdown of his costs made in any way that he feels will aid him in controlling and budgeting these costs.

On the lower portion of this report appears the productive labor in hours and amount at standard with the variances from standard being shown. Productive labor is shown on this report because the foreman is responsible for the efficiency of the productive labor even though he is not responsible for establishing the budget of productive labor.

EXHIBIT 8-4
ABC MANUFACTURING COMPANY
Drill Press Costs
(Foreman)

	Amount		(Over) or under Budget	
	This Month	Year to Date	This Month	Year to Date
Controllable expenses				
Supervision	$ 350	$ 2,100	$ —	$ —
Setup	175	910	(10)	40
Repair and rework	230	1,215	20	35
Overtime premium	215	1,145	(25)	(215)
Supplies	95	545	(10)	(5)
Small tools	115	625	20	(35)
Other	285	1,620	40	85
Total	$1,465	$ 8,160	$ 35	($ 95)

	Standard		Variance	
	This Month	Year to Date	This Month	Year to Date
Productive labor				
Amount	$2,550	$14,250	$ 250	$ 400
Hours	1,700	9,500	50	90
Per hour	$ 1.50	$ 1.50	$0.15	$0.05

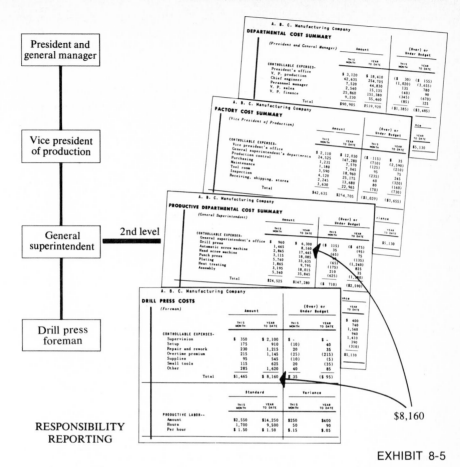

President and general manager

Vice president of production

General superintendent — 2nd level

Drill press foreman

RESPONSIBILITY
REPORTING

EXHIBIT 8-5

In Exhibit 8-5 one sees that the totals for the drill press department have been carried forward into a report for the general superintendent who is designated as the second level of reporting or responsibility. Now proceed to the report directed at the general superintendent.

In Exhibit 8-6, one sees the total amount of $8,160 representing the total controllable costs for the year to date for the drill press department. Likewise it will be noted that controllable cost totals have been carried forward for the other productive departments for which the general superintendent is held responsible. Also one sees listed, under summarized controllable expenses, the cost of the general superintendent's own office, and it is also supported by a detailed statement which is not shown here.

The general superintendent can have, and probably will want, statements from each of the foremen responsible to him. In the bottom section of the report, the productive labor for which the general superintendent is responsible has been summarized by areas of responsibility, the drill press department being one of these areas.

As shown by the anchor chart (Exhibit 8-7), one sees that the third level of reporting is the vice-president in charge of production and that the total controllable costs under the general superintendent have been carried forward from the second level to form a part of the responsibility costs of the vice-president in charge of production.

The report in Exhibit 8-8 for the vice-president in charge of production has been labeled "Factory Cost Summary." Here one sees that the total amount of controllable costs of the general superintendent has been carried forward as one of the areas of responsibility for which the vice-president in charge of production is to be held responsible. These other areas of re-

EXHIBIT 8-6
ABC MANUFACTURING COMPANY
Productive Departmental Cost Summary
(General Superintendent)

	Amount		(Over) or under Budget	
	This Month	Year to Date	This Month	Year to Date
Controllable expenses				
General superintendent's office	$ 960	$ 6,300	($115)	($ 675)
Drill press	1,465	8,160	35	(95)
Automatic screw machine	2,845	17,445	(65)	75
Hand screw machine	3,115	18,085	90	(135)
Punch press	5,740	33,635	(65)	(1,240)
Plating	1,865	9,795	(175)	825
Heat treating	3,195	18,015	210	35
Assembly	5,340	35,845	(625)	(1,380)
Total	$24,525	$147,280	($710)	($2,590)

	Standard		Variance	
	This Month	Year to Date	This Month	Year to Date
Productive labor				
Drill press	$ 2,550	$ 14,250	$ 250	$ 400
Automatic screw machine	1,310	7,890	110	740
Hand screw machine	5,240	31,760	540	1,560
Punch press	3,720	23,850	215	940
Plating	1,410	7,370	155	1,410
Heat treating	1,630	8,510	180	390
Assembly	11,260	68,340	1,570	(310)
Total	$27,120	$161,970	$3,020	$5,130

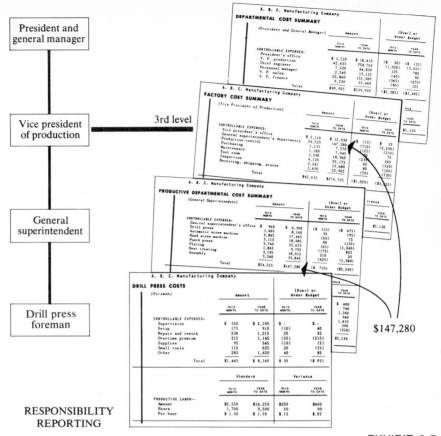

President and general manager

Vice president of production — 3rd level

General superintendent

Drill press foreman

RESPONSIBILITY REPORTING

$147,280

EXHIBIT 8-7

sponsibility, mainly service departments, which report directly to the vice-president would also be supported, as was the general superintendent's statement, by detailed statements of the costs of the respective areas.

Again one sees that the cost of the vice-president's own office is set forth in total and that when it is combined with the controllable costs of all the other areas of responsibility, one arrives at the total controllable costs for which the vice-president is held accountable. The productive labor has also been carried forward directly from the previous report. Undoubtedly the vice-president will also want to see the detailed statements supporting his summary.

In Exhibit 8-9 it is evident that the fourth level of reporting is a summary of departmental controllable costs. This report is prepared for the president and the general manager of the company. Here one notes that the total controllable costs of $254,705 for which the vice-president of production is held responsible, have been brought up to this top level as one of the major responsibility areas of the president and general manager.

Summary Report

The statement in Exhibit 8-10, which summarizes controllable costs by responsible departments, is the responsibility report for the top level of management, the president and general manager of the company. This statement concisely summarizes for the top executives the performance of the entire company with respect to controllable costs by comparing actual against budget by responsibility areas. If the system of responsibility reporting has been correctly tailored, these side captions will relate directly to the original organization chart. Remember that the major areas were the president and general manager, vice-president in charge of production, chief engineer, personnel manager, vice-president in charge of sales, and vice-president of finance. Also note that productive labor has again been carried forward from the previous statement as a separate item.

Finally, Exhibit 8-11 sets forth the complete buildup of controllable costs from the lowest level, which was the drill press department, up to the highest or top level of reporting.

EXHIBIT 8-8
ABC MANUFACTURING COMPANY
Factory Cost Summary
(Vice President of Production)

	Amount		(Over) or under Budget	
	This Month	Year to Date	This Month	Year to Date
Controllable expenses				
Vice president's office	$ 2,110	$ 12,030	($ 115)	$ 35
General superintendent's departments	24,525	147,280	(710)	(2,590)
Production control	1,235	7,570	(125)	(210)
Purchasing	1,180	7,045	95	75
Maintenance	3,590	18,960	(235)	245
Tool room	4,120	25,175	60	(320)
Inspection	2,245	13,680	80	(160)
Receiving, shipping, stores	3,630	22,965	(70)	(730)
Total	$42,635	$254,705	($1,020)	($3,655)

	Standard		Variance	
	This Month	Year to Date	This Month	Year to Date
Productive labor	$27,120	$161,970	$3,020	$5,130

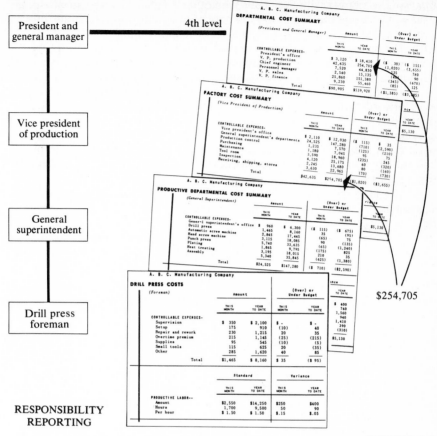

President and general manager

4th level

Vice president of production

General superintendent

Drill press foreman

RESPONSIBILITY REPORTING

$254,705

EXHIBIT 8-9

To review this buildup in detail, it will be recalled that we started with a statement prepared for the drill press department which set forth all of the controllable costs of operating the drill press department and compared these costs as originally budgeted with actual, showing the over and under budget in each case.

The total controllable costs of the drill press department were then carried forward into a statement for the general superintendent. When the total cost of the drill press department was combined with the costs of the other areas for which the general superintendent had responsibility, including the costs of running his own office, one arrived at the total controllable costs for which the general superintendent was responsible.

The total cost of the second level of responsibility was then carried forward in total as one of the areas of responsibility in the third level, which in this case was the vice-president in charge of production. Again when this total was combined with the cost of the other areas for which the vice-president was responsible, including the cost of operating his own office, one arrived at the total costs of the third level of responsibility.

The total of this third level was then carried forward as one of the departments in the top level summary where all expenses of the company were summarized by departments responsible for the incurrence of the costs.

The productive labor in each of these areas has been shown and carried forward from one level to the other. This buildup is not particularly complicated. It is basically simple, and one does not have to be an accountant to understand it. It should be enough to emphasize that what has been done is simply to have placed reporting of costs in phase with the responsibility for the incurrence of the costs. To say it another way, cost reporting has been put in phase with budgeting.

The ingredients of product costs are inherent in such a system of responsibility accounting, whether the company uses a system of job order costing, process costing, or some combination of the two.

The process of reshuffling these costs and blending them for purposes of determining product costs is relatively simple, but beyond the scope of this

EXHIBIT 8-10
ABC MANUFACTURING COMPANY
Departmental Cost Summary
(President and General Manager)

	Amount		(Over) or under Budget	
	This Month	Year to Date	This Month	Year to Date
Controllable expenses				
President's office	$ 3,120	$ 18,410	($ 30)	($ 155)
Vice president, production	42,635	254,705	(1,020)	(3,655)
Chief engineer	7,520	44,830	135	780
Personnel manager	2,540	15,135	(40)	90
Vice president, sales	25,860	151,380	(345)	(670)
Vice president finance	9,230	55,460	(85)	125
Total	$90,905	$539,920	($1,385)	($3,485)

	Standard		Variance	
	This Month	Year to Date	This Month	Year to Date
Productive labor	$27,120	$161,970	$3,020	$5,130

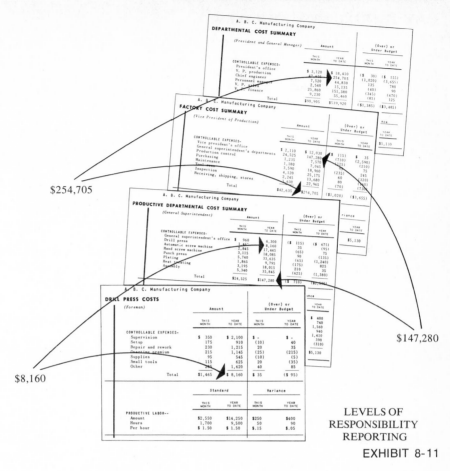

$254,705

$8,160

$147,280

LEVELS OF
RESPONSIBILITY
REPORTING

EXHIBIT 8-11

discussion. The important emphasis here is on the cost control aspects of the management function.

Summary

To summarize, then, responsibility accounting does not involve a drastic change in accounting theory or principles. It is for the most part a change in emphasis from product cost to the cost control aspects of accounting wherein the statements to management emphasize the control of costs by reporting and summarizing them on the basis of "who did it" before they are adjusted and blended for product cost purposes to obtain the conventional financial statements. To say it another way, it is a system which emphasizes the information that is useful to operating management and deemphasizes the accounting and bookkeeping aspects that clutter up so many of our financial statements today.

KEY WORDS AND PHRASES

control by domination   cost center
management by objectives   profit center
motivation   investment center
responsibility accounting   anchor chart

DISCUSSION QUESTIONS

1. Explain the relationship among division of labor, accountability, and control.
2. "To speak of executive control apart from performance standards or some plan of action is impossible." Comment.
3. Why do responsible people in an organization tend to accept budgetary control in theory but resist it in practice?
4. Discuss "control" in terms of management by objectives and management by domination.
5. Name and explain a few typical organizational objectives.
6. Name and comment upon a few personal objectives typical of an individual member of an organization.
7. List and comment on a few of the key conditions which are likely to frustrate the effectiveness of a budgetary control system.
8. List and comment upon some of the conditions usually found in a well-functioning system of budgetary control.
9. What are the key elements in the motivation of an effective manager? Explain.
10. How does a system of responsibility accounting implement the efforts of a manager to control by objectives?
11. How does responsibility accounting differ from conventional cost accounting?
12. How can an accounting system provide responsibility reports as well as conventional product cost reports and financial statements without the necessity of keeping "two sets of books"?
13. Does a responsibility reporting system provide for reporting all the costs incurred throughout the company in a given period, or just selected controllable costs?

PROBLEMS

8-1. A partial organizational chart of the Arrow Company is as follows:

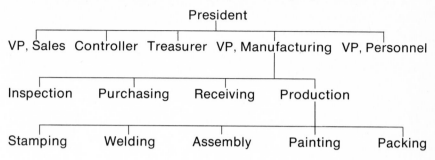

The costs associated with various offices and departments of the Arrow Company for the year just ended are as follows:

	Budget	Actual
Stamping department	$23,000	$22,500
Welding department	17,000	16,900
Assembly department	24,900	25,100
Painting department	10,600	11,100
Packing department	9,000	8,500
Inspection division	15,000	14,900
Purchasing division	22,000	22,900
Receiving division	24,000	24,500
Vice president, Sales	56,000	56,300
Controller	40,000	41,500
Treasurer	38,000	39,000
Vice president, Personnel	29,000	30,300
Administrative costs		
Production division	6,000	6,500
Vice president, Manufacturing	9,000	8,900
President	18,000	19,200

Required:
Prepare the responsibility accounting reports for the president, for the vice president, manufacturing, and for the supervisor of the production division.

8-2. John Peterson and Mike Lins are plant supervisors. John is a production supervisor and Mike a maintenance supervisor. They have been good friends and competitors ever since they played against each other on their high school football teams. John would like to see supervisors evaluated on the number of production units each produces, but Mike feels the only good comparison lies in the trend of historical cost figures.

Required:
1. What would be the purpose of comparing the performance of the two supervisors? What would be the purpose of comparing John with another production supervisor?

2. Do you think that all production supervisors could agree on a single basis of evaluation? Explain.
3. What are some alternatives to the use of a single basis of evaluation?

8-3.   Robert Anderson has just been appointed vice president, manufacturing, of the Arrow Company (see problem 8-1). The president of the company informs him that his first and most important responsibility will be to improve company profits for next year by 10 percent.

Required:
1. What alternatives does Anderson have in this situation?
2. Discuss the president's order from its motivational aspects.

8-4.   College professors are often evaluated by administrators in three areas — teaching, research, and community and university service.

Required:
1. As a student, which of these three areas do you consider most important?
2. If you were a department head interested in developing a nationally known faculty, which area would you consider most important?
3. What are some specific evaluation techniques which could be used in each of these three areas?
4. Comment briefly on each evaluation technique you have listed. How would it affect the professor's behavior if it were used as a basis for promotion?

8-5.†   George Johnson was hired on July 1, 1969, as assistant general manager of the Botel Division of Staple, Inc. It was understood that he would be elevated to general manager of the division on January 1, 1971, when the then-current general manager retired, and this was duly done. In addition to becoming acquainted with the division and the general manager's duties, Mr. Johnson was specifically charged with the responsibility for development of the 1970 and 1971 budgets. As general manager in 1971, he was, obviously, responsible for the 1972 budget.

The Staple Company is a multiproduct company which is highly decentralized. Each division is quite autonomous. The corporation staff approves division-prepared operating budgets but seldom makes major changes in them. The corporate staff actively participates in decisions requiring capital investment (for expansion or replacement) and makes the final decisions. The division management is responsible for implementing the capital program. The major method used by the Staple Corporation to measure division performance is contribution return on division net investment. The budgets presented here were approved by the corporation. Revision of the 1972 budget is not considered necessary even though 1971 actual departed from the approved 1971 budget.

BOTEL DIVISION (000 omitted)

	Actual			Budget	
Accounts	1969	1970	1971	1971	1972
Sales	1,000	1,500	1,800	2,000	2,400
Less division variable costs:					
Material and labor	250	375	450	500	600
Repairs	50	75	50	100	120
Supplies	20	30	36	40	48
Less division managed costs:					
Employee training	30	35	25	40	45
Maintenance	50	55	40	60	70
Less division committed costs:					
Depreciation	120	160	160	200	200
Rent	80	100	110	140	140
Total	600	830	871	1,080	1,223
Division net contribution	400	670	929	920	1,177
Division investment:					
Accounts receivable	100	150	180	200	240
Inventory	200	300	270	400	480
Fixed assets	1,590	2,565	2,800	3,380	4,000
Less: Accounts and wages payable	(150)	(225)	(350)	(300)	(360)
Net investment	1,740	2,790	2,900	3,680	4,360
Contribution return on net investment	23%	24%	32%	25%	27%

Required:
1. Identify Mr. Johnson's responsibilities under the management and measurement program described here.
2. Appraise the performance of Mr. Johnson in 1971.
3. Recommend to the president any changes in the responsibilities assigned to managers or in the measurement methods used to evaluate division management based upon your analysis.

(IMA adapted)

8-6. The Alton Company is going to expand its punch press department. It is about to purchase three new punch presses from Equipment Manufacturers, Inc. Equipment Manufacturers' engineers report that their mechanical studies indicate that for Alton's intended use, the output rate for one press should be 1,000 pieces per hour. Alton has very similar presses now in operation. At the present time, production from these presses averages 600 pieces per hour.

A study of the Alton experience shows the average is derived from the following individual outputs.

Worker	Daily Output
L. Jones	750
J. Green	750
R. Smith	600
H. Brown	500
R. Alters	550
G. Hoag	450
Total	3,600
Average	600

Alton management also plans to institute a standard cost accounting system in the very near future. The company engineers are supporting a standard based upon 1,000 pieces per hour, the accounting department is arguing for 750 pieces per hour, and the department supervisor is arguing for 600 pieces per hour.

Required:
1. What arguments would each proponent be likely to use to support each case?
2. Which alternative best reconciles the needs of cost control and the motivation of improved performance? Explain why you made that choice.

(IMA adapted)

8-7. The supervisor of the assembly department of the Esco Manufacturing Company received the following summary report on the department's activity in June:

	Allowed Cost	Incurred Cost	Over (under) Allowed
Direct labor	$ 7,920	$ 8,050	$130
Department burden	11,520	11,895	375
	$19,440	$19,945	$505

He took the report to one of the members of the controller's department. "Gee, I didn't think I had done so badly last month," he said. The controller's assistant replied, "Well, sit down and we'll check it." She noted the following:

Standards:
   Labor time—2 hours per unit of product
   Labor rate—$2.20 per hour
   Departmental burden rate—$3.20 per direct labor hour
Normal capacity: 2,000 units of product
Budget of departmental burden (at normal):

Variable	$ 8,000
Fixed	4,800
	$12,800

June production: 1,800 units of product
Direct labor hours worked in June: 3,500

Required:
As the controller's assistant, analyze the labor and burden variances. Assuming that the supervisor has no control of the wage rates paid in the department nor of the level of production volume, give an appraisal of his June performance.

8-8. A wildcat strike among the workers in the assembly department of the Electronic Components Division of Megalectric Corporation interrupted departmental operations in the second week in November 19x1. The divisional factory manager appealed to the manager of design engineering for temporary assistance in the crisis. The response to the appeal resulted in the manning of assembly operations in the department by fifteen junior design engineers for the two weeks that the regular workers were out. Normal operations were restored the first week in December.

The Megalectric Corporation paid its productive department supervisors an annual bonus based primarily on volume of production and control of costs. The latter was measured by the determination of certain variances from standard costs as revealed by the company's standard cost system.

The report for the assembly department at the end of November appeared as follows:

MEGALECTRIC CORPORATION
Electronic Components Division,
Supervisor: Joe Btszplk

	Assembly Department	
	Variance: (Over) Under	
	Month	Year to Date
Material usage	($ 650)	$ 200
Labor rate	(2,500)	(1,000)
Labor efficiency	(400)	600
Overhead spending	(150)	300
Overhead efficiency	(600)	200
Overhead capacity	(500)	(100)
Total variance	($4,800)	$ 200

The plant superintendent, the assembly supervisor's immediate supervisor, called him in shortly after the November reports were issued. "Tough luck, Joe. You had a pretty good bonus built up, but this month just about kills it."

"Whaddya mean? You ever try to get production from a bunch of slipstick jockeys? Why should two weeks of this kind of monkeyshines wipe out a whole year of good performance?"

"Now, Joe, take it easy. You know the system. The standards aren't tight—the budgets are fair. If you can't chalk up a pretty good record working with these, maybe you don't rate a bonus."

Required:
1. Discuss the merits of Joe's case.
2. How might the variances be explained?
3. In your opinion, is a bonus system such as the one used here likely to be effective? Any suggestions?
4. If the bonus is determined as 60 percent of what the supervisor saved the company, what would you recommend as a bonus for Joe through November?

8-9.† R. U. Kidding graduated from a leading Midwestern university with a liberal arts degree. Despite his lack of a business background, his uncle took him into his established business, the Containo Container Corporation. When his uncle retired, R. U. succeeded him as president. The corporation is a leading manufacturer of beer bottles. In addition to the bottles, they also must make the cartons and boxes in which the bottles are transported to the customer's brewery. They buy precut cardboard cartons direct from another manufacturer and only have to shape them.

One day in April the supervisor of the package department came into R. U.'s office and asked for a raise. He argued his point with figures from the first-quarter summary. He argued that he was operating below his budget in six of nine categories and was right on budget in another, and that he had saved the company $1,100 overall in only three months.

R. U. did not like the idea of handing out a raise, but at the same time he wanted to be fair with his supervisor. Since he did not have a business degree, the figures meant little to him, so he told the supervisor that he would discuss it with the company's accountant.

THE CONTAINO CONTAINER CORPORATION
Performance Report, Package Department
For Three Months Ended March 31, 19x6

	Budgeted, Fixed	Budgeted Variable, 5,000 DLH*	Budget Total	Actual	(Over) Under Budget
Direct material		$ 4,000	$ 4,000	$ 4,000	
Direct labor		20,000	20,000	19,750	$ 250
Indirect labor		10,000	10,000	9,500	500
Indirect material		2,000	2,000	2,800	(800)
Power	$1,500	6,000	7,500	8,500	(1,000)
Maintenance†	500	6,000	6,500	6,000	500
Depreciation	6,000		6,000	5,000	1,000
General burden		8,000	8,000	7,500	500
Scrap wastage		1,500	1,500	1,350	150
Total	$8,000	$57,500	$65,500	$64,400	$1,100

* Direct labor hours.
† Maintenance:

Material		$4,500	$4,500	$2,000	$2,500
Labor	$500	1,500	2,000	4,000	(2,000)
Total	$500	$6,000	$6,500	$6,000	$ 500

Required:

As the accountant, you are asked to examine the summary and tell Mr. Kidding just what the figures mean. Whether or not the supervisor gets a raise is more or less up to you. What would your decision be when confronted with the preceding performance report?

The direct material consists mainly of the precut cardboard. Indirect labor includes the supervisor's salary and the cost of getting the material to the workers. Indirect material consists mainly of wire and small motors for the stapling machines and glue for the gluing machines. General burden is applied equally to each department.

8-10. The personnel director at the Switchtronics Plant of General Journal, Inc., called in the supervisor of the automation department one day shortly after the beginning of the year.

"Elwood," she began, "we here at old Switcheroo are positively astonished at the improvement in cost control last year in your department. Up until last year, we felt that somehow you weren't really trying to be part of the team—somehow you weren't getting your shoulder to the wheel; somehow you weren't driving for that extra yard after you were stopped. But last year, Elwood, you turned the tide; you showed the stuff of which you're made; you scored when the chips were down; you reached back for that extra stuff—in a word, Elwood, you showed the mark of a true champion—you've proved to be a real competitor.

"Thank you, P. D." Elwood blushed modestly. "But you must realize my true motivation. Formerly I distrusted the company and my organizational superiors. Somehow their whole approach struck me more as management by domination than management by objectives. Somehow I failed to see the harmony between company objectives and my personal objectives. But that's all changed now, P. D. I see things in a different perspective: I realize that, basically, I am seeking stimulation and satisfaction, self-realization, growth and greater personal effectiveness, the recognition of my fellows, and identification with a worthwhile undertaking, in addition to reasonable compensation. All these goals I will achieve, ma'am, in the harmonious climate which the enlightened management of my company has established."

"Well spoken, Elwood," the personnel director beamed. "Your grateful company will not allow your positive attitude to go unrewarded."

In such a euphoric glow, Elwood returned to his office in the plant clutching his performance report with its gleaming gold star. It read:

	Current Year: 19x2			Last Year: 19x1		
	Actual	Budget	Variance	Actual	Budget	Variance
Direct labor				$120,000	$ 90,000	($30,000)
Indirect labor	$ 10,000	$ 9,500	$ (500)	80,000	60,000	(20,000)
Indirect material	12,000	10,000	(2,000)	45,000	35,000	(10,000)
Power	50,000	48,000	(2,000)	5,000	4,000	(1,000)
Maintenance	60,000	62,000	2,000	5,500	6,000	500
Depreciation	100,000	150,000	50,000	10,000	10,000	
Allocated general burden		5,000	5,000	15,000	10,000	(5,000)
Total	$232,000	$284,500	$52,500	$280,500	$215,000	($65,500)

Required:
Comment at some length on the reclamation of Elwood.

8-11. The supervisor of the welding department of the St. Joseph Manufacturing Company received the following report for the month of September:

	Budget	Actual	Variance
Welding labor	$42,000	$41,875	$ 125 F
Materials handling labor	3,200	5,950	2,750 U
Supplies	4,600	4,700	100 U
Power	3,900	6,100	2,200 U
Heat, light	1,000	1,050	50 U
Repairs	6,000	7,250	1,250 U
Depreciation on equipment	4,500	4,500	-0-
Insurance and taxes	2,100	2,050	50 F
Miscellaneous	500	395	105 F
Totals	$67,800	$73,870	$6,070 U

The welding department supervisor has been in charge of this department for only three months. A young and hardworking employee, he has experienced small favorable variances in the previous two months. He consulted the supervisor of the budget area and determined the following:

1. Total costs of operating the company's power plant are prorated to each department based on total labor costs in the various departments. There was a strike in the assembly department during September, which meant that the rest of the producing departments had to bear relatively more of the total costs.
2. The total costs of the repair department are prorated to the various departments on the basis of the amount of time repair department employees spend in each producing department.
3. The increase in materials handling labor costs was the result of one large order being reworked. This order had been sent back from the inspection department for rewelding. The materials handling costs had been charged to the welding department. The original welding job on this order was incorrect because of a mistake in the blueprints received from the engineering department.

The supervisor was quite disappointed in his findings. He felt that his efforts at keeping costs down were not being appreciated because of the way certain costs were being charged to his department. Do you agree with the supervisor? How should the above costs be treated in the monthly reports?

8-12. An important concept in management accounting is that of responsibility accounting.

Required:
1. Define the term "responsibility accounting."
2. What are the conditions that must exist for there to be effective responsibility accounting?
3. What benefits are said to result from responsibility accounting?
4. Listed below are three charges found on the monthly report of a division which manufactures and sells products primarily to outside companies. Division performance is evaluated by the use of return on investment, i.e., division profit divided by capital invested in the division. You are to state which, if any, of the following charges are consistent with the responsibility accounting concept. Support each answer with a brief explanation.
   a. A charge for general corporation administration at 10 percent of division sales.
   b. A charge for the use of the corporate computer facility. The charge is determined by taking actual annual computer department costs and allocating an amount to each user on the ratio of its use to total corporation use.
   c. A charge for goods purchased from another division. The charge is based upon the competitive market price for the goods.
      (IMA adapted)

8-13. The Fillep Company operates a standard cost system. The variances for each department are calculated and reported to the department manager. It is expected that the managers will use the information to improve their operations and will recognize that it is used by their superiors for performance evaluation.

Joan Smith was recently appointed manager of the assembly department of the company. She has complained that the system, as designed, is disadvantageous to her department. Included among the variances charged to the departments is one for rejected units. The inspection occurs at the end of the assembly department. The inspectors attempt to identify the cause of the rejection so that the department where the error occurred can be charged with it. Not all errors can be easily identified with a department. These are totaled and apportioned to the departments according to the number of identified errors. The variance for rejected units in each department is a combination of the errors caused by the department plus a portion of the unidentified causes of rejects.

Required:
1. Is Joan Smith's claim valid? Explain the reason(s) for your answer.
2. What would you recommend the company do to solve its problem with Joan Smith and her complaint?

(IMA adapted)

8-14. You are the supervisor in a manufacturing department that has been assigned a large number of workers and large amounts of equipment. You are paid a base salary that is very low compared with the pay for this type of work in other companies, but you also receive a monthly bonus. The bonus is computed as $500 each time the budget is met plus $2\frac{1}{2}$ percent of the amount under budget. No bonus is received if the budget is not met.

The department's experience has been as follows for the first six months of the current year:

	Jan.	Feb.	Mar.	Apr.	May	June
Budget	$100,000	$100,000	$ 99,500	$99,500	$99,000	$99,000
Actual	100,500	99,000	100,000	98,100	99,200	98,000
Variance	$ 500 U	$ 1,000 F	$ 500 U	$ 1,400 F	$ 200 U	$ 1,000 F
Bonus	-0-	$ 525	-0-	$ 535	-0-	$ 525

Required:
1. What would you do if had this information, were starting the job all over again from the beginning of the year, and wanted to increase the amount of your bonus?
2. What, if anything, would you recommend be done to the system if you are now promoted to a new job and are required to handle the bonus system in your old department?

8-15.† The Parsons Company compensates its field sales force on a commission and year-end bonus basis. The commission is 20 percent of standard gross margin (planned selling price less standard cost of goods sold) contingent upon collection of the account. Customer's credit is approved by the company's credit department. Price concessions are granted on occasion by the top sales management, but sales commissions are not reduced by the discount. A year-end bonus of 15 percent of commissions earned is paid to salespeople who equal or exceed their annual sales target. The annual sales target is usually established by applying approximately a 5 percent increase to the prior year's sales.

Required:
1. What features of this compensation plan would seem to be effective in motivating the salespeople to accomplish company goals of higher profits and return on investment? Explain why.
2. What features of this compensation plan would seem to be counter-effective in motivating the sales staff to accomplish the company goals of higher profits and return on investment? Explain why.

(IMA adapted)

8-16. The president of Taylor School Supply Company, a wholesaler, presents you with a comparison of distribution costs for two salespeople and wants to know if you think the sales compensation plan is working to the detriment of the company. He supplies you with the following data:

	Salespeople	
	McKinney	Sim
Gross sales	$247,000	$142,000
Sales returns	$17,000	$2,000
Cost of goods sold	$180,000	$85,000
Reimbursed expenses (e.g., entertainment)	$5,500	$2,100
Other direct charges (e.g., samples distributed)	$4,000	$450
Commission rate on gross sales dollars	5%	5%

Required:
1. The compensation plan encourages the salesperson to work to increase the measure of performance to which compensation is related. List the questionable sales practices that might be encouraged by basing commissions on gross sales.
2. *a.* What evidence that the compensation plan may be working to the detriment of the company can be found in the data?
   b. What other information should the president obtain before reaching definite conclusions about this particular situation? Why?

(AICPA adapted)

8-17.* Early in January 19x9, the cost report shown here was submitted to Mr.

Comparison of Manufacturing Costs, Metal Frame Department

	19x7	19x8	Variance, 19x8 over 19x7
Raw materials	$535,000	$616,000	$81,000
Direct labor	130,000	135,000	5,000
Department overhead:			
Indirect labor	50,000	10,000	(40,000)
Supervision	10,000	10,000	
Power	4,100	4,750	650
Depreciation	15,000	50,000	35,000
General burden	116,000	132,250	16,250
Total	$860,100	$958,000	$97,900

Peter Dawkins, president of the Dawkins Manufacturing Company. This report was for the frame department which was one of the primary producing departments in the company. Mr. Dawkins was alarmed by the report because of the increase in cost. He commented that the only area of efficiency seemed to be in the use of indirect labor. Mr. Dawkins requested an investigation of the situation, which produced the following additional information.

The department made two types of metal frames which were used in the construction industry. The primary difference in the types was their size. The larger size of frame, called the J frame, required more material than the small frame (S frame), but less direct labor time was required because of an automatic assembly process which had not yet been adapted to the small frames. The department supervisor said that the J frame required about two units of raw material (primarily metal stripping), whereas the S frame required only one unit. The supervisor indicated that these quantities were based on normal operating efficiency. An investigation of the storeroom records showed that 560,000 units of raw materials had been issued during 19x8, whereas 535,000 units had been issued during 19x7.

The direct labor requirement was the opposite of the raw material. The J frame required about one half the amount of labor time as did the S frame. The foreman estimated that, under normal working conditions, the department should produce about ten J frames per labor hour. The direct labor in the department was about the same insofar as the level of skill required, and the average wage rate per hour was $2.50. Failure to schedule work properly and failure to provide adequately for absenteeism (primarily the responsibility of the personnel department) sometimes resulted in a night shift which was paid a 10 percent premium. The policy of the company was to avoid night shift work if at all possible.

While the price of raw materials had gone up in 19x8 about 10 percent (a unit of raw material cost $1.00 in 19x7), the basic direct labor rate stayed about the same. An investigation of the payroll showed that about 52,000 direct labor hours were actually paid for during 19x8, while about 50,500 hours had been paid in 19x7. The actual direct labor rate did vary from the $2.50 rate because of some night shift work and also because in February 19x8 some workers were transferred into the frame department to cover excess absenteeism due to a mild influenza epidemic. These transferred workers received a wage rate somewhat higher than the average for the frame department.

An investigation of the general burden revealed that this cost was an assigned cost. The company's practice was to assign the general administration burden (the cost of such departments as accounting, personnel, general factory management, engineering, etc.) to producing departments on the basis of total direct and indirect labor dollars (excluding supervision). The total general burden for the company was $575,000 in 19x8 and $580,000 in 19x7. The total direct and indirect labor cost for all producing departments was $900,000 in 19x7 and $630,000 in 19x8.

During 19x8, the company purchased and installed some portable conveyors which made it possible to release several material handlers who made up the largest element of indirect labor. The desirability of the equipment had been assessed by using a ten-year economic life, and this period was chosen for depreciation purposes. A full year's depreciation had been included for 19x8.

The power cost was assigned to the frame department by using the unit cost of power as determined by the power service department. In 19x7, this cost was 0.8 cents ($0.008) per kw-hr, whereas the rate went up to 0.9 cents in 19x8 because of an increase in the cost of fuel used to make the power. The foremen of the power department and the frame department agreed that power consumption was highly dependent on direct labor hours. The frame department foreman said that a fairly good rule of thumb that had been used in the past was ten kw-hrs of power for every hour of direct labor. He said that if power were used efficiently this rate of consumption should be attainable.

A check of the production reports showed that production of completed frames for each of the two years was as follows:

	19x7	19x8
S frames	150,000	150,000
J frames	180,000	200,000

Required:

1. Explain, insofar as possible, the significance of and reasons for the increase in costs.
2. In general, how would you rate the efficiency of the metal frame department in 19x8?
3. Can you suggest a better way of reporting costs for the department in the future?

8-18. The Renown Manufacturing Company manufactures and distributes an extremely wide variety of products. It manufactures products for warehouse stock and to customer specifications. The products of the company are sold to customers classified as domestic, commercial, and industrial.

The company has ten different plants located in the area bounded by Chicago, St. Louis, Richmond, and Boston.

The chief operating executive at each plant is the works manager. Each works manager is responsible to and directly under the vice president in charge of production and the general superintendent, both of whom are located at the home office.

Because of the magnitude of this concern and the diversity of its products, production problems of an infinite variety arise daily at every plant. For many years these problems were handled at each plant by an operating policy committee consisting of the works manager, production engineer, departmental engineers, and shop supervisors. In the majority of instances, the production problems were satisfactorily solved, but large losses occurred recently at several plants on many jobs. As a result, the vice president in charge of production called a meeting of all the works managers to determine causes and reasons for what the vice president considered a defective work and production loss problem that was increasing at an alarming rate.

After a two-day conference, it was brought to light that the two principal reasons for this situation were (1) shop supervisor dissatisfaction and (2) the lack of effectiveness of responsibility accounting at shop and other supervisory levels. The first had arisen because in the past two years shop supervisor salaries had not increased proportionately with the earnings of the laborers. The second reason seemed to be the inadequacy of the production cost control, resulting from the department head's lack of understanding of the nature, use, purpose, and value of the direct labor and overhead expense cost reports. A standard production cost system had been put into use which had displaced the exclusive use of an actual production cost system prior to that time.

At the termination of the two-day conference, the vice president in charge of production said that the biggest problem in management was that of organization, personnel, and industrial relations; and that the biggest problem in factory accounting was educating the supervisors and department heads as to the value and use of cost reports to enable them to exercise a greater degree of cost control.

Four of the works managers attending the conference stated that the experience at their respective plants had been that the supervisors and department heads had not been sold on the new standard cost system because they thought that the standard cost reports were too complicated. They said that this was true even though they had attended ten hours of meetings on the subject of the value and interpretation of standard cost reports at the time the new cost system had become operative. Five other works managers said that the supervisor-salary problem and the inauguration of the new standard cost system seemed to be a combination that had developed an apathetic attitude in the minds and actions of the supervisors and department heads. No action was taken at this conference as to the possible remedy of the situation. However, for the next meeting of the general executive committee, the vice president in charge of production asked that this problem be given first place on the agenda. The general executive committee included the president, vice president in charge of production, secretary, treasurer, controller, general superintendent, and general sales manager.

At the next meeting of the general executive committee, the vice president presented a summary of the two-day conference of the works managers. Among the remedies suggested was one for the development of a bonus incentive plan. The vice president said that a sliding-scale bonus based upon degree of good production attainment or on increasing net profit would give the department heads and supervisors an incentive to improve production and control production costs. This suggestion appealed to the president, who then requested that each member of the executive committee give the idea further concentrated thought and that another general executive committee meeting be held two weeks later for sole consideration of the idea. The vice president added that four factors should be given consideration in developing the bonus idea, namely, the basis for the bonus, the participants, the proportionate shares, and the method of payment.

At the next meeting of the general executive committee, three bonus plans were presented. Plan I was developed by the vice president in charge of production. Plan II was designed by the general superintendent. Plan III was planned by the controller. Each of the three plans is outlined with regard to basic details:

Plan I
1. Basis for determination of bonus amount payable to participants. The sum of the following:
    a. Eighty percent of the dollar amount of the favorable controllable overhead expense variance (saving between budget allowance and actual overhead expense) as determined for each specific manufacturing and service department.
    b. Forty percent of the dollar amount of the favorable direct labor time variance (saving between standard allowed direct labor cost and actual direct labor cost) on direct labor operations as determined for each specific manufacturing department.
2. Participants in bonus payments:
    Salaried personnel as named in the supervisory classification presently in existence.
3. Proportionate shares of participants:
    a. The exact amounts of the shares to be determined in separate committee meetings, the personnel of which would consist of the vice president in charge of production, the works manager, and the supervisory personnel at each specific department.
    b. The personnel of each department to share only in the bonus earned in that department.
    c. Some examples of the participants and their proportionate

shares in the bonus plan in four selected departments at a given plant might be as follows:

	Bonus Distribution among Departments (in Percent)			
	Manufacturing		Service	
Position	100 Form- ing	107 Trim- ming	201 Mainte- nance	204 Store- room
General supervisor	15			
Supervisor		40		
Assistant supervisor, first turn	15	40		
Assistant supervisor, second turn	15			
Assistant supervisor, third turn	15			
Chief inspector	10			
Inspector		20		
Assistant inspector, first turn	10			
Assistant inspector, second turn	10			
Assistant inspector, third turn	10			
Maintenance engineer			$66\frac{2}{3}$	
Assistant maintenance engineer			$33\frac{1}{3}$	
Storekeeper				75
Assistant storekeeper				25
	100	100	100	100

4. Method of payment of bonus:
   a. One-half of the bonus earned each month to be paid on the 15th of the following month.
   b. The remaining one-half of the bonus earned each month to be placed in a reserve, which would be reduced by any unfavorable controllable overhead variances or unfavorable direct labor time variances that might occur in some months.
   c. Any favorable balance in the reserve at the end of the fiscal year to be paid to participants fourteen days after the end of the fiscal year.
   d. Any unfavorable balance in the reserve at the end of the fiscal year not to be carried over to the next fiscal year.

Plan II
1. Basis for determination of bonus amounts payable to participants: the sum of *a* and *b*:
   a. One hundred percent of the dollar amount of the favorable controllable overhead expense variance of all manufacturing departments combined.
   b. One hundred percent of the dollar value of the favorable direct labor time variance of all manufacturing departments combined.
   c. The total bonus of all departments to be pooled for distribution to all participants in all manufacturing departments.
2. Participants in bonus payments:
   Salaried personnel of manufacturing departments only as named in the supervisory classification presently in existence.

3. Proportionate shares of participants:

    a. Each staff and supervisory executive to be point-graded as to his or her relative importance in production and cost control, the point grades to be determined by a special committee for the purpose.

    b. Each staff and supervisory executive in all departments to receive a pro rata share of the total combined bonuses earned in all departments in relation to the combined total points in all departments.

    c. Some examples of the participants and their proportionate shares in the bonus plan in four selected departments of a given plant might be as follows:

Bonus Distribution among Departments
(in Points)
Manufacturing

Position	Total Points	100 Form-ing	107 Trim-ming	109 Test-ing	111 Packag-ing
General supervisor		6			6
Supervisor			5	5	5
Assistant supervisor, first turn		4	4	4	4
Assistant supervisor, second turn		4			4
Assistant supervisor, third turn		4			4
Chief inspector		3			
Inspector			2		
Assistant inspector, first turn		1			
Assistant inspector, second turn		1			
Assistant inspector, third turn		1			
Total points	67	24	11	9	23

Explanation: General supervisor of department 100 would be entitled to $\frac{6}{67}$ of the pooled bonus available; supervisor of department 107, entitled to $\frac{5}{67}$ of pooled bonus.

4. Method of payment of bonus:

    a. The favorable variance available for bonus distribution in each month would be paid in its entirety on the 15th of the following month.

    b. If an unfavorable variance resulted in any month, no bonus would be payable for that month.

Plan III

1. Basis for determination of bonus amount payable to participants:

    a. Product division basis:

        The final annual net profit, after deductions for federal and state corporate income taxes, as identified with three divisions—domestic products, commercial products, and industrial products—is the basis for determining the amount of the bonus, payable on a sliding-scale basis as follows:

Net Profit as Stated		Bonus on Annual Base Salary
Under	$ 499,999	1%
$ 500,000–	999,999	2%
1,000,000–	1,499,999	3%
1,500,000–	1,999,999	4%
2,000,000–	2,999,999	5%
Over	3,000,000	6%

    b. No bonus to be paid unless dividends have been declared from current year's profits on the preferred stock and on the common stock to the amount of the minimum regular $1 a share dividend.

2. Participants in bonus payments:

All management and supervisory salaried employees from president to supervisors as specified in the supervisory classification as listed at present.

3. Proportionate shares of participants:

    a. Each of the three product group divisions (domestic, commercial, and industrial) will then divide its respective bonus to the operating divisions on the relative weights of four factors, as determined by a bonus committee headed by the general superintendent, as follows:

(1) Profit contribution	50%
(2) Factory overhead expense favorable controllable variance and direct labor time variance	30
(3) Management development	15
(4) Position and performance in the industry	5
	100%

    b. Each operating division, in turn, will divide its allowed bonus to the division personnel on the basis of their development, progress, and economies as observed by a special bonus committee in each plant headed by the works manager; for example:

    (1) Manufacturing personnel factors:

        (a) Factory overhead expense favorable controllable variance

        (b) Direct labor time favorable variance

        (c) Personnel management ability

        (d) Defective work loss control

    (2) Sales personnel factors:

        (a) Volume of sales achieved

        (b) Position in the industry

        (c) Personnel management ability

        (d) Favorable marketing variable expense control

    (3) Accounting and other administrative service personnel factors:

        (a) Simplification of systems and paper work

        (b) Presentation of accounting and cost reports on dates scheduled

        (c) Cooperation with manufacturing and sales departments

        (d) Favorable variable expense control of accounting and other administrative departments

4. Method of payment of bonus:

Bonus payable as computed for each year to be made available to participants on or before March 15 of the following year; as specified

by participants, bonus to be paid either in cash or in payment on
subscribed capital stock issues of company either at par value or at
current market value of no-par stock.

The merits and disadvantages of each of the three bonus plans were
discussed at four meetings of the general executive committee before
final action was taken, at the last meeting, on a bonus plan to be adopted.

Required:
Which plan should be adopted, if any? Support your conclusion with a
thorough analysis of all relevant factors.

TECHNIQUES
FOR SPECIAL
MANAGEMENT
DECISIONS

CHAPTER

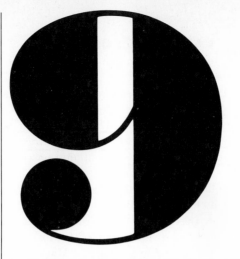

VARIABLE COSTING

THE PLAN OF THIS CHAPTER
One important result of building cost-volume-profit analysis directly into the accounting system is to permit the construction of an income statement which highlights the contribution margin. In discussing one method of costing that builds cost-volume-profit analysis into the accounting system, the following topics will be taken up:

The distinction between the absorption and variable costing notions of product cost

How reported net income differs under the two methods of costing when production differs from sales volume in a given period

The advantages of variable costing for certain management purposes

The current controversy over variable costing

MEANING OF VARIABLE COSTING

One of the key determinants of business profit is the volume at which operations are carried on. The more effectively a firm utilizes its capacity, the more thinly the cost of this capacity is spread over the resulting units of product, and the greater is the net profit realized per unit.

Variable costing is a method of recording and reporting costs which regards as product costs only those manufacturing costs which tend to vary directly with volume of activity. Conventional costing, it will be recalled, considers all manufacturing costs—fixed as well as variable—as product costs.

One of the difficulties in discussing the subject of variable costing stems from the terminology employed. Because it is still a comparatively new area in the accounting field, there is no single set of terms to which everyone completely agrees. The term "direct costing," for example, is probably used more widely than the term "variable costing." "Marginal costing" is another term which emphasizes the contribution concept. The expression "variable costing" is preferable, however, because it is more accurate. Direct costing implies that only direct material and direct labor are to be included as product costs. However, in most cases where the technique is employed, variable overhead is also considered part of product cost. Marginal costing focuses on the other side of the equation: the margin which results from subtracting variable costs from the revenue factor.

Another reason for preferring the term "variable costing" lies in the fact that the primary purpose in the system is to separate costs according to their behavior in relation to volume. Some nonvariable costs, such as engineering salaries, machinery and tool depreciation, or plant manager's salary, can be identified as "direct" with such segments of a company as a product division or a branch plant, but they are not classed as product costs under variable costing.

There is also some difficulty in the terminology describing nonvariable costs. The terms "fixed costs," "capacity costs," and "period costs" have been used variously to describe the class of factory overhead costs typified by such items as factory rent, plant superintendent's salary, and property taxes. "Period cost" denotes the fact that most of such costs are incurred as a function of a period of time rather than of volume of production. "Capacity cost" conveys a notion of costs incurred to provide a certain capacity to produce, which explains their stability and independence of any short-term changes in volume of activity.

Probably the most misleading of the terms descriptive of the nonvariable type of cost is "fixed cost." The most common and logical impression it conveys to the nonaccountant is that such costs do not change. Obviously, such is not the case—the plant superintendent may be granted a raise; the taxing body may raise the millage rate (costs can change upward as well as downward); or a decision to reduce capacity may result in discontinuing the rental of a building. In fact, many fixed costs are "programmed" or "discretionary" costs, which can be changed at management's wishes. Examples of such costs are advertising, preventive maintenance, research and development, employee education, and travel.

In this book, however, the term "fixed cost" is used, despite its inaccuracy, to describe nonvariable costs. Because it is by far the most commonly used of these terms, confusion might result if we used an otherwise more preferable one. The term "period cost" will refer to those costs which are not considered product costs.

VARIABLE AND ABSORPTION COSTING COMPARED

As a method of matching expense against revenue for a fiscal period, variable costing differs from the conventional method, described earlier in the book, in which fixed factory overhead is *absorbed* into (i.e., applied to) product costs. The conventional method (generally known as *absorption costing*) regards unit product cost as consisting of direct material, direct labor, variable factory overhead, and fixed factory overhead. Variable costing excludes the fixed overhead and limits product costs to the variable cost elements. Product costs, in turn, follow the units of product into either cost of goods sold or inventory, depending on whether the period's production was sold or not during the period.

Under absorption costing, fixed factory overhead incurred in any period's production is identified with the production of that period; under variable costing, such incurred fixed overhead is identified with the sales of that period, since it is not considered a part of product cost but is written off entirely against operations of the period. Therefore, in any period in which *production* volume differs from *sales* volume, the net income reported under variable costing will differ from that reported under absorption costing.

A simple example with figures may help clarify the difference. Suppose a company regularly incurs fixed factory overhead of $1,000 per month. In March, 1,000 units of product were *produced* but only 900 units were *sold*. Assume that all other costs matched to March revenue amounted to $24,000 and that the revenue from the sale of 900 units was $27,000. Under absorption costing, the net income would be determined as follows:

Net sales		$27,000
Fixed factory overhead (900/1,000 × $1,000)	$ 900	
All other costs	24,000	
Total costs		24,900
Net income for March		$ 2,100

Under variable costing the net income would be determined thus:

Net sales		$27,000
Fixed factory overhead (incurred)	$ 1,000	
All other costs	24,000	
Total costs		25,000
Net income for March		$ 2,000

Why $100 more net income under absorption than under variable costing? Revenue for the period is the same under both methods of reporting. The difference, then, lies in $100 less cost recognized in March under absorption costing. All other costs being the same, the difference is in the amount of fixed factory overhead cost written off in March operations.

Since $1,000 of such fixed cost was incurred (and written off under variable costing), the question comes down to this: What happened to the other $100 of fixed factory overhead under absorption costing? Ask another logical question: What happened to the 100 units produced that were not sold? The answer is the same for both: They remained in the *ending inventory*.

Since fixed factory overhead is considered a product cost (at $1 per unit in March) under absorption costing, the $1,000 incurred in March attaches to the 1,000 units produced in March. Thus the $900 attaching to the 900 units sold was written off against March revenue, and $100 attaching to the 100 units added to inventory remained in the inventory value at the end of March.

Under variable costing, the fixed factory overhead is considered a cost of the period and does not attach to units of product. Thus no part of it will be deferred in inventory. All of it will be matched against revenue in the period in which incurred, regardless of sales or production volume. In this case, it would not matter whether sales had been 500, 1,000, or 1,500 units; it would not matter what level of volume the production had reached within the relevant range established by $1,000 per month fixed cost: the $1,000 will be written off as incurred.

DIFFERENCES IN VOLUME OF SALES AND PRODUCTION

A schematic view of the similarities and differences between variable and absorption costing is shown in Exhibit 9-1. Here the major cost elements are seen to be the same under both methods of costing. The sole difference between variable and absorption costing lies in the treatment of fixed factory overhead as period cost under the former and as product cost under the latter.

Before going into detailed examples, it may be useful to examine the basic nature of the differences between the two costing methods in terms of their effect on income reporting. Most manufacturing concerns have some fixed overhead in their cost structure. If all their overhead costs were variable, the results as reported under variable and absorption costing would be identical. Obviously, the following discussion does not apply to the unlikely firm which has no fixed overhead costs.

Since fixed factory overhead incurred is identified with production under absorption costing and is written off to sales under variable costing, it follows that there will be *no difference* in net income reported under the two methods when the sales volume and the production volume in a period are *equal*.

Hence, there are basically only two sets of conditions which cause a difference in the reported net income for the same period under the two costing methods:

1. Production exceeds sales volume.
2. Sales exceed production volume.

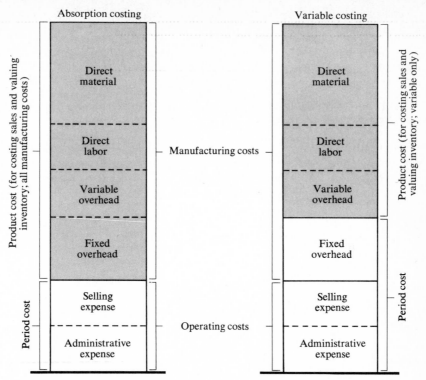

Note: Shaded areas indicate cost elements included as inventoriable product cost.

EXHIBIT 9-1   Schematic comparison of absorption and variable costing

Under the first stated set of conditions (production greater than sales), there will be an increase of units in inventory—ending over beginning. Under the second, the reverse will hold—the number of units in inventory will be *reduced* during the period.

If we remember that fixed factory overhead is considered product cost under absorption costing, then, under condition (1), the portion of such fixed overhead attaching to the period's production which stays in the ending inventory (the excess of production over sales) is deferred until some later period. In this case, the cost of goods sold is relieved of part of the incurred cost, making the net income for the period *higher* than that reported under variable costing.

When goods are sold out of beginning inventory (sales exceeding production), as in condition (2), some of the fixed factory overhead cost from a preceding period is added to that incurred in the current period to arrive at this period's cost of goods sold. In this situation, the net income reported under absorption costing will be *less* than that under variable costing.

In summary, then, two generalizations can be made concerning the nature of the differences between net income reported under the two costing methods:

1. When production exceeds sales volume, net income as reported under absorption costing will be *greater* than under variable costing.

2. When sales exceed production volume, net income as reported under absorption costing will be *less* than under variable costing.

VARIABLE AND ABSORPTION COSTING COMPARED: AN ILLUSTRATION

Perhaps the differences between the results reported under variable and absorption costing for the same firm in the same periods can best be understood if we examine a set of simple examples.

Let us assume that the Abso-Var Company, a small, single-product manufacturer, produces one model of a large steel wastebasket. In successive years, 19x1 through 19x4, the Abso-Var Company experienced fluctuations between production and sales volume as follows:

	In Units	
Year	Sales	Production
19x1	100,000	100,000
19x2	100,000	110,000
19x3	90,000	110,000
19x4	110,000	80,000
Total—four years	400,000	400,000

The Abso-Var Company operates under a standard cost system. Its normal capacity for annual production is 100,000 units of product. Sales price per unit of product is $1.

Manufacturing costs *at normal capacity* are budgeted as follows:

	Total	Per Unit
Material	$40,000	$0.40
Labor	15,000	0.15
Variable overhead	10,000	0.10
Fixed overhead	15,000	0.15
Total manufacturing cost	$80,000	$0.80
Total variable manufacturing cost	$65,000	$0.65

None of the above price, cost, or normal-capacity factors changes over the four-year period.[1] The figure of 80 cents per unit total manufacturing cost will be used to value inventory under absorption costing, and 65 cents per unit of variable manufacturing cost will be used for variable costing.

---

[1] In effect, this chapter assumes fixed overhead remains constant from period to period. If this is not the case, then the difference in income reported under the two methods will depend on the inventory method used (LIFO, FIFO, average, standard costs, etc.) as well as on the relationship between sales and production. See Ijiri, Jaedicke, and Livingstone, "The Effect of Inventory Costing Methods on Full and Direct Costing," *Journal of Accounting Research*, Spring 1965, pp. 63–74.

Sales Equal Production

In the year 19x1, sales and production were equal — 100,000 units each. Assume beginning inventory to be 10,000 units; fixed factory overhead incurred, $15,000; and selling and administrative expenses incurred, $10,000.

Exhibit 9-2 reports the results of operations for the year 19x1 on an absorption costing basis; Exhibit 9-3 reports the same data on a variable costing basis. Three important points stand out in the comparison of the two income statements:

1. The reported net income is the same under both methods.

2. Both beginning and ending inventories show a higher valuation under absorption than under variable costing.

3. The form of the income statement is different under the two methods.

The explanation for (1) is quite simple, as we reflect on the basic cause of differences between the two costing methods: Production and sales were equal, and there was no change between beginning and ending inventories.

The explanation for the higher inventory valuations under absorption costing mentioned in (2) lies in the inclusion of the standard fixed overhead factor of 15 cents in the 80-cent unit product cost factor under absorption costing. The value attaching to 10,000 units in inventory (both beginning and ending in 19x1) under absorption costing at 80 cents each was $8,000; under variable costing, the same 10,000 units were valued at only 65 cents each, a total of $6,500. The difference of $1,500 can be identified as 10,000 units at 15 cents per unit.

An interesting new form for reporting income statement data is introduced in Exhibit 9-3. It will be recalled from our original study of cost-volume-profit analysis that the variable margin between sales and variable costs was

EXHIBIT 9-2
ABSO-VAR COMPANY
Income Statement, Absorption Costing Basis
For the Year 19x1

Net sales			$100,000
Cost of goods sold:			
Beginning inventory (10,000 units @ $0.80)		$ 8,000	
Add:			
Direct material	$40,000		
Direct labor	15,000		
Variable overhead	10,000		
Fixed overhead	15,000	80,000	
Total cost of goods available		$88,000	
Less: Ending inventory (10,000 units @ $0.80)		8,000	80,000
Gross margin			$ 20,000
Less: Selling and administrative			10,000
Net income for period			$ 10,000

EXHIBIT 9-3
ABSO-VAR COMPANY
Income Statement, Variable Costing Basis
For the Year 19x1

Net sales			$100,000
Cost of goods sold:			
Beginning inventory (10,000 units @ $0.65)		$ 6,500	
Add:			
Direct material	$40,000		
Direct labor	15,000		
Variable overhead	10,000	65,000	
Total cost of goods available		$71,500	
Less: Ending inventory (10,000 units @ $0.65)		6,500	65,000
Contribution margin			$ 35,000
Less: Fixed cost:			
Manufacturing overhead		$15,000	
Selling and administrative		10,000	25,000
Net income for period			$ 10,000

named the contribution margin, because it represented that portion of the period's revenue which remained, after variable costs were met, as the contribution to fixed costs and profit for the period.

In Exhibit 9-3, the form of the income statement has been adapted to emphasize the contribution margin, the variable nature of cost of goods sold, and the role of fixed costs in the determination of net income. In this example it is assumed, for simplicity's sake, that all selling and administrative expense is fixed. In practice, some is variable. Where this condition exists, it is customary to deduct such variable selling and administrative expense from revenue along with variable manufacturing cost in arriving at contribution margin. It is also common in such cases to show the difference between sales and variable cost of goods sold as manufacturing contribution margin (or manufacturing variable margin) before deducting variable selling and administrative expense to arrive at contribution margin. In effect, the variable costing income statement is cost-volume-profit analysis "built in" to basic accounting.

In comparing such an income statement with the one prepared on an absorption costing basis (Exhibit 9-2), it is important to recognize that the conventional gross margin is quite different, in both magnitude and concept, from the manufacturing contribution margin of variable costing. Once again, the difference arises out of the differing treatment of fixed factory overhead between the two methods: gross margin under absorption costing has been *reduced* by the amount of fixed overhead absorbed in the cost of goods sold for the period; manufacturing contribution margin under variable costing will always be *larger* than gross margin, since variable cost of sales excludes fixed overhead.

Production Exceeds Sales

The next comparison of net income reporting under absorption and variable costing considers the differences which occur when production volume exceeds

EXHIBIT 9-4
ABSO-VAR COMPANY
Income Statement, Absorption Costing Basis
For the Year 19x2

Net sales			$100,000
Cost of goods sold:			
Beginning inventory (10,000 units × $0.80)		$ 8,000	
Add:			
Direct material (110,000 × $0.40)	$44,000		
Direct labor (110,000 × $0.15)	16,500		
Variable overhead (110,000 × $0.10)	11,000		
Fixed overhead (110,000 × $0.15)	16,500	88,000	
Total standard cost of goods available		$96,000	
Less: Ending inventory (20,000 × $0.80)		16,000	
Total standard cost of goods sold		$80,000	
Less: Overabsorbed fixed overhead		1,500	
Actual cost of goods sold			78,500
Gross margin			$ 21,500
Less: Selling and administrative			10,000
Net income for period			$ 11,500

EXHIBIT 9-5
ABSO-VAR COMPANY
Income Statement, Variable Costing Basis
For the Year 19x2

Net sales			$100,000
Cost of goods sold:			
Beginning inventory (10,000 units × $0.65)		$ 6,500	
Add:			
Direct material (110,000 × $0.40)	$44,000		
Direct labor (110,000 × $0.15)	16,500		
Variable overhead (110,000 × $0.10)	11,000	71,500	
Total cost of goods available		$78,000	
Less: Ending inventory (20,000 × $0.65)		13,000	65,000
Contribution margin			$ 35,000
Less: Fixed cost:			
Manufacturing overhead		$15,000	
Selling and administrative		10,000	25,000
Net income for period			$ 10,000

sales. Our schedule of sales and production for the Abso-Var Company indicated that 110,000 units were produced in 19x2 but only 100,000 were sold, with a resulting increase of 10,000 units in inventory. Exhibits 9-4 and 9-5 present the results of operations for 19x2 on an absorption costing basis and a variable costing basis, respectively.

Comparison of the income statements for 19x2 with their counterparts in 19x1 reveals the following:

1. The total incurred manufacturing costs were greater in 19x2 than in 19x1.

2. The absorption costing basis reflects an overabsorbed fixed cost of $1,500 in 19x2.

3. The net income for the period 19x2 was $1,500 greater on the absorption costing basis than on a variable costing basis ($11,500 − $10,000).

The increase in total incurred manufacturing costs cited in item (1) is measured in the *variable* elements of cost which had to be incurred to produce 10,000 more units than had been made in 19x1.

In the case of (2), a simple review of the mechanics of a standard cost system on an absorption costing basis should provide the reason. Fixed factory overhead is absorbed into production on the basis of a standard unit cost established at the normal capacity volume. In the case of the Abso-Var Company, that rate is 15 cents, having been established at a normal capacity of 100,000 units. In 19x2, 110,000 units were produced, absorbing $16,500 of fixed overhead at the standard rate. However, only $15,000 fixed overhead was actually incurred, leaving it overabsorbed to the extent of $1,500 (10,000 units in excess of normal × 15 cents).

It will be noted that this overabsorbed overhead is deducted from *standard* cost of goods sold in arriving at *actual* cost of goods sold, thus canceling out its effect on actual gross margin. The effect of this reporting device is to demonstrate that production was carried on during the period at a volume higher than normal, before adjusting cost of goods sold to an actual basis.

Let it be emphasized in this regard *that over- or underabsorbed overhead is not a factor causing a difference in reported net income between absorption and variable costing.*[2]

Comparison of Exhibits 9-2 and 9-4 shows that net income for 19x2 on an absorption costing basis was $1,500 greater than it had been in 19x1. The *sole reason* for this is that 15 cents per unit of fixed overhead had followed 10,000 units of production into the ending inventory.

EXHIBIT 9-6
ABSO-VAR COMPANY
Analysis of Inventory Change,
Absorption and Variable Cost Valuations
Compared for the Year 19x2

	Beginning Inventory	Ending Inventory	Increase
Units	10,000	20,000	10,000
Absorption basis−$0.80/unit	$ 8,000	$16,000	$ 8,000
Variable basis−$0.65/unit	6,500	13,000	6,500
Difference−fixed cost − $0.15/unit	$ 1,500	$ 3,000	$ 1,500

[2] If over- or underabsorbed overhead is deferred on interim (e.g., monthly) balance sheets instead of being written off on the income statement, an additional difference is created. This is a spurious difference, however, and is not based on fundamental absorption or variable cost methods.

Exhibit 9-6 presents a somewhat more detailed examination of this change. The beginning inventory of 10,000 units contained $1,500 of fixed cost on an absorption basis; ending inventory of 20,000 units contained $3,000 of the same, the additional $1,500 being attached to the 10,000 units produced and not sold in 19x2; this came out of $15,000 fixed overhead incurred in 19x2; the remaining $13,500 was written off in cost of goods sold in 19x2. Under variable costing, the entire $15,000 was written off against income. The analysis of this difference in fixed cost on the respective income statements is shown in Exhibit 9-7.

EXHIBIT 9-7
ABSO-VAR COMPANY
Analysis of Difference in Fixed Cost Recognized as Expense in 19x2,
Absorption and Variable Costing Compared

Standard manufacturing fixed overhead — absorption basis (110,000 units @ $0.15)	$16,500
Less: Overabsorbed fixed overhead (10,000 @ $0.15)	1,500
Fixed overhead incurred	$15,000
Add: Fixed overhead in beginning inventory (10,000 @ $0.15)	1,500
Fixed overhead in goods available for sale	$16,500
Less: Fixed overhead in ending inventory (20,000 @ $0.15)	3,000
Fixed overhead in cost of goods sold — absorption basis	$13,500
Fixed overhead incurred — written off to income — variable basis	15,000
Difference — lower cost, higher profit — absorption basis	($ 1,500)

To summarize, when production exceeds sales volume, the net income reported under absorption costing will exceed that reported under variable costing. *The difference will be the amount of fixed overhead cost attributable to the unsold production of the period which is deferred in the ending inventory.*

Sales Exceed Production

We observe that, in 19x4, sales amounted to 110,000 units, but production dropped to 80,000, causing inventory to decline by 30,000 units over the year. From what we already know about what causes the difference in reported net income between absorption and variable costing, we correctly infer that this year it will be less under absorption than under variable costing. Moreover, the difference will amount to $4,500, since 30,000 units were sold from inventory, carrying with them 15 cents each of capacity cost deferred from an earlier period.

Exhibits 9-8 and 9-9 indicate the accuracy of these inferences. These exhibits contain comparative income data reported under both absorption and variable costing for the four years 19x1 through 19x4, under the varying conditions of sales and production volume set forth at the beginning of this example. For greater ease in comparison, the selling and administrative expenses (which are the same for both) have been eliminated on both forms, with the income statement ending at the gross-margin level. A gross-margin figure is derived on the variable costing statement merely by deducting fixed factory overhead incurred from the contribution margin.

EXHIBIT 9-8
ABSO-VAR COMPANY
Comparative Income Statement, Absorption Costing Basis
Four Years, 19x1 through 19x4

	19x1	19x2	19x3	19x4	Total
Units:					
Net sales	100,000	100,000	90,000	110,000	400,000
Production	100,000	110,000	110,000	80,000	400,000
Net sales	$100,000	$100,000	$ 90,000	$110,000	$400,000
Cost of goods sold:					
Beginning inventory	$ 8,000	$ 8,000	$ 16,000	$ 32,000	$ 8,000
Add:					
Direct material	40,000	44,000	44,000	32,000	160,000
Direct labor	15,000	16,500	16,500	12,000	60,000
Variable overhead	10,000	11,000	11,000	8,000	40,000
Fixed overhead	15,000	16,500	16,500	12,000	60,000
Standard cost of goods available	$ 88,000	$ 96,000	$104,000	$ 96,000	$328,000
Less: Ending inventory	8,000	16,000	32,000	8,000	8,000
Total standard cost of goods sold	$ 80,000	$ 80,000	$ 72,000	$ 88,000	$320,000
(Over) underabsorbed overhead	–	(1,500)	(1,500)	3,000	–
Actual cost of goods sold	$ 80,000	$ 78,500	$ 70,500	$ 91,000	$320,000
Gross margin	$ 20,000	$ 21,500	$ 19,500	$ 19,000	$ 80,000
Percentage of gross margin to sales	20%	21.5%	21.7%	17.3%	20%
Inventory change, units: increase (decrease)	–	10,000	20,000	(30,000)	–
Standard fixed cost per unit	–	$ 0.15	$ 0.15	$ 0.15	–
Fixed cost in inventory change	–	$ 1,500	$ 3,000	($ 4,500)	–

EXHIBIT 9-9
ABSO-VAR COMPANY
Comparative Income Statement, Variable Costing Basis
Four Years, 19x1 through 19x4

	19x1	19x2	19x3	19x4	Total
Net sales	$100,000	$100,000	$ 90,000	$110,000	$400,000
Cost of goods sold:					
Beginning inventory	$ 6,500	$ 6,500	$ 13,000	$ 26,000	$ 6,500
Add:					
Direct material	40,000	44,000	44,000	32,000	160,000
Direct labor	15,000	16,500	16,500	12,000	60,000
Variable overhead	10,000	11,000	11,000	8,000	40,000
Standard variable cost of goods available	$ 71,500	$ 78,000	$ 84,500	$ 78,000	$266,500
Less: Ending inventory	6,500	13,000	26,000	6,500	6,500
Variable cost of goods sold	$ 65,000	$ 65,000	$ 58,500	$ 71,500	$260,000
Contribution margin	$ 35,000	$ 35,000	$ 31,500	$ 38,500	$140,000
Less: Fixed overhead	15,000	15,000	15,000	15,000	60,000
Gross margin	$ 20,000	$ 20,000	$ 16,500	$ 23,500	$ 80,000
Percentage of contribution margin to sales	35%	35%	35%	35%	35%
Percentage of gross margin to sales	20%	20%	18.3%	21.4%	20%
Gross margin – absorption basis					
(Exhibit 9-8)	$ 20,000	$ 21,500	$ 19,500	$ 19,000	$ 80,000
Gross margin – variable basis	20,000	20,000	16,500	23,500	80,000
Difference – absorption greater (less)	–	$ 1,500	$ 3,000	$ (4,500)	–
Fixed cost in inventory change –					
absorption basis (Exhibit 9-8)	–	$ 1,500	$ 3,000	$ (4,500)	–

Once again, the only difference between the two methods of reporting lies in the inclusion of fixed overhead in absorption inventory and its exclusion under variable costing. At the bottom of Exhibit 9-8, an analysis of inventory changes is shown, and at the bottom of Exhibit 9-9, the differences in gross margin are tied directly to these inventory changes. Note particularly that the difference in gross margin under the two methods is equal to the amount of fixed overhead cost attributable to the change in inventory and that this difference in gross margin is not related to the over- or underabsorbed overhead.

The four years demonstrated the three different relationships between sales and production:

1. 19x1: Sales and production are equal.

2. 19x2 and 19x3: Production exceeds sales.

3. 19x4: Sales exceed production.

We are able to reconfirm that:

1. When sales and production are equal, income as reported under absorption and variable costing will be the same.

2. When production exceeds sales, absorption costing will report greater income than variable costing.

3. When sales exceed production, absorption costing will report less income than variable costing.

Other Comparisons

The comparative income data for these years point up certain other interesting relationships between the two costing methods. For example, it is readily discernible that gross margin can vary at the same sales volume under absorption costing. For purposes of the Abso-Var Company example, "all other things were equal"; only physical volume of sales and production varied over the entire four-year period. Should not management expect (other things being equal) that gross margin would be the same when sales volume is the same and would rise and fall as sales volume rises and falls?

Reference to Exhibit 9-8 indicates that this is not so under absorption costing. Here is what did happen:

Year	Sales	Gross Margin	Gross Margin, Percent
19x1	$100,000	$20,000	20.0
19x2	100,000	21,500	21.5
19x3	90,000	19,500	21.7
19x4	110,000	19,000	17.3

It is evident from these comparisons that gross margins were responding to changes in factors other than sales volume.

The erratic behavior of gross margin is, in fact, related more closely to fluctuations in production than to changes in sales volume, as is evident from the following comparison:

Year	Sales	Production	Gross Margin
19x1	$100,000	100,000	$20,000
19x2	100,000	110,000	21,500
19x3	90,000	110,000	19,500
19x4	110,000	80,000	19,000

In the first two years, while sales were at the same volume, gross margin fluctuated with production volume; only when production was constant (in 19x2 and 19x3) did the gross margin fluctuate with sales volume.

It is understandable that management could be confused by such figures. How much clearer, then, are the same operations reported in Exhibit 9-9, in which the relationship of both contribution margin and gross margin to sales volume is highlighted. We may summarize the comparison thus:

Year	Sales	Contribution Margin	Contribution Margin, Percent	Gross Margin	Gross Margin, Percent
19x1	$100,000	$35,000	35	$20,000	20.0
19x2	100,000	35,000	35	20,000	20.0
19x3	90,000	31,500	35	16,500	18.3
19x4	110,000	38,500	35	23,500	21.4

Because the contribution margin is a fixed relationship between sales, which vary, and variable costs, which vary in direct relationship to sales, it is clear that its percentage relationship to sales should be the same at all levels of sales volume. Since "other things are equal" in this example, its undeviating relationship of 35 percent prevails over all four years.

On the other hand, the ratio of gross margin to sales must change as sales volume changes, since it reflects the recovery of an unvarying amount of fixed overhead each period. Thus, when sales volume is normal, gross margin will be normal in amount and percent (as in the first two years); when volume is down, so is gross margin (year 19x3); when volume is up, so is the gross margin (year 19x4).

This fluctuation of gross margin (or net income) with sales is just what management expects: After all, when sales volume is below normal, profits should be down—the company is paying for idle capacity; when sales volume rises above normal, profits ought to be higher—the company is utilizing capacity at greater than expected efficiency.

FUTURE COST AVOIDANCE: THE TEST

In theory, the question of the deferral of a cost in inventory ought to turn on the point of future cost avoidance. An advocate of variable costing does not believe a cost should be deferred as an asset unless its incurrence now will prevent its incurrence in a future period. As one author explains it:[3]

> The issue lies in the definition of an asset. According to the most widely accepted definition, costs are assets if they can justifiably be carried forward to the future, if they bear revenue-producing power, if they are beneficial to future operations—if they possess service potential. Thus, the justification for treating fixed factory overhead as an asset must meet the test of service potential. The issue becomes service potential versus no service potential. . . .
>
> Variable cost proponents maintain that *a cost has service potential, in the traditional accounting sense, if its incurrence now will result in future cost avoidance in the ordinary course of business.* In other words, assets (unexpired costs) ordinarily represent costs whose reincurrence is unnecessary in the future. If future cost incurrence will be unaffected by the cost in question, the cost has no relevance to future events and therefore cannot represent any benefit, any future service.

Clearly, variable costs meet the test of future cost avoidance. The specific costs of direct material, the labor operations, and the variable (avoidable) factory overhead attaching to specific units of product in inventory will not be incurred again, but they possess an inherent revenue-producing power which will likely be realized in the future.

Fixed overhead, however, is incurred independently of any specific production; its incurrence is usually based on the calendar; whether or not productive capacity is utilized fully has no bearing on the amount incurred. After the property tax bill has been paid in one year, after the plant superintendent's last paycheck for the year has been received, the company can look forward to more of the same the following year. It is not likely that the owner of the factory building will allow a credit against *next* year's rent for that portion of *this* year's rent deferred in the ending inventory.

Thus, in the normal course of business, fixed overhead possesses no service potential in the sense of future cost avoidance.[4] For this reason, advocates of variable costing see no justification for deferring any portion of it in inventory.

ADVANTAGES TO MANAGEMENT OF VARIABLE COSTING

From the standpoint of management, variable costing presents numerous advantages.

Less Confusing

Over- or underabsorbed overhead is no insurmountable obstacle to the reporting of income. However, to the nonaccountant manager, it can be a source of con-

---

[3] Charles T. Horngren, *Cost Accounting: A Managerial Emphasis*, 2d ed., Englewood Cliffs, N.J.: Prentice-Hall, Inc., 1967, p. 322.

[4] In the exceptional case where management foresees a sales volume in the coming period in excess of its capacity to produce, it may decide to produce for inventory in the current period rather than lose future sales. Under such circumstances, a portion of the current period's fixed costs may be considered to have service potential. Many accountants justify deferral of fixed cost to inventory in such a case, but many others would still regard the variable costing method as preferable.

fusion and misunderstanding. As mentioned earlier, its presence on the income statement enables the accountant to report a standard cost of goods sold as well as an actual one (in effect, the absorption variance is inserted and then canceled out).

It has been argued, however, that such information on the income statement benefits the accountant more than the manager. The income statement on a variable costing basis is simpler, more direct, and therefore more understandable to the typical nonaccountant. The effects of operating the plant at a volume other than normal capacity can be reported elsewhere—in an analysis of variances as a separate report, for example.

Net Income Fluctuates with Sales

Generally speaking, management thinking is properly attuned to the economic fact that volume is a fundamental factor in profit making; within the relevant range of cost for basic capacity, profits increase with increased volume and decrease as volume declines.

The absorption costing income statement will, on the contrary, often report deceptively high net income when sales volume is low but production is high during a period of inventory building. Conversely, when sales volume is high in a period when inventory is being reduced, net income will be reported unduly low.

Variable income statements will report net income as following the fluctuations in sales volume, since fixed costs are written off each period in their entirety.

Built-in Break-even Analysis

With the chart of accounts constructed on the basis of the behavior of costs in relation to volume and with the income statement designed to emphasize the contribution margin, break-even analysis is greatly facilitated.

Several additional analyses useful to management are possible within the framework of variable costing. First, cost-volume-profit data are available within the account structure as a starting point for planning purposes. Second, the actual accounting results will be available in the same form, with the cost-volume-profit relationships built in, for direct comparison with the planning budgets. Third, the break-even analyses for the current month and for year to date are readily available. All this information makes it possible to observe trends in break-even points and to make basic comparisons with planned performance.

Product-line Profit Performance

Variable costing helps sharpen management appraisal of the profit performance of product lines, divisions, branch plants, sales territories, and other meaningful segments of the company.

Essentially, there are two problems under absorption costing which tend to obscure the performance of different lines in a multiproduct firm:

1. The effect on net income of the fixed-cost factor in inventory increases and decreases

2. The distortion resulting from the need to allocate indirect costs to product divisions.

Variable costing provides a remedy for each of these two problems. First, because it regards variable manufacturing costs as product costs, variable costing eliminates the problem of the influence on reported net income of fixed costs in inventory. Second, product profitability under variable costing is based primarily on the respective contribution margins of the various lines. Certain fixed costs, such as special equipment and tooling, engineering, supervision, and the like, are frequently identified *directly* with specific product *divisions* (not *units* of product) and can therefore add a degree of refinement to the analysis of product profitability beyond the contribution margin; but the allocation of general, indirect expenses only distorts and confuses.

For illustration, consider the Multi-Pro Company, which manufactures and sells three lines of product: A, B, and C. The following facts concern the company's operations in the year 19x1:

	Product Line		
	A	B	C
Selling price per unit	$ 5.00	$10.00	$ 1.00
Standard manufacturing costs:			
Variable	$ 3.00	$ 6.00	$ 0.70
Fixed	1.00	2.00	0.10
Total standard manufacturing costs	$ 4.00	$ 8.00	$ 0.80
Beginning inventory, 19x1, units	2,000	3,000	5,000
Production, units	4,000	1,000	70,000
Available for sale, units	6,000	4,000	75,000
Ending inventory, 19x1, units	2,000	1,000	25,000
Sales, units	4,000	3,000	50,000
Fixed factory overhead cost incurred (allocated to product divisions on a predetermined basis)	$4,000	$6,000	$5,000
Selling and administrative expense (allocated to product divisions on the basis of dollars of sales)	$2,000	$3,000	$5,000

Exhibit 9-10 compares the income statements by product divisions on the basis of absorption and variable costing. Several interesting things stand out in this analysis.

On an absorption costing basis, it appears that product B is unprofitable and that product C is the most profitable of the three. However, B's production was only 1,000 units, while its sales were 3,000. The absorption costing effect of this inventory change may be seen in the analysis at the bottom of the exhibit. In the case of B, it was necessary to sell 2,000 more units than were produced. These 2,000 units came out of inventory, where they carried a value, at $2 per unit of $4,000 fixed cost from the prior period. Thus the cost of goods sold of $28,000 contained $4,000 of cost from a prior period and reduced the net income for 19x1 by a like amount. If this $4,000 were added back to the $1,000 net loss reported, a net income of $3,000, or 10 percent of its net sales, would be the result for product B.

On the other hand, product C appeared to be the best of the three on an absorption costing basis, with a net income of 14 percent of its net sales. However, its production exceeded its sales — 70,000 to 50,000 — resulting in an increase to inventory of 20,000 units. Each of these units carried a unit fixed cost of 10 cents, or $2,000 total, with it into inventory. Without this help, C would have shown a net income of only $5,000, or 10 percent. Thus, on the basis of adjusting for fixed cost in inventory alone, B and C appear to be equally profitable.

One more thing should be observed, however. If the fixed factory overhead cost assigned to the various products was on the basis of some allocation of the

EXHIBIT 9-10
THE MULTI-PRO COMPANY
Income Statement by Product Lines, Absorption and Variable Costing Compared
For the Year 19x1

	Absorption Costing				Variable Costing			
	Total	A	B	C	Total	A	B	C
Net sales	$100,000	$20,000	$30,000	$50,000	$100,000	$20,000	$30,000	$50,000
Cost of goods sold:								
Beginning inventory	$ 36,000	$ 8,000	$24,000	$ 4,000	$ 27,500	$ 6,000	$18,000	$ 3,500
Add: Costs incurred in production:								
Variable costs	67,000	12,000	6,000	49,000	67,000	12,000	6,000	49,000
Fixed overhead	15,000	4,000	6,000	5,000				
Cost of goods available	$118,000	$24,000	$36,000	$58,000	$ 94,500	$18,000	$24,000	$52,500
Less: Ending inventory	36,000	8,000	8,000	20,000	29,500	6,000	6,000	17,500
Total cost of goods sold	$ 82,000	$16,000	$28,000	$38,000	$ 65,000	$12,000	$18,000	$35,000
Gross margin	$ 18,000	$ 4,000	$ 2,000	$12,000				
Contribution margin					$ 35,000	$ 8,000	$12,000	$15,000
Less: Fixed cost:								
Manufacturing overhead					$ 15,000			
Selling and administrative*	$ 10,000	$ 2,000	$ 3,000	$ 5,000	10,000			
Total fixed cost	$ 10,000	$ 2,000	$ 3,000	$ 5,000	$ 25,000			
Net income for period	$ 8,000	$ 2,000	($ 1,000)	$ 7,000	$ 10,000			
Percentage of net income to sales	8%	10%	(3.3%)	14%	10%			
Percentage of contribution margin to sales						35%	40%	40%	30%
Fixed cost in beginning inventory	$ 8,500	$ 2,000	$ 6,000	$ 500	*Percent total fixed cost to net sales*			
Fixed cost in ending inventory	6,500	2,000	2,000	2,500				
Net change — increase (decrease)	($ 2,000)	—	($ 4,000)	$ 2,000	25%†			

* Allocated on the basis of sales dollars.
† Indicative of minimum level at which the contribution margin of a product contributes enough to meet a proportionate share of the company fixed cost.

general indirect costs of the factory, then product C got another break under absorption costing.

This is revealed in the variable costing analysis, which ignores allocations of indirect fixed costs and allows the analysis of product profitability to rest at the contribution-margin level. Here it can be seen that products A and B each contributed 40 percent of its respective sales volume to the recovery of company fixed cost and net income. Product C's contribution was only 30 percent. All three were above the 25 percent total fixed-cost level for the company as a whole. Nevertheless, the product (C) which appeared to be the most profitable on an absorption costing basis turns out to offer the smallest relative contribution to overall company profitability.

There may be many other factors affecting the profit performance of the various product lines in a multiproduct firm, and management needs all the relevant information it can get concerning the profit performance. However, management certainly ought to be aware of the effects on reported profits by product line of the costing method used and allocation of indirect fixed costs.

Pricing

With regard to pricing, variable costing offers substantially the same advantages as it does in the realm of segment profitability analysis. Emphasis is on the contribution margin, which is unaffected by allocations of indirect cost. This margin offers a simple, clear portrayal of the relationship between specific product costs and the different possible selling prices being considered. This issue will be developed in more detail in Chapter 12.

Compatibility with Standard Cost Accounting

Since variable costing consists primarily in recognizing, within the chart of accounts and the financial reports to management, the fundamental behavior of costs in relation to volume, it can apply to any cost accounting system. However, it seems to fit especially well into a system based on standard costs and flexible budgets. Standards, it will be recalled, are most appropriate to the prime costs and variable overhead. Flexible budgeting permits adaptation to the fixed overhead items. Indeed, flexible budgeting is a form of variable costing, used by some companies for many years without being labeled as such.

CONTROVERSY

Since it is the primary purpose of this book to explore, on an introductory basis, various quantitative techniques rooted in accounting which have proved useful for certain management decisions, we do not feel it necessary to examine in detail all the variations and exceptions involved in the application of such techniques. Nevertheless, we must point out that, at the time of this writing, variable costing is the subject of widespread controversy in accounting circles.

Essentially, opposition to the integration of variable costing into the basic accounting systems of business firms is based on its use for *external reporting,* i.e., reports to stockholders, Internal Revenue, lenders, various government agencies, and the general public.

At the present time, the Securities and Exchange Commission and the Internal Revenue Service do not recognize variable costing as an acceptable accounting practice, although the IRS has allowed a very few companies to use it where variable costing has been consistently used for a number of years.[5] Both the SEC and the IRS base their opposition to variable costing mainly on the fact that the American Institute of Certified Public Accountants does not recognize it as a "generally accepted accounting principle." Thus it would seem that, as long as variable costing is unacceptable to the AICPA for external reporting, the IRS and the SEC will not allow its use by reporting companies either.

It is held that, by not including fixed overhead in inventory, the asset value on the balance sheet is understated. In its Accounting Research Bulletin 43, Chapter 4 on Inventory Pricing, the AICPA states that "the primary basis of accounting for inventories is cost, which has been defined generally as the price paid or the consideration given to acquire an asset. As applied to inventories, cost means, in principle, the sum of the applicable expenditures and charges directly or indirectly incurred in bringing an article to its existing condition and location." Later, the AICPA becomes more specific: ". . . it should also be recognized that the exclusion of all overheads from inventory costs does not constitute an accepted accounting procedure."[6]

The essential point, apparently, is its being "an accepted accounting procedure." Historically, most accounting practices have come to be accepted when they are "generally accepted"—in other words, if enough people do it, a practice is "accepted." In recent years, more and more companies have adopted variable costing for internal management purposes. If the present trend toward more widespread use of this sytem continues, it will eventually become "an accepted accounting practice."

COMPROMISE

One reason that companies which use variable costing have not become too exercised over the failure of AICPA, IRS, and the SEC to accept the practice for external reporting has been that they can virtually "have their cake and eat it too." Conversion from a variable costing to an absorption costing basis for external reporting purposes is generally a matter of a few minutes of work once a year (or oftener, depending on the periodicity of external reporting).

For example, in the case of the Abso-Var Company at the end of 19x1, the conversion would be on the basis of unit cost of fixed overhead times the number of units in inventory, added to the inventory on the variable costing basis, thus:

Inventory—variable costing (10,000 units × $0.65)	$6,500
Add: Fixed overhead (10,000 units × $0.15)	1,500
Inventory—absorption costing (10,000 units × $0.80)	$8,000

[5] See R. W. Hirschman, "Direct Costing and the Law," *The Accounting Review,* January 1965, pp. 176–83, and "Current Application of Direct Costing," *NAA Research Report No. 37,* 1961, pp. 86–107.
[6] *Restatement and Revision of Accounting Research Bulletins,* Committee on Accounting Procedure, American Institute of (Certified Public) Accountants, Accounting Research Bulletin No. 43, New York: 1953.

The same approach could be used whether the fixed overhead is expressed as a percentage of direct labor cost, a rate per direct labor hour, a rate per machine hour, or any other factor. For example, suppose that fixed overhead is 150 percent of direct labor cost. Assume the ending inventory on a variable costing basis to be made up of the following:

Direct material	$10,000
Direct labor	8,000
Variable overhead	6,000
Total inventory — variable costing	$24,000
Add: Fixed overhead (150% × $8,000)	12,000
Total inventory — absorption costing	$36,000

It is obvious that the conversion of any inventory from a variable to an absorption costing basis requires that total overhead be split into its variable and fixed components. But then, this is essential to the operation of a variable costing system, so the availability of the necessary ingredients is automatic.

SUMMARY

Variable costing is a method of recording and reporting costs which regards as product costs only those which tend to vary directly with volume of activity. Thus direct material, direct labor, and variable manufacturing overhead are taken into inventory, while fixed manufacturing overhead is regarded as a period cost and is written off against operations each period. In effect, variable costing is the result of building cost-volume-profit relationships into basic accounting records and reports.

The only difference between conventional, or absorption, costing and variable costing lies in their respective treatment of fixed manufacturing cost. Absorption costing regards it as a part of product cost. Variable costing does not.

Inventories are determinants of reported net income on the income statement. When inventories change from the beginning to the end of the period because production volume differs from sales volume, the net income reported on an absorption costing basis will differ from that reported on a variable costing basis for the same period.

This disparity comes about as a result of the deferral of fixed overhead into inventory under absorption costing, as contrasted with its write-off under variable costing. Under each of three possible conditions of production and sales, the following will result:

1. When sales volume and production volume are equal, net income reported under absorption and variable costing will be the *same*. The reason is that the amount of fixed overhead written off to operations is the same under each method, and also because there is no change in the amount of fixed overhead in the absorption inventory.

2. When production exceeds sales volume, net income reported under absorption costing will be *greater* than that under variable costing. This result occurs because part of the period's production went to increase inventory, and under absorption costing, part of the period's fixed overhead was deferred along with it.

3. When sales exceed production volume, net income reported under absorption costing will be *less* than that under variable costing. The reason is that part of the period's sales came out of beginning inventory, which, under absorption costing, carried with it a portion of the prior period's fixed overhead.

The nature of the absorption costing method causes net income to vary with *production*, whereas net income will vary with *sales* under variable costing.

Among the advantages to management resulting from the use of variable costing are these:

1. It is less confusing — there is no over- or underabsorbed overhead to be concerned about.

2. Reported net income follows logically the fluctuations of sales rather than production.

3. Cost-volume-profit analysis and break-even analysis are "built in."

4. The performance of product lines or other segments of the business can be appraised in terms of relative contribution margin, without the need for arbitrary allocations of fixed costs.

5. Analysis of costs relevant to pricing is simplified and sharpened.

6. Variable costing is compatible with standard cost accounting and flexible budgeting.

Variable costing is still the center of considerable controversy over its use for external reporting, the contention being that assets (inventory) are being understated and that it is not accepted accounting practice. The AICPA maintains this position, and IRS and SEC are in agreement.

Until variable costing becomes a generally accepted accounting practice, companies who wish to use it must convert inventory and cost of goods sold figures to an absorption costing basis for external reporting. This conversion, however, is a relatively simple process in most cases and is no deterrent to the use of variable costing for internal management purposes.

KEY WORDS AND PHRASES

variable costing	programmed (discretionary) cost
conventional costing	product cost
period cost	cost avoidance

DISCUSSION QUESTIONS

1. Distinguish variable costing and absorption (conventional) costing.
2. Unscramble the terminology problem involving (a) variable costing; (b) direct costing; (c) marginal costing; (d) fixed costs; (e) capacity costs; and (f) period costs. First, what have they in common? Second, what are the obvious groupings? Third, what are the fine distinctions between alternative terms within each group?

3. What is the sole and essential distinction between the absorption costing concept of product costs and that of variable costing?

4. Explain what happens to reported net income under absorption costing and variable costing under the following conditions:
   a. Sales and production volume for the period are equal.
   b. Sales exceed production volume for the period.
   c. Production exceeds sales volume for the period.

5. What is meant by the statement "The variable costing income statement is simply built-in break-even analysis"?

6. Explain the role of contribution margin in reporting net income under variable costing.

7. How are over- and underabsorbed overhead treated under variable costing?

8. Is over- or underabsorbed overhead a factor in the difference between net income as reported under absorption costing and net income reported under variable costing? Why?

9. What has future cost avoidance to do with the theoretical justification for variable costing?

10. Explain some of the advantages to management claimed for variable costing.

11. How can you assess product profitability properly without allocating to each product its fair share of indirect costs?

12. "That variable costing is dynamite. Can't you imagine what my salespeople would do to our prices if they thought they were playing with a margin of 30 percent based on direct costs only, instead of with our regular gross margin of 12 percent based on the full costs?" Can this company president's fears be calmed?

13. "Flexible budgeting is a form of variable costing." Comment.

14. Explain the opposition to the use of variable costing for external reporting.

15. How can the key data under variable costing for internal purposes be converted to absorption costing for external reporting?

PROBLEMS

9-1. During its first year of operation, the Pichler Company produced 10,000 units of a product and sold 7,000 units at a sales price of $9 each. Variable costs for the year totaled $25,000 and fixed costs totaled $10,000. Using this information, construct two income statements for the firm, one using absorption costing and the other using variable costing.

9-2. On the basis of the following information, calculate the net income for the year and the value of the finished goods inventory on hand at the end of the year, using absorption costing and variable costing.

Sales	$350,000
Cost of goods manufactured:	
Variable	$180,000
Fixed	$ 45,000
Selling and administrative expenses:	
Variable	$ 65,000
Fixed	$ 50,000
Finished goods inventory:	
Beginning	-0-
Ending	5,000 units
Work in process inventories	-0-
Budgeted and actual production	20,000 units

Supporters of direct costing have contended that it provides management with more useful accounting information than conventional costing does. Critics of direct costing believe that its negative features outweigh its contributions.

Required:
1. Describe direct costing. How does it differ from conventional absorption costing?
2. List the arguments for and against the use of direct costing.
3. Indicate how each of the following conditions would affect the amounts of net profit reported under conventional absorption costing and direct costing:
   a. Sales and production are in balance at standard volume.
   b. Sales exceed production.
   c. Production exceeds sales.

(AICPA adapted)

 Following are data pertaining to a year of operations (000 omitted):

Units produced	600
Units sold	500
Direct material incurred	$900
Direct labor incurred	$300
Variable factory overhead incurred	$750
Fixed factory overhead incurred	$1,200
Selling and administrative expenses (fixed)	$275
Selling price per unit	$6.00
Raw materials inventory—beginning	$100
Raw materials inventory—ending	$100
Work in process inventories—beginning and ending	—
Finished goods inventory—beginning	—

(handwritten: 1.50 / .50 / 1.25 / 2.00 } A.B. Costing. 5.25   3.25 Var. Costing)

Required:
1. Determine the valuation of ending finished goods inventory under the absorption and variable costing methods.
2. Prepare income statements, using absorption and variable costing methods.
3. Determine the break-even point, in units.

9-5.† The Bendit Manufacturing Company showed the following results for the four quarters of 19x1:

	1Q	2Q	3Q	4Q
Sales, units	40,000	60,000	60,000	30,000
Production, units	70,000	50,000	60,000	10,000

Selling price per unit	$ 10
Variable manufacturing cost per unit	$ 4
Fixed manufacturing cost per quarter	$150,000
Selling and administrative cost—fixed—per quarter	$ 90,000
Normal capacity per quarter, units	50,000
No work in process inventories; level of raw materials inventory constant throughout	

Required:
1. Prepare comparative condensed quarterly and year's total income statements:

     a. On absorption costing basis, showing over- and underabsorbed overhead as adjustment to cost of goods sold

     b. On a variable costing basis

2. Comment on the differences in results as reported under the two methods.

9-6. On a graph whose horizontal axis represents time and whose vertical axis shows dollars, plot all the following figures for a company that started operations at the beginning of year 1971:

Year	Sales	Direct Costing Contribution Margin	Direct Costing Profit	Absorption Costing Profit
1971	$ 750,000	$150,000	$ -0-	$ 25,000
1972	750,000	150,000	-0-	25,000
1973	800,000	160,000	10,000	33,333
1974	1,000,000	200,000	50,000	66,667
1975	1,500,000	300,000	150,000	150,000
1976	3,000,000	600,000	450,000	400,000

Required:

State the conclusions you can draw from an inspection of your graph.

9-7. The XYZ Company was organized on January 2, 1972. The company's financial position, prepared at the end of each of its first three years, was as follows:

	1972	1973	1974
Cash	$11,000	$ 6,000	$20,000
Inventories	-0-	15,000*	5,000†
	$11,000	$21,000	$25,000
Capital stock	$10,000	$10,000	$10,000
Retained earnings	1,000	11,000	15,000
	$11,000	$21,000	$25,000

* Includes $4,000 of fixed overhead.

† Includes $1,500 of fixed overhead.

Required:

1. What were the reported incomes for 1972, 1973, 1974, assuming that no dividends were paid?

2. What would the income have been if variable costing had been used instead of absorption costing for these three years?

9-8. The Wilson Company began operations on January 1, 1972. Following is a summary of its operations for the first three years of its existence:

	1972	1973	1974
Volume in units			
Sales	25,000	30,000	20,000
Production	30,000	35,000	15,000
Selling price per unit	$33	$33	$33
Variable costs per unit			
Selling	$ 4	$ 4	$ 4
Production	$12	$12	$12
Fixed costs per year			
Selling	$125,000	$125,000	$125,000
Production	$225,000	$225,000	$225,000

Fixed overhead is applied under the absorption costing method, based on a normal volume of 25,000 units per year.

Required:
1. Compute the income in each of the three years under absorption costing and then under variable costing.
2. Explain the differences in reported income in each year and for the three-year period.
3. Which costing method do you believe presents the more useful statement of the company's income? Why?

9-9. The following annual flexible budget has been prepared for use in making decisions relating to product X:

	100,000 Units	150,000 Units	200,000 Units
Sales volume	$800,000	$1,200,000	$1,600,000
Manufacturing costs:			
Variable	300,000	450,000	600,000
Fixed	200,000	200,000	200,000
	500,000	650,000	800,000
Selling and other expenses:			
Variable	200,000	300,000	400,000
Fixed	160,000	160,000	160,000
	360,000	460,000	560,000
Income (or loss)	$ (60,000)	$ 90,000	$ 240,000

The 200,000 unit budget has been adopted and will be used for allocating fixed manufacturing costs to units of product X; at the end of the first six months, the following information is available:

	Units
Production completed	120,000
Sales	60,000

All fixed costs are budgeted and incurred uniformly throughout the year and all costs incurred coincide with the budget.

Over- and underapplied fixed manufacturing costs are deferred until year-end.

Required:
1. Compute the amount of fixed factory costs applied to product during the first six months under absorption costing.
2. Compute the net income (or loss) for the first six months under absorption costing.
3. Compute the net income (or loss) for the first six months under direct costing.

(AICPA adapted)

9-10. Norwood Corporation is considering changing its method of inventory valuation from absorption costing to direct costing, and it has engaged you to determine the effect of the proposed change on the 19x8 financial statements.

The corporation manufactures Gink, which is sold for $20 per unit.

The ingredient, Marsh, is added before processing starts, and labor and overhead are added evenly during the manufacturing process. Production capacity is budgeted at 110,000 units of Gink annually. The standard costs per unit of Gink are:

Marsh, 2 lb	$3.00
Labor	6.00
Variable manufacturing overhead	1.00
Fixed manufacturing overhead	1.10

A process cost system is used, employing standard costs. Variances from standard costs are now charged or credited to cost of goods sold. If direct costing were adopted, only variances resulting from variable costs would be charged or credited to cost of goods sold.

Inventory data for 19x8 follow:

	Units	
	January 1	December 31
Marsh (pounds)	50,000	40,000
Work in process		
Two-fifths processed	10,000	
One-third processed		15,000
Finished goods	20,000	12,000

During 19x8, 220,000 pounds of Marsh were purchased and 230,000 pounds were transferred to work in process. Also, 110,000 units of Gink were transferred to finished goods. Actual fixed manufacturing overhead during the year was $121,000. There were no variances between standard variable costs and actual variable costs during the year.

Required:
1. Prepare schedules which present the computation of:
   a. Equivalent units of production for material, labor, and overhead
   b. Number of units sold
   c. Standard unit costs under direct costing and absorption costing
   d. Amount, if any, of over- or underapplied fixed manufacturing overhead
2. Prepare a comparative statement of cost of goods sold, using standard direct costing and standard absorption costing.

(AICPA adapted)

9-11.† Flear Company has a maximum productive capacity of 210,000 units per year. Normal capacity is regarded as 180,000 units per year. Standard variable manufacturing costs are $11 per unit. Fixed factory overhead is $360,000 per year. Variable selling expenses are $3 per unit and fixed selling expenses are $252,000 per year. The unit sales price is $20.

The operating results for 19x1 are as follows: sales, 150,000 units; production, 160,000 units; beginning inventory, 10,000 units; and net unfavorable variance for standard variable manufacturing costs, $40,000. All variances are written off as additions to (or deductions from) standard cost of sales.

Required:

(For items 1 to 3, assume no variances from standard for manufacturing costs.)

1. What is the break-even point expressed in dollar sales?
2. How many units must be sold to earn a net income of $60,000 per year?
3. How many units must be sold to earn a net income of 10 percent on sales?
4. Prepare formal income statements for 19x1 under (*a*) conventional costing; (*b*) direct costing.
5. Briefly account for the difference in net income between the two income statements.

(AICPA adapted)

9-12. Ray Baker began manufacturing operations in a small plant at the beginning of 1974. At the end of that year, his accountant prepared the following income statement:

BAKER BREAD COMPANY
Income Statement
Year Ended December 31, 1974

Sales (80,000 units)		$81,000
Variable expenses:		
Manufacturing	$39,200	
Marketing	16,000	55,200
Contribution margin		25,800
Fixed expenses		
Manufacturing	22,500	
Other	6,500	29,000
Net loss		$ (3,200)

Baker became very discouraged as a result of seeing this income statement. His wife, however, who was working for her M.B.A. at the university, suggested that his mistake was in using variable costing to prepare the income statement. She thought that a switch to absorption costing would be profitable for Baker. Income taxes do not need to be considered since the company is not incorporated. Production for 1974 totaled 150,000 units of final product.

Required:

1. Recompute the company's 1974 income, using absorption costing. Was Mrs. Baker correct? Explain.
2. Assume that Baker produces 120,000 units in 1975 and sells 190,000 units. Assuming that all costs and expenses adhere to the same pattern as in 1974 and that the unit selling price does not change, which costing method will result in the higher net income in 1975? Support your answer with calculations.

9-13.* The Aero O-Two Company separates oxygen from the air, freezes it, and sells it in its solid form. Thus, its raw material is free and it incurs only production costs, all of which are fixed, since the plant is fully automated. These production costs amount to $300,000 per year. The oxygen is sold at $40 per unit.

The company has made two forecasts of sales for the next two years, one optimistic and one pessimistic:

	Units	
	1975	1976
Optimistic sales forecast	10,000	30,000
Pessimistic sales forecast	10,000	10,000

The company president has decided that production during the next two years would be 20,000 in each year under the optimistic forecast. Under the pessimistic forecast, however, production would be 20,000 in 1975 but zero in 1976, even though fixed costs would continue.

Required:
1. Compute income before taxes in dollars and as a percentage of sales revenue under both absorption costing and variable costing for both sales forecasts.
2. Which costing method should the company use? Why?

9-14. Some firms use variable costing for internal reports to management and absorption costing for external reports to stockholders and others.

Required:
1. Indicate what steps are required to convert from variable costing reports to absorption costing reports, where the absorption costing reports are based on FIFO costing.
2. Indicate what steps are required to convert from variable costing reports to absorption costing reports, where the absorption costing reports are based on standard costs and all variances are charged against income in the current period.

9-15. The Burke Company, following two years of losing operations, decided in 19x3 to install a profit-sharing plan in the hope of minimizing inefficiencies, thereby reducing costs and building a profitable operation.

Basic data in 19x2 were as follows:

Sales price per unit	$12
Sales volume, units	1,800,000
Total fixed manufacturing costs	$8,000,000
Total fixed selling and administrative costs	$1,000,000
Variable manufacturing cost per unit	$4.80
Variable selling expense per unit	$2.40
Normal capacity, units	2,500,000

There were no opening inventories in 19x3.

* This problem is adapted from an article by R. P. Marple, appearing in *Accounting Review,* July 1956.

The profit-sharing plan called for the establishment of a pool to be distributed in cash to all employees according to a preestablished formula. This pool would amount to 20 percent of net profits before taxes as determined by the company's CPA firm in accordance with generally accepted principles. It would be deductible for tax purposes.

Payment was to be made to the profit-sharing pool, however, only after the payment of a dividend of 20 cents a share on the company's 1 million outstanding shares. This dividend, not deductible for tax purposes, would require that the firm earn approximately 40 cents per share before taxes to cover it. Recent losses had about used up the balance of retained earnings, so dividends would have to be related to earnings in the current period.

To add incentive to the sales and production forces alike, the president decided to push for greater volume, both in sales and in the plant. She launched an intensive sales campaign, supplemented by an additional advertising expenditure of $600,000. The plant produced 2,500,000 units; the sales force sold 2 million units. "Looks as if we're on our way," exulted the president.

The operating results for 19x3, as certified by the company's audit firm, were as follows:

Sales (2,000,000 units)		$24,000,000
Manufacturing cost of sales:		
Variable (2,500,000 × $4.80)	$12,000,000	
Fixed	8,000,000	
Available for sale	$20,000,000	
Less: Finished goods ending inventory		
(500,000 × $8)	4,000,000	
Total manufacturing cost of sales		16,000,000
Gross margin		$ 8,000,000
Selling and administrative expense:		
Variable	$ 4,800,000	
Fixed	1,600,000	6,400,000
Income before profit sharing and taxes		$ 1,600,000
Less: Profit-sharing pool —20%		320,000
Income before taxes		$ 1,280,000
Less: Income tax —50%		640,000
Net income		$ 640,000
Less: Dividends ($0.20 on 1,000,000 shares)		200,000
Net income retained in the business		$ 440,000

Required:

As a member of the board of directors:

1. How would you appraise the effectiveness of the profit-sharing plan in the first year?
2. Would you approve the distribution of the profit-sharing pool to the employees, as well as the declaration of dividends?
3. How optimistic would you be about the outlook for 19x4?
4. What recommendations would you be prepared to make at the next board meeting?

9-16.† The S. T. Shire Company uses direct costing for internal management purposes and absorption costing for external reporting purposes. Thus, at the end of each year, financial information must be converted from direct costing to absorption costing in order to satisfy external requirements.

At the end of 1971, it was anticipated that sales would rise 20 percent the next year. Therefore, production was increased from 20,000 units to 24,000 units to meet this expected demand. However, economic conditions kept the sales level at 20,000 units for both years.

The following data pertain to 1971 and 1972:

	1971	1972
Selling price per unit	$30	$30
Sales (units)	20,000	20,000
Beginning inventory (units)	2,000	2,000
Production (units)	20,000	24,000
Ending inventory (units)	2,000	6,000
Unfavorable labor, materials, and variable overhead variances (total)	$5,000	$4,000

Standard variable costs per unit for 1971 and 1972:

Labor	$ 7.50
Materials	4.50
Variable overhead	3.00
	$15.00

Annual fixed costs for 1971 and 1972 (budgeted and actual):

Production	$ 90,000
Selling and administrative	100,000
	$190,000

The overhead rate under absorption costing is based upon practical plant capacity, which is 30,000 units per year. All variances and under- or overabsorbed overhead are taken to cost of goods sold.

All taxes are to be ignored.

Required:
1. Present the income statement based on direct costing for 1972.
2. Present the income statement based on absorption costing for 1972.
3. Explain the difference, if any, in the net income figures. Give the entry necessary to adjust the book figures to the financial statement figure, if one is necessary.
4. The company finds it worthwhile to develop its internal financial data on a direct cost basis. What advantages and disadvantages are attributed to direct costing for internal purposes?
5. There are many who believe that direct costing is appropriate for external reporting and many who oppose its use for external reporting. What arguments for and against the use of direct costing are advanced for its use in external reporting?

(IMA adapted)

9=17. The Clark Company has a contract with a labor union that guarantees a minimum wage of $500 per month to each direct labor employee having at least twelve years of service. One hundred employees currently qualify for coverage. All direct labor employees are paid $5 per hour.

The direct labor budget for 1970 was based on the annual usage of 400,000 hours of direct labor times $5, or a total of $2 million. Of this amount, $50,000 (100 employees times $500) per month (or $600,000 for the year) was regarded as fixed. Thus the budget for any given month was determined by the formula:

$50,000 + $3.50 × direct labor hours worked

Data on performance for the first three months of 1970 follow:

	January	February	March
Direct labor hours worked	22,000	32,000	42,000
Direct labor costs budgeted	$127,000	$162,000	$197,000
Direct labor costs incurred	$110,000	$160,000	$210,000
Variance (U—unfavorable; F—favorable)	$17,000 F	$2,000 F	$13,000 U

The factory manager was perplexed by the results, which showed favorable variances when production was low and unfavorable variances when production was high, because he believed his control over labor costs was consistently good.

Required:
1. Why did the variances arise? Explain and illustrate, using amounts and diagrams as necessary.
2. Does this direct labor budget provide a basis for controlling direct labor cost? Explain, indicating changes that might be made to improve control over direct labor cost and to facilitate performance evaluation of direct labor employees.
3. For inventory valuation purposes, how should per-unit standard costs for direct labor be determined in a situation such as this? Explain, assuming that in some months fewer than 10,000 hours are expected to be utilized.

(AICPA adapted)

9-18. The Lindale Company reported the following operating results for December 1975:

Sales (units)	62,000
Selling price (per unit)	$10
Production (total units)	66,000
Cost of production:	
Variable (per unit)	$6
Fixed (total)	$79,200
Selling and administrative costs:	
Variable (per unit sold)	$1.50
Fixed (total)	$26,000
Work in process inventories	-0-

Required:
Prepare an income statement for December 1975, using (1) absorption costing, and (2) variable costing, under each of the following assumptions:
a. There is no beginning inventory of finished goods.
b. The beginning inventory of finished goods consists of 5,000 units with a full cost of $7.50 per unit ($6.10 of which is variable manufacturing costs). The company uses FIFO.
c. The beginning inventory of finished goods is as described above, but the company uses LIFO.

CHAPTER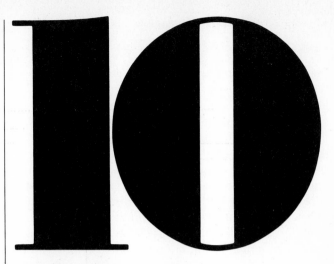

RETURN ON CAPITAL USED

THE PLAN OF THIS CHAPTER
The core importance of a simple ratio —
return on capital used — as a device for
appraising management performance can be
demonstrated. In doing so, we shall examine
the following:

Investors' ratio

The ratio of earnings to capital used

The role of asset turnover

The appraisal of segment rates of return

The problems of allocating assets and costs

The problem of fixed-asset valuation

The measurement of periodic changes in rates
of return

The concept of residual income

CONCEPT

Inasmuch as undertaking business activity involves risk, and money is scarce, the investor in business enterprise expects a return commensurate with the risk he or she assumes. Economic analysis suggests that the scarcer the funds available for investment in relation to the demand for investment, the higher the rate they command; the greater the degree of risk involved in the venture, the higher the return expected.

Because investment in business enterprise generally involves a higher degree of risk than investment in bank savings accounts or government bonds, the purchaser of corporate shares usually expects a somewhat higher rate of return. The source of that return is the profit earned from the operation of the business. Therefore, the corporate shareholder tends to judge corporate management according to the amount of profit earned relative to the capital the shareholders have provided.

INVESTORS' RATIO

The return on the common shareholders' equity, commonly called the "investors' ratio," has long been a recognized measure of the relative attractiveness of a share of common stock as an investment. The common shareholders' equity is the residual equity in a corporation; net income after taxes is the residual income for the period. The investors' ratio logically measures the relationship between the two, which finds expression in the formula

$$\text{Return} = \frac{\text{net income after taxes}}{\text{shareholders' equity}}$$

Thus, if the net income added to retained earnings for a given year amounted to $150,000 and the average shareholders' equity for the year amounted to $1 million, the company earned 15 percent on its shareholders' capital.

The investors' ratio will ordinarily be different from the market yield on the company's common stock. This yield is usually defined as the ratio of dividends plus stock price appreciation to the stock price at the beginning of the period. The market yield is heavily influenced by investors' expectations regarding the firm's future economic performance. The investors' ratio, on the other hand, is based on historical accounting data and not subject to direct influence from stock market changes.

In addition to serving as a measure of investment worth of the company's common stock, the investors' ratio has also been found to be significantly related to company bond ratings and to be useful as a predictor of company failure.[1] Thus this ratio, while of particular concern to stockholders, is also of interest to bondholders and to company management as well.

[1] See James Horrigan, "The Determination of Long-Term Credit Standing with Financial Ratios," and William Beaver, "Financial Ratios as Predictors of Failure," *Empirical Research in Accounting: Selected Studies, 1966,* Supplement to *Journal of Accounting Research,* IV (1966).

THE RATIO OF EARNINGS TO CAPITAL USED

Since a large segment of economic activity is carried on by firms managed by professional managers on behalf of absentee shareholders, modern management is even more acutely aware of the importance of maximizing long-term return. Hence, considerable attention is focused on the means by which this is accomplished.

It was pointed out in an earlier chapter that management pursues the economic goals of the business by combining, in the most effective manner possible, the scarce human and nonhuman (capital) resources at its disposal. This chapter is concerned primarily with the capital resources (or assets) and their effective use.

The assets available to management typically derive from three sources: creditors, owners (direct investment), and retained earnings. The last two sources reflect claims by owners on the assets of the business. Capital from borrowers ordinarily is repaid with a return calculated at a contractual rate in the form of interest.

Management uses the assets from *all* sources to carry on the operations of the business; a borrowed dollar buys as much as one belonging to the owners. Management must first maximize the return from its operations on *all* the assets used before the residual return to shareholders can be maximized. Hence, management has come to recognize that the relationship of *profit from operations* to the *total assets used* is an extremely important gauge of the effectiveness of its performance in the pursuit of the ultimate economic goals.

Thus we derive a second ratio based on the return on capital concept: the return on capital used, variously known as return on investment (ROI), return on assets used, or return on capital employed. In its most common form, the basic ratio is expressed thus:

$$\text{Return} = \frac{\text{net income from operations}}{\text{total operating assets}}$$

At this point, let us emphasize the distinction, in both form and meaning, between the investors' ratio and the return on capital used. Essentially, the return on capital used depicts the effectiveness of all the *operating* decisions, from the routine to the critical, made by management at all levels of the organization from shop supervisor to president; for example:

Production decisions: plant layout, acquisition of automated equipment, product redesign, testing and quality control, purchasing, production and inventory control, employee welfare plans, relocation of a plant, etc.

Marketing decisions: the marketing plan, hiring and training of sales representatives, sales promotion, advertising campaigns, etc.

Administrative decisions: installation of standard cost system, installation of electronic data processing equipment and systems, executive development programs, etc.

These and a myriad of other decisions aimed at improving organizational performance and maximizing profits must be made continually.

The return on capital used, then, takes as its numerator a profit figure which represents the revenues realized from the regular operations of the business, reduced by the manufacturing, selling, and administrative expenses incurred to produce them—the *net profit from operations.* As the denominator, a figure is used that embraces all the assets employed in the operation of the business—the cash, receivables, inventories, plant, property, and equipment. The resulting ratio purports to measure the effectiveness of management in its operating decisions.

Responsible corporate management must also see to it that sufficient capital is provided for carrying on its operations. To the extent that it is necessary and desirable to augment equity capital with borrowing, management must make certain financial decisions to back up its operating decisions. Shrewd financing is no less a factor in profit maximization than the introduction of a profitable new product or the opening of a fertile new sales territory. The results of financial decisions are not reflected directly in the return on capital used, however. Rather, their final impact is felt in the investors' ratio; the cost of borrowed capital—interest—has been deducted in arriving at net income to retained earnings (the numerator), while creditors' claims have been deducted from the investment base.

DISTINCTION ILLUSTRATED

To illustrate the distinction between the form and function of the investors' ratio and the return on capital used, assume the following facts from the condensed balance sheet and income statement for the Returno Company:

RETURNO COMPANY
Balance Sheet
As of December 31, 19x1

Assets		Equities	
Total operating assets	$1,000,000	Total liabilities	$ 500,000
		Common shareholders' equity	500,000
	$1,000,000		$1,000,000

Income Statement
For the Year Ended December 31, 19x1

Net sales	$1,000,000
Total manufacturing and other operating expenses	800,000
Net income from operations	$ 200,000
Interest and income taxes	110,000
Net income to common shareholders	$ 90,000

Calculation of return on capital[2]

$$\text{Investors' ratio} = \frac{\text{net income to common shareholders}}{\text{common shareholders' equity}} = \frac{\$90,000}{\$500,000} = 18\%$$

$$\text{Return on capital used} = \frac{\text{net income from operations}}{\text{total operating assets}} = \frac{\$200,000}{\$1,000,000} = 20\%$$

Clearly, there is a direct relationship between the investors' ratio and the return on capital used. However, the 18 percent investors' ratio cannot be compared directly with the 20 percent return on the assets. The factors in the two ratios are different, and are to be interpreted differently.

Suppose the results for 19x1 are compared under the following assumptions: (A) the same as above, with interest on the $500,000 liabilities at an average rate of 4 percent; (B) no borrowed capital was used, with operating assets limited to the $500,000 supplied by common shareholders.

Net income from operations	A	B
A — 20 percent on $1,000,000 total assets	$200,000	
B — 20 percent on $500,000 total assets		$100,000
Less: Interest under A — 4 percent on $500,000	20,000	
Net income before income taxes	$180,000	$100,000
Less: Income taxes at 50 percent	90,000	50,000
Net income to common shareholders	$ 90,000	$ 50,000
Investors' ratio (on $500,000)	18%	10%

Now let us examine the implications of the different results under (A) and (B). Management's operating efficiency was the same under both assumptions — 20 percent on its operating assets. The tax rate was also the same; moreover, the tax-rate factor is beyond management's control. The best it can hope to do about the income tax liability is to attempt to minimize it by means of certain policies suggested by the company's tax experts.

The key to the difference in the two investors' ratios lies in the fact that management was able to return 20 percent from operations on *all* assets — including the borrowed funds for which it was paying only 4 percent interest. The resulting difference of 8 percent (18 percent minus 10 percent) represents the *after-tax* benefit to the shareholders, resulting from the use of $500,000 of borrowed capital.

Management thus has exhibited both financial acumen in borrowing at 4 percent and operating acumen in earning 20 percent (a phenomenon known to financiers as "trading on the equity" or "financial leverage"). It should be recognized that management's *financial* performance and its *operating* performance are two different things. Moreover, it would be well to observe that the operating performance is the independent variable in the relationship; unless

[2] Note that the calculation uses balances of assets and stockholders' equity as of the *end* of the period. This is done purely for purposes of simplicity. It is theoretically more accurate to average the *beginning* and *ending* balances, inasmuch as net income is earned over the entire period, utilizing the capital available at any time from beginning to end.

management is able to return something greater than the 4 percent it is paying for borrowed funds, there is no financial benefit.

EXPANSION OF THE FORMULA

Throughout the rest of this chapter, we shall focus attention on return on capital used as a measure of management performance. To facilitate the analysis of the causes of change in rates of return, we break down the basic formula into two component parts.

Return on capital used may be considered as a function of both percent of net operating income on net sales and the turnover of operating assets in net sales. The relationships may be expressed thus:

$$\frac{\text{Net operating income}}{\text{Operating assets}} = \frac{\text{net operating income}}{\text{net sales}} \times \frac{\text{net sales}}{\text{operating assets}}$$

or, more simply,

Return on capital used = percentage of net income to net sales × asset turnover

The term "net sales" in the denominator of the first ratio and in the numerator of the second may be canceled out algebraically, and the result is the original ratio. However, our purpose is more refined analysis, and the factors of net income percentage to sales and asset turnover open up insights not apparent in the basic formula.

The new term "asset turnover" is an expression of the number of sales dollars supported by one dollar of operating assets or, put another way, the number of times the operating assets are "recovered" in the sales of the period. The percentage of net income to sales is already familiar. Expressed in this manner, it becomes more evident that the harder the assets are worked (i.e., the higher their turnover in sales volume), the more times the net income percentage is earned on them. For example, if a company earns 10 percent on its net sales and turns its assets twice in the year, the return on capital used is 20 percent (10 percent times 2).

EXHIBIT 10-1
Return on Capital Used, Comparison of Three Companies

	Company A	Company B	Company C
Net sales	$400,000	$400,000	$800,000
Net operating income	$ 40,000	$ 40,000	$ 40,000
Total operating assets	$200,000	$400,000	$400,000
Percent net operating income to net sales	10%	10%	5%
Turnover—operating assets in net sales	2	1	2
Return on capital used	20%	10%	10%

These relationships and their underlying significance might be better understood in the light of a simple example. Exhibit 10-1 compares the net sales, net operating income, and total operating assets, together with the resulting ratios, for three companies in the same industry. Let us see what inferences can be drawn from a brief analysis thereof.

To begin with, all three have earned the same net operating income — $40,000. From the viewpoint of return on capital used, the management of company A has been the most effective of the three, earning 20 percent. This company does not appear to be the largest in the industry, since both the others have more capital invested in operating assets ($400,000 compared with $200,000), and one of them has considerably more sales ($800,000 compared with $400,000). However, company A has earned 10 percent on its net sales and turned its assets twice in sales, with the result that its return is 20 percent on the capital employed.

Company B has the same volume and operating income as A ($400,000 and $40,000); therefore its percentage based on sales is the same — 10 percent. However, some sluggishness is apparent in the fact that operating assets turned over only once in net sales. Management in company B, therefore, cannot be adjudged as effective as that of A, despite equaling its performance in terms of income to sales, because company B management needed twice as much in the way of assets to do it, thus showing only 10 percent return on capital used.

This analysis suggests an investigation of the composition of the assets, since they seem too high in relation to the performance of their two competitors. Perhaps there has been overinvestment in inventory, or too many slow-moving items; accounts receivable may be past due; plant capacity may be underutilized, suggesting the need for partial liquidation of fixed assets or vigorous sales efforts to build volume back to normal capacity; there may be a large idle cash balance, suggesting the need to pay a larger dividend to stockholders or perhaps to invest in product diversification to broaden the operating base of the business.

Company C has realized 10 percent on its assets and has turned them twice in its sales for the period. However, the 5 percent net operating margin on sales is inferior to that of the other two. Since it is probably already pricing its products at the competitive levels of the other companies in the industry, management of company C ought to look to its operating costs as the cause of difficulty, as well as the direction of improved performance.

GRAPHIC ANALYSIS

In Exhibit 10-2, the relative positions of companies A, B, and C are plotted on a chart which highlights the effects of the percentage of net income to sales and the asset turnover on return on capital used. The slightly unusual form of this chart results from the inclusion of three variables instead of the customary two suggested by the two-dimensional scope.

In order to read this chart with some facility, one ought to familiarize oneself first with the interrelationships of the variables plotted on the horizontal (x) and vertical (y) axes. They are, respectively, percentage of operating income to net sales, and operating-asset turnover in net sales. It is thus possible to plot a point representing a company's income-to-sales percentage and turnover, the location of which is an expression of that company's return on capital used (the third, or resultant, variable).

The curved lines on the chart result from connecting a series of points which indicate, within the scope of the x and y scales, various combinations of the two variables which produce the *same* rate of return on capital used. For example, a point placed at the intersection of 10 percent on the x-axis and the turnover of 1 on the y-axis designates one combination which produces a 10 percent rate of return. A few of the other combinations yielding the same 10 percent rate are listed below:

(1) Turnover	× (2) Percentage of Income to Sales	= (3) Rate of Return, in Percent
0.50	20.0	10
1.00	10.0	10
1.25	8.0	10
1.50	6.7	10
2.00	5.0	10
2.50	4.0	10
3.00	3.3	10

When the points are plotted and connected, the resulting curve is the one labeled 10 percent on both the upper margin and the right-hand margin on the chart. The other lines have been similarly calculated and respectively designated.

For the companies used in our example, it can be seen that the company A return was superior to that of companies B and C, and that the last two show the same rate. However, one of the distinctive features of the chart lies in the fact that, although B and C both show a rate of return of 10 percent, they arrive at the same result in *distinctly* different ways. The significance of the difference in the component factors has already been discussed.

The point that should be emphasized here is the visual impact of such a graphic representation. Comparisons between companies or segments within a company are readily grasped, and the most promising direction of improvement is highlighted. For example, its position on the chart suggests that the approach more likely to raise company C's rate to 20 percent is income-to-sales rate improvement, presently only 5 percent, inasmuch as increasing turnover from two to three times will raise the rate of return to only 15 percent. Moreover, such an increase in turnover would entail substantial increases in sales volume, decrease in investment in operating assets, or both.

In the case of company B, however, there appears to be considerable merit in an upward push in turnover. Not only does a turnover of assets once a year appear sluggish, but the rate of net income to sales seems reasonable by industry standards. To reach the 20 percent rate of return on capital by increas-

Percent operating profit on operating assets (return on capital used)

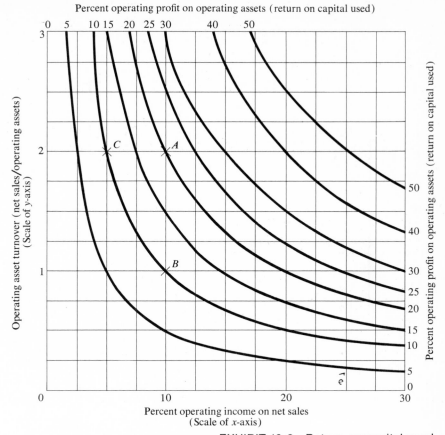

EXHIBIT 10-2   Return on capital used

ing its margin on sales to 20 percent, company B would have to achieve rather spectacular cost reductions or attempt to impose some price increases or both. The former would require that it outperform company A, a seemingly efficient producer. The latter might cause a reduction in volume which could eliminate the potential gain in margin percentage.

In any case, the graphic presentation in Exhibit 10-2 offers the same fundamental rate-of-return information as Exhibit 10-1 in a clear, simple form which many management people find more appealing than figures on a sheet of paper.

APPLICATION OF RETURN ON CAPITAL USED

On the surface, there appears to be no problem in setting up the return on capital used formula; just take the appropriate figures from the balance sheet and the income statement, plug them into the formula, and crank out the answer.

Once again, however, the question of purpose arises. If the purpose is to measure the performance of the company as a whole, the problem is different from that of measuring the performance of company segments. Furthermore,

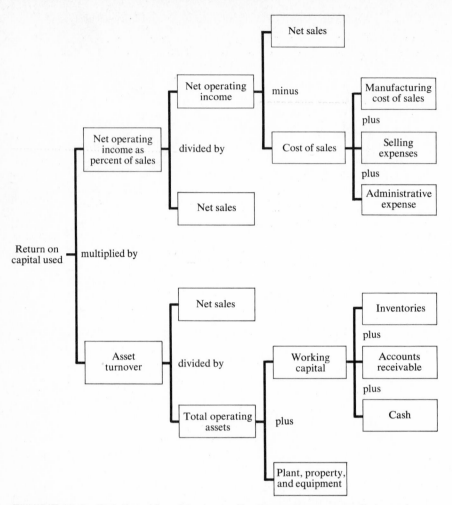

EXHIBIT 10-3   Relationship of factors affecting return on capital used

the purpose for which this information will be used affects the type and valuation of factors making up operating assets and net operating income. If the purpose is the motivation of operating managers, the approach might be different from that used for profit planning or for pricing.

The focus of the remainder of this chapter will be on the use of return on capital to evaluate the performance of operating management in segments of a company, such as product divisions, branch plants, sales territories, and the like. Its use for capital expenditure decisions, pricing, decisions among alternative choices, etc., will be discussed in later chapters.

The breakdown of the component parts of the return on capital used calculation is presented schematically in Exhibit 10-3. E. I. du Pont de Nemours & Co. pioneered in the use of this technique for appraising the performance of its segment managers, and this approach has been widely adopted in recent years.

PROBLEMS OF SEGMENT RATES OF RETURN

Four problems must be met before return on capital used can be employed effectively for motivating and evaluating the operating performance of segment managers:

1. Asset allocation

2. Cost allocation

3. Pricing transactions between segments within the company

4. Fixed-asset valuation

Motivation and Management

A key to the resolution of these problems lies once more in an examination of the purpose for employing return on capital used. When applied to the appraisal of segment management performance, it parallels closely the purpose of responsibility accounting and control budgeting. Top management usually wishes to employ an effective means both for measuring results against predetermined norms (i.e., standards) and for motivating responsible managers to behavior which will foster the achievement of company and personal goals.

Insofar as division or plant managers can recognize the harmony between their personal and company objectives and they can see the means of measuring their performance as essentially fair, the climate is favorable for good motivation. On the other hand, if they fear the effect of one or another of the yardsticks by which they are judged by their superiors, the edge of motivation is blunted. When either costs or assets are assigned to managers arbitrarily; when they are required to sell to or purchase from other company divisions at prices that are not comparable to those available outside the company; if their fixed assets are valued at unrealistic levels—in short, if they are to be held responsible for factors in rate of return over which they have no control—they are likely to feel threatened. Thus, the concept of the return on capital used is likely to be most effective in evaluating managers of investment centers— where the manager has control over revenues, costs, and investment.

Managers' negative responses, with varying degrees of subtlety, will often take the form of passive resistance, alibis, harshness with subordinates, attempts to shift the blame for poor performance to others, "tampering" with the figures, or, perhaps worst of all, making decisions which may make them look good in the short run but which are likely to be in conflict with the long-run goals of the company.

Asset Allocation

Operating assets are generally understood to be the sum of current and fixed assets. Thus, cash, receivables, inventories, and prepaid expenses, as well as plant, property, and equipment, are the capital tools with which management carries on its operations. The development of the base of capital to be used in a segment of a company, then, entails some measurement of those assets which comprise the segment manager's capital tool kit.

Cash   Separate cash accounts are not always established under the manager's control. Top management may wish to assign cash to a segment in some standard amount geared to the capacity, expected volume, and amount of cash expenses to be incurred.

Accounts Receivable   Under modern machine-accounting methods, frequently it is possible to identify receivables by product division or plant even if such records are not kept in the offices of the segment itself. Sometimes top management may wish to allocate receivables on the basis of credit sales or some other appropriate measure.

Inventories   Generally such records are kept at the plant or division location, or can otherwise be directly identified. Sometimes, however, top management may deem it advisable to assign raw materials common to more than one segment on some sort of usage basis.

Prepaid Expenses   This type of item is often quite "sticky," especially when it consists of such things as supplies inventory, rent, insurance premiums, and the like, the benefit of which is broad and indirect as to segments. Frequently this type of asset is not included in capital used by segments, because it is insignificant in amount and allocations are usually rather arbitrary.

Plant, Property, and Equipment   If segments are decentralized, or if the fixed assets of one are clearly distinct from those of others, the problem of their assignment to appropriate segments is not difficult. Often, more than one segment may occupy the same building or utilize equipment in common. Top management may deem it necessary to allocate such assets by using floor space and machine or worker-hours of usage as a basis.

Cost Allocation

To the extent that costs can be identified directly with the segment, no problem of cost assignment arises. Prime costs in manufacturing, factory overhead generated in a branch plant or directly in connection with manufacturing the products of a division, direct costs of selling the segment's products, costs of staff, and supplies and services incurred in administering the segment can all be identified with the segment in the normal course of cost accounting—indeed, the segment may do its own cost accounting.

The problem arises when top management deems it necessary, in applying return on capital used to segments, to dispose of all the company's costs among the operating segments of the company. When the factory building, productive facilities, offices, cafeterias, etc., are shared by more than one segment, some means of allocation may be used. Even where segments are decentralized and self-contained, top management may wish to assign to each a portion of "home office" costs, company advertising programs, professional services, research and development costs, and the like. Various bases are employed for allocation purposes, such as sales volume, value of total operating assets, number of employees, or square feet of floor space.

It is readily apparent that, whether dealing with assets or costs, the problem of allocation of indirect factors to segments bears a strong resemblance to that of allocating indirect factory overhead and factory service department costs for product costing purposes. Like the allocation of overhead, such allocations are all more or less arbitrary, and seldom can the bases and methods be immune from criticism.

Indeed, it might well be recommended that allocations, whether of costs or of assets, be avoided altogether. In recognition of the intention to motivate as well as to measure performance, it would seem best to base the return on capital for segment management only on *costs* and *assets* under the manager's direct control.

Transfer Pricing

A problem common to most companies operating with decentralized segments is that of placing a fair value upon exchanges of goods and services between segments within the company—the problem of transfer pricing. Frequently the number and volume of such transactions are such as to have a profound effect on the operations of a segment, and management must clearly understand the impact of transfer prices in order to use the segment rate of return most effectively. The general topic of transfer prices is considered in Chapter 12.

Fixed-Asset Valuation

The problem of fixed assets as a factor in rate of return calculations includes the problem of valuation as well as assignment to segments. Three possibilities have been suggested: net depreciated cost, gross cost, and cost adjusted to current prices.

Net Depreciated Cost   The book value for accounting purposes constitutes a logical valuation base for fixed assets, and it is widely used. However, its use involves certain problems.

It will be recalled that depreciation is an accounting device the purpose of which is to apportion the original cost of a long-term asset in some equitable manner to the individual periods which make up its useful life. The depreciation in a given period is regarded as partial expiration of asset value. Thus, the expired portion constitutes an expense of producing revenue in that period on the one hand, and reflects a corresponding reduction in the value of the asset on the other.

The depreciation charge, as a proper expense of the period, acts to reduce that period's income; but since it does not require the outlay of cash in the period, the cash derived from the operating revenues of the period is greater in that amount. If such additional cash were not reinvested in fixed assets, the net effect on the balance sheet (with other things equal) would be a decrease in fixed assets and an increase in cash in the amount of the depreciation. To the extent that cash is reinvested in capital assets in an amount at least equal to the period's depreciation, or is held as cash or converted to some other asset (such as inventory), the total operating asset base for rate of return calculations is unchanged.

Suppose, however, that instead of holding or reinvesting the cash thus generated, management chose to pay off a debt, declare extra dividends to stockholders, or purchase treasury shares. The result would be a lowering of the operating asset base, which (other things being equal) would increase the rate of return on capital. To pursue such a practice for very long would be tantamount to liquidating the fixed assets, a policy of questionable long-term benefit to the going concern.

Such a problem tends to be more theoretical than practical insofar as it affects the evaluation of the performance of the company as a whole. Prudent top management typically will adopt the long-range attitude favoring reinvestment in capital equipment. It will recognize that as equipment gets older, maintenance costs tend to increase; this, coupled with the likelihood that the older equipment is less efficient than what competitors may be using, will likely cause the net income figures to be lower and will thus offset somewhat the more favorable effects of the smaller asset base on the rate of return. Hence top management is unlikely to allow the fixed-asset base to deteriorate. Under such conditions, the use of net depreciated value for fixed assets is considered quite satisfactory.

When included in the base for determining segment rate of return, however, net depreciated value can raise certain difficulties. For example, a certain manager who is authorized to make a good share of the division's capital expenditures may be tempted to postpone needed capital expenditures, thus jeopardizing the long-term competitive position of the division and the company as a whole, in favor of a better short-range showing in his or her own divisional return on capital.

Blunting the edge of managerial motivation is another danger in the use of net depreciated value for divisional fixed assets. For example, suppose top management decides to replace a substantial portion of the old, highly depreciated equipment of one of its divisions with new, high-priced machines. The manager of this division, having no voice in such a decision, may see two personal disadvantages in this change:

1. The manager may fear that the gain in productive efficiency due to the new machines may not begin to offset the reduction in the return rate caused by such an increase in the fixed-asset base.

2. Whereas this manager's rate of return formerly may have compared favorably with that of another divisional manager whose asset base likewise contains a high percentage of well-depreciated fixed assets, the return rate will now show to considerable *disadvantage* as a result of the considerably *increased fixed-asset base,* even though the manager may be contributing as much or more to the company's *operating profit* performance.

Gross Cost   Gross cost (i.e., cost without deduction of accumulated depreciation) is widely used in valuing fixed assets for calculating the return on capital for segments of companies.

One reason sometimes given for using gross cost is that changing price levels render the net depreciated values less reflective of the real worth of fixed assets as time goes by. The use of gross cost tends to offset this distortion in periods of inflation.[3]

It is also argued that the gross-cost base enables a more equitable comparison among divisions, plants, or other segments of the company, the fixed assets of which were purchased at different times. Thus the plant with a larger proportion of older equipment does not show an artificially high rate of return in comparison with the newer plant with less accumulated depreciation. In fact, the tendency for older, less efficient equipment to depress net income, and thus the rate of return, will be even more apparent.

There is an inherent drawback to the use of gross cost, however. The buildup of cash from operations resulting from the use of noncash depreciation expense as a determinant of income is not offset by a corresponding decrease in the value of the fixed assets out of which it arose. Hence there will be duplication of asset values unless some adjustment is made. For example, if the additional cash is reinvested in new fixed assets, there is duplication of dollar value (if not in the physical assets) in fixed assets as well as total assets.

In choosing between net or gross cost as a basis for valuing fixed assets, management can once again take its cue from the idea of using different costs for different purposes. In an authoritative research report on this subject, an NAA committee states:[4]

> Over a period of years, [top] management aims to direct capital into activities which offer the best opportunity for profits, and to withdraw capital from activities which have a declining profit potential. The *net asset base* reflects the over-all result of depreciation and investment policies established by top management because capital recovered from sales revenues and reinvested tends to offset the reduction of asset values by depreciation.
>
> On the other hand, management in charge of a division, plant, or other segment of a company is responsible only for earning a return on the specific assets entrusted to its control. The effect of depreciation and reinvestment policies on the rate of return from a limited segment of the company's assets tends to distort rate of return from a limited segment of a company's assets because increases in the allowance for depreciation may not be offset by *reinvestment of recovered capital in the same segment.* Therefore, a more useful rate of return may be secured by using *gross assets* as the investment base. [Emphases added.]

Cost Adjusted to Current Prices   A third method involves the use of a valuation for fixed assets based on original cost figures converted to current prices minus accumulated depreciation, also based on current prices. This method is not widely used, primarily because of the difficulties in developing acceptable conversion factors, as well as the considerable clerical work involved in annual revisions.

---

[3] The advocates of the net-asset base counter this argument with the assertion that two wrongs will not make a right—while net depreciated values (based on original cost) may not reflect present price levels, neither is there anything in the gross cost which is inherently related to these current levels. The similarity, if any, is purely accidental.

[4] *Return on Capital as a Guide to Managerial Decisions,* National Association of Accountants, Research Report 35, New York, 1959, p. 16.

The use of current values nevertheless is capable of answering a number of the objections to the other two methods. First, differences due to the variety of acquisition values among the company segments are eliminated. Second, the problem of duplication associated with the gross-cost method is avoided. Finally, the advantage of the shrinking-asset base associated with the net-depreciated-asset method is minimized as current economic values are annually assessed.

One noted writer on this subject (measurement of segment rate of return) has cited cases in which manipulation of other valuation methods leads to decisions by segment managers which are in conflict with the goals of the company as a whole. In developing his proposals for improving measurement of rate of return by segments, he says: "It is my belief that the only completely satisfactory method for assigning values to divisional facilities is one that uses replacement values and is not tied directly into the books of account."[5]

It would not be practical, within the scope of this book, to delve more deeply into this controversy. It is clear that no single approach to fixed-asset valuation is without its limitations. We shall merely stress once more that management's purpose should be the principal guide to the method chosen, and that great care should be exercised in its implementation.

MEASUREMENT OF CHANGES

Much of the practical difficulty in this regard can be avoided. If top management will disabuse itself of the supposed need to compare one manager directly with another and to use only (and all) the figures which appear in company accounting records, it might find return on capital used a more effective tool for its purpose.

Instead of comparing one manager with another and allocating costs and assets among them more or less arbitrarily, some companies have focused attention on the changes which managers effect in their own segments over a period of time. Working toward preestablished standards for the key factors of return on capital used, and being charged only with costs and assets under their direct control, the managers are better able to concentrate on improving their performance period by period.

A simplified example of the type of analysis by which the causes of change and improvement are evaluated appears in Exhibit 10-4. Division X of A Company is assigned certain assets, and its net income is reported as the difference between its net sales and all direct divisional costs.

Operations of Division X are located in Midwest City, 1,000 miles from the company's home office. It has its own divisional sales manager and sales staff, as well as manufacturing staff, design engineering, personnel, and accounting functions. It has a local bank account and pays all its own payrolls and bills. The general manager is allowed to expend funds for fixed assets up to $20,000 per year without home office approval. Fixed assets, for purposes of the rate of return calculation, are reported at gross cost. The division bene-

[5] John Dearden, "Problem in Decentralized Profit Responsibility," *Harvard Business Review* (May–June 1960), p. 86.

EXHIBIT 10-4
A COMPANY
Comparison of Divisional Rate of Return, Division X
For the Years 19x1 and 19x2

	19x1	Change—Increase (Decrease)			Incremental Effect on Return	19x2
		Assets	Sales	Costs		
Assets						
Cash	$ 50,000	—				$ 50,000
Accounts receivable	100,000	$10,000				110,000
Inventory	250,000	5,000				255,000
Plant, property, and equipment	200,000	10,000				210,000
Total assets	$ 600,000	$25,000			($ 25,000)	$ 625,000
Net income						
Net sales	$1,000,000		$250,000		$250,000	$1,250,000
Variable manufacturing costs	$ 500,000			$125,000		$ 625,000
Variable selling expense	50,000			12,500		62,500
Divisional fixed factory overhead	200,000			—		200,000
Divisional fixed selling and administrative	130,000			95,000		225,000
Total expenses	$ 880,000			$232,500	($232,500)	$1,112,500
Net income	$ 120,000				$ 17,500	$ 137,500
Percentage net income to sales	12%					11%
Turnover of assets	1.67					2
Return on assets used	20%					22%
Change in return—19x1 to 19x2						+2%

fits from the company advertising, research and development, legal, labor relations, and other staff services along with other operating divisions of the company, but it receives no allocation of their costs.

Exhibit 10-4 shows the analysis of the key asset, revenue, and expense factors comprising the return on capital used for Division X for the years 19x1 and 19x2, as well as the changes in 19x2. The company has set standards for the division of 15 percent net income on sales, a turnover of two per year for operating assets, and a return on capital used of 30 percent.

In 19x1, the manager of Division X fell short of standard net income by 3 percent (15 percent standard minus 12 percent realized), of turnover by 0.33 times (2.00 standard minus 1.67 realized), and of return on capital by 10 percent (30 percent standard minus 20 percent realized). In 19x2, she showed only 11 percent net income to sales (4 percent off standard) but had improved turnover until it matched standard (two times), with the result that return on capital was improved from 20 to 22 percent (still 8 percent short of standard).

In seeking reasons for these changes, the manager of Division X looks at changes in the three key factors — assets, sales volume, and costs. She notes that she has increased her investment in total assets by $25,000 (from $600,000 to $625,000) while expanding sales volume by $250,000 (from $1,000,000 to $1,250,000), which accounts for the improvement of turnover rate from 1.67 to 2.0 times per year.

Detailed analysis indicates some of the reasons for this. The expanded volume has required no increase in the cash account. The 25 percent increase in sales has required only a 10 percent increase in receivables ($10,000 increase on $100,000) and a 2 percent increase in inventory ($5,000 increase on $250,000).

The manager has invested $10,000 in fixed assets, partly for increased capacity and partly for the special tools needed to produce a redesigned model of product. Both of these, she believes, have contributed to the increased sales volume.

Upon examining the details of her net operating income, she finds the following:

Variable manufacturing costs increased in proportion to the increased volume.

Variable selling expenses increased in proportion to the increased volume.

The divisional fixed factory overhead cost remained the same.

The divisional fixed selling and administrative cost increased by $95,000.

Closer examination of the last category of cost revealed that a special advertising and sales promotion campaign instituted by her divisional sales manager to introduce the new product models to the market accounted for the bulk of the increase. The campaign has been judged a success in the light of increased sales volume, but the added *contribution* from increased sales was insufficient to cover its cost and still provide the desired additional profit. This cost factor was the chief cause of the decline in total net income to sales from 12 to 11 percent.

The general manager concluded that, while the beneficial effects of the promotional campaign might extend into future years (in a sense, the cost might be considered a form of investment), she was determined that, in the future, more constraints would be placed on such costs.

Thus, while top management might be inclined to applaud the overall improvement in Division X performance—from 20 to 22 percent return on capital used—the manager will probably begin planning her attack on operating costs for the coming year.

This example tends to highlight what we believe is one of the better applications of the return on capital used concept to the appraisal of segment performance. Instead of stressing the *absolute size* of the measurements shown in comparison with *other segments*, this approach emphasizes *relative* change *within* the segment from period to period, and conformity to top management norms. The NAA study previously cited describes how one company employs this approach:[6]

> The company, emphasizing *change* in return on capital employed, presents a quarterly "report card" to top management. On this "report card," each division is rated for its performance in terms of seven different measures of financial performance. One of the most important of these measures is return on capital employed. Return on capital employed is not, however, presented as an absolute figure. Like the other seven measures, the percentage change in return on capital from the previous quarter is shown. The assistant controller pointed out that, in this way, no division can complain because the investment base does not reflect replacement cost, or that allocations are unrealistic. Each division is compared not with another division's performance, but with its own performance in a prior period. Accordingly, the capital employed base and the allocation methods are completely comparable between periods. The division that shows the greatest improvement in return on capital employed for the quarter is ranked first for return on capital even though the absolute size of the return on capital figures may be far less than another division's. Similar rankings are prepared for the other six measures of financial performance. Then the rankings for each division for each of the seven measures are totaled to give a total rank for financial performance during the month. The division having the lowest total score "stands at the head of the class." Thus, if one division stands first in all seven measures, it will have a total score of seven. Considerable competitive spirit is generated by the division managers in their attempts to score best for the overall standing, and also to score best in certain measures, such as return on capital employed. A poll of top management and division managers revealed that none ranked return on capital less than second most important of the seven different measures.

RESIDUAL INCOME

Focusing on changes in the divisional return on capital used, as just described, avoids many of the problems otherwise associated with the use of this ratio.

[6] *Return on Capital as a Guide to Managerial Decisions*, op. cit., pp. 31, 32.

However, there remains one disadvantage which has caused some companies to modify its use in practice. The divisional return on capital used is an average of the return earned on all the division's assets. If a division has an opportunity to invest in an undertaking which returns less than this average, the overall return on capital used will be decreased even though the undertaking is advantageous to the company as a whole.

An illustration of this problem appears in Exhibit 10-5. Division Y of A Company has control over certain assets, and its net income is considered to be the difference between its net sales and direct divisional costs.

As shown in Exhibit 10-5, Division Y has decreased its return on capital used from 26 percent to 25 percent by increasing its net income $20,000 as a result of an increased investment of $100,000. If the divisional manager's performance is evaluated using changes in return on capital used, it would appear that

EXHIBIT 10-5
A COMPANY
Comparison of Divisional Rate of Return, Division Y,
For the Years 19x2 and 19x3

	19x2	Incremental Effect on Return	19x3
Divisional assets	$500,000	($100,000)	$600,000
Net sales	$2,000,000	$500,000	$2,500,000
Direct costs	1,870,000	(480,000)	2,350,000
Net income	$ 130,000	$ 20,000	$ 150,000
Percentage net income to sales	6.5%		6.0%
Turnover of assets	4.0		4.17
Return on assets used	26%		25%
Change in return – 19x2 to 19x3			–1%

EXHIBIT 10-6
A COMPANY
Comparison of Rate of Return
For the Years 19x2 and 19x3

	19x2	Incremental Effect on Return	19x3
Total assets	$2,000,000	($100,000)	$2,100,000
Net sales	$6,000,000	$500,000	$6,500,000
Total costs	5,700,000	(480,000)	6,180,000
Net income	$ 300,000	$ 20,000	$ 320,000
Percentage net income to sales	5%		4.9%
Turnover of assets	3.0		3.1
Return on capital used	15%		15.2%

19x3's performance was not as good as the previous year's. As far as Company A as a whole is concerned, however, a return on capital used of 20 percent ($20,000/$100,000) may represent a very desirable investment. This is illustrated in Exhibit 10-6, which indicates that A Company's return on capital used increased slightly because of the additional investment, even though Division Y's return decreased. The problem faced by top management of A Company is to ensure that the manager of Division Y continues to make such investments, even though it lowers the divisional return.

One method of doing this is to employ the concept of residual income. Residual income is defined as net income in excess of a desired or budgeted return on capital used. For example, assume that top management of Company A and the manager of Division Y agree that a 15 percent return on capital used is a fair measure of the cost of capital used in that division. The computation of residual income in 19x2 and 19x3 for Division Y would then be as follows:

	19x2	19x3
Divisional assets	$500,000	$600,000
Minimum desired return on capital used	15%	15%
Minimum desired net income	$ 75,000	$ 90,000
Actual net income	130,000	150,000
Residual income	$ 55,000	$ 60,000

Division Y's residual income has increased by $5,000, which represents the difference between the income from the additional investment in 19x3 and a 15 percent return on that investment ($20,000 minus $15,000). By focusing on changes in residual income, top management can evaluate division managers through using a performance measure which encourages these managers to make decisions which are best for the division and for the company as a whole. Residual income will always increase if an additional investment yields a return higher than the desired minimum, regardless of the average return on capital used reported by the division.

Useful as the residual income concept is, however, it is based on the same data as in the return on capital used, and it is thus subject to many of the same problems regarding allocations, transfer prices, and valuation. Once again, though, focusing on changes in residual income is one way to avoid many of these problems.

SUMMARY

The return on capital concept is not new. It has, however, come in for considerable attention in recent years as an effective tool for appraising management performance. There is much similarity in the use of the return on capital concept as applied to the evaluation of an investment — a *financial* purpose — and its use in *measuring managerial effectiveness*. The former is known as the investors' ratio, the latter as the return on capital used. For the investors' ratio, the net income and investment figures used are residual — net income to common stockholders and common stockholders' equity.

Management, however, wants to know how well it has done through the employment of *all* the operating assets of the business, regardless of source. Moreover, it considers the net income from operations as the most sensitive gauge of its profit-making ability. Thus, the managerial return on capital concept focuses on the amount of *net operating income* management produces with the total *operating assets* at its disposal. The resulting measure is return on capital used.

The key factors in return on capital used are the percentage of net operating income to net sales and the turnover of operating assets in net sales. The components of net operating income include the net sales and the manufacturing, selling, and administrative expenses. The net operating assets might include the main current assets, cash, receivables, inventories and prepaid items, and the plant, property, and equipment used in the company's operations. By close attention to the interaction of these components, management is better able to influence the return on capital used.

One sticky problem is the choice of the valuation base for fixed assets. Various companies prefer and use one of three possible bases: net depreciated cost of assets; gross cost of assets; cost adjusted to current prices. In general, there seems to be good reason for using net depreciated value for computing return on capital used for the *company as a whole*, whereas the gross-cost value seems better suited to measurement of *segment* rates of return. On the other hand, there are some who believe that cost adjusted to current price valuation is superior to both.

In the last analysis, management's purpose should be the principal guide to the method of applying techniques such as return on capital used or residual income. They are generally regarded as good devices, along with a number of others, for both motivating and measuring the performance of segment management. When such techniques are used for such a sensitive purpose, their limitations and pitfalls must be borne in mind. It has been shown how the results of using certain asset valuation bases tend to inject a conflict between the self-interest of the manager and the goals of the company. Another danger lies in the allocation of assets and costs to segments where such items cannot be identified directly with the segment. Like the problem of the allocation of indirect manufacturing overhead costs to productive cost centers in a plant, such allocation poses a threat to responsible managers in the form of implied responsibility for factors over which they have no control. It is recommended that allocations be avoided altogether.

One approach to minimizing the dangers of faulty measurement and negative motivation is the reporting of return on capital used and residual income for a segment manager in terms only of changes in his or her own segment over a period of time. In this way, unfair comparisons with other segments of the company are avoided, and managers may still be ranked in terms of their ability to effect changes in their own segment as measured against company standards and past performance.

KEY WORDS AND PHRASES

investors' ratio
market yield
return on capital used
trading on the equity
financial leverage
asset turnover

net income to net sales
segments of a business
residual income
net depreciated cost
gross cost

DISCUSSION QUESTIONS

1. Distinguish between the concepts of investors' ratio and return on capital used.
2. Explain the interrelationship of good operating management and good financial management in maximizing return on stockholders' equity.
3. Why separate return on capital used into calculations of percentage of net profit on sales and asset turnover?
4. Which is preferable, high percentage of profit on sales or rapid asset turnover? Are there pitfalls in either?
5. Characterize each of the following in terms of net profit percentage and asset turnover as being relatively high, moderate, or low:
   a. A meat packer
   b. A manufacturer of pharmaceutical products
   c. A food supermarket
   d. A manufacturer of aerospace components
   e. A commercial airline
   f. A filling station
   g. A jewelry store
   h. A commercial television station
   i. A basic petroleum producer
   j. A manufacturer of computers
6. Why is the problem of return on capital measurement different for segments than for the company as a whole?
7. What are the most important problem areas in segment measurement?
8. Comment on the similarities and differences in the assignment of assets and costs to segments of a firm.
9. Discuss segment management motivation vis-à-vis asset and cost allocation.
10. Explain transfer pricing. Why should it be a problem?
11. Discuss the merits of the residual income concept.
12. Why should the valuation of fixed assets constitute a problem in the measurement of return on capital used?
13. Discuss advantages and disadvantages of valuing fixed assets at (a) gross cost; (b) net depreciated cost; and (c) cost adjusted to current prices.
14. Must all factors in the measurement of return on capital used "tie in" to the official financial statements of a company? Why?
15. Discuss the relative merits of measuring a segment manager's performance both against that of other managers in absolute terms, and in comparison with his or her own in terms of relative change over a period of time.

PROBLEMS

10-1. Janet Monet is considering purchasing one of two businesses. The following estimates have been made for these businesses as representing average yearly results:

	Business No. 1	Business No. 2
Investment required (purchase price of business)	$100,000	$ 50,000
Sales revenue	300,000	200,000
Net income after tax	8,000	5,000

Required:
1. Compute the asset turnover, percentage return on sales, and return on capital used for each business.
2. Which business should Janet Monet purchase? Why?

10-2. The Edson Company has income of $75,000 and assets of $500,000. Its net sales were $900,000. In considering next year's budget, management has made five different forecasts, shown below:

1. Sales will increase by $20,000 with no change in the income or assets.
2. Income will increase $5,000 and investment will increase $10,000.
3. Income will increase $5,000 and investment will decrease by $10,000.
4. Income will decrease $5,000 and investment will decrease by $10,000.
5. Sales will increase by $20,000 and income will increase by $5,000.

Required:
1. Compute the profit percentage, asset turnover, and return on capital used for the Edson Company last year.
2. Considering each of the five forecasts separately (they are not related), compute the profit percentage, asset turnover, and return on capital used of the Edson Company under the various forecasts.
3. Which of these forecasts appears to be most favorable? Why?

10-3.† Three companies — Wynken Corporation, Blynken Limited, and Nod Consolidated Industries — are competitors in the sleeping-bag industry. Basic comparative statistics for the year 19x1 are as follows:

	Net Sales	Operating Costs	Operating Assets
Wynken	$5,000,000	$4,600,000	$2,500,000
Blynken	3,000,000	2,700,000	6,000,000
Nod	960,000	912,000	240,000

Required:
1. Which is the largest company in the industry?
2. Which was the best performer in 19x1?
3. Did any of the three leave nothing to be desired in 19x1 performance? Why?

4. Make recommendations regarding the areas most in need of improvement for each company.

10-4. Prepare a graph similar to Exhibit 10-2, including curved lines for rates of return of 5 percent, 10 percent, and 20 percent. Plot on that chart the following three divisions of the Vigers Company:

	Division A	Division B	Division C
Net sales	$100,000	$ 50,000	$400,000
Operating income	10,000	10,000	10,000
Operating assets	50,000	100,000	200,000

Required:
Top management is well pleased with the performance of Division A. What suggestions do you have for Divisions B and C in order that their performance be improved?

10-5. James and Edward Toben are brothers each of whom owns a business. James owns a department store in the downtown area and has sales of $500,000 per year with an investment of $250,000. Edward has a discount store in the suburbs which does annual sales of $2 million on an investment of $200,000. The two brothers are trying to determine which business is more profitable. James believes that his is more profitable because his sales margin is 10 percent compared with Edward's 2 percent. Edward argues that his business is more profitable because of his high turnover rate of ten times per year.

Required:
Comment on the brothers' arguments, and support your comments with appropriate calculations.

10-6. Shown below are the income and financial position statements for two companies for year 19x1.

	Company A	Company B
Total assets	$100,000	$200,000
Current liabilities	$ 10,000	$ 20,000
Bonds payable	10,000	80,000
Stockholders' equity	80,000	100,000
Total equities	$100,000	$200,000
Net sales	$200,000	$200,000
Operating expenses	(186,000)	(176,000)
Bond interest expense	(1,000)	(10,800)
Income tax expense	(6,500)	(6,600)
Net income	$ 6,500	$ 6,600

Required:
Is either company trading on the equity—that is, does either company exhibit financial leverage? Explain.

10-7. James Rochelle, newly hired management accountant, has suggested to the vice president—controller of the Largly Company that using return on investment as a divisional performance measure would reduce investments in idle resources in those divisions. The controller replied that there were no idle resources in the divisions because of a sure-fire way the controller had of eliminating them. Once a year he makes a personal visit to each division. If any idle equipment or other resources are found, the manager of the division is fired on the spot. In the first year of these visits, two of the six division managers were fired. In the four years since that time, not one manager has been discharged for this reason, although the controller has continued these inspections. The controller cites this as evidence that his method is working well.

Required:
1. Do you think the controller's method is really working well? Explain.
2. As James Rochelle, how could you justify using return on investment in this situation?

10-8. The Joyce Manufacturing Company, presently operating at its practical capacity, is considering the next step in its vigorous growth trend. An extension of physical plant and equipment is a must, but such a move seems certain to change the cost-volume-profit relationship, rate of return on capital used, and probably the selling price.

The following are condensed financial statements for 19x2:

INCOME STATEMENT

Sales (500,000 × $6)		$3,000,000
Cost of sales:		
Variable manufacturing costs	$1,800,000	
Fixed manufacturing costs	480,000	
Total cost of sales		2,280,000
Gross margin		$ 720,000
Operating expenses:		
Variable selling and administrative	$ 200,000	
Fixed selling and administrative	160,000	
Total operating expenses		360,000
Net operating profit		$ 360,000

BALANCE SHEET
Assets

Cash	$ 100,000
Receivables	200,000
Inventories	500,000
Plant, property, equipment (net)	1,200,000
Total assets	$2,000,000

Equities

Accounts payable	$ 250,000
Mortgage payable	750,000
Stockholders' equity	1,000,000
Total equities	$2,000,000

The contemplated expansion would effect the following changes:

Increase in practical capacity over present	100%
Increase in normal capacity (based on 3- to 5-year projection) over present practical capacity	50%
Increased investment in plant, property, and equipment	$800,000
Increase in cash	50,000
Increase in receivables	100,000
Increase in inventories	250,000
Increase in annual fixed manufacturing costs	320,000
Increase in annual fixed selling and administrative costs	40,000

Required:

1. For the year 19x2, determine (*a*) percentage operating profit on sales; (*b*) operating-asset turnover; (*c*) rate of return on capital used; and (*d*) break-even point.

2. Assuming that 19x3 operations would be at the level of the new normal capacity, prepare a pro forma income statement.

3. On the same basis, determine operating-profit percentage, asset turnover, return on capital used, and break-even point for 19x3.

4. Assuming no change in selling price, determine the level of volume necessary to restore the 19x2 rate of return for 19x3 operations.

5. With an operating level at the new normal capacity in 19x3, what selling price would have to be charged to restore the 19x2 rate of return on capital used?

6. If operations were at the new *practical* capacity, what selling price would yield the 19x2 rate of return on capital used?

10-9. The Germaine Corporation has three divisions sharing the facilities of its one location. Comparative balance sheets for the total company show:

	December 31, 19x1	December 31, 19x2
Assets		
Cash	$ 235,000	$ 325,000
Receivables	180,000	220,000
Raw materials inventories	150,000	90,000
Finished goods inventories	320,000	280,000
Land and buildings	430,000	410,000
Equipment	1,380,000	1,500,000
Total assets	$2,695,000	$2,825,000
Equities		
Payables	$ 225,000	$ 205,000
Stockholders' equity	2,470,000	2,620,000
Total equities	$2,695,000	$2,825,000

Divisional income statements for 19x2 show:

		Division		
	Total	I	II	III
Sales	$2,800,000	$1,400,000	$1,000,000	$400,000
Cost of sales:				
Material	$ 700,000	$ 280,000	$ 210,000	$210,000
Labor	500,000	300,000	170,000	30,000
Burden	800,000	460,000	300,000	40,000
Total cost of sales	$2,000,000	$1,040,000	$ 680,000	$280,000
Gross margin	$ 800,000	$ 360,000	$ 320,000	$120,000
Selling and administrative	650,000	350,000	230,000	70,000
Net profit	$ 150,000	$ 10,000	$ 90,000	$ 50,000

The controller wishes to measure divisional return on capital used. The accounting system already provides for assignment of revenues and expense, including allocations of indirect burden and selling and administrative expense, with results as shown. The next step would be to assign operating assets to divisions. He analyzes the data as follows:

	Basis
Cash	Sales
Receivables	Direct
Raw materials inventories	Material in cost of sales
Finished goods inventories	Direct
Land and buildings	Square feet of floor space
Equipment	Direct labor hours

		Division		
Basis	Total	I	II	III
Direct charges:				
Receivables	100%	50%	35%	15%
Finished goods inventory	100%	60%	25%	15%
Square feet of floor space	150,000	75,000	50,000	25,000
Direct labor hours	240,000	160,000	70,000	10,000

Assignments of operating capital to divisions will be based on average asset balances.

Required:

1. Calculate divisional and total company profit-to-sales percentages, asset turnover, and return on capital used.
2. Are you satisfied with the validity of the results? Would you praise or blame division managers, expand or drop product lines, or take other action on the basis of your calculations? Explain.

10-10.† The management of the Southern Cottonseed Company has engaged you to assist in the development of information to be used for managerial decisions.

The company has the capacity to process 20,000 tons of cottonseed per year. The yield of a ton of cottonseed is as follows:

	Average Yield per Ton of Cottonseed	Average Selling Price per Trade Unit
Oil	300 lb	$ 0.15/lb
Meal	600 lb	50.00/ton
Hulls	800 lb	20.00/ton
Lint	100 lb	3.00/cwt
Waste	200 lb	

A special marketing study revealed that the company can expect to sell its entire output for the coming year at the listed average selling prices.

You have determined the company's costs to be as follows:

Processing costs:
  Variable: $9 per ton of cottonseed put into process
  Fixed: $108,000 per year
Marketing costs:
  All variable: $20 per ton sold
Administrative costs:
  All fixed: $90,000 per year

From the above information, you have prepared and submitted to management a detailed report on the company's break-even point. In view of conditions in the cottonseed market, management told you that it would also like to know the average maximum amount that the company can afford to pay for a ton of cottonseed.

Management has defined this as the amount that would result in the company's having losses no greater when operating than when closed down under the existing cost and revenue structure. Management states that you are to assume that the fixed costs shown in your break-even-point report will continue unchanged even when the operations are shut down.

Required:

1. Compute the average maximum amount that the company can afford to pay for a ton of cottonseed.
2. You also plan to mention to management the factors, other than the costs that entered into your computations, that it should consider in deciding whether to shut down the plant. Discuss these additional factors.
3. The stockholders consider the minimum satisfactory return on their investment in the business to be 25 percent before corporate income taxes. The stockholders' equity in the company is $968,000. Compute the maximum average amount that the company can pay for a ton of cottonseed to realize the minimum satisfactory return on the stockholders' investment in the business.

(AICPA adapted)

10-11. As the chief executive officer of Begamma Industries, you have been given the following data regarding the performance of three of Begamma's divisions:

Division	Net Book Value of Assets	Net Replacement Value of Assets	Net Income
East	$10,000	$10,000	$1,800
Midwest	20,000	35,000	3,000
West	30,000	33,000	4,200

Required:

1. For each of the divisions, compute the rate of return and the residual income based first on net book value and then on net replacement value. To compute residual income, use 10 percent as the minimum desired return on capital used.
2. Rank the performance of each division under each of the four measures computed in part 1.
3. What does this ranking tell you about the performance of the division managers and the divisions?

10-12. The appliance division of the Northern Electric Company reports the following assets on its divisional balance sheet:

Original cost	$48,000,000
Accumulated depreciation	19,200,000
Book value	$28,800,000

These assets have an estimated current replacement cost of $42 million.

The division's income statement for 1972 appears below in summary form:

Sales	$60,000,000
Direct division expenses	(45,000,000)
Allocated from home office	(7,500,000)
Income before taxes	$ 7,500,000

Required:
1. Compute the rate of return on investment in the division's assets based on book value, gross cost, and replacement cost.
2. Which of these rates of return would be most useful for the company's managers? Why?

10-13. The Solomon Company uses only one type of asset. This asset has a useful life of four years, costs $10,000 to acquire, brings in revenues of $10,500 per year for those four years, and requires an expenditure of $7,680 per year for those four years for labor, maintenance, and other costs (excluding depreciation). The company assumes no salvage value and uses the straight-line method.

Required:
1. Prepare schedules computing the return on capital used of this asset over its four-year life, using first net assets and then gross assets.
2. Assume that the Solomon Company began operations in 1971 by purchasing one such asset and has continued to purchase one new asset at the beginning of every year. Prepare schedules computing the return on capital used which would be reported by the company for 1971 through 1976, using first net assets and then gross assets.

10-14. The Brownell Company has made the following budgets for its three divisions for the coming year. The company charges each division a 5 percent return on its average current assets and a 10 percent return on its average fixed assets and uses residual income for measuring division managers.

	Division A	Divison B	Division C
Budgeted profit	$ 90,000	$ 50,000	$ 55,000
Budgeted current assets	100,000	200,000	300,000
Budgeted fixed assets	400,000	400,000	500,000
Budgeted sales	900,000	250,000	350,000

Required:
Listed below are four management actions. For each of these independent situations, calculate the effect of the action on residual income and on the return on capital used for each division.

1. An investment in fixed assets is made which increases fixed assets by $100,000 and profits by $12,000.
2. An investment in working capital is made which increases current assets by $100,000 and profits by $12,000.
3. An investment in fixed assets is made which increases assets by $100,000 and profits by $7,000.
4. A plant is closed down and sold. Fixed assets are reduced by $75,000, current assets are increased by $75,000, and profits are decreased by $7,500.

10-15. The Acme Manufacturing Company is a decentralized company with several operating divisions. The general manager of the Consumers Division is considering the following projects requiring capital investment in the division:

Project	Required Investment	Annual Return
1	$1,000,000	$160,000
2	800,000	100,000
3	700,000	75,000
4	500,000	40,000
5	200,000	35,000

In addition to the above, the Consumers Division manager expects a return of $12\frac{1}{2}$ percent on $10 million invested in other projects. The cost of invested capital to the company is 10 percent.

Required:
1. What will be the total investment, total return, return on capital used, and residual income of the rational division manager under the following situations:
   a. The company has a rule that all projects promising at least 15 percent should be undertaken.
   b. The division manager is evaluated on his ability to maximize his return on capital used.
   c. The division manager is evaluated on his ability to maximize residual income of his division.
2. Which of the three approaches in part 1 will encourage the investment policy which is best for the company as a whole? Why?

10-16† Bill Sweet was manager of the Pacific Division of Admiral Motors. His operations comprised the manufacture and sale of controls for automatic equipment. The division was virtually autonomous, including manufacturing, sales, engineering, personnel, accounting, and financial functions. Bill was allowed to manage the division as would the president of an independent company, with only two constraints: adherence to broad company policy and achievement of a satisfactory return on operating assets.

His results for the year 19x1 are summarized thus (000 omitted):

OPERATING ASSETS

	December 31, 19x1	Average for Year
Cash	$ 400	$ 500
Receivables	1,600	1,500
Inventories	2,400	2,500
Plant and equipment	6,100	5,500
Total	$10,500	$10,000

INCOME STATEMENT

Sales		$18,000
Cost of sales:		
Variable manufacturing	$7,920	
Fixed manufacturing	4,000	
Total cost of sales		11,920
Gross margin		$ 6,080
Selling and administrative:		
Variable divisional selling and administrative	$2,880	
Fixed divisional selling and administrative	1,400	
Allocated home office cost	270	
Total selling and administrative		4,550
Net operating income		$ 1,530

Fixed assets are valued at gross cost. Home office expenses include a share of total company research and development, major advertising, and corporate administration. This cost is allocated to all operating divisions on the basis of total employees.

In 19x2, Bill undertook to increase volume and increase productive efficiency. He added $600,000 to the advertising budget and added $1,200,000 of modern equipment in the plant.

The results were: Sales increased 25 percent; the percentage of variable manufacturing costs to sales decreased by 4 percent; the fixed manufacturing costs increased $1,530,000; operating asset balances at December 31, 19x2, were (000 omitted):

Cash	$ 500
Receivables	1,700
Inventories	2,500
Plant and equipment	7,300
Total	$12,000

Home office cost allocated was $740,000.

Required:
1. Calculate Bill Sweet's profit percentage, asset turnover, and return on capital used for 19x1 (average asset balances are used to determine turnover).
2. Calculate the same information for 19x2.
3. Compute the change in the break-even point from 19x1 to 19x2.
4. Discuss the effect of including fixed assets at gross cost and the allocation of home office cost.

10-17. Dan Rancid manages the Turbulent Division of Admiral Motors and Nan Neutral manages the Insipid Division.

Top management compares the profit performance of all its division managers after the close of each year. The pertinent data for 19x1 and 19x2 are as follows (000 omitted):

	Turbulent		Insipid	
	19x1	19x2	19x1	19x2
Average investment				
Current assets	$30,000	$31,500	$400	$310
Plant and equipment	20,000	20,500	500	500
Total	$50,000	$52,000	$900	$810
Condensed income statements				
Sales	$50,000	$52,000	$3,600	$3,400
Variable cost of sales	$30,000	$30,856	$2,400	$2,248
Fixed cost of sales	5,000	5,000	622	622
Variable selling and administrative	3,500	3,640	180	170
Fixed selling and administrative	2,000	2,000	200	200
Home office cost allocated	950	624	25	27
Total costs	$41,450	$42,120	$3,427	$3,267
Net operating income	$ 8,550	$ 9,880	$ 173	$ 133

Required:
1. Calculate profit percentages, asset turnovers, and rates of return for the two divisions for the two years.
2. Make a comparison of all three divisions, Turbulent, Insipid, and Pacific (problem 10-16), on the basis of the system presently in effect. Do you feel that this comparison gives a fair appraisal of the relative performances of the three managers? Why?
3. Recast the comparison on a basis which you believe would be equitable.

10-18. You have been engaged to assist the management of the Stenger Corporation in arriving at certain decisions. The Stenger Corporation has its home office in Philadelphia and leases factory buildings in Rhode Island, Georgia, and Illinois. The same single product is manufactured in all three factories. The following information is available regarding 19x4 operations:

	Total	Rhode Island	Illinois	Georgia
Sales	$900,000	$200,000	$400,000	$300,000
Fixed costs:				
Factory	$180,000	$ 50,000	$ 55,000	$ 75,000
Administrative	59,000	16,000	21,000	22,000
Variable costs	500,000	100,000	220,000	180,000
Allocated home office				
expense	63,000	14,000	28,000	21,000
Total costs	$802,000	$180,000	$324,000	$298,000
Net profit from operations	$ 98,000	$ 20,000	$ 76,000	$ 2,000

Home office expense is allocated on the basis of units sold. The sales price per unit is $10.

Management is undecided whether to renew the lease of the Georgia factory, which expires on December 31, 19x5, and which, if renewed, will require an increase in rent of $15,000 per year. If the Georgia factory is shut down, the amount expected to be realized from the sale of the equipment is greater than its book value and would cover all termination expenses.

If the Georgia factory is shut down, the company can continue to serve customers of the Georgia factory by one of the following methods:

1. Expanding the Rhode Island factory, which would increase fixed costs by 15 percent. Additional shipping expense of $2 per unit would be incurred on the increased production.
2. Entering into a long-term contract with a competitor who would serve the Georgia factory customers and who would pay the Stenger Corporation a commission of $1.60 per unit.

The Stenger Corporation is also planning to establish a subsidiary corporation in Canada to produce the same product. Based on estimated annual Canadian sales of 40,000 units, cost studies produced the following estimates for the Canadian subsidiary:

	Total Annual Cost	Percentage of Total Annual Cost That Is Variable
Material	$193,600	100
Labor	90,000	70
Overhead	80,000	64
Administrative	30,000	30

The Canadian production will be sold by manufacturer's representatives, who will receive commissions of 8 percent of the sales price. No portion of the United States home office expense will be allocated to the Canadian subsidiary.

Required:
1. Prepare a schedule computing the Stenger Corporation's estimated net profit from United States operations under each of the following procedures:
   a. Expansion of the Rhode Island factory
   b. Negotiation of long-term contract on a commission basis
2. Management wants to price its Canadian product to realize a 10 percent profit on the sales price. Compute the sales price per unit that would result in an estimated 10 percent profit on sales.
3. Assume that your answer to part 2 is a sales price of $11 per unit. Compute the break-even point in sales dollars for the Canadian subsidiary.

(AICPA adapted)

CHAPTER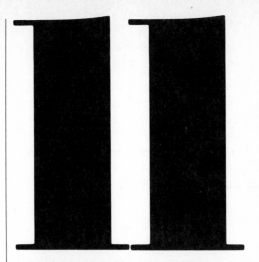

DECISIONS INVOLVING ALTERNATIVE CHOICES

THE PLAN OF THIS CHAPTER
The concept of "different costs for different purposes" will be applied to a series of specific types of management decisions. Attention will be focused on the following topics:

Futurity and difference as determinants of the relevance of costs

The meaning of differential costs

Relevant costs and the equipment-replacement decision

Relevant costs and the decision to process joint products

Relevant costs and the decision to drop a product line

Relevant costs and the decision to accept a special order

Relevant costs and the decision to make or buy

RELEVANT COSTS: A CLOSER LOOK

Different costs for different purposes has been our core concept since the beginning of our study of management accounting. Webster informs us that the term "relevant" means "pertinent; applying to the case at hand." Thus, the relevance of cost and revenue data is determined by the purpose for which they are used.

When management's purpose is a decision involving alternative choices (such as whether to manufacture a part or to purchase it from an outside supplier), the relevancy of cost data takes on a special meaning. Essentially, relevant costs exhibit two fundamental characteristics:

1. They are *future* costs.
2. They will be *different* for each alternative.

Futurity

Not *all* future costs are necessarily relevant to alternative-choice decisions, and they are not relevant *unless* they are future. This important point ought to be self-evident, but it is frequently misunderstood. Past costs are the result of past decisions; no current or future decision can change what has already happened.

On this point, however, we must make an important distinction. It is true that the past, *as* past, is irrelevant. The past as history, though, can be significant insofar as we learn from it and thus are able to make more intelligent decisions affecting the future. Frequently the best guide to likely future happenings will be a study of past events. Past experience can condition management thinking with respect to normal capacity, standard costs, flexible budgets, break-even points, sales forecasts, and the like.

Manifestly, future cash flows in and out of the business will respond to changes in general business conditions, product design, manufacturing methods and tooling, wage and salary increases, material price changes, and a host of other uncertain events. No matter how heavily management may depend upon information from past experience to formulate planning decisions, *the past as such is irrelevant.*

Difference

To be relevant for decision making, costs must clear two hurdles: They must be *future* and they must *differ* between alternatives. That they must pass these two tests in the order stated is also clear. Since all past costs are irrelevant, it matters not they they may have given different results under given conditions in the past. Not all future costs are necessarily relevant to alternative-choice decisions, however. Only those which may be expected to differ between alternatives are relevant.

Suppose a young couple were planning an evening out to have dinner at a restaurant and go to the opera, leaving the children in the care of a baby-sitter. They had done the same thing a year ago, and that time they had driven their own car. The entire evening, including dinner, tickets to the opera, baby-sitter, out-of-pocket costs of driving the car, and parking, had cost $35. While they regarded this as interesting information, they realized that it was irrelevant to the cost of this year's excursion.

Although the ticket prices, baby-sitter rates, and the distances had not changed, the parking rates and gasoline prices had, and also it was unlikely that they would select the same restaurant or meals that they had before. Besides, they were considering the advisability of taking the bus from their suburban home instead of driving their own car. The question really was, "How much *difference* will it make in the cost of *this* year's night out if we take the bus instead of driving?"

Only those costs expected to be different would be relevant. Obviously, which mode of transportation they chose would have no bearing on the cost of the opera tickets or the meal. The costs of these items, though large in the total, are irrelevant. However, if they took the bus and incurred the cost of two fares, they would not incur out-of-pocket driving costs or parking fee. They would probably also take a cab from the restaurant to the opera house. Finally, because of the inflexibility of bus schedules, they would probably have to leave home earlier and arrive back later than if they drove the car, which would increase the cost of the baby-sitter.

Analysis of these latter costs would reveal which of the proposed modes of transportation would result in the lower total costs. The decision might not be based solely on the lower of the two costs, however. Such intangibles as the relaxation afforded by riding the bus as compared with fighting the traffic and finding suitable parking, or the personal satisfaction and the flexibility of scheduling inherent in driving one's own car, or the insistence by the parents of the baby-sitter that he be home by a certain hour might swing the decision to the higher cost alternative. Nevertheless, a reliable estimate of the difference in cost between two alternatives such as these would doubtless be weighed carefully before a decision was reached.

In summary, costs relevant to the making of decisions among alternative choices are future costs which are expected to differ between the alternatives. Two distinct tests are to be applied: the first draws the line between past and future costs, and the second separates those costs which will be different from those which will not.

Assume that a decision must be made concerning the substitution of a piece of automatic equipment for the slower, higher labor cost method now being employed in a chemical process. The material consumption would not change, but conversion cost per unit of product would decrease. If the unit product cost under the present method is $2 for direct material and $5 for conversion, while under the proposed method these costs are expected to be $2 and $3 respectively, the determination of relevant costs may be viewed schematically as follows:

	TEST 1: Futurity		TEST 2: Difference
Past Costs	Future Costs		
	Present Method	Proposed Method	Result
Direct material $2	$2	$2	Irrelevant
Conversion cost $5	5	3	Relevant
(On this side of first line, *always* irrelevant, though sometimes indicative and helpful)			

DIFFERENTIAL COSTS

In the development of our analysis for alternative-choice decisions, the relevant costs as discussed above will be compared as a means of measuring the total difference in cost between alternatives. These cost differences have appropriately been termed *differential* or *incremental*[1] costs. One of the earlier writers in this field, the economist J. M. Clark, describes the concept of differential costs in this manner:[2]

When a decision has to be made involving an increase or decrease of n-units of output, the difference in cost between two policies may be considered to be the cost really incurred on account of these n-units of business, or of any similar units. This may be called the *differential* cost of a given amount of business. It represents the cost that must be incurred if that business is taken and which need not be incurred if that business is not taken.

In general, the economic advantage in decisions of this type will lie with the alternative which will maximize the profit (or minimize the loss) for the firm as a whole, in terms of both the periodic dollar profit and the return on capital. So the comparison of the relevant costs of available alternatives should reveal the incremental (or differential) profit provided by the most favorable alternative and, when measured against the incremental capital which must be invested to produce it, the incremental return.

TYPES OF DECISIONS

One of the more important decisions involving alternative choices is whether or not to buy new capital equipment. Generally, the economic advantage offered by such an investment is the realization of operating-cost savings which are translated into increased net profits. We need some means of applying relevant costs to the measurement of such increased profit and, in turn, to the incremental capital investment.

Of particular significance in this chapter is the determination of just which costs *are* relevant. The means for measuring the return on capital of various alternatives, as well as for appraising the relative attractiveness of a number of investment opportunities, will be treated in more detail in Chapter 13.

Another problem requiring differential cost analysis has to do with adding or dropping a product line in a multiproduct company. Variable costing is a useful method of appraising the respective profit contributions of the several products in a company's line, but insofar as this method is used to report *past* income, the information is irrelevant. What is needed is an analysis of the effects on the *future* profits of the company of a decision to drop (or add) a product. If a product is eliminated, its sales revenues and certain costs will also be eliminated; if a product is added, the reverse will occur. The problem is to determine

---

[1] The same terms apply to the revenue differences, profit differences, and capital investment differences between alternatives.
[2] J. M. Clark, *The Economics of Overhead Costs,* Chicago: The University of Chicago Press, 1923, p. 49.

the incremental data attributable to the product line in question and measure their probable effects on future company profits.

Frequently the management of a company is offered a special order for one of its products, usually at a price lower than its customary selling price. When a firm is operating at something lower than its normal volume, such a special order can be attractive to a degree depending on the effect of incremental revenues and costs on overall company profits. Here again, relevant costing provides a useful means for assessing the economic benefits of such an opportunity.

Some variations on the same theme include decisions with respect to manufacturing or purchasing a certain part or product; purchasing or leasing a building or piece of equipment; and selling products direct to customers through a company-employed sales force or marketing through wholesalers. In this chapter we shall explore some of these problems by using a few simplified examples.

Equipment-Replacement Decision

Assume that a company purchased a machine two years ago at a cost of $60,000; it is depreciating this new equipment on a straight-line basis over a six-year life with no anticipated salvage value. The machine has no disposal value at present.

Management learns that a new machine can be purchased at a cost of $80,000 to do the same job, having an expected economic life of four years with no salvage value. The advantage of the new machine lies in its greater operating efficiency: It promises to reduce variable operating expenses from the present level of $165,000 to $130,000 per year. Sales volume is expected to continue at $200,000 per year for the next four years.

A natural tendency on the part of many accountants and managers would be to reject the proposal. After all, the present machine is functioning well and is expected to perform its useful services for another four years; to scrap it now (since it has no disposal value at present) would mean writing off the undepreciated book value of $40,000 as a "loss on disposal of fixed assets."

The difficulty here is grasping the idea that the book value of the old machine is *irrelevant;* it represents a cost incurred as a result of a decision made two years ago. The *depreciation expense* merely reflects the apportionment of that past cost[3] over the fiscal periods whose income benefits from the use of the asset. As such, book value should be eliminated as a factor in the decision whether to buy the new machine. Furthermore, its accounting treatment as an immediate write-off of $40,000 or as depreciation of $10,000 per year for four years results in no difference in total cost and before-tax profits for the next four years taken as a whole.

Since the book value of the old machine is irrelevant, it ought to be ignored in arriving at the decision to buy the new machine or not; instead, the cost of the new machine and the operating-cost savings should be considered. Exhibit 11-1 demonstrates the relevant cost analysis by which an accurate appraisal of the proposal may be made.

---

[3] Economists refer to the historical and basically irrecoverable costs of long-term assets as "sunk" costs.

EXHIBIT 11-1

COMPARISON OF ALTERNATIVES, REPLACEMENT OF EQUIPMENT
(Covering Entire Four-Year Period)*

	Alternative 1, Present Machine	Difference	Alternative 2, New Machine
Sales	($200,000 × 4) $800,000	–	$800,000
Expenses:			
Variable operating	($165,000 × 4) $660,000	($140,000)	($130,000 × 4) $520,000
Old machine:			
Depreciation	40,000 ⎫	–	⎧
Write-off	⎭		⎩ 40,000
New machine – depreciation	–	80,000	80,000
Total expenses	$700,000	($ 60,000)	$640,000
Net income – four years	$100,000	$ 60,000	$160,000
Average annual incremental income		$ 15,000	
Incremental investment		$ 80,000	
Accounting rate of return		18.75%	

* The same analysis can be made on an average annual basis if the write-off on the old machine is pro-rated over the four years, $10,000 per year.

It will be noted that the book value of the old machine was included in the analysis. This was done merely to emphasize the irrelevance of the item; in terms of the four-year time span involved, it is clear that there is no difference in overall before-tax profits, whether the $40,000 is written off immediately or taken as depreciation of $10,000 per year for four years. The relevant costs are the four-year operating-cost savings of $140,000 against the cost of $80,000 for the new machine, which would net the company an additional $60,000 of before-tax profits for the four years, an average of $15,000 per year.[4] This represents an accounting rate of return of 18.75 percent before taxes, based on the incremental investment of $80,000. (The accounting rate of return and other methods of evaluating investment proposals are discussed in Chapter 13.) Notice, too, that of the three columns used for this analysis, only the middle — "difference" — column is needed; all relevant information is to be found there. This form of analysis will be used throughout the chapter.

Relevance of Salvage Value While the book value of old equipment is irrelevant to the replacement decision, any realizable salvage or disposal value of

[4] Whether the book value of the old machine is treated as depreciation (i.e., if the first alternative is chosen) or as loss on disposal (under the second alternative) will make a slight difference in the amount and timing of income tax payments. Thus, the tax factor will be relevant, and management will usually wish to consider it in the decision. The determination of such tax effects is beyond the scope of this book. Nevertheless, the basic proposition remains the same: Although the income tax factor is relevant, the treatment of the book value of the old machine will result in no difference in overall before-tax profits; therefore, that book value is irrelevant per se.

that equipment *is* relevant. The reason is that the realization of the amount of the disposal value is conditioned upon choosing one of the alternatives rather than the other—cash flow will be different in that amount, depending on the alternative chosen.

Let us modify the preceding example: Assume that the company pondering the replacement decision is offered $10,000 as a trade-in allowance (in reality a salvage value) on the old machine. The results may be seen in Exhibit 11-2.

Note that the factor of $10,000 representing salvage value appears as a negative cost (actually, it will reduce the total depreciation of the new machine) in the "difference" column, highlighting the fact that its benefit is to be realized only if alternative 2 is chosen. If the present machine is kept, the company forgoes the benefit of this $10,000, since the machine is expected to have no salvage value at the end of four years. This relevant cost is sometimes referred to as an *opportunity cost* of choosing alternative 1.

"Opportunity cost" is the economist's term for the monetary benefit one must forgo if one rejects an alternative. For example, if a person has $20,000 cash and decides to use it to purchase a house, the decision may be advantageous. However, by choosing to put the money in the house, the home buyer forgoes the opportunity to invest it in government bonds at 6 percent. This $1,200 per year ($20,000 at 6 percent) may not represent an actual interest payment, but it is the sacrifice of income that is accepted as a cost of rejecting the alternative investment in government bonds.

Another differentiating effect of the $10,000 salvage value may be observed in the reduction of the incremental investment in alternative 2 from $80,000 to

EXHIBIT 11-2
COMPARISON OF ALTERNATIVES, REPLACEMENT OF EQUIPMENT
(Showing Relevance of Salvage Value)

	Alternative 1, Present Machine	Difference	Alternative 2, New Machine
Sales	$800,000	—	$800,000
Expenses:			
Variable operating	$660,000	($140,000)	$520,000
Old machine:			
Depreciation	40,000	—	40,000
Write-off			
Salvage value		(10,000)	(10,000)
New machine—depreciation	—	80,000	80,000
Total expenses	$700,000	($ 70,000)	$630,000
Net income—four years	$100,000	$ 70,000	$170,000
Average annual incremental income		$ 17,500	
Incremental investment		$ 70,000	
Accounting rate of return		25%	

$70,000. The fundamental value of alternative 2 should be measured in terms of the *net* return (savings) in relation to the *net* (incremental) investment required to attain it. If the old machine had possessed no salvage value at the time of the purchase of the new machine, the incremental investment would be the $80,000 purchase price; however, we are told that it does have a salvage value of $10,000. Hence, the company need invest only $70,000 more capital to acquire it. The relevant investment figure is the net *incremental* investment of $70,000.

The salvage value of the old machine is relevant on two counts: as additional cost savings under alternative 2 (opportunity cost of alternative 1) and as a reduction in incremental investment. The combined effect of this factor, then, is to increase the accounting rate of return on the incremental investment from the 18.75 percent shown in Exhibit 11-1 to 25 percent.

We may sum up by saying that where a decision must be made regarding the economic advantages of replacing a piece of equipment, the undepreciated book value of the old equipment is irrelevant, but the salvage value, if any, is a relevant factor. This concept is difficult to grasp at first, and to understand it thoroughly one must keep in mind the two essential tests of relevancy: futurity and difference. Book value of fixed assets must be irrelevant merely because they are past costs, incurred by past decisions. Moreover, their accounting treatment in the future will result in no difference in overall company profits. Salvage value, on the contrary, is realized in the future, and only if one particular alternative is chosen.

The difficulty in this matter is compounded by the fact that people hate to admit their mistakes—and many managers look upon a substantial income statement item titled "loss on disposal of fixed assets" as a blatant black mark against their judgment. The point, however, is that it is foolish to incur another mistake to cover an old one. Writing off a past cost as *depreciation*—a well-known ordinary and necessary expense of doing business—may be more palatable than calling it *loss on disposal*, but it does not change the fact that the impact on future profits will be the same regardless of what you call it. If management wishes to pursue the economic objective of maximizing long-term profits, it must disregard irrelevant past costs (however painful the realization that it may have erred in previous judgment) and concentrate on *future* costs which will be influenced by pending decisions.

Decision to Process Joint Products

Joint products are those products that are produced by a single process but are not identifiable as individual products until some definite point in the manufacturing process. Industries producing joint products include petroleum refining, chemicals, meat packing, dairies, sawmills, soap making, and flour milling. For example, a dairy cannot produce skim milk only; it must start with raw whole milk which can then be separated into various dairy products—milk, skim milk, cream, butter, etc.

Joint product costs are those costs associated with the products before they reach the split-off point—the point in the process where they become separate, identifiable products. Such costs are usually allocated to final products in the ratio of market values. Suppose that a company produces two products, X and Y, from a joint manufacturing process. The joint costs are $200,000 per batch, and each batch yields 100,000 gallons of X (selling for $1 per gallon) and 200,000 gallons of Y (selling for $1.50 per gallon). Such a process can be diagramed as follows:

Joint costs = $200,000

100,000 gallons X = $100,000 (market value)

200,000 gallons Y = $300,000 (market value)

For product costing purposes, X would be assigned 25 percent of the joint costs since it accounts for 25 percent of the total market value ($100,000 out of $400,000). This means that X would be costed for inventory purposes at 50 cents per gallon. Product Y accounts for 75 percent of the total market value and would thus be allocated $150,000 of the joint costs, or 75 cents per gallon for inventory costing purposes.

The accounting for joint costs as just described is necessary to allocate production costs to ending inventories so that periodic income may be measured following generally accepted accounting principles. The resulting inventory costs, however, are not applicable to decisions regarding what happens to the joint products *after* the split-off point.

Suppose that a new processing technique now makes it possible to transform product X into a new product, Z, which sells for $3 per gallon. Processing costs amounting to $175,000 will need to be added to convert 100,000 gallons of product X to product Z. These costs would be incurred after the split-off point. Exhibit 11-3 shows that such a step would increase company gross profits by $25,000 per batch. An examination of Exhibit 11-3 indicates that the joint costs of $200,000 are not relevant to this decision—that is, they do not change between the two alternatives. Exhibit 11-3 also shows the relevant cost analysis

EXHIBIT 11-3
COMPARISON OF ALTERNATIVES,
FURTHER PROCESSING OF JOINT PRODUCTS
(Original Batch: 300,000 Gallons)

	Alternative 1, No Further Processing				Alternative 2, Further Processing		
	X (100,000 gal)	Y (200,000 gal)	Total	Total Difference	Z (100,000 gal)	Y (200,000 gal)	Total
Sales	$100,000	$300,000	$400,000	$200,000	$300,000	$300,000	$600,000
Joint costs	50,000	150,000	200,000	-0-	100,000	100,000	200,000
Additional processing	-0-	-0-	-0-	175,000	175,000	-0-	175,000
Total costs	50,000	150,000	200,000	175,000	275,000	100,000	375,000
Gross profit	$ 50,000	$150,000	$200,000	$ 25,000	$ 25,000	$200,000	$225,000

in such a decision. In this case, there are also relevant revenues — future revenues which are expected to change between alternatives:

Increase in revenues (100,000 gallons times an extra $2/gallon)	$200,000
Increase in costs	175,000
Net benefit of further processing per batch	$ 25,000

An examination of Exhibit 11-3, however, also indicates the danger of using joint costing allocations in the decision process. If only product X and product Z income statements were prepared, it would appear that further processing is not economical because the gross profit of Z is $25,000 less than that of X. This is misleading, however, since the allocation of joint costs is also different between the two alternatives because the market values have now changed. Product Z is now assumed to account for 50 percent of the total value, and thus is allocated $100,000 of the joint costs. An increase in X's allocation, of course, must result in a decrease in Y's, since the total of $200,000 does not change between the alternatives. An analysis of the income statements of X and Z alone would ignore the increased gross profit of Y as a result of further processing of X. By examining the total sales and costs, however, it is possible to see the clear advantage of further processing.

In this example the joint cost allocations *result from* management's decisions and should not be used as an *input to* those decisions. Accountants concerned with reporting periodic income have questioned the usefulness of such joint cost allocations, claiming that they can be confusing if not interpreted correctly. Other methods have been used to allocate joint costs — such as allocations based on physical quantities and allocations based on sales value at the split-off point — but all allocations must in essence be somewhat arbitrary and may therefore not be useful for managerial decision making. Although there are many complexities in joint cost allocations and in decisions involving joint products which are beyond the scope of this book, it is clear that relevant cost analysis can be used to focus management's attention on the critical factors involved in the choice between alternatives.

Decision to Drop a Product Line

For the purpose of examining other decisions from alternative choices, let us consider a comprehensive example.

Assume a manufacturer of toys — the M. Larks Toy Company — which produces three product lines: electric trains, dolls, and games. In Exhibit 11-4 are listed the standard costs of each product by major cost elements, the selling prices of each product, and the normal production capacity upon which standard costs are based.

In the year 19x1, the results of operations were as shown in the conventional product income statement, Exhibit 11-5. It will be noted that all three product lines operated at less than normal capacity. Sales for the total company amounted to $960,000, and net income was $19,000 before taxes, representing 2 percent of net sales. By product lines, results were varied. The Trains Division showed a loss of $24,000 (6.9 percent of net sales), while the Dolls Division recorded a $30,000 profit on sales (6.7 percent) and Games Division a profit of $13,000 (8.1 percent).

In reviewing these results, management quite naturally raised the question, "Should we drop the Trains line?" The answer to this question would depend on a number of factors, a principal one being the effect of such a decision on overall company profits.

As the first step in his analysis, the management accountant broke down the standard overhead into its fixed and variable factors. These are shown, together with the total fixed and variable overhead costs budgeted at normal

EXHIBIT 11-4
M. LARKS TOY COMPANY
Standard Unit Costs

	Trains	Dolls	Games
Direct material	$ 5	$ 1	$1.00
Direct labor	2	3	1.00
Factory overhead	10	3	1.00
Total manufacturing costs	$17	$ 7	$3.00
Selling and administrative costs	5	2	0.50
Total costs	$22	$ 9	$3.50
Selling price	$25	$10	$4.00
Normal capacity	20,000	50,000	50,000

EXHIBIT 11-5
M. LARKS TOY COMPANY
Income Statement by Products
For the Year Ended December 31, 19x1

	Trains	Dolls	Games	Total
Units sold	14,000	45,000	40,000	
Net sales	$350,000	$450,000	$160,000	$960,000
Standard cost of goods sold:				
Direct material	$ 70,000	$ 45,000	$ 40,000	$155,000
Direct labor	28,000	135,000	40,000	203,000
Factory overhead	140,000	135,000	40,000	315,000
Total standard cost of goods sold	$238,000	$315,000	$120,000	$673,000
Standard gross margin	$112,000	$135,000	$ 40,000	$287,000
Less: Unabsorbed factory overhead	36,000	5,000	2,000	43,000
Actual gross margin	$ 76,000	$130,000	$ 38,000	$244,000
Less: Selling and administrative expenses	100,000	100,000	25,000	225,000
Net income	($ 24,000)	$ 30,000	$ 13,000	$ 19,000
Percentage net income to net sales	(6.9%)	6.7%	8.1%	2%

capacity, by product, in Exhibit 11-6. This analysis confirmed the composition of the overhead reported in the product income statement as follows:

For Trains:

Variable overhead (14,000 @ $4)	$ 56,000
Fixed overhead (14,000 @ $6)	84,000
Total standard overhead (14,000 @ $10)	$140,000
Add: Unabsorbed overhead (6,000 units under normal capacity @ $6 standard fixed rate)	36,000
Total overhead assigned to trains	$176,000

For Dolls:

Variable overhead (45,000 @ $2)	$ 90,000
Fixed overhead (45,000 @ $1)	45,000
Total standard overhead (45,000 @ $3)	$135,000
Add: Unabsorbed overhead (5,000 @ $1)	5,000
Total overhead assigned to dolls	$140,000

For Games:

Variable overhead (40,000 @ $0.80)	$ 32,000
Fixed overhead (40,000 @ $0.20)	8,000
Total standard overhead (40,000 @ $1)	$ 40,000
Add: Unabsorbed overhead (10,000 @ $0.20)	2,000
Total overhead assigned to games	$ 42,000

This analysis further confirmed the total amounts of fixed overhead to be as shown in Exhibit 11-6, made up of the standard fixed overhead for the volume attained plus the unabsorbed overhead which represented the cost of idle capacity [e.g., for Trains, $84,000 standard (for 14,000 units) + $36,000 unabsorbed = $120,000 total].

Armed with this information, the management accountant proceeded to recast the product operating results on a variable costing basis, as shown in Exhibit 11-7. This report revealed the highly significant factor of contribution

EXHIBIT 11-6
M. LARKS TOY COMPANY
Analysis of Fixed and Variable Factory Overhead Costs

	Standard Costs per Unit			Total Costs at Normal Capacity			
	Trains	Dolls	Games	Trains	Dolls	Games	Total
Units at normal capacity	20,000	50,000	50,000				
Factory overhead cost:							
Variable	$ 4	$2	$0.80	$ 80,000	$100,000	$40,000	$220,000
Fixed	6	1	0.20	120,000	50,000	10,000	180,000
Total	$10	$3	$1.00	$200,000	$150,000	$50,000	$400,000

EXHIBIT 11-7

M. LARKS TOY COMPANY
Income Statement by Products, Variable Costing Basis
For the Year Ended December 31, 19x1

	Standard per Unit			Total for Year			
	Trains	Dolls	Games	Trains	Dolls	Games	Total
Net sales	$25	$10	$4.00	$350,000	$450,000	$160,000	$960,000
Variable cost of goods sold:							
Direct material	$ 5	$ 1	$1.00	$ 70,000	$ 45,000	$ 40,000	$155,000
Direct labor	2	3	1.00	28,000	135,000	40,000	203,000
Factory overhead	4	2	0.80	56,000	90,000	32,000	178,000
Total variable cost of goods sold	$11	$ 6	$2.80	$154,000	$270,000	$112,000	$536,000
Contribution margin	$14	$ 4	$1.20	$196,000	$180,000	$ 48,000	$424,000
Fixed costs:							
Factory overhead (as allocated at normal capacity)				$120,000	$ 50,000	$ 10,000	$180,000
Selling and administrative expenses (as allocated at normal capacity)				100,000	100,000	25,000	225,000
Total fixed costs				$220,000	$150,000	$ 35,000	$405,000
Net income				($ 24,000)	$ 30,000	$ 13,000	$ 19,000
Percentage contribution margin to net sales	56%	40%	30%				

margin and its relationship to sales. Seeing that Trains were making the largest contribution to company fixed costs and profits ($196,000 and 56 percent of net sales) of any of the products, he paused to consider the reason for the net loss shown on Exhibit 11-5.

Fixed costs of $220,000 ($120,000 factory overhead and $100,000 selling and administrative) had been assigned to Trains from a pool of $405,000 of such costs for the company as a whole. These costs represented the cost of the company's basic capacity to produce and sell products and to manage itself. Assignment of $220,000 of the total to Trains was by allocation. The startling fact was that for the short term, these costs would continue to be incurred whether Trains were kept or dropped. The economic effect of dropping Trains is seen rather clearly in the differential analysis shown in Exhibit 11-8.

It is likely that no prudent management would drop a line occupying as large a portion of the firm's capacity as Trains does in this case without eventually either trying to fill it with other products or trying to cut back its capacity substantially. Nevertheless, in the short term, the loss of the present contribution made by Trains would turn the total company profit into a substantial loss.

The misleading effects of allocating indirect fixed (capacity) costs are quite evident here. In simple truth, Trains cannot be said to have incurred a loss in 19x1. As indicated by Exhibit 11-7, its contribution margin is the highest percentage rate of the three product lines. Since all allocations of indirect costs are more or less arbitrary, it would not be difficult to manipulate the figures for the fixed costs to show a net profit before taxes for the Trains Division in 19x1.

Let us emphasize, however, that the relevant data for a decision on dropping the line are to be found in the *differential analysis*, not in the product-line income statements (which report past — therefore irrelevant — results). Two points should be borne in mind: first, it was a misleading product-line income statement which raised the question of dropping the Trains Division in the first place; second, much clearer, more meaningful information concerning the profit performance of product lines is available from the income statement on the variable costing basis, since it emphasizes each product's contribution to the cost of overall company capacity and profit.

Before a decision can be made on the question of dropping a product line, factors other than immediate profit maximization must be considered. For ex-

EXHIBIT 11-8
M. LARKS TOY COMPANY
Effects of Dropping Product Line

	Keep Trains	Difference	Drop Trains
Net sales	$960,000	($350,000)	$610,000
Variable costs	$536,000	$154,000	$382,000
Fixed costs	405,000	–	405,000
Total costs	$941,000	($154,000)	$787,000
Net income	$ 19,000	($196,000)	($177,000)

ample, it is evident that volume in the Trains line is substantially below normal. The long-term prospects for this product line must be assessed. If it is in a serious decline with no reasonable prospect for increased volume, a cutback in capacity may be necessary even if the line is not dropped immediately. The conditions of competition in the market must be considered. Such things as the trend of prices, the number and caliber of competitors, the rate of innovation (changes in design of products, introduction of new products, etc.), the attitude of customers and particularly of those buying in large quantities, changes in manufacturing methods and equipment, and capital requirements must all be taken into account.

Among all the factors to be considered, volume is probably as important as any. The consequences of a decision to drop a product line at a time when volume is below normal capacity differ considerably from those of the same decision under conditions of crowded capacity. Almost any product which contributes to the cost of overall capacity can be justified when a good deal of it is idle. Alternatively, to drop a line which may be using one-third of the firm's capacity suggests that another product ought to be available to take its place or a more or less permanent cutback in *total* capacity should be considered. In the last analysis, a differential cost study ought to be a key factor in arriving at such a decision.

Decision to Accept a Special Order

Frequently, the opportunity arises for management to consider an order for a quantity of its regular product at a special price (usually less than that charged regular customers). When there is idle capacity, such an offer may be attractive. Once again the basic question is, "What difference will it make in the overall profit of the company?" Essentially, if there is idle capacity the special order is advantageous if the price amounts to more than out-of-pocket costs.

Suppose the Larks Toy Company receives an offer from a large mail-order house for 5,000 trains at $15 apiece. There is to be a slight modification in the design so as to differentiate it from the same product sold to regular customers, but it will not affect the direct product costs. Larks Company expects to incur its regular unit variable costs, and, in addition, it must absorb $5,000 as the cost of freight to the customer's central warehouse. Exhibit 11-9 presents the differential cost analysis depicting the effect the special order will have on total company profit if operations are assumed to be at the same level as in 19x1.

It can be seen that the $15 price not only covers the variable manufacturing costs but the freight costs as well, leaving an incremental net income of $15,000 on the order for 5,000 units. It has been estimated that an additional investment in working capital (inventories and receivables) will be required in an amount of $10,000 during the period over which the order is being filled. The $15,000 net income before taxes represents an accounting rate of return of 150 percent on this additional investment. Other things being equal, the order should be accepted.

As with all such decisions, factors other than the profit effect must be considered. The Robinson-Patman Act (discussed in the next chapter) places restrictions on management's right to sell merchandise to different customers

EXHIBIT 11-9
M. LARKS TOY COMPANY
Effects of Special Order

	Without Special Order	Difference		With Special Order
Net sales	$960,000	(5,000 × $15)	$75,000	$1,035,000
Direct material	$155,000	(5,000 × $ 5)	$25,000	$ 180,000
Direct labor	203,000	(5,000 × $ 2)	10,000	213,000
Variable overhead	178,000	(5,000 × $ 4)	20,000	198,000
Fixed overhead	180,000		—	180,000
Total manufacturing costs	$716,000		$55,000	$ 771,000
Gross margin	$244,000		$20,000	$ 264,000
Selling and administrative expenses	225,000	(Freight)	5,000	230,000
Net income	$ 19,000		$15,000	$ 34,000
Incremental investment:				
Receivables			$ 6,000	
Inventories			4,000	
Fixed assets			—	
Total incremental investment			$10,000	
Accounting rate of return on incremental investment before taxes ($15,000/10,000)			150%	

at different prices. Whenever the opportunity to fill a special order such as this one presents itself, management must consider these legal implications.

In this instance, the company has idle capacity which enables it to take on additional business without adding to its fixed costs. Under other conditions, however, more than variable costs may be relevant (i.e., different under the new alternative). If the company is already operating at or above normal capacity, it may be necessary to work overtime, add a second shift, rent additional space, hire new workers and supervision, increase its cost of maintenance, and incur a host of other possible costs beyond the ordinary variable product costs. Extra care must be exercised in putting together the differential cost analysis under such circumstances.

If the company is operating at or above normal capacity when it receives the opportunity to consider a special order, management may not wish to add to its capacity because of the temporary, "one-shot" nature of the order. In such a case, it must displace some of the company's regular business to be able to accommodate the special order. Under these conditions, the opportunity cost of the lost business becomes a relevant cost and must be taken into account.

A variety of other factors may affect the decision: the possibility of cultivating the permanent patronage of the new customer; the possibility of having to lower the company's regular price to other customers because of competitive pressures, which would change the entire price-cost-volume-profit structure of the company; or the need to put business into the plant to avoid the necessity of laying off a valuable working force. The wise management will weigh all the factors carefully in the light of the profit impact revealed by the differential cost analysis.

Decision to Make or Buy

The Larks Company is considering an opportunity to subcontract the production of a certain component part of its Trains product to another manufacturer. This subcontractor has submitted a bid to produce the part for $1.80. The outside firm believes that it has the special equipment, the skilled work force, and the productive efficiency in this type of work, based on its specialized type of operations, to be able to meet not only its direct product costs but the costs of general factory overhead, selling, and administration, and still make a profit at a selling price of $1.80.

Larks, on the other hand, considers the part a nuisance to make. It constitutes a bottleneck in the flow of its production and requires a type of manufacturing which is not in accord with Larks' special skills. It is perfectly possible that it would be to the company's advantage to subcontract it.

The management accountant makes a study of the costs and discovers that:

The standard unit cost of material is 50 cents.

The direct labor cost per unit should be 25 cents.

The variable overhead is estimated to be $1 per unit.

It is believed by the plant superintendent that supervision in the amount of $2,000 per year can be eliminated if the job is subcontracted and that the cost of special tools will be reduced by $500 per year.

The results of the differential cost analysis based on these estimates are shown in Exhibit 11-10.

It will be noted that no change in volume or selling price is assumed, so revenue is not a relevant factor. The benefit lies purely in cost savings. The purchase price of the subcontracted part is substituted for the accumulated material, labor, variable overhead, and avoidable fixed overhead costs which can be eliminated if the 14,000 units of the part are purchased from the outside rather than manufactured in the Larks plant. The apparent benefit at this level of volume is $1,800.

As is the case with other types of alternative-choice decisions, the impact of other factors might upset the economically beneficial one. Since the company and the division are operating at less than normal capacity, the small monetary advantage (based on estimates) offered by this opportunity may not be considered sufficient to offset the ill effects of laying off more of the work force.

EXHIBIT 11-10
M. LARKS TOY COMPANY
Effects of Make-or-Buy Decision

	Trains Division			
	Make	Difference		Buy
Net sales	$350,000		$ —	$350,000
Direct material	$ 70,000	(14,000 × $0.50)	($ 7,000)	$ 63,000
Purchased parts	—	(14,000 × 1.80)	25,200	25,200
Direct labor	28,000	(14,000 × 0.25)	(3,500)	24,500
Variable overhead	56,000	(14,000 × 1.00)	(14,000)	42,000
Fixed overhead	120,000	(Supervision $2,000; tools $500)	(2,500)	117,500
Total manufacturing costs	$274,000		($ 1,800)	$272,200
Selling and administrative costs	100,000		—	100,000
Total costs	$374,000		($ 1,800)	$372,200
Net income	($ 24,000)		$ 1,800	($ 22,200)

On the other hand, a company might find it necessary, at or near full capacity operations, to subcontract such an item even at a slight cost disadvantage if the cost of farming out other components would be even greater or if
the company were to run the risk of losing sales as a result of keeping the work
in its own plant. Even under present conditions, there might be a long-range
advantage to feeding such work to the outside firm in order to acquire and keep
a dependable, low-cost source of supply open for those times in the future when
it might be sorely needed. Whatever the impact of the nonquantitative factors,
however, the differential cost analysis remains at the core of the make-or-buy
decision.

SUMMARY

When it comes to decisions involving alternative choices, relevant costs are
essential to an accurate quantitative analysis directed toward long-term profit
maximization. For costs to be relevant to the purpose of choosing among alternatives, they must pass two tests: They must be *future* costs, and they must
be *different* between alternatives.

Not all future costs are relevant; but to be relevant, they must be future.
Past costs in themselves are irrelevant, although they may be helpful in making estimates of what future costs may be. If a cost passes the test of futurity,
it must still be different between alternatives to be relevant. Costs which will
remain unchanged regardless of the decision rendered, even though they be
future costs, are irrelevant.

The differences between future costs under different alternatives are
called *differential or incremental costs.* The net effect of all the differential

costs is the focal point of the economic benefit or disadvantage of one alternative compared with another.

One of the most difficult areas for differential cost analysis is the equipment-replacement decision. For accurate appraisal of alternatives, the *undepreciated book value* of existing equipment must be recognized as being irrelevant. This is true simply because it is a past cost, based on a past decision the result of which it is impossible to change. In addition to being irrelevant as a past cost, it is irrelevant because it would make no difference in costs or profits over the remaining life of the asset whether the entire book value is written off immediately as a loss if it is replaced or written off as depreciation if it is retained.

On the other hand, salvage value on old equipment is likely to be relevant because its possible realization is in the future and it will make a difference in costs and profits as between the alternatives. The reluctance of managers to accept this concept might be interpreted as an unwillingness to admit a past error in judgment, preferring the "normal" recognition of depreciation to the unpleasant connotations of "loss on disposal." Nevertheless, past costs ought not to cloud the equipment-replacement issue when the relevant factors indicate where the economic advantage lies.

Differential cost analysis operates in a similar manner to evaluate the economic advantage or disadvantage in processing a joint product further, adding or dropping a product line, accepting or rejecting a special order, or making or purchasing a product or a component part. In each such case, estimates must be made of the future costs to be incurred under each of the alternatives, and then an examination made of which of these will be different as between the alternatives.

In all such decisions, other, nonquantitative factors must be taken into account before management takes final action. Nevertheless, long-run profit maximization as the central economic goal remains at the core of these decisions.

KEY WORDS AND PHRASES

relevant costs	opportunity cost
differential (incremental) cost	joint product costs
salvage value	split-off point

DISCUSSION QUESTIONS

1. What is the essential meaning of "relevant"?
2. What tests must cost and revenue data pass to be regarded as "relevant" for purposes of deciding among alternative choices?
3. Are all future costs relevant? Why?
4. Why is the past, as such, irrelevant?
5. Why is undepreciated book value on existing fixed assets irrelevant to the decision to replace them?
6. Why is the salvage value of existing fixed assets a relevant factor in the decision to replace them?
7. What are (a) differential costs; (b) sunk costs; (c) opportunity costs?

8. The controller comments, "To dispose of fixed assets before they are fully depreciated is economic waste! If we are in business to maximize profits (or minimize losses), how can you possibly justify disposing of fixed assets at a loss when to keep them and depreciate them over the remainder of their useful life would avoid such a loss?" Do you agree? Why?

9. What is the most accurate criterion of the relative profitability of product lines or other segments of a business?

10. Can a sound decision as to whether to drop a product line be made without determining the line's full costs (including its share of overall capacity costs)?

11. Under what conditions may it be advantageous for a firm to accept a special order? What pitfalls should be considered?

12. Why relate the incremental profit from equipment replacement, acceptance of a special order, adding a product line, etc., to the incremental capital investment required?

13. What conditions might impel a company to investigate the advisability of subcontracting a portion of its business activity?

14. Give examples of factors which might deter management from choosing an alternative, despite the fact that relevant cost analysis indicates the economic desirability of doing so, in each of the following:
    a. Buy new equipment.
    b. Drop a product line.
    c. Reject an opportunity for a special order.
    d. Continue to make, rather than buy, an item.

PROBLEMS

11-1. Sullivan's Men's Store has 3,000 men's shirts in last year's style left over after its annual "going-out-of-business" sale. These shirts cost an average of $6.50 each. Management is considering the following alternatives:

1. Return the shirts to the manufacturer for restyling. This would cost $4 each, but the shirts could then be sold for $9.
2. Sell the shirts to a discount chain for $6 each.
3. Donate them to charity.
4. For a storage cost totaling $1,500, the shirts could be retained and sold at next year's sale for $5 each.

Required:
Which alternative is most desirable? Why? (Ignore taxes.)

11-2. Under normal operating conditions, the Brady Machine Company manufactures 6,000 units of a particular product in a six-month period. Each unit contributes $100 to fixed overhead costs and to profits. The fixed overhead costs for six months amount to $450,000. Strikes at other companies that buy this product have cut sales to a rate of 300 units a month. The company management is considering closing the plant for six months, anticipating that the market will be back to normal at the end of that time. The fixed overhead costs could be reduced to $250,000 for the six months the plant is closed, but the additional costs to protect the facilities and to start the plant up again have been estimated to total $50,000.

Required:
Should the plant be closed? If not, what is the lowest volume of sales for the next six months which would justify keeping the plant open?

11-3.† The president of the Horngren Manufacturing Company, ever alert to the economic advantages of automation, is considering replacing the present semiautomatic assembly line with a new, completely automated, computer-controlled setup.

The old equipment was purchased six years ago at a cost of $122,000. It was estimated at that time to have a useful life of ten years and a salvage value of $2,000. The supplier of the new equipment has offered a "trade-in" allowance of $20,000 toward the purchase price of the new equipment, costing $170,000. At present, the old equipment is estimated to have no salvage value at the end of its useful life.

The new equipment is estimated to offer savings in direct labor and other manufacturing costs in an amount of $45,000 per year over its expected life of four years. At the end of four years it is expected to have no salvage value.

The controller points out to the president that the trade-in allowance offered on the old equipment is substantially below its book value, with the result that a sizable loss on disposal will be incurred if it is to be replaced by the new equipment.

Required:
Assume no increased volume over the next four years. Ignore income taxes.
1. Analyze the effects of the two alternatives (*a*) on an annual basis; (*b*) taking the four years as a whole.
2. Is there any economic advantage to replacing the old equipment?
3. Suppose the president wishes to realize 10 percent annual return on the incremental investment. What should his decision be?

11-4. The Dent Products Company manufactures products S and T jointly. Pertinent figures regarding production and sales of the products are as follows:

Joint manufacturing costs	$33,000
Output of S, 10,000 lb., total market value	30,000
Output of T, 10,000 lb., total market value	15,000

The company can process product T for an additional cost of $17,000 to obtain 8,000 pounds of product W, which can be sold for $4.10 per pound.

Required:
1. Allocate the joint costs to S and T.
2. Should T be further processed? Show computations.

11-5. Two separate products emerge from a process as follows:

	Market Value
Product X: 20,000 lb	$10 per lb
Product Y: 50,000 lb	1 per lb

The joint manufacturing costs of this process are $140,000.

Management is considering the further processing of product Y, from which would emerge product Z, whose market price is $4 per pound. The yield of this new process will be 80 percent; that is, for each input of 10 pounds of product Y, only 8 pounds of product Z will be derived.

For a study of this problem, management had the following schedules prepared:

Allocation of joint costs of $140,000:		
Product X (20/70 of $140,000)		$ 40,000
Product Y (50/70 of $140,000)		100,000
		$140,000
Net income to be derived from product Z:		
Revenue (40,000 lb at $4)		$160,000
Cost of producing product Z		
Allocated joint costs	$100,000	
Additional processing	125,000	
Total		225,000
Loss from further processing Y		$ 65,000

Required:
Before making its final decision, management calls you in as a consultant to check these figures and to make recommendations. What do you suggest?

11-6. The controller of the Jones Manufacturing Company asks for your advice and assistance regarding the problem of whether to replace the firm's A machines with new and advanced B machines. B machines are capable of doubling the present annual capacity of the A machines. At present, the annual finished production of the A machines is $2\frac{1}{2}$ million good units. You are to assume that the increased production can be sold at the same profitable price.

The A machines are being depreciated by the Jones Manufacturing Company under the straight-line method, using a salvage value of 10 percent and a useful life of eight years. The A machines cost the Jones Manufacturing Company $175,000 plus freight and insurance of $25,000. The raw materials as they are fed into the machines are subject to heavy pressure; because of this there is a 20 percent waste factor on an annual basis. The waste materials have no value and are scrapped for nominal value. Direct labor costs are equal to 60 percent of prime cost at the present time (labor and materials are considered prime cost).

The company has been purchasing its raw materials in small lots at a cost of $50 per 1,000 units. Factory overhead, exclusive of depreciation, is applied to the manufacturing process at the rate of 20 percent of direct labor costs.

If the company purchases the B machines, certain economies will be gained. Material costs will decrease 20 percent because the company will be able to buy in larger quantities. In addition, the new machines have been perfected to such an extent that the waste factor will be reduced by 50 percent. However, because the B machine is much larger than the A machine, direct labor cost will be expected to increase by 20 percent. Direct labor will continue to be 60 percent of prime cost before the increase of 20 percent in direct labor cost is applied. In addition, it is expected that factory overhead rate will increase by 10 percent. The life of the new machines is expected to exceed the life of the A machines by one-fourth, and the salvage value of the B machines will be in the same ratio as the salvage value of the A machines. The cost of the B machines, including freight and insurance of $35,000, will amount to $500,000. The company is aware of the fact that dismantling costs and installation costs will be involved; however, it does not wish to consider this factor at the present time.

Required:
1. Prepare a statement of estimated cost comparisons on an annual basis. (Round to the nearest dollar.)
2. List additional factors that should be considered in deciding upon the replacement.
3. Comment briefly on the usefulness and validity of the comparisons made in part 1.

(AICPA adapted)

11A. The Croteau Food Company has two divisions: the Tea Division and the Crumpets Division. The divisional income statement for the year ended December 31, 19x1, follows (000 omitted):

	Tea	Crumpets	Total
Sales	$5,000	$1,000	$6,000
Costs:			
Direct material	$2,000	$ 200	$2,200
Direct labor	500	90	590
Variable overhead	400	70	470
Fixed overhead	750	500	1,250
Variable selling and administrative	100	40	140
Fixed selling and administrative	400	200	600
Total costs	$4,150	$1,100	$5,250
Net income	$ 850	($ 100)	$ 750

The two divisions are housed in a single facility; and if management should decide to curtail or drop one or the other activity, it is doubtful that total capacity would be reduced.

The selling price for Tea is $2.50 per case; for Crumpets, $1 per case.

Required:

1. Revise the form of the income statement to make it more meaningful for the purpose of appraising divisional profitability.
2. Compute break-even points for (*a*) Tea; (*b*) Crumpets; and (*c*) total company.
3. Should the company drop Crumpets? Why?
4. Comment on other factors which might influence your decision in this case.

11-8. The management of Bay Company is considering a proposal to install a third production department within its existing factory building. With the company's present production setup, raw material is passed through department I to produce materials A and B in equal proportions. Material A is then passed through department II to yield product C. Material B is presently being sold "as is" at a price of $20.25 per pound. Product C has a selling price of $100 per pound.

The per pound standard costs currently being used by the Bay Company are as follows:

	Department I (Materials A and B)	Department II (Product C)	(Material B)
Prior depart-			
ment costs	$ —	$53.03	$13.47
Direct material	20.00	—	—
Direct labor	7.00	12.00	—
Variable overhead	3.00	5.00	—
Fixed overhead:			
Attributable	2.25	2.25	—
Allocated (2/3, 1/3)	1.00	1.00	—
	$33.25	$73.28	$13.47

These standard costs were developed by using an estimated production volume of 200,000 pounds of raw material as the standard volume. The company assigns department I costs to materials A and B in proportion to their net sales values at the point of separation, computed by deducting subsequent standard production costs from sales prices. The $300,000 of common fixed overhead costs are allocated to the two producing departments on the basis of the space used by the departments.

The proposed department III would be used to process material B into product D. It is expected that any quantity of product D can be sold for $30 per pound. Standard costs per pound under this proposal were developed by using 200,000 pounds of raw material as the standard volume. They are as follows:

	Department I (Materials A and B)	Department II (Product C)	Department III (Product D)
Prior depart-			
ment costs	—	$52.80	$13.20
Direct material	$20.00	—	—
Direct labor	7.00	12.00	5.50
Variable overhead	3.00	5.00	2.00
Fixed overhead:			
Attributable	2.25	2.25	1.75
Allocated (1/2,			
1/4, 1/4)	.75	.75	.75
	$33.00	$72.80	$23.20

Required:

1. If (*a*) sales and production levels are expected to remain constant in the foreseeable future, and (*b*) there are no foreseeable alternative uses for the available factory space, should the Bay Company install department III and thereby produce product D? Show calculations to support your answer.

2. Instead of constant sales and production levels, suppose that under the present production setup $1 million in additions to the factory building must be made every ten years to accommodate growth. Suppose, also, that proper maintenance gives these factory additions an infinite life and that all such maintenance costs are included in the standard costs presented in the text of the problem. How would the analysis that you performed in part 1 be changed if the installation of department III shortened the interval at which the $1 million factory additions are made from ten years to six years? Be as specific as possible in your answer.

(IMA adapted)

11-9.† The officers of Bradshaw Company are reviewing the profitability of the company's four products and the potential effect of several proposals for varying the product mix. An excerpt from the income statement and other data follow:

	Totals	Product P	Product Q	Product R	Product S
Sales	$62,600	$10,000	$18,000	$12,600	$22,000
Cost of goods sold	44,274	4,750	7,056	13,968	18,500
Gross profit	18,326	5,250	10,944	(1,368)	3,500
Operating expenses	12,012	1,990	2,976	2,826	4,220
Income before income taxes	$ 6,314	$ 3,260	$ 7,968	$ (4,194)	$ (720)
Units sold		1,000	1,200	1,800	2,000
Sales price per unit		$10.00	$15.00	$7.00	$11.00
Variable cost of goods sold per unit		$2.50	$3.00	$6.50	$6.00
Variable operating expenses per unit		$1.17	$1.25	$1.00	$1.20

Each of the following proposals is to be considered independently of the other proposals. Consider only the product changes stated in each proposal; the activity of other products remains stable. (Ignore income taxes.)

Required:

1. If product R is discontinued, what will be the effect on income?

2. If product R is discontinued and a consequent loss of customers causes a decrease of 200 units in sales of Q, what will be the total effect on income?

3. If the sales price of R is increased to $8 with a decrease in the number of units sold to 1,500, what will be the effect on income?

4. The plant in which R is produced can be utilized to produce a new product, T. The total variable costs and expenses per unit of T are

$8.05, and 1,600 units can be sold at $9.50 each. If T is introduced and R is discontinued, what will be the total effect on income?

5. Part of the plant in which P is produced can easily be adapted to the production of S, but changes in quantities may make changes in sales price advisable. If production of P is reduced to 500 units (to be sold at $12 each) and production of S is increased to 2,500 units (to be sold at $10.50 each), what will be the total effect on income?

6. Production of P can be doubled by adding a second shift, but higher wages must be paid, increasing variable cost of goods sold to $3.50 for each of the additional units. If the 1,000 additional units of P can be sold at $10 each, what will be the total effect on income?

(AICPA adapted)

11-10. The Loebl Company is considering the submission of a bid to an agency of the Defense Department for 50,000 units per month of its battery-powered fingernail clippers. The design and manufacturing operations for this item for the armed forces would be the same as for the company's standard commercial line, which sells at $1.75 per unit.

Geared to a normal capacity of 400,000 units per month, the Loebl Company has been operating for the last few months at about 300,000 units.

Management has learned informally that competitive bids are ranging in price from $1.30 to $1.45 per unit. It believes that if it can bid $1.25 per unit, the company can land the contract. It is to quote a price with terms net, f.o.b. company's plant.

Pertinent data for current monthly activity are:

Cost Item	Costs Incurred Last Month (300,000 Units)	Budget at Normal Capacity (400,000 Units)
Direct material	$135,000	$180,000
Direct labor	75,000	100,000
Indirect labor	45,000	60,000
Heat, light, power	28,000	36,000
Supervision	55,000	70,000
Depreciation	40,000	40,000
Engineering	20,000	20,000
Sales commissions	21,000	28,000
Packing costs	15,000	20,000
Freight out	15,000	20,000
Office expense	15,000	15,000
Advertising	19,000	22,000
Miscellaneous administrative	6,000	6,000
Total costs	$489,000	$617,000

Required:

1. Determine the desirability of submitting a bid of $1.25 per unit.

2. At what price should the contract be bid to bring monthly total company operating profit to a level equal to a return of 15 percent on average monthly operating assets of $350,000 (i.e., average balance of $4,200,000 divided by 12)?

3. Comment on other factors affecting the decision.

AN ACCOUNTING ACCOUNTING*

or

Through the Jungle of Accounting Logic with Gun and Camera

A Tragedy in One Act

The Scene: A small store deep in the jungle of accounting logic.
The Time: Today—and tomorrow, if you aren't careful.
The Cast: Joe, owner and operator of a small store-restaurant in the jungle; an accounting-efficiency-expert.

As the curtain rises, we find Joe dusting his counter and casting admiring glances at a shiny new rack holding brightly colored bags of peanuts. The rack sits at the end of the counter. The store itself is like all small store-restaurants in the jungle of accounting logic. It is a clean, well-lighted joint patronized by the neighborhood residents and an occasional juvenile delinquent. As Joe dusts and admires his new peanut rack, he listens almost uncomprehendingly to the earnest speeches of the accounting-efficiency-expert.

EFF. EX: Joe, you said you put in these peanuts because some people ask for them, but do you realize what this rack of peanuts is *costing* you?

JOE: It ain't gonna cost. 'Sgonna be a profit. Sure, I hadda pay $25 for a fancy rack to holda bags, but the peanuts cost 6¢ a bag and I sell'em for 10¢. Figger I sell 50 bags a week to start. It'll take $12\frac{1}{2}$ weeks to cover the cost of the rack. After that I gotta clear profit of 4¢ a bag. The more I sell, the more I make.

EFF. EX: That is an antiquated and completely unrealistic approach, Joe. Fortunately, modern accounting procedures permit a more accurate picture which reveals the complexities involved.

JOE: Huh?

EFF. EX: To be precise, those peanuts must be integrated into your entire operation and be allocated their appropriate share of business overhead. They must share a proportionate part of your expenditures for rent, heat, light, equipment depreciation, decorating, salaries for waitresses, cook—

JOE: The cook? what's he gotta do wit' peanuts? He don't even know I got 'em.

---

* Used with the permission of Rex H. Anderson, Vice-president, Life Insurance Company of North America.

EFF. EX: Look, Joe, the cook is in the kitchen, the kitchen prepares the food, the food is what brings people in, and while they're in,
they ask to buy peanuts. That's why you must charge a portion of the
cook's wages, as well as a part of your own salary to peanut sales. This
sheet contains a carefully calculated cost analysis which indicates the
peanut operation should pay exactly $1,278 per year toward these gen-
eral overhead costs.

JOE: The peanuts? $1,278 a year for overhead? Thatsa NUTS!

EFF. EX: It's really a little more than that. You also spend money
each week to have the windows washed, to have the place swept out
in the mornings, keep soap in the washroom and provide free colas to
the police. That raises the total to $1,313 per year.

JOE: (Thoughtfully) But the peanut salesman said I'd make money
—put 'em on the end of the counter, he said—and get 4¢ a bag profit—

EFF. EX: (With a sniff) He's not an accountant. Do you actually
know what the portion of the counter occupied by the peanut rack is
worth to you?

JOE: Ain't worth nothing—no stool there—just a dead spot at the
end.

EFF. EX: The modern cost picture permits no dead spots. Your
counter contains 60 square feet and your counter business grosses
$15,000 a year. Consequently, the square foot of space occupied by the
peanut rack is worth $250 per year. Since you have taken that area away
from general counter use, you must charge the value of the space to the
occupant.

JOE: You mean I gotta add *$250 a year* more to the peanuts?

EFF. EX: Right. That raises their share of the general operating
costs to a grand total of $1,563 per year. Now then, if you sell 50 bags
of peanuts per week, these allocated costs will amount to 60¢ per bag.

JOE: (Incredulously) What?

EFF. EX: Obviously, to that must be added your purchase price of
6¢ a bag, which brings the total to 66¢. So you see, by selling peanuts
at 10¢ per bag, you are losing 56¢ on every sale.

JOE: Something's crazy!

EFF. EX: Not at all! Here are the figures. They prove your peanut operation cannot stand on its own feet.

JOE: (Brightening) Suppose I sell lotsa peanuts — thousand bags a week 'stead of fifty?

EFF. EX: (Tolerantly) Joe, you don't understand the problem. If the volume of peanut sales increased, your operating costs will go up — you'll have to handle more bags, with more time, more general overhead, more everything. The basic principle of accounting is firm on that subject: "The bigger the operation the more general overhead costs must be allocated." No, increasing the volume of sales won't help.

JOE: Okay. You so smart, *you* tell *me* what I gotta do.

EFF. EX: (Condescendingly) Well — you could first reduce operating expenses.

JOE: How?

EFF. EX: Take smaller space in an older building with cheaper rent. Cut salaries. Wash the windows biweekly. Have the floor swept only on Thursday. Remove the soap from the washrooms. Cut out the colas for the cops. This will also help you decrease the square-foot value of your counter. For example, if you can cut your expenses 50%, that will reduce the amount allocated to peanuts from $1,563 down to $781.50 per year, reducing the cost to 36¢ per bag.

JOE: (Slowly) That's better?

EFF. EX: Much, much better. However, even then you would lose 26¢ per bag if you charge only 10¢. Therefore, you must also raise your selling price. If you want a net profit of 4¢ per bag, you would have to charge 40¢.

JOE: (Flabbergasted) You mean even after I cut operating costs 50%, I still gotta charge 40¢ for a 10¢ bag of peanuts? Nobody's that nuts about nuts! Who'd buy 'em?

EFF. EX: That's a secondary consideration. The point is, at 40¢, you'd be selling at a price based upon a true and proper evaluation of your then reduced costs.

JOE: (Eagerly) Look! I gotta better idea. Why don't I just throw the nuts out — put 'em in the ash can?

EFF. EX: Can you afford it?

JOE: Sure, all I got is about 50 bags of peanuts — cost about three bucks — so I lose $25 on the rack, I'm outa this nutsy business and no more grief.

EFF. EX: (Shaking head) Joe, it isn't quite that simple. You are IN THE PEANUT BUSINESS! The minute you throw those peanuts out, you are adding $1,563 of annual overhead to the rest of your operation. Joe — be realistic — *can you afford to do that?*

JOE: (Completely crushed) It'sa unbelievable! Last week I wasa make money. Now I'm in-a trouble — justa because I think peanuts onna counter is a gonna bring me some extra profit — justa because I believe 50 bags of peanuts a week is-a easy.

EFF. EX: (With raised eyebrow) That is the reason for modern cost studies, Joe — to dispel those false illusions.

Required:
1. Joe says, "Something's crazy." Is it Joe? Explain.
2. If Joe loses money on the peanut operation, as the accountant claims, how much would his loss be in the first year?
3. As a management accountant who understands relevant costs, explain this situation to Joe.

11-12. George Jackson operates a small machine shop. He manufactures one standard product available from many similar businesses and he also manufactures products to customer order. His accountant prepared this annual income statement:

	Custom Sales	Standard Sales	Total
Sales	$50,000	$25,000	$75,000
Material	$10,000	$ 8,000	$18,000
Labor	20,000	9,000	29,000
Depreciation	6,300	3,600	9,900
Power	700	400	1,100
Rent	6,000	1,000	7,000
Heat and light	600	100	700
Other	400	900	1,300
	$44,000	$23,000	$67,000
	$ 6,000	$ 2,000	$ 8,000

The depreciation charges are for machines used in the respective product lines. The power charge is apportioned on the estimate of power consumed. The rent is for the building space which has been leased for ten years at $7,000 per year. The rent, and heat and light are apportioned to the product lines based on amount of floor space occupied. All other costs are current expenses identified with the product line causing them.

A valued custom parts customer has asked Mr. Jackson if he would manufacture 5,000 special units for him. Mr. Jackson is working at capacity and would have to give up some other business in order to take this order. He can't renege on custom orders already agreed to, but he can reduce the output of his standard product by about one-half for one year while producing the specially requested custom part. The customer is willing to pay $7 for each part. The material cost will be about $2 per unit and the labor will be $3.60 per unit. Mr. Jackson will have to spend $2,000 for a special device which will be discarded when the job is done.

Required:
1. Calculate and present the following costs related to the 5,000-unit custom order:
    a. The incremental cost of the order
    b. The full cost of the order
    c. The opportunity cost of taking the order
2. Should Mr. Jackson take the order? Explain your answer.

(IMA adapted)

11-13. The Largo Manufacturing Company makes a single product, Vostex, and sells it through normal marketing channels. You have been asked by its president to assist in determining the proper bid to submit for a special manufacturing job for the Aztec Sales Company. Below is the information you have collected.

1. The special job is for Mofac, a product unlike Vostex, though the manufacturing processes are similar.
2. Additional sales of Mofac to the Aztec Sales Company are not expected.
3. The bid is for 20,000 pounds of Mofac. Each 1,000 pounds of Mofac requires 500 pounds of material A, 250 pounds of material B, and 250 pounds of material C.
4. Largo's materials inventory data follow:

Material	Pounds in Inventory	Acquisition Cost per Pound	Current Replacement Cost per Pound
A	24,000	$0.40	$0.48
B	4,000	0.25	0.27
C	17,500	0.90	0.97
X	7,000	0.80	0.85

Material X may be substituted for material A in Mofac. Material X, made especially for Largo under a patent owned by Largo, is left over from the manufacture of a discontinued product, is not usable in Vostex, and has a current salvage value of $180.
5. Each 1,000 pounds of Mofac requires 180 direct labor hours at $3 per hour (overtime is charged at time and a half). However, Largo is working near its two-shift capacity and has only 1,600 hours of regular time available. The production manager indicates that he can keep the special job on regular time by shifting the production of Vostex to overtime if necessary.
6. Largo's cost clerk informs you that the hourly burden rate at normal production is as follows:

Fixed element	$0.20 per direct labor hour
Variable element	0.80 per direct labor hour
Total hourly burden rate	$1.00 per direct labor hour

7. The bid invitation states that a performance bond must be submitted with the bid. A local agent will bond Largo's performance for 1 percent of the total bid.

Required:
1. Prepare a schedule to compute the minimum bid (i.e., the bid that will neither increase nor decrease total profits) that Largo Manufacturing Company may submit.
2. Largo's president also wants to know what his new competitor, Melton Manufacturing Company, probably will bid. You assume that Melton's materials inventory has been acquired very recently and that Melton's cost behavior is similar to Largo's. You know that Melton has ample productive capacity to handle the special job on regular time.

Prepare a schedule to compute the minimum bid (i.e., the bid that will neither increase nor decrease total profits) that Melton Manufacturing may submit.

(AICPA adapted)

11-14. The Ace Publishing Company is in the business of publishing and printing guidebooks and directories. The board of directors has engaged you to make a cost study to determine whether the company is economically justified in continuing to print, as well as publish, its books and directories. You obtain the following information from the company's cost accounting records for the preceding fiscal year:

	Departments			
	Publishing	Printing	Shipping	Total
Salaries and wages	$275,000	$150,000	$25,000	$ 450,000
Telephone and telegraph	12,000	3,700	300	16,000
Materials and supplies	50,000	250,000	10,000	310,000
Occupancy costs	75,000	80,000	10,000	165,000
General and administrative	40,000	30,000	4,000	74,000
Depreciation	5,000	40,000	5,000	50,000
	$457,000	$553,700	$54,300	$1,065,000

Additional data:
1. A review of personnel requirements indicates that if printing is discontinued, the publishing department will need one additional clerk at $4,000 per year to handle correspondence with the printer. Two layout artists and a proofreader will be required at an aggregate annual cost of $17,000; other personnel in the printing department can be released. One mailing clerk, at $3,000, will be retained; others in the shipping department can be released. Employees being released will receive immediately, on the average, three months' termination pay, which will be amortized over a five-year period.
2. Long-distance telephone and telegraph charges are identified and distributed to the responsible department. The remainder of the

telephone bill, representing basic service at a cost of $4,000, is allocated in the ratio of 10 to publishing, 5 to printing, and 1 to shipping. The discontinuance of printing is not expected to have a material effect on the basic service cost.

3. Shipping supplies consist of cartons, envelopes, and stamps. It is estimated that the cost of envelopes and stamps for mailing material to an outside printer will be $5,000 per year.

4. If the printing is discontinued, the company will retain its present building, but will sublet a portion of the space at an annual rental of $50,000. Taxes, insurance, heat, light, and other occupancy costs will not be significantly affected.

5. One cost clerk will not be required ($5,000 per year) if printing is discontinued. Other general and administrative personnel will be retained.

6. Included in administrative expenses is interest expense on a 5 percent mortgage loan of $500,000.

7. Printing and shipping-room machinery and equipment having a net book value of $300,000 can be sold without gain or loss. These funds in excess of termination pay will be invested in marketable securities earning 5 percent.

8. The company has received a proposal for a five-year contract from an outside printer, under which the volume of work done last year would be printed at a cost of $550,000 per year.

9. Assume continued volume and prices at last year's level.

Required:

Prepare a statement setting forth in comparative form the costs of operations of the printing and shipping departments under the present arrangement and under an arrangement in which inside printing is discontinued. Summarize the net saving or extra cost in case printing is discontinued.

(AICPA adapted)

11-15.

X MANUFACTURING COMPANY
Income Statement
For the Year Ended December 31, 19x1

Sales (100,000 units at $5)		$500,000
Variable costs:		
Direct material	$ 90,000	
Direct labor	100,000	
Factory burden	50,000	
Total manufacturing variable cost	$240,000	
Selling expense	10,000	
Total variable costs		250,000
Contribution margin		$250,000
Fixed costs:		
Factory burden	$100,000	
Selling expense	30,000	
Administrative expense	70,000	
Total fixed costs		200,000
Net profit		$ 50,000

Management has negotiated a 10 percent increase in wage rates with the union, effective January 1, 19x2, applicable to the following:

1. All direct labor
2. Indirect labor, representing 40 percent of variable factory burden in 19x1
3. Additional indirect labor in fixed factory burden, amounting to $20,000 in 19x1

In view of the increased labor and burden cost anticipated in 19x2, management is seeking an opportunity to subcontract a major component which X Company is presently manufacturing.

The direct labor cost per unit for this component at 19x1 wage rates was 27.3 cents. Variable burden bears the same relationship to the cost of this component as it does to the unit cost of the end product. It is assumed that if X Manufacturing decides to subcontract the item, it will purchase the direct material for delivery to the supplier and will subcontract only the conversion cost and supplier's profit. The X Company will not expect to reduce its fixed costs if it decides to subcontract the component.

Required:
1. What is the highest price per unit the X Company could pay for the component which would still yield an advantage over making it within the company?
2. Assume that it is management's goal to restore the dollar profit earned in 19x1 without increasing the selling price of its product. What unit price for subcontracting the component would accomplish this?

(Round all computations of unit cost to three digits.)

11-16.† When you had completed your audit of The Scoopa Company, management asked for your assistance in arriving at a decision whether to continue manufacturing a part or to buy it from an outside supplier. The part, which is named Faktron, is a component used in some of the finished products of the company.

From your audit working papers and from further investigation, you develop the following data as being typical of the company's operations:

1. The annual requirement for Faktrons is 5,000 units. The lowest quotation from a supplier was $8 per unit.
2. Faktrons have been manufactured in the precision machinery department. If they are purchased from an outside supplier, certain machinery will be sold and will realize its book value.
3. The following were the total costs of the precision machinery department during the year under audit when 5,000 Faktrons were made:

Material	$67,500
Direct labor	50,000
Indirect labor	20,000
Light and heat	5,500
Power	3,000
Depreciation	10,000
Property taxes and insurance	8,000
Payroll taxes and other benefits	9,800
Other	5,000

4. The following precision machinery department costs apply to the manufacture of Faktrons: material, $17,500; direct labor, $28,000; indirect labor, $6,000; power, $300; other, $500. The sale of the equipment used for Faktrons would reduce the following costs by the amounts indicated: depreciation, $2,000; property taxes and insurance, $1,000.

5. The following additional precision machinery department costs would be incurred if Faktrons were purchased from an outside supplier: freight, 50 cents per unit; indirect labor for receiving, materials handling, inspection, etc., $5,000. The cost of the purchased Faktrons would be considered a precision machinery department cost.

Required:

1. Prepare a schedule showing a comparison of the total costs of the precision machinery department (*a*) when Faktrons are made, and (*b*) when Faktrons are bought from an outside supplier.

2. Discuss the considerations in addition to the cost factors that you would bring to its attention when assisting management to arrive at a decision whether to make or buy Faktrons. Include in your discussion the considerations that might be applied to the evaluation of the outside supplier.

(AICPA adapted)

11-17. The Vernom Corporation, which produces and sells to wholesalers a highly successful line of summer lotions and insect repellents, has decided to diversify in order to stabilize sales throughout the year. A natural area for the company to consider is the production of winter lotions and creams to prevent dry and chapped skin.

After considerable research, a winter products line has been developed. However, because of the conservative nature of the company management, Vernom's president has decided to introduce only one of the new products for this coming winter. If the product is a success, further expansion in future years will be initiated.

The product selected (called Chap-off) is a lip balm that will be sold in a lipstick-type tube. The product will be sold to wholesalers in boxes of 24 tubes for $8 per box. Because of available capacity, no additional fixed charges will be incurred to produce the product. However, a $100,000 fixed charge will be absorbed by the product to allocate a fair share of the company's present fixed costs to the new product.

Using the estimated sales and production of 100,000 boxes of Chap-off as the standard volume, the accounting department has developed the following costs:

Direct labor	$2.00 per box
Direct materials	$3.00 per box
Total overhead	$1.50 per box
Total	$6.50 per box

Vernom has approached a cosmetics manufacturer to discuss the possibility of purchasing the tubes for Chap-off. The purchase price of the empty tubes from the cosmetics manufacturer would be 90 cents per 24 tubes. If the Vernom Corporation accepts the purchase proposal, it is estimated that direct labor and variable overhead costs would be reduced by 10 percent and direct material costs would be reduced by 20 percent.

Required:
1. Should the Vernom Corporation make or buy the tubes? Show calculations to support your answer.
2. What would be the maximum purchase price acceptable to the Vernom Corporation for the tubes? Support your answer with an appropriate explanation.
3. Instead of sales of 100,000 boxes, revised estimates show sales volume at 125,000 boxes. At this new volume, additional equipment, at an annual rental of $10,000, must be acquired to manufacture the tubes. However, this incremental cost would be the only additional fixed cost required even if sales increased to 300,000 boxes. (The 300,000 level is the goal for the third year of production.) Under these circumstances, should the Vernom Corporation make or buy the tubes? Show calculations to support your answer.
4. The company has the option of making and buying at the same time. What would be your answer to part 3 if this alternative was considered? Show calculations to support your answer.
5. What nonquantifiable factors should the Vernom Corporation consider in determining whether it should make or buy the lipstick tubes?

(IMA adapted)

11-18. Marshall Manufacturing, Inc., has produced two products, Z and P, at its Richmond plant for several years. On March 31, 1973, P was dropped from the product line. Marshall manufactures and sells 50,000 units of Z annually, and this activity is not expected to change. Unit material and direct labor costs are $12 and $7, respectively.

The Richmond plant is in a leased building; the lease expires June 30, 1977. Annual rent is $75,000. The lease provides Marshall the right of sublet; all nonremovable leasehold improvements revert to the lessor. At the end of the lease, Marshall intends to close the plant and scrap all equipment.

P has been produced on two assembly lines which occupy 25 percent of the plant. The assembly lines will have a book value of $135,000 and a remaining useful life of seven years as of June 30, 1973. This is the only portion of the plant available for alternative uses.

Marshall uses one unit of D to produce one unit of Z. D is purchased under a contract requiring a minimum annual purchase of 5,000 units. The contract expires June 30, 1977. A list of D unit costs follows:

Annual Purchases (Units)		Unit Cost
5,000 to	7,499	$2.00
7,500 to	19,999	1.95
20,000 to	34,999	1.80
35,000 to	99,999	1.65
100,000 to	250,000	1.35

Alternatives are available for using the space previously used to manufacture P. Some may be used in combination. All can be implemented by June 30, 1973. Should no action be taken, the plant is expected to operate profitably, and manufacturing overhead is not expected to differ materially from past years when P was manufactured. Following are the alternatives:

1. Sell the two P assembly lines for $70,000. The purchaser will buy only if he can acquire the equipment from both lines. The purchaser will pay all removal and transportation costs.
2. Sublet the floor space for an annual rental of $12,100. The lease will require that the equipment be removed (cost nominal) and leasehold improvements costing $38,000 be installed. Indirect costs are expected to increase $3,500 annually as a result of the sublease.
3. Convert one or both P assembly lines to produce D at a cost of $45,500 for each line. The converted lines will have a remaining useful life of ten years. Each modified line can produce any number of units of D up to a maximum of 37,000 units at a unit direct material and direct labor cost of 10 cents and 25 cents respectively. Annual manufacturing overhead is expected to increase from $550,000 to $562,000 if one line is converted and to $566,000 if both lines are converted.

Required:
Prepare a schedule to analyze the best utilization of the following alternatives for the four years ended June 30, 1977. (Ignore income taxes and the time value of money.)
1. Continue to purchase D; sell equipment; rent space.
2. Continue to purchase D; sell equipment.
3. Produce D on two assembly lines; purchase D as needed.
4. Produce D on one assembly line; purchase D as needed.

Set up your workpaper allowing one column for the evaluation of each alternative. The columns should be numbered 1, 2, 3, and 4.

(AICPA adapted)

11-19.   The Columbus Hospital operates a general hospital but rents space and beds to separate entities for specialized areas such as pediatrics, maternity, and psychiatry. Columbus charges each separate entity for such common services to its patients as meals and laundry and for administrative services including billings and collections. All uncollectible accounts are charged directly to the entity. Space and bed rentals are fixed for the year.

For the entire year ended June 30, 1973, the Pediatrics Department at Columbus Hospital charged each patient an average of $65 per day, had a capacity of 60 beds, operated 24 hours per day for 365 days, and had revenue of $1,138,800.

Expenses charged by the hospital to the Pediatrics Department for the year ended June 30, 1973, were as follows:

	Basis of Allocation	
	Patient Days	Bed Capacity
Dietary	$ 42,952	
Janitorial		$ 12,800
Laundry	28,000	
Laboratory, other than direct charges to patients	47,800	
Pharmacy	33,800	
Repairs and maintenance	5,200	7,140
General administrative services		131,760
Rent		275,320
Billings and collections	40,000	
Bad debt expense	47,000	
Other	18,048	25,980
	$262,800	$453,000

The only personnel directly employed by the Pediatrics Department are supervising nurses, nurses, and aides. The hospital has minimum personnel requirements based on total annual patient days. Hospital requirements beginning at the minimum expected level of operation follow:

Annual Patient Days	Aides	Nurses	Supervising Nurses
10,000–14,000	21	11	4
14,001–17,000	22	12	4
17,001–23,725	22	13	4
23,726–25,550	25	14	5
25,551–27,375	26	14	5
27,376–29,200	29	16	6

These staffing levels represent full-time equivalents, and it should be assumed that the Pediatrics Department always employs only the minimum number of required full-time equivalent personnel.

Annual salaries for each class of employee are: supervising nurses, $18,000; nurses, $13,000; and aides, $5,000. Salary expense for the year ended June 30, 1973, for supervising nurses, nurses, and aides was $72,000, $169,000, and $110,000, respectively.

The Pediatrics Department operated at 100 percent capacity during 111 days for the past year. It is estimated that during 90 of these capacity days, the demand averaged 17 patients more than capacity and even went as high as 20 patients more on some days. The hospital has an additional twenty beds available for rent for the year ending June 30, 1974.

Required:

1. Calculate the *minimum* number of patient days required for the Pediatrics Department to break even for the year ending June 30, 1974, if the additional twenty beds are not rented. Patient demand is unknown, but assume that revenue per patient day, cost per patient day, cost per bed, and employee salary rates will remain the same as for the year ended June 30, 1973. Present calculations in good form.

2. Assuming for purposes of this problem that patient demand, revenue per patient day, cost per patient day, cost per bed, and employee salary rates for the year ending June 30, 1974, remain the same as for the year ended June 30, 1973, should the Pediatrics Department rent the additional twenty beds? Show the annual gain or loss from the additional beds. Present calculations in good form.

(AICPA adapted)

CHAPTER

12

PRICING POLICIES

THE PLAN OF THIS CHAPTER
An important task for most managements is the setting of prices for the firm's products and services. In discussing the various methods and techniques which can be used, we shall examine the following topics:

Objectives of pricing policies

Marginal analysis and pricing

Full-cost pricing

Contribution approach to pricing

Transfer prices

Two of the most important long-run strategic decisions management must make are the selection of appropriate investment projects and the setting of prices for the company's products and services. These decisions have a direct impact on the financial position, profitability, and funds flow of the company and are often difficult and costly to change after they are put into effect. Thus, a study of accounting for management would be incomplete without an examination of accounting data as input to these decisions. Various aspects of the pricing decision are discussed in the current chapter, and the selection of investment projects is covered in Chapter 13.

OBJECTIVES OF PRICING POLICIES

Some companies do not need to make pricing decisions and are therefore not concerned with pricing policies. A farm corporation, even a very large one, can do very little about changing the price of wheat, for example. Instead, market forces determine the price and the wheat grower must react to expected future prices by deciding the quantity of wheat to plant and the methods to be used in producing it. The vast majority of firms, however, do have some discretion in the setting of prices and thus should formulate an explicit pricing policy. This policy may be quite simple—such as meeting the price of the industry "price leader"—or it may be incredibly complex. The important point is that management should decide on a formal policy in such a critical area as pricing.

A pricing policy consists of a broad philosophy and the specific methodology to implement it. Ideally, top management—e.g., the board of directors—should formulate, or at least approve, this broad philosophy as part of its strategic planning, so that it can be integrated into the company's overall goals. In order to stay in business, a company must, of course, make sufficient profits and also satisfy the various constraints of government regulation. Thus, these two factors must always be considered. Furthermore, specific companies may have additional goals to be considered in establishing a pricing policy—growth rate of sales, share of the market, community and labor relations, etc. Once again, it is essential that top management formulate this broad pricing philosophy so that operating management can then implement it with respect to specific products and services.

The previous chapter has emphasized that, while long-run profit maximization remains as the basic corporate objective, it is not always possible to quantify every aspect of a decision. There are always nonquantitative factors which must be taken into account. This applies equally well to the pricing decision. Accounting data—specifically cost data—can be used to develop what appears to be a profit-maximizing price. This price, however, should be considered a starting point from which management can consider the other objectives in the pricing policy.

MARGINAL ANALYSIS AND PRICING

The profit-maximizing price for a particular product or service is that price which produces the largest difference between total revenues and total costs.

It is natural, then, to begin an analysis of the profit-maximizing price by considering total revenues and total costs.

Demand Functions

Suppose that the marketing division of the Zero Company estimates that the relationship between the selling price of its new product and the quantity which could be sold per year is that shown in the first two columns of Exhibit 12-1. This relationship can be graphed as is done in Exhibit 12-2. The line *DD* represents the demand curve for the Zero Company's new product—it shows the quantity which would be sold per year at various prices.

Two additional important economic concepts are illustrated in Exhibits 12-1 and 12-2. The third column of Exhibit 12-1 indicates the total revenue estimated by the marketing division. Notice that it increases for some price increases but not for others. As was pointed out in Chapter 4, this concept is known as the *price elasticity of demand*—it represents the *relative* change in quantity caused by a change in price. For example, when price is raised from $2 to $3, a 50 percent increase, quantity is estimated to decrease from 80,000 to 70,000 units per year, only a $12\frac{1}{2}$ percent decrease. Since the relative price change is greater than the relative quantity change, total revenues increase. Demand at this point is considered *inelastic*. An increase in price from $6 to $7, however, gives the opposite result—a $16\frac{2}{3}$ percent rise in price leads to a 25 percent decrease in quantity, from 40,000 to 30,000 units per year, and thus a decrease in total revenue results. The demand curve at this point would be considered *elastic*.

The elasticity of demand is related to another economic concept called *marginal revenue*, which is defined as the change in total revenue resulting from a one-unit increase in quantity. Marginal revenue is shown in the fourth column

EXHIBIT 12-1
ZERO COMPANY
Estimated Sales

Selling Price per Unit	Estimated Units to Be Sold per Year	Estimated Sales Revenue per Year	Marginal Revenue
$2	80,000	$160,000	
			−$5
3	70,000	210,000	
			− 3
4	60,000	240,000	
			− 1
5	50,000	250,000	
			+ 1
6	40,000	240,000	
			+ 3
7	30,000	210,000	
			+ 5
8	20,000	160,000	

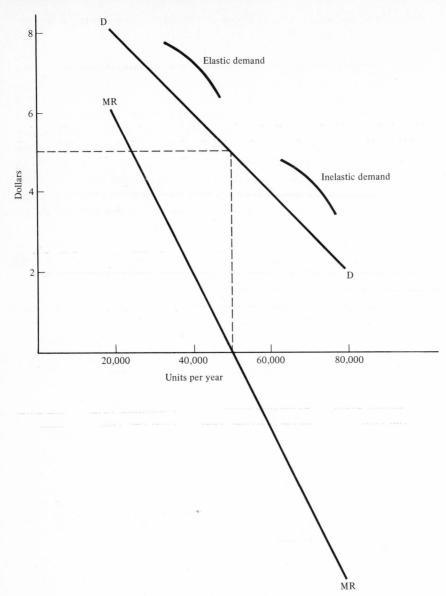

EXHIBIT 12-2 Demand and marginal revenue

of Exhibit 12-1 and as the line MR in Exhibit 12-2. When price is decreased from $4 to $3, for example, the estimated quantity to be sold increases by 10,000 units per year and total revenue *decreases* by $30,000 per year. The reason for this $30,000 decrease is that the firm's revenues are *reduced* by $60,000 because of the decrease in price of $1 on the original 60,000 units, while the firm's revenues are *increased* by $30,000 because of the extra 10,000 units sold at $3 each. Marginal revenue is computed as −$3 by dividing the net lost revenue ($30,000) by the increase in volume (10,000). This −$3 is an average amount representing the revenue lost by increasing volume from 60,000 to 70,000 units per year. It can be seen that <u>marginal revenue will be negative when demand is inelastic because revenue will be reduced with an increase in volume. By the same token, marginal revenue will be positive when demand is elastic.</u>

Marginal Cost

The profit-maximizing price cannot be determined from demand data alone, of course. Cost information is equally important. Suppose that the manufacturing division of Zero Company estimates that the fixed costs of its new product will total $80,000 per year and that variable costs will amount to $3 per unit. The estimated total costs are shown in the third column of Exhibit 12-3. The fourth column of that exhibit shows marginal costs, which are defined as the change in total costs resulting from a one-unit increase in quantity. Marginal costs in this example are constant at $3, equal to the variable costs.

Economic Theory of Pricing

One way to determine the profit-maximizing price from demand and cost data is to compute the estimated profit at various price-output combinations. This is done in Exhibit 12-4, where a maximum estimated profit of $40,000 results from selling 40,000 units at $6 *or* 30,000 units at $7 each.

EXHIBIT 12-3
ZERO COMPANY
Estimated Costs

Selling Price per Unit	Estimated Units to Be Sold per Year	Estimated Total Cost per Year	Marginal Cost
$2	80,000	$320,000	
3	70,000	290,000	+$3
4	60,000	260,000	+ 3
5	50,000	230,000	+ 3
6	40,000	200,000	+ 3
7	30,000	170,000	+ 3
8	20,000	140,000	+ 3

EXHIBIT 12-4
ZERO COMPANY
Estimated Profits

Selling Price per Unit	Estimated Units to Be Sold per Year	Estimated Total Revenues per Year	Estimated Total Cost per Year	Estimated Profit per Year	MR	MC
$2	80,000	$160,000	$320,000	−$160,000		
3	70,000	210,000	290,000	− 80,000	−5	+3
4	60,000	240,000	260,000	− 20,000	−3	+3
5	50,000	250,000	230,000	+ 20,000	−1	+3
6	40,000	240,000	200,000	+ 40,000	+1	+3
7	30,000	210,000	170,000	+ 40,000	+3	+3
8	20,000	160,000	140,000	+ 20,000	+5	+3

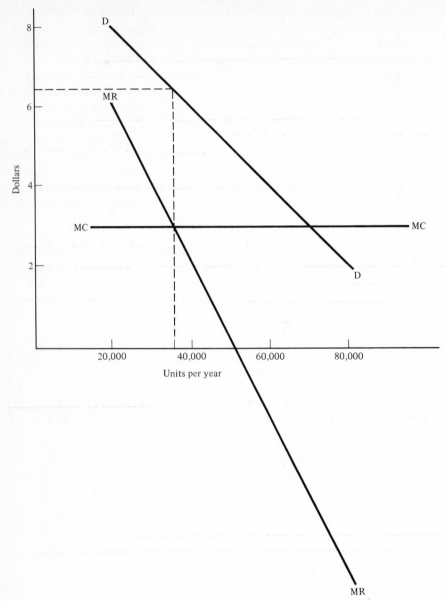

EXHIBIT 12-5 Marginal analysis

The more traditional economic analysis, however, considers the marginal amounts, rather than total revenues and total costs. Economic theory concludes that the most profitable price-output combination will be the one where marginal revenue and marginal costs are equal. Exhibit 12-4 indicates that this is so in the case of the Zero Company. Marginal revenue and marginal costs are equal at a price between $6 and $7 a unit and an output between 30,000 and 40,000 units per year. These same relationships are graphed in Exhibit 12-5, where the marginal costs (MC) and the marginal revenue (MR) curves intersect at the most profitable price-volume combination.

It is easy to see why the marginal analysis is an attractive method of attacking the price-output decision. If marginal costs and marginal revenue were not equal, a change in the price-output combination could increase profits. Suppose that the Zero Company decided to sell its new product at $5 per unit (instead of $6) in order to maximize total revenues. Exhibit 12-4 shows that the marginal revenue between 40,000 and 50,000 units is +$1, while marginal costs are +$3. Thus, increasing output at this point does result in increased total revenue, but it also results in an even larger increase in total costs. Therefore, profits are lower at a price of $5 than at $6 even though total revenues are greater at the $5 price. On the other hand, suppose that the Zero Company sets the price at $8 per unit. According to Exhibit 12-4, marginal revenue between 20,000 and 30,000 units is +$5, while marginal costs are still +$3. Reducing output will reduce total costs, but at this point on the demand curve, the reduction in total revenues is even greater and thus profits are reduced. Only when marginal revenue and marginal costs are equal is there no possibility to increase profits by changing the price-output combination.

The economic theory of pricing, then, sees the firm's management as picking that price-output combination which equates marginal revenue and marginal costs. Such a combination will maximize the firm's profits.

Limitations of Marginal Analysis

Although the marginal analysis as just described is conceptually appealing, it does have some practical limitations. The most obvious, and damaging, disadvantage is that demand and cost factors must be estimated by management. If such factors were known with certainty, marginal analysis would be fairly straightforward and simple to apply to a variety of price-output decisions. Unfortunately, demand factors are rarely known with any significant degree of certainty, and cost factors can also be subject to some uncertainty.

Compounding this problem of uncertainty is the fact that a relatively small error in estimating quantity demanded can result in a very large error in estimating marginal revenue. If the marketing department of the Zero Company had estimated the number of units to be sold at $3 would be 65,000 per year (instead of 70,000), for example, total revenue at that price would be estimated at $195,000. Marginal revenue would have been −$9 instead of −$3 between a price of $3 and $4 $\left(\dfrac{\$195,000 - \$240,000}{65,000 - 60,000} = \dfrac{-\$45,000}{5,000} = -\$9\right)$, a substantial difference.

Because of these shortcomings, most firms apparently set prices without *explicitly* making a marginal analysis such as described here. Most research into the question of actual pricing practices indicates that firms use "cost-plus" pricing, where a "markup" for overhead and profit is added to the direct costs.[1] This does not mean that demand factors are or should be ignored. Instead, it

[1] See R. L. Hall and C. J. Hitch, "Price Theory and Business Behavior," in *Oxford Economic Papers,* Oxford: The Clarendon Press, 1939; and Kaplan, Dirlam, and Lanzillotti, *Pricing in Big Business,* Washington: The Brookings Institution, 1958.

means that cost factors are considered more explicitly than are demand factors because they are usually known with more certainty. Demand is then considered as a moderating factor or constraint in setting the price for the product or service.

FULL-COST PRICING

Full-cost pricing, or *cost-plus pricing,* as it is also called, sets the price of a product or service at an amount equal to its budgeted (or standard) manufacturing cost plus a "normal" markup. This markup is intended to cover marketing and administrative costs and net profit before taxes. Thus, full-cost pricing is based on the concept of absorption costing, discussed in Chapter 9, where product costs include an allocation of fixed manufacturing overhead.

Suppose that the Zero Company uses full-cost pricing to set a tentative price for its new product. The company may have computed this price in the following way:

Per Unit:	Manufac-turing	Other	Total
Variable costs	$2.00	$1.00	$3.00
Fixed costs, based on 40,000			
units per year	1.75	.25	2.00
Total	3.75	$1.25	$5.00
Normal markup of 60 percent	2.25		
Tentative selling price	$6.00		

If the Zero Company had made these computations, the resulting selling price would have been the price-output combination determined to maximize profits, using marginal analysis. Of course, several key factors in the cost-plus or full-cost pricing computation were assumed to make the selected price end up just that way! First, it was assumed that fixed costs would be spread out over 40,000 units per year—this 40,000 figure was picked because of the marginal analysis previously performed. There is a definite possibility of circular reasoning here, as this 40,000-unit figure has to be picked before total cost is determined and thus before the price is determined by management using full-cost pricing. But if price is not determined, how can an estimate of sales volume be made?

This problem of volume being a variable in the determination of cost under the full-cost pricing method is a very difficult one to solve. In effect, a trial-and-error approach can be taken—a volume is picked to allocate costs, and the reasonableness of that volume level is then reconsidered in light of the resulting selling price. For example, assume that the Zero Company had initially made the following computations:

	Per Unit
Variable manufacturing costs	$2.00
Fixed manufacturing costs, based on a volume of 70,000 units per year	1.00
Total manufacturing costs	3.00
Normal markup of 60%	1.80
Tentative selling price	$4.80

The marketing department would then be consulted to determine if it is reason-able to expect sales of 70,000 units per year at a price of $4.80. In this case, the department would undoubtedly say that $4.80 is too high a selling price for that volume. Reference to the demand curve in Exhibit 12-5 indicates that just over 50,000 units per year is a reasonable expectation at that price, assuming the demand curve is accurate as originally estimated. The Zero Company's man-agement could then go through a similar calculation, based on another volume level, to see if it results in a selling price which could generate the assumed vol-ume. This methodology is obviously time-consuming and indicates the arbitrari-ness of the "normal" markup percentage.

ROI Pricing

How is this normal markup determined? In the preceding examples, the markup was based on manufacturing cost, but it could also be based on other cost figures as well — a 20 percent markup on the total full cost of $5 would also result in a selling price of $6. Some method must be used to establish this normal markup percentage. Some companies have a traditional percentage which they try to maintain, whereas others may use some sort of past average.

One practical approach to the determination of the normal markup per-centage is to base it on the required *return on investment* (ROI). For example, if the Zero Company must invest an additional $250,000 in order to produce its new product and if its cost of raising capital is 16 percent, the following analysis may be made:

	Per Unit
Total variable costs	$3.00
Total fixed costs, based on 40,000 units per year	2.00
Total costs per unit	5.00
Desired return on investment	1.00*
Tentative selling price	$6.00

$$* \left(\frac{\$250,000 \times .16}{40,000} \right)$$

This approach does not solve the problem of allocating fixed costs, but it does establish a definite methodology for computing the markup. (The problem of determining the cost of raising capital is discussed in the next chapter.)

However the selling price is determined using full-cost pricing techniques, it must be considered tentative at best. Management of course desires to recover all costs and to earn profits, but merely using full-cost pricing will in no way assure achievement of these objectives. In a competitive environment, the reac-tions of customers and competitors must always be considered. This is the point where some type of demand analysis must be used. Competitive pressure and demand elasticities can lead to different markups for different products or for different years for the same product. The important fact is that the price deter-mined using full-cost pricing must not be considered the final price — it may be necessary to deviate from it substantially because of demand factors.

Full-Cost Pricing and Government Regulation

One area where full-cost pricing is widely used is in dealing with government agencies. Many government contracts are awarded on a cost-plus basis. That is, a final selling price is not included in the contract; instead, it calls for the seller to be reimbursed for all costs incurred plus a profit amount. Such contracts are frequently the subject of congressional concern because of cost overruns — where the seller incurs more cost that was anticipated and the government is committed to reimbursing all costs.

Regulatory agencies, such as the Federal Power Commission and the Federal Communications Commission, generally use full-cost pricing in establishing a maximum rate schedule for the utilities under their jurisdiction. Typically, these agencies allow utilities to set their rates in such a way that total revenues are expected to equal total costs plus an amount for their cost of debt and equity capital. Once again, however, there is no guarantee that such rates will in fact cover all these factors.

An aspect of governmental regulation of interest to all businesses is the Robinson-Patman Act. Basically, this act makes it illegal for a seller to quote different prices to competing customers unless such "price discrimination" is based on some difference in manufacturing, marketing, or transportation costs. Decisions of the Federal Trade Commission (FTC), which administers the act, are based on full-cost pricing. Companies which charge different prices to different customers need to be aware of the necessity of keeping adequate records to substantiate their prices. When attempting to justify such price discrimination, of course, it is more convincing if careful cost comparisons were made before the sale, rather than after the FTC has initiated an inquiry!

CONTRIBUTION APPROACH TO PRICING

As has been stressed earlier, the price derived from application of a full-cost pricing methodology must be considered a tentative price — one from which deviations will be made as a result of the actions of customers and competitors. One problem with the methodology as discussed here is that it does not supply management with the proper information needed to adjust the price in view of market conditions. Management would like to know, in particular, how low the price could be before profits would actually be lowered as a result of the sale. Fortunately, this kind of information can be built into the pricing decision, using tools and techniques we have already discussed.

Differential Costs and Pricing

Chapter 11 discussed the concept of differential costs — the total difference in costs between alternatives. It was seen that an analysis of the relevant costs involved in a proposed alternative was a proper and legitimate procedure to follow in evaluating alternatives. Relevant costs by definition include only those future costs which will change as a result of the alternative under consideration and thus are definitely important to the decision. This same type of analysis can give management an idea of the minimum acceptable price — that price which just covers the differential costs involved.

EXHIBIT 12-6
M. LARKS TOY COMPANY
Cost Effects of Special Order

Direct material (5,000 × $5)	$25,000
Direct labor (5,000 × $2)	10,000
Variable overhead (5,000 × $4)	20,000
Increase in manufacturing costs	55,000
Selling and administrative	
expenses (freight)	5,000
Total differential costs	$60,000

Referring back to the example of the Larks Toy Company in Chapter 11, we note that the company was given the opportunity to supply a large mail-order house with 5,000 toy trains. An analysis of the differential costs associated with producing this order was prepared in Exhibit 11-9 and is partially reproduced in Exhibit 12-6. It will be recalled that the mail-order house offered to purchase the trains at $15 each in the example from Chapter 11. Suppose, instead, that no price was mentioned and that the Larks Toy Company (along with other manufacturers) was asked to submit a bid price to the mail-order house. The company supplying the lowest bid would presumably stand the best chance of getting the order. Management of Larks Toy Company can use the relevant costs shown in Exhibit 12-6 to assist it in deciding on the price to bid on this special order.

Seeing that this order, if obtained, would increase total costs by $60,000, management may very well decide that this is the minimum amount of extra revenue which should be generated by the special order. If this is the decision, the minimum price to be considered by management would be $12 each ($60,000 divided by 5,000). This price would probably be accepted by the mail-order house, since it is doubtful that any of the Larks Toy Company's competitors would bid lower unless they were much more efficient than the Larks Company or unless they were willing to take a loss now in order to build up a future business relationship with the mail-order house. This probability does not mean that the company should make a $12 bid, however, because to do so would commit the company to an order on which no profit and no rate of return will be earned. Management must balance desired profits and rate of return against the chance of obtaining the order.

Suppose the company estimates that an additional investment in working capital of $10,000 will be needed if this order is to be accepted. If management would be willing to accept a 5 percent before-tax return—a lower-than-average return—in order to increase the chance of getting the order, the price to be bid can be calculated as follows:

Total differential costs	$60,000
Desired profit (.05 × $10,000)	500
Necessary total revenues	$60,500
Number of units in order	5,000
Price per unit to bid	$12.10

Obviously, the Larks Company would be happier with a higher price because it would mean higher profits—*if* the company could still get the order at that higher price.

By looking at differential costs, management is focusing its attention on desired *contribution margins*. Any contribution margin greater than zero will increase profits over what they would otherwise have been. The price at which the contribution margin is zero ($12 each, in the current example) thus represents the *minimum* price acceptable in most situations. This same type of analysis can be used for all situations where management has some discretion in establishing selling prices. The price which just covers differential costs would represent the minimum acceptable price. The full-cost price, on the other hand, represents the *maximum* price which the firm could ordinarily expect, since it includes a full allowance for profit as well as total cost recovery. With this range of prices in mind, management would then be in a better position to judge what discount is possible from the price based on full costs. Competitive conditions may require management to charge a price less than one which would lead to "normal" profits, and the contribution approach to pricing allows management to judge the effect on profits of various possible prices.

Relationship of Full-Cost and Contribution Pricing

An important point to remember is that the contribution approach and the full-cost approach to pricing are not necessarily competing methods. Instead, they should be considered as complementing each other. The full-cost approach gives management an idea of the price which is necessary to obtain "normal" profits with a normal volume. The contribution approach shows the effect on company profits of deviating from that price-volume combination. As was pointed out earlier, some companies in effect combine both approaches by basing the markup on variable costs rather than on total manufacturing costs. In any case, prices determined from cost data must always be considered tentative and subject to adjustments as a result of changing market conditions.

TRANSFER PRICES

One aspect of the pricing problem faced by large, decentralized companies deserves special consideration. Chapter 10 discussed the role that the return on capital used has in the evaluation and motivation of segment managers. It was there pointed out that segment managers are most likely to be highly motivated and thus to perform best when they are held responsible only for those factors over which they have control. If some of their costs or revenues are arbitrarily assigned to them, they are likely to regard the return on capital used as an unfair evaluator. In a decentralized company which has substantial interdivisional sales, the appropriate price for such sales is thus of great concern to the division managers and to top management.

The price of interdivisional sales will affect the selling division's sales and the buying division's costs. The sale itself, of course, will not have any direct effect on company profits, because its effect on one division's costs is exactly offset by its effect on another division's revenues. The *transfer price policy,* however, can greatly affect company profits indirectly by influencing the decisions of the division managers.

For example, if one segment (say Division A) sells a component part to another segment (Division B), it may be required by company policy to price the item at its own cost. Under such circumstances, the manager of A is involved in a *profitless* transaction, with the accompanying adverse effect on the division's performance. On the other hand, the manager of Division B gets a profit break. The more volume A does with B, the better B's performance looks and the worse A's looks. Even if this interdivisional sale is quite profitable to the company, the manager of Division A has an incentive to discourage it and concentrate on profitable sales. On the other hand, even if this sale is not profitable for the company, the manager of Division B has tremendous incentive to encourage it because of the favorable effect on the division's profits. This situation is exactly opposite to the one described in Chapter 10 as desirable — managers in this situation are not motivated to behavior which will foster company goals.

Economics of Transfer Pricing

From the preceding discussion, it is apparent that transfer prices should be set at a level which will motivate both the selling and the buying divisions to follow the course of action which is best for the company as a whole. Division managers are more likely to do so if the action is also in their own best interests. The transfer price must be one, therefore, which makes the company's, the division's, and the manager's goals compatible. To a large extent, the appropriate transfer price under this definition depends on the type of market existing for the goods being transferred. If there is a definite outside market for the transferred product, so that the buying division can easily satisfy its needs by buying in that market at the prevailing price or so that the selling division can easily sell its output in that market at the prevailing price, the market price of the product is also the appropriate transfer price.

Transfer Price with an Outside Market

Assume that the Jensen Company has two divisions, Producing and Marketing. For a number of years in the past the Producing Division has manufactured a custom line of pipe fittings, which it sells to the Marketing Division. Similar pipe fittings cannot be obtained by the Marketing Division from other manufacturers. The Producing Division has now embarked upon a program of manufacturing standard as well as custom fittings. Exhibit 12-7 shows the standard costs of producing fitting no. 1033, which has just been added to the Jensen Company's product line. This is not a custom fitting but a standard one produced by several other companies as well.

In the past, the Producing Division has sold its output to the Marketing Division at a price equal to 150 percent of full standard costs. Such a policy would call for a transfer price of $9 for fitting no. 1033 (1.5 × $6). The Marketing Division, however, objects to this price, pointing out it can obtain the same fitting from any one of a number of other suppliers for $8 per unit and that its normal final selling price is only $9.50. The variable costs incurred by the Marketing Division would amount to $1 per unit, but no additional fixed costs would be in-

EXHIBIT 12-7
JENSEN COMPANY
Producing Division
Fitting No. 1033

Standard cost per unit:	
Direct material	$1.50
Direct labor	2.00
Variable overhead	1.00
Fixed overhead*	1.50
Total manufacturing cost	$6.00

* Based on a projected volume of 10,000 units
per year and sufficient available excess capacity.

curred. Because of the change in manufacturing policies, top management is reconsidering its transfer price policy.

Top management should establish a transfer price policy which will encourage division managers to act in the best interests of the company, but which will, at the same time, not detract from their authority and autonomy. Suppose it arbitrarily sets a transfer price higher than the intermediate market price of $8 — say $8.75. This will be fine with the Producing Division,[2] but the Marketing Division would refuse to purchase from the Producing Division and would, instead, want to buy from other suppliers at $8. Suppose, on the other hand, top management sets a price below the market price — say $7.50. The Marketing Division would now be anxious to purchase fitting no. 1033 from the Producing Division, but the Producing Division would rather sell its output to other wholesalers, since they will be willing to buy at the $8 price. Thus, at any price other than the market price, there is a conflict between division managers, one wanting to sell although the other refuses to buy or one wanting to buy when the other refuses to sell. If the price is set at $8 by top management, however, this conflict disappears. The Producing Division would be just as willing to sell to the Marketing Division as to any other buyer, and the Marketing Division would be as willing to buy from the Producing Division as from any other seller. If the Producing Division cannot or will not supply the Marketing Division with all its requirements, the Marketing Division can simply purchase its supply from other manufacturers at the same $8 price. If the Marketing Division for some reason will not purchase the Producing Division's output, it can be sold to other wholesalers at that $8 price.

Thus, where one exists, the *competitive market price* is the appropriate transfer price.[3] Only the market price will do away with conflicts between division managers and allow these managers to operate their divisions with the de-

[2] It is assumed that the manager of the Producing Division realizes that any price over the variable costs of $4.50 will contribute to the division's profits.

[3] A competitive market price is one which is set in a perfect market. If the external market is an imperfect one, declining marginal revenues must be considered. In such a case, the marginal costs of the Producing Division would be more appropriate as the transfer price, as in the case of a product with no intermediate market, which is discussed later. See Jack Hirschleifer, "On the Economics of Transfer Pricing," *Journal of Business,* July 1956, pp. 172–184; and "Economics of the Divisionalized Firm," *Journal of Business,* April 1957, pp. 96–108. These articles are considered the classical exposition of the transfer pricing problem.

gree of autonomy required by a true decentralization system. In addition, the use of an outside market price as the transfer price establishes the discipline of the market on the division managers. The outside price represents a clear standard to measure the performance of the division managers because it represents a price under which other manufacturers and wholesalers are able to operate profitably. The Zero Company should expect its division managers to be able to operate profitably when they must sell or buy at that price, too.

Transfer Price with No Outside Market

Assume now that there is no outside market for the intermediate product—and thus no market price. Fitting no. 1033 is now assumed to be another custom fitting manufactured by the Producing Division and available only from the Jensen Company. Top management now has the task of setting a transfer price policy without benefit of a recognized market price to use as a guide.

Since the Marketing Division manager does not have an alternative source of supply and the Producing Division manager does not have an alternative market for fitting no. 1033, there is no one price that they can both look to as representing their opportunity costs. When an intermediate market existed, the price in that market represented just that. If the Producing Division transferred units to the Marketing Division, the company had given up the opportunity of selling those units to other wholesalers at the $8 market price. On the other hand, if the Marketing Division received units from the Producing Division, the company had given up the opportunity of obtaining those units from other manufacturers at the $8 market price. In any case, the $8 market price represented the opportunity cost to the divisions and to the company. If there is no intermediate market, however, the divisions do not have alternative sources of supply or alternative buyers. Thus, the divisions do not have a single price which can be considered their opportunity cost.

There is, however, an opportunity cost to the company of producing and marketing these units. That opportunity cost can be considered to be equal to the variable costs of production and marketing. Thus, for the company as a whole, the production and sale of fitting no. 1033 will be profitable if the selling price is greater than $5.50 ($4.50 plus $1). Top management now must come up with a transfer price policy which will encourage the Marketing Division to make sales when the price is greater than $5.50 and which will discourage it from making sales when the price is less than $5.50. Since the Marketing Division manager is presumably aware of the division's variable costs, the most direct way of motivating him to make decisions in the company's interest is to charge $4.50 per unit as the transfer price. If this is done, the Marketing Division's total variable costs, including the transfer price, will be $5.50, and it will be in the manager's own interest to do what is also best for the company.

Unfortunately, a transfer price equal to variable manufacturing costs means that the Producing Division will not earn any contribution on fitting no. 1033. If all its products are transferred at their variable manufacturing costs, the Producing Division will report a loss equal to its fixed costs. Obviously, the manager of this division would not want to be evaluated using profit or return on capital used under such circumstances. If he were so evaluated, he would refuse to sell at a price just equal to variable cost. Top management may then be forced to impose this price and to require the Producing Division to manufacture the units and to transfer them to the Marketing Division at variable cost. Obviously, the concept of *decentralization*—where division managers make their own decisions and where they are consequently highly motivated—has all but disappeared in such a situation. The Producing Division manager should then be evaluated through using cost budgets and performance reports, as described in Chapters 7 and 8.

Dilemma of Transfer Pricing

The preceding examples have demonstrated that the most appropriate transfer price is the competitive market price where it exists and variable costs where there is no intermediate price. There are definite disadvantages in using variable costs as the transfer price, because decentralization will not work well at all under such a system. Unfortunately, most transfers are made where no competitive market price exists. This does not mean that decentralization is abandoned, however. Instead, it merely means that transfer prices are usually not the ideal prices they could be under other circumstances. Some compromise has to be made. In some companies, transfer prices are negotiated between buying and selling divisions, with top management being the ultimate arbitrator. In other companies, transfer prices are established using some variation of the full-cost pricing rules discussed earlier in this chapter. In such cases, top management must give serious consideration to the trade-off between the benefits of decentralization and the costs of having some division managers make decisions not in the best interests of the company as a whole.

SUMMARY

One of the most important responsibilities of management is the setting of prices for the firm's products and services. How well management carries out this responsibility will have great impact on the success or failure of the firm in fulfilling its long-range objectives.

Economic theory indicates that the profit-maximizing price is that price at which marginal revenue and marginal costs are equal. Because of the difficulty in measuring these marginal factors in realistic business situations, however, most firms use some form of full-cost pricing, where a percentage markup is added to total manufacturing costs to obtain the tentative selling price. The major problem with full-cost pricing is that the inclusion of fixed costs in the pricing formula means that the volume estimate used to allocate these costs is a critical factor in the computation.

This volume factor can be eliminated by using a contribution margin approach to pricing. If the markup is based on variable costs alone, volume does not enter directly into the price computation. An additional benefit of using the contribution approach is that total variable costs represent a minimum price that management would ordinarily be willing to accept, and the contribution approach focuses on that relevant number.

In pricing goods transferred to other divisions, the decentralized firm is faced with a dilemma. The appropriate transfer price is the competitive market price, if one exists. Ordinarily, however, there will not be such a market price available. Under these circumstances, the appropriate transfer price appears to be the variable costs of the selling division. The use of this price would make the selling division incur losses on intercompany sales and would in all likelihood destroy the concept of decentralization. This dilemma is not easily solved — some compromise is necessary in setting the transfer price or in the application of the principles of decentralization.

All prices set with regard only to cost data must be considered tentative. The reactions of customers and competitors require that prices be constantly reevaluated. There is no escape from the fact that competitive conditions will affect the firm's prices and therefore its profits.

KEY WORDS AND PHRASES

pricing policy
marginal analysis
demand functions
inelastic demand
elastic demand
cost-plus pricing
full-cost pricing

markup
ROI pricing
contribution pricing
transfer price
"competitive market price"
decentralization

DISCUSSION QUESTIONS

1. Who should establish a company's pricing policies?
2. What is a demand function?
3. What is the most important limitation of marginal analysis as a method of pricing?
4. "Prices computed from cost data should be considered tentative." Why?
5. What problems would a decision maker face in setting prices if costs (fixed and variable) were known with certainty?
6. Describe the allocation problem encountered in full-cost pricing.
7. Will net profit be maximized if the contribution margin is maximized? Explain.
8. What is the major advantage of the contribution approach to pricing?
9. Why is the percentage markup on cost always higher than the gross profit percentage?
10. Explain the difference between full-cost pricing and the contribution approach to pricing.
11. What is a transfer price?
12. List the ways in which a transfer price may be established.
13. What are the advantages of using market price as the transfer price?
14. What are the disadvantages of using market price as the transfer price?

PROBLEMS

12-1. The Harwood Toy Company is introducing a new toy called the Whis-
bee, and because the product is new, management cannot be sure how
the market will accept it. The marketing department, however, has
made the following estimates of sales volume at various prices:

Price	Estimated Volume in Units
$ 0.50	3,000
1.00	2,800
2.00	2,600
3.00	2,500
4.00	2,375
5.00	2,250
6.00	1,875
7.00	1,625
8.00	1,500
9.00	1,250
10.00	1,000
12.00	800
15.00	500

The company expects to incur fixed costs of $4,875 per year and vari-
able costs of $1.20 per unit.

Required:
1. Prepare a table showing for each possible price the total revenue,
   total cost, and total profit or loss.
2. Compute the marginal revenue for each possible price.
3. Select the price which will maximize profits and compute the break-
   even point in units at that price.

12-2. The French Company is introducing a new product and wants your
advice on setting the tentative price. An estimated demand schedule
is as follows:

Price	Quantity Demanded (in Units)
$1.00	200,000
1.05	190,000
1.10	180,000
1.15	170,000
1.20	156,000
1.25	140,000
1.30	120,000

Estimated costs:	
Fixed manufacturing	$24,000
Direct materials	$0.40 per unit
Direct labor	$0.10 per unit
Variable overhead	$0.10 per unit
Selling expenses	10% of sales
Administrative expenses	$18,000

Required:
Prepare a schedule to determine the price that should be tentatively
set for the new product.

12-3. Refer to problem 12-1. Assume the Harwood Toy Company sets its
tentative price by adding a normal markup of $66\frac{2}{3}$ percent to total costs.

Using this formula, determine a selling price which could generate the volume assumed in the cost calculation. (This will have to be done by trial and error.)

12-4. Refer to problem 12-2. Assume that the French Company sets its tentative price by adding a normal markup of 50 percent to full manufacturing costs. Using this formula, determine a selling price which could generate the volume assumed in the cost calculation. (This will have to be done by trial and error.)

12-5.† The Wilson Company is attempting to compute costs for its three products for pricing purposes. The company has annual fixed manufacturing costs of $492,000. The variable costs of the company's products are as follows:

Product	Variable Costs of Manufacture (per Unit)
X	$ 6
Y	9
Z	12

The company expects to produce and sell 60,000 units of X, 80,000 units of Y, and 100,000 units of Z annually. Company policy is to add a markup of 30 percent to each product's total manufacturing costs to compute the tentative selling price.

Required:
1. Compute the selling price of each product if fixed costs are allocated on the basis of number of units produced.
2. Compute the selling price of each product if fixed costs are allocated on the basis of total variable costs.
3. Recompute the prices in parts 1 and 2, assuming that the company's policy is to add a markup of 50 percent to each product's variable manufacturing costs.

12-6. A mail-order house has offered to buy 25,000 units of the Whitmore Company's product at 50 cents each and will pay for the shipping expenses. The president of Whitmore is reluctant to accept this order because the 50-cent price is less than the factory unit cost of 68.75 cents. The current operating level, which is below full capacity of 120,000 units per year, shows the following results for the year:

	Total	Per Unit
Sales—80,000 units	$80,000	$1.0000
Manufacturing cost of goods sold*	55,000	.6875
Gross profit	25,000	.3125
Selling and other expenses†	20,000	.2500
Net income	$ 5,000	$ .0625

* Includes fixed costs of $25,000.
† Includes fixed costs of $16,000; the remaining costs consist only of shipping expenses.

Required:

1. Should the mail-order house's offer be accepted? Show computations.
2. What is the minimum price the Whitmore Company would ordinarily accept under the circumstances?

12-7. The Edmunt Company and the Elelamp Company both make television sets. The Edmunt Company purchases most of the parts and subassemblies and assembles them into a final product, whereas the Elelamp Company manufactures almost all the product's components. Each company sells 10,000 units per year.

Cost per Unit

	Edmunt	Elelamp
Direct material	$50	$20
Direct labor	20	30
Overhead*	10	30
Total	$80	$80

* Overhead for both companies is fixed.

Required:

1. If the companies each charge 200 percent of variable cost, what would be their tentative prices?
2. If the companies each charge 150 percent of full cost, what would be their tentative prices?
3. What markups on variable costs will allow each company to earn $200,000 per year?

12-8. The Adam Company has been selling a product for $25. This price was originally calculated from cost data and then cut 10 percent to reflect competitors' prices:

Variable costs	$12.85
Allocated fixed costs	8.00
Total costs	20.85
Markup — one-third	6.95
Tentative selling price	27.80
Competitive discount	2.80
Selling price	$25.00

The controller contends that the price should be reduced to $20, estimating that $6 of the allocated fixed costs in the past was related to a machine which has now been fully depreciated, and thus allocated fixed costs in the future will be that much less. The marketing department estimates that sales would increase from 10,000 units to 13,000 units if the price reduction is made.

Required:

1. Show how the controller obtained the $20 selling price.
2. Should the price be reduced to $20? Show computations.
3. Comment carefully on the controller's argument.

12-9.† E. Berg and Family build custom-made pleasure boats which range in price from $10,000 to $250,000. For the past thirty years, Mr. Berg, Sr., has determined the selling price of each boat by estimating the costs of material, labor, a prorated portion of overhead, and adding 20 percent to these estimated costs.

For example, a recent quotation was determined as follows:

Direct materials	$ 5,000
Direct labor	8,000
Overhead	2,000
	$15,000
Plus 20 percent	3,000
Selling price	$18,000

The overhead figure was determined by estimating total overhead costs for the year and allocating them at 25 percent of direct labor.

If a customer rejected the price and business was slack, Mr. Berg, Sr., would often be willing to reduce his markup to as little as 5 percent over estimated costs. Thus, average markup for the year is estimated at 15 percent.

Ms. Sally Berg has just completed a course on pricing and believes the firm could use some of the techniques discussed in the course. The course emphasized the contribution margin approach to pricing and Sally feels such an approach would be helpful in determining the selling prices of the company's custom-made pleasure boats.

Total overhead, which includes selling and administrative expenses for the year, has been estimated at $150,000, of which $90,000 is fixed and the remainder is variable in direct proportion to direct labor.

Required:
1. Assume the customer in the example rejected the $18,000 quotation and also rejected a $15,750 quotation (5 percent markup) during a slack period. The customer countered with a $15,000 offer.
   a. What is the difference in net income for the year between accepting or rejecting the customer's offer?
   b. What is the minimum selling price Ms. Berg could have quoted without reducing or increasing net income?
2. What advantages does the contribution margin approach to pricing have over the approach used by Mr. Berg?
3. What pitfalls are there, if any, to contribution margin pricing?
                                                            (IMA adapted)

12-10. The Booker Company services washing machines and clothes dryers. It charges customers on a time and material basis, with the same markup on both types of costs. The company has three employees, each earning $10,000 per year and spending 1,000 hours per year on service calls. It sells parts that cost $25,000 annually. The company has other costs of $18,000 a year, which is allocated two-thirds to labor and the remainder to material.

Required:
1. Assuming that the company has a target profit of $15,000 per year,

what should be the price it charges for labor? What should be its markup on parts?

2. Suppose that the Booker Company wants to earn a 25 percent return on its investment of $82,000. What price should it charge for labor and what markup should be applied to parts?

12-11. The Monroe Company has several divisions, the managers of which have been delegated profit responsibility and the authority to accept or reject interdivisional transfers at the established transfer price. Division X produces a major subassembly for one of the company's products; this subassembly is incorporated into the final product by Division Y. Both the subassembly and the final product are sold in competitive markets, and the transfer price for the subassembly has been set at the market price.

The following data are available to each division manager:

Selling price for final product	$1,200
Selling price for subassembly	700
Variable cost for completion in	
Division Y	600
Variable cost in Division X	520

The manager of Division Y argues that Division X should transfer the subassembly at a price lower than the market price because Division Y cannot make a profit at that price even though the company's profit on the final product would be increased by $80 per unit if the transfers were made.

Required:

1. Compute Division Y's profit contribution if transfers are made at market. Show how the division manager computed the $80.
2. Assuming that Division X can sell its entire production of subassemblies in the intermediate market, should transfers be made? Is the market price the appropriate transfer price?
3. Suppose that Division X can sell only one-half of its capacity in the intermediate market and that a 20 percent reduction in price on all units sold would be necessary to sell its full capacity. Assuming that transfers could be made to Division Y without affecting market prices, should these transfers be made? At what price? Division X can produce 1,000 units per month.

12-12. The Ajax division of Gunnco, operating at capacity, has been asked by the Defco division of Gunnco Corporation to supply it with electrical fitting no. 1726. Ajax sells this part to its regular customers for $7.50 each. Defco, which is operating at 50 percent capacity, is willing to pay $5 each for the fitting. Defco will put the fitting into a brake unit which it is manufacturing on essentially a cost plus basis for a commercial airplane manufacturer.

Ajax has a variable cost of producing fitting no. 1726 of $4.25. The cost of the brake unit as being built by Defco is as follows:

Purchased parts—outside vendors	$22.50
Ajax fitting no. 1726	5.00
Other variable costs	14.00
Fixed overhead and administration	8.00
	$49.50

Defco believes the price concession is necessary to get the job.

The company uses return on investment and dollar profits in the measurement of division and division manager performance.

Required:
1. Consider that you are the division controller of Ajax. Would you recommend that Ajax supply fitting no. 1726 to Defco? (Ignore any income tax issues.) Why or why not?
2. Would it be to the short-run economic advantage of the Gunnco Corporation for the Ajax division to supply Defco division with fitting no. 1726 at $5 each? (Ignore any income tax issues.) Explain your answer.
3. Discuss the organizational and manager behavior difficulties, if any, inherent in this situation. As the Gunnco controller, what would you advise the Gunnco Corporation president to do in this situation?

(IMA adapted)

12-13.† The Large Charge Corporation has a policy of allowing its divisions to negotiate transfer prices for interdivisional transactions in the light of competitive market prices from outside suppliers. Another policy is for each division to maximize its profit to the extent that it does not reduce total company profit.

Division A uses a certain magnetic material from department M as an essential component in its major product line. The negotiated interdepartmental price which prevailed during 19x3 was $3 per pound.

Department M had a practical annual capacity to produce 6,000 tons of the material. In 19x3 it produced and sold this entire capacity, two-thirds to outside, small-quantity users at $3.75 per pound and the remaining one-third to Division A.

At the beginning of 19x4, the manager of Division A received an offer from an outside supplier willing to enter a contract to supply his full needs for the year at a price of $2.75.

The manager of Division A offered the manager of department M a chance to meet the $2.75 price. Checking his costs, manager M noted the following:

Variable manufacturing costs	$2.50/lb
Fixed manufacturing costs—total	$9,000,000

"I'm selling to you below my cost the way it is," he concluded.

Required:
If he cannot expect to sell the Division A volume to outsiders, what effect will manager M's refusal to negotiate the $2.75 price have (1) on his own departmental profit; (2) on Division A profit; (3) on total company profit.

12-14. The A. N. Allisis Company follows a policy of transfer pricing for inter-departmental sales at full manufacturing cost plus 20 percent. Managers of using departments are permitted to purchase from outside suppliers when it is to their advantage to do so.

The screw machine department incurs total fixed costs of $20,000. Fixed costs are applied to units on the basis of normal capacity, which is rated at 100,000 total units per month. Unit variable costs and corresponding outside prices by part number are as follows:

Part No.	Unit Variable Costs	Outside Price
2 × 14	$0.35	$0.70
2 × 18	0.50	1.00
6 × 20	0.30	0.60
6 × 25	0.25	0.50
8 × 2	0.60	1.20

The manager of the assembly department buys parts from the screw machine department in the following average monthly quantities:

Part No.	Quantity
2 × 14	5,000
2 × 18	7,000
6 × 20	12,000
6 × 25	20,000
8 × 2	2,000

Required:

1. For the parts produced in the screw machine department, develop the set of prices according to company policy.
2. As manager of the assembly department, compare interdepartmental prices with outside prices and decide which parts to purchase outside.
3. As manager of the screw machine department, reallocate your fixed costs on the assumption that the lost assembly business cannot be replaced. Recalculate your price list.
4. Comment critically on the present transfer pricing system. Any suggestions?

12-15.* A large manufacturing concern is vertically integrated to the extent that several fabricating divisions produce parts and subassemblies for assembly into the finished product by the end-product divisions. This organization naturally entails the problems of intracompany sales and, specifically, the determination of prices to be used for the intracompany sales.

It has been determined that the several divisions of the company should be set up as "independent" businesses, to the extent that the operations of each should be measured in terms of its individual sales, costs, profits, and return on investment. The determination of sales is dependent, obviously, on the resolution of the problem of intracompany prices. The basic philosophy on this question has been defined as that of the competitive pricing concept. Thus the selling price for a particu-

* Copyright by Professor Leo A. Schmidt. Reproduced by permission.

lar part would be determined by the price for that part if bought from outside competition.

In a particular division of the company, the measurement of prices against "competition" has not proved altogether satisfactory. For many parts produced, no outside competitive parts exist in sufficient degree of comparability.

In other cases, the competition that does exist is not always competitive in itself, in terms of being an efficient, low-cost producer. For these reasons, the pricing philosophy has been modified to the extent that "competitive" pricing is determined on the basis of the costs of an "efficient, modern producer."

Plant A of the division is a new plant which will be going into production in 1972. As a new plant with the latest equipment, the assumption is that its labor and overhead costs will be in line with the costs of an "efficient, modern producer." The development of prices at Plant A, therefore, has proceeded along the lines of projecting labor, material, and overhead costs in 1972 at a "standard volume," which is used for pricing and budgeting purposes. These prices, including a profit markup, will provide Plant A with revenue which is sufficient to show an adequate return on investment as a going operation.

However, Plant A incurred starting costs in its first months of operation which the prices are not designed to recover. This fact became obvious to management when certain profit figures were presented which showed an expected return of 9 percent on investment as against a return of 15 percent, which is considered standard for the industry. Divisional management is now of the opinion that these starting costs should be recovered in 1972 pricing.

Required:
1. Comment on the equitability of pricing on the basis of a "modern, efficient producer." How would such a pricing structure affect an old plant operating with aged equipment? What advantages are inherent in such pricing to the end-product divisions, in pointing up excess-cost areas?
2. Within the pricing philosophy as set forth, is the recovery of starting costs justified? Would an outside producer recover these costs as such? How might the expected return on investment be modified in the initial year?

12-16.* In order to preserve some of the advantages of cost and profit pressures which characterize the operations of independent businesses, the X Motor Company has decentralized its divisional and plant accounting on a profit-center basis. Because of the integrated nature of the company's operations, a large percentage of the production of its various plants goes to other plants for further processing and for final assembly.

Under these conditions, it is very necessary that the prices at which products are transferred from plant to plant be determined with great care, so that the resulting profit shown by each plant may reflect the efficiency of its operations. Since these decentralized plant profits are an important element in determining management compensation through annual salary bonuses, the plant managers are very sensitive to the processes of intracompany price determination. The original basic philosophy was that the price to be used in each case would simply be "the amount for which the goods at that stage could be purchased or sold in the open, arms-length, market." This ideal was found difficult to apply because there were no actual "arms-length" purchases and sales for many stages of the product. It is quite probable that more or less parallel difficulties will be encountered by any industry attempting a decentralization program. After some years of experience, the X Motor Company found that its products at various stages fell into four groups with respect to the intracompany pricing problem. These groups were as follows:

1. Products for which there is an active outside market and which are in fact sometimes purchased and sold "at arms length." Such products made up about 5 percent of intracompany sales.
2. Products for which competitive prices are obtainable that possess a sufficient degree of comparability with intracompany products to be useful. Such products, making up about 25 percent of intracompany sales, were, however, not purchased or sold outside the company.
3. Products for which outside comparisons do not exist realistically but which are produced by two or more of the company's own plants and which can therefore be priced on the basis of the costs and the investment of the most efficient plant within the company. The group represents 40 percent.
4. Products which are essentially unique to the producing plant. For the transfers of such products, the use of competitive market prices is impractical. Control and attainment of efficiency must be accomplished on other bases — engineered standards and normal standard cost techniques, for instance. These products constitute about 30 percent of intracompany sales.

Required:
1. Do these four categories adequately blanket the possible situations, or will further experience and closer examination reveal other intraplant price relationships?
2. Visualize the problem of profit-center decentralization for a large food processor with 40 plants in 10 states and 157 different food products. To what extent would the pricing of intracompany sales parallel that of the X Motor Company?

12-17. Assume that you are on the staff of the State Public Utility Commission. The Big City Power Company has petitioned the Commission to allow a rate increase to account for increased cost of labor and fuel. The Commission has determined that the following statements are to be used in establishing a fair rate schedule:

BIG CITY POWER COMPANY
Budgeted Average Assets and Equities
Year Ended July 15, 1976
(Thousands of Dollars)

Utility properties (net)	$1,250	Stockholders' equity	$ 625
Current assets	150	Long-term debt	675
Other assets	25	Current liabilities	125
Total assets (net)	$1,425	Total equities	$1,425

BIG CITY POWER COMPANY
Budgeted Operating Expenses
Year Ended July 15, 1976

Payrolls	$100,000
Fuel	95,500
Maintenance	65,500
Depreciation	40,500
Taxes	85,000
Total operating expenses	$386,500

The Commission has decided that the Big City Power Company is to be allowed a return of 8 percent on stockholders' equity, 12 percent on long-term debt, and 6 percent on current liabilities.

Required:
Compute the total revenues the Commission is allowing the Big City Power Company.

12-18. Refer to problem 12-17. Assume that the Big City Power Company is again asking for a rate increase. The Commission determines that stockholders' equity has increased 20 percent, long-term debt has decreased 4 percent, and current liabilities have not changed since the estimates made in problem 12-17. The company forecasts increased payroll costs of 15 percent and increased fuel costs of 20 percent. All other operating costs are expected to remain unchanged from the earlier estimates.

Required:
Assuming that the Commission accepts the company's forecasts, compute the total revenues the company will be allowed to earn. The Commission will allow a return of 10 percent on stockholders' equity, 12 percent on long-term debt, and 4 percent on current liabilities.

CHAPTER 13

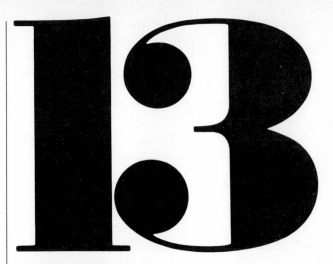

CAPITAL EXPENDITURE DECISIONS

THE PLAN OF THIS CHAPTER
The problems of planning the long-term
investment of relatively large sums of capital
are intricate. In this chapter, using the
criterion of long-term maximization of return
on capital as our guide, we shall examine
the following factors:

The purpose of capital investments

The methods of evaluating capital investment
proposals, including:
Payback period
Accounting method—rate of return
Time-adjusted rate of return
Excess present value

Depreciation and the tax shield

The cost of capital

BUDGETING WITH A DIFFERENCE

The term "capital budgeting" contains two words with which we are now quite familiar: "capital"—the relatively scarce, nonhuman resources of productive enterprise; and "budgeting"—the detailed, quantified planning which guides the future activities of the enterprise toward the achievement of its profit goals. Capital budgeting, then, consists in planning the deployment of available capital for the purpose of maximizing the long-term profitability (return on investment) of the firm.

Capital budgeting is budgeting with a difference, however.

1. While the typical *comprehensive planning budget* projects the details of the firm's activities over near-term fiscal periods, the *capital budget* looks to the longer-range future; the consequences of investment in plant, property, equipment, product development, and the like will ordinarily affect the welfare of the firm for many years.

2. Most capital expenditure decisions involve substantially larger sums of money than do the day-to-day operating decisions of the firm.

Uncertainty is a part of any decision—but the further into the future its effects are projected, the greater the degree of that uncertainty. When this heightened uncertainty is combined with the commitment of large sums of money to irreversible[1] projects, the importance of the decision is greatly magnified. It is understandable, then, that such decisions are usually made at a rather high level in the organization—many, indeed, by the board of directors.

CLASSES OF PROJECTS

Most capital projects can be classed in one of the following ways:

1. *Replacement.* When certain basic machines or equipment wear out, they are replaced in kind. Urgency is frequently the motive for choosing a replacement-type project. If a boiler bursts or a bridge crane suffers an irreparable breakdown, replacement must be made quickly if normal operations are not to be unduly interrupted. Replacement of old punch presses or engine lathes may be carried out under less urgent circumstances, but generally the purpose is simply to maintain operations at status quo, ordinarily without applying the test of future profit improvement.

2. *Product or process improvement.* Of special importance in capital expenditure plans are those which are intended to produce additional revenue or to realize cost savings. New special-purpose or automatic equipment to transform a predominantly manual operation into a more mechanized one may be considered if the projected cost savings are considered adequate. A change in the design of the product, or the development of a new one, may

---

[1] While the commitment of capital to long-term projects is indeed *irreversible*, it need not be *irrevocable.* The fact that a project may be foreshortened, however, does not change the inherent risk in the capital expenditure decision. Thus, a piece of productive equipment may be sold before its useful life has expired, but generally at a considerable loss; a product development project may be dropped when it is deemed a failure but, in most cases, only after the expenditure of much time and money.

require the investment of considerable sums of money; it would likely be undertaken with the expectation that increased revenues in future years would yield a satisfactory return on the investment.

3. *Expansion.* The growing firm typically is faced with decisions concerning the form and rate of their expansion. Large investments may be made in opening a branch plant; in enlarging a building and adding equipment; in acquiring another firm by merger; or in undertaking a large-scale advertising campaign. All such investments contemplate the enhancement of long-term returns inherent in increased profitable volume.

Because funds for long-term capital investment are essentially scarce, the various investment projects open to management at any given time are likely to be in competition with one another. The alert, progressive management will always be on the lookout for ways of improving the profit-making capacity of the company by wise investment of available capital. Apart from projects given priority because of urgency, each of the alternatives should be evaluated, ranked, and chosen in terms of the relative long-term advantage it promises.

METHODS OF EVALUATION

The more commonly used methods of evaluating capital investment proposals are classed as follows:

1. Payback period
2. Accounting rate of return
3. Discounted cash flow

Each of these methods has certain advantages and disadvantages. Each has its proponents. Inasmuch as none of them is very complex, it is well to know them all and to be able to compare the results of each as applied to any capital proposal. (An example illustrating the various methods is given in the chapter appendix.)

For our illustrative purposes, let us assume that the Investo Company has the opportunity to purchase a piece of automatic equipment; the details of the proposal include:

Original cost, installed (no salvage value)	$6,000
Estimated annual cash savings (after taxes)	$2,000
Estimated useful life	5 years

Payback Period

To relate monetary benefits (return, savings) to the investment which produces them is one basic way of measuring the worth of that investment. Management has long been quick to see the need to recoup a capital expenditure as soon as possible out of the return it yields. The question "What is the *payback* on this investment?" demands an answer in terms of the length of time required to equate cash return with initial cost. The mathematics of the technique is simple; the calculation is

$$P = \frac{I}{C}$$

where P = payback period
      I = original investment
      C = annual cash inflows (cash savings after taxes)

For the example of the Investo Company, payback is determined thus:

$$P = \frac{\$6,000}{\$2,000} = 3 \text{ years}$$

The chief advantage in the payback method of evaluating a capital expenditure is its simplicity. For most proposals, nearly anyone can approximate the payback period with a mental calculation. Furthermore, it is almost universally understood: The sooner an investment is recovered, the shorter the period of uncertainty regarding its worth.

The disadvantages are grave, however. The emphasis of the payback method is on *liquidity*; it gives no effect to *profitability*, which is management's basic economic objective. It gives the impression that if cash savings accumulate to the amount of the initial investment, that is enough. This, clearly, is misleading; if the $6,000 machine which the Investo Company is contemplating should prove worthless after the three-year payback period, the company would have recovered its cost through cash savings, but it would have been wiser to invest the money in bonds at 3 percent interest.

Thus, although the payback method relates an investment to the monetary benefits it provides, it offers no measure of its true contribution to the profit goals of the firm.

Accounting Method

The accounting method is so called because it determines the *return* by accrual methods. As a rate of return, the resulting percentage is a measure of profitability, overcoming the major disadvantage of the payback method. The accounting method, like the payback, is comparatively simple.

The formula is

$$R = \frac{C - D}{I}$$

where R = accounting rate of return
      C = annual cash inflows (cash savings after taxes)
      I = original investment
      D = depreciation

With the figures from the Investo Company example, the rate of return is determined thus:

$$R = \frac{\$2,000 - \$1,200}{\$6,000} = \frac{800}{6,000} = 13.3\%$$

This calculation bases return on the *original* investment in the project. Since the investment in this example is in a depreciable asset, estimated to have a five-year useful life with no salvage value, it could be argued that the investment base for calculating the rate of return ought to be the *average* of the undepreciated value of the asset over its useful life. Since the annual depreciation would be $1,200 on a straight-line basis, the undepreciated balances and their average appear as follows:

Original investment	$ 6,000
Undepreciated balances:	
End of year 1	4,800
End of year 2	3,600
End of year 3	2,400
End of year 4	1,200
End of year 5	—
Total of balances	$18,000
Average undepreciated balance (÷6)	$ 3,000

As a shortcut, when there is no estimated salvage value, the average undepreciated balance over the economic life of the asset may be assumed to be one-half its original cost; in this case, $6,000/2 = $3,000. Thus, the rate of return based on average investment would be

$$R = \frac{C - D}{I/2} = \frac{\$2,000 - \$1,200}{\$6,000/2} = \frac{800}{3,000} = 26.7\%$$

Where there is no salvage value and the average investment is one-half the original investment, the rate of return will be double the rate calculated on the original investment.

In addition to the basic simplicity of the method, the accounting rate of return places the emphasis on the profitability of the project, rather than on liquidity, as in the case of the payback method.

However, the accounting method also has drawbacks. In averaging all earnings, regardless of how far in the future they may be realized, this method overlooks the fundamental *time value of money*. Moreover, when future earnings from capital projects are realized in an uneven flow, the accounting method is incapable of measuring the precise effects on overall profits because it is essentially an averaging technique.

The weaknesses in the accounting method arise out of the fact that accrual methods were developed primarily for purposes of income determination and reporting financial position and not to measure the desirability of capital projects. Whereas both payback and accounting methods provide rough-and-ready estimates of the worth of investment proposals, their limitations suggest the use of more appropriate and accurate methods.

Discounted Cash Flow

The determination of the potential profitability of capital expenditure proposals by discounted cash-flow methods is based on the concept of the time value of money, implemented by some simple mathematical techniques. The time value of money is rooted in its fundamental scarcity, combined with its economic function as a commodity. Very simply, when you need more money than you possess, you borrow it. What you must pay for the use of borrowed funds is a function of three factors:

1. The *amount* borrowed

2. The interest *rate* (rate of return, from the point of view of the lender)

3. The *time* period during which borrowed money is used

   If you borrow $100 for one year at 6 percent, you must repay $106 a year from now. This tells you that under the conditions stated, a year's time makes a $6 difference in the value of the money. Obviously, if you borrow under these conditions, you regard $100 today to be worth as much to you as $106 a year from now. It's the old "bird in the hand—two in the bush" idea. The value of money changes with time.

   An example may help to clarify this fact. Assume that a man needs to borrow a sum of money to build an addition to his home. The bank agrees to lend him $3,169 at 10 percent interest on the unpaid balance for a period of four years, with repayments on the mortgage of $1,000 at the end of each year. The schedule of repayments, including interest (return) is as follows:

Balance Beginning of Period	Applied to Interest (10%)	Applied to Principal	Total Payment	Unpaid Balance after Payment
$3,169	$317	$ 683	$1,000	$2,486
2,486	249	751	1,000	1,735
1,735	174	826	1,000	909
909	91	909	1,000	
	$831	$3,169	$4,000	

From the standpoint of the bank, investing its money at 10 percent, the total of $4,000 repayments, received at different times over the term of the loan, amounted to enough to recover the initial investment and to provide a return of 10 percent on the amount of money invested at all times. To summarize:

Cost (initial investment)	$3,169
Return (time-adjusted—10%)	831
Total cash inflows	$4,000

   The bank, in setting up its schedule of payments to yield 10 percent on the unpaid balance for four years, would consult certain mathematical tables, called "present value tables" (see Tables I and II on pages 426–427).

   Suppose the problem is to determine how much money the bank can lend at the *present time* if the borrower agrees to make four annual repayments of $1,000 each, representing a rate of return of 10 percent to the bank. The bank would refer to Table I. Here the factors are arranged by years, as indicated in the extreme left column, and by rates of return, as shown in the column headings across the page. These factors represent the *present value* of $1 under the given rate for as many years as are indicated in the "years" column.

For instance, $1 one year from now is worth $0.91 (0.909 rounded) at present, using the 10 percent rate. This is the same as saying that 91 cents invested now at 10 percent will be worth $1 one year from now. The same holds true for the other factors in the 10 percent column. The process of reducing future values according to the factors shown to determine the present value is called *discounting.*

The determination of the present value of any amount of future dollars at a given rate for a given number of years consists in determining the present value factor from the table, representing the present value of $1, and multiplying by the number of future dollars being discounted. Thus, the bank would discount a future amount of $1,000 at 10 percent by multiplying the appropriate present value factor from Table I by $1,000. Since there are four such future payments of $1,000 in the example, the four discounting calculations would be:

Year	Present Value Factor	Payment	Present Value
1	0.909	$1,000	$ 909
2	0.826	1,000	826
3	0.751	1,000	751
4	0.683	1,000	683
Total			$3,169

Whenever the annual cash payments are *equal* in amount, as in this case, a simpler method of determining the present value is available through Table II. Taking the same example, the bank could look in the 10 percent column at the line for four years in Table II and find a factor of 3.169. Multiplying by $1,000, they would find the present value to be the same $3,169 as determined by the longer method using Table I. Table II contains factors which represent the present value of $1 *received annually* for the given number of years (this form of cash flow is commonly known as an *annuity*). The relationship to Table I is clear from the following analysis:

From Table I:
Present value of $1 for first year @ 10%	0.909
Present value of $1 for second year @ 10%	0.826
Present value of $1 for third year @ 10%	0.751
Present value of $1 for fourth year @ 10%	0.683

Equals: From Table II:
Present value of $1 *per year* for four years @ 10%	3.169

To visualize better the cash flow and the time-adjusted value of money represented in the foregoing example, consider the following schematic description:

TABLE I
PRESENT VALUE OF $1

Years	5%	6%	8%	10%	12%	14%	15%	16%	18%	20%	22%	24%	25%
1	0.952	0.943	0.926	0.909	0.893	0.877	0.870	0.862	0.847	0.833	0.820	0.806	0.800
2	0.907	0.890	0.857	0.826	0.797	0.769	0.756	0.743	0.718	0.694	0.672	0.650	0.640
3	0.864	0.840	0.794	0.751	0.712	0.675	0.658	0.641	0.609	0.579	0.551	0.524	0.512
4	0.823	0.792	0.735	0.683	0.636	0.592	0.572	0.552	0.516	0.482	0.451	0.423	0.410
5	0.784	0.747	0.681	0.621	0.567	0.519	0.497	0.476	0.437	0.402	0.370	0.341	0.328
6	0.746	0.705	0.630	0.564	0.507	0.456	0.432	0.410	0.370	0.335	0.303	0.275	0.262
7	0.711	0.665	0.583	0.513	0.452	0.400	0.376	0.354	0.314	0.279	0.249	0.222	0.210
8	0.677	0.627	0.540	0.467	0.404	0.351	0.327	0.305	0.266	0.233	0.204	0.179	0.168
9	0.645	0.592	0.500	0.424	0.361	0.308	0.284	0.263	0.225	0.194	0.167	0.144	0.134
10	0.614	0.558	0.463	0.386	0.322	0.270	0.247	0.227	0.191	0.162	0.137	0.116	0.107
11	0.585	0.527	0.429	0.350	0.287	0.237	0.215	0.195	0.162	0.135	0.112	0.094	0.086
12	0.557	0.497	0.397	0.319	0.257	0.208	0.187	0.168	0.137	0.112	0.092	0.076	0.069
13	0.530	0.469	0.368	0.290	0.229	0.182	0.163	0.145	0.116	0.093	0.075	0.061	0.055
14	0.505	0.442	0.340	0.263	0.205	0.160	0.141	0.125	0.099	0.078	0.062	0.049	0.044
15	0.481	0.417	0.315	0.239	0.183	0.140	0.123	0.108	0.084	0.065	0.051	0.040	0.035
16	0.458	0.394	0.292	0.218	0.163	0.123	0.107	0.093	0.071	0.054	0.042	0.032	0.028
17	0.436	0.371	0.270	0.198	0.146	0.108	0.093	0.080	0.060	0.045	0.034	0.026	0.023
18	0.416	0.350	0.250	0.180	0.130	0.095	0.081	0.069	0.051	0.038	0.028	0.021	0.018
19	0.396	0.331	0.232	0.164	0.116	0.083	0.070	0.060	0.043	0.031	0.023	0.017	0.014
20	0.377	0.312	0.215	0.149	0.104	0.073	0.061	0.051	0.037	0.026	0.019	0.014	0.012

TABLE II
PRESENT VALUE OF $1 RECEIVED ANNUALLY FOR N YEARS

Years (N)	5%	6%	8%	10%	12%	14%	15%	16%	18%	20%	22%	24%	25%
1	0.952	0.943	0.926	0.909	0.893	0.877	0.870	0.862	0.847	0.833	0.820	0.806	0.800
2	1.859	1.833	1.783	1.736	1.690	1.647	1.626	1.605	1.566	1.528	1.492	1.457	1.440
3	2.723	2.673	2.577	2.487	2.402	2.322	2.283	2.246	2.174	2.106	2.042	1.981	1.952
4	3.546	3.465	3.312	3.169	3.037	2.914	2.855	2.798	2.690	2.589	2.494	2.404	2.362
5	4.330	4.212	3.993	3.791	3.605	3.433	3.352	3.274	3.127	2.991	2.864	2.745	2.689
6	5.076	4.917	4.623	4.355	4.111	3.889	3.784	3.685	3.498	3.326	3.167	3.020	2.951
7	5.786	5.582	5.206	4.868	4.564	4.288	4.160	4.039	3.812	3.605	3.416	3.242	3.161
8	6.463	6.210	5.747	5.335	4.968	4.639	4.487	4.344	4.078	3.837	3.619	3.421	3.329
9	7.108	6.802	6.247	5.759	5.328	4.946	4.772	4.607	4.303	4.031	3.786	3.566	3.463
10	7.722	7.360	6.710	6.145	5.650	5.216	5.019	4.833	4.494	4.192	3.923	3.682	3.571
11	8.306	7.887	7.139	6.495	5.937	5.453	5.234	5.029	4.656	4.327	4.035	3.776	3.656
12	8.863	8.384	7.536	6.814	6.194	5.660	5.421	5.197	4.793	4.439	4.127	3.851	3.725
13	9.394	8.853	7.904	7.103	6.424	5.842	5.583	5.342	4.910	4.533	4.203	3.912	3.780
14	9.899	9.295	8.244	7.367	6.628	6.002	5.724	5.468	5.008	4.611	4.265	3.962	3.824
15	10.380	9.712	8.559	7.606	6.811	6.142	5.847	5.575	5.092	4.675	4.315	4.001	3.859
16	10.838	10.106	8.851	7.824	6.974	6.265	5.954	5.669	5.162	4.730	4.357	4.033	3.887
17	11.274	10.477	9.122	8.022	7.120	6.373	6.047	5.749	5.222	4.775	4.391	4.059	3.910
18	11.690	10.828	9.372	8.201	7.250	6.467	6.128	5.818	5.273	4.812	4.419	4.080	3.928
19	12.085	11.158	9.604	8.365	7.366	6.550	6.198	5.877	5.316	4.844	4.442	4.097	3.942
20	12.462	11.470	9.818	8.514	7.469	6.623	6.259	5.929	5.353	4.870	4.460	4.110	3.954

Year	Present Value Factor ($1 @ 10%)	Present Value	Time in Years			
		0	1	2	3	4
1	0.909	$ 909 ← $1,000				
2	0.826	826 ← $1,000				
3	0.751	751 ← $1,000				
4	0.683	683 ← $1,000				
Total		$3,169				

This description indicates that four annual payments of $1,000 each are worth progressively less *at present* as their realization becomes more remote. From the point of view of the management, which is considering an investment costing $3,169 which produces cash inflows of $1,000 per year for four years, the rate of return will be 10 percent, and the initial investment will be recovered systematically.

Discounted cash-flow methods for evaluating capital expenditure proposals are of two types:

1. The time-adjusted rate of return on the investment (TAR)

2. The excess present value, also called net present value

Time-adjusted Rate of Return   The time-adjusted rate is used when the cost of the investment and the annual cash inflows are known and the unknown rate of earnings is to be determined. The time-adjusted rate is described as that rate which equates the present value of the future cash inflows with the cost of the investment which produces them.

With the use of Table I or II, the TAR may be approximated when the initial investment and future cash inflows are known, as in the case of the Investo Company example. With the initial cost of the equipment given as $6,000 and the cash inflows for five years estimated at $2,000 each year, the TAR is determined in two steps:

1. Calculate the factor to be located in Table II (the annuity table). This factor (symbol F) reflects the same relationships of investment and cash inflow as does the payback calculation:

$$F = \frac{I}{C} = \frac{\$6,000}{\$2,000} = 3.000$$

2. Locate the factor thus calculated — 3.000 — in Table II on the line representing five years (the estimated life of the asset). It is found to be smaller than the factor in the 18 percent column (3.127) and larger than that in the 20 percent column (2.991).

In most cases, there will be no factor on the appropriate "years" line which corresponds exactly to the calculated factor. However, its location *between* the two factors *nearest* it means that our calculated factor reflects a TAR for the equipment proposal which is greater than 18 percent but less than 20 percent.

It is possible to interpolate to a more specific rate between 18 and 20 percent. Considering the fact that both future cash inflows and useful life of assets are based on estimates, such resulting "accuracy" must be regarded as spurious. It will ordinarily be enough for management to know that this proposal promises a return of slightly under 20 percent.

Excess Present Value The second discounted cash-flow method for capital expenditure evaluation is known as excess present value. Generally, management has established a "target" — a minimum rate below which a proposal would be rejected as undesirable in the light of profit goals and above which it could be considered favorably.

Using the same mathematical methods and tables, this method seeks to determine whether the present value of estimated future cash inflows at management's desired rate of return will be greater or less than the cost of the proposal. In this method, the cash inflows, initial investment, and desired rate of return will be given; the present value of the cash inflows and its deviation from initial investment are to be determined.

This is accomplished in two simple steps, as in the case of the Investo Company equipment proposal:

1. Compute the present value of the stream of cash savings from the equipment at management's desired minimum rate (given as 15 percent after taxes):

PV = present value
 C = annual cash inflows ($2,000)
 F = factor (Table II) for 5 years @ 15% (3.352)
 I = investment ($6,000)
PV = C × F = $2,000 × 3.352 = $6,704

2. Subtract the investment from the present value of cash savings thus determined (excess present value = EPV):

EPV = PV − I = $6,704 − $6,000 = $704

The equipment proposal is seen to be attractive according to this method of evaluation. In effect, management is told that if it desires to earn 15 percent after taxes on capital investments, it is getting a bargain in this instance. It would be willing to pay $6,704 for a stream of cash payments of $2,000 each for five years; it can buy it for only $6,000. The difference, or savings in present dollars, of $704 represents excess present value: the present worth of the future cash inflows exceeding the initial investment by this amount.

A further step in the refinement of the excess present value approach, known as the *excess present value index* (sometimes called the *profitability index*), reflects the *percentage relationship* between the present value of the stream of future payments at the desired rate of return and the initial investment. In the example of the Investo Company equipment proposal, the excess present value index is determined thus:

$$\text{EPV index} = \frac{\text{PV}}{\text{I}} = \frac{\$6,704}{\$6,000} = 1.117, \text{ or } 111.7\%$$

The chief advantage in the use of the excess present value index lies in the ready comparability it affords between investment proposals of different magnitudes. For example, at a certain desired rate of return, one investment costing $100,000 may show excess present value of $13,000, while another costing $10,000 might show only $2,000 excess present value. The second would be viewed as the more favorable, however, in view of an excess present value index of 120 percent as compared with 113 percent for the first. Under such circumstances, it is conceivable that, if there were enough smaller proposals having excess present value indices higher than 113 percent, the one costing $100,000 with an index of 113 percent would be rejected.

DEPRECIATION AND THE TAX SHIELD

The cash inflows in the foregoing examples are assumed to be after income taxes. By definition, depreciation is not a factor in discounted cash-flow techniques. Nevertheless, depreciation, as well as income tax, is a factor in the determination of the net cash inflows. This results from the fact that depreciation is deductible as a regular business expense in the determination of the income tax.

Because depreciation does not require the repeated outlay of cash over the useful life of the asset, it does not reduce the *cash* earnings from a particular investment. But the *incremental* earnings from such an investment are taxed at the prevailing rate, and the *incremental* tax payment (paid in cash) reduces cash earnings. Since depreciation on the asset is a tax deduction, thereby reducing the tax payment, it does act to "shield" part of the cash inflow from the tax burden.

An illustration based on the automatic equipment proposal of the Investo Company should demonstrate clearly how this works: Assume the annual cash savings from using the automatic equipment to be $2,800 *before* taxes; the depreciation (straight-line) will be the same as before: $1,200, based on the initial cost of $6,000, no salvage value, five-year life; the tax rate will be assumed to be 50 percent. The calculation is as follows:

	Tax Purposes	Cash Inflow
Gross annual cash cost savings	$2,800	$2,800
Less: Depreciation	1,200	
Net incremental income subject to tax	$1,600	
Income tax @ 50% (payment in cash)	800	800
Net cash inflow after taxes		$2,000

Had depreciation not been deductible, the incremental income tax on $2,800 would have been $1,400 and the net incremental cash inflow $1,400. As it is, $600 of cash flow is retained; the tax rate (50 percent) applied to the depreciation deduction ($1,200) is thus regarded as a "tax shield."

LIMITATIONS IN CAPITAL BUDGETING TECHNIQUES

Frequently there is danger in assuming that mathematically exact techniques always produce highly accurate answers. Caution must be exercised in the application of methods described in this chapter to problems of capital expenditures. The degree to which the results are dependent upon estimated factors must be borne in mind constantly.

There are essentially three factors in the quantitative techniques for capital budgeting decisions: (1) capital investment; (2) return; (3) time.

The first of these—capital investment—can be determined in some cases with a high degree of accuracy (e.g., the purchase price and installation cost of a piece of equipment). In other cases (e.g., development of a new product; opening a new sales territory), the amount can only be approximated.

The return factor (cash savings, earnings) nearly always depends on estimates. Determining the amount of cash savings from the use of labor-saving equipment requires that an experienced engineer or production executive estimate the number of labor worker-hours to be saved, the increase or decrease in maintenance cost, the effects on power consumption, the insurance and property tax rates, and a host of other factors. Estimates of the contribution margin on increased sales volume, resulting from the introduction of a new product, the opening of a new market, or an augmentation of the advertising program, are always highly speculative. Even the forecast of rental income from investment in an office building depends on someone's estimate of the rate of occupancy, the number of new buildings to be built in the area, and the "going rate" for office space in the area.

Finally, the useful, or economic, life of an investment is an integral determinant of its worth. The estimate of this factor, however, is probably the most tenuous of all. An educated engineering guess as to the useful *physical* life of a productive asset may be fairly reliable, but estimates as to the rate of technological development and obsolescence complicate the picture. The profitable career of a new product depends upon customer acceptance and competitors' reactions—both highly speculative phenomena. Certain techniques based on the statistics of probability are helpful in minimizing the errors of estimating under such conditions of uncertainty, but they cannot eliminate uncertainty, and therefore error, entirely.

COST OF CAPITAL

The use of excess present value techniques for capital budgeting purposes requires the use of a desired minimum rate of return. Basically, there are two ways in which this rate may be established:

1. By using a rate reflective of operating performance in the company itself or the industry with which it is associated — a rate reflective of *internal* factors

2. By basing the rate on the company's "cost of capital" — a rate reflective of factors *external* to the firm

The former method is the more subjective of the two. Management may regard its own operating experience as a satisfactory standard; if industry experience is better, management may decide to adopt this higher level for goal-setting purposes; in some cases, it may be the wish of management to set a "desired" rate for cutoff purposes which is independent of either and reflective of a level of future profits intended to improve on both.

Cost of capital, on the other hand, places the minimum level of profit maximization at a point determined by what it costs the company for money in the market. Various methods are available for determining cost of capital, and no unanimity of opinion exists as to which is the best.[2] The inclusion of the interest rate for borrowed funds is fairly obvious, and readily determinable. The cost of equity funds is less clear. The stated rate of dividends on preferred stock may be a guide to the cost of this type of capital, but capital from preferred stock bears many of the same characteristics as borrowed funds.

A more difficult problem lies in the treatment of common shareholders' equity, particularly retained earnings. Some say that capital from this source has no cost, being internally generated. The more persuasive argument holds, however, that the cost of earnings retained in the business is an opportunity cost: If such capital cannot earn a satisfactory return by being plowed back into the operations of the business, it ought to be paid to the stockholders in dividends. One measure of this opportunity cost would be the returns which stockholders could earn by investing such dividends (after personal income taxes), which returns they must forgo if funds are retained in the business instead.

In practice, when a company's stock is listed on an organized exchange, the market price will usually reflect the earnings per share (after taxes) currently being earned by the company. The company's practice with respect to dividend payment and retention of earnings will also have an influence on the market price. Thus, one method of determining the cost of common equity capital for the firm with listed shares is to relate its earnings per share to the market value of the stock.

The company's cost of capital is a dynamic thing, affected by its current capital structure, its financing plans for the future, and any changes in its rate of earnings. To determine an average cost of capital for a firm, it is necessary to include some provision for capital structure, the expected cost of borrowed funds, and the market-established cost of equity capital.

To illustrate, assume a company with 40 percent of its capital structure composed of bonds (paying 10 percent interest) and 60 percent of common equity; able to borrow at 10 percent; and showing a market value of $25 on

---

[2] See Hunt, Williams, and Donaldson, *Basic Business Finance: Text*, Homewood, Ill.: Richard D. Irwin, Inc., 1974, chap. 10.

its common shares, reflecting current earnings per share (after taxes) of $5. Cost of capital determined by weighted average would be:

Type of Capital	Weight	After-Tax Rate	Weighted Average
Bonds	40%	5	2%
Common stock	60%	20	12%
Total	100%		14%

In this calculation, the rate of 5 percent for bonds is the effective cost of interest after taxes, since interest is a deductible expense for tax purposes (i.e., ten percent rate before taxes × 50 percent assumed tax rate). The effective rate of 20 percent for common stock ($5 earnings per share/$25 market price) is also taken after taxes, so the weighted average of fourteen percent is an after-tax rate. In this case, management presumably would reject capital expenditure proposals promising less than fourteen percent return after taxes. Acceptance of those indicating higher returns would, of course, be subject to whatever other constraints management might impose, such as total budget limitations.

SUMMARY

Effective deployment of capital over the long term is one of the key means by which management achieves profit maximization. Decisions affecting investment in long-term capital projects, however, are fraught with uncertainty. The further into the future the effects of a decision are projected, the greater is the likely margin of error. Typically, capital investment projects involve large commitments of funds. Therefore, management finds considerable need for methods of analysis which will enable it to rank and choose intelligently among proposals competing for essentially scarce long-term funds.

The methods in most common use at present are (1) the payback period, (2) the accounting rate of return, and (3) discounted cash-flow techniques.

The payback is a "rough-and-ready" means of estimating how long it will take to recoup the original investment from the flow of cash earnings produced by the project. It suffers from the serious drawback that it provides no measure of profitability — only the relative liquidity of the investment.

The accounting method, based on an accrual determination of the conventional rate of return, is readily understood, easily determinable, but subject to serious limitations. It averages cash flows, failing to distinguish between projects with long lives and those with shorter lives and between those with uneven cash flows. Moreover, it overlooks the all-important time value of money.

The time value of money, rooted in its use as a commodity and in its fundamental scarcity, is the truly accurate element in measuring returns on long-term investments. The discounted cash-flow techniques are of two basic types: (1) the time-adjusted rate of return, and (2) the excess present value of cash inflows. The former is the rate of return which discounts the stream of future cash inflows to the original cost of the investment which produces them. The latter employs some desired rate of return as a discount factor in determining the present value of the cash inflows; the desirable investment should show an excess of present value at the desired rate over the cost to secure it.

The excess present value index is the percentage relationship between present value of the cash inflows discounted at the desired rate and the cost of the investment. This device offers ready comparability between projects of unlike size and duration. In general, discounted cash-flow techniques provide the most reliable appraisals of alternative investment proposals. The use of present value tables makes these techniques reasonably simple to employ.

Certain limitations underlie all capital budgeting appraisals, however. The three basic factors of the quantitative analytical techniques—investment, return, and time—are all, to varying degrees, the results of estimates. Certain statistical techniques have been developed which help to narrow the margin of error of such estimates, but uncertainty continues to characterize the entire process, and the deceptively precise mathematical answers provided by capital budgeting techniques must be interpreted in that light.

The use of depreciation as a tax deduction provides a tax shield to a portion of the cash inflow from certain types of capital investments. As a noncash expense, depreciation does not reduce cash *inflow* from a capital asset. But it does reduce the amount of cash *outflow* for income taxes. In this way it preserves part of the before-tax inflow from the inevitable tax drain.

Management's desired minimum rate of return for deriving excess present values may be arrived at from internal sources, such as past returns on operating assets, or from external sources, such as the cost of capital. The calculation of the latter is based upon the proportions of debt and equity in the firm's capital structure, the rate at which it must pay interest on borrowed money, and the rate of return to common shareholders reflected in the percentage of earnings per share to the market value of the stock. The weighted average of these factors provides a rate against which to measure the returns promised by various capital expenditure proposals.

When management approaches the capital budgeting decision in a manner which thus systematically evaluates capital investment proposals according to time-adjusted rates of return, it provides the basis for making each decision a building block in the long-term process of maximizing profits.

APPENDIX: ILLUSTRATIVE EXAMPLE

Given the assortment of methods for evaluating capital expenditure proposals described in this chapter, let us examine a series of proposals that might be submitted to the Investo Company, from which it might formulate its capital budget.

With the original assumption that management desires a minimum return of 15 percent after taxes on all its investments and that it will be limited to total investments of $35,000, the following proposals are to be considered:

Nature of Investment	Cost	Form of Return	Year	Annual Cash Inflow	Dura- tion, Years
1. Automatic equipment (no salvage value)	$ 6,000	Savings in labor cost		$ 2,000	5
2. Product development— subcontract to industrial research firm—to be in- troduced 2 years hence; estimated sales are for years 2 through 6	25,000	Contribution mar- gin from sales	1 2 3 4 5 6	— 5,000 8,000 12,000 15,000 15,000	6
3. New boiler (no salvage value)	10,000	Cost savings—fuel consumption and mainte- nance		2,500	10
4. Purchase of small ma- chine shop to add to pro- ductive capacity	18,000	Profits after taxes		5,000	10

NOTE: All cash inflows are assumed to be after taxes.

EXHIBIT 13-1

Proposal 1.	Automatic Equipment	Investment: $6,000

Payback

$$P = \frac{\$6,000}{\$2,000} = 3 \text{ years}$$

*Accounting rate of return**

$$R = \frac{\$2,000 - \$1,200}{\$6,000} = \frac{800}{6,000} = 13.3\%$$

Time-adjusted rate of return

$$F = \frac{\$6,000}{\$2,000} = 3.000$$

TAR (3.000 for 5 years—Table II) = 20 − % (slightly less than 20%)

Excess present value (desired rate—15%)

F (5 years @ 15%) = 3.352 (Table II)

PV = $2,000 × 3.352 = $6,704

EPV = $6,704 − $6,000 = $704

$$EPV \text{ index} = \frac{\$6,704}{\$6,000} = 111.7\%$$

---

* In each of the examples shown, accounting rate of return will be based on original investment.

Exhibits 13-1 to 13-4 show the calculations for the various methods of evaluation in connection with each of the four proposals.

Ranking of Proposals in Exhibits 13-1 to 13-4

Exhibit 13-5 shows how the four proposals would be ranked in accordance with the comparative values shown under each of the methods of evaluation used.

EXHIBIT 13-2

Proposal 2.　　Product Development　　Investment: $25,000

Payback

Because of uneven cash flow, payback is determined by deducting each year's cash inflow in sequence from the unrecovered balance of the previous year, thus:

Initial balance	$25,000
Cash inflow—year 1	—　　—
Balance—end of year 1	$25,000
Cash inflow—year 2	—　5,000
Balance—end of year 2	$20,000
Cash inflow—year 3	—　8,000
Balance—end of year 3	$12,000
Cash inflow—year 4	—　12,000

Payback = 4 years

Accounting rate of return

Because of uneven cash inflows, the accounting method will average the inflows over the projected life of the investment. Note that this investment involves no depreciation; therefore, cash inflow alone is the measure of return for the numerator of the calculation:

Cash inflow—year 1	$　—
Cash inflow—year 2	5,000
Cash inflow—year 3	8,000
Cash inflow—year 4	12,000
Cash inflow—year 5	15,000
Cash inflow—year 6	15,000
Total cash inflows	$55,000
Average—6 years	$ 9,167

$$R = \frac{\$9,167}{\$25,000} = 36.7\%$$

Time-adjusted rate of return

Determination of TAR with uneven cash inflows is by trial and error. In the following calculation, an attempt was made using first 18 percent, then 20 percent. Present value for each annual cash inflow must be determined separately from Table I.

With the budget constraint of $35,000, the following would be accepted, depending on the method used:

Payback:	Proposals 1, 4, and 3
Accounting rate of return:	Proposal 2
Time-adjusted rate of return:	Proposals 4, 3, and 1
Excess present value index:	Proposals 4 and 3

    Now let us take a closer look at how each method rates the various proposals.

EXHIBIT 13-2 *(Continued)*

Year	Cash Inflow	First Attempt: 18 Percent PV Factor	PV	Second Attempt: 20 Percent PV Factor	PV
1	$ —	—	—	—	—
2	5,000	0.718	3,590	0.694	3,470
3	8,000	0.609	4,872	0.579	4,632
4	12,000	0.516	6,192	0.482	5,784
5	15,000	0.437	6,555	0.402	6,030
6	15,000	0.370	5,550	0.335	5,024
Total			$26,759		$24,940
Investment			25,000		25,000
Difference			$ 1,759		($ 60

TAR = 20 − %

The first attempt yielded a present value substantially higher than the investment; hence another attempt, at a higher rate, was in order, since the TAR is the rate which *equates* the present value of cash inflows with the investment. Twenty percent brings the two figures within $60 of each other; it is unlikely that any other rate in the table will bring them any closer, so 20 percent is the approximation of the TAR on this proposal.

Excess present value (desired rate — 15%)

Year	Cash Inflow	15 Percent PV Factor*	Present Value
1	$ —	—	$ —
2	5,000	0.756	3,780
3	8,000	0.658	5,264
4	12,000	0.572	6,864
5	15,000	0.497	7,455
6	15,000	0.432	6,480
Total			$29,843
Investment			25,000
Excess present value			$ 4,843

$$\text{EPV index} = \frac{\$29,843}{\$25,000} = 119.4\%$$

* Table I.

EXHIBIT 13-3

Proposal 3.　　New Boiler　　Investment: $10,000

Payback

$$P = \frac{\$10,000}{\$2,500} = 4 \text{ years}$$

Accounting rate of return

$$R = \frac{\$2,500 - \$1,000}{\$10,000} = \frac{1,500}{10,000} = 15\%$$

Time-adjusted rate of return

$$F = \frac{\$10,000}{\$2,500} = 4.000$$

TAR (4.000 for 10 years – Table II) = 22 – %

Excess present value (desired rate – 15%)

F (10 years @ 15%) = 5.019 (Table II)
PV = $2,500 × 5.019 = $12,548
EPV = $12,548 – $10,000 = $2,548

$$\text{EPV index} = \frac{\$12,548}{\$10,000} = 125.5\%$$

EXHIBIT 13-4

Proposal 4.　　Purchase Machine Shop　　Investment: $18,000

Payback

$$P = \frac{\$18,000}{\$5,000} = 3.6 \text{ years}$$

Accounting rate of return

$$R = \frac{\$5,000}{\$18,000} = 27.8\%$$

Time-adjusted rate of return

$$F = \frac{\$18,000}{\$5,000} = 3.600$$

TAR (3.600 for 10 years – Table II) = 25 – %

Excess present value (desired rate – 15%)

F (10 years @ 15%) = 5.019 (Table II)
PV = $5,000 × 5.019 = $25,095
EPV = $25,095 – $18,000 = $7,095

$$\text{EPV index} = \frac{\$25,095}{\$18,000} = 139.4\%$$

Payback The payback periods for all proposals are so closely clustered that no meaningful cutoff is possible on this basis. The budget constraint seems to eliminate the second proposal, though. It must be remembered that payback is not a measure of profitability. It merely discloses how soon the initial investment may be recovered out of cash inflows. In relying solely on payback, therefore, management takes the persistent risk of rejecting more profitable proposals for the sake of faster recoupment of cost. Clearly, such is not in the interest of long-term profit maximization.

Accounting Rate of Return Suddenly, proposal 2 rises from bottom to top. Indeed, in view of the budget constraint, it will be the only project chosen under this method of evaluation. The accounting method places the emphasis where it belongs — on profitability — but it possesses two obvious weaknesses. First, it averages the returns, obscuring the differences between projects with short lives and those with long lives, and between those with equal cash flows and those offering heavier returns either earlier or later in their economic lives. Second, and more important, it ignores the time value of money.

Time-adjusted Rate of Return A comparison of the rankings under TAR with

EXHIBIT 13-5
RANKING OF PROPOSALS

	Proposal No.	Cost of Investment	Cumulative Investment
Payback			
3.0 years	1	$ 6,000	$ 6,000
3.6 years	4	18,000	24,000
4.0 years	3	10,000	34,000
4.0 years	2	25,000	59,000
Accounting rate of return			
36.7%	2	$25,000	$25,000
27.8%	4	18,000	43,000
15.0%	3	10,000	53,000
13.3%	1	6,000	59,000
Time-adjusted rate of return			
25 – %	4	$18,000	$18,000
22 – %	3	10,000	28,000
20 – %	1	6,000	34,000
20 – %	2	25,000	59,000
Excess present value index			
$ Index			
$7,096 139.4%	4	$18,000	$18,000
2,548 125.5%	3	10,000	28,000
4,843 119.4%	2	25,000	53,000
704 111.7%	1	6,000	59,000

those under the accounting method raises questions regarding cause. First, proposal 2, with the top-ranked accounting rate of 36.7 percent, is rejected by the TAR, with the lowest-ranked rate of 20— percent. This rate does exceed management's desired minimum of 15 percent, but there just is not enough capital to go around in this case, and other opportunities promise greater returns. Notice, too, that proposal 4, which failed to make the cutoff under the accounting method, ranks as potentially the most profitable of the group under TAR. Proposal 3 also shows to better advantage when ranked according to its TAR.

What accounts for these differences? First, the effect of averaging the returns under the accounting method greatly distorts the effect of the rather gradual buildup of cash inflows over the life of proposal 2, where the greater returns are deferred until the later years. The TAR, on the other hand, gives effect to the time value of money and, in discounting more heavily the larger returns in the more distant years, reveals the greater risk inherent in this type of proposal.

Another discrepancy between time-adjusted rates and accounting rates lies in their markedly different numerical values. For example, proposal 4 has an accounting rate of 27.8 percent but a TAR of only 25— percent, and proposal 2 drops from 36.7 to 20— percent. On the other hand, proposals 1 and 3 increase respectively from 13.3 to 20— percent and from 15 to 22— percent. Remember at this point that only the TAR is the *true* rate; the accounting calculation gives as much weight to $1 of cash return ten years hence as it does to $1 today, by means of the averaging techniques employed (e.g., under proposal 2, the expected cash inflow of $15,000 in year 6 carries the full weight of $15,000; under TAR, it turns out to have a present value of only $5,025).

Furthermore, the accounting method discriminates against investment proposals involving purchase of depreciable assets. Now the accounting purpose of recording depreciation is to provide for the apportionment of the original cost of the investment in a depreciable asset over its useful life. But this accrual adjustment grew out of the need for proper income determination. The capital budgeting purpose is different. Not all capital investment projects involve depreciable assets. For those which *do not*, the accounting method provides no means for recovering the original investment, but shows, instead, that the entire cash inflow is return. This is, of course, erroneous.

The corollary to depreciation in the discounted cash-flow technique (but certainly not the *same* as depreciation) is the measured recovery of the original investment through the cash inflows. The way this is accomplished is reflected in the rather simple example of the mortgage payments shown earlier in this chapter, in which it is seen that both the original investment *and* the return are included in the cash payment. Indirectly at least, it could be said that the purpose of accrual accounting depreciation—the systematic write-off of the original investment—is achieved in the discounted cash-flow method. This is done in a manner which is appropriate to its own purpose, however— that of measuring the profitability of an investment by its own true (time-adjusted) rate of return.

Moreover, this method may be applied to any investment yielding a measurable return, whether it is a depreciable asset or not. Thus, where the accounting method does not provide means of recovering the original investment of proposals 2 and 4, the TAR computation does.

Excess Present Value and Excess Present Value Index   The rankings according to excess present value, being a form of the discounted cash-flow approach, are substantially similar to those under TAR. Certain differences do occur, however. In this example, proposals 1 and 2 show the same TAR of 20— percent. Nevertheless, proposal 2 is distinctly superior on the basis of the excess present value index.

This superiority comes about for two reasons. First, proposal 2 offers cash inflows heavily weighted toward the later years, while proposal 1 shows an equal annual stream of payments. The mechanics of discounted cash flow tip the balance in favor of proposal 1 from the standpoint of TAR, because earlier cash flows are discounted *less* than later ones. Put another way, if the total of $55,000 of cash inflows over the six-year life of proposal 2 were to be realized in equal annual amounts (an average of $9,167), the TAR would be much higher (viz., 28+ percent). The lower rate of 20— percent reflects the higher risk factor in the distribution of cash inflows which are so heavy in the later years.

Second, the fact that proposal 2 is the longer-lived of the two means that it delivers its return, which is in excess of the minimum of 15 percent required by management, for one year longer than proposal 1. The effect of this will be reflected in the excess present value calculation, whereas it will not show in the TAR. The reason is that the TAR is computed independently of any other rate, and depends only on the internal relationship of the factors in the proposal it is measuring. The excess present value, on the other hand, depends for its evident "leverage" on the minimum desired rate of return specified by management, which provides the basis on which *excess* present value (at the *true* rate) is determined. Thus, when the TARs between two proposals are equal and higher than the desired minimum rate, the one with the longer life will possess the higher excess value index.

It is beyond the scope of this book to explore the subtleties of this distinction between the results under TAR and excess present value methods any further. It is sufficient to note that where such differences do appear, sophisticated management tends to choose the proposals favored by the excess present value index method.

KEY WORDS AND PHRASES

capital budgeting
payback period
accounting rate of return
time-adjusted rate of return
present value

excess present value
excess present value index
tax shield
cost of capital

DISCUSSION QUESTIONS

1. Analyze the meaning of capital budgeting. Differentiate from operating budget.
2. Examine the different classes of capital projects and explain why they are often approached differently.
3. Explain the concept of the payback period.
4. Why does payback enjoy such popularity among business executives? What are its limitations?
5. Explain the accounting concept of "rate of return."
6. Is accounting method a satisfactory measure of the worth of an investment proposal? Why?
7. What is meant by the time value of money?
8. Explain how a woman, for example, would determine the amount of money she should save each year to accumulate a specified amount at retirement age. Explain how a man would determine how much he would need at retirement age if he knew that he wanted to receive equal monthly payments of a certain amount for a specified number of years thereafter (do not set up figures for the calculation—just discuss concept and method).
9. What is the meaning of time-adjusted rate of return?
10. Are time-adjusted rate and payback related? Explain.
11. What is meant by excess present value?
12. Why is an excess present value index considered useful?
13. "Discounted cash flow techniques may be fine for some projects, but they have one flaw—they ignore depreciation. Depreciation is an important factor in some types of capital investment. Therefore discounted cash flow methods are useless when considering investment in depreciable assets." Discuss the logic of this position.
14. How does depreciation act as a tax shield?
15. What are the essential limiting factors in the reliability of capital budgeting measurement techniques, including discounted cash flow?
16. Explain the concept of "cost of capital" as a device for establishing a cutoff point for capital investment proposals.
17. "Retained earnings is one form of capital that has no cost." Comment.

PROBLEMS

1. How much money would you have to deposit in a savings account today in order to have $1,000 in that account at the end of five years if the bank pays an 8 percent return? How much would you have to deposit if you wanted to have $2,500 after five years?

2. How much money would you have in a savings account after seven years if you deposited $1,000 today and the bank were paying a 6 percent rate? How much would you have after seven years if you deposited $4,500 today?

3. Suppose you have won the grand prize in the state lottery. You have the opportunity to pick one of two prizes:

Prize A: $50,000 a year for the next ten years, paid on December 31 of each year

Prize B: $350,000 cash paid today, January 1

Assuming both prizes are tax-free and that you can earn an interest return of 6 percent on your money (also tax-free), which prize would you pick? Which prize would you pick if you could earn 10 percent on your money? At about what interest rate would you consider the two prizes to be of equal value to you?

4. Determine how much money a bank can lend at the present time if the borrower agrees to make five annual repayments of $1,000 each, representing a rate of return of 14 percent. Prepare a schedule of repayments similar to the one shown on page 424.

5. A bank loans out $6,850 for three years and requires a rate of return of 15 percent. Determine the amount of the annual repayment which the borrower would have to make to repay the loan over a three-year period. Prepare a schedule of repayments similar to the one shown on page 424.

 The Deadson Company is planning the purchase of a new, computerized production machine. The company's cost of capital is 12 percent. Data regarding the machine follow (ignore income taxes):

Cost	$160,000
Estimated life	8 years
Annual savings	$34,000
Salvage value	$10,000

Required:
1. What is the accounting rate of return?
2. What is the payback period?
3. What is the time-adjusted rate of return?
4. What is the net present value?

 The Dincolo Company is considering the purchase of an automatic turning machine for one of its production departments. Engineering estimates indicate that an annual saving of $1,500 in cash operating expenses will be realized over a ten-year period if this machine is used. It will cost $7,500 and have no salvage value at the end of its estimated ten-year life.

The company appraises capital investment opportunities at a minimum desired rate of return of 15 percent.

Required:
Determine:
1. The payback period
2. The accounting rate of return, on both initial and average investment
3. The time-adjusted rate of return
4. The excess present value index
(NOTE: Round all calculations to the nearest dollar. Disregard income tax.)

13-4.† The Ruth Company estimates that it can save $5,600 a year in cash operating expenses for the next ten years if it buys a new machine at a cost of $22,000. No salvage value is expected at the end of the ten years. The Ruth Company uses a 14 percent rate of return. Income taxes are to be ignored.

Required:
(Round all computations to the nearest dollar.)
1. Compute the payback period.
2. Compute the accounting rate of return on initial investment.
3. Compute the accounting rate of return on average investment.
4. Compute the net present value.
5. Compute the time-adjusted rate of return.
6. Should the project be accepted? Why?

13-5. The Powell Company has the opportunity to purchase for $150,000 a machine which will generate net cash inflows before taxes of $50,000 per year for each of the next five years. The company has a desired minimum rate of return of 11 percent.

Required:
1. What is the net present value of the machine assuming that there is no income tax?
2. Assuming that the income tax rate is 50 percent and that the company uses straight-line depreciation for tax purposes, what is the net present value of the machine?
3. Assuming that the income tax rate is 50 percent and that the company uses the sum-of-the-years'-digits method for tax purposes, what is the net present value of the machine?

13-6. The BD Company is considering the following investment projects:

X: Cost, $10,000; annual cash savings, $3,400

Y: Cost, $30,000; annual cash savings, $9,200

Both projects have an expected useful life of five years. The BD Company's cost of capital is 10 percent.

Required:
1. What is the time-adjusted rate of return for each project?
2. Assuming that one, but only one, of the projects must be undertaken, which should be picked? Why?

13-7. The Johnston Company has the opportunity to invest in one of the following investment projects:

Project	Cost	Salvage Value	Annual Cost Savings	Useful Life
A	$10,000	-0-	$3,700	5
B	10,000	-0-	2,000	10

The Johnston Company's minimum desired rate of return on such projects is 10 percent.

Required:
1. Which project has the higher time-adjusted rate of return?
2. Which project has the higher net present value?
3. Which project should be accepted? Are there any circumstances under which the other project should be accepted?

13-8. The Whit Company has used the net present value method in making capital investment decisions. The company rejected an offer of an equipment sales representative who had convincing evidence that her $20,000 materials handling equipment would save the company $5,000 in cash operating expenses each year for the next ten years. There was no disposal value of the machine after that ten-year period. In computing the net present value, the company did not consider income taxes. The computations resulted in a negative net present value of $385.

Required:
What was the minimum desired before-tax rate of return?

13-9. The England Company must replace an important machine in its production line. Two alternatives are available.

1. Machine A is being offered at a special price of $100,000, with an estimated life of seven years and a salvage value of $2,000. The cash operating expenses would amount to $60,000 annually, and the machine would require major repairs every two years at a cost each time of $10,000.

2. Machine B is available for a price of $150,000, with an estimated useful life of seven years and a salvage value of $10,000. The cash operating expenses would amount to $52,000 annually, with a major repair costing $7,000 required every third year.

Both machines will perform satisfactorily, so the choice between them will not affect the firm's revenues. The company desires a minimum rate of return of 10 percent.

Required:
Compute the present value of the costs of each machine. Which one should be purchased?

13-10. The business manager at Stroganoff University is reviewing the operations of some of its auxiliary enterprises. One of them involves a lunch counter in the basement of the library building which is operated for the convenience of students, faculty, and employees working in or utilizing library facilities.

The opportunity has arisen to replace the entire operation with automatic vending machines. Sales representatives of the vending machine manufacturer have assured the business manager that (1) everything now being served at the lunch counter can be handled by the machines; and (2) the amount of floor space devoted to the operation can be cut in half, releasing valuable space for storage, office space, or the like.

The annual results of the present operations are as follows:

Receipts		$80,000
Costs (all cash):		
Food, beverage, merchandise	$50,000	
Salaries	9,000	
Other direct costs	16,000	75,000
Margin		$ 5,000

It is assumed that there will be no change in the volume of business nor in the level of prices charged.

If vending machines are installed, food, beverage, and merchandise costs are expected to remain the same. Salaries for present employees will be eliminated, and other cash direct costs will be reduced by $12,000 per year. Twenty-five hundred dollars will be incurred annually as salary cost for part of one person's time spent in stocking machines and removing coins. Maintenance cost is estimated at $3,500 per year. Cleaning and janitor services will be charged in the amount of $2,000 per year.

The machines cost $68,000 and are estimated to have a useful life of ten years, with $8,000 salvage value at the end of ten years. The seller will allow a trade-in value of $3,000 on present lunch-room equipment, presently carried on the books at zero.

Required:
1. Prepare a projected condensed income statement for vending-machine operations.
2. Determine:
   a. The payback period
   b. The accounting rate of return, initial and average investments
   c. The time-adjusted rate of return
   d. The excess present value index
   (Assume 10 percent to be the desired rate of return for capital decision purposes.)
3. What other factors might affect this decision?

13-11. The president of the Powell Corporation is considering three capital expenditure proposals:

1. To purchase new automatic equipment in assembly — $450,000
2. To bring a new product to market — $360,000
3. To buy a small company to diversify business — $500,000

Proposal 1. This new equipment, costing $450,000, will reduce the number of direct labor workers in the assembly department and cut other operating costs, effecting a total cash savings on direct departmental costs in an estimated annual amount of $100,000. It is assumed that volume will not change significantly over the anticipated eight-year life of the equipment and that there will be no residual value at that time.

Proposal 2. An engineer has developed a product which has proved functional in the laboratory but for which no known market exists. If the decision is made to introduce this product in the current year, market testing, initial advertising commitment, immediate establishment of a nucleus of sales outlets, and tooling and preproduction costs in the plant are expected to total $360,000 of almost immediate investment. Once operations on the product have begun, investment is considered complete, and cash flows by way of operations start to be realized. The best estimates of the sales and accounting departments as to future cash flows from these operations are:

Year 1 (cash loss)	($44,000)
Year 2 (cash loss)	(12,000)
Year 3	36,000
Year 4	90,000
Year 5	150,000
Year 6	170,000
Year 7	190,000
Year 8	200,000

Proposal 3. Powell Corporation has been negotiating with Fremgen Manufacturing Company for a merger. Fremgen has indicated a willingness to sell at $500,000. If Powell purchases, the expectation is to build up cash inflows, in the form of after-tax cash retention from profitable operations, from the present low levels, on a scale as follows:

Year 1	$ 25,000
Year 2	75,000
Year 3	125,000
Years 4 through 8	200,000

Assume that all cash flows are after taxes. The president has a maximum of $500,000 to invest, and desires a 12 percent return after taxes for all capital commitments.

Required:
Select the proposal which will be the most economically beneficial for the eight-year period, giving consideration to (1) payback; (2) accounting rates of return; and (3) discounted cash flow.

13-12.† By purchasing and installing a small computer, the Mittleman Company expects to realize certain cash savings in its data processing operations.

Direct cash expenses per month under the present manual--bookkeeping-machine system are:

Salaries – bookkeeping and clerical (15 people)	$5,250
Forms and supplies	500
Overtime, payroll taxes, fringes	1,250
Total	$7,000

Existing furniture and equipment are fully depreciated on the books of the company.

The computer costs $110,000, including alterations, installation, and accessory equipment.

The department will be staffed as follows:

	Per Year
Data processing supervisor	$10,000
Machine operator	6,000
Programmer	6,500
Key-punch operators (2 @ 4,500)	9,000
Other payroll costs	6,500

It is expected that forms and supplies costs will remain unchanged.

The computer is expected to be obsolete in five years, having a salvage value of $10,000 at that time.

Assume a 50 percent tax rate.

Required:
1. Determine the annual cash flow, reflecting the tax shield.
2. Decide whether or not to purchase the computer, using discounted cash flow, assuming a desired rate of return of 10 percent after taxes.

13-13. The Finnan Company wishes to determine its cost of capital as a means of establishing minimum cutoff points for testing capital expenditure proposals.

At present the long-term capital of the firm shapes up as follows:

Mortgage payable (4%)	$ 2,000,000
Convertible debentures (7%)	3,000,000
Capital stock (1,000,000 shares)	5,000,000
Retained earnings	2,000,000
Total long-term capital	$12,000,000

In the year just ended, Finnan Company earned $2,290,000 before interest and taxes. The latest quotation for the stock was $8 per share.

Required:
With a 50 percent tax rate, what is the Finnan Company's present cost of capital after taxes? (Considering all percentages as decimals, round all calculations to four places.)

13-14. The capital budget committee of the Walton Corporation was established to appraise and screen departmental requests for plant expansions and improvements at a time when these requests totaled $10 million. The committee thereupon sought your professional advice and help in establishing minimum performance standards which it should demand of these projects in the way of anticipated rates of return before interest and taxes.

The Walton Corporation is a closely held family corporation in which the stockholders exert an active and unified influence on the management. At this date, the company has no long-term debt and has 1 million shares of common capital stock outstanding. It is currently earning $5 million (net income before interest and taxes) per year. The applicable tax rate is 50 percent.

Should the projects under consideration be approved, management is confident that the $10 million of required funds can be obtained either (1) by borrowing, via the medium of an issue of $10 million, 4 percent, 20 years' bond; or (2) by equity financing, via the medium of an issue of 500,000 shares of common stock to the general public. It is expected that the ownership of these 500,000 shares would be widely dispersed and scattered.

The company has been earning $12\frac{1}{2}$ percent return after taxes. The management and the dominant stockholders consider this rate of earnings to be a fair capitalization rate (8 times earnings) as long as the company remains free of long-term debt. An increase to 15 percent, or $6\frac{2}{3}$ times earnings, would constitute an adequate adjustment to compensate for the risk of carrying $10 million of long-term debt. They believe that this reflects, and is consistent with, current market appraisals.

Required:
1. Prepare columnar schedules comparing maximum returns, considering interest, taxes, and earnings ratio which should be produced by each alternative to maintain the present capitalized value per share.
2. What minimum rate of return on new investment is necessary for each alternative to maintain the present capitalized value per share?

(AICPA adapted)

13-15.* Mr. H. C. Caldwell, manager of the production department of the Bevis Petroleum Company, was considering a proposal that involved the purchase by Bevis of producing oil property owned by R. M. Bentley. Mr. Bentley offered to sell the property for $2,340,000, but for tax reasons he wished this amount paid to him annually over a ten-year period.

A schedule of expenditures and estimated receipts for this property is shown on page 450. Explanation of the columns is as follows:

Column 1 is the schedule of payments to Mr. Bentley. Assuming the deal is closed at the end of 1955 the first payment, $390,000, would be made at the end of 1955, and other payments would be made at the end of the years specified. When the deal is closed, Bevis would give Mr. Bentley a noninterest bearing note for $2,340,000.

Column 2 is the estimated capital expenditures that good engineers say should be made "within the next five years" to improve the property. The amount is fairly definite (subject to price changes), but the timing depends on circumstances. The timing of the expenditures, shown in the schedule, is at the end of the year indicated, and is conservative.

Column 3 is the estimated cash inflow, consisting of sales revenue from crude oil sold, less cash lifting, moving, and selling costs and less income taxes. Columns 1 and 2 have been used in the income tax calculations, but do not otherwise influence column 3 figures. The property was producing crude oil in 1955. The quantity of crude oil remaining in the property was based on good geological estimates. The selling price estimate of course depends on future market conditions. Cost estimates are based on good experience. In short, the figures in column 3 are as good as, but no better than, competent, experienced people can make them.

Columns 4 and 5 are self-evident.

Bevis had recently borrowed $150 million on 30-year sinking fund debentures, at 4 percent (2 percent after taxes). The company desired to earn at least 15 percent after taxes on funds invested in producing oil properties.

BEVIS PETROLEUM COMPANY
(000 Omitted)

	Col. 1 Payments to Seller	Col. 2 Additional Expenditures	Col. 3 After-tax Cash Income	Col. 4 (Col. 3 less Col. 2)	Col. 5 Net Cash Flow
1955	390	350		(350)	(740)
1956	130	50	387	337	207
1957	130		377	377	247
1958	130		351	351	221
1959	130		351	351	221
1960	130		338	338	208
1961	130		338	338	208
1962	130		338	338	208
1963	130		325	325	195
1964	130		234	234	104
1965	780		143	143	(637)
1966			143	143	143
1967			143	143	143

Mr. Caldwell explained that he had considered the following possible approaches:

1. Our first thought was to find the time-adjusted discount rate which would bring the present value of column 5 to zero. This turns out to be around 22 percent.
2. At the time the deal is closed, however, Bevis would have to give the seller a note for $2,340,000 payable without interest on the schedule indicated in column 1. This would be a fixed obligation irrespective of the performance of the producing properties and would have to be carried as a memorandum note on our balance sheet.

    In effect, therefore, we are "borrowing" $2,340,000 from the seller, just as we would from a bank or other lending institution and are investing the proceeds of the "loan" in the purchase of these properties. The situation (except for the zero interest rate) is thus no different from some other project which might make use of the funds secured from our $150 million 30-year sinking fund debentures.

Following this line of thought, the $2,340,000 is "spent" at the time the deal is made, and we should find the discount rate which makes the present value of column 4 equal to $2,340,000. This turns out to be around 5 percent.

3. The "loan" of $2,340,000 is peculiar in that it carries no interest charge. It might be said, however, that it relieves us of the need for borrowing an equivalent amount at a cost of 4 percent or 2 percent after taxes. By discounting column 1 at 2 percent, we can get the present value of our future obligation to the seller. This turns out to be $2,080,000. We may then find the discount rate which makes the present value column 4 equal to this, which is about 7 percent.

Required:

1. What is the expected return on this investment? (NOTE: If you conclude that none of the methods described in the case gives the expected return, indicate how you would make the calculation and what the approximate result would be. You are *not* asked to make the actual calculations. Assume that the arithmetic leading to all figures given in the case is correct.)
2. Should the property be purchased?
3. What procedure should the company follow in the future in analyzing investment proposals of the type described in the case?

13-16. The Gercken Corporation sells computer services to its clients. The company completed a feasibility study and decided to obtain an additional computer on January 1, 19x5. Information regarding the new computer follows:

1. The purchase price of the computer is $230,000. Maintenance, property taxes, and insurance will be $20,000 per year. If the computer is rented, the annual rent will be $85,000 plus 5 percent of annual billings. The rental price includes maintenance.
2. Because of competitive conditions, the company feels it will be necessary to replace the computer at the end of three years with one which is larger and more advanced. It is estimated that the computer will have a resale value of $110,000 at the end of three years. The computer will be depreciated on a straight-line basis for both financial reporting and income tax purposes.
3. The income tax rate is 50 percent.
4. The estimated annual billing for the services of the new computer will be $220,000 during the first year and $260,000 during each of the second and third years. The estimated annual expense of op-

erating the computer is $80,000 in addition to the expense mentioned above. An additional $10,000 of start-up expenses will be incurred during the first year.

5. If it decides to purchase the computer, the company will pay cash. If the computer is rented, the $230,000 can be otherwise invested at a 15 percent rate of return.

6. If the computer is purchased, the amount of the investment recovered during each of the three years can be reinvested immediately at a 15 percent rate of return. Each year's recovery of investment in the computer will have been reinvested for an average of six months by the end of the year.

7. The present value of $1 due at a constant rate during each year and discounted at 15 percent is:

Year	Present Value
0–1	$0.93
1–2	0.80
2–3	0.69

The present value of $1 due at the end of each year and discounted at 15 percent is:

End of Year	Present Value
1	$0.87
2	0.76
3	0.66

Required:

1. Prepare a schedule comparing the estimated annual income from the new computer under the purchase plan and under the rental plan. The comparison should include a provision for the opportunity cost of the average investment in the computer during each year.

2. Prepare a schedule showing the annual cash flows under the purchase plan and under the rental plan.

3. Prepare a schedule comparing the net present values of the cash flows under the purchase plan and under the rental plan.

4. Comment on the results obtained in parts 1 and 3. How should the computer be financed? Why?

(AICPA adapted)

13-17. The Baxter Company manufactures toys and other short-lived items of the fad type.

The research and development department came up with an item that would make a good promotional gift for office equipment dealers. Aggressive and effective effort by Baxter's sales personnel has resulted in almost-firm commitments for this product for the next three years. It is expected that the product's value will be exhausted by that time.

In order to produce the quantity demanded, Baxter will need to buy additional machinery and rent some additional space. It appears that about 25,000 square feet will be needed. Space of 12,500 square feet, presently unused but leased, is available now. (Baxter's present lease with ten years to run costs $3 a foot.) There is another 12,500 square feet adjoining the Baxter facility which Baxter will rent for three years at $4 per square foot per year if it decides to make this product.

The equipment will be purchased for about $900,000. It will require $30,000 in modifications, $60,000 for installation, and $90,000 for testing; all these activities will be done by a firm of engineers hired by Baxter. All the expenditures will be paid for on January 1, 1973.

The equipment should have a salvage value of about $180,000 at the end of the third year. No additional general overhead costs are expected to be incurred.

The following estimates of revenues and expenses for this product for the three years have been developed:

	1973	1974	1975
Sales	$1,000,000	$1,600,000	$800,000
Material, labor, and incurred overhead	400,000	750,000	350,000
Assigned general overhead	40,000	75,000	35,000
Rent	87,500	87,500	87,500
Depreciation	450,000	300,000	150,000
	$ 977,500	$1,212,500	$622,500
Income before tax	$ 22,500	$ 387,500	$177,500
Income tax (40%)	9,000	155,000	71,000
	$ 13,500	$ 232,500	$106,500

Required:

1. Prepare a schedule which shows the incremental, after-tax, cash flows for this project.
2. If the company requires a two-year payback period for its investment, would it undertake this project? Show your supporting calculations clearly.
3. Calculate the after-tax accounting rate of return for the project.
4. A newly hired business school graduate recommends that the company consider the use of the net present value analysis to study this project. If the company sets a required rate of return of 20 percent after taxes, will this project be accepted? Show your supporting calculations clearly. (Assume all operating revenues and expenses occur at the end of the year.)

(IMA adapted)

13-18. **COMPREHENSIVE REVIEW PROBLEM**

One of the directors of the Rocca Company became concerned over the seeming inability of the company to make a reasonable profit on what he considered to be a fairly satisfactory sales volume (about $1.3 million) and to return a reasonable yield on the capital employed in the business, a substantial part of which represented borrowings from a bank with which the director was associated.

He asked the management services supervisor of the company's CPA firm to make a preliminary survey of the company's situation and report findings as a basis for a possible consulting engagement. He had at hand an audit report covering the fiscal year most recently concluded. This report disclosed that there were actually two companies which were operated by the same management. The subsidiary (100 percent owned) had been acquired about three years earlier, formerly having been in about the same type of business. The consolidated balance sheet (condensed) reflected the following:

Assets
Current:

Cash	$ 12,000
Receivables (less allowance for doubtful)	141,000
Inventories	182,000
Prepaid items	13,000
Total current	$348,000
Sundry assets	4,000
Machinery, equipment, and leasehold improvements (net)	94,000
	$446,000

Liabilities and capital
Current:

Unsecured short-term bank loan	$ 7,000
Current maturities of long-term debt	25,000
Trade payables	166,000
Accrued items	34,000
Total current	$232,000
Long-term debt	166,000
Credit arising from bargain purchase of subsidiary	26,000
Stockholders' equity	22,000
	$446,000

The audit report also showed a consolidated net profit of $4,500 for the year. A loss had been sustained in the prior year.

The director had serious doubts as to whether the management knew what its product costs were, since when he had asked whether a particular segment of the business (there were two) was profitable, and to what extent, management could not provide a satisfactory answer.

The problem, then, was to analyze the operation over all to find out what was wrong. This process was initiated by an interview with the president, who provided the following general information:

There were two product lines: (1) job-shop wire products such as fan guards, barbecue grills, and french-fry baskets (this line accounted for about 70 percent of the volume); (2) pegboard hooks made from wire which was generally of smaller dimension than that used in job-shop items (this line accounted for about 30 percent of the volume; however, it accounted for 50 percent of the inventory investment).

The business was highly competitive with a lot of "alley shops" in existence. It was not an especially profitable industry, and there had been several business failures in recent years.

The job-shop customers were, by and large, well-established concerns making both consumer and industrial products. There were about 16 large-volume customers and about 100 small ones.

The hook line was distributed through jobbers to hardware stores, specialty stores, etc. It was intended to be a fill-in line since it could be produced by using much the same equipment as that used for job-shop items. One jobber handled more than 50 percent of the output.

Freight considerations limited the marketing area to a 700-mile radius from the plant.

No sales representatives were employed. The president and the vice president made calls on certain large customers; however, basically the selling was done through others who were compensated on a 5 percent basis (job item) and 10 percent basis (hooks). About two-thirds of the job item business was "house" business (no commission).

The market potential was unknown. (There was no trade association, and the company itself had not attempted to gather information bearing on this point.)

Incoming orders for the job-shop line were sizable, and some concern was expressed regarding ability to meet delivery schedules. The hook items were back-ordered to a serious degree.

As a general rule, the job-shop customers were reasonable about paying higher prices when the need was demonstrated to their satisfaction.

Two inside people handled phone inquiries from customers and did all the estimating and price quoting.

The caliber of help was poor, basically because the business was in a low-pay industry. Most of the plant force were poorly educated, many were of foreign extraction, and absenteeism and turnover were major problems.

Personnel difficulties had been experienced as a result of acquiring the subsidiary, many of whose key employees had not adapted to their new employer too well and had ultimately left the company.

The accounting personnel consisted of one person, whose experience had been in public accounting (three years), plus two clerks.

It had been the practice to prepare operating statements on a quarterly basis; however, at the time, such statements were being prepared monthly.

The job-shop operation characteristically involved the building of samples, which was done by three toolroom employees who worked on one sample at a time. Some tooling charges were made to customers in this connection.

Sales administration, in the conventional sense, was virtually non-existent. The company more or less waited for business to come to it through the efforts of its independent representative.

Purchasing of wire (the principal raw material) was handled by the president. Other items were purchased by one of the inside people.

Production scheduling was handled by the vice president, who worked closely with the plant supervisor.

There were a total of about 120 employees, about 9 of whom could be classified as administrative. The others were in-plant personnel.

Individual interviews were next arranged with certain key persons, during which interview records were inspected, job responsibilities were explored, and miscellaneous inquiries were made, yielding the following additional facts:

From the accountant:

Inventories were taken once a year, although a midyear physical had been attempted, but since it "did not look right," it was never finished.

Monthly cost-of-sales figures were derived by applying a fixed percentage to sales covering material and labor. Plant overhead was expensed as incurred.

Labor reporting was limited to in and out (clock card) time.

There were no perpetual records pertaining to inventories.

Virtually all the hooks produced were sent outside for plating and then returned to stock.

The accountant considered the accounting system somewhat primitive but explained she had been with the company only about fifteen months and had inherited a system which was little more than a record of receipts and disbursements. She would like to do a much better job, particularly in the cost area, but could do only so much with the available staff.

She had recently been keeping memo records in an attempt to segregate certain direct costs applicable to the hook line. However, she had not been able to segregate wire purchases, and, of course, she had no means of segregating labor.

From the inside people:

Their principal duties were estimating for price quotations, handling customer inquiries regarding status of orders, working with sales representatives, and, in general, "customer relations."

Both had a general rule of thumb that costs (including administrative and selling) should equal 75 percent of the selling price.

The estimating involved four principal factors: materials, toolroom time, setup time, and running time.

Although they quoted on the basis of the operations routing and sequence as they visualized them, they did not know whether the plant supervisor adhered to their "plan." The plant supervisor did not know what prices were quoted.

There was no way for them to determine how actual costs compared with their estimates.

Estimates of time requirements were made on the basis of general experience rather than on studied or standardized performance tables.

Each person had an in-process file of from forty to sixty jobs covering activities from the customer's first inquiry to ultimate receipt of order.

These employees were responsible for tooling procurement, either within the plant or outside. In effect, they scheduled toolroom production.

From the plant supervisor:

Duties included:

Scheduling production to specific machines or work centers (had recently started a production control board but was having difficulty in getting it used properly)

Hiring and firing of help

Looking after needed equipment repairs

Directing the plant force through ten "supervisors"

In general, "running the plant"

Major problems were:

Poor-caliber help (see previous mention of this)

Difficulty in getting full cooperation from supervisors

Crowded plant and poor working conditions

Resistance at management level in implementing ideas which he thought would reduce costs

Little consultation with management when quotations were given or delivery promises made

There were normally about fifty jobs in process at all times

From other observation and inquiry:

A certain amount of cost data (particularly regarding hooks) was on hand. However, it was obviously out of date and incomplete.

The accountant had neither the time nor the capability to install a good cost system, nor could the company afford either the time or the cost to have it done by professionals.

The chart of accounts in use did not provide enough information to segregate hook costs from job-shop costs and could not be properly modified to do so without going into a complete cost system.

Some semblance of budgeting had been recently introduced; however, it was quite informal and primitive.

Monthly statements were late in preparation.

Management was very cost-conscious and watched expenditures closely. There were no obvious frills or unnecessary expenses, and all salary levels, expense reporting, etc., were modest.

Required:

As management services supervisor, analyze the information thus uncovered and prepare a preliminary report with recommendations.

GLOSSARY

Absorption costing:
See *Conventional costing.*

Accountability:
The obligation of management to report to the ownership of the firm its progress toward the attainment of the economic goals of the company. The concept of accountability attaching to delegated duties forms the basis of responsibility accounting and budgetary control.

Accounting method:
A measure of rate of return as a method of evaluating capital investment proposals. It is derived from accrual accounting methods for income determination. As a rate of return, the resulting percentage is a measure of the profitability of a capital proposal.

Activity base:
Some measure of operating activity within a department, plant, or company. It is often used as a basis for distributing indirect costs.

Actual costs:
See *Incurred costs.*

Asset turnover:
An expression of the number of sales dollars supported by one dollar of operating assets, or the number of times the operating assets are "recovered" in the sales of the period. It is determined by dividing net sales by operating assets.

Attained volume:
The level of activity (production, sales, or other activity) actually reached during the fiscal period.

Break-even point:
That point at which total expenses (fixed and variable) associated with a certain level of sales are exactly matched by the revenues generated by the level of sales, leaving no profit.

Budget:
As a noun, a detailed, integrated plan used by the management of a firm as a guide to its operations in the near future; as a verb, to plan.

Budget factor:
A cost factor used to determine the amount of cost allowed under given operating conditions. It is used especially in a system of flexible budgeting for cost control purposes.

Capacity costs:
Expenses incurred on the basis of a certain amount per period of time, independently of the number of units that might be produced during that period. Generally such costs are incurred in order to provide a certain capacity for the firm's production and sales activities. Also called *fixed costs* and *period costs.*

Capacity variance:
The variance that arises when the attained level of activity is anything other than

normal capacity. It represents the difference between the total standard fixed overhead applied to attained volume of production and the budgeted fixed overhead for the period.

Capital budgeting:
Planning the deployment of available capital (the relatively scarce, nonhuman resources of productive enterprise) for the purpose of maximizing the long-term profitability of the firm.

Capital investment:
Procurement by the firm of the relatively scarce, nonhuman resources of productive enterprise.

Cash-flow budget:
A projection of cash receipts and disbursements and resulting cash balances based on the budgeted activity of the firm. The purpose of this statement is to highlight the highs and lows in the short-term flows of cash through the business; foreknowledge of shortages of cash will facilitate borrowing arrangements, and anticipation of large cash balances will facilitate temporary investment of these balances.

Comprehensive budget:
Detailed schedules appropriate to each of the key functions in the organization, together with the entire company's plan, summarized in a projected cash-flow budget and *pro forma* financial statements.

Contribution margin:
The margin per unit or excess of sales price over unit variable cost, contributing to the recovery of fixed expenses and the realization of profit in that order.

Contribution pricing:
An approach to pricing which emphasizes the contribution margin and the behavior of costs and revenues with respect to changes in volume.

Controllable costs:
Expenses which are, to a major extent, the responsibility of a specific individual or department within an organization.

Controller:
The top management accountant in an organization.

Conventional costing:
The conventional method of recording and reporting costs for income determination (matching expense against revenue of a fiscal period) which regards unit product cost as consisting of direct material, direct labor, variable factory overhead, and fixed factory overhead. Also called *absorption costing.* (For a comparison of conventional and variable costing, refer to Chapter 9.)

Conversion cost:
The sum of the cost of direct labor and overhead cost incurred in the process of changing or converting the raw material into the finished product.

Cost:
Value forgone for the purpose of achieving some economic benefit which will promote the profit-making ability of the firm.

Cost adjusted to current prices:
Original cost converted to current prices by means of some economic index, minus accumulated depreciation also based on current prices. It is one of the various possibilities for the valuation of fixed assets, to be used in rate-of-return calculations.

Cost center:
A department or other organizational unit which forms a natural clustering point for the accumulation of costs.

Cost control:
The ability of responsible managers to influence certain costs for the purpose of maintaining them within acceptable limits. Performance reports compare incurred with allowed costs, highlighting differences and helping pinpoint causes for off-standard conditions in order that corrective action may be taken.

Cost of capital:
The cost of raising capital in the market. It may include interest on borrowed money or the relation of a company's earnings to the market value of its equity securities.

Cost of equity funds:
Funds arising from the sale of stock in the company, or the use of retained earnings. Costs associated with the use of such funds are dividends, or the opportunity cost to stockholders if funds are retained in the business instead of paid as dividends. Cost of equity funds is part of *cost of capital* (see above).

Cost-plus pricing:
See *Full-cost pricing.*

Delegation:
The passing downward of administrative power from the owners to responsible management and, within the firm, from top management to lower organizational levels.

Differential costs:
See *Incremental costs:*

Direct costing:
See *Variable costing.*

Direct labor cost:
The cost of any operation performed by a productive worker directly on any part of the product which contributes to its finished form.

Direct material cost:
The cost of material which becomes a part of the finished product.

Discounted cash flow:
A measure of rate of return as a method of evaluating capital investment proposals, based on the concept of the time value of money.

Discounting:
A reduction of some future amount of money to a present value at some appropriate rate, in accordance with the concept of the time value of money.

Discretionary costs:
Fixed costs which result from a management decision to undertake a particular program and which can be changed at management's wishes. Also called *programmed costs.*

Elasticity of demand:
The economic notion that lowering the price of a product causes an increase in its sales volume sufficient to increase the total revenue over that realized at the former (higher) price, or that total revenue decreases if the price is raised.

Equivalent completed units:
The number of units of product which could have been completed with the costs incurred to bring a larger number of units to a degree of partial completion. It is a cost concept used in process costing.

Equivalent units:
The sum of the completed units transferred out and the equivalent completed units in ending work-in-process inventory.

Estimated annual volume:
Capacity determined each year in the light of forecast volume. It is useful for planning material purchases, manpower needs, and cash requirements.

Exception principle:
A management principle which specifies that the manager will maximize his or her efficiency by concentrating on those operational factors which are deviations from the plan.

Excess present value:
A technique of discounted cash flow for capital expenditure evaluation. It seeks to determine whether the present value of estimated future cash inflows at management's desired rate of return is greater or less than the cost of the proposal.

Expired cost:
The basic notion of an expense. It is the measure of the value of an economic service which was used up during a fiscal period and which helped produce the firm's revenue during that period.

Factors of cost:
The two basic determinants of cost: quantity and the rate or cost per unit, useful in the establishment of standards for cost control and budget purposes.

Factory burden:
See *Factory overhead.*

Factory overhead:
A major manufacturing cost element containing all manufacturing expenses other than direct material and direct labor. Also called *factory burden.*

Favorable variance:
The variance existing when incurred costs are less than standard costs.

Fixed budget:
A plan of operations drawn up for only one level of estimated annual volume.

Fixed costs:
See *Capacity costs.*

Flexible budgeting:
A method of planning operations, for purposes of cost control, which permits allowed costs to be adjusted to the attained level of volume.

Flexible budgeting formula:
An expression of the composition of a mixed cost element as a variable rate and a fixed cost amount. The budget allowance for an expense equals the fixed cost plus the unit variable cost multiplied by the number of units.

Forecast volume:
The level of activity (production, sales, or other activity) anticipated by management for the coming fiscal period and around which the fixed budget is constructed.

Full-cost pricing:
A method which sets the price of a product at an amount equal to its budgeted manufacturing cost plus a normal markup. Also called *cost-plus pricing*.

Gross cost:
The acquisition value of a fixed asset (with no reduction for accumulated depreciation) used in calculating return on capital.

Incremental costs:
Costs incurred as a result of taking on an additional piece of business, which would be avoided if that piece of business were forgone. Also called *differential costs*.

Incurred costs:
Expenses for which the company paid or actually received benefits during the period. Also called *actual costs*.

Incurred overhead rate:
The relationship of the overhead cost incurred in a given period and the appropriate activity base.

Indirect labor:
The cost of labor, other than direct labor, incurred in facilitating the production process.

Indirect material:
The cost of material which is not classified as becoming a part of the product (i.e., direct material) but which facilitates the production process.

Investment center:
A segment of a company whose manager has control over the amount of investment in the center as well as over revenues and costs.

Investors' ratio:
A measure of the relative attractiveness of a share of common stock as an investment by expressing the relationship between net income after taxes and shareholders' equity.

Job lot costing:
See *Job order costing*.

Job order costing:
The technique of accumulating costs for types of manufacturing activity charac-

terized by the production of certain items to the unique specifications of the customer or by the performance of some specified activity under a negotiated contract. Under this costing method, the job is the costing unit. Also called *job lot costing.*

Joint products:
Products that are produced by a single process but are not identifiable as individual products until some definite point in the manufacturing process.

Labor efficiency variance:
The variance resulting from a difference between the actual time worked, priced at standard labor rates, and the standard quantity (based on realized production), also priced at standard rates. This is a quantity variance and results from efficient or inefficient use of labor.

Labor rate variance:
The variance resulting from the difference between the actual labor rates paid for time actually worked, and the same time period at standard labor rates. This is a spending variance and results from paying labor at rates other than the standard rate set for the job.

Management by domination:
A philosophy of managing based on coercion by higher management of persons in subordinate positions.

Management by objectives:
A philosophy of running a business which seeks to harmonize the goals and objectives of the business with those of the employee.

Marginal analysis:
The process of considering the relationship between marginal revenues and marginal costs in establishing the profit-maximizing price.

Marginal cost:
The change in total costs resulting from a one-unit increase in quantity produced.

Marginal costing:
See *Variable costing.*

Marginal revenue:
The change in total revenue resulting from a one-unit increase in quantity sold.

Material price variance:
The variance resulting from the difference between the actual price paid for materials purchased (actual quantity or number of units) and the standard price paid for the same quantity. This is a spending variance and results from purchasing material at any price other than the standard price.

Material usage variance:
The variance resulting from the difference between the actual quantity of materials used, valued at standard prices, and the standard quantity for the production realized, also valued at standard prices. This is a quantity variance and results from efficient or inefficient use of materials by the workers.

Mixed cost:
A cost (whether single expense, cost element, or total class of costs) made up of both variable and fixed factors.

Motivation:
The combination of recognized conditions which influences an individual to act as he or she does.

Net cost:
The book value of a fixed asset (as determined by accrual methods), which constitutes one basis for the valuation of fixed assets in rate of return calculations.

Noncontrollable costs:
Costs which cannot be controlled in a given department, although they may be controlled at a higher level of management.

Normal capacity:
That level of factory operations which is considered the norm in view of market constraints over the period of the next three to five years.

Opportunity cost:
The monetary benefit one must forgo if he or she rejects an alternative. It is an economic term.

Overapplied overhead:
The amount by which the overhead applied to attained production at a predetermined rate exceeds the overhead actually incurred during the period.

Overhead efficiency:
The variance resulting from a difference between the actual quantity factor of overhead cost (e.g., time worked) incurred, priced at the standard variable overhead rate, and the standard quantity (based on realized production), also priced at the standard variable overhead rate. This is a quantity variance and results from efficient use of variable productive resources.

Overhead spending:
The variance resulting from the difference between the actual variable costs incurred and the allowed variable costs at standard rate for the production volume attained. This is a spending variance, similar to material price and labor rate variances, resulting from the incurred overhead rate being different from the standard rate.

Payback period:
The length of time required to equate cash return with the initial cost of a capital investment. It is determined by dividing the original investment by the annual cash inflows (cash savings after taxes).

Period costs:
See *Capacity costs.*

Planning budget:
The detailed plan of operations based on one level of forecast volume.

Practical capacity:
Theoretical engineering capacity reduced by the internal natural constraints of factory realities, such as the ordinary and expected interruptions, delays, and other normal deterrents to worker productivity, as well as vacations, holidays, and inventory shutdowns.

Predetermined overhead rate:
A rate developed by dividing anticipated overhead costs by some appropriate ac-

tivity base. It is useful for pricing and assessing the profitability of jobs before the end of the fiscal period.

Present value:
The amount of money which, if invested immediately at a stated rate, would yield one or more future payments reflecting the increased value of the investment in accordance with the time value of money. Conversely, it may be considered the value of a future stream of payments discounted at a given rate to the present time.

Prime cost:
The sum of the two manufacturing cost elements known as direct labor and direct material.

Process costing:
A technique of accumulating costs when the production is large quantities of similar or identical units of standardized product.

Productive departments:
Departments which perform operations contributing directly to the conversion of raw materials to finished product.

Profit:
The excess of a firm's operating revenue over the expenses of producing that revenue in a given fiscal period.

Profit center:
A segment of a company whose manager has control over revenues and costs but not over the amount of investment in the segment.

Pro forma financial statements:
Literally, "according to form" financial statements. They are the basic financial statements projected to the end of the next fiscal period in accordance with the provisions of the planning budget.

Programmed costs:
See *Discretionary costs.*

Ratio of earnings to capital used:
See *Return on capital used.*

Relevant costs:
Costs which are pertinent or apply to the case at hand. The relevance of costs is determined by the purpose for which they are to be used.

Relevant range:
Generally, the range of production (and sales) volume over which a firm's fixed costs will remain stable; also applied to the range over which variable costs remain stable.

Residual income:
Net income in excess of a desired or budgeted return on capital used.

Responsibility accounting:
A system of accounting designed to facilitate control of expenditures by meaningful reports to the individuals in the company or organization who are responsible for their control. The reporting system usually provides a series of summaries from

one level of the organization to the next, culminating in a report of total costs at the top management level.

Return on assets used:
See *Return on capital used.*

Return on capital:
The concept which relates income to investment as a means of measuring the effectiveness with which risk capital has been managed.

Return on capital employed:
See *Return on capital used.*

Return on capital used:
The ratio of net income from operations to total operating assets. It is used to measure the effectiveness of all operating decisions, from the routine to the critical, made by management at all levels of the organization from shop foreman to president. Also called *ratio of earnings to capital used, return on assets used, return on capital employed,* and *return on investment.*

Return on investment:
See *Return on capital used.*

Revenue:
The inflow of economic values resulting from a firm's operations.

Sales mix:
The composition of the total sales of a multiproduct firm in terms of the relative sales of each product line.

Salvage value:
The residual value of a depreciable asset at the end of its useful life.

Service departments:
Departments which help the productive departments perform more efficiently but do not themselves perform any operations directly on the product.

Standard cost:
A measure of acceptable performance, established by management as a guide to certain economic decisions; a reflection of what management thinks costs ought to be.

Standard overhead rate:
An overhead rate for a cost center, department, or entire plant which includes both fixed and variable expenses in a single costing factor. It is determined by dividing total overhead cost budgeted at normal capacity by base activity at normal capacity.

Theoretical capacity:
Full engineered capacity; the maximum production of which the plant is capable, running full tilt, with no interruptions.

Time-adjusted rate of return:
That rate which equates the present value of the future cash inflows with the cost of the investment which produces them. It is a form of discounted cash flow.

Transfer price:
The price established on interdivisional sales in a decentralized company.

Underapplied overhead:
The amount by which actual overhead costs exceed the amount of overhead applied to production at a predetermined overhead rate.

Unexpired cost:
Stored-up service potential to be realized as economic benefit in the future. It represents asset value.

Unfavorable variance:
The variance existing when incurred costs are more than standard costs.

Unrecovered fixed costs:
The excess of fixed costs over contribution margin; it amounts to the net loss from operations sustained by the firm in a period where sales volume was insufficient to build contribution margin to the level equating total fixed costs.

Variable costing:
A method of recording and reporting costs which regards as product costs only those manufacturing costs which tend to vary directly with volume of activity, i.e., direct material, direct labor, and variable factory overhead. Also called *direct costing* and *marginal costing*.

Variable costs:
Costs which are dependent upon the level of activity for the amount of their incurrence. They increase as activity increases, and vice versa.

Variance:
The difference between incurred costs and standard costs.

Variance analysis:
The breakdown by major cost elements of variances of incurred costs from standard in order to pinpoint the factors causing them and to assess responsibility for their control.

APPENDIX: SOLUTIONS TO SELECTED PROBLEMS

2-2. **Y COMPANY**
Comparative Income Statements
For the Years 19x1 and 19x2

	19x1	19x2
Net sales	$100,000	$110,000*
Cost of goods sold (see Schedule 1)	70,000	80,000
Gross margin on sales	30,000*	30,000
Operating expenses	20,000	18,000*
Income from operations	10,000*	12,000
Interest expense	1,000	1,000
Income before taxes	9,000*	11,000*
Income tax expense	4,500	5,500
Net income	$ 4,500*	$ 5,500*
Schedule 1		
Stores, beginning inventory	$ 1,000	$ 2,000*
Purchases	10,000*	12,000
Cost of material available	11,000	14,000*
Stores, ending inventory	2,000	1,000*
Cost of material used	9,000*	13,000
Direct labor	25,000	27,000*
Factory overhead	40,000*	41,000
Manufacturing costs incurred	74,000	81,000*
Work in process, beginning inventory	15,000	14,000*
Cost of work in process	89,000*	95,000
Work in process, ending inventory	14,000*	16,000
Cost of goods manufactured	75,000	79,000*
Finished goods, beginning inventory	20,000	25,000*
Cost of goods available for sale	95,000*	104,000*
Finished goods, ending inventory	25,000	24,000
Cost of goods sold	$ 70,000*	$ 80,000*

* Problem unknowns.

2-9. 1. WILSON CORPORATION
Comparative Income Statement
For the Years Ended
December 31, 1974 and 1975

	1974	1975
Sales	$330,000	$400,000
Less: Material	$150,000	$160,000
Labor	75,000	90,000
Overhead	60,000	110,000
Total	285,000	360,000
Income before taxes	$ 45,000	$ 40,000

2. WILSON CORPORATION
Average Manufacturing Costs
For the Years 1974 and 1975

	1974	1975
Material	$5.00	$4.00
Labor	2.50	2.25
Overhead	2.00	2.75
Total	$9.50	$9.00

MORAL: Reducing average costs does not always increase profits—even with increased volume.

2-17. THE PIPE COMPANY

1.

	18-inch	24-inch	30-inch	Total
a. Feet produced	7,200	10,200	6,320	
Pounds per foot	150	250	400	
Pounds produced	1,080,000	2,550,000	2,528,000	6,158,000

Cost of production:

Raw material purchases			$17,657	
Add: Freight in			2,447	
Raw material available			$20,104	
Less: Raw material inventory 12/31			1,630	
Cost of raw material used				$18,474
Direct labor			$13,255	
Manufacturing overhead				
Depreciation—factory		$ 600		
Depreciation—machinery		3,000		
Electric power—factory		1,519		
Shop supplies		2,550		
Repairs and maintenance—factory		2,175		
Other factory expenses		760		
Total manufacturing overhead			$10,604	23,859
Total cost of production				$42,333

Material cost:
Raw material cost ÷ pounds produced: $18,474/6,158,000 = $.003/pound

	18-inch	24-inch	30-inch	Total
Feet produced/year	7,200	10,200	6,320	
Feet produced/day	120	100	80	
Productive days	60	102	79	241

Conversion cost/day:
Conversion cost ÷ productive days:
23,859/241 = $99/day

Summary:

	18-inch	24-inch	30-inch	Total
Pounds produced	1,080,000	2,550,000	2,528,000	6,158,000
Material cost @ $.003/lb	$3,240	$7,650	$7,584	$18,474
Productive days	60	102	79	241
Conversion cost @ $99/day	$5,940	$10,098	$7,821	$23,859
Total production cost	$9,180	$17,748	$15,405	$42,333
Cost per foot	$1.275	$1.740	$2.4375	
b. Selling price/ft	$2.2000	$3.0000	$4.0000	
Production cost/ft	1.2750	1.7400	2.4375	
Gross profit/ft	$.9250	$1.2600	$1.5625	
Percentage gross profit to selling price	42.0%	42.0%	39.1%	
c. Inventory, 12/31, units (ft)	1,000	2,080	1,320	
Unit cost (ft)	$1.2750	$1.7400	$2.4375	
Inventory value, 12/31	$1,275	$3,619	$3,218	$8,112

2.

Cost of one day's production: 36″ pipe

Production—pounds: 64 ft × 500 lb	32,000
Material cost @ $.003/lb	$96
Conversion cost/day	99
Cost of one day's production	$195
Cost/ft for 64 ft	$3.0469
Selling price/ft	$5.0000
Production cost/ft	3.0469
Gross profit/ft	$1.9531
Percentage gross profit	39.1%

Comparison of gross profit by size per day:

	18-inch	24-inch	30-inch	36-inch
Gross profit per ft	$.9250	$1.2600	$1.5625	$1.9531
Feet per day	120	100	80	64
Gross profit per day	$111	$126	$125	$125

3-5. SNAPPY TOOL AND DIE COMPANY
Job No. 682

	Direct Material	Direct Labor	Factory Burden	Total
Inventory—June 1	$ 75	$ 20	$ 23	$118
Add: Input—department 1	350	50	42	442
Input—department 2	–	75	90	165
Total cost of finished job	$425	$145	$155 =	$725

Summary analysis:
Manufacturing cost (75%)	$725
Selling and administrative (10%)	97
Profit (15%)	145
Billing price	$967

3-8. THE WEN COMPANY
1. Predetermined rate

Estimated factory overhead cost: $\dfrac{\$360,000}{144,000}$ = $2.50/direct labor hour
Estimated direct labor hours:

2. Over (under) applied overhead

Factory overhead incurred	$338,000
Factory overhead applied (121,500 direct labor hours)	303,750
Underapplied factory overhead	$ (34,250)

3. General ledger

Factory overhead control	$338,000	
Vouchers payable		$338,000
Work in process	303,750	
Factory overhead applied		303,750

Subsidiary ledger

Factory supervision	51,000	
Indirect labor	99,000	
Inspection	73,000	
Maintenance	39,000	
Indirect materials	20,000	
Heat, light, power	18,000	
Depreciation	35,000	
Miscellaneous factory overhead	3,000	
Vouchers payable		$338,000

For application of overhead to jobs, each job sheet will be debited for the appropriate amount, the total equalling the $303,750 credit to factory overhead applied.

4. Incurred rate: $338,000/121,500 = $2.782/direct labor hour

Several factors could have caused the result seen:
a. Actual volume failed to reach the level estimated.
b. Labor efficiency proved greater than estimated, causing the base to be smaller relative to incurred overhead, resulting in a higher rate per hour.
c. Overhead costs may have been poorly controlled.
d. If there is a diversity of products, the mix realized in production may have been different from that estimated.

3-14. THE BILTIMAR COMPANY

	Total	Transferred In	Material	Conversion
Physical flow				
Work in process 7/1	10,000			
Transferred in	40,000			
Total units in process	50,000			
Units finished	35,000			
Units in process 7/31	15,000			
Total units in process	50,000			
Equivalent units				
Units finished	35,000	35,000	35,000	35,000
Units in process 7/31	15,000			
Transferred-in and material, completed		15,000	15,000	
Conversion, one-third completed				5,000
Equivalent units		50,000	50,000	40,000
Costs in process				
Work in process 7/1	$140,500	$ 38,000	$21,500	$ 81,000
Current costs	502,600	140,000	70,000	292,600
Total costs in process	$643,100	$178,000	$91,500	$373,600
Cost per equivalent unit	$14.73	$3.56	$1.83	$9.34

Summary
1. Completed and transferred to finished goods (35,000 @ $14.73) $515,550
2. Work in process 7/31
   Transferred-in cost (15,000 @ $3.56) $53,400
   Material (15,000 @ $1.83) 27,450
   Conversion (5,000 @ $9.34) 46,700 127,550
   Total costs in process $643,100

4-3. **TIMELESS INSTRUMENT COMPANY**

Basic operations

Sales (500,000 @ $2)	$1,000,000
Variable costs (500,000 @ $1.60)	800,000
Contribution margin	$ 200,000
Fixed costs	150,000
Net profit	$ 50,000

	(1) 10% Increase Selling Price	(2) $0.25 Decrease Selling Price	(3) $0.20 Increase Variable Cost	(4) 10% Decrease Variable Cost
Sales	$1,100,000	$ 875,000	$1,000,000	$1,000,000
Variable costs	800,000	800,000	900,000	720,000
Contribution margin	$ 300,000	$ 75,000	$ 100,000	$ 280,000
Fixed costs	150,000	150,000	150,000	150,000
Net profit	$ 150,000	($ 75,000)	($ 50,000)	$ 130,000
Change from basic net profit	$ 100,000	($ 125,000)	($ 100,000)	$ 80,000
Percentage change from basic net profit	200%	(250%)	(200%)	160%

	(5) $20,000 Increase Fixed Cost	(6) 10% Decrease Fixed Cost	(7) 10% Increase Sales Volume	(8) 20% Decrease Sales Volume
Sales	$1,000,000	$1,000,000	$1,100,000	$ 800,000
Variable costs	800,000	800,000	880,000	640,000
Contribution margin	$ 200,000	$ 200,000	$ 220,000	$ 160,000
Fixed costs	170,000	135,000	150,000	150,000
Net profit	$ 30,000	$ 65,000	$ 70,000	$ 10,000
Change from basic net profit	($ 20,000)	$ 15,000	$ 20,000	($ 40,000)
Percentage change from basic net profit	(40%)	30%	40%	(80%)

	(9) 10% Decrease Selling Price 10% Increase Sales Volume	(10) 10% Increase Selling Price 10% Decrease Sales Volume	(11) $0.20 Decrease Selling Price $0.04 Decrease Variable Cost	(12) 10% Increase Fixed Cost 10% Increase Sales Volume
Sales	$ 990,000	$ 990,000	$ 900,000	$1,100,000
Variable costs	880,000	720,000	780,000	880,000
Contribution margin	$ 110,000	$ 270,000	$ 120,000	$ 220,000
Fixed costs	150,000	150,000	150,000	165,000
Net profit	($ 40,000)	$ 120,000	($ 30,000)	$ 55,000
Change from basic net profit	($ 90,000)	$ 70,000	($ 80,000)	$ 5,000
Percentage change from basic net profit	(180%)	140%	(160%)	10%

	(13) $50,000 Increase Fixed Cost 10% Decrease Variable Cost
Sales	$1,000,000
Variable costs	720,000
Contribution margin	$ 280,000
Fixed costs	200,000
Net profit	$ 80,000
Change from basic net profit	$ 30,000
Percentage change from basic net profit	60%

4-12. THE CAREY COMPANY

1.

Unit selling price	$20
Unit variable cost	14
Unit contribution margin	$ 6

Total fixed costs	$ 792,000

Break-even point in units ($792,000/$6)	$ 132,000
Unit selling price	20
Break-even point in dollars	$2,640,000

2.

Total fixed costs	$792,000
Desired profit before taxes	60,000
Desired contribution margin (CM)	$852,000

Number of units yielding desired CM ($852,000/$6)	142,000

3.

Total fixed costs	$792,000
Desired profit before taxes ($90,000/.6)	150,000
Desired contribution margin	$942,000

Number of units yielding desired CM ($942,000/$6)	157,000

4.

Old total variable costs	$14.00
Labor cost percentage	.5
Old total variable labor costs	$ 7.00
Percentage increase	.1
Increase in variable costs	$ .70
Old contribution margin	6.00
New contribution margin	$ 5.30

Old total fixed costs	$792,000
Labor cost percentage	.2
Old total fixed labor costs	$158,400
Percentage increase	.1
Increase in fixed costs	$ 15,840
Old total fixed costs	792,000
New total fixed costs	$807,840

Break-even point in units ($807,840/$5.30)	152,423

4-17. CLIENT ANALYSIS

1. Computation of selling price per unit

	Amount	Ratio
Material	$4.00	
Direct labor	.60	
Burden	1.00	
Administrative expense	1.20	
Profit	1.02	
	$7.82	85%
Selling expense at 15% of selling price		
($7.82 ÷ 85% = $9.20)	1.38	15%
Selling price	$9.20	100%

2. Projected profit and loss statement (using 24,000 units)

Sales		$220,800
Cost of sales:		
Material	$ 96,000	
Direct labor	14,400	
Burden	24,000	
Total cost of sales		134,400
Manufacturing profit		$ 86,400
Operating expenses:		
Selling	$ 33,120	
Administrative	28,800	
Total operating expenses		61,920
Net income		$ 24,480

3. Computation of break-even point

		Amount	Percentages
Sales		$220,800	100%
Variable costs:			
Material	$96,000		
Labor	14,400		
Selling	33,120		
Total variable costs		143,520	65%
Contribution margin		$ 77,280	35%
Fixed costs:			
Burden		$ 24,000	
Administrative		28,800	
Total fixed costs		$ 52,800	

Break-even: Fixed cost/contribution margin: 52,800/.35 = $150,857
in units: $150,857/$9.20 = 16,398 units

5-3.   TOMLINSON RETAIL COMPANY

	May	June
Unit sales	11,900	11,400
Ending inventory desired	14,820	15,600
Inventory requirements	26,720	27,000
Beginning inventories	15,470	14,820
Required purchases in units	11,250	12,180
Unit cost	$20	$20
Budgeted purchases	$225,000	$243,600
Sales in dollars	$357,000	$342,000
Selling, general, and administrative expense percentage	.15	.15
Total S., G., and A. expense	$ 53,550	$ 51,300
Less: depreciation	2,000	2,000
S., G., and A. expense requiring current cash outlay	$ 51,550	$ ·49,300

1. Budgeted cash disbursements during June:

May purchases (46% of $225,000)	$103,500
May S., G., and A. (46% of $51,550)	23,713
June purchases (54% of $243,600)	131,544
June S., G., and A. (54% of $49,300)	26,622
Total	$285,379

2. Budgeted collections during May:

9% of March sales	$ 31,860
60% of April sales	217,800
Less: Discount on $217,800	(6,534)
25% of April sales	90,750
Total	$333,876

3. Budgeted purchases during July:

Unit sales	12,000
Ending inventory desired	15,860
Inventory requirements	27,860
Beginning inventory	15,600
Required purchases in units	12,260

5-7.   JAZBO COMPANY

Production budget	× 10	× 20	× 30
Sales forecast	26,000	32,000	18,000
Add: Inventory 12/31/x1	1,000	1,500	800
Requirements—4Q	27,000	33,500	18,800
Less: Inventory 9/30/x1	1,200	1,600	900
Production required—4Q	25,800	31,900	17,900

					Cartons		
Purchasing budget	Produc-tion	Steel	Paint	Handles	p	r	s
× 10	25,800	51,600	25,800	51,600	25,800		
× 20	31,900	95,700		127,600		31,900	
× 30	17,900	89,500	35,800	71,600			17,900
Production requirements		236,800	61,600	250,800	25,800	31,900	17,900
Add: Inventory—12/31/x1		16,000	7,200	7,000	2,000	2,000	2,000
Total requirements		252,800	68,800	257,800	27,800	33,900	19,900
Less: Inventory—9/30/x1		20,000	9,600	9,000	4,000	6,000	4,000
Required purchases		232,800	59,200	248,800	23,800	27,900	15,900
In purchasing units		116.4	7,400	248,800	23,800	27,900	15,900

5-12. THE APPLIANCE BUSINESS
Summary of Budgeted Receipts, Disbursements, and Additional
Cash Investments For the Six-Month Period Ending June 30

	Jan.	Feb.	Mar.	Apr.
Minimum balance	$15,000	$15,000	$15,000	$15,000
Cash receipts	15,500	26,300	31,800	40,700
Total	$30,500	$41,300	$46,800	$55,700
Cash disbursements	23,700	30,150	35,150	43,840
Difference	$ 6,800	$11,150	$11,650	$11,860
Minimum balance	15,000	15,000	15,000	15,000
Additional cash investment	$ 8,200	$ 3,850	$ 3,350	$ 3,140

	May	June	Summary
Minimum balance	$15,000	$15,000	$ 15,000
Cash receipts	68,800	71,400	254,500
Total	$83,800	$86,400	$269,500
Cash disbursements	73,900	73,960	280,700
Difference	$ 9,900	$12,440	($ 11,200)
Minimum balance	15,000	15,000	15,000
Additional cash investment	$ 5,100	$ 2,560	$ 26,200

Schedule of cash receipts

	Jan.	Feb.	Mar.	Apr.
Cash sales	$ 5,000	$ 8,000	$ 9,000	$11,000
Down payments (10% of installment sales)	1,500	2,400	2,700	3,300
Installments and interest collected		1,500	3,900	6,600
Loans on pledged installment contracts	9,000	14,400	16,200	19,800
	$15,500	$26,300	$31,800	$40,700

	May	June	Total
Cash sales	$19,000	$18,000	$ 70,000
Down payments (10% of installment sales)	5,700	5,400	21,000
Installments and interest collected	9,900	15,600	37,500
Loans on pledged installment contracts	34,200	32,400	126,000
	$68,800	$71,400	$254,500

Schedule of cash disbursements

	100	160	180	220
	Jan.	Feb.	Mar.	Apr.
Other fixed expenses	$ 1,200	$ 1,200	$ 1,200	$ 1,200
First purchase	5,000			
Inventory replacement	12,500	20,000	22,500	27,500
Commissions and other variable expenses	5,000	8,000	9,000	11,000
Loan repayments		900	2,340	3,960
Interest payments		50	110	180
	$23,700	$30,150	$35,150	$43,840

	380	360	1,400
	May	June	Total
Other fixed expenses	$ 1,200	$ 1,200	$ 7,200
First purchase			5,000
Inventory replacement	47,500	45,000	175,000
Commissions and other variable expenses	19,000	18,000	70,000
Loan repayments	5,940	9,360	22,500
Interest payments	260	400	1,000
	$73,900	$73,960	$280,700

5-12. THE APPLIANCE BUSINESS (continued)

Schedule of cash sales and installment contracts

		Total	Cash (25%)	Installment (75%)	Down Payment	Installment Contract, 10 months × $20/month	Unearned Carrying Charges
January	100	$ 20,000	$ 5,000	$ 15,000	$ 1,500	$ 15,000	$ 1,500
February	160	32,000	8,000	24,000	2,400	24,000	2,400
March	180	36,000	9,000	27,000	2,700	27,000	2,700
April	220	44,000	11,000	33,000	3,300	33,000	3,300
May	380	76,000	19,000	57,000	5,700	57,000	5,700
June	360	72,000	18,000	54,000	5,400	54,000	5,400
	1,400	$280,000	$70,000	$210,000	$21,000	$210,000	$21,000

Schedule of installments and interest collected
($20 per month per contract)

		Feb.	Mar.	Apr.	May	June	Total
On January sales	75	$1,500	$1,500	$1,500	$1,500	$ 1,500	$ 7,500
On February sales	120		2,400	2,400	2,400	2,400	9,600
On March sales	135			2,700	2,700	2,700	8,100
On April sales	165				3,300	3,300	6,600
On May sales	285					5,700	5,700
On June sales	270						
		$1,500	$3,900	$6,600	$9,900	$15,600	$37,500

Schedule of bank loan and interest payments

Loan Schedule	New Bank Loan, 60% Installment Note	Repayments, 60% of Collections	Cumulative Loan Balance	Interest Payment
January	$ 9,000		$ 9,000	
February	14,400	$ 900	22,500	$ 50
March	16,200	2,340	36,360	110
April	19,800	3,960	52,200	180
May	34,200	5,940	80,460	260
June	32,400	9,360	103,500	400
	$126,000	$22,500		$1,000

Schedule of cash payments for inventory replacements

	Units × Price	
January sales	100 × $125	$ 12,500
February sales	160 × 125	20,000
March sales	180 × 125	22,500
April sales	220 × 125	27,500
May sales	380 × 125	47,500
June sales	360 × 125	45,000
Total		$175,000

6-5. SIEGFRIED COMPANY

Bill of materials for forecast sales:

	Ein (20,000)		Zwei (10,000)		Drei (2,000)		Total Requirements for Year
	Q/Unit	Total	Q/Unit	Total	Q/Unit	Total	
A	12	240,000	40	400,000	25	50,000	690,000
B	4	80,000	–	–	8	16,000	96,000
C	–	–	1	10,000	20	40,000	50,000
D	5	100,000	10	100,000	–	–	200,000

1. Selection of material price standards:

	Total Year	Standard Purchase Quantity	Turnover	Standard Price
A	690,000	50,000	13.8	$ .90
B	96,000	15,000	6.4	2.00
C	50,000	50,000	1.0	8.00
D	200,000	50,000	4.0	4.00

2. Standard material cost per unit:

	Ein	Zwei	Drei
A	$10.80	$36.00	$ 22.50
B	8.00		16.00
C	–	8.00	160.00
D	20.00	40.00	–
Total	$38.80	$84.00	$198.50

6-9. OSBERGER CORPORATION

1. *Material variances:*

AQ (purchase) × AP
32,000 × $1.18 = $37,760 } Price variance $640 F
AQ (purchase) × SP
32,000 × $1.20 = $38,400 }

Budget variance $1,120 F

AQ (used) × SP
25,600 × $1.20 = $30,720 } Usage variance $480 F
SQ × SP
26,000 × $1.20 = $31,200 }

Labor variances:

AQ × AR
20,000 × $1.75 = $35,000 } Rate variance $1,000 F
AQ × SR
20,000 × $1.80 = $36,000 }

Budget variance $100 F

Eff. variance $900 U

SQ × SR
19,500 × $1.80 = $35,100 }

Factory overhead:

Actual incurred − standard applied = total overhead variance
$12,500 − (19,500 × $.60) 11,700 = $800 U

2. Cost = $12/unit
SP = $12 + .4 SP
.6 SP = $12
SP = $20

Net sales ($20 × 6,000)		$120,000
Standard cost of goods sold ($12 × 6,000)		72,000
Standard gross margin		$ 48,000
add: Variance from standard*		
Material price variance	$640	
Material usage variance	480	
Labor rate	1,000	
Labor efficiency	(900)	
Factory overhead	(800)	420
Actual gross margin		$ 48,420

* Parentheses indicate unfavorable variances.

6-14. **THE DEARBORN COMPANY**
Material:

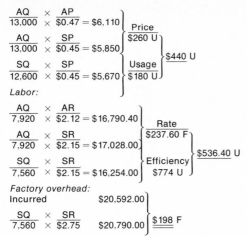

$$\begin{array}{l}
\dfrac{AQ}{13,000} \times \dfrac{AP}{\$0.47} = \$6,110 \\[6pt]
\dfrac{AQ}{13,000} \times \dfrac{SP}{\$0.45} = \$5,850 \\[6pt]
\dfrac{SQ}{12,600} \times \dfrac{SP}{\$0.45} = \$5,670
\end{array}$$

Price $260 U
Usage $180 U
$440 U

Labor:

$$\begin{array}{l}
\dfrac{AQ}{7,920} \times \dfrac{AR}{\$2.12} = \$16,790.40 \\[6pt]
\dfrac{AQ}{7,920} \times \dfrac{SR}{\$2.15} = \$17,028.00 \\[6pt]
\dfrac{SQ}{7,560} \times \dfrac{SR}{\$2.15} = \$16,254.00
\end{array}$$

Rate $237.60 F
Efficiency $774 U
$536.40 U

Factory overhead:

Incurred	$20,592.00
$\dfrac{SQ}{7,560} \times \dfrac{SR}{\$2.75}$	$20,790.00

$198 F

1. Material cost was above standard for two reasons:
    a. The purchase of 13,000 pounds at 2 cents per pound over standard price, adding $260
    b. The waste in production, of 400 pounds, worth 45 cents per pound, adding $180
2. Labor was paid an average of $2.12 per hour, 3 cents less than standard, for 7,920 hours, saving $237.60; however, 360 hours were wasted in production, adding $774 at $2.15 standard rate per hour.
3. Overhead, applied at standard rate of $2.75 per hour for 7,560 standard hours, was $20,790. Overhead incurred was only $20,592, resulting in a saving of $198.
4. Labor-AQ: $20,592/2.60 = 7,920

7-1. **OSBERGER CORPORATION**

1.

Units per month	7,000
Labor hours per unit	3
Labor hours per month	21,000
Overhead rate per hour	$0.60
Budgeted overhead per month	$12,600
Fixed overhead percentage	$33\frac{1}{3}$
Budgeted fixed overhead per month	$ 4,200

Total overhead per month = $4,200 + $0.40 (DLH)

2.

	Variable	Fixed	Total	
Incurred	?	?	$12,500	Spending variance $300 U
AQ × BA				
V (20,000 × $0.40)	$8,000		$12,200	
F ($4,200)		$4,200		Efficiency variance $200 U
SQ × BA				
V (19,500 × $0.40)	$7,800		$12,000	
F ($4,200)		$4,200		Capacity variance $300 U
SQ × SR				
V (19,500 × $0.40)	$7,800		$11,700	
F (19,500 × $0.20)		$3,900		

7-7.   **JONES FURNITURE COMPANY**

1,200 units produced

Material:

$$\frac{AQ}{132,000} \times \frac{AP}{\$0.12} = \$15,840 \left.\right\} \begin{array}{l} \text{Price} \\ \hline \$3,960 \text{ F} \end{array}$$

$$\frac{AQ}{132,000} \times \frac{SP}{\$0.15} = \$19,800$$

$$\frac{SQ}{120,000} \times \frac{SP}{\$0.15} = \$18,000 \left.\right\} \begin{array}{l} \text{Usage} \\ \hline \$1,800 \text{ U} \end{array}$$

Labor:

$$\frac{AQ}{5,100} \times \frac{AR}{\$2.60} = \$13,260 \left.\right\} \begin{array}{l} \text{Rate} \\ \hline \$510 \text{ U} \end{array}$$

$$\frac{AQ}{5,100} \times \frac{SR}{\$2.50} = \$12,750$$

$$\frac{SQ}{4,800} \times \frac{SR}{\$2.50} = \$12,000 \left.\right\} \begin{array}{l} \text{Efficiency} \\ \hline \$750 \text{ U} \end{array}$$

Standard burden:	Normal (4,000 hr)	Std/hr	Budget Allowance
Variable	$6,000	$1.50	$1.50/unit
Fixed	3,000	.75	$3,000
Total	$9,000	$2.25	

Burden:

		V	F	Total	
Incurred		?	?	$10,560	Spending
					$90 F
	$\dfrac{AQ}{5,100} \times \dfrac{BA}{\$\ 1.50} =$				
Variable	5,100 × $ 1.50 =	7,650			
Fixed	$3,000		3,000	10,650	Efficiency
					$450 U
	$\dfrac{SQ}{4,800} \times \dfrac{BA}{\$\ 1.50} =$				
Variable	4,800 × $ 1.50 =	7,200			
Fixed	$3,000		3,000	10,200	
					Capacity
	$\dfrac{SQ}{4,800} \times \dfrac{SR}{\$\ 1.50} =$				$600 F
Variable	4,800 × $ 1.50 =	7,200			
Fixed	4,800 × $ 0.75 =		3,600	10,800	

7-13. **THE BRONSON COMPANY**

    1. Materials price variance:

Actual cost of materials purchased		$1,044,000
Materials purchased at standard cost:		
Miracle mix	$1,000,000	
Drums	94,000	1,094,000
		$ 50,000 F

    2. Materials usage variance:

Actual materials used at standard cost:		
Miracle mix	$1,300,000	
Drums	80,000	$1,380,000
Standard usage: 80,000 × $17		1,360,000
		$ 20,000 U

    3. Labor rate variance:

Actual direct labor cost	$414,100
Actual hours at standard rate: 82,000 × $5	410,000
	$ 4,100 U

    4. Labor usage variance:

Actual hours at standard rate	$410,000
Standard hours at standard rate: 80,000 × $5	400,000
	$ 10,000 U

    5. Overhead budget variance:

Actual factory overhead costs	$768,000
Budgeted factory overhead costs	760,000
	$ 8,000 U

    6. Overhead capacity variance:

Budgeted factory overhead at September production level	$760,000
Factory overhead applied: 80,000 × $6	480,000
	$280,000 U

8-5. GEORGE JOHNSON

1. Mr. Johnson is responsible for the current operating results of his division; this includes revenue development, pricing, and physical volume, cost incurrence for manufacturing and distributing the product, for maintenance of the facilities, and for development of work force. He is also responsible for contributing to the capital investment program for his division and for implementing the approved capital programs. The inclusion of certain balance sheet items, Inventory, Accounts receivable, and Accounts and wages payable and the Contribution return on division net investment, imply responsibility for the management of some assets and liabilities.

2. The first impression is that Mr. Johnson has done a fine job. His return is 32 percent, compared with a budgeted return of 25 percent for 1971 and average return of 25 percent for the three-year period of 1969–1971. Careful analysis of the data suggests that this record was achieved by manipulation of activities which resulted in an overstatement of Division net contribution and an understatement of Division net investment.

a. Items affecting contribution:

   (1) Sales — $200,000 below budget
   (2) Repairs — $40,000 below their normal relationship to sales
   (3) Managed costs — $35,000 below budgeted amounts and $25,000 below last year
   (4) Depreciation and rent below budget amounts [see item b(1)].

b. Items affecting investment:

   (1) Fixed assets $580,000 below budget — capital plan not implemented (note rent also low, suggesting leased capacity not acquired according to plan)
   (2) Accounts and wages payable $70,000 above normal relationship to material and labor
   (3) Inventory $90,000 below normal relationship with sales

8-5.   GEORGE JOHNSON (continued)

All the items within his control (sales excepted) varied from normal relationships (relationships he accepted and embodied in the budgets he recommended) in directions which enhanced his division return. This suggests he took action to improve the return in the short run at the expense of the longer run. He appears to have deferred repairs, maintenance, employee training, and capital improvements. Each should have detrimental effect upon future performance of the division and the firm.

3.   The responsibilities of Mr. Johnson seem quite appropriate for a manager of an autonomous division. The use of the Contribution return on division net investment for overall performance measurement is a good start for autonomous divisions. In addition to this measure, additional activities should be reported:

a.   Budget for implementation of capital programs compared to actual implementation

b.   Budgeted operating costs and revenues compared to the actual figures

c.   Comparison of level of controlled assets to budgeted levels

The reports should be accompanied by explanations of significant differences. This information, plus the return on investment, would provide a good measure of the division manager's performance.

8-9.   CONTAINO CONTAINER CORPORATION

Controllable Costs	Budget at 5,000 DLH	Actual 3 Months	(Over) Under Budget	Budget at 4,940 DLH	(Over) Under Budget
Direct material	$ 4,000	$ 4,000		$ 3,952	($ 48)
Direct labor	20,000	19,750	$ 250	19,760	10
Indirect labor	10,000	9,500	500	9,880	380
Indirect material	2,000	2,800	(800)	1,976	(824)
Power – variable	6,000	7,000	(1,000)	5,928	(1,072)
Maintenance labor – variable	6,000	5,500	500	5,928	428
Scrap wastage	1,500	1,350	150	1,482	132
Total	$49,500	$49,900	($ 400)	$48,906	($ 994)
Noncontrollable Costs					
Power – fixed	$ 1,500	$ 1,500			
Maintenance labor – fixed	500	500			
Depreciation	6,000	5,000	$1,000		
General burden	8,000	7,500	500		
Total	$16,000	$14,500	$1,500		
Total	$65,500	$64,400	$1,100		

The decision would be, in all likelihood, not to allow the supervisor his raise if the only basis for it is good performance. He is responsible only for controllable costs, and when these items are studied, his claimed $1,100 favorable variance is in reality a $400 unfavorable variance. When the budget is adjusted to 4,940 hours, his performance is seen to have resulted in a $994 unfavorable variance.

8-15. THE PARSONS COMPANY

1. The Parsons Company sales compensation plan does provide financial motivation to sales representatives to make profitable sales. First, sales commissions are contingent upon the collection of accounts receivable. Thus, salespersons are discouraged from selling to high-credit-risk customers merely to generate sales volume (a double-edged condition; see 2). The sales commission is based upon product profitability. This motivates salespeople to direct their efforts toward the most profitable products in the line. Third, the sales force is not penalized if price concessions are considered necessary and desirable to attract certain customers. Finally, the substantial year-end bonus provides a strong economic stimulus to sales representatives to meet their annual sales quota.

2. The Parsons Company sales compensation plan does have several major deficiencies. Most notably, the flat 15 percent bonus for meeting or exceeding the annual sales quota does not stimulate a sales representative to exceed the quota by more than a slight safety margin. The sales staff is further discouraged from making sales far in excess of the quota due to the method of setting sales quotas. By setting the annual quota at 105 percent of prior year's sales, a salesperson increases his or her quota for the following year by making sales well in excess of the current year's quota. If the sales representatives have achieved their respective quotas near the end of the year, they would be motivated to hold back sales until the following year. Second, the commission/collection policy could discourage the sales staff from contacting prospective customers who would be classified as slow, but collectible. Third, the standard gross margin is not necessarily a good measure of product profitability. Product contribution margin would be a better measure. The standard gross margin does not reflect cost-volume-profit relationships. Nor does it consider directly traceable marketing costs. Finally, the reward system is apparently limited to monetary rewards. The system does not provide for higher-order rewards such as recognition by peers or superiors.

9-5.   1.   BENDIT MANUFACTURING COMPANY
Income Statement (Absorption Basis)
For the Year of 19x1

	1 Q	2 Q	3 Q	4 Q	Total
Sales	$400,000	$600,000	$600,000	$300,000	$1,900,000
Variable manufacturing costs ($4/unit)	160,000	240,000	240,000	120,000	760,000
Fixed manufacturing costs ($3/unit)	120,000	180,000	180,000	90,000	570,000
Total standard mfg. cost	$280,000	$420,000	$420,000	$210,000	$1,330,000
Add: (Over-) Underabsorbed	(60,000)	—	(30,000)	120,000	30,000
Cost of sales	$220,000	$420,000	$390,000	$330,000	$1,360,000
Gross margin	$180,000	$180,000	$210,000	($ 30,000)	$ 540,000
Less: Selling and administrative expense	90,000	90,000	90,000	90,000	360,000
Net income	$ 90,000	$ 90,000	$120,000	($120,000)	$ 180,000

BENDIT MANUFACTURING COMPANY
Income Statement (Variable Costing Basis)
For the Year of 19x1

	1 Q	2 Q	3 Q	4 Q	Total
Sales	$400,000	$600,000	$600,000	$300,000	$1,900,000
Variable manufacturing costs	160,000	240,000	240,000	120,000	760,000
Contribution margin	$240,000	$360,000	$360,000	$180,000	$1,140,000
Fixed costs:					
Manufacturing	$150,000	$150,000	$150,000	$150,000	$ 600,000
Selling and administrative	90,000	90,000	90,000	90,000	360,000
Total fixed costs	$240,000	$240,000	$240,000	$240,000	$ 960,000
Net income	-0-	$120,000	$120,000	($ 60,000)	$ 180,000

2.   In the first quarter, when production exceeded sales, net income reported under absorption costing was greater than that under variable costing. Conversely, in the second and fourth quarters, when sales volume was greater than production, the reported net income was larger under the variable than under the absorption costing method. In the third quarter, when sales and production were equal, there was no difference in net income reported under the two methods. When production volume exceeds sales, the unit fixed costs of such excess follow such units into inventory under absorption costing. Conversely, such fixed costs in inventory flow into cost of goods sold in periods where sales volume is greater than production. Under variable costing, however, such fixed costs do not move in and out of inventory, but are written off against income in the period in which they are incurred.

9-11.   1.   FLEAR COMPANY

Fixed costs:

Manufacturing		$ 360,000
Selling		252,000
Total		$ 612,000
Selling price per unit		$ 20
Less variable costs:		
Manufacturing	$11	
Selling	3	14
Contribution margin		$ 6

Break-even point:

Units to be sold ($612,000 ÷ $6)	102,000
Sales dollars (102,000 × $20)	$2,040,000

2.

Break-even point in unit sales	102,000
Unit sales over break-even point required to earn desired net income ($60,000 ÷ $6)	10,000
Total units to be sold to earn $60,000 net income	112,000

3.

Contribution margin	$ 6
Less net profit per unit required to produce a 10% net income on sales	2
Contribution margin which will produce a net income of 10% on sales	$ 4
Units to be sold to earn 10% net income on sales ($612,000 ÷ $4)	153,000

4.   (*a*)   Conventional costing income statement:

FLEAR COMPANY
Income Statement

Sales	$3,000,000
Less cost of sales:	
Beginning inventory	130,000
Manufacturing costs:	
Fixed	360,000
Variable	1,760,000
Variation from standard variable manufacturing costs	40,000
Total	2,290,000
Ending inventory	260,000
Total cost of sales	2,030,000
Gross profit from operations	970,000
Less selling expenses:	
Fixed	252,000
Variable	450,000
Total selling expenses	702,000
Net income for year	$ 268,000

(*b*)   Direct costing income statement:

9-11. 4. FLEAR COMPANY (continued)

Income Statement

Sales	$3,000,000
Less direct costs and expenses:	
Manufacturing:	
Beginning inventory	110,000
Variable manufacturing costs	1,760,000
Variation from standard variable manufacturing costs	40,000
Total	1,910,000
Ending inventory	220,000
Total direct manufacturing cost	1,690,000
Selling expenses variable	450,000
Total direct costs and expenses	2,140,000
Income before period costs	860,000
Period costs:	
Manufacturing	360,000
Selling	252,000
Total period costs	612,000
Net income	$ 248,000

5. Analysis of variation in net income:

Net income per direct costing income statement	$ 248,000
Less excess of beginning inventory under conventional costing as compared with direct costing	20,000
Remainder	228,000
Add excess of ending inventory under conventional costing as compared with direct costing	40,000
Net income per conventional costing income statement	$ 268,000

9-16. THE S. T. SHIRE COMPANY

1.

Sales		$600,000
Variable cost of goods sold		
(20,000 × $15)	$300,000	
Manufacturing variances	4,000	304,000
Contribution margin		$296,000
Less period costs		
Production	90,000	
Selling and administrative	100,000	190,000
Net Income		$106,000

2.

Sales		$600,000
Cost of goods sold		
(20,000 × $18)	$360,000	
Manufacturing variances	22,000*	382,000
Gross margin		$218,000
Less selling and administrative costs		100,000
Net income		$118,000
* Manufacturing variances—variable costs		$ 4,000
Capacity variance (6,000 × $3)		18,000
Total		$22,000

3. Inventory increased 4,000 units. Each added unit absorbs $3 in allocated fixed overhead, or a total of $12,000.

The assumption in the problem is that the books are maintained on a direct cost basis. Therefore, an adjustment to the book figures would need to be made to recognize the fixed costs in inventory for all units.

Inventory	$72,000	
Cost of goods sold	60,000	
Unabsorbed fixed overhead	18,000	
Period production costs		$90,000
Retained earnings		60,000

If just the current year needs to be adjusted (the beginning inventory of 1972 was charged with the appropriate fixed overhead), the entry would be:

Inventory	$12,000	
Cost of goods sold	60,000	
Unabsorbed fixed overhead	18,000	
Period production costs		$90,000

9-16. THE S. T. SHIRE COMPANY (continued)

   4. *Advantages:*

     a. The fixed costs are reported at incurred values (and not absorbed), thus increasing the likelihood of better control of those costs.

     b. Profits are directly influenced by changes in sales volume (and not influenced by building for inventory).

     c. The impact of fixed costs on profits is emphasized.

     d. The income statements are in the same form as the cost-volume-profit relationship.

     e. Product line, territory, marginal contribution, etc., are emphasized and more readily ascertainable.

   Disadvantages:

     a. Total costs may be overlooked when considering problems.

     b. Distinction between fixed and variable costs is arbitrary for many costs.

     c. Emphasis on variable cost may cause managers to ignore fixed costs.

   5. *Advantages:*

     a. Statements would readily reflect the direct impact of sales volume on profits.

     b. The consequences of fixed costs would be more obvious.

     c. Inventory swings would not influence profits.

   Disadvantages:

     a. Costs are not matched to revenues.

     b. The difficulty in separating fixed and variable costs might cause statements to be misleading.

     c. Statements would confuse investors accustomed to absorption costing statements.

     d. Confidential information (on nature of costs) could be disclosed to competitors.

10-3. WYNKEN, BLYNKEN, AND NOD CORPORATIONS

1. It depends on how bigness is measured. Wynken has largest sales volume and market share; Blynken has largest asset structure.

2. The best performance, when employing return on capital used criteria, was Nod with a 20 percent return:

	Wynken	Blynken	Nod
Net sales	$5,000,000	$3,000,000	$960,000
Operating costs	4,600,000	2,700,000	912,000
Net operating income	$ 400,000	$ 300,000	$ 48,000
Net operating income = Net sales	$ 400,000 $5,000,000	$ 300,000 $3,000,000	$ 48,000 $960,000
(A) Net operating income as percentage of sales	8%	10%	5%
Net sales ÷ operating assets =	$5,000,000 $2,500,000	$3,000,000 $6,000,000	$960,000 $240,000
(B) Asset turnover	2	.5	4
Return on capital used (A × B) =	16%	5%	20%

Questions 3 and 4

All three firms seem to have some ills, even though the return on capital used was fairly high for two of them.

Wynken's net operating income as a percentage of net sales was 8 percent. The industry's high was 10 percent, indicating that perhaps a little more efficiency could possibly be introduced. Wynken's asset turnover was 2 (the industry's high was 4), indicating that a study of the composition of the assets might be warranted.

Blynken's net operating income as a percentage of net sales was high, 10 percent; however, further analysis reveals that the asset turnover is extremely low, at .5 per year. A close study of the assets, their composition and efficiency, seems necessary. A streamlining here is apparently needed.

Nod's net operating income as a percentage of sales is quite low. However, this low is offset by a high turnover in assets, indicating that the low value of the operating assets yielding a high turnover figure could possibly be responsible for the higher costs of operations.

Not enough is known about the industry and the three firms, but from the analysis here, it seems that a return on capital of 40 percent (10 percent profit/sales times 4 turns) is possible. It may be that this is still not the ultimate attainable. Management must set its own goals.

10-10. SOUTHERN COTTONSEED COMPANY

1. Revenue from production:

Per ton of cottonseed:	Number of Pounds	Price per Pound	Amount
Oil	300	$.15	$ 45
Meal	600	.025	15
Hulls	800	.01	8
Lint	100	.03	3
Total			$ 71
Production at the rate of 20,000 tons per year			$1,420,000

Fixed costs and maximum loss:		
Processing		$ 108,000
Administrative		90,000
Total		$ 198,000

Computation of maximum price to be paid per ton of cottonseed:

Total revenue		$1,420,000
Less:		
Variable processing costs ($9 × 20,000)	$180,000	
Fixed processing costs	108,000	
Marketing costs ($20 × 90% of 20,000)	360,000	
Administrative costs	90,000	738,000
Profit from production before material costs		682,000
Maximum loss		198,000
Maximum amount to be paid for 20,000 tons of cottonseed		$ 880,000
Maximum amount to be paid for 1 ton of cottonseed		$ 44

2. Factors to be considered by management in its decision as to whether the plant should be shut down:

   a. The computation in part 1 has assumed that all fixed costs will continue when operations are shut down, although certain fixed costs, such as administrative salaries, could be eliminated during a plant shutdown. The elimination of such costs lowers the maximum loss and consequently lowers the average amount to be paid for cottonseed.

   b. The company would permanently lose a portion of the company's experienced operating and supervisory personnel. The resumption of operations would necessitate the training of inexperienced help who would temporarily lack the efficiency of present personnel.

   c. The company would permanently lose a portion of its present customers, since they would seek new suppliers during the shutdown.

   d. The maximum loss permissible resulting from a shutdown should be related to the company's financial ability to sustain such losses.

   e. The company should consider the possibility of utilizing the present facilities for the production of products other than cottonseed.

3. Computation of maximum price to be paid per ton of cottonseed that will realize the minimum satisfactory return on investment:

Profit from production before material costs (from part 1)	$682,000
Minimum profit (25% of $968,000)	242,000
Maximum amount to be paid for 20,000 tons of cottonseed	$440,000
Maximum amount to be paid for 1 ton of cottonseed	$ 22

10-16.   BILL SWEET

1.   19x1

$$\text{Profit percentage} = \frac{\text{net operating income}}{\text{net sales}} = \frac{1{,}530}{18{,}000} = 8.5\%$$

$$\text{Asset turnover} = \frac{\text{net sales}}{\text{operating assets}} = \frac{18{,}000}{10{,}000} = 1.8$$

Return on capital used = profit percentage × asset turnover = 15.3%

2.   19x2   Revised income statement

Sales (125% of $18,000)		$22,500
Cost of sales:		
Variable manufacturing (40% of sales)	$9,000	
Fixed manufacturing	5,530	
Total cost of sales		14,530
Gross margin		$ 7,970
Selling and administrative:		
Variable divisional selling and administrative (16% of sales)	$3,600	
Fixed divisional selling and administrative		
(including advertising increase)	2,000	
Allocated home office cost	740	
Total selling and administrative		6,340
Operating income		$ 1,630

$$\text{Profit percentage} = \frac{\text{net operating income}}{\text{sales}} = \frac{1{,}630}{22{,}500} = \underline{7.2\%}$$

$$\text{Asset turnover} = \frac{\text{sales}}{\text{average operating assets}} = \frac{22{,}500}{11{,}250} = \underline{\underline{2}}$$

Return on capital used = profit percentage × asset turnover = 14.4%

3.   Break-even point, 19x1

X = break-even sales = $.44x + .16x + \$5{,}670$
$.4x = \$5{,}670$
$x = \$14{,}175$

Break-even point, 19x2

X = break-even sales = $.40x + .16x + \$8{,}270$
$.44x = \$8{,}270$
$x = \$18{,}795$
Increase in break-even point: $18,795
    14,175
$ 4,620

4.   The inclusion of fixed assets at gross cost has the tendency to off-set the distortion of the worth of fixed assets as time goes by in periods of inflation. The inherent drawback of using gross cost, however, is that the buildup of cash from operations resulting from the use of noncash depreciation expense as a determinant of income is not offset by a corresponding decrease in the value of the fixed assets out of which it arose. Unless some adjustment is made, therefore, there will be duplication of asset values. The allocation of home office costs to segments bears a strong resemblance to that of allocating indirect factory overhead and factory service costs for product costing purposes. These allocations seem to be more or less arbitrary and easily open to criticism. It would therefore seem best to base the return on capital for segment management only on costs and assets under the particular manager's direct control.

11-3. THE HORNGREN COMPANY

1. (a)

Annual Basis

	Semiautomated	Difference	Automated
Operating costs	$45,000	$ (45,000)	—
Equipment:			
Old: Depreciation*	12,500		
Write-off (avge. 4-yr)		—	$12,500
New (one-fourth of $170,000)	—	42,500	42,500
Disposal (one-fourth of $20,000)	—	(5,000)	(5,000)
Total	$57,500	$ (7,500)	$50,000
Incremental investment		$150,000	
Percentage return on incremental investment		5%	

* Cost	$122,000
Less: Salvage	2,000
Depreciation base	$120,000
Annual depreciation (10-yr life)	$ 12,000
Accumulated depreciation (6 yrs)	$ 72,000
Book value: $122,000– 72,000 =	$ 50,000

Average depreciation—4 years (assuming no salvage value): $50,000/4 = $12,500

(b)

Four Years

	Semiautomated	Difference	Automated
Operating costs	$180,000	$(180,000)	—
Equipment:			
Old: Depreciation	50,000	—	
Write-off			$ 50,000
New	—	170,000	170,000
Disposal	—	(20,000)	(20,000)
Total	$230,000	$ (30,000)	$200,000
Incremental investment		$ 150,000	
Percentage return		20%	

2. There is economic advantage to the extent of 5 percent average return over the next four years.

3. Obviously, the return is insufficient to meet the president's goals.

11-9. THE BRADSHAW COMPANY

1.
Selling price of R	$ 7.00
Unit variable cost of R	7.50
Contribution margin per unit of R	$(.50)
Units sold of R	1,800
Increase in profits if R is discontinued	$ 900

2.
Selling price of Q	$15.00
Unit variable cost of Q	4.25
Contribution margin per unit of Q	$10.75
Lost sales in units	200
Lost contribution margin from Q	$2,150
Less: Effect of discontinuing R	900
Decrease in profits	$1,250

3.
New selling price of R	$ 8.00
Unit variable cost of R	7.50
New contribution margin per unit of R	$ .50
New number of units sold	1,500
New total contribution margin from R	$ 750
Old total contribution margin from R	(900)
Increase in income	$1,650

4.
Selling price of T	$ 9.50
Unit variable cost of T	8.05
Contribution margin per unit of T	$ 1.45
Number of T to be sold	1,600
Total contribution margin from T	$2,320
Old total contribution margin from R	(900)
Increase in income	$3,220

5.
	Old P	New P	Old S	New S
Selling price	$10.00	$12.00	$11.00	$10.50
Unit variable cost	3.67	3.67	7.20	7.20
Unit contribution margin	$ 6.33	$ 8.33	$ 3.80	$ 3.30
Units to be sold	1,000	500	2,000	2,500
Total contribution margin	$6,330	$4,165	$7,600	$8,250
Decrease from P		$2,165		
Increase from S				$650
Total decrease in income			$1,515	

6.
Selling price of additional P	$10.00
Unit variable cost of additional P	4.67
Contribution margin per additional unit of P	$ 5.33
Additional units of P	1,000
Increase in income	$5,330

11-16. THE SCOOPA COMPANY

1. Comparison of precision machinery department costs:

	With Manufacture of Factrons	Factrons Purchased from Supplier
Materials	$ 67,500	$ 50,000
Direct labor	50,000	22,000
Indirect labor	20,000	14,000
Light and heat	5,500	5,500
Power	3,000	2,700
Depreciation	10,000	8,000
Property taxes and insurance	8,000	7,000
Payroll taxes and other benefits (14% of labor costs or ratio of total cost of payroll taxes and other benefits to total labor costs)	9,800	5,040
Other	5,000	4,500
Additional costs resulting from outside purchases:		
Material		40,000
Freight		2,500
Indirect labor		5,000
Payroll taxes and other benefits (14% of labor costs)		700
Total	$178,800	$166,940

2. Items to be considered by management in its decision on whether to make or buy Factrons:

a. Purchases from outside supplier would result in annual saving of approximately $12,000.

b. The disposition of machinery would provide additional working capital.

c. Would the elimination of manufacturing Factrons upset present production schedules of the department and result in slack periods within the department?

d. Can the plant area occupied by Factron production be effectively utilized in other production?

e. Is the supplier adequately capitalized? Are the supplier's production facilities adequate to maintain a production schedule that will minimize the investment in inventory or will there be an increase in the investment in inventory? If a larger inventory is required, would plant area be available for the larger quantity?

f. What is the supplier's reputation among its customers as to meeting production schedules?

g. Would the quality standards of the outside supplier be equal to those of the department?

h. Would the supplier's price and production requirements be fixed by contracts? What is the potential for obsolescence which might give rise to the required purchase, due to a contract, of obsolete parts?

i. Should the company rely on only one supplier or should the work be distributed to two suppliers in order to protect against interruptions due to strikes or other delays? Would the original supplier's quotation be increased if the work was distributed between two suppliers rather than going to only the one supplier?

12-5. THE WILSON COMPANY

		X	Y	Z	Total
1.	Total fixed costs				$492,000
	Number of units	60,000	80,000	100,000	240,000
	Fixed cost per unit	$ 2.05	$ 2.05	$ 2.05	$2.05
	Variable cost per unit	6.00	9.00	12.00	
	Total unit cost	$ 8.05	$11.05	$14.05	
	Markup – 30%	2.415	3.315	4.215	
	Selling price	$10.465	$14.365	$18.265	
2.	Number of units	60,000	80,000	100,000	
	Variable cost per unit	$6	$9	$12	
	Total variable cost	$360,000	$720,000	$1,200,000	$2,280,000
	Share of total variable cost	.1579	.3158	.5263	1.00
	Allocated fixed costs	$ 77,687	$155,373	$ 258,940	$ 492,000
	Fixed cost per unit	$ 1.295	$ 1.942	$ 2.589	
	Variable cost per unit	6.00	9.00	12.00	
	Total unit cost	$ 7.295	$ 10.942	$ 14.589	
	Markup – 30%	2.189	3.283	4.377	
	Selling price	$ 9.484	$ 14.225	$ 18.966	
3.	Variable cost per unit	$6.00	$ 9.00	$12.00	
	Markup – 50%	3.00	4.50	6.00	
	Selling price	$9.00	$13.50	$18.00	

12-9. E. BERG AND FAMILY

1. a. An *increase* in income of $1,200 (before taxes) would result from accepting the $15,000 offer.

    b. The minimum price needed to have no effect on profit is $13,800.

$$\frac{\text{Variable overhead}}{\text{Total overhead}} = \text{percentage of overhead variable}$$

$$\frac{\$60,000}{\$150,000} = 40\%$$

Overhead rate × percentage of overhead variable = variable overhead rate per direct labor

$$25\% \times 40\% = 10\%$$

Variable costs of quoted boat

Direct material	$ 5,000
Direct labor	8,000
Variable overhead (10% × 8,000)	800
	$13,800

Customer's offer	$15,000
Variable costs	13,800
Contribution to profit	$ 1,200

2. The contribution margin approach focuses on the relationship between the costs to be incurred as a result of taking an order and the revenue the order will produce. The impact of a specific order on profits can be estimated and the lower limits on price can be observed.

3. The major pitfall to the contribution margin approach to pricing is its failure to recognize explicitly the fixed costs. Although they can be overlooked in the short run, the fixed costs must be covered in the long run if the business is to continue.

12-13.   1.   THE LARGE CHARGE CORPORATION
Department M Operations
19x3

	Outside	Division A	Total
Sales—pounds	8,000,000	4,000,000	12,000,000
Selling price per pound	$3.75	$3.00	
Sales revenue	$30,000,000	$12,000,000	$42,000,000
Less: Variable manufacturing			
costs ($2.50/lb)	20,000,000	10,000,000	30,000,000
Contribution margin	$10,000,000	$ 2,000,000	$12,000,000
Fixed manufacturing costs—total			9,000,000
Gross profit			$ 3,000,000

If the manager of department M refuses to sell to Division A at the $2.75 price, he will lose $2 million in contribution margin. If department M's sales to outsiders are not increased and if fixed costs do not change as a result of a one-third reduction in production, the department's gross profit will also decrease by $2 million:

Sales (8,000,000 @ $3.75)	$30,000,000
Variable costs (8,000,000 @ $2)	20,000,000
Contribution margin	$10,000,000
Fixed costs	9,000,000
Gross profit	$ 1,000,000

On the other hand, if the manager of department M does sell to Division A at the $2.75 price, these sales will contribute an additional $1 million to profits:

Sales—pounds	4,000,000
Selling price per pound	$2.75
Sales revenue	$11,000,000
Variable costs	10,000,000
Contribution margin	$ 1,000,000

Assuming no changes in fixed costs, the manager of department M will report higher profits by making sales to Division A at any price greater than the variable costs of $2.50 per pound.

2.   The $2.75 price will result in a 25 cents per pound increase in profits to Division A, regardless of from whom he purchases.

Total savings = 2,000 × 2,000 × .25 = $1,000,000 increase

3.   For the company as a whole:

If M refuses to sell department profits fall by	($2,000,000)
When A purchases, division profits increase by	1,000,000
Profit change for the company as a whole	($1,000,000)

13-1. PRESENT VALUE CALCULATIONS

1.

Factor from Table I	.681	.681
Desired amount	× $1,000	× $2,500
Required deposit—present value	$ 681	$1,702.50

2.

Deposit—present value	$1,000	$4,500
Factor from Table I	÷ .665	÷ .665
Future amount	$1,503.76	$6,766.92

3.

Interest rate	6%	10%
Factor from Table II	7.360	6.145
Annual payment	× $50,000	× $50,000
Present value of prize A	$368,000	$307,250

At a 6 percent rate, prize A is more attractive; but at a 10 percent rate, prize B is more worthwhile. The interest rate at which the two prizes would be approximately equal can be found by interpolation:

Interest rate	6%	8%
Factor from Table II	7.360	6.710
Annual payment	× $50,000	× $50,000
Present value of prize A	$368,000	$335,500

Since the present value of prize A must be $350,000 to be equal to prize B, we see that the rate is between 6 percent and 8 percent. Interpolation yields a rate of 7.1 percent.

$$\left[.06 + \left(\frac{368,000 - 350,000}{368,000 - 335,500}\right) \times (.02)\right]$$

4.

Factor from Table II	3.433
Annual payments	× $1,000
Amount of loan—present value	$3,433

Balance, Beginning of Year	Applied to Interest (14%)	Applied to Principal	Total Payment	Unpaid Balance after Payment
$3,433	$ 481	$ 519	$1,000	$2,914
2,914	408	592	1,000	2,322
2,322	325	675	1,000	1,647
1,647	230	770	1,000	877
877	123	877	1,000	-0-
	$1,567	$3,433	$5,000	

5.

Amount of loan—present value	$6,850
Factor from Table II	÷ 2.283
Annual payments (rounded)	$3,000

Balance, Beginning of Year	Applied to Interest (15%)	Applied to Principal	Total Payment	Unpaid Balance after Payment
$6,850	$1,027	$1,973	$3,000	$4,877
4,877	732	2,268	3,000	2,609
2,609	391	2,609	3,000	-0-
	$2,150	$6,850	$9,000	

13-4. THE RUTH COMPANY

1. $P = \dfrac{I}{C} = \dfrac{\$22,000}{\$5,600} = 3.9$ years

2. $R = \dfrac{C - D}{I} = \dfrac{\$5,600 - \$2,200}{\$22,000} = .155$

3. $R = \dfrac{C - D}{I/2} = \dfrac{\$3,400}{\$11,000} = .309$

4.
Factor from Table II	5.216
Annual savings	$\times$ $5,600
Present value of savings	$29,209.60
Original cost	22,000.00
Net present value	$ 7,209.60

5.
Original cost	$22,000.00
Annual savings	$\div$ $5,600.00
Factor to be located in Table II	3.929

Time-adjusted rate of return is approximately 22 percent.

6. Yes, its net present value is positive and its time-adjusted rate of return is greater than the desired minimum.

13-12. THE MITTLEMAN COMPANY

1.

	Tax Purposes	Cash Inflow
Gross annual cash cost savings	$40,000	$40,000
Less: Depreciation	20,000	
Net incremental income subject to tax	$20,000	
Income tax (50% rate)	10,000	10,000
Net cash inflow after taxes (a.t.)		$30,000

2. Discounted cash flow:

$$\dfrac{TAR}{100,000} = \text{PV of annuity of 30,000 at X\% for 5 yrs}$$

$$100,000 = 30,000 \, F$$

$$F = 3.33 \text{ (payback)}$$

TAR (30,000 for 5 yrs — Table II) = 15+%

EPV		EPV index:
F (5 yrs @ 10%)	3.791	
cash inflow (a.t.)	$\times$ $30,000	
	$113,730	$\dfrac{113,730}{110,000} = 103.4\%$
Investment	110,000	
EPV	$ 3,730	

According to this test, the company's desired rate of return of 10 percent after taxes seems to be exceeded and the computer should be purchased.

INDEX

INDEX